T0309632

MARKET-ORIENTED GRID AND UTILITY COMPUTING

MARKET-ORIENTED GRID AND UTILITY COMPUTING

Edited by

RAJKUMAR BUYYA, PhD
The University of Melbourne and Manjrasoft Pty Ltd, Australia

KRIS BUBENDORFER, PhD
Victoria University of Wellington, New Zealand

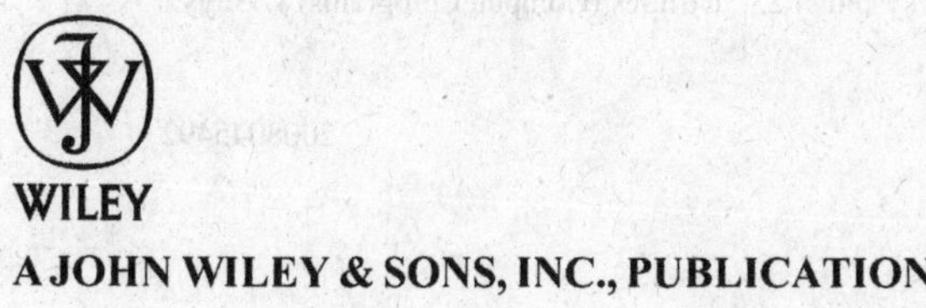

A JOHN WILEY & SONS, INC., PUBLICATION

Published by John Wiley & Sons, Inc., Hoboken, New Jersey
Published simultaneously in Canada

For general information on our other products and services or for technical support, please contact our Customer Care Department within the United States at (800) 762-2974, outside the United States at (317) 572-3993 or fax (317) 572-4002.

Wiley publishes in a variety of print and electronic formats and by print-on-demand. Some material included with standard print versions of this book may not be included in e-books or in print-on-demand. If this book refers to media such as a CD or DVD that is not included in the version you purchased, you may download this material at http://booksupport.wiley.com. For more information about Wiley products, visit www.wiley.com.

Library of Congress Cataloging-in-Publication Data:

Market-oriented grid and utility computing / edited by Rajkumar Buyya, Kris Bubendorfer.
p. cm.
Includes bibliographical references and index.
ISBN 978-0-470-28768-2 (cloth)
1. Computational grids (Computer systems) 2. Utilities (Computer programs) I. Buyya, Rajkumar, 1970- II. Bubendorfer, Kris.
QA76.9.C58M37 2009
004'.36–dc22 2008045492

10 9 8 7 6 5 4 3 2 1

CONTENTS

PART IV RESOURCE ALLOCATION AND SCHEDULING MECHANISMS

CONTRIBUTORS

David Abramson Clayton School of Information Technology, Monash University, Clayton, Melbourne, VIC 3800, Australia [e-mail: david.abramson@infotech.monash.edu.au]

Jörn Altman Computer Networks and Distributed Systems, International University, Campus 3, 76646 Bruchsal, Germany [e-mail: jorn.altmann@acm.org]

Nazareno Andrade Departamento de Sistemas e Computação, Universidade Federal de Campina Grande, Av. Aprígio Veloso, 882 Bodocongó, Bloco CO 58109-970, Campina Grande, PB, Brazil [e-mail: nazareno@dsc.ufcg.edu.br]

Alvin AuYoung Department of Computer Science and Engineering, University of California San Diego, 9500 Gilman Drive, MC 0404, La Jolla, CA 92093, USA [e-mail: alvina@cs.ucsd.edu]

Pavan Balaji Mathematics and Computer Science Division, Argonne National Laboratory, 9700 South Cass Avenue, Argonne, IL 60439, USA [e-mail: balaji@mcs.anl.gov]

Siegfried Benkner Institute of Scientific Computing, University of Vienna, Nordbergstraße 15, 1090 Vienna, Austria [e-mail: sigi@par.univie.ac.at]

José Luis Bosque Facultad de Informática, Universidad Politécnica de Madrid, Campus de Montegancedo S/N 28.660 Boadilla del Monte, Madrid, Spain [e-mail: joseluis.bosque@unican.es]

Ivona Brandic Institute of Scientific Computing, University of Vienna, Nordbergstraße 15, 1090 Vienna, Austria [e-mail: brandic@par.univie.ac.at]

Francisco Brasileiro Universidade Federal de Campina Grande, Departamento de Sistemas e Computação, Av. Aprígio Veloso, 882 Bodocongó, Bloco CO 58109-970, Campina Grande, PB, Brazil [e-mail: fubica@dsc.ufcg.edu.br]

Kris Bubendorfer School of Mathematics, Statistics, and Computer Science, Victoria University of Wellington, Kelburn Parade, Wellington, New Zealand [e-mail: kris@mcs.vuw.ac.nz]

Phil Buonadonna Intel Research Berkeley, 2150 Shattuck Avenue, Suite 1300, Berkeley, CA 94704, USA [e-mail: pbuonadonna@archrock.com]

Rajkumar Buyya Department of Computer Science and Software Engineering, The University of Melbourne, Parkville, Melbourne, VIC 3010, Australia [e-mail: raj@csse.unimelb.edu.au]

Kyle Chard School of Engineering and Computer Science, Victoria University of Wellington, Kelburn Parade, Wellington, New Zealand [e-mail: Kyle.Chard@mcs.vuw.ac.nz]

Kenneth Chiu Department of Computer Science, State University of New York (SUNY) at Binghamton, Binghamton, NY 13902, USA [e-mail: kchiu@cs.binghamton. edu]

Brent N. Chun Intel Research Berkeley, 2150 Shattuck Avenue, Suite 1300, Berkeley, CA 94704, USA [e-mail: bnc@theether.org]

Walfredo Cirne Departamento de Sistemas e Computação, Universidade Federal de Campina Grande, Av. Aprígio Veloso, 882 Bodocongó, Bloco CO 58109-970, Campina Grande, PB, Brazil [e-mail: walfredo@dsc.ufcg.edu.br]

Karim Djemame School of Computing, University of Leeds, Leeds LS2 9JT, UK [e-mail: karim@comp.leeds.ac.uk]

Rubing Duan Institut für Informatik, Universität Innsbruck, Technikerstraße 21a, A-6020 Innsbruck, Austria [e-mail: Rubing.Duan@uibk.ac.at]

Iain Gourlay School of Computing, University of Leeds, Leeds LS2 9JT, UK [e-mail: iain@comp.leeds.ac.uk]

Andrew S. Grimshaw Department of Computer Science, Thornton Hall, University of Virginia, Charlottesville, VA 22903, USA [e-mail: grimshaw@cs.virginia.edu]

Andrea Guarise Istituto Nazionale di Fisica Nucleare—Sezione di Torino, Via Pietro Giuria 1, 10125 Torino, Italy [e-mail: guarise@to.infn.it]

Jordi Guitart Barcelona Supercomputing Center, c/Jordi Girona 29, Edifici Nexus II, 3ª planta, E08034 Barcelona, Spain [e-mail: jguitart@ac.upc.edu]

Pilar Herrero Facultad de Informatica, Universidad Politecnica de Madrid, Campus de Montegancedo S/N 28.660 Boadilla del Monte, Madrid, Spain [e-mail: pherrero@fi.upm.es]

H. Howie Huang Department of Electrical and Computer Engineering, School of Engineering and Applied Science, The George Washington University, 801 22nd Street NW, Washington, DC 20052, USA [e-mail: howie@gwu.edu]

Mohammad Islam Department of Computer Science and Engineering, 595 Dreese Lab, 2015 Neil Avenue, Ohio State University, Columbus, OH 43210, USA [e-mail: islammo@cse.ohio-state.edu]

Odej Kao Technische Universitat Berlin, Department of Telecommunication Systems, Einsteinufer 17, 10587 Berlin, Germany [e-mail: Odej.Kao@tu-berlin.de]

Bastian Koller University of Stuttgart, High Performance Computing Center, Nobelstrasse 19, D-70569 Stuttgart, Germany [e-mail: koller@hlrs.de]

Yu-Kwong Kwok Department of Electrical and Computer Engineering, Colorado State University, Fort Collins, CO 80523, USA [e-mail: Ricky.Kwok@colostate.edu]

Richard Lowe IT Innovation Centre, University of Southampton, 2 Venture Road, Southampton SO16 7NP, UK

Mario Macías Barcelona Supercomputing Center, c/Jordi Girona 29, Edifici Nexus II, 3ª planta, E08034, Barcelona, Spain [e-mail: mario.macias@bsc.es]

Dan Cristian Marinescu School of Electrical Engineering and Computer Science, University of Central Florida, 4000 Central Florida Boulevard, Orlando, FL 32816, USA [e-mail: dcm@cs.ucf.edu]

Paul McKee Centre for Information and Security Systems Research, BT Adastral Park, British Telecom, Ipswich IP5 3RE, UK [e-mail: paul.mckee@bt.com]

John Patrick Morrison Computer Science Department, University College, Cork, Ireland [e-mail: J.Morrison@cs.ucc.ie]

Miranda Mowbray Hewlett-Packard Laboratories Bristol, Filton Road, Stoke Gifford, Bristol BS34 8QZ, UK [e-mail: miranda.mowbray@hp.com]

Chaki Ng School of Engineering and Applied Science, Harvard University, Maxwell Dworkin 229, 33 Oxford Street, Cambridge, MA 02138, USA [e-mail: chaki@eecs.harvard.edu]

Eduardo Oliveros Telefónica I + D, Emilio Vargas, 6, Madrid 28043, Spain [e-mail: eod@tid.es]

James Padgett School of Computing, University of Leeds, Leeds LS2 9JT, UK [e-mail: jamesp@comp.leeds.ac.uk]

Ben Palmer School of Engineering, and Computer Science, Victoria University of Wellington, Kelburn Parade, Wellington, New Zealand [e-mail: Benjamin.Palmer@mcs.vuw.ac.nz]

David C. Parkes School of Engineering and Applied Science, Harvard University, Maxwell Dworkin 229, 33 Oxford Street, Cambridge, MA 02138, USA [e-mail: parkes@eecs.harvard.edu]

María S. Pérez Facultad de Informática, Universidad Politécnica de Madrid, Campus de Montegancedo S/N 28.660 Boadilla del Monte, Madrid, Spain [e-mail: mperez@fi.upm.es]

Rosario M. Piro Istituto Nazionale di Fisica Nucleare – Sezione di Torino, Via Pietro Giuria 1, 10125 Torino, Italy [e-mail: piro@to.infn.it]

Sabri Pllana Institute of Scientific Computing, University of Vienna, Nordbergstraße 15, 1090 Vienna, Austria [e-mail: pllana@par.univie.ac.at]

Radu Prodan Institut für Informatik, Universität Innsbruck, Technikerstraße 21a, A-6020 Innsbruck, Austria [e-mail: radu@dps.uibk.ac.at]

Dang Minh Quan Computer Networks and Distributed Systems, International University, Campus 3, 76646 Bruchsal, Germany [e-mail: quandm@upb.de]

Kotagiri Ramamohanarao Department of Computer Science and Software Engineering, The University of Melbourne, Parkville, Melbourne, VIC 3010, Australia [e-mail: rao@csse.unimelb.edu.au]

Omer Rana School of Computer Science, Cardiff University, Queen's Buildings, Newport Road, Cardiff CF24 3AA, UK [e-mail: o.f.rana@cs.cardiff.ac.uk]

Rajiv Ranjan Department of Computer Science and Software Engineering, The University of Melbourne, Parkville, Melbourne, VIC 3010, Australia [e-mail: rranjan@csse.unimelb.edu.au]

Ponnuswamy Sadayappan Department of Computer Science and Engineering, 595 Dreese Lab, 2015 Neil Avenue, Ohio State University, Columbus, OH 43210, USA [e-mail: saday@cse.ohio-state.edu]

Alfonso Sánchez-Macián IT Innovation Centre, University of Southampton, 2 Venture Road, Southampton SO16 7NP, UK [e-mail: asm@it-innovation.soton.ac.uk]

Björn Schnizler Institute of Information Systems and Management (IISM), Universität Karlsruhe (TH), Englerstraße 14, D-76131 Karlsruhe, Germany [e-mail: Schnizler@iism.uni-karlsruhe.de]

Jeff Shneidman School of Engineering and Applied Science, Harvard University, Maxwell Dworkin 229, 33 Oxford Street, Cambridge, MA 02138, USA [e-mail: jeffsh@eecs.harvard.edu]

Howard Jay Siegel Department of Electrical and Computer Engineering, Colorado State University, Fort Collins, CO 80523, USA [e-mail: HJ@ColoState.edu]

Alex C. Snoeren Department of Computer Science and Engineering, University of California, San Diego, 9500 Gilman Drive, MC 0404, La Jolla, CA 92093, USA [e-mail: snoeren@cs.ucsd.edu]

Tiberiu Stef-Praun Computation Institute, University of Chicago, 5640 S. Ellis Ave, Chicago, IL 60637, USA [e-mail: tiberius@ci.uchicago.edu]

Yibo Sun San Diego Supercomputer Center, University of California, San Diego, 10100 Hopkins Drive, MC 0505, La Jolla, CA 92093, USA [e-mail: sunyibo@gmail.com]

Mike Surridge IT Innovation Centre, University of Southampton, 2 Venture Road, Southampton, SO16 7NP, UK

Steve Taylor IT Innovation Centre, University of Southampton, 2 Venture Road, Southampton, SO16 7NP, UK [e-mail: sjt@it-innovation.soton.ac.uk]

Wayne Thomson School of Engineering and Computer Science, Victoria University of Wellington, Kelburn Parade, Wellington, New Zealand [e-mail: Wayne.Thomson@mcs.vuw.ac.nz]

Ruppa K. Thulasiram Department of Computer Science, University of Manitoba, Winnipeg, MB R3T 2N2, Canada [e-mail: tulsi@cs.umanitoba.ca]

Sameer Tilak San Diego Supercomputer Center, University of California, San Diego, 10100 Hopkins Drive, MC 0505, La Jolla, CA 92093, USA [e-mail: sameer@sdsc.edu]

Amin Vahdat Department of Computer Science and Engineering, University of California, San Diego, 9500 Gilman Drive, MC 0404, La Jolla, CA 92093, USA [e-mail: vahdat@cs.ucsd.edu]

Srikumar Venugopal Department of Computer Science and Software Engineering, The University of Melbourne, Parkville, Melbourne, VIC 3010, Australia [e-mail: srikumar@csse.unimelb.edu.au]

Kerstin Voss Paderborn Center for Parallel Computing, University of Paderborn, Furstenallee 11, 33102 Paderborn, Germany [e-mail: kerstinv@upb.de]

Philipp Wieder Dortmund University of Technology, ITMC, Campus South, GB V, Room 101, August-Schmidt-Str. 12, 44227 Dortmund, Germany [e-mail:philipp.wieder@udo.edu]

John Wilkes HP Laboratories, 1501 Page Mill Rd., MS 1139, Palo Alto, CA 94304, USA [e-mail: john.wilkes@hp.com]

Ramin Yahyapour Dortmund University of Technology, ITMC, Campus South, GB V, Room 101, August-Schmidt-Str. 12, 44227 Dortmund, Germany [e-mail: ramin.yahyapour@udo.edu]

Chee Shin Yeo Department of Computer Science and Software Engineering, The University of Melbourne, Parkville, Melbourne, VIC 3010, Australia [e-mail: csyeo@csse.unimelb.edu.au]

Jia Yu Department of Computer Science and Software Engineering, The University of Melbourne, Parkville, Melbourne, VIC 3010, Australia [e-mail: yujia_mail@yahoo.com]

Wolfgang Ziegler Fraunhofer-Institut für Algorithmen, und Wissenschaftliches Rechnen SCAI, Schloss Birlinghoven, 53754 Sankt Augustin, Germany [e-mail: Wolfgang.Ziegler@scai.fraunhofer.de]

PREFACE

The growing popularity of the Internet and Web, and the availability of powerful computers and high-speed networks as low-cost commodity components, are changing the manner in which computing, communication, and business are carried out. These technological advances enable the coupling of a wide variety of geographically distributed resources, such as supercomputers, storage systems, databases, sensors, scientific instruments, and software services, to establish the next-generation paradigm for distributed computing, called *Grid computing*. The interest in creating Grids for sharing resources from multiple, "autonomous" organizations is growing due to the potential for solving large-scale problems that cannot be typically tackled using resources in a single organization. There are several initiatives and projects all over the world that are actively exploring the design and development of Grid technologies, service, and applications, and the infrastructure to support them.

The Grid is analogous in concept to the power (electricity) Grid. It aims to couple distributed resources, and offers consistent and inexpensive access to them irrespective of their physical location. Thus, Grid computing is enabling the delivery of computing as the fifth utility to users after water, gas, electricity, and telephone. Such a model of computing is popularly called "utility computing" in the business world where service providers maintain and supply information technology (IT) services to consumers, and receive payment in return.

As the Grid matures, a vision of a truly global Grid infrastructure has started to emerge. In this global Grid, computational resources are acquired on demand and provided with an agreed-on quality of service. Participation is open to all, and resources may be used or potentially provided by institutions, companies, or the general public. Such a global Grid will motivate the establishment of new marketplaces for trading application, computation, bandwidth, and storage services. These marketplaces will help enhance the value of utility delivered to the end users.

Ultimately, Grid computing requires a paradigm shift, whereby resources are traded, negotiated, allocated, provisioned, and monitored according to users' quality of service requirements. The *market-oriented Grid* will underpin the evolution of the Grid from a collection of computational islands into a global computational environment capable of delivering different levels of services, with efficient handling of risks and costs, depending on the preferences of the user. At the same time, it will provide economic "incentives" for service providers for sharing resources and encourage the delivery of services that meet users' quality-of-service expectations.

Such a market-oriented Grid will create value for all participants. Resource providers can generate revenue, allowing long-term investments in their resources, and thus, outsourcing of peak loads can be automated. Users can better express their preferences, trade costs against performance, access to a larger pool of resources, and negotiate service-level agreements (SLAs) to enhance the observed stability of their applications.

The purpose of this book, entitled *Market-Oriented Grid and Utility Computing*, is to capture the state of the art in both market-oriented Grid and utility computing research, and to identify potential research directions and technologies that will facilitate creation of a global commercial Grid system. We expect the book to serve as a reference for large audiences such as systems architects, practitioners, developers, new researchers, and graduate-level students. This book will also come with an associated Website (hosted at http://www.gridbus.org/gridmarket/) containing pointers to advanced online resources and teaching material.

ORGANIZATION OF THE BOOK

This book contains chapters authored by several leading experts in the field of market-oriented Grid and utility computing. The book is presented in a coordinated and integrated manner starting with the fundamentals, and followed by the technologies that implement them.

The contents of the book are organized into four parts:

I. Foundations
II. Business models
III. Policies and agreements
IV. Resource allocation and scheduling mechanisms

Part I presents fundamental concepts of market-oriented computing, introduces various market mechanisms along with their implications on global Grids followed by the issues and challenges in allocating resources in a decentralized computing environment. It also presents utility functions capturing goals of users and service providers, and various types of markets, such as options and commodity markets, for computing resources.

Part II covers business models for services providers and brokers supporting different types of distributed applications. It also presents business-rules-based models for managing virtual organizations, and for accounting operations and services in Grid computing environments.

Part III introduces policies, agreements, and specifications for the negotiation and establishment of contracts between providers and consumers. It also covers different approaches for resource allocation, based on SLAs and management of risks associated with SLA violations.

Part IV presents market-oriented resource allocation mechanisms and various technologies supporting different market models. It covers economic models, such as commodity models, reciprocation, auctions, and game theory, and middleware technologies such as Nimrod-G and Gridbus for market-oriented Grid computing and utility-oriented resource allocation.

ACKNOWLEDGMENTS

First and foremost, we are grateful to all the contributing authors for their time, effort, and understanding during the preparation of the book.

We thank Professor Albert Zomaya, editor of Wiley book series on parallel and distributed computing, for his enthusiastic support and guidance during the preparation of book and enabling us in easily navigating through Wiley's publication process.

We thank our family members Smrithi, Soumya, and Radha Buyya; and Andrea, Gretchen, and Katja Bubendorfer for their love and understanding during the preparation of the book.

Finally, we would like to thank the staff at Wiley, particularly Paul Petralia (Senior Editor), Anastasia Wasko, Michael Christian (Editorial Assistants), and Sanchari Sil (at Thomson Digital). They were wonderful to work with!

RAJKUMAR BUYYA

The University of Melbourne and Manjrasoft Pty Ltd, Australia

KRIS BUBENDORFER

Victoria University of Wellington, New Zealand

ACRONYMS

AAA	authentication, authorization, and accounting
AC	activity class; alternating current
aet	average execution time
ANC	average normalization cost
ANT	average normalized time
AO	agreement offer
API	application program interface
ASP	application service provider
AT	agreement template
BES	basic execution service
BFS	breadth-first search
BIC	Bayesian incentive compatibility
BLO	business-level objective
BoT	bag of tasks
BPEL	business process execution language
BT	backtracking
B2B	business-to-business (business–business)
B2C	business-to-consumer (business–consumer)
CAM	collaborative/cooperative awareness management/model
CAP	combinatorial allocation problem; catallactic access point
CCS	command–control subsystem
CD	cost distribution
CDE	CAM data extension
cdf	cumulative distribution/density function
CORA	coallocative oversubscribing resource allocation

COVITE	collaborative virtual team(s)
CP	control partition
CRH	collaborative resolution history
CSCW	computer-supported cooperative work
CSF	community scheduler framework; critical success factor
DAC	directed acyclic graph
DBC	deadline/budget-based constraint
DEISA	Distributed European Infrastructure for Supercomputing Applications
DF	derivative-following (algorithm)
DFS	depth-first search
DGAS	distributed Grid accounting system
DHT	distributed hash table
dl	deadline
DNS	domain name service
DRIVE	distributed resource infrastructure for a virtual economy
DSIC	dominant strategies incentive compatibility
DSS	database search service
EDL	encourage/discourage, linear
EDN	encourage/discourage, nonlinear
eet	expected execution time
EGEE	Enabling Grids for E-sciencE (proprietary name)
EMH	efficient market hypothesis
EN	enterprise network
EPIC	ex post incentive compatibility
EPIR	ex post individual rationality
EPR	endpoint reference
FCFS	first come–first serve
FLVM	first-level virtual machine (SLVM, TLVM = second-, third-level VM)
FQAN	fully qualified attribute name
FSK	frequency shift key(ing)
GA	genetic algorithm
GAF	general auction framework
GASA	Grid accounting services architecture
GASS	global access to secondary storage
GC	global constraint; greedy cost
GCC	Grid compute commodity
GFA	Grid-Federation agent
GIIS	Grid Information Indexing Service
GIS	Grid Information Service
GMD	Grid Market Directory
GMM	Grid market manager
GMP	Grid marketplace
GOC	Grid operations center

GP	guest partition
GPM	GMD portal manager
GQWS	GMD query Web service
GRAAP	Grid Resource Allocation Agreement Protocol
GRACE	Grid architecture for computational economy
GrADS	Grid Application Development Software
GRAM	Grid/Globus resource allocation management
GRASP	greedy randomized adaptive search procedure
GRB	Grid resource broker
GSC	Grid service customer
GSI	Globus security infrastructure
GSP	Grid service provider
GTS	Grid trade server/Trading Service
GUI	graphical user interface
HEFT	heterogeneous earliest finish time
HP	host partition
HPC	high-performance computing
HPCC	high-performance computing center
IaaS	infrastructure as a service
IBV	integrated bid vector
ICE	IntercontinentalExchange (proprietary)
ICNIP	iterated contract-net interaction protocol
IETF	Internet Engineering Task Force
IP	integer programming
IPR	intellectual property right
IRB	Intel Research Berkeley
iRODS	Internet Rule Oriented Data System (proprietary)
iSCSI	Internet small-computer systems interface
ISM	industrial–scientific–medical (RF band)
ISP	Internet service provider
IT	information technology
JSDL	job submission description language
KPI	key performance indicator
(L)APW	(linearized) augmented plane wave
LCG	LHC computing Grid
LEAD	linked environments and atmospheric discovery
LHC	Large Hadron Collider
LO	local orbital
LRM	local resource manager
MA	market authority
MACE	multiattribute combinatorial exchange
MAP	MACE allocation problem
MAUT	multiattribute utility theory
MCDM	multicriteria decisionmaking
MCT	minimum completion time

MDFA	metadata flow analyzer
MDS	message delivery service; monitoring and discovery service; metacomputing directory service
MDV	metadata variable
MET	minimum execution time
MFSS	maxillofacial surgery simulation
MGS	master Grid service
MRT	modified real time
MSB	modified slack-based
MTTF	mean time to failure
MTTR	mean time to respond
NAA	numerical aerodynamic application
NGS	National Grid Service (UK)
NP	nonparametric
OASIS	Organization for Advancement of Structural Information Standards
OC	opportunity cost
OCEAN	Open Competition Exchange and Arbitration Network
OGF	Open Grid Forum
OGSA	open Grid service(s) architecture
OGSI	open Grid service(s) infrastructure
OLB	optimistic load balancing
OSG	Open Science Grid
P&L	profit and loss
pdf	probability distribution/density function
PLC	PlanetLab Center
PoF	probability of failure
PSA	parameter sweep application
PSHA	probabilistic seismic hazard analysis
P2P	peer-to-peer (P^3 = parallel P2P)
PV	payload variable
QoE	quality of experience
QoPS	QoS for parallel (job) scheduling (VQoPS = value-aware QoPS; DVQoPS = dynamic VQoPS)
QoS	quality of service
QoWL	QoS-aware (Grid) workflow language
QWE	QoS-aware (Grid) workflow engine
RA	risk assessment
RI	reputation index
RLQ	resource lookup query
RM	risk management
rms	root mean square
RMS	resource management system
ROI	return on investment
RPC	remote procedure call

RSS	resource selection service
rt	ready time
RUQ	resource update query
RUS	resource usage service
SaaS	software as a service
SAGE	storage accounting for Grid environments
SAM	SLA action manager
SB	slack-based
SCEC	Southern California Earthquake Center
SCS	social choice function
SD	supplier database; Storage@desk
SDT	service description term
SF	slack factor
SGVA	secure generalized Vickrey auction (vSGVA = verifiable SGVA)
SGT	strain green tensor (seismic index used by SCEC)
SLA	service-level agreement
SLI	service-level indicator
SLO	service-level objective
SMI	special model of interaction
SOA	service-oriented architecture
SOAP	Simple Object Access Protocol (proprietary)
SOI	service-oriented infrastructure
SP	service provider/profile
SPEC	Standard Performance Evaluation Corporation
SPMD	single program–multiple data
SRM	storage resource management
SSL	Secure Sockets Layer (proprietary)
SVM	standard virtual machine
TD	time distribution
TF	tolerance factor
TFE	task-farming engine
TL	temporary list
UCITA	Uniform Computer Information Transaction Act
UETA	Uniform Electronic Transaction Act
UI	user interface
UNCITRAL	United Nations Commission on International Trade Law
UR	usage record
USP	unique selling point
VCG	Vickrey-Clarke-Groves
VE	virtual enterprise
VGE	Vienna Grid Environment
VLDB	very large database
VM	virtual machine
VO	virtual organization
VOMS	virtual organization membership service

VPOT	verifiable proxy oblivious transfer
WAP	wireless access point
WfMC	Workflow Management Coalition
WORM	write once–read many
WQ	work queue
WS	workstation; Web services
WSAS	Web Services Agreement Specification
WSC	Web services consumer
WSLA	Web Service Level Agreement
WSP	Web services provider
WSRF	Web services resource framework
WWG	World Wide Grid
WWW	World Wide Web
XML	eXtensible Modeling Language
XPML	eXtended Parametric Modeling Language

PART I

FOUNDATIONS

1

MARKET-ORIENTED COMPUTING AND GLOBAL GRIDS: AN INTRODUCTION

RAJKUMAR BUYYA AND SRIKUMAR VENUGOPAL

1.1 INSPIRATION

Following Alessandro Volta's invention of the electric battery in 1800, Thomas Edison and Nikola Tesla paved the way for electricity's widespread use by inventing the electric bulb and alternating current (AC), respectively. Figure 1.1 shows Volta demonstrating the battery for Napoleon I in 1801 at the French National Institute, Paris. Regardless of whether Volta envisioned it, his invention evolved into a worldwide electrical power Grid that provides dependable, consistent, and pervasive access to utility power and has become an integral part of modern society [1].

Inspired by the electrical power Grid's pervasiveness, ease of use, and reliability, computer scientists in the mid-1990s began exploring the design and development of an analogous infrastructure, called the *computational power Grid* [4], for wide-area parallel and distributed computing [6]. The motivation for computational Grids was initially driven by large-scale, resource (computational and data)-intensive scientific applications that require more resources than a single computer [PC, workstation (WS), supercomputer, or cluster] could provide in a single administrative domain. A Grid enables the sharing, selection, and aggregation of a wide variety of geographically distributed resources, including supercomputers, storage systems, data sources, and specialized devices owned by different organizations for solving large-scale resource-intensive problems in science, engineering, and commerce. Because of its potential to make impact on the twenty-first century as much as the electric power

Market-Oriented Grid and Utility Computing Edited by Rajkumar Buyya and Kris Bubendorfer

Figure 1.1 Volta demonstrates the battery for Napoleon I at the French National Institute, Paris, in 1801. The painting (by N. Cianfanelli, 1841) is from the Zoological Section of "La Specula" at the National History Museum, Florence University, Italy.

Grid did on twentieth century, Grid computing has been hailed as the next revolution after the Internet and the Web.

These developments foreshadow the realization of the vision of Leonard Kleinrock, one of the chief scientists of the original Advanced Research Projects Agency Network (ARPANET) project that seeded the Internet, who said in 1969 [3]: "As of now, computer networks are still in their infancy, but as they grow up and become sophisticated, we will probably see the spread of '*computer utilities,*' which, like present electric and telephone utilities, will service individual homes and offices across the country."

Utility computing is envisioned to be the next generation of information technology (IT) evolution that depicts how computing needs of users can be fulfilled in the future IT industry [13]. Its analogy is derived from the real world, where service providers maintain and supply utility services, such as electrical power, gas, and water to consumers. Consumers in turn pay service providers according to their usage. Therefore, the underlying design of utility computing is based on a service provisioning model, where users (consumers) pay providers for using computing power only when they need to.

1.2 GRID COMPUTING

Grid computing follows the service-oriented architecture and provides the hardware and software services and infrastructure for secure and uniform access to heterogeneous resources and enables the formation and management of virtual organizations (VOs). It also supports application and services composition, workflow expression, scheduling, and execution management and service-level agreement (SLA)-based allocation of resources.

As there are a large number of projects around the world working on developing Grids for different purposes at different scales, several definitions of Grid abound. The Globus project (Argonne National Laboratory, USA) defines Grid as "an infrastructure that enables the integrated, collaborative use of high-end computers, networks, databases, and scientific instruments owned and managed by multiple organizations." Another utility notion-based Grid definition put forward by the Gridbus project (University of Melbourne, Australia) is "Grid is a type of parallel and distributed system that enables the sharing, selection, and aggregation of geographically distributed 'autonomous' resources dynamically at runtime depending on their availability, capability, performance, cost, and users' Quality of Service (QoS) requirements."

The development of the Grid infrastructure, both hardware and software, has become the focus of a large community of researchers and developers in both academia and industry. The major problems being addressed by Grid developments are the social problems involved in collaborative research:

- Improving distributed management while retaining full control over locally managed resources
- Improving the availability of data and identifying problems and solutions to data access patterns
- Providing researchers with a uniform user-friendly environment that enables access to a wider range of physically distributed facilities improving productivity

A high-level view of activities involved within a seamless and scalable Grid environment is shown in Figure 1.2. Grid resources are registered within one or more

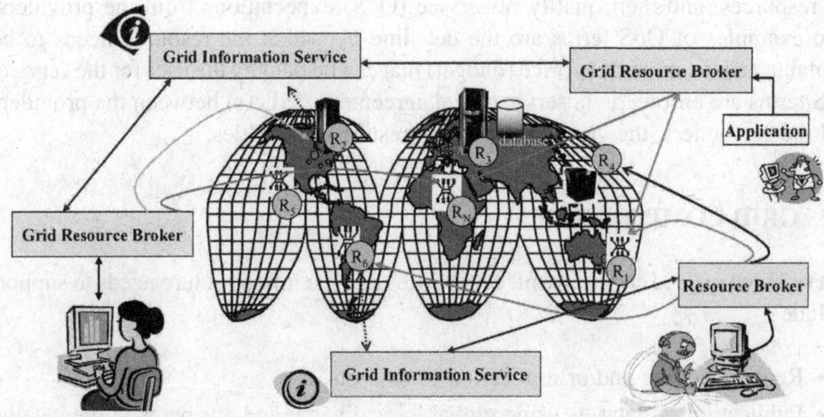

Figure 1.2 A worldwide Grid computing environment.

Grid information services. The end users submit their application requirements to the Grid resource broker, which then discovers suitable resources by querying the information services, schedules the application jobs for execution on these resources, and then monitors their processing until they are completed. A more complex scenario would involve more requirements and therefore, Grid environments involve services such as security, information, directory, resource allocation, application development, execution management, resource aggregation, and scheduling. Software tools and services providing these capabilities to link computing capability and data sources in order to support distributed analysis and collaboration are collectively known as *Grid middleware*.

In order to provide users with a seamless computing environment, the Grid middleware systems need to solve several challenges originating from the inherent features of the Grid [8]. One of the main challenges is the heterogeneity that results from the vast range of technologies, both hardware and software, encompassed by the Grid. Another challenge involves the handling of Grid resources that are spread across political and geographic boundaries and are under the administrative control of different organizations. It follows that the availability and performance of Grid resources are unpredictable as requests from within an administrative domain may gain higher priority over requests from outside. Thus, the dynamic nature of Grid environment poses yet another challenge.

To tackle these challenges, a Grid architecture has been proposed based on the creation of virtual organizations (VOs) [9] by different physical (real-world) organizations coming together to share resources and collaborating in order to achieve a common goal. A VO defines the resources available for the participants and the rules for accessing and using the resources. Within a VO, participants belonging to member organizations are allocated resource shares according to the urgency and priority of a request as determined by the objectives of the VO. Another complementary Grid architecture [10] is based on economic principles in which resource providers (owners) compete to provide the best service to resource consumers (users) who select appropriate resources according to their specific requirements, the price of the resources, and their quality-of-service (QoS) expectations from the providers. Two examples of QoS terms are the deadline by which the resource needs to be available and the maximum price (budget) that can be paid by the user for the service. QoS terms are enforced via service-level agreements (SLAs) between the providers and the consumers, the violation of which results in penalties.

1.3 GRID COMPONENTS

In a worldwide Grid environment, capabilities that the infrastructure needs to support include

- Remote storage and/or replication of datasets
- Publication of datasets using global logical name and attributes in the catalog
- Security—access authorization and uniform authentication

- Uniform access to remote resources (data and computational resources)
- Publication of services and access cost
- Composition of distributed applications using diverse software components including legacy programs
- Discovery of suitable datasets by their global logical names or attributes
- Discovery of suitable computational resources
- Mapping and scheduling of jobs (aggregation of distributed services)
- Submission, monitoring, and steering of job execution
- Movement of code/data between user desktop computers and distributed Grid resources
- Enforcement of QoS requirements
- Metering and accounting of resource usage

These capabilities in Grid computing environments play a significant role in enabling a variety of scientific, engineering, and business applications. Various Grid components providing these capabilities are arranged into layers. Each layer builds on the services offered by the lower layer in addition to interacting and cooperating with components at the same level (e.g., resource broker invoking secure process management services provided by core middleware). Figure 1.3 shows four layers of the hardware and software stack within a typical Grid architecture: fabric, core middleware, user-level middleware, and applications/portals layers. Adaptive management capabilities are supported by implementing principles of market-oriented resource management mechanisms in different horizontal layers.

The *Grid fabric* layer consists of distributed resources such as computers, networks, storage devices, and scientific instruments. The computational resources

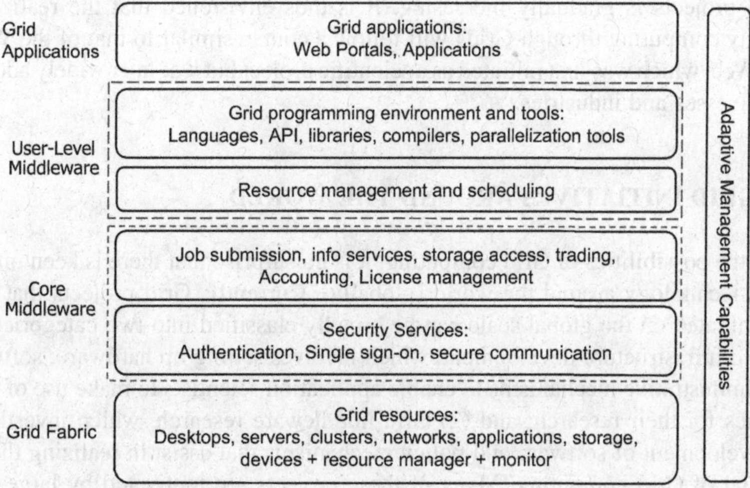

Figure 1.3 A layered Grid architecture and components.

represent multiple architectures such as clusters, supercomputers, servers, and ordinary PCs that run a variety of operating systems (such as UNIX variants or Windows). Scientific instruments such as telescopes and sensor networks provide real-time data that can be transmitted directly to computational sites or are stored in a database.

The *core Grid* middleware offers services such as remote process management, coallocation of resources, storage access, information registration and discovery, security, and aspects of QoS such as resource reservation and trading. These services abstract the complexity and heterogeneity of the fabric level by providing a consistent method for accessing distributed resources.

The *user-level Grid* middleware utilizes the interfaces provided by the low-level middleware to provide higher-level abstractions and services. These include application development environments, programming tools, and resource brokers for managing resources and scheduling application tasks for execution on global resources.

Grid applications and portals are typically developed using Grid-enabled programming environments and interfaces and are deployed on Grids using brokering and scheduling services provided by user-level middleware. An example application, such as parameter simulation of a grand-challenge problem, would require computational power and access to remote datasets, and may need to interact with scientific instruments. Grid portals offer Web-enabled application services, where users can submit their jobs to remote resources and collect results from them through the Web.

The design aims and benefits of Grids are analogous to those of utility computing, thus highlighting the potential and suitability of Grids to be used as utility computing environments. The current trend of implementing Grids based on open standard service-based architectures to improve interoperability is a step toward supporting utility computing. Even though most existing Grid applications are scientific research and collaboration projects, the number of applications in business and industry-related projects is gradually increasing. It is thus envisioned that the realization of utility computing through Grids will follow a course similar to that of the World Wide Web, which was first initiated as a scientific project but was later widely adopted by businesses and industries.

1.4 GRID INITIATIVES AROUND THE WORLD

Given the possibilities of Grid computing, it is no surprise that there is keen interest in this technology around the world (globally). Currently, Grid projects that have been initiated on the global scale can be broadly classified into two categories [8]: (1) Grid infrastructure development, which involves setting up hardware, software, and administrative mechanisms to enable application scientists to make use of these facilities for their research; and (2) Grid middleware research, which investigates the development of software and policy mechanisms that assist in realizing the full potential of Grid computing. Many of these projects are motivated by large-scale scientific projects that will involve the production and analysis of data at an unprecedented scale. One frequently cited such large-scale scientific project is the Large Hadron Collider (LHC) experiments [11] at the European Organisation for Nuclear Research (CERN), which began data production in 2008. The volume of data generated by these experiments is in the petabyte (PB) range, for distribution to physicists around the world for analysis. As the Grid has been mandated as the IT infrastructure for handling the massive workloads of LHC experiments, all the collaborating nations are setting up Grid infrastructure in one form or another. In the following sections, we will describe some of the major Grid infrastructure and middleware projects around the world.

1.4.1 United States of Amercia (USA)

Production Grid testbeds for various application domains have been deployed over physical (hardware) Grid infrastructure such as the National Science Foundation (NSF)-funded TeraGrid [17] in the United States, which provides over 40 tera-floating-point operations per second (Tflops) of computing power at eight sites around the country with 2 PB of available storage interconnected by a network operating at a speed of 10–30 gigabits per second (Gbps). The BioInformatics Research Network (BIRN) is another testbed for the purpose of furthering biomedical science by sharing data stored in different repositories around USA. The NEESGrid enables scientists in the earthquake engineering community to carry out experiments in distributed locations and analyse data through a uniform interface.

Of the Grid middleware efforts in the United States, the Globus toolkit from the Globus Alliance led by Argonne National Laboratory is the most widely known. Other notable efforts are the Condor project (University of Wisconsin, Madison) for high-throughput computing mechanisms, and "i Rule Oriented Data Systems" (iRODS) [58] from the San Diego Supercomputing Center (SDSC) for Grid data management. In addition, several commercial organizations such as IBM, Sun Microsystems, Hewlett-Packard (HP), and Oracle are actively involved in the development of enterprise and global utility Grid technologies.

1.4.2 Europe

Two pioneering Grid efforts in Europe, started in early 2001, were the United Kingdom (UK)'s e-Science program [5] and the European Union (EU)-funded Data Grid project [11]. The latter was succeeded by the EGEE (Enabling Grids for E-sciencE) project, which aims to create a Grid infrastructure available to scientists and to develop robust middleware for application deployment. CERN manages the LHC Computing Grid (LCG) project, which has created a production Grid infrastructure for researchers involved in the experiments using the LHC.

Other notable EU-funded projects include GridLab [53], providing a Grid application development toolkit; Cactus framework, for scientific programming; GridSphere, for creating a Web portal environment for Grid users; P-Grade, providing a visual environment for application development; Triana, for workflow formulation; and OGSA-DAI, for integration of relational databases in Grid environments.

1.4.3 Asia–Pacific

Several countries in the Asia–Pacific region have started national Grid programs similar to those initiated in the United States and Europe. In addition, countries such as Australia, China, Japan, South Korea, and Singapore are active participants in worldwide Grid projects such as the LCG. Some of the notable Grid programs are the National Research Grid Initiative (NAREGI) in Japan, China National Grid in China, K*Grid in South Korea, and Garuda National Grid in India.

Prominent Grid middleware projects include the Ninf project (Tokyo Institute of Technology) for building a Grid-based remote procedure call (RPC) system [29], the Grid Datafarm (Gfarm) project (AIST, Japan) for providing a petascale data storage–processing system, the Nimrod/G project (Monash University, Australia) for parametric computations on Grid resources [28], and the Gridbus project (University of Melbourne, Australia) for market-oriented Grid and utility computing [54].

1.4.4 Standardization Efforts

Given the large amount of middleware development happening in this area of research, standardization is important to ensure interoperability between different products and implementations. Grid standardization efforts led by the Open Grid Forum (OGF) [12] have produced standards for almost all aspects of Grid technology. Work at the OGF has produced the open Grid service infrastructure (OGSI) specification and its successor, the Web services resource framework (WSRF), which have paved the way for integration of Web services within Grid architecture. This is important as Web services allow Grid developers to take advantage of standard message formats and mechanisms such as HTTP and XML for communicating between heterogeneous components and architectures. Other standardization bodies such as World Wide Web Consortium (W3C), Organization for Advancement of Structured Information Standards (OASIS), and Internet Engineering Task Force (IETF) also produce standards relevant to aspects of Grid Computing.

1.5 MARKET-ORIENTED GRID RESOURCE MANAGEMENT

Resource management and scheduling in Grid environments is a complex undertaking. The geographic distribution of resources owned by different organizations with different usage policies, cost models, and varying load and availability patterns is problematic. The *producers* (resource owners) and *consumers* (resource users) have different goals, objectives, strategies, and requirements. Classical Grids are motivated by an assumption that coordinated access to diverse and geographically distributed resources is valuable. However, this paradigm needs mechanisms that allow not only such coordinated access but also sustainable, scalable models and policies that promote utility-oriented sharing of Grid resources.

To address these resource management challenges, several groups of researchers have proposed a distributed computational economy-based[1] framework [10,14,50,56], for resource allocation and to regulate supply and demand of the available resources. This economy-based framework offers an incentive to resource owners for contributing and sharing resources, and motivates resource users to think about tradeoffs between the processing time (e.g., deadline) and computational cost (e.g., budget), depending on their QoS requirements. It can be observed that, even in electricity Grids, bid-based electricity trading over the Internet has been adopted to develop competitive forces in the electricity marketplace [20].

Resource management and scheduling systems for Grid computing need to manage resources and application execution depending on resource consumers' and owners' requirements, and they need to continuously adapt to changes in the availability of resources. This requirement introduces a number of challenging issues that need to be addressed, namely: site autonomy, heterogeneous substrate, policy extensibility, resource allocation or coallocation, online control, resource trading, and QoS-based scheduling.

1.5.1 Assessing Wants and Needs

In an economy-based Grid computing environment, resource management systems need to provide mechanisms and tools that allow resource consumers (end users) and providers (resource owners) to express their requirements and facilitate the realization of their goals. Resource consumers need

- A utility model to determine how consumers demand resources and their preference parameters
- A broker that supports resource discovery and strategies for application scheduling on distributed resources dynamically at runtime depending on their availability, capability, and cost along with user-defined QoS requirements

Resource providers need

- Tools and mechanisms that support price specification and generation schemes to increase system utilization
- Protocols that support service publication, trading, and accounting

For the market to be competitive and healthy, coordination mechanisms are required to help reach equilibrium price—the market price at which the supply of a service equals the quantity demanded.

1.5.2 Computational Economy and Its Benefits

Like all systems involving goals, resources, and actions, computations can be viewed in economic terms. With the proliferation of networks, high-end computing systems

[1]The terms "economic/economy-based" and "market-based" are synonymous and interchangeable.

architecture has moved from centralized toward decentralized models of control and action; the use of economy-driven market mechanisms would be a natural extension of this development. The ability of trade and price mechanisms to combine local decisions by diverse entities into globally effective characteristics reflect their value for organizing computations in large systems such as Internet-scale computational Grids.

The need for an economy-driven resource management and scheduling system comes from the answers to the following questions:

- What constitutes the Grid, and who owns its resources?
- What motivates resource owners to contribute their resources to the Grid?
- Is it possible to have access to all resources in the Grid by contributing our resource?
- If not, how do we have access to all Grid resources?
- If we have access to resources through collaboration, are we allowed to use them for any other purposes?
- Do resource owners charge the same or a different price for different users?
- Is access cost the same for peak and off-peak hours?
- How can resource owners maximize their profits?
- How can users solve their problems within a minimum cost?
- How can a user get high priority over others?
- If the user relaxes the deadline by which results are required, can solution cost be reduced?

Several individuals or organizations that have contributed resources to the Grid have been motivated largely by the public good, prizes, fun, fame, or collaborative advantage. This is clearly evident from the construction of private Grids (but on volunteer resources) or research testbeds such as SETI@Home [18], Condor pool [38], and TeraGrid [17]. The chances of gaining access to such computational testbeds for solving commercial problems are low. Furthermore, contributing resources to a testbed does not guarantee access to all the other resources in that testbed.

Commercial companies such as Entropia, ProcessTree, Popular Power, United Devices, and DataSynapse are exploiting idle central processing unit (CPU) cycles from desktop machines to build a commercial computational Grid infrastructure based on peer-to-peer (P2P) networks [19]. These companies are able to develop large-scale infrastructure for Internet computing and use it for their own financial gain by charging for access to CPU cycles for their customers, without offering fiscal incentive to all resource contributors. However, in the long run, this model does not support the creation of a maintainable and sustainable infrastructure, as the resource contributors have no incentive for their continued contribution. Therefore, a Grid economy seems a better model for managing and handling requirements of both Grid providers and consumers. The benefits of economy-based resource management include the following:

- It helps in building a large-scale Grid as it offers incentive for resource owners to contribute their (idle) resources for others to use and profit from.
- It helps in regulating the supply and demand for resources.
- It offers an economic incentive for users to back off when solving low-priority problems and thus encourages the solution of time-critical problems first.
- It removes the need for a central coordinator (during negotiation).
- It offers uniform treatment of all resources; that is, it allows trading of everything including computational power, memory, storage, network bandwidth/latency [22], data, and devices or instruments.
- It allows users to express their requirements and objectives.
- It helps in developing scheduling policies that are user-centric rather than system-centric.
- It offers an efficient mechanism for allocation and management of resources.
- It helps in building a highly scalable system as the decisionmaking process is distributed across all users and resource owners.
- It supports a simple and effective basis for offering differentiated services for different applications at different times.
- Finally, it places the power in the hands of both resource owners and users, enabling them to make their own decisions to maximize the utility and profit.

1.6 REQUIREMENTS FOR ECONOMY-BASED GRID SYSTEMS

To deliver value to users greater than that possible with traditional systems, economy-based resource management systems need to provide mechanisms and tools that allow resource consumers (end users) and providers (resource owners) to express their requirements and facilitate the realization of their goals. In other words, they need (1) the means to express their requirements, valuations, and objectives (*value expression*); (2) scheduling policies to translate them into resource allocations (*value translation*); and (3) mechanisms to enforce selection and allocation of differential services, and dynamic adaptation to changes in their availability at runtime (*value enforcement*). Similar requirements are raised [2] for market-based systems in a single-administrative-domain environment such as clusters, and they are limited to cooperative economic models since they aim for social welfare. Grids need to use *competitive economic models* as different resource providers and resource consumers have different goals, objectives, strategies, and requirements that vary with time.

Essentially, resource consumers need a *utility model* to allow them to specify resource requirements and constraints. For example, the Nimrod/G broker allows users to specify the deadline and budget constraints along with optimization parameters such as optimizing for time (*value expression*). They need *brokers* that provide strategies for choosing appropriate resources (*value translation*) and dynamically adapt to changes in resource availability at runtime to meet user requirements (*value enforcement*). The resource owners need mechanisms for *price generation schemes* to increase system utilization and *protocols* that help them offer competitive services (*value expression*). For the market to be competitive and healthy, coordination mechanisms are required that help the market reach an equilibrium price—the price at which the supply of a service equals the quantity demanded. Grid resources have their schedulers (e.g., OS or queuing system) that allocate resources (*value translation*). A number of research systems have explored QoS-based resource (e.g., CPU time and network bandwidth [22,23]) allocation in operating systems and queuing systems, but the inclusion of QoS into mainstream systems has been slow-paced (e.g., the Internet mostly uses the best effort allocation policy [24], but this is changing with IPv6 [25]). Some research systems support resource reservation in advance (e.g., reserving a slot from time t_1 to t_2 using the Globus Architecture for Reservation and Allocation (GARA) [21] and binding a job to it) and allocate resources during reserved time (*value enforcement*).

1.7 MARKET-ORIENTED GRID ARCHITECTURE

A reference service-oriented architecture for market-oriented Grids is shown in Figure 1.4. The key players in a market-oriented Grid are the Grid user, Grid resource broker, Grid middleware services, and Grid service providers (GSPs). The Grid user wants to make use of Grids to complete their applications. Refactoring existing applications is thus essential to ensure that these applications are Grid-enabled to run on Grids [26]. The Grid user also needs to express the service requirements to be fulfilled by GSPs. Varying QoS parameters, such as a deadline for the application to be completed and budget to be paid on completion, are defined by different Grid users,

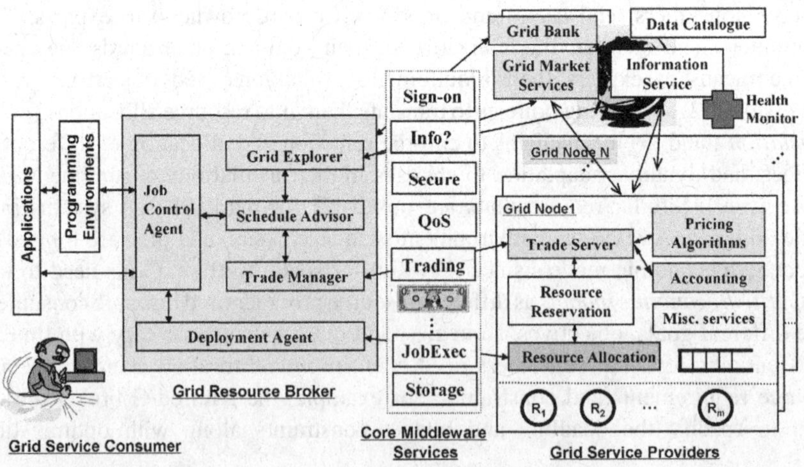

Figure 1.4 A reference service-oriented architecture for utility Grids [1].

thus resulting in dynamic fluctuation of peak and nonpeak service demands. The Grid resource broker then discovers appropriate Grid middleware services on the basis of these service demand patterns and QoS requirements, and dynamically schedules applications on them at runtime, depending on their availability, capability, and costs. A GSP needs tools and mechanisms that support pricing specifications and schemes so they can attract users and improve resource utilization. They also require protocols that support service publication and negotiation, accounting, and payment.

The Grid resource broker comprises the following components:

- *Job control agent*—interacts with users to determine the application profile that is used to create jobs that are executed on the Grid resources. These jobs are then input to the schedule advisor. The control agent also ensures that the jobs are persistent and their status is properly maintained.
- *Grid explorer*—discovers computational and data resources, including their current and future status, and also their prices.
- *Schedule advisor*—receives the list of jobs from the control agent and the list of resources from the Grid explorer. It uses these inputs to assign jobs to the suitable Grid resources such that the users' requirements are satisfied. It keeps track of the progress of execution and makes changes in the schedule accordingly.
- *Trade manager*—negotiates with resources and services selected by the schedule advisor and forms SLAs with them using pricing information gathered from the market directory and past history. It then monitors the compliance of these agreements.
- *Deployment agent*—executes jobs on the selected resources according to the assignment performed by the schedule advisor. If any advance reservations have been negotiated by the trade manager, this component also claims the nodes allocated before submitting jobs. It monitors job execution and reports job status periodically.

Traditional core Grid middleware focuses on providing infrastructure services for secure and uniform access to distributed resources. Supported features include security, single signon, remote process management, storage access, data management, and information services. An example of such middleware is the Globus toolkit [27], which is a widely adopted Grid technology in the Grid community. Market-oriented Grids require additional service-driven Grid middleware infrastructure, which includes

- *Grid market directory*—allows GSPs to publish their services so as to inform and attract users.
- *Trade server*—negotiates with Grid resource broker on the basis of pricing algorithms set by the GSP and sells access to resources by recording resource usage details and billing the users according to the agreed on pricing policy.
- *Pricing algorithms*—specifies prices to be charged to users on the basis of the GSP's objectives, such as maximizing profit or resource utilization at varying times and for different users.

- *Accounting and charging*—records resource usage and bills the users according to the terms negotiated and agreed to between Grid resource broker and trade server.

An end-to-end realization of market-oriented Grid supported by the Gridbus middleware is discussed in Chapter 26.

1.8 OPERATIONAL FLOW IN A MARKET-ORIENTED GRID

Figure 1.5 shows how services are assembled on demand in a market-oriented Grid. The application code is the legacy application to be run on the market-oriented Grid. Users first compose their application as a distributed application such as a parameter sweep using visual application composer tools (step 1). The parameter sweep model creates multiple independent jobs, each with a different parameter. This model is well suited for Grid computing environments wherein challenges such as load volatility, high network latencies, and high probability of individual node failures make it difficult to adopt a programming approach that favors tightly coupled systems. Accordingly, a parameter sweep application has been termed as a "killer application" for the Grid [28].

Visual tools allow rapid composition of applications for Grids by hiding the associated complexity from the user. The user's analysis and QoS requirements are submitted to the Grid resource broker (step 2). The Grid resource broker first discovers

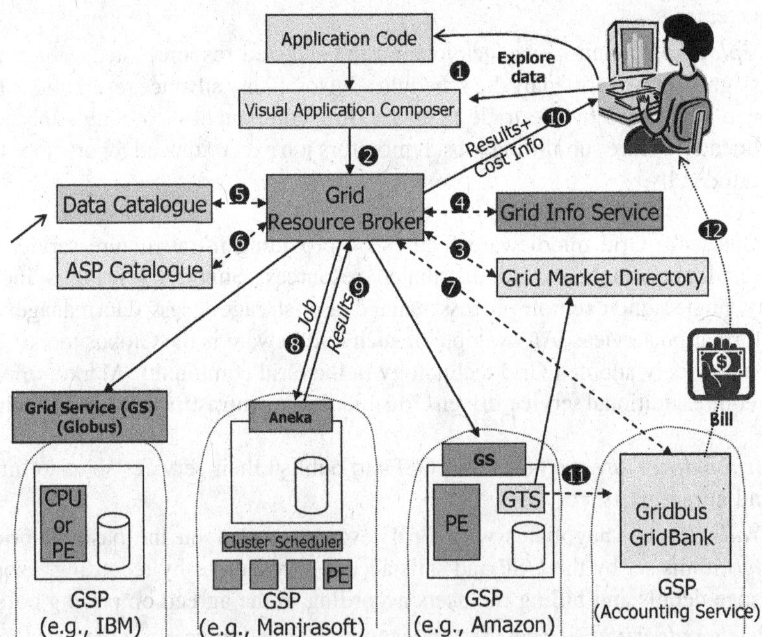

Figure 1.5 On-demand assembly of services in a utility Grid.

suitable Grid service providers (step 3) and capabilities of their services to meet QoS requirements of users, including price (step 4) using the Grid Market Directory and Grid Information Services, respectively. The broker then identifies the list of data sources or replicas through a data catalog and selects the optimal ones (step 5). The broker also identifies the list of GSPs that provides the required application services using the application service provider (ASP) catalog (step 6). The broker checks that the user has the necessary credit or authorized share to utilize the requested Grid services (step 7). The broker scheduler assigns and deploys jobs to Grid services that meet user QoS requirements (step 8). The broker agent on the Grid resource at the GSP then executes the job and returns the results (step 9). The broker consolidates the results before passing them back to the user (step 10). The metering system charges the user by passing the resource usage information to the accounting service (step 11). The accounting service reports remaining resource share allocation and credit available to the user (step 12).

1.9 MARKET-ORIENTED SYSTEMS IN PRACTICE

Economics has a long history both as a set of mechanisms by which human commerce is enacted and as a field of study involving analysis and research of these mechanisms of commerce (resource allocation and management). As these mechanisms have evolved with society, they tend to be resilient and flexible, and offer much that is directly applicable for use in computer systems. Various economic theories and models, including micro- and macroeconomic principles that can be applied for Grid computing [16], include the following:

- Commodity market models
- Posted-price models
- Bargaining models
- Tendering or contract-net models
- Auction models
- Bid-based proportional resource-sharing models
- Cooperative bartering models
- Monopoly and oligopoly

Various criteria used for judging the effectiveness of a market model [55] are social welfare (global good of all), Pareto efficiency (global perspective), individual rationality (better off by participating in negotiation), stability (mechanisms that cannot be manipulated, i.e., that behave in the desired manner), computational efficiency (protocols should not consume too much computation time), and distribution and communication efficiency (communication overhead to capture a desirable global solution).

Several research systems (see Table 1.1) have explored the use of different economic models for trading resources to manage resources in different application

TABLE 1.1 Computational Economy–Based Distributed Resource Management Systems

System Name	Economic Model	Platform	Remarks
Mariposa [47] (UC Berkeley)	Bidding (tendering/contract-net); pricing based on load and historical information	Distributed database	Supports budget-based query processing and storage management
Mungi [48] (Univ. New South Wales)	Commodity market (renting storage space that increases as available storage runs low, forcing users to release unneeded storage)	Storage servers	Supports storage objects based on bank accounts from which rent is collected for storage occupied by objects
Popcorn [40] (Hebrew Univ.)	Auction (highest bidder gets access to resource and it transfers credits from buyer to the seller account)	Web browsers (*popcorn parallel code* runs within a browser of provider)	Popcorn API-based parallel applications need to specify a budget for processing each of its modules
Java Market [41] (Johns Hopkins Univ.)	QoS-based computational market [resource owner receives $f(j,t)$ award for completing f in time t]	Web browsers (JavaMarket runs *standard Java applets* within a browser)	One can sell CPU cycles by pointing Java-enabled browser to portal and allow execution of applets
Enhanced MOSIX [42]	Commodity market (resource cost of each node is known)	Clusters of computers (Linux PCs)	Supports process migration such that overall cost of job execution is kept low
Xenoservers [44] (Cambridge Univ.)	Bidding (proportional resource sharing)	Single computer	Accounted execution of untrusted code
D'Agents [45] (Dartmouth College)	Bidding (proportional resource sharing)	Single computer or mobile agents	Agent's bid function is proportional to benefit
Rexec/Anemone [46] (UC Berkeley)	Bidding/auction (for proportional resource sharing)	Clusters (a market-based cluster batch queue system)	Users assign utility value to their application and system allocates resources proportionally
Spawn [39] (Xerox PARC)	Second-price/Vickery auction (uses sponsorship model for funding money to each task depending on some requirements)	Network on workstations; each WS executes a single task per time slice	Supports execution of concurrent program expressed in the form of hierarchy of processes that expand and shrink size depending on the resource cost

CSAR supercomputing center [52] (Manchester)	Commodity market and priority-based model (they charge for CPU, memory, storage, and human support services)	MPPs, Crays, clusters, and storage servers	Any application can use this service, and QoS is proportional to user priority and scheduling mechanisms
Nimrod-G [15] (Monash Univ.)	Supports economy models such as commodity market, spot market, and contract-net for price establishment	Worldwide Grid (resources Grid-enabled using Globus middleware)	A *real* system that supports deadline and budget constrained algorithms for scheduling task-farming and data parallel applications on global Grids.
G-Commerce [49] (UC Santa Barbara)	Commodity and auctions	Simulates hypothetical consumers and produces	Explores strategies for pricing Grid resources to enable resource trading
OCEAN [51] (Univ. Florida)	Continuous double auction	A Java-based platform with distributed PCs	Explores the use of continuous double auction for trading computational resources
Stanford Peers [49] (Stanford Univ.)	Auctions with cooperative bartering in a cooperative sharing environment	Simulates storage trading for content management	Demonstrates distributed resource trading policies based on auctions by *simulation*
Gridbus [54] (Univ. Melbourne)	Both commodity and auction models for clusters, computational and data Grids	Clusters, clouds, and Grids	Provides services for ensuring end-to-end QoS at various levels for users in cluster and Grid environment
CatNets [57] (Europe)	Interconnected markets of providers and consumers	Grid and service-oriented computing	The approach is to have free markets of participants wherein consumers procure services on the basis of dynamic price changes caused by market processes.
SORMA [59] (Europe)	Market-based system consisting of self-interested resource brokers and user-agents	Open Grid market on top of existing resource management systems	The open Grid market matches users and brokers; resource allocation is mediated via SLAs
GridEcon [60] (Europe)	Markets for trading of resources between small and medium enterprises	Resources managed by commercial service providers	At the time of writing, the project is researching into a viable business model for trading services in an open market

domains: CPU cycles, storage space, database query processing, and distributed computing. They include Spawn [39], Popcorn [40], JavaMarket [41], Enhanced MOSIX [42], JaWS [43], Xenoservers [44], D'Agents [45], Rexec/Anemone [46], Mariposa [47], Mungi [48], Stanford Peers [49], G-Commerce [50], OCEAN [51], Nimrod/G [15], Gridbus [54], CatNets [57], SORMA [59], and GridEcon [60]. These systems have been targeted to manage single or multiple resources for application domains as follows:

- *Single-domain computing systems*—enhanced MOSIX and Rexec/Anemone
- *Agent-based systems*—Xenoservers and D'Agents
- *Distributed database management system*—Mariposa
- *Shared storage management system*—Mungi
- *Storage space trading system*—Stanford Peers
- *Web-based distributed systems*—Popcorn and Java Market
- *Multidomain distributed Grid systems*—Nimrod-G and Gridbus Broker

Many of the resource management systems presented in Table 1.1 follow a single model for resource trading. They have been designed with a specific goal in mind, for either CPU or storage management. In order to use some of these systems, applications have to be designed using their proprietary programming models, which is generally discouraging, as applications need to be specifically developed for executing on those systems. Also, resource trading and job management modules have been developed using monolithic system architecture that limits their extensibility.

Multidomain Grid systems such as Nimrod/G and Gridbus brokers separated these two concerns through a layered design approach to support different middleware technologies that coexist with trading strategies and user-level resource brokers. The resource trading services are offered as core services and can be used by different higher-level services such as resource brokers and resource-aware applications.

Typically, in a Grid marketplace, the resource owners and users can use any one or more of these models or even combinations of them in meeting their objectives [14]. Both have their own expectations and strategies for being part of the Grid. The resource consumers adopt the strategy of solving their problems at a low cost within a required timeframe. The resource providers adopt the strategy of obtaining the best possible return on their investments while trying to maximize their resource utilization by offering a competitive service access cost in order to attract consumers. The resource consumers can choose providers that best meet their requirements.

Both GRBs and GSPs can initiate resource trading and participate in the interaction depending on their requirements and objectives. GRBs may invite bids from a number of GSPs and select those that offer the lowest service costs and meet their deadline and budget requirements. Alternatively, GSPs may invite bids in an auction and offer services to the highest bidder as long as its objectives are met. Both GSPs and GRBs have their own utility functions that must be satisfied and maximized. The GRBs perform a cost–benefit analysis depending on the deadline (by which the results are required) and budget available (the amount of money that the user is willing to invest for solving the problem). The resource owners decide their pricing on the basis of various factors. They may charge different prices for different users using the same service depending on the specific user demands. Resources may have different prices on the basis of environmental influences such as the availability of larger core memory and better communication bandwidth with the outside world.

Grid brokers (note that each user has his/her own broker as his/her agent in a Grid environment) may have different goals (e.g., different deadlines and budgets), and each broker tries to maximize its own good without concern for the global good. This needs to be considered in building automated negotiation infrastructure. In a *cooperative distributed computing or problem-solving environment* (like a cluster of computers), the system designers impose an *interaction protocol* (possible actions to take at different points) and a *strategy* (a mapping from one state to another and a way to use the protocol). This model aims for global efficiency as nodes cooperate toward a common goal. On the other hand, in Grid systems, brokers and GSPs are provided with an interaction protocol, but they choose their own private strategy (as in multiagent systems), which cannot be imposed from outside. Therefore, the negotiation protocols need to be designed assuming a *noncooperative, strategic* perspective. In this case, the main concern is what social outcomes follow given a protocol, which guarantees that each broker/GSP's desired local strategy is best for her/him and hence that she/he will use it.

1.10 CHALLENGES OF UTILITY COMPUTING MODELS FOR GRIDS

The adoption of utility computing requires a change in the manner in which many IT operations are planned and performed in the enterprise. This induces many challenges that need to be addressed both technologically and culturally. One challenge is that both providers and users need to redraft and reorganize their current IT-related procedures and operations to incorporate the usage of services from external providers [30]. New IT policies need to be negotiated and agreed on between providers and users, compared to the previous situation where providers and users owned and controlled their standalone policies. Providers must also understand specific service needs and requirements of users in order to design suitable policies for them.

The end user in an organization must not be able to perceive a difference between an internal, dedicated service and one that is sourced from an external provider. Therefore, the utility computing experience has to be seamless and should increase the flexibility of service consumption. This motivates the need for appropriate software interfaces and toolkits that enable an organization to expand and contract its service usage at will without causing disruptions in the users' workflows. Currently, toolkits such as Amazon Web Services and Google App Engine allow a measure of flexibility for external users deploying services on the companies' infrastructure. However, these are provider-specific and are short of features such as variable, demand-driven usage pricing models, and integration with business processes. True utility computing requires vendors and providers to move away from proprietary services toward open standards so that users and producers experience fewer difficulties and complexities in integrating technologies and working together, thus reducing associated costs.

As seen so far, in a utility computing scenario, the users cede much of their abilities to control dedicated resources. Therefore, the only way that they can obtain guarantees to meet their QoS requirements is through binding SLAs with service providers. Such SLAs have penalty clauses that are triggered when the guarantees are violated. Providers therefore need strategies for selecting SLAs such that the risk of violations is minimized [31,32]. Improved service-oriented policies and autonomic controls [33,34] are essential for achieving this.

Financial risk management for utility computing [35] consist of two factors: delivery risk and pricing risk. *Delivery risk* factors examine the risks concerned with each possible scenario in which a service can be delivered. *Pricing risk* factors study the risks involved with pricing the service with respect to the availability of resources. Given shorter contract durations, lower switching costs, and uncertain customer demands in utility computing environments, it is important to have dynamic and flexible pricing schemes to potentially maximize profits and minimize losses for providers [36]. Also, current providers have rigid SLAs that do not offer flexibility to allow tradeoff of lower QoS requirements for lower charges. Such ability would enable providers to supply services to satisfy a range of users, thereby increasing the profitability of their enterprise. Therefore, this motivates the adoption of different negotiation mechanisms through which providers and consumers can arrive at mutually agreeable terms in SLAs. This would also require both parties to adopt sophisticated negotiation strategies that mirror interactions between humans in real marketplaces.

There are also potential nontechnical obstacles to the successful adoption of utility computing such as cultural and people-related issues that will require organizations to change their current stance and perceptions [37]. The most worrying issues that are perceived are loss of control or access to resources, risks associated with enterprisewide deployment, loss or reduction of budget dollars, and reduced priority of projects. Also important are concerns about security, particularly with regard to maintaining the confidentiality of data while they are being processed on providers' resources. Regulations governing confidentiality and disclosure may prohibit many applications from accessing utility computing services. Ultimately, applications dealing with sensitive areas such as national security and health may be forever confined to dedicated resources. Yet, overcoming these nontechnical obstacles is extremely critical and requires the dissemination of correct information to all levels of management within organizations to prevent the formation of misperceptions.

1.11 SUMMARY AND CONCLUSION

To summarize, we have presented the emergence of Grid computing as a platform for next-generation parallel and distributed computing. We have covered some of the major Grid efforts around the world and discussed the Grid software stack with two sample technologies. We have identified various challenges in managing Grid resources owned by different organizations. We have introduced computational economy, that is, a market-oriented model for tackling challenges of resource management within large-scale Grids. We have discussed the reference architecture for market-oriented Grids and presented a scenario for its operation. Various approaches followed by representative works in market-oriented resource management and application scheduling are also discussed.

It can be observed that while significant effort has been devoted to development of Grid technologies, still more must be achieved in terms of Grids providing computing utilities in the same manner as power utilities supply electric power. The Grid resource management systems must dynamically trade for the best resources according to a metric of the price and performance available, and schedule computations on these resources such that they meet user requirements. The Grid middleware needs to offer services that help resource brokers and resource owners to trade for resource access. Market-based Grid systems need to pay attention to the reputation of service providers, where regular offenders are penalized and additional incentives are provided for good services [61]. Ultimately, this would require the development of richer services and applications on top of existing ones so that Grid computing can move beyond scientific applications into the mainstream IT infrastructure.

ACKNOWLEDGMENTS

This chapter is partially derived from the authors' past work, especially from the PhD thesis [1] of the first author. We would like to thank various colleagues, especially David Abramson (Monash University), with whom we have investigated market-oriented Grid computing. We would also like to thank Chee Shin Yeo for his comments on this chapter.

REFERENCES

1. R. Buyya, *Economic-Based Distributed Resource Management and Scheduling for Grid Computing*, PhD thesis, Monash Univ., Melbourne, Australia, April 2002.
2. B. Chun, *Market-Based Cluster Resource Management*, PhD dissertation, Univ., California, Berkeley, CA, Oct. 2001.
3. L. Kleinrock, A vision for the Internet, *ST Journal of Research* **2**(1):4–5 (Nov. 2005).
4. I. Foster and C. Kesselman, eds., The Grid: Blueprint for a Future Computing Infrastructure, Morgan Kaufmann, San Francisco, 1999.
5. T. Hey and A. Trefethen, The UK e-Science Core Programme and the Grid, *Journal of Future Generation Computer Systems* **18**(8):1017–1031 (2002).
6. M. Chetty and R. Buyya, Weaving computational grids: How analogous are they with electrical Grids?, *Computing in Science and Engineering* **4**(4):61–71 (July–Aug. 2002).
7. F. Berman, G. Fox, and A. Hey, eds., Grid Computing: Making the Global Infrastructure a Reality, Wiley, Hoboken, NJ, 2003.

8. M. Baker, R. Buyya, and D. Laforenza, Grids and Grid technologies for wide-area distributed computing, *Software: Practice and Experience* **32**(15):1437–1466 (Dec. 2002).
9. I. Foster, C. Kesselman, and S. Tuecke, The anatomy of the Grid: Enabling scalable virtual organizations, *International Journal of High Performance Computing Applications*, **15**(3):200–222 (2001).
10. R. Buyya, D. Abramson, and J. Giddy, An economy driven resource management architecture for global computational power Grids, *Proc. 7th International Conf. Parallel and Distributed Processing Techniques and Applications*, Las Vegas, June 26–29, 2000.
11. W. Hoschek, J. Jaen-Martinez, A. Samar, H. Stockinger, and K. Stockinger, Data management in an international data Grid project, *Proc. 1st IEEE/ACM International Workshop on Grid Computing, Bangalore, India, Dec.* 2000.
12. Open Grid Forum, http://www.ogf.org.
13. M. Rappa, The utility business model and the future of computing services, *IBM Systems Journal* **43**(1):32–42 (2004).
14. R. Buyya, D. Abramson, and J. Giddy, A case for economy Grid architecture for service-oriented Grid computing, *Proc. IPDPS, 10th IEEE International Heterogeneous Computing Workshop*, San Francisco, CA, April 23, 2001.
15. R. Buyya, D. Abramson, and J. Giddy, Nimrod-G: An architecture for a resource management and scheduling system in a global computational Grid, *Proc. 4th International Conf. High Performance Computing in Asia-Pacific Region, Beijing, China, May* 2000.
16. R. Buyya, D. Abramson, J. Giddy, and H. Stockinger, Economic models for resource management and scheduling in Grid computing, *Concurrency and Computation: Practice and Experience* **14**(13–15):1507–1542 (Nov.–Dec. 2002).
17. C. Catlett, P. Beckman, D. Skow, and I. Foster, Creating and operating national-scale cyberinfrastructure services, *CTWatch Quarterly* **2**:2–10 (2006).
18. W. T. Sullivan, III, D. Werthimer, S. Bowyer, J. Cobb, D. Gedye, and D. Anderson, A new major SETI project based on Project Serendip data and 100,000 personal computers, *Proc. 5th International Conf. Bioastronomy*, 1997.
19. R. Buyya, Grid and peer-to-peer (P2P) commercial companies, *Grid Computing Information Centre*, http://www.gridcomputing.com/, 2000–2008.
20. ISO New England, Electricity trading over the Internet begins in six New England states, *Business Wire*, http://industry.java.sun.com/javanews/stories/story2/0,1072,15093,00.html, May 13, 1999.
21. I. Foster, A. Roy, and V. Sander, A quality of service architecture that combines resource reservation and application adaptation, *Proc. IEEE/IFIP 8th International Workshop on Quality of Service (IWQOS 2000)*, Pittsburgh, PA, June 2000.
22. R. Cocchi, S. Shanker, D. Estrin, and L. Zhang, Pricing in computer networks: Motivation, formulation, and example, *IEEE/ACM Transactions on Networking* **1**(6):614–627 (Dec. 1993).
23. A. Lazar and N. Semret, *Auctions for Network Resource Sharing*, Technical Report TR 468-97-02, Columbia Univ., Feb. 1997.
24. L. W. McKnight and J. Boroumand, Pricing Internet services: Approaches and challenges, *IEEE Computer* **33**(2):128–129 (Feb. 2000).

25. B. Carpenter, IPv6 and the future of the Internet, *The Internet Society Member Briefing*, July 23, 2001. http://www.isoc.org/briefings/001/.
26. IBM developerWorks, Six strategies for Grid application enablement, http://www.ibm.com/developerworks/grid/library/gr-enable (accessed Nov. 2006).
27. The Globus Alliance, The Globus toolkit, http://www.globus.org/toolkit (accessed Nov. 2006).
28. D. Abramson, J. Giddy, and L. Kotler, High performance parametric modeling with Nimrod/G: Killer application for the global Grid?, *Proc. 14th International Parallel and Distributed Processing Symp.* (*IPDPS 2000*), Cancun, Mexico, May 2000.
29. Y. Tanaka, H. Nakada, S. Sekiguchi, T. Suzumura, and S. Matsuoka, Ninf-G: A reference implementation of RPC-based programming middleware for Grid computing *Journal of Grid Computing* **1**(1):41–51 (2003).
30. R. Buyya, T. Cortes, and H. Jin, Single system image, *International Journal of High Performance Computing Applications* **15**(2):124–135 (summer 2001).
31. M. Buco, R. Chang, L. Luan, C. Ward, J. Wolf, and P. Yu, Utility computing SLA management based upon business objectives, *IBM Systems Journal*, **43**(1):159–178 (2004).
32. C. S. Yeo and R. Buyya, Integrated risk analysis for a commercial computing service, *Proc. 21st IEEE International Parallel and Distributed Processing Symp.* (*IPDPS 2007*), Long Beach, CA, March 26–30, 2007.
33. J. Kephart and D. Chess, The vision of autonomic computing, *IEEE Computer* **36**(1):41–50 (Jan. 2003).
34. R. Murch, Autonomic Computing, Prentice-Hall, 2004.
35. C. Kenyon and G. Cheliotis, Elements of financial risk management for Grid and utility computing, in *Handbook of Integrated Risk Management for E-Business: Measuring, Modeling, and Managing Risk*, A. Labbi, ed., J. Ross Publishing, 2005.
36. G. Paleologo, Price-at-risk: A methodology for pricing utility computing services, *IBM Systems Journal* **43**(1):20–31 (2004).
37. Platform computing, the politics of Grid, http://www2.platform.com/adoption/politics (accessed Nov. 2006).
38. J. Basney and M. Livny, Deploying a high throughput computing cluster, *High-Performance Cluster Computing*, R. Buyya, ed., Prentice-Hall PTR, May 1999.
39. C. Waldspurger, T. Hogg, B. Huberman, J. Kephart, and W. Stornetta, Spawn: A distributed computational economy, *IEEE Transactions on Software Engineering* **18**(2):103–117 (Feb. 1992).
40. N. Nisan, S. London, O. Regev, and N. Camiel, Globally distributed computation over the Internet: The POPCORN project, *Proc. 18th International Conf. Distributed Computing Systems*, Amsterdam, The Netherlands, May 26–29, 1998.
41. Y. Amir, B. Awerbuch, and R. Sean Borgstrom, A cost-benefit framework for online management of a metacomputing system, *Proc. 1st International Conf. Information and Computational Economy*, Charleston, VA, Oct. 25–28, 1998.
42. Y. Amir, B. Awerbuch., A. Barak A., S. Borgstrom, and A. Keren, An opportunity cost Approach for job assignment in a scalable computing cluster, *IEEE Transactions on Parallel and Distributed Systems* **11**(7):760–768 (July 2000).
43. S. Lalis and A. Karipidis, An open market-based framework for distributed computing over the Internet, *Proc. 1st IEEE/ACM International Workshop on Grid Computing* (*Grid 2000*), Bangalore, India, Dec. 17, 2000.

44. D. Reed, I. Pratt, P. Menage, S. Early, and N. Stratford, Xenoservers; accounted execution of untrusted code, *Proc. 7th Workshop on Hot Topics in Operating Systems* (*HotOS-VII*), Rio Rico, AZ, March 28–30, 1999.
45. J. Bredin, D. Kotz, and D. Rus, *Utility Driven Mobile-Agent Scheduling*, Technical Report CS-TR98-331, Dartmouth College, Hanover, NH, Oct. 3, 1998.
46. B. Chun and D. Culler, *Market-Based Proportional Resource Sharing for Clusters*, Technical Report CSD-1092, Univ. California, Berkeley, Jan. 2000.
47. M. Stonebraker, R. Devine, M. Kornacker, W. Litwin, A. Pfeffer, A. Sah, and C. Staelin, An economic paradigm for query processing and data migration in Mariposa, *Proc. 3rd International Conf. Parallel and Distributed Information Systems*, Austin, TX, Sept. 28–30, 1994.
48. G. Heiser, F. Lam, and S. Russell, Resource management in the Mungi single-address-space operating system, *Proc. Australasian Computer Science Conf., Perth, Australia, Feb. 4–6*, 1998.
49. B. Cooper and H. Garcia-Molina, Bidding for storage space in a peer-to-peer data preservation system, *Proc. 22nd International Conf. Distributed Computing Systems* (*ICDSC 2002*), Vienna, Austria, July 2–5, 2002.
50. R. Wolski, J. Plank, J. Brevik, and T. Bryan, Analyzing market-based resource allocation strategies for the computational grid, *International Journal of High-Performance Computing Applications* **15**(3):258–281 (fall 2001).
51. P. Padala, C. Harrison, N. Pelfort, E. Jansen, M. Frank, and C. Chokkareddy, OCEAN: The Open Computation Exchange and Arbitration Network, a market approach to meta computing, *Proc. 2nd International Symp. Parallel and Distributed Computing, Ljubljana, Slovenia, Oct.* 2003.
52. J. Brooke, M. Foster, S. Pickles, K. Taylor, and T. Hewitt, Mini-grids: Effective test-beds for Grid application, *Proc. 1st IEEE/ACM International Workshop on Grid Computing* (*Grid 2000*), Bangalore, India, Dec. 17, 2000.
53. G. Allen, T. Goodale, T. Radke, M. Russell, E. Seidel, and K. Davis, Enabling applications on the grid: A Gridlab overview, *International Journal of High-Performance Computing Applications* **17**(4):449–466 (2003).
54. R. Buyya and S. Venugopal, The Gridbus toolkit for service oriented Grid and utility computing: An overview and status report, *Proc. 1st IEEE International Workshop on Grid Economics and Business Models* (*GECON 2004*), Seoul, South Korea, April 23, 2004.
55. T. Sandholm, Distributed rational decision making, in *Multi-Agent Systems: A Modern Introduction to Distributed Artificial Intelligence*, G. Weiss, ed., The MIT Press, Cambridge, MA, 2000.
56. R. Buyya, D. Abramson, and S. Venugopal, The Grid economy, *Proceedings of the IEEE* **93**(3):698–714 (March 2005).
57. T. Eymann, M. Reinicke, et al., Catallaxy-based Grid markets, *Multiagent and Grid Systems* **1**(4):297–307 (2005).
58. A. Rajasekar, M. Wan, R. Moore, and W. Schroeder, A prototype rule-based distributed data management system, *Proc. Workshop on Next Generation Distributed Data Management: 15th ACM/IEEE International Symp. High Performance Computing, Paris, May* 2006.

59. D. Neumann, J. Stoesser, A. Anandasivam, and N. Borissov, SORMA—building an open Grid market for Grid resource allocation, *Proc. 4th International Workshop of Grid Economics and Business Models* (*GECON 2007*), Rennes, France, Aug. 28, 2007.

60. J. Altmann, C. Courcoubetis, J. Darlington, and J. Cohen, GridEcon–the economic-enhanced next-generation Internet, *Proc. 4th International Workshop of Grid Economics and Business Models* (*GECON 2007*), Rennes, France, Aug. 28, 2007.

61. J. Broberg, S. Venugopal, and R. Buyya, Market-oriented Grids and utility computing: The state-of-the-art and future directions, *Journal of Grid Computing* **6**(3):255–276 (2008).

2

MARKETS, MECHANISMS, GAMES, AND THEIR IMPLICATIONS IN GRIDS

YIBO SUN, SAMEER TILAK, RUPPA K. THULASIRAM, AND KENNETH CHIU

2.1 INTRODUCTION

Grid computing, at its root, is a method for concatenating and allocating computing resources whose ownership is diffuse. Hence, in addition to technical issues of how to synchronize data, route communications, optimize distributed performance, and so on, Grid computing raises the economic issue of how to induce the people who own and use the distributed resources to cooperate with each other. Experience has demonstrated that many people's incentives are not perfectly aligned with those of the Grid computing organizations in which they participate, so their cooperation cannot be taken for granted. In this chapter we provide an introduction to three economic paradigms that are available with which to study these issues, and we provide a view of the Grid computing literature through lenses colored by these paradigms.

2.2 BACKGROUND

The economic content of Grid computing can be boiled down to two stylized functions: the allocation of resources and the availability of resources. Grid computing organizations allocate computing resources among users, and in the process must weigh the benefits that each user might gain from using resources that other users also want to use. Grid computing organizations also need access to computing resources; these may be purchased by the organization itself, or provided by donors. In the first

Market-Oriented Grid and Utility Computing Edited by Rajkumar Buyya and Kris Bubendorfer

case, there is the problem of deciding which resources to purchase; in the second case, there is the problem of motivating donors to provide useful resources.

Although allocation and availability are interrelated, it is often helpful to separate them for purposes of analysis; that is, holding availability fixed, how should resources be allocated? Also, holding allocation as a function of availability fixed, which resources should be made available? These kinds of questions are familiar in elementary economics, where availability corresponds to "supply" and allocation corresponds to "demand." However, the problem is typically not elementary, because there is the complication of private information. When allocating resources, we would like to know how they are valued by each user, so that they can be allocated in a way that maximizes value. When making resources available, we would like to know how much they cost each donor to provide, so that they can be provided in a way that minimizes cost.

In economics, there are three main paradigms for handling these kinds of issues: markets, mechanisms, and games. These three paradigms are ordered along at least two dimensions of interest: large to small, and naive to strategic. Market theory applies to Grid computing organizations with many small users and donors, as well as to situations in which users and donors are naive, docile, or under the direct control of the organization. Game theory [1,2] applies to situations with small numbers of strategic users or donors, when the Grid computing organization is unable to commit in advance to formal rules. The theory of mechanism design fits in between; it applies when the agents may be strategic, but the Grid computing organization commits in advance to formal rules. A significant portion of the economic theory discussed in this chapter can be found, with much greater rigor, in good graduate microeconomics textbooks. For interested readers, we particularly suggest the text by Mas-Colell et al. [4] for markets and mechanisms, and Osborne and Rubinstein [7] for games.

2.3 MARKETS

In a market, supply and demand reach equilibrium via a price that may be adjusted. Agents treat the price as given externally. Consider, for example, a market for compute cycles, assuming that all cycles are identical and infinitely divisible, and that there is a posted price for cycles. Potential users and suppliers observe the price, and decide how many to buy or sell. (Note that any given agent may sell if the price is high and buy if the price is low, so users and suppliers are not fixed roles.) Holding the price fixed, each agent makes a simple, nonstrategic decision: given her/his pools of money and cycles, optimize the number of cycles she/he buys or sells. We say that the market is in equilibrium if, given the price, the resulting number of cycles bought exactly equals the number of cycles sold. If the market is not in equilibrium, then the decisions of the individual agents are mutually incompatible; more cycles cannot be bought than sold, nor vice versa.

The key task for a Grid computing organization using market principles is to determine the correct price. In this section we investigate various considerations to this determination process, starting with some basic tools of market theory.

2.3.1 Basic Tools

Market theory relies on marginal costs and benefits, respective to some utility function, which maps resources and money to some abstract notion of how much satisfaction a consumer might derive from the given entity. A user's marginal benefit on receiving x units of a resource is the derivative of that user's utility at x. Similarly, a supplier's marginal cost when providing y units of a resource is the derivative of that supplier's cost at y. In equilibrium, the marginal benefits and marginal costs of all users and suppliers equal the price. (Any agent for whom this was not true would benefit by adjusting the quantity she/he uses or provides.)

A demand curve gives the number of units that an agent will buy as a function of the price; a supply curve gives the number of units that an agent will sell as a function of the price. At the point of intersection between these two curves, the quantity supplied and purchased are the same for the given price.

Consumer surplus is the benefit received by users for being able to purchase a resource for an amount less than what they are willing to pay. It is the area between the demand curve and the price. Producer surplus is the amount that suppliers benefit from being able to sell at a price that is higher than what they would be willing to sell for. It is the area between the supply curve and the price. Social surplus is the sum of consumer surplus and producer surplus. We say that the outcome is "efficient" if the social surplus is maximized.

2.3.2 Price Adjustment

Market theory relies on the assumption that the price will adjust to achieve equilibrium. Economists have long sought to support this assumption for decentralized markets. An informal justification is usually taught at the undergraduate level, and is as follows: a price that is higher than the equilibrium price will result in an excess supply, and suppliers who do not have buyers will "push" the price down; a price that is lower than the equilibrium price will create excess demand, and the consumers who are unable to buy will "push" the price up. Note that when thinking strictly in terms of market theory, we do not include any kind of "bidding," because we assume that price is given exogenously, and consequently agents cannot directly control the price. It does not adjust as the consequence of any agents' direct actions.[1]

In a distributed system, a central organization may control the price, and raise or lower prices to balance supply and demand. Users and providers, if they are cooperative, may make decisions as if the price is not affected by how much they buy or sell. Or, if all users and providers are small relative to the organization, then none of them can significantly affect the price, so even strategic, selfish agents base decisions on an exogenous price.

[1]We explain later that auctions can be viewed as a mechanism that can adjust prices.

2.3.3 Efficiency

A market equilibrium is *Pareto-efficient* if there is no way to reallocate resources such that everyone will be better off. A well-known result in economics is that if all agents cannot directly affect the price (known as "price takers") and there are no externalities (see below), then a market equilibrium is Pareto-efficient. In other words, at market equilibrium, resources cannot be reallocated in a way that would make everyone better off. In the simple market described above, the proof is by contradiction. Assume that the equilibrium is not Pareto-efficient, in which case there must be some pair of agents, one with a marginal valuation higher than the other. One of these marginal valuations must be strictly more or strictly less than the price, thus reflecting excess supply or excess demand. This contradicts the assumption that the market is in equilibrium. This result is applicable to a large number of market situations, where all agents are price takers, each good is infinitely divisible, and agents have no fixed costs. For example, Pareto efficiency applies (by appropriately extending the basic assumptions) to economies with multiple goods, or with labor and input markets. The result also extends to economies that behave stochastically over time, as long as security markets are complete.[2]

Of course, the assumption that agents are price takers is not always valid. For instance, perhaps some agents simply do not know that a particular good is available, effectively treating that good as having an infinite price. Pareto efficiency thus depends on all agents being able to perfectly observe all prices. In the real world, this is, of course, unrealistic. Likewise, we assume that no large, strategic agents exist, since such an agent could exert a nonnegligible effect on the price, and make decisions accordingly.

2.3.4 Rationing

When a market is not in equilibrium, there is excess demand or excess supply, implying that there are some agents that are willing to transact, but unable due to a lack of buyers or sellers. Rationing is thus required to determine which agents may transact. Often rationing results in inefficiencies due to inconvenience. For example, some agents may rush to market in order to beat others. This inefficiency raises the effective price for buyers, or lowers the effective price for sellers, since the cost of the inefficiency must be accounted for. Those agents whose valuations do not allow for this inefficiency are essentially priced out of the market. Since inconvenience has no benefit, and even those who are able to transact must incur the same inefficiency, rationing that induces inconvenience is not desirable.

Any economics-based computer system based on market principles must address rationing, unless it includes mechanisms that can adjust prices to reach equilibrium instantaneously.

[2]Security markets are complete if, for every possible future state of the economy, there exists a security that pays off only in that state and that can be bought or sold in any quantity at any time prior to the realization of that state.

2.3.5 Altruism

Up to now, we have assumed that agents are completely selfish, which may not always be the case. Agents may also be altruistic to varying degrees. If all agents are completely altruistic, then none of them have any preferences. Thus all agents will unanimously agree to any allocation and outcome, obviating the need for markets. In fact, there is no economic problem at all.

The more likely case is that agents are partially altruistic, taking into consideration both their own well-being and the well-being of others. This altruism induces agents to supply more than they might otherwise, or demand less than they might otherwise. The result is a lower equilibrium price, but equilibrium analysis can still be used.

Altruism can be used to explain the success of a number of unpriced Grid computing projects that rely on altruistic suppliers to provide cycles without compensation.

Technically, these projects are not in market equilibrium if the price is zero, however, since there would be excess demand. A number of projects try to increase the effective price paid to suppliers by rewarding them nonmonetarily. For example, the projects may hold competitions to give recognition to suppliers.

2.3.6 Monopoly

In a monopoly situation, a single large strategic agent dominates the market. Market theory can still be used if we assume that all remaining agents are purely price takers. Of course, the market will be efficient (except for one caveat described below). Consider the case of a monopolist donor interacting with price-taking users.

If the monopolist knows the valuations of all the users but must set a uniform price, then the problem is a simple optimization. The optimal monopoly price is higher than the efficient market price. The proof is as follows. At the efficient price, the marginal supplier cost and the marginal buyer's benefit both equal the price. If the price were increased, fewer units would be sold, but at lower unit cost, and at a higher price. If the amount of increase is small, the supplier's profit would increase.[3]

If the monopolist knows the valuations of all the users and can charge a separate price to each user (known as "third-degree price discrimination"), the result is somewhat surprising—the equilibrium condition is an efficient market. The reason is that the optimal pricing is to charge each user exactly that user's value for each unit of the good. Since all users receive zero payoffs, the monopolist obtains all of the social surplus in the market, thus maximizing the social surplus and resulting in an efficient market. In practice, a monopolist cannot know the valuations of all users. Even if asked, they would not tell the truth, since they would have strong incentive not to do so.

Usually, the monopolist observes only the quantity that can be sold at the current price. In this case, the monopolist will experiment with small variations in price in order to maximize profits. If the market conditions are static, this process will

[3]The supplier loses the small difference between the value for the last unit and the price times the small magnitude of the last unit but gains the small change in the price times the large number of remaining units.

converge quickly, but in rapidly changing conditions, the process can be computationally challenging. A Grid computing organization that controls its resources and provides them to a large number of small users can be analyzed as a monopolist. Such an organization would set the price to maximize its profits, resulting in a market at equilibrium but not an efficient one.[4] In the inverse situation, a Grid computing organization that is the exclusive user of resources provided by a large number of small providers is also in the position of a monopsonist—a monopolist buyer. This might correspond to certain situations such as SETI@Home, at least during some historical periods. For a monopsonist, the optimal price is below the efficient price, resulting in fewer of the resource being provided.

2.3.7 Externalities

An *externality* occurs when one agent can affect another agent through its actions. Economists distinguish two types of externalities: pecuniary and nonpecuniary. Pecuniary externalities occur when an agent is large enough so that its actions affect prices. Nonpecuniary externalities are other effects. In distributed systems, such effects might include packet congestion, spam, domain squatting, and intrusive advertising. Market theory assumes that participants make decisions only on the basis of price, so externalities are ignored when deciding how much to buy or sell. If the provision or use of a resource has a negative impact on other agents, it is termed a *negative externality*, and in equilibrium too much of the resource is provided, relative to maximizing overall social good. For example, if the use of a resource causes network congestion to affect other users, then a greater overall good could be obtained if the amount of resource used were reduced from the market equilibrium. In some rare cases, the provision or use of a resource actually benefits other agents. This is known as a *positive externality*, and more of the resource should be provided than at market equilibrium.

Altruism can be relevant when addressing externalities. Altruistic agents may be persuaded to reduce activities that have detrimental impact on other agents, and increase activities that benefit other users.

2.3.8 Indivisibility and Complementarity

The market may not converge to an equilibrium when there are multiple, indivisible, complementary goods. In such cases, there is no vector of prices that results in equilibrium between supply and demand for each good simultaneously. Thus, surpluses or shortages of some goods are inevitable. In Grid computing, many goods may be complements, although indivisibility may not be an issue.

[4]Bear in mind that resources like Websites that are provided for free often derive their income from advertising and tie-ins, and are therefore best regarded as selling the attention of consumers to advertisers, rather than selling Website content to viewers. With regard to advertising, see Section 2.3.7, below.

2.4 MECHANISMS

In a mechanism, the transactions are determined according to formal rules by an authority known as the "center." Note that the existence of such an authority does not necessarily imply a centralized algorithm. The center publicly commits to the rules and is bound to follow them. The rules specify how the center queries agents, and they specify the transaction that will be executed as a function of the agents' replies.

More formally, a mechanism is a message space and an outcome function. The outcome function selects the transaction to occur as a function of the messages received from the agents. Typically, the transaction involves allocations and availability, and a set of payments (often called *transfers*).

In a mechanism, unlike in a market, prices are not determined exogenously, but rather directly as a result of the rules. Mechanisms can have advantages because agents often have private information about their own supply and demand. A mechanism can extract this in such a manner that the desired outcome can be selected directly, rather than attempting to use pricing to hope that the market will reach an efficient equilibrium on its own. With the use of algorithms and networking, mechanism implementation can be straightforward, at least in principle.

One common class of mechanisms is auctions, and these can be applied to Grid computing to determine the allocation and provisioning of resources. In this section, we elaborate on some of the issues of mechanism design and implementation, focusing primarily on auctions.

2.4.1 Incentive Compatibility

In an arbitrary mechanism, agents may not reveal private information truthfully. If an agent can improve its outcome by submitting false information, the theoretical assumption is that it will in fact do so. Therefore, a successful mechanism should be designed so that agents have incentives to truthfully reveal private information. A mechanism is considered incentive compatible when the agent obtains the best possible outcome for itself when it submits truthful information.

It should be emphasized that nonincentive compatible mechanisms can be designed, but in such cases, many agents will submit false information, and the outcome of the mechanism will not comport to the overall desired result.

Two types of incentive compatibility are commonly discussed in modern economics: Bayesian incentive compatibility (BIC) and ex post incentive compatibility (EPIC) [6]. In a BIC mechanism, the incentives of agents are compatible when they know their own private information and the expected private information of all the other players. Unfortunately, BIC requires the assumption that the joint probability distribution of the private information of all other agents is commonly and publically available. In Grid computing, this would typically be the private costs and benefits of using and providing resources, and would most likely not be known to others. BIC is likely difficult to implement in distributed computing.

On the other hand, in an EPIC mechanism compatibility is achieved even if agents already do not know the private information of all other agents.[5] Under EPIC, the probability distribution over private information does not need to be known. Under EPIC, since we assume that private information does not affect compatibility, messages can be made public.

2.4.2 The Revelation Principle

The revelation principle states that any EPIC mechanism (using any arbitrary messages) can be transformed into a direct revelation mechanism that also satisfies EPIC and implements the same outcome function. When using such a mechanism, each agent's message to the center simply states his/her private information. An outline of the proof is as follows: Consider an EPIC mechanism with arbitrary messages. Transform the messages to simply be the agents' private information. The outcome function is chosen so that exactly the same outcome is selected as the original mechanism with the original messages. Since the original mechanism conformed to EPIC, the transformed outcome function will also be EPIC.

Direct revelation mechanisms facilitate analysis, but may have heavy communication requirements, due to the amount of private information that may need to be communicated. One approach to address this is to construct a direct revelation mechanism for easy analysis, and then once the desired properties are proved, find an equivalent mechanism with a simpler set of messages.

2.4.3 Individual Rationality

Agents may have the choice to withdraw from the mechanism in most applications. This may occur even after the outcome has been chosen. In such situations, successful operation requires that the mechanism give the agents enough incentive not to withdraw. This is framed as a constraint, and is known as individual rationality. One type is known as *ex post individual rationality* (EPIR), and states that even after knowing the outcome, no agent will choose to withdraw. Since most distributed systems organizations have cooperative, nonbinding memberships, EPIR is probably the best individual rationality constraint for Grid computing.

2.4.4 Vickrey Auctions and Groves Mechanisms

A common example of an EPIC mechanism is the Vickrey, or "second price" auction. Assume that a single, indivisible object is up for auction. Each agent knows her/his own value of the object, which is the private information. Each agent then bids money for the object. The highest bidder wins the object, but in the Vickrey auction, the actual

[5]EPIC is sometimes confused with the older notion of dominant strategies incentive compatibility (DSIC). EPIC is weaker than DSIC, because under EPIC an agent need not be willing to tell the truth when other agents do not tell the truth. When there are no externalities, EPIC and DSIC turn out to be equivalent. However, when there are externalities, DSIC is so strong as to rule out virtually any mechanism of interest.

amount paid is the bid of the second highest bidder. A game-theoretic analysis of this mechanism shows that each agent will bid exactly his value.

The Vickrey auction mechanism complies with EPIC. If an agent bids more than the value of the object to that agent, the amount paid is the same. The only possible benefit is that the agent might win the object in situations it otherwise might not. But those situations are exactly those in which there was some other bid higher than the value of the object. Since the price paid is the second highest bid, the agent would end up paying more than the value of the object. Likewise, bidding less than the actual value of the object has no benefit to an agent. Furthermore, since agents bid exactly their values, the agent with the highest value wins the object, and thus the Vickrey auction is efficient. Groves mechanisms are a generalization of the idea underlying Vickrey auctions, and cover more arbitrary settings. When using such a mechanism, all agents reveal their private information to the center, which chooses an efficient physical outcome. After a transaction, each agent i receives a payment in two parts; the first part is equal to the sum of the payoffs that agents i receive from the physical outcome, and the second part is an arbitrary amount that does not depend on agent i's private information (although it may depend on the other agents' information).[6] Since each agent receives his/her own payoff through the physical outcome plus the payoffs of all other agents through his/her payment, that agent's incentives are aligned with those of the center. Since the center chooses an efficient physical outcome if the agents tell the truth, each agent is willing to tell the truth.

2.4.5 Budget Balance

When operating under many EPIC mechanisms, including Groves mechanism, if the center paid only the first part of each agent's payment (which is the sum of all other payoffs), the amount could be quite substantial. The second part of each agent's payment, on the other hand, has no impact on incentives to truthfully reveal private information, simply because it does not depend on each agent's own private information. Therefore, balancing the budget can be assisted by the second part of the payment.

Unfortunately, Groves mechanisms, in general, cannot have balanced budgets ex post. In other words, no method exists to guarantee that the center's payments sum to zero for all possible combinations of the agents' private information. If the probability distribution over the agents' private information is known, however, the expected budgeted can often be balanced, as long as the EPIR constraints are not too restrictive.

A budget-balanced EPIC mechanism cannot, in general, also be efficient. The first part of the payments are constructed using the envelope theorem [5], which is beyond the scope of this chapter. Usually, linear programming can be used to construct the EPIC balanced-budget mechanism.

[6] In the Vickrey auction, the second part of agent i's payment is minus the highest bid among the other players. Hence the winning bidder pays the second highest bid, while the losing bidders pay zero.

2.4.6 Combinatorial Auctions

Combinatorial auctions [3] may be especially applicable to Grid computing. In these auctions, agents bid on combinations of items. This is especially significant when there are complementarities (goods that are often consumed together), such as among memory, storage, and CPU cycles. The theory behind combinatorial auctions is still being developed, but ascending combinatorial auctions have been found to work well on the basis of experimental evidence and theoretical underpinnings.

Such an auction can be implemented by allowing each agent to submit a list of bids, one for each possible bundle of goods. After the bids have been submitted, the center selects the outcome so as to maximize its own revenue given the bids, and announces this outcome as tentative. Agents are then given a chance to increase their bids. The cycle repeats until no agents increase their bids. When this point is reached, the tentative outcome is declared to be final, and each agent then pays the final bid for whatever bundle he or she requested.

Although this mechanism seems complex and dynamic, the equilibrium choice is actually for each agent to bid straightforwardly. In each iteration, one (i.e., the agent) will increase one's bid on any bundle that one is not currently winning, and that would increase one's payoff in the event of a win. Straightforward bidding minimizes the number of bundles that the agent needs to evaluate, because one bundle needs to be considered in each iteration.

Combinatorial auctions can be computationally challenging, however. Computing the revenue-maximizing outcome for a given set of bids is NP-hard. Furthermore, in an ascending combinatorial auction, such computations would need to be repeated until the auction concludes. A number of modifications can be made to reduce the computational complexity.

2.4.7 Double Auctions

Under conditions of many providers and users (such as a securities exchange), a double auction is required. Providers and users both post bids. The center then sorts the buy bids in descending order, and the sell bids in ascending order. The highest quantity at which the marginal buy bid is higher than the marginal sell bid is then identified. If a uniform price is desired, the price is set somewhere between the buy and sell bids, and all sellers who bid below that price and all buyers who bid above the price trade at that price. Under a variety of real-world conditions, large double auctions will converge to the market equilibrium as the number of bidders grows. This provides a real-world foundation for the market price mechanism. The current effective price in a double auction, which is based on the equilibrium set by the bids of large bidders, can be used as price quote to small bidders, similar to the way that ordinary investors think of a stock priçe, while stockbrokers and finance firms consider the entire order set. Currently, combinatorial double auctions are an area that remains to be explored.

2.4.8 Auctions with "Funny" Money

For some projects, using real money poses difficulties. One common response is to use virtual money, or "funny money." Each user is given an initial supply of funny money with which to bid on resources. Game theory analysis, however, shows that auctions with funny money do not yield efficient outcomes.

For illustration, consider an ascending combinatorial auction for $n \geq 2$ unrelated items, and suppose that there are $n + 1$ bidders, each of whom values each of the items at more than zero. In the auction, any bidder can bid on any bundle of items, but can win only one bundle. For simplicity, assume that ties are broken according to some deterministic rule. Each bidder has one unit of funny money, which can be used only to bid in the auction. Consider the perspective of bidder i in an arbitrary round. There are several possible scenarios:

- Bidder i already has the tentative winning bid on some bundle, with a bid of 1. In this case, bidder i has exhausted her funny money budget, and can do nothing in this round.
- Bidder i already has the tentative winning bid on some bundle, with a bid less than 1. Since funny money has no use other than to bid in these auctions, bidder i should hold her remaining funny money for future rounds in case some other bidder outbids her on this bundle.
- Bidder i does not have any tentative winning bid. Then bidder i's entire budget of funny money is available. She should bid on one of the bundles, with a bid high enough to become the tentative winning bidder of that bundle if possible.

It is clear from these strategies that in the final round of the auction each bundle must theoretically have a winning bid of 1, and that the allocation awards n of the bidders a bundle containing just one item. Which bidders receive which items depends entirely on the tiebreaking rule. Hence such an auction can do no better than simply asking the bidders which items they want and then allocating the items according to the tiebreaking rule, without collecting any payments.

The problem is that spending funny money is costless. Hence an auction with funny money is a kind of mechanism without any payments. To make an auction with an artificial currency work, the bidders must be able to trade the currency for items of value outside the auction. For instance, such trades might arise informally around an auction with funny money if bidder 1, who values a particular auction item more than bidder 2 values any of the auction items, gives something of value to bidder 2 in exchange for her funny money. Such a trade enhances efficiency, since it helps bidder 1 attain whichever item he values particularly highly, while bidder 2, who does not particularly value any of the auction items, obtains an alternative benefit that she values highly. "Secondary markets" of this kind are already widely observed with respect to the artificial currencies in massive multiplayer online role-playing games. A Grid computing organization that wants to run auctions with artificial currency can benefit from supporting the secondary market with some sort of centralized bartering system, so that bidders who can make mutually beneficial trades can find each other more easily.

2.5 GAMES

Game theory [7] is a method of analyzing strategic behavior that was founded by von Neumann and Morgenstern [9]. Deardorff defines game theory as [8] "The modeling of strategic interactions among agents, used in economic models where the numbers of interacting agents (firms, governments, etc.) is small enough that each has a perceptible influence on the others," whereas a game can be defined as [8] "a theoretical construct in game theory in which players select actions and the payoffs depend on the actions of all players." In essence, game theory considers an interactive environment and studies the choice of optimal behavior when costs and benefits of individual options are not fixed, but depend on the choices made by other individuals. Players and strategies are defined as follows:

Player—any participant in a game who (1) has a nontrivial set of strategies (more than one) and (2) selects among the strategies based on payoffs.

Strategy—a set of moves or actions that a player will follow in a given game. A strategy must be complete, defining an action in every contingency, including those that may not be attainable in equilibrium.

2.5.1 Dominance and Rationalizability

In a game setting, each player has a number of possible strategies, or plans of how to play the game. A strategy s_i for player i is dominated if there is some other strategy (possibly randomized) that gives player i payoffs strictly higher than s_i for every possible set of strategies that the other players could choose. In the example at the beginning of this section, contributing any amount greater than zero to the common good is a dominated strategy.

The most expansive definition of "rationality" is that a player who does not play dominated strategies is rational. This is a weak enough definition that if we observe someone playing a strategy that seems to be dominated on the basis of the resulting material payoffs, we should infer that his/her preferences include nonmaterial payoffs under which the strategy is not dominated.

Rationalizability takes the next logical step. If player i knows that the other players are rational, then player i knows that other players will not play dominated strategies. So player i can consider just the reduced game that is left over after eliminating dominated strategies for all players. Then, player i, being rational, should not play any strategy that is dominated in the reduced game.

If in addition player i knows that the other players know that player i is rational, player i can consider the further reduced game that is left over after eliminating dominated strategies from the first reduced game. Naturally, player i should not play any strategy that is dominated in this further reduced game. If this process of reducing the game continues iteratively, it will converge to a set of strategies that are rationalizable. If it is common knowledge that all the players are rational, it follows that all players must choose rationalizable strategies.

Common knowledge, as discussed in the previous section, is a strong assumption that is difficult to justify in practice. In laboratory games, subjects commonly play strategies that seem not to be rationalizable in terms of their material payoffs. Although we cannot rule out the possibility that these strategies are rationalizable under the subjects' preferences, it is also perfectly plausible that the players do not have common knowledge of rationality.

2.5.2 Nash Equilibrium

A strategy for player *i* is called a "best response" if, taking a particular probability distribution over the other players' strategies, it maximizes player *i*'s expected utility. A common definition of rationality is that if player *i*'s belief about what other players will do can be represented as a probability distribution over their strategies, then player *i* must play a best response to her belief. Two assumptions underly the Nash equilibrium: correct beliefs and common knowledge of rationality. By common knowledge of rationality, of course, a Nash equilibrium must be rationalizable. Because all players have correct beliefs and are playing best responses, no player can gain by unilaterally deviating from the equilibrium. Hence an equivalent definition of Nash equilibrium is a set of strategies, one for each player, such that no player has a profitable deviant strategy.

Common knowledge of rationality is, of course, a strong assumption, but correct beliefs is yet stronger. In particular, if there are multiple Nash equilibria in the game, why should any player have correct beliefs about what the other players will do? Because many people form beliefs on the basis of experience, Nash equilibrium is more appropriate when the players have experience playing (or observing play of) the particular game under study.

Resource management in such large-scale distributed systems is a daunting task. Game theory brings two important benefits to bear on such problems: (1) it provides a set of tools for constructing and evaluating equilibria in Grids, and (2) it provides a method for analyzing the human and institutional motives that underly the use of Grids.

2.6 ARCHITECTURE

We now describe common architectural functionalities that we believe any economics-based Grid computing system must provide:

- *Resource Organization.* The resources in a Grid system are widely distributed and in different administrative domains and hence often have their own access policy, cost, mechanism, and scheduling algorithm. A middle layer should be provided to organize heterogeneous resources; provide a set of generic interfaces such as general service information, runtime resource status, and price query; and conduct the local scheduler on resource providers to allocate specific resource.

- *Request and Resource Matching (the Mechanism).* The goal of adopting a certain kind of mechanism is not simply to match the demand and the supply of the resource, but to maximize utility of both resource owners and users. It collects private information from both consumers and service providers (resource discovery) and applies specific resource-matching algorithms corresponding to the mechanism that the system uses, such as double auction. Since the price might change on the fly with the change of resource status, it also needs to provide resource status and price monitoring.
- *Job Scheduling and Execution.* After resource matching, an accepted requested will be scheduled, and later dispatched to corresponding resourceholder and executed.
- *QoS Control.* To ensure that a certain level of service quality is maintained, if a user does not have a QoS requirement or a service provider cannot ensure it, the system will often adapt a best-effort model.
- *Interface for Resource Consumers and Providers.* The system must provide interfaces for consumers to express their resource needs and the price that they are willing to pay; specify QoS requirement such as deadline, bandwidth, and budget; and ensure access to the "bought" resources later. Also, a set of interfaces should be provided for resource providers to announce how many resources they can provide, the cost of resources or per piece of resource corresponding to each QoS level, and make local resource open for use under system scheduling.

We next take GRACE [10] as an example illustrating how these requirements are organized and fulfilled. GRACE is a distributed Grid architecture for computational economy developed by Buyya et al. and generic for different kinds of Grids such as computational, data, and service-oriented. The four key components of GRACE are

- Grid service providers (GSPs)
- Grid services middleware (GSM)
- User-level middleware, such as Grid resource broker (GRB)
- User application

Grid service providers use the GRACE interface to define their resource amount, QoS level, and pricing and are posted to the Grid market directory in GSM. The user application interacts with the Grid by defining their requirements through GRB. GRB then submits request to the Grid trading service in GSM, which then explores the Grid market directory to identify GSPs that meet the requirements. In the case described above, the functionalities of the mechanism are put in GSM, but that is not the only place. They can also be implemented in either the GRB or the GSP, depending on the specific mechanism adopted. For example, the GRB may initiate an auction and select the best offer from the bidding GSPs that both meets their requirements and has the minimum cost. Alternatively, the GSP can initiate an auction and offer services to the highest bidder.

2.7 CASE STUDIES

In this section we study a number of economics-based systems in the context of markets, mechanisms, and games.

2.7.1 Bellagio

In this work, the authors consider the problem of allocating combinations of heterogeneous, distributed resources among self-interested parties in the context of a large-scale distributed system spanning multiple administrative domains [11]. Their solution is based on the combinatorial auctions technique described in Section 2.3.6. The authors assume that the end users derive utility from receiving a share of resources and that the goal of the system is to allocate resources in a way that maximizes aggregate end-user utility. The salient feature of this work is the ability to support allocation of combinations of heterogeneous goods in a flexible and economically efficient manner. Each end user expresses personal preferences for these resources over time and space in the form of combinatorial auction bids using a simple bidding language. Resource allocation is conducted by a centralized auctioneer by running a period auction. Further details about the bidding language and empirical evaluations can be found in the paper by AuYoung et al. [11].

The authors claim that the auction-based model was chosen since it simplifies the overall system architecture. More specifically, since the end users submit bids, the system does not need to compute the value (price) of combinations of goods, which on its own can be an expensive computational task. The system uses the Vickrey, or second-price, auction technique described in Section 2.3.4 to ensure that the end users reveal their true valuation for resources. As noted in Section 2.3.4, a Vickery auction is efficient.

2.7.2 CatNet

The authors evaluate a decentralized mechanism for resource allocation in large-scale distributed systems such as Grid or peer-to-peer systems, which are fairly dynamic [12]. For example, both the demand and the supply of resources in these systems can change at a rate that cannot be handled by a central arbitrator. To that end, CatNet proposes a distributed framework based on agent-based computational economics. The goal of the system is to the maximum social welfare criterion—maximize the sum of all utilities of the participating nodes. Social welfare maximizing solutions are a subset of Pareto efficiency (described in Section 2.2.3). In this framework, software agents responsible for various resources can buy and sell access to a network service using a heuristic and adaptive negotiation strategy.

To account for the changes in prices for various services as a result of fluctuations in demand and supply, information is propagated throughout the network. The resource providers and consumers use the latest information about the resource prices and adapt their strategies about where to buy and sell, and thus in turn continuously change the state of the network.

2.7.3 G-Commerce

G-commerce [13] compares commodities markets and auctions in four aspects:

- Gridwide price stability
- Market equilibrium
- Application efficiency
- Resource efficiency

Price stability directly affects performance stability as the resource/request matching and scheduling should adapt to price changes, and hence leads to poor performance if it changes frequently. The equilibrium metric determines whether prices are fair or whether the Grid is doing its job. Application efficiency measures the effectiveness of implementation of the mechanism, and resource efficiency measures how well the Grid service middleware couples the resource provider and manages the resources.

In evaluating the commodities market, G-commerce adopts an exchange economy model. A central pricing algorithm module is provided to calculate the prices after collecting vectors of demand and supply of each commodity; and *the First Bank of G* scheme, an approximation of *Smale's method,* is used to adjust the prices.

In evaluating the auction mechanism, a "second-price auction" model is adopted. A central auctioneer takes information of commodity and bids from users during each cycle, then decides who is the winner and the winning price.

The final conclusion is that markets using Smale's method of price determination offer better equilibrium than do auctions, and better efficiency in most cases except in overdemand.

2.8 FUTURE RESEARCH DIRECTIONS

Use of economic theories to deal with service-oriented markets such as the Grid might not provide efficient results. In such cases where QoS becomes important, economic theories expect the agents to be altruistic; this is not realistic, especially in the Internet age, where business happens at the speed of a mouse click. Moreover, since the Grid resources are generally treated as nonstorable commodities, concepts such as discounted cash flows and net present value do not capture the underlying issues of the problem well. One direction to explore in Grid resources pricing is finance models. There are already a few studies reported in the literature using the finance concept, especially using options. In this section we provide an overview of some of the current work and end the section with possible future direction.

2.8.1 A Primer on Options

A financial option is defined (see, e.g., the text by Hull [14]) as the right to buy or to sell an underlying asset (e.g., a stock) that is traded in an exchange for an agreed-on sum. The right to buy or sell an option may expire if the right is not exercised on or before a specific period and the option buyer forfeits the premium paid at the beginning of the contract. The exercise price (*strike price*) specified in an option contract is the stated price at which the asset can be bought or sold at a future date. A *call option* grants the holder the right to purchase the underlying asset at the specified strike price. On the other hand, a *put option* grants the holder the right to sell the underlying asset at the specified strike price. An *American option* can be exercised at any time during the life of the option contract; a *European option* can be exercised only at expiry. An option is a derivative security because its value is a derived function from the price of some underlying asset on which the option is written. Options are also risky securities because the price of their underlying asset at any future time may not be predicted with certainty. This means that the optionholder has no assurance that the option will be "in the money" (i.e., will yield a nonnegative reward) before expiry. As with all risky securities, an important question one might want to ask is how such a security might be valued a priori. The value of an option may be determined using a number of variables that relates to the underlying assets. These include the current value of the underlying asset S, the strike price of the options X, the time to expiration T, volatility of the underlying asset during the option's life σ, expected dividends on assets d, and the risk-free interest rate during the option's life r. In a Grid the underlying assets could be CPU cycles, memory, network bandwidths, throughput, computing power, disks, processor, software, and various measurements and instrumentation tools. They can be collectively called *Grid compute commodities* (GCCs).

2.8.2 Factor Influencing Option Value

The value of the option is calculated at the time of maturity. Suppose that asset price given as S is less than the strike price of the option X (i.e., $S < X$), and that the holder of a call option does not want to exercise the option. This is because the same asset could be bought from the market at a lower price. However, if $S > X$, the holder can buy the asset for X and sell it immediately at price S. At maturity, the difference between the asset price and the strike price is called the *payoff*. But at any time before the maturity, this difference is called the *intrinsic value* of a call option. The general form for the value of a call option at maturity is given as

$$C = \max(0;\ S - X)$$

It can be observed that a higher asset price implies a higher call option value and the lower the strike price, the higher the call option value. The converse is true for a put option. Since there is every possibility for a future exercise of the option value, we say that both the American and the European options have value before the maturity. Another factor that greatly influences option value is the volatility in the asset price. The asset price volatility measures the uncertainty in the future asset price movements. With an increasing volatility, there is a higher chance that the asset will do either well or poorly. This is because the assetholder has a limited downside risk. (The equation displayed above illustrates this point.) To recap, six important factors affect the value of options: current asset price S, strike price K, time to maturity T, volatility σ, risk-free rate r, and dividend yield. Financial options represent the right to either buy or sell an asset. On the other hand, real options deal with the possibility of chosing two either for or against an investment decision without necessarily binding oneself upfront. Real options have distinct characteristic behavior when compared with financial options. Because of the flexible opportunity in asset prices that fit well with Grid computing commodities (GCCs), one can treat the GCCs as real assets and develop a model for pricing them.

2.8.3 Pricing Grid Commodities as Real Options

The current literature on real option approaches to valuing projects presents real options framework in eight categories [15]: option to defer, time-to-build option, option to alter, option to expand, option to abandon, option to switch, growth options, and multiple integrating options. Our particular case of a real option for pricing Grid resources could be expressed as a component of three of the categories listed above: the option to defer, the option to alter, and the option to abandon. There are also efforts reported toward improving the selection and decision methods used in the prediction of the capital that an investment may consume. Carlsson and Fullér [16] apply a hybrid approach to valuing real options. Their method incorporates real option and fuzzy logic and some aspects of probability to account for the uncertainty involved in the valuation of future cash flow estimates. The results of the research efforts given by Gray et al. [15] and Carlsson and Fullér [16] have no formal reference to the QoS that characterize a decision system. Carlson and Fullér [16] apply fuzzy methods to measure the level of decision uncertainties; however, there is a lack of indication on how accurate the decisions could be. Other notable studies [17,18] have evaluated real options and applied it to spot pricing. These research efforts are tuned toward pricing real options in the finance industry. They did not consider the development of a price-based grid infrastructure as a means to capture the value of the GCC. In a Grid system, resources are nonstorable and a user who predicts that she might need more computing power in the future must pay upfront today to hold the right to exercise the option when she needs the computing resources in the stated future date. By formulating and translating the Grid resources pricing problem as a real option pricing problem, the concepts described above can be applied and a deterministic approach to price options can be modeled. A preliminary effort [19] in this direction has shown some promise.

2.9 CONCLUSION

Market theory, mechanisms, and game theory provide powerful aspects for analysis and development of market-based grid computing systems. Although in any real system, it may be difficult to point to any one component and classify it into one of these categories, these aspects nonetheless provide a useful context through which to view Grid systems. We have also discussed a number of representative systems in these terms, and provided some insight into possible future research directions.

REFERENCES

1. C. F. Camerer, T. H. Ho, and J. K. Chong, A cognitive hierarchy model of games, *Quarterly Journal of Economics* **119**(3):861–898 (Aug. 2004).
2. M. A. Costa-Gomes and V. P. Crawford, Cognition and behavior in two-person guessing games: An experimental study, *American Economic Review* **96**:1737–1768 (Dec. 2006).
3. P. Cramton, Y. Shoham, and R. Steinberg, *Combinatorial Auctions*, MIT Press, 2006.
4. A. Mas-Colell, M. D. Whinston, and J. R. Green, *Microeconomic Theory*, Oxford Univ. Press, New York, 1995.
5. P. R. Milgrom and I. Segal, Envelope theorems for arbitrary choice sets, *Econometrica* **70**(2):583–601 (March 2002).
6. D. A. Miller, The dynamic cost of ex post incentive compatibility in repeated games of private information, Working Paper, http://dss.ucsd.edu/~d9miller/papers/d9miller_EPPPE.pdf, Nov. 2007.
7. M. J. Osborne and A. Rubinstein, *A Course in Game Theory*, MIT Press, Cambridge, MA, 1994.
8. A. Deardorff, *Terms of Trade: Glossary of International Economics*, World Scientific Publishing Company, Sina, July 2006.
9. O. Morgenstern and J. von Neumann, *The Theory of Games and Economic Behavior*, Princeton Univ. Press, 1953.
10. R. Buyya, D. Abramson, and S. Venugopal, The Grid Economy, *Proceedings of the IEEE* **93**(3):698–714 (March 2005).
11. A. AuYoung, B. N. Chun, A. C. Snoeren, and A. Vahdat, Resource allocation in federated distributed computing infrastructures, *Proc. 1st Workshop on Operating System and Architectural Support for the On-Demand IT Infrastructure*, Oct. 2004.
12. T. Eymann, M. Reinicke, O. Ardaiz, P. Artigas, L. Dmaz de Cerio, F. Freitag, R. Messeguer, L. Navarro, and D. Royo, Decentralized vs. centralized economic coordination of resource allocation in Grids, *Proc. 1st European Across Grids Conf.*, Feb. 2003.
13. R. Wolski, J. S. Plank, J. Brevik, and T. Bryan, Analyzing market-based resource allocation strategies for the computational Grid, *International Journal of High-Performance Computing Applications* **15**(3):258–281 (2001).
14. J. C. Hull, *Options, Futures, and Other Derivatives*, 6th ed., Prentice-Hall, 2006.
15. A. A. Gray, P. Arabshahi, E. Lamassoure, C. Okino, and J. Andringa, *A Real Option Framework for Space Mission Design*, Technical Report, Jet Propulsion Laboratory, NASA JPL, Pasadena, CA, Aug. 2004.

16. C. Carlsson and R. Fullér, A fuzzy approach to real option valuation, *Fuzzy Sets and Systems* **39**:292–312 (2003).
17. A. Gupta, L. Zhang, and S. Kalyanaraman, Simulation for risk management: A two-component spot pricing framework for loss-rate guaranteed internet service contracts, *Proc. 35th Conf. Winter Simulation*, 2003.
18. M. Amico, Z. J. Pasek, F. Asl, and G. Perrone, Simulation methodology for collateralized debt and real options: A new methodology to evaluate the real options of investment using binomial trees and Monte Carlo simulation, *Proc. 35th Conf. on Winter Simulation*, 2003.
19. D. Allenotor and R. K. Thulasiram, G-FRoM: Grid resources pricing—a fuzzy real option model, *Proc. 3rd IEEE International Conf. eScience and Grid Computing*, Bangalore, India, Dec. 10–13, 2007.

3

OWNERSHIP AND DECENTRALIZATION ISSUES IN RESOURCE ALLOCATION MECHANISMS

TIBERIU STEF-PRAUN

3.1 INTRODUCTION

The ever-increasing complexity of the systems and applications employed in all aspects of human activities, and the associated steep growth of the effort involved in developing such systems and applications have led to an increased popularity of distributed systems design. Distributed systems are no longer characterized only by the physical distribution of their components; they also need to reconcile interconnectivity aspects of independently designed components and to address the goals and expected payoff of the owners of these autonomous components. This chapter focuses on the decentralization and ownership aspects of the components of a distributed system and on how the economics dimension changes the design process in distributed environments.

The combination of spatially distributed components and the selfish and independent nature of the owners of these components lead to a design environment characterized by *information decentralization.* In order to assemble applications in such an environment, the system designer has to locate components in both the time and space domains (through some searching function) and to extract the relevant information from the components' owners that will allow them to choose the proper (cost-effective) alternative (through some efficient information elicitation mechanism).

Market-Oriented Grid and Utility Computing Edited by Rajkumar Buyya and Kris Bubendorfer

In practice we are interested in building mechanisms that address this information decentralization and enable cooperation on resources/services consumption in distributed systems, and we are providing the participants in such interactions with win–win interaction strategies.

Further complicating the design environment, the evolution of software systems brings with it an increase in both the demand for resources and the complexity of the functionality provided. In high-performance computing, the standard solution for hardware resource provisioning is to build computational Grids that can support resource-hungry applications by employing time multiplexing. At the software resource (components) level, application complexities translate into requiring cooperation of independent software modules. This leads to a scenario where the applications consist of loosely coupled independent components, supported by powerful Grids.

3.1.1 Example and Model

At this point we are ready to introduce the model that we use to prototype the Grid services environment and the mechanisms that we put in place to obtain an efficient (defined later) functionality of applications in this environment.

Consider an application developer who wants to mesh together some services provided by other entities on the Internet. One of the projects which we have been involved with consists of using a mapping application programing interface (API) service for displaying socioeconomic survey data in combination with using Grid computing services to produce model-derived data such as the distribution of entrepreneurial and occupational choice in Thailand [1]. Having to combine plain (non-Grid) Web services with computational (Grid) models (also made available as services) makes an excellent case for the issues we are addressing in this chapter.

Some other examples could be

- Providing on-demand Grid infrastructure with the GridWay [2] or market-oriented metaschedulers such as the Gridbus broker [16], with the resources being farmed from independent providers (academic Grids, Amazon EC2 virtual infrastructure, etc.)
- Consolidating related services through a brokering mechanism (e.g., using various stockmarket indicators in parallel, and providing a "best estimate" from all of the predicted outcomes)

The model that we consider here consists of three major participants: (1) the *users* (also the application developers), who are the consumers of the components that are made available in the (Internet) environment as services, and who will locate and use these services in the applications that they are building and/or using; (2) the *owners* of the components—possibly the algorithms developers—who make the components available for consumption by the users, and which, henceforth, we will refer to as *service providers*; and (3) the physical *resource providers* who offer hosting and execution support for the components mentioned above.

The model also defines the canonical *interactions* between the components. On one hand, the users interact only with component owners to acquire and use those software components; on the other hand, the component owners interact with the resource providers to acquire the resources needed to run their components on behalf of the users.

3.1.2 Design Goal

The independently owned nature of software services that are demanded by consumer applications led to the use of economic theory for the design of mechanisms for this allocation process.

The service and the resource allocation problems can be expressed in economic terms as the design of two markets, one focused on services and the other on resources. The two markets will have to support an efficient allocation of the resources in the sense that the spatio-temporal and ownership fragmentation should be transparent for the users trying to utilize these services. Since the users requesting services also need resources for those services, we address this extra complication by hiding the resource components acquisition behind the service components acquisition.

The goal is to obtain an environment where the user sees everything as a service and where the shared ownership of the service (resulting from ownership of the code implemented as a service and ownership of the resources used for execution of the service) is transparent to the service consumers.

To implement the transparency property, services will have to acquire for themselves the resources they need. By acting as a *proxy* for the user, the services can completely isolate the user from the actual resource acquisition. Having the services act on behalf of the user to acquire the resources that they need for execution yields two main benefits. On one hand, pushing the complexity of resource acquisition to the service provider significantly facilitates the task of the user interested in combining several services; on the other hand, the system exports a very simple interface to the user (the amount the user is willing to allocate for each service) and that ensures interoperability with non-Grid-enabled, single-owner services (ones that include the supporting execution resource), which are usually characterized by a similar single-price label.

3.1.3 Background and Related Work

To enable an interaction built on services valuation and competitive acquisition by the users, we are making use of mechanism design theory [3], a powerful tool used for designing protocols and rules for systems in which participants have conflicting goals. Mechanism design uses economic and game-theoretic principles such as utility, social choice function, and strategy to ensure that the participants in the interaction reach an efficient equilibrium in terms of the distribution of the value of the services environment among themselves. The result of mechanism design is usually a special kind of auction mechanism whose outcome fulfills the goals of the system/market designer.

Most of the work in mechanism design (with applications in computer science), as summarized by Jackson [4], de Vries and Vohra [5], Dash et al. [6], and others has focused on efficient, strategyproof allocations of single or multiple items under boundary conditions such as computational load, budget, or required information. In the specific domain of auctions for reusable digital services, probably the closest to our setting is the work of Hajiaghayi [7], who addressed truthful allocations for online auctions. However, they focused only on the individual auctions efficiency without considering marketwide allocation efficiency, which is our main design goal. Their maximum-weight matching allocation with a Vickrey–Clarke–Groves (VCG)-like pricing is a generalized solution, which is supported by our proposed solution in the Web services setting.

In the Grid market, the possible alternative for having the service as a resource acquisition proxy (which is our solution) would be to design a market for combinatorial auctions where the user can ask for bundles of services and resources. This is a widely addressed topic [5,8], with a well-known intractable complexity for computing the market allocation (as in the celebrated VCG [9–11] scheme or in the iterative version thereof [12]).

In addition to the complexity of combinatorial settings for auctions, the complication comes from the dynamic nature of this services environment. The participants can come and leave at any point in time, as described in the *online mechanism design* and analyzed first by Friedman and Parkes [13]. They use as a resource model the WiFi channels provided at Starbucks, and they prove that the strategyproofness is related to offline allocation optimality. They also show that an online optimal Bayesian mechanism supports a VCG mechanism that will guarantee Bayes–Nash incentive compatibility. Further research of the online allocation mechanism is due to Porter [14], who analyzes details of a job scheduling mechanism that needs to maximize the sum of values of the jobs completed by their respective deadlines, given the user-declared job submission, job length, deadline and job value parameters. He shows that, to ensure allocation optimality, the resource provider should always run the job with the higher priority (defined in terms of declared value, time spent on the processor, value density, and ratio of value densities across jobs). Further improvement of the online allocation mechanism is due to Hajiaghayi [7], who proposes a randomization of the allocation and goes with the same VCG pricing style. They support both synchronous and asynchronous (preemptive) service, with a greedy weighting scheme to choose the client to be allocated to the resource.

3.1.4 Contributions toward Enabling Grid Services Markets

Our contribution for the services allocation market is the design of a solution (which we call the *WS-auction* mechanism) that solves a systemwide market-based allocation problem in a completely decentralized services setting. We do this by extending individual auction mechanisms to support systemwide bidding decisions. Creating an efficient allocation at both the individual component (service) and the whole-market levels qualifies this work as an instance of a *metamechanism design*. Using mechanism design theory and simulations, we design and show that an *indirect second-price auction* that exposes *historical* winning bids and provides *provisional* allocation information is the necessary mechanism for such an efficient allocation to be possible.

We also show that in the setting of a distributed services market, the equilibrium strategy for everybody is to *bid their true valuation* of the service *at the earliest time* they start participating in the auctions. These qualities make the mechanism strategyproof with respect to both valuation and timing; thus, we can qualify WS-auction as an online mechanism.

In the Grid resources market, our contribution goes toward designing the proxy mechanism for the services, to be used for acquiring physical resources for their own execution on behalf of the user. We are focusing on market-efficient strategies for distributing the payment submitted by the user between the service owner and the resource provider such that the overall allocation of the payment is fair marketwide ("fairness" is defined later). We show that the dominant strategy of the services owner is to charge a *fixed* (as in nonvariable, or nonproportional) amount from the bids submitted by the users and bid the rest for the resources acquisition. We also argue that using the service as an intermediary introduces a constant computational and communication overhead, and that a dual-market (one for the services and one for resources) remains strategyproof and efficient, when each component market has been designed to be strategyproof and efficient.

3.1.5 The Dual-Market Model of the Grid

The Grid services market has two allocation components (see Fig. 3.1), each of which can be addressed and solved *independently* of the other one. The first component of the allocation is modeled by the interaction between the users and the services, and it has its own social choice function SCF_{US}, which focuses on maximizing the allocation

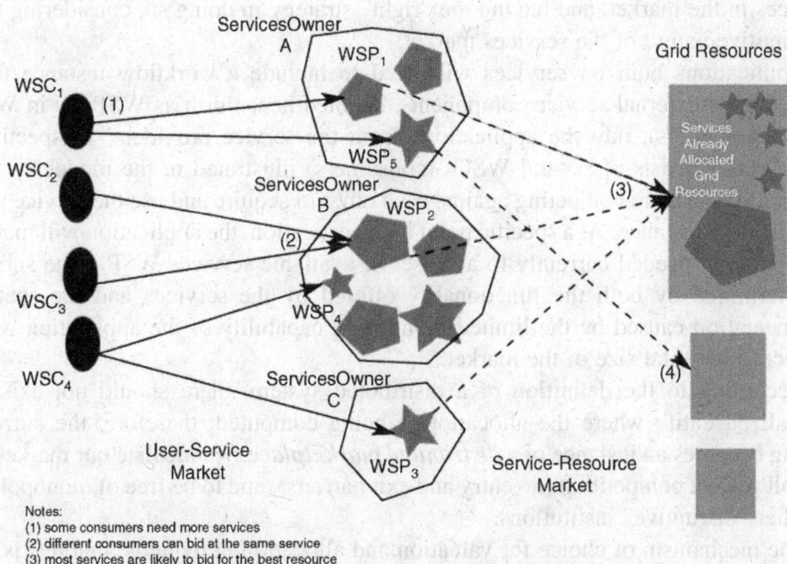
ServicesOwner
A
WSP1
Grid Resources
WSC1
(1)
Services Already Allocated Grid Resources
WSP5
WSC2
ServicesOwner
B
(3)
WSP2
(2)
WSC3
WSP4
(4)
WSC4
ServicesOwner
C
User-Service Market
WSP3
Service-Resource Market
Notes:
(1) some consumers need more services
(2) different consumers can bid at the same service
(3) most services are likely to bid for the best resource
(4) some resources might fit better specific services
(5) service owner could have multiple instances of the same service, and multiple distinctive services

Figure 3.1 Services and resources market.

in the market in the presence of spatial fragmentation (caused by the distributed, independent nature of the services). We define the user service market social choice function as *the total value of the current winning allocations as given by a snapshot of the ongoing allocation process.*

The social choice function SCF_{SR} of the second allocation component—the resource market—is concerned with mirroring the user preferences as described by the bid values onto the resources. We define a *preference ordering property* (measured in terms of the bid amounts) that the services will have to consider when bidding for resources.

The model has partial information made available at each service provider, resulting in a decentralized *preferences organization problem*. On the resource side, the distributed resource setting is mirrored in structure by the decentralized services market, and therefore the same design and discussion applies.

We continue next with the modeling and design of the services market, and show how to address the spatial decentralization with respect to bidding for services.

3.2 SPATIAL DECENTRALIZATION

Let's review again the distributed environment modeled in Figure 3.1. It consists of a set of independently-owned services, loosely classified by their common functionality, and using physical resources for execution from the resource market. Applications and systems built on such an environment will need to address, among other issues, the problem of the decentralized service acquisition procedure: choosing the "right" (according to some criteria defined below) service from the available services in the market, and having the "right" strategy in doing so, considering the competitive nature of the services market.

Applications built on services will need to include a workflow instance that connects the external service components, denoted henceforth as WSP (as in Web service providers), into the application. From the service providers' perspective, the market consists of several WSCs (consumers) illustrated in the model by the applications that are competing against each other to acquire and use the service at a specific time instance. At a specific point in the execution, the application will match the operation needed currently to a subset of available services WSP_t. The subset is determined by both the functionality offered by the services and the spatial fragmentation caused by the limited monitoring capability of the application with respect to the total size of the market.

According to the definition of a distributed system, there should not exist a centralized entity where the allocation is being computed; therefore, the current setting becomes an instance of a *distributed marketplace*. We idealize our market to exhibit perfect competition (no entry and exit barriers), and to be free of monopolies or other "disruptive" institutions.

The mechanism of choice for valuation and allocation in dynamic markets is an *auction*. Our goal is to design an auction, which, when used by all the market participants, produces an allocation outcome that *maximizes the allocation in the whole market*. In other words, we are extending the auction mechanisms used by each service provider to support bidding strategies that can produce an efficient outcome, similar to what a centralized auctioning allocation mechanism would produce in the same market.

Accordingly, our design effort goes into supporting optimal service selection (for bidding purposes) mechanisms that should, in practice, hide the decentralized nature of the services market.

3.2.1 The Agent Model

In the distributed model of the allocation, agents are characterized by information, preferences, and behavior. In the mechanism design context, the term *information* $\theta(i, n)$ refers to the value that agent i has for service n. It is very important to mention at this point that the information function of each agent depends on several parameters, which we group under the generic term *quality of service* (QoS). Essentially, we assume that this QoS parameter is directly related to the service *value* and that it will determine an ordering of the preference of the user across the services available. In the case of digital items (such as Web services), the *private value* model describes better the market because each agent is likely to have his own valuation for the items (regardless of what the value of the item is for the other agents). The general assumption in economics is that the information $\theta(i, n)$ of each agent comes from the same known distribution Θ, allowing agents to use this information in designing their strategies.

The *bidding preferences* are generally given by the *utility function*, a quasilinear equation of the form $u(n,\theta,p) = v(n,\theta) - p$, where v is the agent's valuation function and p is the price to be paid for the item. As v is a measure of θ, the valuation of the items will depend on the ordering preference, and therefore on the QoS. We will use this at the design phase, when we exploit the preference for higher QoS items in producing bidding and pricing strategies for the agents. The utility function is generally private information (because of the item valuation component), and an allocation mechanism that uses utility or valuation in its computation would have to provide incentives for the participants to announce their true values (called "truthful" mechanisms).

Additionally, standard settings assume rational agents with risk-neutral behavior, meaning that rational agents prefer participating in an allocation process (and getting the allocation with some probability $p > 0$) to not participating.

3.2.2 WS-Auction Design

The design problem we are addressing originates in the fact that there are two levels of allocation: (1) one that addresses individual auction-level allocation, and (2) another one that addresses marketwide resources allocation. The decentralized market setting confines us to using and extending the existing individual (peer-wise) auctions, as no centralized entity should exist in the market. We extend the individual auctions so that they can support efficient market-level allocations as well.

We start the design by defining the utility functions that define the social choice for an efficient allocation. At the market level, we will want to maximize the total allocation in the current snapshot:

$$
\begin{aligned}
\mathrm{SCF}_{\mathrm{US}} &= \max \sum_{i=1,\dots,m, j=1,\dots,n} x_{ij} v_{ij} \\
\text{s.t.} &\sum_{i=1\dots m} x_{ij} \leq 1, \forall j \\
\text{s.t.} &\sum_{j=1,\dots,n} x_{ij} \leq 1, \forall i \\
x_{ij} &= \begin{cases} 1, & \mathrm{WSP}_j \xrightarrow{\text{allocated}} \mathrm{WSC}_i \\ 0, & \text{otherwise} \end{cases}
\end{aligned}
\tag{3.1}
$$

The maximization part of Equation (3.1) (where s.t. = subject to) describes the total market allocation, and the following summations describe a single-item allocation. The quantity v_{ij} denotes the valuation of the service or zero if no bid is placed, m is the number of auctioneers, and n is the number of bidders.

We observe that the marketwide allocation inefficiencies are not caused by the individual allocation mechanisms, which are considered efficient (following from the individual auctioneer's goals), but by the incapacity of bidders to find easily the proper place where to bid successfully. We are designing the WS-auction mechanism, which, added to the individual allocation mechanisms, helps the bidders choose to bid at the "proper" place, such that the inefficiencies caused by the decentralized setting are reduced or even eliminated. The goal is to produce an outcome (an allocation) similar to what a centralized allocation mechanism would have produced. Since the centralized allocation is efficient, reproducing the same outcome with a decentralized mechanism also makes that mechanism efficient. As the main beneficiary of our design is a Web services market, we have chosen the term *WS-auction* for the decentralized auctioning mechanism.

Producing a centralized-like allocation in a decentralized setting demands, as we will show next, the auctions to be incremental, indirect, second-price [9] auctions. We show that these auctions also need to expose both the historical winning bids information and the provisional (currently winning) allocation. Such a setting will allow a user to resubmit a bid immediately after it has been outbid, at some other service where a different auction is still ongoing.

The first recommended bidding strategy (whose proof—similar to the Vickrey auction bidding strategy proof—we omit for brevity reasons) is illustrated below:

1. *Bidding the true valuation in the decentralized WS-auction setting is incentive-compatible (maximizes the utility) for rational bidders.* In addition to choosing how much to bid, the bidders also need choose the best auction to bid at. This is the component that addresses the spatial fragmentation of the market. Under the decentralized setting that tries to mimic the outcome of a centralized setting,

as in the case of our model, the optimal place for bidding would be at the auction assigned by a centralized allocation algorithm. As we assume that the bidders come from a common *valuation distribution*, we can use historical allocations to create an *allocation profile* that would allow the bidder to "find" its position in the allocation. We show below that the equilibrium strategy is to bid at the "centralized allocation"-determined auction.

2. Let $E[\cdot]$ represent the expected value of a random variable. Let $V_{(k)}$ represent the kth-order statistic of a random variable V. We will show that: *In a centralized market, an efficient allocation is given by the highest-order statistic bids submitted.* By definition, efficient allocations maximize the total value of the bids submitted into the system. Therefore, given a nondecreasing ordering of the bids, in a market of N items, and M bids drawn from a common distribution V, the allocation produces the following outcome:

$$E[\text{alloc}_{\text{centr}}] = E\left[\sum_{i=1,\ldots,N} V(M-(t-1))\right] = \sum_{i=1,\ldots,N} V(M-(i-1)) \tag{3.2}$$

3. We will also argue that: *Historical information supports the maximization of the allocation.* Given the historical winning information, one can make better decisions on where to submit the bids. Essentially, knowing the previous winning bids allows the current bidders to build a *view* of the "value of the services in the market" (or an approximation for the distribution Θ) as seen by the previous bidders. This information allows the bidders to "arrange" themselves according to that information, as if they were allocated by a centralized mechanism. The strategy for bidding in this setting is described in the following paragraph (item 4 in this list).

4. *Using the bidder's truthful value, bid at an auction that historically has been assigned to similar bids.* Assume a nondecreasing ordering on the previous winning bid set, and assume that the distribution of the previous winning bids has been stable or is changing very slowly. We approximate this historical distribution with that of the currently submitted bids. We also assume that the pricing is truthful, and that the users will reuse the same bid value ("the value of being allocated the service in the current timeframe") across all the services at which they are bidding. If the current bidder bids at an auction with a lower winning price, it has a lower risk of being outbid. However, because of the ordering preference of the auctions according to the winning bids (and implicitly to the value of the services), previously "lower-priced" auctions imply that they might have a lower quality of service (a lower value) and therefore a lower utility. If the bidder bids at an auction that had a higher historical winning price than its bid value, it is likely that some other bidder whose value is in that range will outbid the bidder. This argument shows that the equilibrium strategy is to bid at auctions that had historical bids similar to their current bid.

The strategies for choosing where to bid and how much to bid described above are not efficient for the case when new auctions appear in the market. For such a scenario, and also for outbidding cases, it is a good idea to randomly probe bidding at other auctions, outside the range of the truthful valuation.

Another parameter that affects allocation efficiency is *temporal fragmentation*. Its effect can be observed in the case of outbidding (or *preempting*) existing provisional allocation. This phenomenon creates a potential inefficiency because the currently loosing bidder might have a sufficiently high value to qualify for the final allocation but not enough time to rebid at the right auction. The way to address this is to introduce *provisional allocation* information, which allows for more timely rearrangement of the bids *before other potentially fitting auctions end*. The market need not have synchronized auctions for this information to be useful; provisional allocations simply make best use of the time available before the auctions end.

At this point we are able to illustrate the mechanism that resulted from our design; each individual item should run an incremental, second-price auction (to support local valuation truthfulness). The auctions should also provide historical winning bids information to support the users decision on where to place the bids. The auctions also need to provision for rebidding support, allowing outbid users to find out (from the provisional information) that they have been outbid, so that they can rebid at a different auction, before the current auction expires.

A simple example demonstrates the utility of WS-auction. Let the current provisional allocation be (WSC_1, WSP_A,6), (WSC_2, WSP_B,5). Should a new participant bid (WSC_3, WSP_A,7), the allocation becomes inefficient because WSC_1 will now have to rebid at B. Should historical information be provided, the service consumers are able to construct the distribution for WSP, and WSC_1 would have chosen to bid (WSC_1, WSP_B,6), according to historical evidence of the prices for WSP_A.

3.2.3 Simulation Model and Experiments

For validation purposes, we have built a small, decentralized market model, and we have simulated a centralized and a decentralized bidding for single-item auctions. The bidders have two important decisions to make: where to place the bid, and how much to bid. For each of the bidders' decisions, we have created strategies that either do or do not make use of the WS-auction information for deciding on where to bid. To make the simulation realistic, the random (non-WS-auction) strategies only lack the information provided by WS-auction (previous winner, current allocation) and otherwise make use of the publicly available information (auctions reserve prices). So, they are comparable in intelligence with the WS-auction "strategies." The bidder's model also includes a limit for the highest bid.

To estimate WS-auction performance, we measure the total market allocation value and the number of outbid events (the convergence to the optimal allocation). We compare these measurements for the case of a centralized market, a WS-auction-enabled market, and a distributed market without the provisional and historical information. Measurements have shown that using the information and the suggested WS-auction strategies produces more efficient outcomes.

3.3 OWNERSHIP DECENTRALIZATION

Ownership decentralization refers to the Grid market model, where the service that the user is bidding on has two "owners": (1) the owner of the algorithm provided by the service and (2) the owner of the physical resources that provide execution support (and possibly input data sources) for the service that the user needs to invoke.

3.3.1 Interactions

As described previously, we let the service provider acquire the infrastructure (resources) it needs to run the service; thus, the client will perceive the whole interaction as *a chained proxy-based bidding*. We will start with a simplified case of the interaction, characteristic of a closed environment (a Grid supporting a single service). Then we describe the most general case of interaction and the expected behavior of the system; later we design the resource acquisition mechanism accordingly.

Case 1: All the Bids Go to the Same Service Class. This is a simple scenario that depicts a market consisting of a single service class (which could contain several identical instances) that makes use of Grid resources. Examples include a stochastic optimization service, a rendering farm, and many others.

The allocation mechanism design goal is "fairness": *the higher bid gets a better resource allocation* (across the market consisting of identical service instances). This is by definition the meaning of value-based allocation. Consider only one service class SI. The corresponding subset of potential consumers SC_{SI} will place bids at the service instances SI, and their expectation is that the higher bids should result in better experience, mostly because they expect to get higher-quality resources (the service instances algorithm being the same). We consider this an efficient allocation, where the ordering of the bid values determines quality of service (QoS) (as given by the resource supporting the service execution).

Case 2: Bids Can Go to Different Services. This case generalizes the market model by considering the effect of having other service classes SI_k contending for the same resources in the market, a state of things expected to exist in a real distributed environment.

The fairness design goal is expressed by *maintaining relative ordering on the resources allocated*, according to relative valuation across the whole market, regardless of which services demand the resources. The complexity of implementing this goal is caused by the resource allocation mechanism experiencing market fragmentation, due to different services that are contending over the Grid resources independently of each other.

The single-value bid preference for the service–resource bundle limits the user to express resource valuation directly, and in combination with the selfish nature of the service owners, the resource allocation outcome will be nondeterministic.

3.3.2 Grid–Market Auction Design

We design here an incentive-compatible mechanism (whose winning strategy is to disclose its real valuation for the item) that bids for resources on behalf of users. The service provider uses this mechanism to acquire the resources needed for executing an instance of it. Only one parameter is used to communicate the choice of the user: *the bid value*. This limitation on the communication leaves the choice to the service provider on how much of the initial bid to allocate to acquiring the resource, and how much to keep for itself. This decision has to be made by all service providers independently of each other, in a manner that results in a "fair" mapping of the users' bid values onto the resources acquired.

3.3.2.1 Service–Resource Market Social Choice Function. As the goal of the allocation is to enforce the users preferences as illustrated by their bids, we can see our solution as a *distributed preference aggregation* scheme. The goal of the service-resource market allocation, illustrated by the social choice function $\mathrm{SCF_{SR}}$, is defined as follows: *For any pair of bids submitted into the market, increasing them with the same amount should not result in a reordering of their current allocation onto the resource.*

Formally, let $(\mathrm{SC}_a \cdots \mathrm{SC}_k)$ be the *provisional* winners allocated over the set of resources $\mathrm{RP}_\alpha \cdots \mathrm{RP}_\kappa$. If two winning bidders *i,j* decide to increase their bids with the same amount δ, we denote the new allocation with $(\mathrm{SC}_{a'} \cdots \mathrm{SC}_{k'})$, where $i \to i'$ and $j \to j'$.

The $\mathrm{SCF_{SR}}$ states that their relative ordering across the resource should not change:

$$\texttt{rbid\_SCi} \geq \texttt{rbid\_SCj} \Rightarrow \texttt{rbid\_SCi'} \geq \texttt{rbid\_SCj'}\ \forall\ \texttt{i,j}\ \text{winning bids}$$

In other words, if bidder *i* has an allocation better than or equal to that of bidder *j* in terms of the quality of the resource received, then after they increase their bids with the same quantity, bidder *i* should still have received an allocation better than or equal to that of bidder *j*. The rationale for the ordering requirement is supported by the fact that the money (value) is the absolute means for measuring service satisfaction (QoS). The same amount of bid *change* between two bidders should not change the ordering (or relative quality) of the resources that they are getting, regardless of which services they receive the resource for. If a reordering occurs, the same amount of money will be perceived as not having the same value in terms of service quality from the user's perspective, an undesired characteristic of an allocation mechanism. A short example will illustrate our point.

Assume that two participants, A and B, bid for service $\texttt{sbid}_A = 20$ and $\texttt{sbid}_B = 18$. Assume that service for bidder A charges $\texttt{sc}_A = 0 + 50\% * \texttt{sbid}_A$, whereas service B charges a smaller (or even zero) percentage after a fixed service minimum amount has already been reached $\texttt{sc}_B = 10 + 0\% * \texttt{sb}_B$. At this point the bid for the resource is $\texttt{rbid}_A = 10$ and $\texttt{rbid}_B = 8$. Assuming that both A and B decide to increase their bids by the same amount *5* (let's say in an attempt to get a higher-quality resource), then they end up in a different order: $\texttt{rbid}_A = 12.5$, $\texttt{rbid}_B = 13$. This reordering will be associated with unfairness and uncertainty, as such a variable payment scheme will not maximize their chance of getting the resources that the bidders desire, because of the *greedy nature* of the service providers. This is a negative aspect and will determine the clients' service preference strategies.

3.3.2.2 ***Bidding Strategy Determination.*** We can model this bidding as a game where participants might have different strategies on *how much to allocate for the resource payment from the initial bid.*

One strategy choice for the service provider is to bid a predetermined, fixed amount for the resource. This has disadvantages in terms of (1) not implementing a positive correlation between the user's payment and the resource (QoS) received and (2) its incapacity to compete dynamically to the evolving prices of the resources.

We are left with two strategies: one that assigns a *fixed percentage* of the user's full bid to the resource and keeps for itself the remaining percentage—denoted `proportionalBidStrategy`—as service A in the example above, and the other that assigns the full remaining bid amount to the service, after a constant service payment is charged—denoted `reducedBidStrategy`—as service B in the same example above.

Given the strategies presented above, we can represent in Table 3.1 the normal form of a game where the two strategies are evaluated against each other. Having defined the utility (satisfaction) function to be directly proportional with the quality of the service obtained, the interactions are judged as follows. The players associate fairness with the outcome when their bids are fully utilized to maximize their QoS and associate unfairness with the case where their bids have limited contribution to the QoS.

Using the utility formula given by the strategies above, one can show (omitted for brevity purposes) that the `reducedBidStrategy` is incentive-compatible and strategyproof.

Given the selfish, rational, utility-maximizing profile of the service consumers, it becomes readily apparent that the game described above has the "constant service-charging" price strategy as the equilibrium, and therefore it will be used as the *dominant strategy* for the service providers to use. The `reducedBidStrategy` supports an *order-preserving*, fairness-based allocation, which can be considered *revenue-maximizing* for the service providers under the assumption that service users are capable of detecting deviations from the dominant strategy described above. Verifying that a service charges a constant amount for itself can turn out to be difficult to support in practice, and we will assume that additional mechanisms such as service reservation price and historical resource pricing will support the detection of `proportionalBidStrategy` charges. Details of monitoring the services behavior in the market are considered implementation decisions, and we only assume that they are available.

TABLE 3.1 Bidding Strategy Evaluation Matrix

	`reducedBidStrategy`	`proportionalBidStrategy`
`reducedBidStrategy`	(fair, fair)	(fair, unfair)
`proportionalBidStrategy`	(unfair, fair)	(unfair, unfair)

3.3.3 Resource Manager's Allocation Strategy

The resource market can be either simplified to a centralized model or generalized to model a set of independent resource provider entities. In both cases, we will refer to the resource providing entities as "Grids."

A centralized market will have its own algorithm for evaluating the impact of a new resource request over the existing allocation, and it will have ways to fit the incoming bid onto the resources; several solutions have been explored, some of which are mentioned below.

In a distributed resources market, services will additionally need to employ similar strategies to the WS-auction mechanism to ensure that the decentralized nature of the resources does not affect the allocation adversely.

For each service that bids for resources, we assume that there has been some previous interaction between the service and the resource provider, with the purpose of "profiling" the resource needs (CPU, memory, storage, networking) of those services. Given this information, the bids from the services will need to include, in addition to the bid value, the requested resource characteristics. Having to choose between different service profile (SP) component characteristics (memory, CPU, etc.) submitted by services in combination with a bid price makes the problem an instance of the combinatorial allocation problem, (CAP) which is known to be NP-hard.

In addition to the spatial model of the resource market (either centralized or distributed), the resource market allocation designer has to address the temporal aspect of receiving bids submitted continuously. Fortunately, such cases have been researched in *online mechanism* literature; significant work has gone into designing efficient and truthful mechanisms for online allocation problems [13,14].

Online mechanism solutions suggest having optimal offline allocations (greedy-based) that make the online mechanism truthful, in combination with a form of Vickrey payment. The problem with this is that the payment determination is excessively complex in most cases. The offline greedy allocation results in a truthful scheme that avoids speculations. In order to simulate the commodity nature of resources in terms of pricing, and to implement a fair payment scheme, we propose a uniform-pricing Vickrey model across the same resource class RP_i. Assuming a "services" capacity $SC_i = |RP_i|$, the pricing is a c_ith price Vickrey model, the actual value per each SC_i corresponding to $\mathtt{rval}_i$.

In practice, a greedy-like allocation scheme will need to support a *preemptive service model*, a model that is currently available in some large resource pool such as computational Grids servicing extremely large resource requirements. For the nonpreemptive services case, the Grid resource market could support simpler (yet inefficient) allocation schemes, such as computing a fixed "cost" of the requested resources, or even more complex schemes where the resource manager takes into account the "overhead cost" on the performance of the already accepted services and discounts their payment according to the "load" introduced by the new service. We plan to research practical aspects of these schemes in future work.

For the special case of accommodating variable-runtime services, actual resource payment will depend on the amount of time the resources are used. The payment will also depend on some policy to account for variations in using the resource attributes defined above. In practice, being unable to determine beforehand the amount of usage, the payment scheme will either have to consider credits, or request continuous payments.

3.3.4 Market Efficiency Supporting Infrastructure

An efficient environment functioning as two markets connected through the brokering behavior of the service providers needs specific pieces of information disclosed and a set of mechanisms that would use such information and would ensure an efficient and strategyproof functionality. We are referring to the historical and provisional information supporting the users to submit bids at the service (or respectively by services bidding for resources) that maximizes their utility N: risk ratio (as dictated by the WS-auction design) and to verification mechanisms that can be used to detect deviations from the strategy recommended by our design. These can be considered implementation aspects, and we will not discuss them here.

3.4 CONCLUSIONS

We have shown elsewhere [15] that in the primary services market, the complexity of computing each individual allocation is $O(m)$, depending on the number of bidders m that can end up at some auction. The complexity of the user's bidding in the market is linear $O(n)$ in the size n of the group of services in which the user is interested. This complexity is not propagated onto the second market because of the insulating effect of the service acting as a proxy.

In the secondary resource market, after the service has decided the amount to bid for the resource, the bidding complexity is constant for the centralized resource model or $O(k)$ in the distributed case, following the same WS-auction argument. The resource allocation computation is generally much more complex, due to the combinatorial nature of the resources demanded (some amount of memory, and some amount of CPU, etc.), but several solutions cited above already exist.

A very important characteristic of our model is the *strategyproofness* of the bidding entities. According to WS-auction, in the service market, in order to minimize the risk of loosing the resource allocation, the user's strategy will be to bid truthfully at the "right" service (the best one that historically had the highest chance of accepting a bid such as the user's). In the resource market, we argued earlier that the service's strategy is to subtract a fixed amount for itself, and bid the rest for the resource. Having both truthful strategies and efficient resulting allocations in both the services and the result market allows us to declare the overall experience for the users to be strategyproof and efficient.

In the combined market, we can generalize the rule for allocating the user's bid as follows. Given the SCF_{SR} function discussed earlier, the strategy for splitting the bid across the owners of the components that make up the service (in this case the algorithm and the physical resource) indicates the following rule:

There can be differentiated two classes of resource types, according to their contribution to the utility function of the user:

- *Fixed-Utility Providers.* Items providing constant utility (QoS) should charge *fixed* amounts in order to be perceived as fair by the user. For example, correct and optimal algorithmic implementations of the services are independent from the QoS perceived by the user.
- *Variable-Utility Providers.* Items providing variable utility (QoS) should charge *proportional* amounts, in order to be perceived as fair by the user. For example, the characteristics of the resources that are used for executing the services are directly proportional to the QoS delivered.

The generalization that follows dictates that a broker who needs to bid on a set of resources on the user's behalf needs to allocate fixed costs to fixed-utility providers (algorithmic services) and to bid the rest fully toward variable-utility providers (computational resources), in the proportion that they contribute to the final QoS perceived by the user.

Comparing the Grid–auction model with a Grid commodity market shows the advantages of the auction model. The centralized commodity market needs to compute the market equilibriums for determining the prices, but the environment is too dynamic (no fixed allocation computation point) because jobs differ in requirements and timespan. It is also generally costly to compute the commodity equilibrium price. On the other hand, without a dynamic computation of the commodity price, inefficient allocations will result. Having auctions determine dynamically the *commodity price* as the *n*th *Vickrey price* (e.g., in the simple single-resource case) is the most efficient solution in terms of computation overhead and outcome fairness.

REFERENCES

1. G. A. Madeira and R. M. Townsend, Endogenous groups and dynamic selection in mechanism design, *Journal of Economic Theory* **142**(1):259–293 (2008).
2. E. Hudo, R. S. Montero, and I. M. Llorente, The GridWay framework for adaptive scheduling and execution on Grids, *Scalable computing: Practice and Experience (SCPE)* **6**(3):1–8 (Sept. 2005).
3. A. Mas-Colell, M. Whinston, and J. Green, *Microeconomic Theory*, Oxford Univ. Press, New York, 1995.
4. M. Jackson, Mechanism theory, in *The Encyclopedia of Life Support Systems*, Ulrich Derigs, ed., EOLSS Publishers, Oxford, UK, 2003.
5. S. de Vries and R. Vohra, Combinatorial auctions: A survey, *INFORMS Journal on Computing* **15**(3):284–309 (2003).
6. R. Dash, D. Parkes, and N. Jennings, Computational mechanism design: A call to arms, *IEEE Intelligent Systems* **18**(6):40–47 (2003).

7. M. Hajiaghayi, Online auctions with re-usable goods, *Proc. 6th ACM Conf. Electronic Commerce*, New York, Oct. 25–27, 2004.
8. N. Nisan, Bidding and allocation in combinatorial auctions, *Proc. 2nd ACM Conf. Electronic Commerce*, Minneapolis, MN, Oct 17–20, 2000.
9. W. Vickrey, Counterspeculation, auctions, and competitive sealed tenders, *Journal of Finance* **16**:8–37 (1961).
10. E. Clarke, Multipart pricing of public goods, *Journal of Public Choice* **11**:17–33 (1971).
11. T. Groves, Incentives in teams, *Econometrica* **41**:617–633 (1973).
12. D. C. Parkes, An iterative generalized Vickrey auction: Strategy-proofness without complete revelation, *Proc. AAAI Spring Symp. Game Theoretic and Decision Theoretic Agents.* AAAI Press, March 2001.
13. E. Friedman and D. C. Parkes, Pricing WiFi at Starbucks—issues in online mechanism design, *Proc. 4th ACM Conf. Electronic Commerce*, San Diego, CA, June 9–12, 2003.
14. R. Porter, Mechanism design for online real-time scheduling, *Proc. 5th ACM Conf. Electronic Commerce*, New York, May 17–20, 2004.
15. T. Stef-Praun and V. Rego, WS-Auction: Mechanism design for a web-services market, *Proc. ICDCS 2006—Incentive Based Computing Workshop, Lisbon, Portugal, July 4–7*, 2006.
16. S. Venugopal, R. Buyya, and L. Winton, A Grid service broker for scheduling e-science applications on global data Grids, *Concurrency and Computation: Practice and Experience* **18**(6):685–699 (May 2006).

4

UTILITY FUNCTIONS, PRICES, AND NEGOTIATION

JOHN WILKES

4.1 INTRODUCTION

This chapter provides an introduction to the use of utility theory with service-level agreements between a computer-based service provider and a client. It argues that a consistent approach to utility, together with a flexible notion of pricing, can go a long way to clarifying some of the hidden assumptions that pervade many existing contracts and decisions around them. The goal is to enhance understanding of a surprisingly tricky area, identify a few consequences for services providers and their clients, suggest a set of terminology that reduces ambiguities, and make some suggestions for future work.

The environment assumed here contains a set of *service providers* that offer computer-based *services* to their clients, which may themselves be service providers. Each service provider is assumed to be an independent entity, motivated by business concerns such as achieving profitability, and so services must be paid for somehow—such as by pay per use, subscription, advertising, or a subsidy from a sponsor. Service providers are assumed to be at least partially self-managing, and thus able to operate autonomously without human intervention, although humans will always be held responsible for the service provider's actions. The purpose of this chapter is to discuss some of the considerations involved when a client and a service provider determine how to agree on a price for a contract between them. To keep things simple, it largely restricts itself to the interactions between one client and one service provider.

Market-Oriented Grid and Utility Computing Edited by Rajkumar Buyya and Kris Bubendorfer

This chapter is meant as a tutorial, rather than a survey, and while there is a great deal of work on using economic mechanisms to control computer systems of various kinds that could be included in such a survey, space limitations preclude discussing most of it here. Nonetheless, a few notable, relevant examples include the following: the paper by Sutherland [30] for one of the earliest uses of economic mechanisms to limit access to a shared resource, Mariposa [29] for a distributed database that used profit to motivate data placement and query execution choices, and Spawn [36] and Tycoon [16] for distributed, spot-auction-based pricing of compute resources. A paper aimed at economists [12] argued for bringing economic mechanisms to bear on distributed control of computer systems, and pointed out some associated perils, such as potential inefficiencies compared to centralized schemes, and oscillations from delayed access to partial information.

The field of self-managing systems (called *autonomics* by some) has been around for a long time. Such systems need clear objectives to achieve, and these have often been specified as "utility" or even more explicitly "profit." A few examples from a crowded field include these papers: [2,13,14,24,37]. The Trading Agent Competition (http://www.sics.se/tac/) pits implementations of autonomous agents against one another in a series of competitive games that foster learning about how such systems should operate.

References to other supporting material are cited in the remaining text of this chapter, which begins with a review of service-level agreements and prices, before an introduction to the notion of utility and how it affects prices and negotiation. This is followed by a discussion of how risks and penalties affect prices and contracts. The chapter concludes with suggested directions for future work, some overall observations, and a summary.

4.2 SERVICE-LEVEL AGREEMENTS (SLAs)

A service provider offers service to a client under the terms of a service-level agreement (SLA), which is a bilateral contract that governs the terms of the interaction between the parties. An SLA is typically negotiated before service will be provided, although some services may be offered under an implicit SLA, which the client is deemed to have agreed to if it uses the service.

For self-managing computer entities, the SLA will take the form of a computer-readable document. It will typically contain some or all of the items listed below (this list is loosely extended from the Web Services Agreement Specification [38]):

1. The identities of the provider and the client.
2. The start and duration of the contract.
3. The service that is to be delivered. This is typically described in an informal manner, although interface specifications may be incorporated directly or by reference (e.g., if they are written in WSDL [8]). Reporting, escalation, and remediation processes belong here, although they are often bundled into "what

happens if things go wrong". See O'Sullivan's thesis [21] for a survey of many aspects of service specification.

4. Service-level indicators (SLIs), which are carefully defined, observable, measures on the service or the behavior of the client or provider. Examples might include "the 95th percentile of the per-second message-arrival rate accumulated over a 5 minute interval" or "the number of discrete 1 second or longer intervals in the last minute in which another (named) SLI had a value of less than 50, when sampled every 100 ms." Sometimes processes for taking the measurements are also defined in an SLA, and may include the use of a particular trusted third party to make the measurements [9].
5. The amount or level of service that is expected, often expressed in the form of service-level objectives (SLOs). These represent bounds on both the client's and service provider's behaviors (e.g., highest load level permitted, target response time, maximum delay before a technician is dispatched if an outage occurs). The term "SLO violation" means that a desired SLO is not being met during the execution of a contract. SLOs are defined in terms of SLIs.[1]
6. The price: how much money will change hands as a result of this SLA being executed. By convention, positive values represent payments from a client to a service provider; negative values, the reverse. Thus, penalties imposed on a service provider are specified as negative values, and added to the price.
7. When payment should occur, such as when or if invoices will be issued (e.g., whichever comes first: SLA completion, monthly, or once the debt exceeds $1000), and how soon payment is expected (e.g., before the service is used, or within 1 minute of an invoice).
8. What happens if things go wrong? For example, it might specify penalties that will be incurred if a party's behavior fails to conform to what is expected. The most common case addresses the service provider failing to meet an SLO, but a good SLA also constrains client behavior. Such penalties are often financial, and can range from a partial rebate of service fees, through recompense for economic damage, to punitive. There may also be implicit penalties, such as damage to a supplier's reputation.[2]
9. Additional conditions such as the jurisdiction in which the agreement is to be interpreted; the use of binding arbitration to adjudicate disputes, confidentiality terms that apply to the SLA itself.
10. Irrefutable evidence that both parties have agreed to the terms of this particular SLA, such as a pair of digital signatures of the SLA's contents.

[1] People often mistakenly talk about "an SLA being violated" when all they mean is that the expected SLOs aren't being met. If the SLA itself is being violated, the usual recourse in the United States is to the law courts.

[2] Although these implicit penalties are rare recorded directly in an SLA, they may be hinted at by attempts to limit them by restrictions on the types of recourse a party is allowed to pursue such as binding arbitration and confidentiality clauses.

SLAs are often simplified by relying on "out of band" terms and conditions that must be interpreted by humans, leaving the SLA to describe only those parts that both sides feel might be mis-interpreted by the other. This has some risks, however, since omitting something from an SLA is tantamount to giving the other party permission to behave in any way it pleases for that part of the agreement.

It helps to assume that the two parties are selfish, i.e., interested in protecting their own interests, mildly distrusting of one another, as well as what economists call rational—taking a dispassionate view of gains and losses. This will motivate them to specify everything in an SLA on which they feel that the other party might adopt a contrary position.

Specificity carries costs (e.g., generating, understanding, and checking clauses), so great thoroughness tends to be employed in an SLA only when the stakes get large. This is just like traditional commerce, where a simple one-off purchase may be done without a contract, but a multi-billion-dollar commercial deal is typically governed by a contract that runs to hundreds of pages, much of which is concerned with handling contingencies and risk mitigation. Such terms may explicitly be included in the SLA itself, or incorporated by reference, or simply assumed. In practice, it is best to think of an SLA as a legally binding contract. If something matters, include it explicitly, or by reference.[3]

4.3 PRICE FUNCTIONS

Most SLAs are written as if the SLOs are the governing terms. Instead, this chapter takes the position that because SLAs are business contracts, what actually matters are the financial consequences to client and service provider of the outcomes that are achieved for an SLA.[4] Those financial consequences are defined by the *price* of each outcome—how much money changes hands between client and service provider for that outcome.

Prices are the governing terms in a contract, not SLOs; an SLO is merely a hint that specifies a desired outcome. How desirable? That's determined by the price—each possible outcome has a single price. This leads naturally to calling this approach *outcome-based pricing*. The range of prices that cover all possible outcomes is represented by means of a *price function*, which maps the space of outcomes to prices (Fig. 4.1).

Since a price function reflects the interests of the service provider and its client across the entire range of potential outcomes, it is typically more complicated than a constant value to represent a simple flat fee. For example, it might include

[3] This often causes surprise, provoking observations of the form "computers cannot generally understand natural-language text." This is immaterial; legal contracts are always interpreted in a larger context, which often includes niceties that are basically incomprehensible to a layperson. What matters is that the details of interest to the parties are accurately, and completely, spelled out in the SLA, and that the actionable elements of the contract are represented in a way that the parties can interpret, preferably automatically.

[4] This chapter uses the word "outcome" to mean everything but the price. Although a case could be made for including the price in the outcome, excluding it simplifies some of the descriptions.

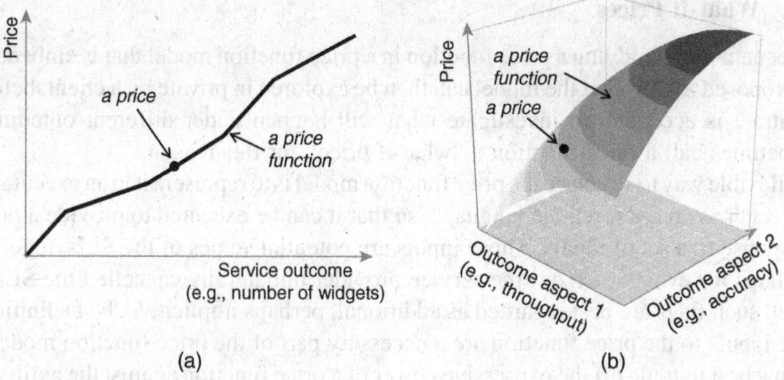

Figure 4.1 A price and a price function for (a) a single-outcome dimension, for which the price function is a line, and (b) two outcome dimensions; with N outcome aspects, it's a surface in an $(N+1)$-dimensional space.

volume-related usage fees, discounts for use of multiple service features at one time (a form of product bundling), a monthly subscription charge, or penalties for misbehavior—or all of these.

The price function can be proposed by the service provider or by the client—as long as they both agree in the end, it doesn't really matter. In practice, many service providers are reluctant to negotiate a pricing structure with each client, so price-setting service providers are more common than clients, especially for services with many clients, although clients may be allowed to specify values for parts of the pricing function, such as penalties. Since client and service provider distrust one another, outcomes, and hence price functions, must be defined over measures that both parties have agreed to and are mutually visible (i.e., SLI values).

A price function is represented in an SLA document by means of a *price function model*, or simply *price model*, which allows the price function to be communicated between the service provider and the client. Limitations in the capabilities of the price model may, in turn, limit the set of price functions that can be supported—for example, it is common to simplify the price model to make it easier to understand or write, such as by formulating it as a sum of independent terms (e.g., a fee for the base service plus any penalties). The complexity of the price function can also be reduced by limiting the range of alternatives that an SLA can describe, such as by imposing constraints on what can go into an SLA.

Outcome-based pricing has several desirable characteristics, especially in the context of self-managing service providers. It eliminates ambiguities about how to make tradeoffs between different alternatives—what if two SLOs are being violated, but only one can be fixed? It provides a numerical scale (a common currency) that can be used to rank-order (the consequences of) different service provider and client behaviors. It also provides a clear input to the objective functions, such as "maximize profitability," that are used when a service provider is determining how to respond to different situations.

4.3.1 What-If Prices

One benefit of embodying a price function in a price function model that is embedded in a proposed SLA is that the model can then be explored in private by a client, before a contract is accepted, to investigate what will happen under different outcomes. I sometimes call a price function a "what-if price" for this reason.

A flexible way to structure the price function model is to represent it in an executable form, such as an interpretable language, so that it can be executed to provide a price in response to a set of inputs. Those inputs are potential values of the SLIs, together with flags for events such as "the service provider unilaterally cancelled the SLA." In fact, such flags are best regarded as additional, perhaps implicit, SLIs. Definitions of the inputs to the price function are a necessary part of the price function model.

How best to trade off the expressive power of a price function against the ability of the recipient to reason about the result is still an open question. If a client cannot understand the behavior of a price function, it should probably not agree to an SLA that contains it. A common, simple pattern is to describe the price function as a sum of independent parts. At the opposite extreme are the complex functions that are needed to describe rich price structures with interdependent parts, such as personal taxes in industrialized nations, with their subsidies, discounts, caps, rebates, and other special cases that reflect a government's policies about wealth (re)distribution.

Executable specifications offer great flexibility, but risk imposing equally great complexity in reverse-engineering their behavior. Perhaps this is the real value of SLOs: they can provide hints about boundaries in the outcome space where the price function model should be expected to emit relatively rapidly changing values.

4.3.2 Setting Prices

There are many ways to determine how to set the price for a service. This chapter approaches the problem from the perspective of a rational, self-interested service provider, which is interested solely in maximizing its profitability in direct negotiations with a single client. For simplicity, it largely elides details of longer-term issues such as market segmentation, building a customer base, competition, and customer retention, all of which might cause a service provider to offer different prices at different times to different clients, and focuses on a single interaction between a client and a service provider.

There are a great many different ways in which services can be priced; O'Sullivan [21] provides a survey, and Section 4.5 touches on the topic of price negotiation. This chapter simply assumes that the service provider has already chosen the structure of its pricing function, which determines what inputs the price function will use for a particular service. For example, the service provider might charge on a per unit basis, plus a flat fee or a monthly retainer; it might offer a subscription service up to some maximum amount of service; it might offer bulk discounts for large purchases or offset some charges against others; it might charge its most loyal customers less (or more); it might allow its clients to select from several different forms of pricing function; and so on. Although the structure(s) may be fixed, there's typically still room to negotiate the parameters and constants used in the pricing function, including the actual rates charged, the breakpoints that correspond to desired service levels (SLO targets), and potential penalties to be paid.

Ultimately, whether a service provider is able to impose its choice on customers depends on the latter's willingness to pay its prices—which, in turn, depends on the number of potential customers and their valuations of its services, as well as the presence of competitors and their behavior. The amount of demand for a service is generally assumed to be a function of the price at which it is offered, with lower prices bringing greater demand—the so-called demand curve of microeconomics, also known as the *elasticity of demand with price*. There is a great deal of literature in this space; Luo et al. [18] provide an approachable introduction to the topic.

Estimating a demand curve is difficult—doubly so in the relatively new market for computer-based services. The *price-at-risk* methodology [23] attempts to control this uncertainty by using estimates of both demand curves and uncertainty in that demand to produce distributions of likely profitability, using models such as Monte Carlo simulations. This approach allows a service provider to make statements of the form "I will accept a contract if the expected return (e.g., gross profit margin) is greater than $X and the likelihood of a loss is less than Y%".[5] More on this below.

4.4 UTILITY

Like many before me, I find the notion of utility a useful one to guide decisions in automated service providers. This section discusses what is meant by utility.

In microeconomics, *agents* (i.e., service providers and their customers) are assumed to have *preferences*, which represent (partial) orderings on outcomes, and those preferences are assumed to guide behaviors; rational agents will always attempt to achieve the outcomes that they most prefer. In many cases, a party's preferences can be mapped to values of *utility*, where higher utility means greater preference. Utility is measured in subjective units, and so it does not make sense to compare or add two parties' utility values, or even to try to normalize them into a common range. A *utility function* is simply a mapping from a space of outcomes onto utility values.

In the simplest possible case (see Fig. 4.2a), the service outcome is fixed and the utility is just a function of the price to be paid—it might be as trivial as a linear function of the profit an agent would expect to make, but many other options are available, especially when people are involved, as Figure 4.2b suggests.[6]

[5] Price at risk is related to *value at risk*, which is used to articulate the amount of risk associated with a trading portfolio. A value-at-risk estimate is a prediction, at a certain confidence level, of the maximum amount of money that might be lost given a model of likely future price movements in a set of financial instruments. Known difficulties include estimating the likelihood of rare events using historical data, and determining the correct models to use [31].

[6] In the United States, "list price" is specified by the car manufacturer, and "invoice price" is what the dealer pays the manufacturer – before any adjustments for volume discounts or other sales incentives. Note that utility dropped as the price got too low because of the implied risk of faulty or counterfeit goods or provider mis-behavior in other areas, such as ability to deliver.

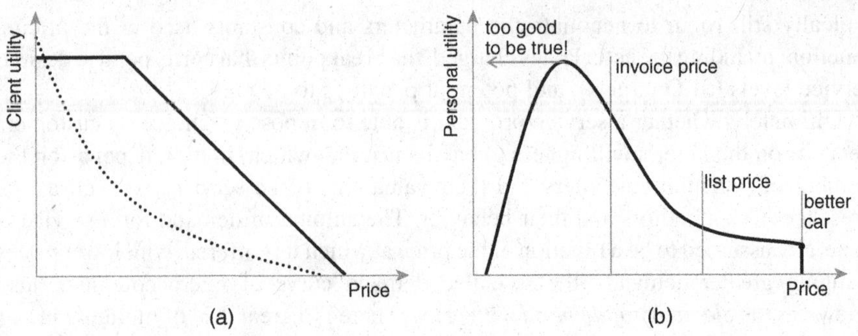

Figure 4.2 Utility functions for a range of prices for a fixed outcome: (a) two simple mappings between price and utility; (b) the author's de facto internal utility function when he last negotiated the price for a car.

For computer services, it is normal to have at least one variable outcome such as response time or throughput, in addition to the price for the service. Indeed, there are often multiple dimensions (or aspects or attributes) to the service outcomes—such as throughput and response time and accuracy for a Web service, or memory and bandwidth and startup delay for a virtual machine rental service. The extension is straightforward: the utility function is defined over all these aspects plus the price, forming a surface in an $(N+2)$-dimensional space for N outcome aspects plus a price (Fig. 4.3).[7]

In what follows, I will use an example with only one kind of outcome to make things easier to visualize. I further simplify the discussion by assuming that contracts are independent, and the parties retain no memory of previous negotiations.

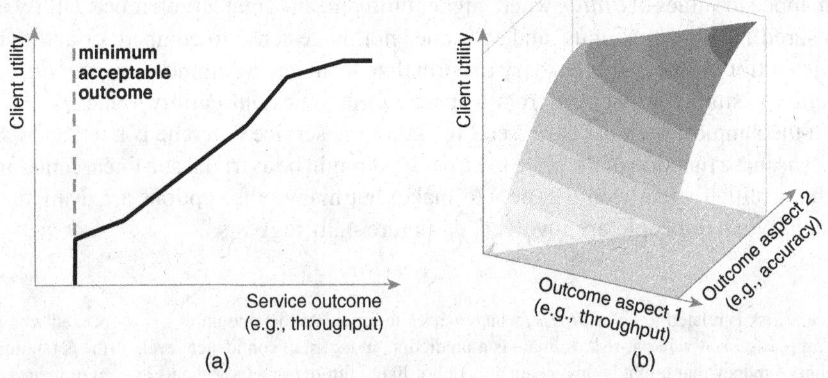

Figure 4.3 Utility functions for (a) a single-dimension outcome and (b) multiple outcome aspects.

[7] The assumption made here is that neither party discovers a significant loophole that allows them to achieve the outcome they desire for a much lower (higher) price, such as by violating an SLO without getting caught.

Soliciting complete multidimensional utility functions from people is difficult, so simpler approaches are often used. For example, multiattribute utility theory (MAUT) [15] typically assumes independence of each outcome aspect or attribute, and generates $N+1$ independent utility functions—one for each outcome aspect, plus one for price. These are weighted and then added together, although other ways of combining the individual values are possible. Obviously, utility functions formulated in this manner are less general than the full form—for example, they cannot readily express a utility function that requires minimal values of several aspects to be satisfied simultaneously—but they may be useful in some circumstances, especially when people are involved.[8] Since the focus of this chapter is automated clients and service providers, I prefer the full formulation for its flexibility and greater capability.

It is common to constrain or approximate the utility function to make it more mathematically tractable, by insisting on features such as smoothness, continuity, and differentiability.

4.4.1 The Client Perspective

Consider the example of a request-processing service, such as a web service or a job execution service, with some appropriate, agreed-on measure of throughput, such as the count of requests completed in some averaging interval. Suppose that there is only one price to be paid at the end of the contract, and this price is determined by a single outcome value measured along one dimension—the request throughput. A client of the service is likely to prefer higher throughputs over lower ones, although there may come a point of diminishing returns on the high end, and there may be a lower bound below which the service becomes unusable (see Fig. 4.4).

When an SLA is negotiated, the client's objective is to persuade the service provider to provide it with the best possible utility—in this case, by maximizing the throughput offered. The client's utility can be expressed as a function of throughput: $\texttt{utility}_{\texttt{client}}\texttt{(throughput)}$.

However, there's no free lunch. It is likely that the service provider will expend more resources to provide a higher throughput, and to maintain profitability it will want to recoup its extra costs by raising the price for the service. Now the client needs to rank-order its preferences over the two-dimensional space of response time and price, which can be accomplished with a utility function $\texttt{utility}_{\texttt{client}}\texttt{(throughput, price)}$.

The client is said to be *indifferent* to (i.e., equally happy with) all outcomes that produce the same value of utility, and the line connecting such a set of points is called an *indifference curve*. The indifference curves might look like those shown in Figure 4.4.

[8] A common form of MAUT in human-to-human interactions is to have each participant write down their per-aspect utility functions in the form of a table, provide weights for summing them, and normalize the result (e.g., into a [0,100] range). The functions and weights are then communicated to a trusted third-party mediator, who can use these data to calculate an "optimal" operating point that maximizes the sum of the overall utility functions for both sides. Although this is makes good sense when it results in an agreement where none was possible before, it relies on many assumptions that I prefer to avoid.

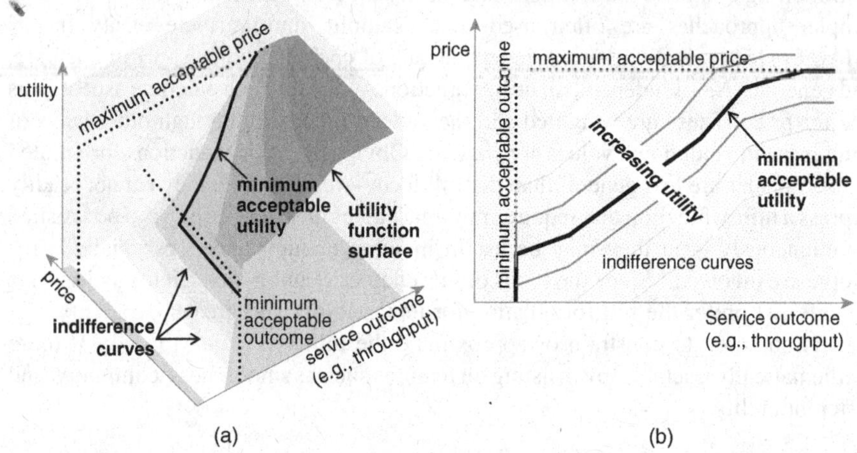

Figure 4.4 A sample utility function: (a) utility as a function of service throughput and price, with indifference curves on the surface representing the function; (b) contour plot of the same utility function projected onto the price versus throughput plane.

A client will only accept contracts that [are likely to] provide at least some minimum utility—the value at which they are indifferent as to whether to accept a contract. Since utility is measured in arbitrary units, and can be rescaled and renormalized at will, it is sometimes convenient to set this minimally acceptable utility value at zero; positive values imply that clients will be happy with the outcome; negative values mean they will be unhappy.

When mapped onto the price–outcome plane of Figure 4.4b, where minimum utility represents a worst-case price curve for the client—it is the *client max price function,* also called the client *price boundary function* and the client *reservation price function.* It is used to define the client's acceptable region during contract negotiation: no contract that lies in a region with lower utility (e.g., a higher price or lower output) will be acceptable. In Figure 4.4b, only the area to the right and below the client's max price function will be acceptable. It is also common—as shown here—for there to be an absolute upper bound on the amount the client is willing to pay, regardless of the amount of service obtained.

For multioutcome utility functions, the same trick can be applied to generate a client max price function from a minimum-acceptable utility indifference curve. With N aspects, the client indifference curves now traverse an $(N+2)$-dimensional surface, and they can be projected down onto an $(N+1)$-dimensional space.

4.4.2 The Service Provider Perspective

A service provider performs a calculation similar to the client's, to calculate its utility for the range of possible outcomes and prices. When these are mapped into the price/outcome space (Fig. 4.5), the result is a *minimum* acceptable price (`min_price`), below which it will not enter into a contract.

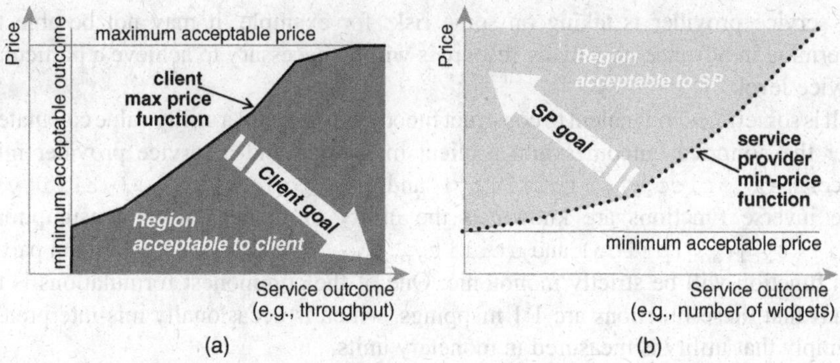

Figure 4.5 The client and service provider (SP) perspectives; each has a viable operating region bounded by a `max_price/min_price` function.

A tenet of outcome-based pricing is that price functions in SLAs must be written only in terms of outcomes that are visible to both parties; it is not acceptable for a price function to depend on "magic values" that the service provider can set to any number they like.

One effect is that although "cost plus" price functions are quite common in human-mediated contracts, they are less likely to be useful in SLAs agreed on between mildly distrusting automated agents; they require the service provider's costs to be made visible and (potentially) audited to check that they are being reported correctly, which is itself expensive. Instead, service provider costs are usually folded into a price function by means of flat fees and service-consumption-related factors of one kind or another.

A second effect is that the service provider's utility function is likely to depend on hidden "outcome" data that only the provider is privy to, and cannot directly be included in an SLA. For example, the service provider will probably estimate its costs for a particular client-visible outcome using a model of client behavior, service provider outlays, and desired service level. Service provider outlays typically fall into two categories: (1) direct costs associated with a particular SLA, such as those for renting resources, license fees, and power and cooling bills; and (2) indirect costs, which include fixed overheads such as resource purchases that must be amortized across many contracts, overheads such as personnel, and additional business expenses such as taxes. A service provider may choose to include other factors in its utility calculation, such as the opportunity cost of tying up a resource (using it now may preclude a lucrative future use of it), and it may demand an adequate rate of return on its investments, not just a nonzero profit. The result will be a private utility function over the service provider's outcome space. Given a minimal acceptable utility value and its associated indifference curve, the service provider can then determine a minimum acceptable price.

Working out how to do this mapping between its hidden utility function and the client-visible price function is one of the hardest parts of determining how to set the price for a service. By using a prediction rather than post facto measurements, the service provider is taking on some risk; for example, it may not be able to determine in advance how many resources will be necessary to achieve a particular service level.

It is sometimes convenient to construct functions to convert a utility value calculated over the nonprice outcomes into a client max price and a service provider min price: `max_price`$_{\texttt{client}}$`(utility)` and `min_price`$_{\texttt{provider}}$`(utility)`. The inverse functions are known as the utility of money, or of consumption: `utility`$_{\texttt{client}}$`(price)` and `utility`$_{\texttt{provider}}$`(price)`. For a rational party, this function will be strictly monotonic. One of the commonest formulations is to assert that these functions are 1:1 mappings, which is occasionally mis-interpreted to imply that utility is measured in monetary units.

4.5 NEGOTIATION

The purpose of SLA negotiation is to arrive at a mutually acceptable contract for both parties, which will contain an *agreed-on price function*. This chapter focuses on bilateral negotiation between a single client and a single service provider. Additional forms of negotiation are certainly possible—auctions are quite popular—but they typically require that clients trust the provider to act as a trustworthy broker, marketmaker, or auctioneer, or require a trusted third party to fill this role.

An underlying assumption is that the agents are self-managing, autonomous computer services that are rational in the economic sense. This distinguishes much of the discussion that follows from research into people-to-people negotiation, where additional aspects such as respect for the other party and relative position power can complicate the issue [17,25].

During a negotiation, each party will try to maximize their excess utility—the additional utility they receive above their minimally acceptable indifference value. To do this, both parties try to drag the final agreed-on price function closer to their own preferred operating regime. For example, in Figure 4.6, the client should try to pull the

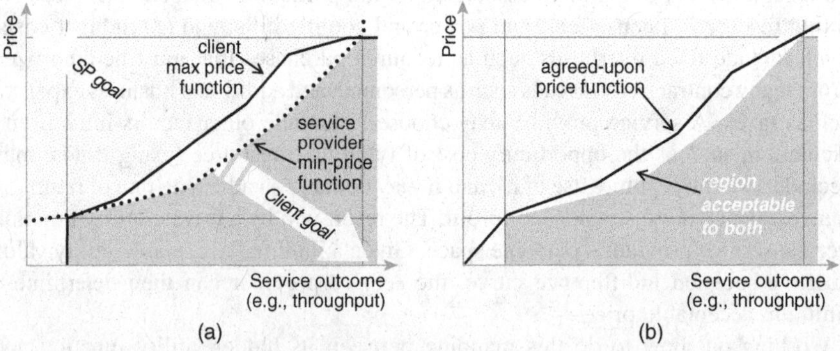

Figure 4.6 The goals of negotiation: (a) maximizing each side's excess utility; (b) a possible acceptable outcome, expressed as a price function that traverses the mutually acceptable region.

price function down and to the right, while the service provider should try to pull it up and to the left.

There is a great deal of existing work on negotiation strategies, tactics, and protocols, and this chapter does not attempt to discuss it in detail; see the studies by Bartolini et al. [3] and Faratin et al. [10] for some representative examples.

Reaching agreement requires guessing—or determining (e.g., by probing)—an approximation to the other side's boundary function. In general, the goal of a negotiation strategy is to extract as much information as possible about the shape of the other's utility function for the minimum concession in the proposer's utility. Faratin et al. [11] describe one way of making tradeoffs during this process under an assumption of mutual benefit, which may or may not apply. Negotiation strategies, such as proposing smaller concessions in later rounds, are ways to communicate (possibly fallacious) hints about the shape of a party's utility function, and how close the party is to reaching agreement, in an attempt to influence the other party's decision-making. The maximum movement toward a desirable outcome for one party will occur in areas where the slope of the utility function for the other party is lowest, and one purpose of negotiation strategies is to find—and exploit—such regions. This is easier if the parties engage in multiple interactions and past history can be used as a guide to future behavior [39].

Mutual exploration of the utility functions of distrusting partners is not always very efficient; it takes time, can result in suboptimal answers, and offers no guarantee of "fairness" or even success. Such is the nature of negotiation. Note that the common expedient of summing the two parties' utility values and solving a differential equation to determine the maximum common utility is not usually possible, because (1) utility values are subjective and thus not directly comparable, and (2) neither side is willing to furnish the other with their utility function in this kind of direct negotiation. A party that volunteers its utility function or price boundary function to the other will "lose" the negotiation, by giving up any ability to achieve a better outcome for itself.[9]

Some systems aim to distribute excess utility more or less "fairly" between the two parties. For example, k-pricing offers one approach [4], by splitting the excess price (not utility) beyond each party's price boundary functions in a fixed ratio between them. It requires a third party to perform the calculation if the client and service provider do not fully trust one another, and hence falls outside this two-party scenario.

Purely rational agents do not need to achieve fairness in order to reach agreement, but fairness is an important property in human-to-human negotiations. People will refuse to enter into an agreement if they view it as sufficiently unfair, even if they would benefit (the ultimatum game [22]). This suggests that future automated agents should offer the option of being programmed to reflect this, on the grounds that their human masters may otherwise come to regret the consequences.

[9] Imagine going into a used car dealership and announcing the highest price you are willing to pay before starting to haggle over the price ....

A negotiation process or mechanism is said to be *incentive-compatible* if it is in the interests of the parties to reveal private information that the process requests. This property is not strictly necessary for reaching agreement, although it may speed up negotiations and increase the likelihood of reaching it.

A service provider might not want to offer a service that is defined at all possible outcomes, but it needs to provide a price function that is valid for all of them. For example, a virtual machine rental service may choose only to offer virtual machines at certain fixed capacity points, even though the underlying virtual machine monitor might be capable of providing a near continuum of offerings. Since the price function deals with outcomes, not desired levels of service, it needs to specify what happens if (say) more or less processor power is made available than was expected. There are many ways it can do so—for this example, it might simply round up the price to that of the next-larger service delivery unit.

A client may want to bias the service provider to offer outcomes that the client would prefer, to speed up the negotiation process or increase the likelihood that a desirable outcome is reached. At the same time, the client must avoid giving away its max-price function. One way to do this is to provide a hint to the service provider about which outcomes the client prefers. A *client ranking function* provides such a hint by ordering some or all of the outcomes in client desirability order [27]. A bigger ranking value should imply the client's willingness to pay a higher price—but no data about how much higher a price. This can be accomplished by a nonlinear mapping from ranking value to the client max-price value for the same outcome.

Sometimes a "good enough" agreement is better than none at all, or better than spending too long trying to get a marginally better one; that is, there is a utility aspect to the negotiation itself. This is captured in the notion of *satisficing*, which can either mean (1) picking an agreement point that is at least minimally acceptable (typically the first), on the grounds that it is likely to be close enough to the optimal; or (2) including the cost of the negotiation process itself in the decision-making about when to end the negotiation process. It may even be the case that the cost of reaching an agreement is greater than the potential value of the result to a party, in which case it isn't worth starting a negotiation.

Fortunately, many situations are relatively straightforward; many service providers will be price-setting, meaning that they will propose a price in response to a request for a particular level of service. Such a price is likely to reflect a previously published skeleton price function that allows clients to estimate what it is reasonable for them to ask for. Typically, a service provider will advertise an SLA template [38] that includes many of the service terms; a client will populate it with the details of their service request and ask for a quote; the service provider will respond with a specific service offering and a price function; and the client will either accept the result, or modify the request and repeat the process until they are satisfied or abandon the attempt to reach an agreement. Many variations of this basic protocol are possible. For example, the client may be the active party, proposing a pricing function in the SLA that they propose; or both parties may make arbitrary modifications to the SLAs that they propose, which may speed up the process of reaching agreement by communicating more information in each round.

4.5.1 Expected Utility and Risk

Never [try to] cross a river because it is on average 4 feet deep.

—Nissam Taleb

An *ideal* agreed-on price function will lie within the acceptable region (boundary function) for both parties across all possible outcomes. These are rare, because (1) SLAs often specify penalties—by definition, these lie outside a preferred operating range; and (2) it is unlikely that a client would be able to persuade a service provider to offer a price function that lies within the client's preferred operating region for all possible outcomes. For example, the service provider might charge too much at high service levels for the client's preference. But if the client doesn't expect those service levels to be reached, that may not matter. What the parties are really trying to maximize is their *expected utility value* over the actual outcomes that they believe will be experienced under the SLA [28].

Conceptually, the expected utility is simple to calculate (Fig. 4.7); over the space of possible outcomes, sum (or integrate) the product of each outcome's likelihood and its utility.[10] In practice, of course, things are not as simple as this suggests.

First, there is likely to be intrinsic uncertainty in the outcomes: Just how many cellphone minutes will I use in a month? How much load will my customers impose on the service? What will the response time be under such load? These are manifestations of *risk*, which is defined as variance in utility across outcomes. Most people associate risk with negative outcomes (i.e., losses compared to an expected outcome), but that is not its strict definition, although the downside risk is often more important.

Client downside risk can be reduced by minimizing the price for each additional unit of service. Service provider downside risk can be reduced by ensuring that the incremental costs for delivering more service are adequately covered. Both parties can reduce their risk by capping the amount of service that is to be delivered (e.g., by throttling or shedding excess load), and by improving the quality of their predictions.

Second, the client and service provider may have asymmetric information: one may know more about the likelihood of certain outcomes than the other. For example, a client may never have used this service before, but the service provider has been in business a long time, and had many clients. Clients can reduce the asymmetry by researching alternate information sources such as reviews, surveys, analyst reports, or reputation ratings from third parties, and they can reduce their downside risk by

[10] The ability to perform this calculation relies on some detailed properties of the agent's preferences: the so-called von Neuman–Morgenstern conditions or axioms [35]. Most observers seem to agree that these conditions are usually reasonably well approximated in practice.

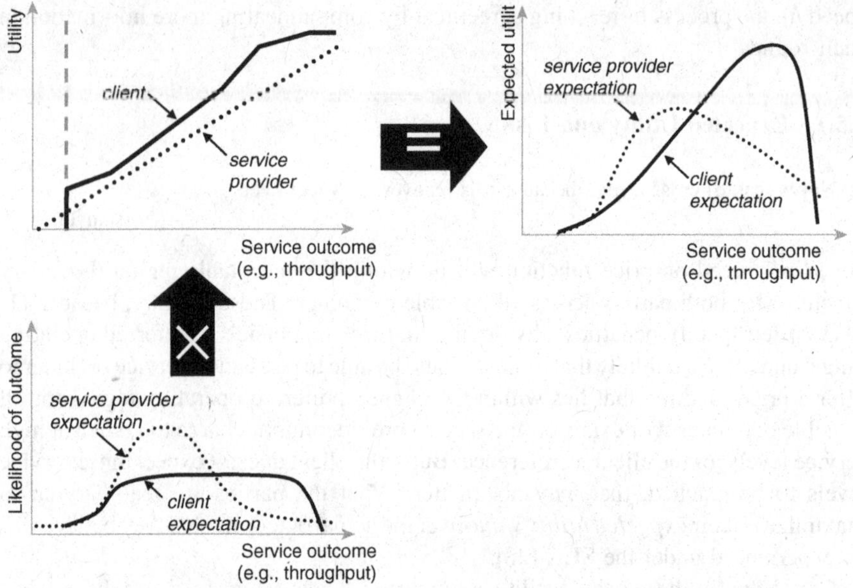

Figure 4.7 Calculating expected utility for a predicted set of outcome likelihoods. The client and service provider lines are shown together on one graph only for convenience; they are each independently—and privately—calculated.

making conservative assumptions about the relative frequencies of undesirable outcomes. Service providers can reduce their risk by pushing for SLAs that bound the downside of mis-estimating their real costs, and penalize undesired client behaviors in order to discourage them.

Third, the formulation offered above assumes that the agents (client and service provider) are indifferent to all outcomes that achieve the same expected utility. In practice, the agent's utility value might itself be affected by the probabilities of the individual outcomes. *Risk aversion* is how this affect can be quantified; it offers a measure of how an agent values sets of possible outcomes in comparison to a fixed single outcome [1].

A classic example of risk aversion occurs with mortgage loans; For instance, a risk-averse borrower may be willing to pay a fixed interest rate that is higher than the expected variable interest rate average, in order to reduce the risk associated with interest rate variation over the lifetime of a loan. Formally, economists talk about how agents react to participating in a *lottery* (a hypothetical game) that offers different outcomes: for example, a 50:50 chance of receiving either \$0 or \$100, or a guaranteed \$40. A risk-averse agent might prefer the latter; a risk-seeking agent might prefer the lottery over a guarantee of \$59. The difference between the expected value and the guaranteed one (\$10 in the first case, –\$9 in the second) is known as the agent's *risk premium* for this lottery: it's a measure of how risk averse they are. Risk aversion may increase or decrease with the size of the potential payout.

When people are involved, behaviors associated with risk quickly get complicated. For example, the common explanation for risk aversion [35] is that the marginal utility of wealth (money) decreases: as a payout gets larger, each additional $1 contributes less utility than the one before it (economists say that the utility of wealth function is concave). But this is insufficient to explain the difference in people's behavior between moderate- and large-scale bets [26]. Cumulative prospect theory [34] attempts to address this, by offering models of people's risk behavior. It accounts for several observed phenomena:

- People are *loss aversive* (they weight a loss as more significant than a gain of the same amount).
- They are more receptive to risk when they are below an expected reference point or target, on the grounds that "I have to try *something* to get ahead," and significantly more averse to risk when they are above the reference.
- People suffer from *long-shot bias* – they overweight very rare, extreme events, such as winning the lottery, a terrorist attack, or a nuclear meltdown, and discount "average" occurrences.

Autonomous service providers may want to take these factors into account when dealing with human clients, and these factors may be a part of the business goals that their owners and operators would like to impose on them. Risk-related behavior will cause both clients and service providers to modify the utility that they associate with a potential SLA away from the straightforward expected utility value. In turn, this moves their boundary functions, and thus changes the pricing functions and SLAs that they will find acceptable.

4.5.2 Losses And Penalties

One particular area where risk is associated with SLAs is when there are sets of outcomes (operating regimes) in which losses or financial penalties occur.[11] No *ideal* price function will include losses or penalties, since no agent is indifferent to loss. For example, the price function in Figure 4.6 is not ideal because it lies outside the acceptable region at the two extremes of service outcome.

It is likely that both the service provider and the client will have to compromise if they are to reach a price function that they can both live with. The degree of risk that each side is willing to accept, plus the likelihoods of the various outcomes, will determine whether agreement is possible.

A common approach to losses is to distribute them between the two parties in some fashion, for example, by using the *k*-pricing technique introduced earlier, but applied to price deficit, rather than excess. Pushing all the losses onto one party or another can introduce *moral hazard*—whereby one party can impose a bad operating point on the

[11] Using financial penalties everywhere simplifies many things, and is not particularly limiting. Other types of penalty, such as additional service in lieu of a payment, can usually be given an economic equivalent, such as the cost to the service provider of providing the additional service.

other and yet is largely insulated from the consequences. Penalties are a special case of this: they are intended to impose an undesirable outcome, so sharing losses makes no sense. The risk of moral hazard means that an agent should be wary of accepting SLAs with penalties unless it largely controls whether the operating point enters a regime that will trigger the penalty.

A penalty is intended to discourage the service provider from operating in a region of outcomes that is undesirable to the client. A penalty will only be effective if it is large enough to make other, reachable, operating points more profitable for the service provider. A strict form of penalty design calls for every incremental movement away from a bad operating point to result in a net benefit to the service provider [4], but this may not be necessary if the control system for the service provider can recognize better outcomes and move to them, even if they are not adjacent to the problematic one.

How should a penalty be priced in an SLA? In exactly the same way as with any other risk. The service provider should make sure that two additional terms are reflected in the price function somehow for each penalty: (1) compensation for the reduction in their expected utility from the expected penalty payout (the product of its likelihood and its size), plus (2) their risk premium. Formulating things in this fashion allows a client to specify the penalties they want in an SLA, as long as the service provider can determine the remainder of the price function. Typically, the higher the penalties, the larger the expected value of the price function.

It may be possible to reduce the effective risk premium by buying insurance against loss. Insurance is a way to pool downside risk across multiple entities; since the likelihood of all the downsides coming true simultaneously is low, the intrinsic cost of loss coverage plus an appropriate profit for the insurer may be less than a single entity's underlying risk premium. Thus, the price function's "risk premium" may be set from the provider's raw risk premium or the cost of insurance—whichever is lower.

To simplify the description, the discussion above focused on penalties paid out by a service provider, but it applies just as well to a client, since an SLA may stipulate penalties for clients too—most commonly if they impose more load on a service than was agreed to, or are tardy in providing payment. The client, too, should make similar calculations about the expected value of the price function as well as any risk premiums it may care about.

4.6 FUTURE RESEARCH DIRECTIONS

There is a long way to go before most autonomous service providers are capable of the kinds of economic analysis presented here. Even a basic approach is beyond many implementations [7], and the use of even moderately advanced financial instruments such as futures and options is still further away. All of these require a clear understanding of the value that the mechanisms and policies are trying to achieve, and how effective they are. There seem to be many opportunities to leverage existing work in other domains and apply it to the field of self-managing systems.

More systematic management of risk in automated service providers and the SLAs they write deserves greater attention. It is not enough to simply measure the outcomes from a contract, or set of contracts; what is needed is for the risk associated with those outcomes to be used as input to the control system for the service provider, and their clients. This may not be enough; existing work tends to assume that decision-making should be rational, but this fails to incorporate models of people's attitudes toward risk, such as cumulative prospect theory. The process of eliciting and representing user preferences in these areas is remarkably difficult, by no means fully understood, and merits further work [18].

There has been much work on human-to-human negotiation, but it's still an open question whether it is a good idea to mimic these processes in automated agents.

Finally, it should be noted that utility theory is not the only form of representing inputs to decision-making under uncertainty. It is appealing for automated systems because it can readily be mapped onto numerical optimization-based approaches, but other formulations, such as target-oriented decisions analysis [33], have been shown to be helpful in getting people to think about their choices [5], and may be applicable to autonomous computer systems, as well.

4.7 CONCLUSION

Individuals, businesses, and other parties or organizations have come to rely heavily on automated computer systems, including service providers and autonomous agents. The trend is likely to continue apace, meaning that more, and larger, decisions will be placed in the hands of such systems. It is becoming increasingly important that we have a clear way to delegate our intentions to these systems, so they can act on our behalf, with some assurance that unpleasant surprises won't occur.

This chapter has attempted to address one aspect of this, by discussing ways to capture the complicated mapping between happiness, service outcomes, and prices. It has provided an introduction to the topic of utility and risk in the management of SLAs for a pair of partially distrusting computer-based systems. It has shown how utility theory provides a basis for automated decision-making for contracts and their prices, including some approaches to handling different types of risk. It has also suggested a number of extensions and opportunities that would allow automated service providers and their automated clients to do a better job of serving their human masters.

The use of utility as a guiding principle for self-managing systems has long been recognized. Nonetheless, fulfilling these opportunities, and putting the ideas into practice, will be a significant challenge for some years to come.

ACKNOWLEDGMENTS

Sharad Singhal provided the impetus to write this chapter, and the basis of the graphical representation used here of the overlap between client/service-provider-acceptable-regions. Elaine Wong implemented a prototype of the executable what-if pricing functions described in Section 4.3.1, and, together with Subu Iyer, acted as a sounding board for several of the ideas presented here. Yang Yinping provided many helpful references and comments on the topic of negotiation. Claudio Bartolini and Kay-Yut Chen helped educate this neophyte author on some of the basics of the economic perspective. Any remaining errors are, of course, entirely my own.

REFERENCES

In addition to the references cited below, Wikipedia (http://wikipedia.org) has several useful articles that cover many of the economics-related topics discussed in this chapter.

1. K. J. Arrow, *Essays in the Theory of Risk-Bearing*, North-Holland, Amsterdam, 1971.
2. A. AuYoung, L. Grit, J. Wiener, and J. Wilkes, Service contracts and aggregate utility functions, *Proc. 15th IEEE International Symp. High Performance Distributed Computing* (*HPDC-15*), *Paris, June* 2006, pp. 119–131.
3. C. Bartolini, C. Preist, and N. R. Jennings, *A Software Framework for Automated Negotiation,* Technical Report HPL–2006–33 (revised and updated), HP Laboratories, Palo Alto, CA, Feb. 2006.
4. M. Becker, N. Borissov, V. Deora, O. Rana, and D. Neumann, Using *k*-pricing for penalty calculation in Grid markets, *Proc. 41st Hawaii International Conf. System Sciences* (*HICSS*), paper 97, Waikoloa, Big Island, HI, Jan. 2008.
5. R. F. Bordley and M. LiCalzi, Decision analysis using targets instead of utility functions, *Decisions in Economics and Finance* **23**(1):53–74 (2000).
6. R. F. Bordley, Teaching decision theory in applied statistics courses, *Journal of Statistics Education* **9**(2) (2001), http://www.amstat.org/publications/jse/v9n2/bordley.html.
7. G. Cheliotis and C. Kenyon, Autonomic economics, *Proc. IEEE International Conf. E-Commerce* (*CEC'03*), Newport Beach, CAL, June 2003, pp. 120–127.
8. E. Christensen, F. Curbera, G. Meredith, and S. Weerawarana,Web Services Description Language (WSDL) 1.1, W3C Note, W3C, Sophia-Antipolis, France, Fujisawa, Japan, and Cambridge, MA, http://www.w3.org/TR/wsdl, World Wide Web Consortium, March 15, 2001.
9. A. Dan, D. Davis, R. Kearney, R. King, A. Keller, D. Kuebler, H. Ludwig, M. Polan, M. Spreitzer, and A. Youssef, Web services on demand: WSLA-driven automated management, *IBM Systems Journal*, **43**(1):136–158 (March 2004).
10. P. Faratin, C. Sierra, and N. R. Jennings, Negotiation decision functions for autonomous agents, *Robotics and Autonomous Systems* **24**(3):159–182 (Sept. 1998).
11. P. Faratin, C. Sierra, and N. R. Jennings, Using similarity criteria to make negotiation trade-offs, *Proc. 4th International Conf. Multi-Agent Systems*, Boston, MA, July 2000, pp. 1–19.
12. B. Huberman and T. Hogg, Distributed computation as an economic system, *The Journal of Economic Perspectives* **9**(1):141–147 (winter 1995).
13. D. E. Irwin, L. E. Grit, and J. S. Chase, Balancing risk and reward in a market-based task service, *Proc. 13th IEEE Symp. High Performance Distributed Computing* (*HPDC*), Honolulu, HI, June 2004, pp. 160–169.

14. J. O. Kephart and R. Das, Achieving self-management via utility functions, *IEEE Internet Computing* **11**(1):40–48 (Jan. 2007).

15. R. L. Keeney and H. Raiffa, *Decisions with Multiple Objectives: Preferences and Value*, Cambridge Univ. Press, 2003.

16. K. Lai, L. Rasmusson, E. Adar, L. Zhang, and B. A. Huberman, Tycoon: an implementation of a distributed, market-based resource allocation system, *Multiagent Grid Systems* **1** (3):169–182 (Aug. 2005).

17. R. J. Lewicki, D. M. Saunders, and J. W. Minton, *Negotiation*, 3rd ed., Irwin/McGraw-Hill, Boston, MA, 1999.

18. X. Luo, N. R. Jennings, and N. Shadbolt, Acquiring user tradeoff strategies and preferences for negotiating agents: a default-then-adjust method, *International Journal of Human-Computer Studies*, **64**:304–321 (2006).

19. R. P. McAfee, *Introduction to Economic Analysis*, version 2.0, July 2006 (available from http://www.introecon.com or Lulu Press, Morrisville, NC, 2006).

20. J. O'Sullivan, D. Edmond, and A. H. M. ter Hofstede, The price of services, *Proc. 3rd International Conf. Service-Oriented Computing* (ICSOC 2005), Amsterdam, Netherlands, Dec. 2005; *Lecture Notes in Computer Science* 3826: 564–569 (Nov. 2005).

21. J. O'Sullivan,*Towards a Precise Understanding of Service Properties*, PhD thesis, Faculty of Information Technology, Queensland Univ. Technology, Australia, 2006.

22. H. Oosterbeek, R. Sloof, and G. van de Kuilen, Differences in ultimatum game experiments: evidence from a meta-analysis, *Experimental Economics* **7**(2):171–188 (June 2004).

23. G. A. Paleologo, Price-at-risk: A methodology for pricing utility computing services, *IBM Systems Journal* **43**(1):20–31 (Jan. 2004).

24. F. I. Popovici and J. Wilkes, Profitable services in an uncertain world, *Proc. Supercomputing* (SC|05), Seattle, WA, Nov. 2005.

25. H. Raiffa, J. Richardson, and D. Metcalfe, *Negotiation Analysis: The Science and Art of Collaborative Decision Making*, Belknap Press (imprint of Harvard Univ. Press), Cambridge, MA, 2002.

26. M. Rabin, Diminishing marginal utility of wealth cannot explain risk aversion, in *Choices, Values, and Frames*, D. Kahneman and A. Tversky, eds., Cambridge Univ. Press, Cambridge, UK, 2002, pp. 202–208.

27. R. Raman, M. Livny, and M. Solomon, Matchmaking: distributed resource management for high throughput computing, *Proc. 7th IEEE International Symp. High Performance Distributed Computing* (*HPDC'98*), Chicago, IL, July 1998, pp. 140–146.

28. L. J. Savage, *The Foundation of Statistics*, Wiley, New York, 1954.

29. M. Stonebraker, P. M. Aoki, W. Litwin, A. Pfeffer, A. Sah, J. Sidell, C. Staelin, and A. Yu, Mariposa: a wide-area distributed database system, *The VLDB Journal* **5**(1):19–34 (Jan. 1996).

30. I. E. Sutherland, A futures market in computer time, *Communications of the ACM* **11**(6):449–451 (June 1968).

31. N. Taleb and A. Pilpel, Epistemology and risk management, *Risk & Regulation* **13**:6–7 (summer 2007).

32. G. E. Tesauro, W. Walsh, and J. O. Kephart, Utility-function-driven resource allocation in autonomic systems, *Proc. 2nd International Conf. Automatic Computing* (*ICAC'05*), Seattle, WA, June 2005, pp. 342–343.

33. I. Tsetlin and R. L. Winkler, On equivalent target-oriented formulations for multiattribute utility, *Decision Analysis Archive* **3**(2):94–99, (June 2006).

34. A. Tversky and D. Kahneman, Advances in prospect theory: cumulative representation of uncertainty, *Journal of Risk and Uncertainty* **5**:297–323 (1992).

35. J. von Neumann and O. Morgenstern, *The Theory of Games and Economic Behavior*, Princeton Univ. Press, 1944 (republished 1980).

36. C. A. Waldspurger, T. Hogg, B. A. Huberman, J. O. Kephart, and W. S. Stornetta, Spawn: a distributed computational economy, *IEEE Transactions on Software Engineering* **18**(2):103–117 (Feb. 1992).

37. W. E. Walsh, G. Tesauro, J. O. Kephart, and R. Das, Utility functions in autonomic systems, *Proc. International Conf. Autonomic Computing* (ICAC'04), New York, NY, May 2004, pp. 70–77.

38. *Web Services Agreement Specification* (*WS-Agreement*), Open Grid Forum (OGF), Joliet, IL, Sept. 2006.

39. D. Zeng and K. Sycara, Bayesian learning in negotiation, *International Journal of Human Computer Studies* **48**(1):125–141 (1998).

5

OPTIONS AND COMMODITY MARKETS FOR COMPUTING RESOURCES

DAN CRISTIAN MARINESCU, JOHN PATRICK MORRISON, AND HOWARD JAY SIEGEL

5.1 INTRODUCTION

In this chapter, we introduce basic concepts regarding the role of commodity markets for computing resources supporting service-based computing and give an overview of Pleiades, an infrastructure for service-based computing. We discuss pricing strategies and the role of option trading in a commodity market for computing resources. Finaly, we review a macroeconomic model for computer services based on utility, satisfaction, and pricing.

The Internet and the World Wide Web have profoundly changed the way our society conducts its business; education, research, healthcare, economy, defense, and virtually all other human activities take advantage of the services and the information accessible through the Internet. The computing and communication infrastructure, which has enabled these changes, is now poised to take advantage of new technologies, and it seems reasonable to expect that the service-based computing economy, already promoted by Amazon.com, Salesforce.com, and others, will expand in the future.

Throughout this chapter the term *service-based computing* is used to mean a World Wide Web of domain-specific services offered by autonomous service providers. A *service-based computing economy* will provide the resources necessary to offer these services, and, in this chapter, we advocate using a commodity market for the provision and acquisition of computing resources.

Market-Oriented Grid and Utility Computing Edited by Rajkumar Buyya and Kris Bubendorfer

Market-oriented grids allow computing and communication resources to be traded; if they become a reality, options-based trading could play a role in Grid computing. However, today's Grid computing is restricted to relatively few users with data-intensive applications requiring vast amounts of computing resources available at only a few sites. Also, Grid resources are owned by a relatively small number of organizations. A commodity market for computing resources may have a greater impact on a service-based computing economy than on Grid computing, simply because it has the potential to reach a much larger audience.

A commodity market for software, hardware, information, and knowledge, coupled with an infrastructure for service-based computing, will support Web-based service providers by guaranteeing that they can call on the resources needed to support their offerings. We believe that this resource provisioning will, in turn, stimulate the further growth of Web-based service delivery in many fields such as education, finance, and consulting. How Grid computing will respond to the challenges posed by a service-based computing economy is a matter of speculation.

The scale of the systems considered here is considerably larger than that of current systems. We postulate a large number of sites with excess computing resources, and, a smaller, but still substantial, cohort of resource-starved service providers. In considering where these resources will come from, we note that the home computer of the future will most likely be a multicore system with tens, if not hundreds, of cores; gigabytes of cache; tens of gigabytes of main memory; and hundreds of gigabytes, if not terabytes, of secondary storage. These machines will be connected to the Internet via high-speed links and will allow owners to (remotely) control and monitor a wide range of appliances, including the home environment and security system. In addition to advances in the home computer, Web-based services are likely to proliferate; service-based computing will be integral to many applications, making them easy to use, and appealing to a very large user population.

The markets that we envision will allow a very large number of owners of home computers to trade their excess resource capacity for a variety of incentives such as monetary rewards, service credits, and software maintenance contracts, all at a much larger scale than that envisioned for Grid computing. It should be clear that sharing of home computer resources can happen only if (1) incentives for owner are substantial, and (2) an infrastructure guaranteeing fast remote access and tight security is in place.

As software systems become increasingly complex and the diversity of application software increases, the cost of software maintenance will dominate the computing costs for the majority of users. The prospect of remote diagnostics, automatic operating system updates, and assurance of compatibility between the operating system and application software may convince personal computer owners to join an infrastructure where these items are included in the incentive package.

Our approach is focused on the role that the options market could play in distributed systems, and, in particular, in a service-based computing economy. An *option* [14,25,27,28] is a binding contract between, in our case, resource providers and resource seekers. Options on indices, futures, currencies, commodities, as well as equity options, are traded on all major exchanges. Options are *derivatives* because they derive their value from an underlying asset.

The concepts discussed here are consistent with the philosophy and the design principles of autonomic computing [15], the semantic Web [17], peer-to-peer computing, and economic models for large-scale distributed systems [19,23,24,29,30], but they push the envelope (extend the limits) of these paradigms and break away from engrained ideas such as the notion that a home computer is a dedicated utility and that its local operating system should be in total control of its resources, including cores and CPU cycles, and primary and secondary storage. Other notions are that

- Contracting out the excess capacity of a home computer and allowing an external entity to control some of the local resources is socially and technically heretical. Note that even specific peer-to-peer systems, which use resources distributed over the Internet, are installed only with the owner's agreement;
- If a service provider does not have total control of the resources necessary to support the service, it is not feasible to provide quality of service (QoS) or security guarantees or to ensure fault-tolerance.

Table 5.1 summarizes important attributes of peer-to-peer systems, autonomic computing, and Pleiades. The next section will address the question of how the Pleiades system will provide QoS and security guarantees while reducing the investments that service providers have to make in hardware and software and, at the same time, reducing the software maintenance costs for the owners of home computers.

The chapter is organized as follows. In Section 5.2 we present the design objectives and the organization of the Pleiades system; the system can benefit from a market-oriented

TABLE 5.1 Comparison of Several Attributes of Peer-to-Peer Systems, Autonomic Computing, and the Planned Pleiades System

	Peer-to-Peer Systems	Autonomic Computing	Pleiades
Reduce investments in hardware systems for service providers	Yes—uses resources scattered over the Internet	To some extent	Yes—uses resources scattered over the Internet
Reduce software maintenance costs for service providers	No	Yes	Yes
Reduce software maintenance costs for home computer owners	No	No	Yes
Provide quality of service (QoS) guarantees	No	Yes	Yes
Provide security guarantees	No	Yes	Yes

economy supporting option trading. Section 5.3 provides an overview of commodity markets for computing resources and pricing strategies. Then, in Sections 5.4 and 5.5 we introduce basic concepts regarding options and option pricing in financial markets. In Section 5.6 we discuss the role of options in a commodity market for computing resources. Finally, in Section 5.7 we provide an overview of a macroeconomic model for commodity markets for computing resources.

5.2 A SERVICE-ORIENTED SYSTEM BASED ON RESOURCE VIRTUALIZATION

Traditionally, a service provider in a service-based distributed system owns, or is in total control of, all the resources needed to provide its service. Peer-to-peer systems are challenging this paradigm with varying degrees of success. For example, Skype, an Internet phone service provider, surreptitiously uses selected sites connected to the system as supernodes to route calls. Napster, a file-sharing system stores data files on individual sites owned by subscribers. Video-on-demand is an application attempting to take advantage of data storage on sites scattered around the Internet.

The strategy used by these applications and others is motivated by the desire to reduce the cost of providing services. Current implementations of this resource-sharing philosophy is plagued by problems such as uncertainty regarding the number of resources available at any instant in time, and the lack of system support at those sites needed to implement those services. As a result, such systems are unable to provide QoS guarantees or to ensure fairness, are vulnerable and prone to catastrophic failures, do not provide security guarantees to either the resources supplier or the system user (who are often the same individual), are restricted to a few services with a simple user interface, and are limited in their ability to use a wide spectrum of resources. The lack of an enabling structure to mediate among suppliers and consumers of resources makes peer-to-peer systems scalable, but the disadvantages of the approach seem to be severely limiting. The next evolutionary step in service-based computing and communication systems could use a distributed infrastructure to mediate QoS and security guarantees, enable interested parties to negotiate reliability and fault tolerance levels, and support graceful performance degradation on the occurrence of catastrophic events.

We consider a service-based computing economy where resources are distributed throughout the network [7–9,16,18,21,31]. The Pleiades system mirrors the realities of financial markets. The component that we call the "market authority" is a distributed infrastructure; one of its functions is to buy computational resources from individuals, bundle them, and sell them to the providers of computing services; thus, service providers no longer need to make costly and often risky investments in very large computing facilities together with their associated high costs of ownership. This strategy is consistent with autonomic computing promoted by IBM, but emphasizes distributed resources rather than resources concentrated in a few sites.

We now examine briefly those attributes of a service-oriented system that we believe to be critical in addressing the problems mentioned above.

- *Self-Organization* A system is self-organizing if its components interact to dynamically achieve a global function or behavior [12]. Self-organizing systems typically have higher-level properties that cannot be observed at the level of the individual components and that can be seen as a product of their interactions (they are more than the sum of their parts). Complex systems exhibit a high degree of self-organization. More recent observations of power-law distributions in the connectivity of complex networks came as a big surprise to researchers steeped in the tradition of random networks. Even more surprising was the discovery that power-law distributions also characterize many biological and social networks. Many attributed a deep significance to this fact, inferring the existence of a "universal architecture" of complex systems. Self-organization can be best explained in terms of the network model of a system [6] where the vertices represent the principals and the links represent the relationships among them. Self-organization implies that the probability that one node of a graph is connected with m other nodes, $P(m)$, decays as a power law when a vertex interacts with m other vertices, $P(m) \approx m^{-\gamma}$ [4], regardless of the type and function of the system, the identity of its constituents, or the relationships between them. This implies that large systems self-organize into a *scale-free* state when $P(m)$ has the expression given above regardless of the number of nodes of the network [2–4]. The term *scale-free*, although linguistically questionable, is widely used in the literature to quantify scalability in the context of a random graph model of a system: *Scale-free means that the probability that one node of the graph is connected with m other nodes, P(m), is independent of the scale of the network, that is, the number N of nodes in the graph.* Empirical data available for social networks, power grids, the Web, and the citation index of scientific papers confirm this trend. As an example of a social network, consider the *collaborative graph* of movie actors, where links are present if two actors were ever cast together in the same movie; in this case $\gamma \approx 2.3$. The power grid of the Western United States has some 5000 vertices representing power generating stations and in this case $\gamma \approx 4.0$. For the World Wide Web, the exponent $\gamma \approx 2.1$; this means that the probability that m pages point to a particular page is $P(m) \approx m^{-2.1}$. More recent studies indicate that for scientific papers; this means that the probability that m papers referring to the same paper is $P(m) \sim m^{-3}$ [4]. The larger the network, the closer is the distribution approximated with a power law with $\gamma = 3.0$, $P(m) \sim m^{-3}$. To be scalable and fair, and to take advantage of temporospatial locality of resources, services, and users, a service-oriented system should be self-organizing.
- *Virtual Organizations* The members of a service-oriented community should be able to form virtual organizations consisting of resource providers, service providers, users of services, or any subset of these categories. In principle, virtual organizations can use the basic mechanisms provided by the system (e.g., contract negotiations protocols, performance evaluation tools, data transport mechanisms) to develop their own security, QoS, and fault tolerance policies, and subsequently behave as autonomous entities—independent of the other communities using the service-oriented framework. Virtual organizations may

be created dynamically and exist only for the duration of a contracted period. The statement that the complexity of a system increases with the number of its elements, the number of interactions among them, the complexity of individual elements, and the complexity of the interactions is generally accepted [10,13,18]. To ensure scalability of our system, we devote particular attention to the algorithms and policies necessary for supporting the formation of virtual organizations. Our virtual organizations are nearly self-sufficient entities; trading outside the organization occurs only when the demand and supply cannot be satisfied within the organization. The members of a virtual organization agree to share resources such as CPU cycles, primary memory, secondary storage, software, information, and data in a dependable, flexible, economical, and secure manner subject to a set of individual constraints. We expect virtual organizations to have a number of benefits: including (1) improved scalability; (2) increased satisfaction levels for both resource suppliers and resource consumers, and support for better matching of contract requirements of suppliers and consumers; and (3) better utilization of resources and lower penalties on defaulted contracts. In general, contracted parties are rewarded for fulfilling contractual obligations and penalized otherwise; by continually meeting contractual obligations, individuals can build up their reputation over time [20,32]. Our preliminary studies indicate that these expectations are well founded. For example, Figure 5.1 shows the "average matching level" function of the population of agents (suppliers and consumers) on the basis of a simulation study that we are now conducting. The *average matching level* measures the absolute value of the difference of corresponding attributes of "call" and "put" contracts (described in Section 5.4) once they are matched together; the lower the value of this discrepancy, the higher the average satisfaction level of the agents involved in the contract. As can be seen in Figure 5.1, the matching level improves when contracts are carried out by the local market authority in each virtual organization, referred to as VO-MA, rather than by the global market authority (the MA).

- *Security and Trust Management* We assume that resource providers, service providers, and users of services have different security constraints and policies. Thus, our system has to provide basic mechanisms for enabling security and trust and to allow individuals to negotiate as appropriate. Security for resource providers metaphorically means that when they "cut a slice" of their resources and offer them to the pool of global resources, they are guaranteed that the functionality of their slice is maintained and no security issues are introduced. This is in stark contrast with existing systems such as the Grid, which requires third party software to be installed on local systems without guaranteeing that the functionality of the local system is maintained, or that the security of the local system is not compromised. Service providers and users of services have to trust that resources distributed throughout the system satisfy their security constraints. For example, a user of a service must trust the service provider to fulfill its obligations regarding security, QoS, and other user policies. In turn, the service provider must trust the suppliers of resources, and so on.

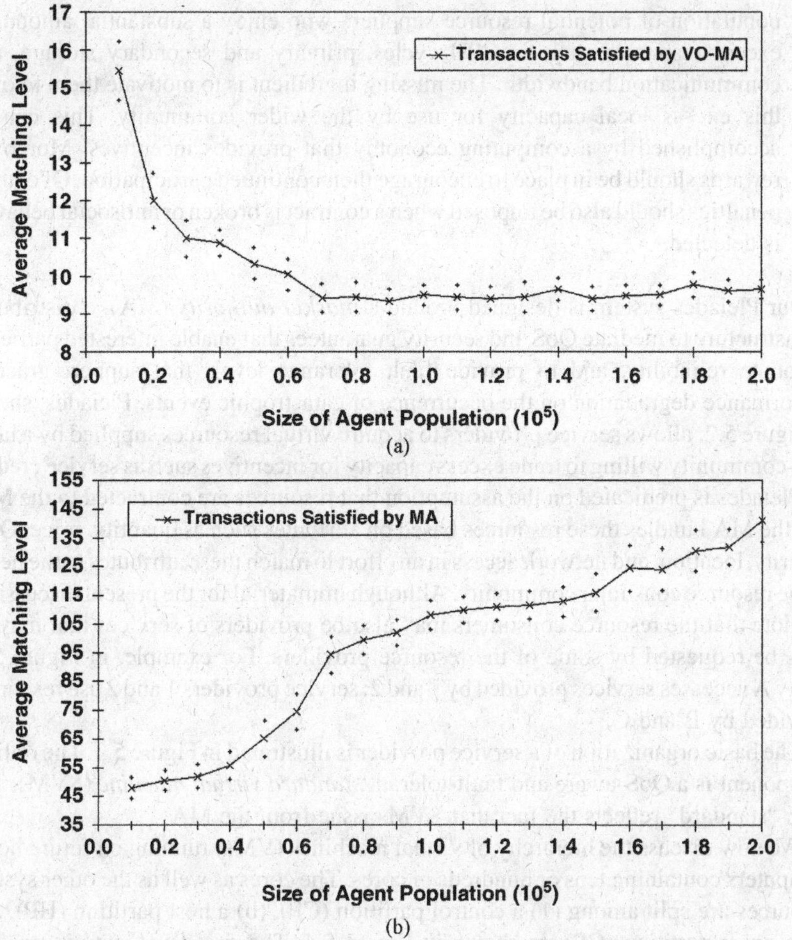

Figure 5.1 The average matching level as a function of the population size with and without virtual organizations, based on a simulation study. The average matching level measures the absolute value of the difference of corresponding attributes of "call" and "put" contracts once they are matched together; the lower the value of this discrepancy, the higher the average satisfaction level of the agents involved in a contract. (a) When each virtual organization has its own market authority, VO-MA, the value of the matching level when contracts are carried out within a virtual organization is better than the case (b) when a global market authority is involved; 95% confidence intervals are shown.

- *Resource Virtualization.* Resource virtualization allows transparent access to resources. In our context, this simply means that the resources available to a service provider are actually distributed throughout the system in a similar way that the pages of a virtual address space are distributed throughout the physical memory.
- *Incentives, Rewards, and Penalties.* Let us assume that we have in place an ideal system with all the ingredients mentioned above and that there is a very large

population of potential resource suppliers who enjoy a substantial amount of excess resources such as CPU cycles, primary and secondary storage, and communication bandwidth. The missing ingredient is to motivate them to offer this excess local capacity for use by the wider community. This can be accomplished by a computing economy that provides incentives. Moreover, rewards should be in place to encourage their continued participation. Of course, penalties should also be imposed when a contract is broken or antisocial behavior is detected.

Our Pleiades system is designed around a *market authority* (MA), a distributed infrastructure to mediate QoS and security guarantees that enable interested parties to negotiate reliability, and to provide fault tolerance levels that support graceful performance degradation on the occurrence of catastrophic events. Pleiades, shown in Figure 5.2, allows service providers to acquire virtual resources supplied by a large user community willing to trade excess capacity for incentives such as service credits.

Pleiades is predicated on the assumption that resources are contracted to the MA, and the MA bundles these resources based on attributes such as quantity, price, QoS, security, location, and network access in an effort to match these attributes to the needs of the resource consumer community. Although immaterial for the present discussion, we note that the resource consumers may also be providers of services that may, in turn, be requested by some of the resource providers. For example, in Figure 5.2, entity A accesses services provided by 1 and 2; service providers 1 and 2 use resources provided by B and C.

The basic organization of a service provider is illustrated in Figure 5.3. The critical component is a QoS-aware and fault-tolerant *standard virtual machine* (SVM). The term "standard" reflects the fact that SVMs issue from the MA.

We now discuss the hierarchy of virtual machines (VMs) running on future home computers containing tens or hundreds of cores. The cores as well as the other system resources are split among (1) a control partition (CP), (b) a host partition (HP), and (c) a guest partition (GP), as shown in Figure 5.4. The *first-level virtual machine* (FLVM) is a tamperproof software component, obtained from the MA, which periodically certifies its compliance to systemwide security standards. Once an FLVM is installed on a local machine, the owner can initiate contract negotiations for the supply of a portion of the local resources and in return for credit that can be used to purchase various services or can be encashed for financial recompense. For the sake of simplicity, we assume that the excess resources are negotiated as a single package with the MA. When a negotiation is completed, the FLVM provides a "capability list" to the *second-level virtual machines* (SLVMs) that control resource allocation in the host and guest partitions. FLVM and SLVM are replicated and provisions for fault tolerance are built into the system. Every FLVM has a unique FLVMId, and at creation time is provided with the information necessary to access the MA. Once a contract is negotiated and agreed between the MA and the host, the FLVM loses control of the local resources subject to that contract. An FLVM can regain control of these resources again only after a renegotiation process, which, in turn, can occur only with the approval of the MA.

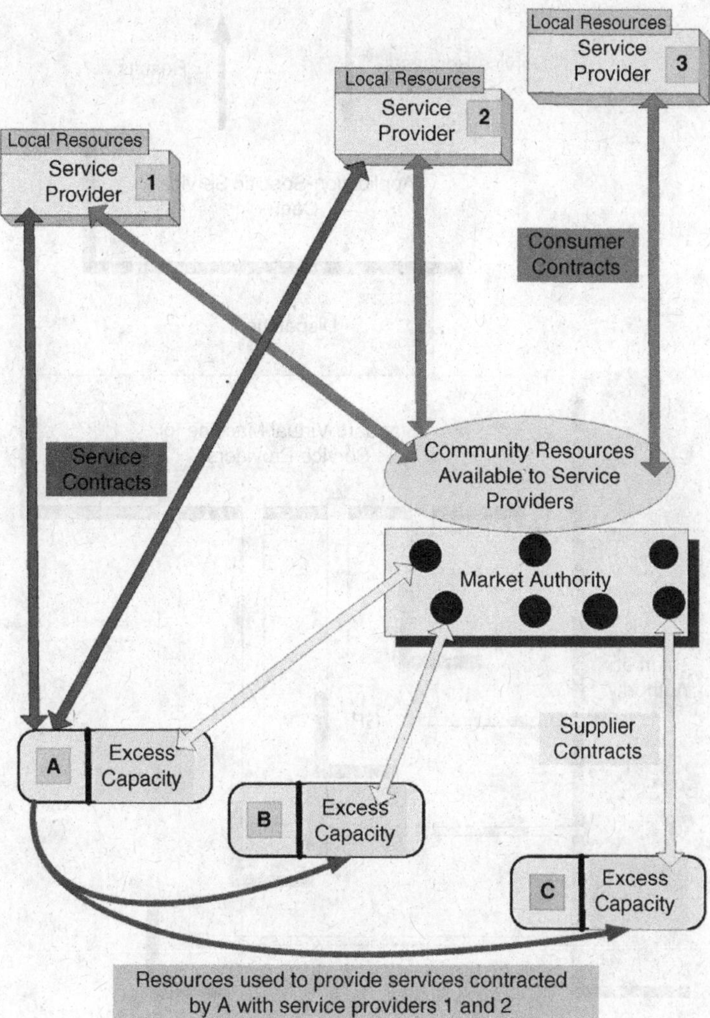

Figure 5.2 Conceptual organization of the Pleiades architecture. The market authority contracts with individual resource suppliers (labeled A, B, C) access to local resources and bundles these resources as needed by service providers (labeled 1, 2, 3). Clients request services; for example, A accesses services provided by 1 and 2; service providers 1 and 2 use resources provided by B and C. Virtual organizations mimic the layout in this figure; they have their own market authority.

The process of bundling resources is called *resource virtualization*. Pleiades' resource virtualization requires special features of the hardware and software that are largely unavailable at present:

1. The strict security model is based on a hierarchy of virtual machines running on individual nodes, supplying resources to a common pool. The FLVM should

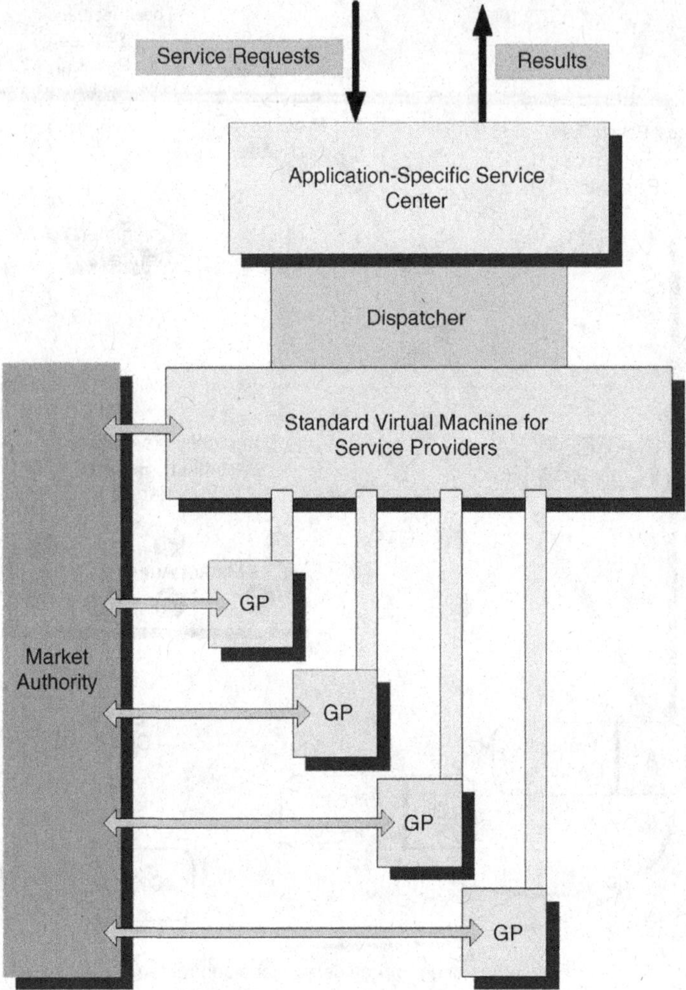

Figure 5.3 A service provider runs application specific software; a dispatcher uses the resources provided by a standard virtual machine (SVM) that interacts with the market authority and guest partitions (GPs) (see Fig.5.4), running at many sites.

ensure an impenetrable security wall between the local resources contracted by the host, the owner of a home computer, and the market authority. This is in stark contrast with existing operating systems that vest total control in local resources.

2. The hardware support for security should include a memory architecture based on multiple virtual spaces, and multiple virtual processors that can be allocated dynamically. A segmented memory, multicore context switching, and access-key-controlled I/O are some of the hardware features required to support strict partitioning of local resources.

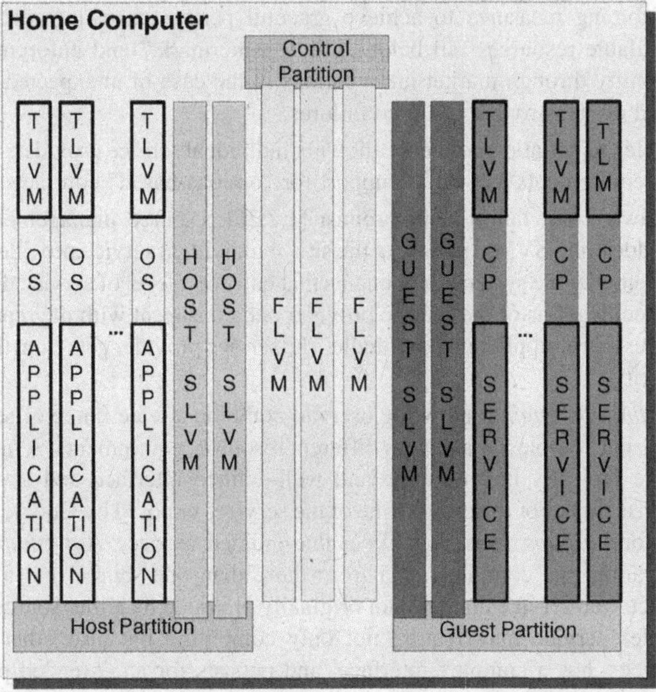

Figure 5.4 The local system configuration of a resource provider. The cores are shared among three partitions: control, host, and guest. The first-level virtual machine (FLVM) controls the resource partitioning and enforces security policies and contracts. The FLVM is certified by the market authority and is replicated on multiple cores to ensure fault tolerance. The host partition is controlled by a second-level virtual machine (SLVM) and is also replicated on several cores. Each core in this partition is controlled by a third-level virtual machine (TLVM) that can load an operating system (OS), or another control program (CP) and run an application. The guest partition also is controlled by an SLVM and cores in this partition run a service under the control of a CP.

3. Different functional components of the market authority perform critical functions for the Pleiades system, such as
   a. Supplying and certifying critical software components: the SVMs for service providers (Fig. 5.3) and the FLVMs for resource providers (Fig. 5.4)
   b. Conducting contract negotiations between parties: conducting contract renegotiations subject to the approval of all parties involved, monitoring strict enforcement of existing contracts, gathering data relating to the reputation of the parties involved, and disseminating reputation information
   c. "Bundling" resources from multiple suppliers so as to match the requirements of service providers
   d. Ensuring fair allocation of resources to service providers
   e. Ensuring fair compensation of resource suppliers

   f. Enforcing measures to achieve graceful performance degradation when available resources fall below a "low watermark," and enforcing system stability through market interventions in the case of unexpected surges of load or catastrophic resource failures
4. Complex negotiation protocols allowing individual service providers to specify QoS requirements as well as support for "options-based" contracts.
5. QoS-aware and fault-tolerant robust [1,7,26] resource management system embedded into SVMs running at the site of individual service providers. SVMs are customizable system components that enforce a level of service dictated by the specifications of the service provider and consistent with the reputation of each resource supplier in the "bundle" the service provider gets from the market authority.
6. *Coordination engines* allowing users to combine a wide range of services of increasing complexity and with different resource requirements. A *lightweight* service typically has a simple and well-defined interface and a very short response time. For example, some of the services exposed by Google map, and used for *mashups,* would qualify as fine-grained services. A *mashup* is a Web application that combines data from more than one source into a new and distinct Web service that was not originally provided by either source. A more complex service may require not only computing but also other types of resources, has a complex interface, and persists for an extended periods of time. For example, a service requiring the manipulation of a network-based instrument (e.g., an electron microscope) qualifies as a coarse-grained service.
7. A versatile abstract machine to express the functions of the hierarchy of Virtual Machines as required in Pleiades, as shown in Figure 5.4.

A catastrophic system failure, detected either by a service provider or by the market authority, results in penalties. The FLVM maintains a log of critical events and can avoid penalties if failure is due to causes outside local control, such as power or network failures. Each core of a partition runs under the control of a third-level virtual machine (TLVM) that may load an operating system or a control program on that core and execute an application.

The system presented in this section relies on a commodity market for computing resources, and the next sections introduce basic concepts regarding commodity markets and option trading in financial markets.

5.3 MARKETS AND COMMODITY PRICING

A market is a meeting place for (1) investors who have excess resources (e.g., cash in case of financial markets), (2) organizations that need additional resources (e.g., companies that issue shares and use the revenue obtained by selling the shares to introduce new technologies, hire more personnel, or increase production capacity), and (3) organizations who mediate the transactions (e.g., exchanges and financial institutions). Investors buy and sell *securities* (such as stocks, bonds, mutual funds, or futures), *commodities* (such as oil, precious metals, or agricultural goods), *currency*, and other valuable items; the prices of the items traded on financial markets reflect the *market hypothesis*. Efficient market hypotheses (EMHs) assert that prices on traded assets, such as stocks, bonds, or property, reflect the collective beliefs of all investors about future prospects.

Computing and communication resources such as CPU cycles and communication bandwidth are perishable commodities that also can be traded. Paradoxically, more recent advances in microprocessors, memory, storage, and communication technology, coupled with widespread Internet access, while significantly increasing the compute resources of the average owner, provide an impetus for the development of a distributed market economy trading these resource, because the need for computing resources among certain sectors (such as service providers) is, and will remain, insatiable.

In this section, we review classical pricing strategies from traditional markets and their applicability to service-based computing [14,25,27,28]. We also discuss the relation between quality and price:

- *Premium pricing* is the application of higher prices when there is uniqueness about the service and a competitive advantage exists. For example, access to a parallel system with a new and very fast interconnection network will be priced higher than a similar system with a more modest interconnection network. Similarly, if a service provides additional guarantees, for instance, guarantees on the response time, it will command a higher price.
- *Penetrating pricing* is the application of reduced pricing to gain market shares, and once the goal is achieved, the price increases. A new service may use this strategy to attract customers.
- *Economy pricing* is the application of reduced pricing to dispose of abundant commodities or services. For example, if a service provider in the Pleiades system has a number of *futures* contracts canceled, under favorable circumstances, it may decide to use economy pricing. Recall that the service provider is a consumer of resources; it "buys" resources it deems necessary and sufficient for the delivery of its services; in addition, it may buy options (see Section 5.4) to guard against the possibility that more resources then initially anticipated are needed.
- *Price skimming* is applied when one has a competitive advantage, but this advantage is somehow not sustainable. Price skimming is a pricing strategy in which a marketer initially sets a relatively high price for a product or service and then lowers the price over time. This allows the supplier to recover its costs quickly before competition steps in and lowers the market price. This policy is effective in situations where a firm has a substantial lead over the competition with a new product or when there is a shortage of services or products. For example, in the Pleiades system a service provider may take advantage of power outages in some regions of the country to increase the price of its services—reflecting increased demand.

- *Product-line pricing* is applied when there is a range of services or products and the price reflects the benefits of parts of the range. A line can comprise related products of various sizes, types, colors, qualities, or prices. Product-line pricing is based on the correlations between the demand for the products of a line, the costs of the products, quality, and so on. For example, a car manufacturer usually has a line of cars and the prices may not reflect the actual costs; profit margins may be smaller for small cars, reflecting a larger volume of sales.
- *Captive product pricing* increases the price when the service or product has attributes that force a customer to use a particular provider. For example, once one installs an operating system on a home computer, application software such as browsers from other software companies may not work well or may not run at all. In the context of the computing services, when the format of the results produced by one service is nonstandard, then the provider of that service may charge a premium price for another service capable of further processing the results.
- *Service bundle pricing* combines multiple services in the same package and charges a smaller price than the sum of the prices charged for individual services; this strategy forces the customer to pay for all services, regardless of use. For example, a cable service provider may bundle several channels.

The concepts from financial markets cannot be applied directly to a commodity market for computing resources for a number of reasons. First, some of the computing resources, such as CPU cycles and bandwidth, are perishable and this will affect their price; if at time t_0 a contract for a resource that becomes available at time t_a is posted, then its price will typically decline slowly at first and then faster as the time approaches t_a. Furthermore, computing resources have attributes that do not exist in traditional commodity markets. An appliance will not distinguish a kilowatt of electricity produced by a windmill from one produced by a nuclear power plant; the electricity supplier can switch from one source to another and mix multiple sources of electricity at will without affecting any appliance connected to the electric Grid. However, computing resources may not be interchangeable, limiting how they can be mixed or substituted transparently; such a substitution requires that some action be carried out at the point of consumption and thus leads to additional overhead. In our system, the MA offers CPU cycles from multiple sources, say, to a service provider, bundled together in the same package. If one of the sources fails, then the MA has to first find another source and then reduce the price per unit of service to compensate for the overhead experienced by the SVMs running at the service provider's site to move data around and possibly to redo some computations at the new site. Moreover, the price of several resources such as CPU cycles and main memory when bundled together should reflect their joint utility to the customer.

In Section 5.7, we discuss two more pricing strategies used to encourage or discourage consumption. To encourage consumption, the unit price is decreased as consumption increases; for example, for the first 1000 kWh of electricity a consumer may be charged 8 ¢/kWh, for the next 1000, the price could be 7 ¢/kWh, and when the consumption exceeds 2000 kWh, a price of 5 ¢/kWh is charged. To discourage consumption, the price per unit could be increased as the consumption increases.

A service provider in the Pleiades system can benefit from contracts that give the right, but not the obligation, to acquire resources. Such contracts enable a service provider to minimize its costs while being able to adapt to sudden change of demand for services. Financial markets support instruments, called "options," the subject of the next sections.

5.4 OPTIONS: BASIC CONCEPTS

An *option* is a financial contract between two or more parties. The value of this contract is determined by fluctuations in some underlying asset(s). In its simplest form, an option is sold by one party (who becomes known as the option *writer*) to another party (who then becomes known as the option*holder*). The contract offers the holder the right, but not the obligation, to buy or to sell (in finance speak: to "call" or "to put") an asset within a specified period of time for a price that is preagreed at the time the contract is made (this price is called the "strike price").

As part of the contract, the writer is paid a sum of money by the holder. This *fee* obliges the writer to honor the contact (i.e., to buy or sell the underlying asset) if the holder decides to exercise her/his option.

An option writer may *sell* either a *call option* or a *put option* (or both, of course). In selling a *call option*, the writer agrees to *sell* the asset to the option holder within the terms of the contract. Likewise, in selling a *put option*, the writer agrees to *buy* the asset from the option holder, also subject to the terms of the contract. (Reciprocally, an optionholder *buys* call options and put options—enabling the buyer to buy or sell, at the buyer's discretion within the terms of the contract.) Option trading is a zero-sum game; the option buyer's grain is the option seller's loss and vice versa.

Options can be used to speculate; an option writer selling a call option is betting that the asset value will fall substantially relative to the strike price during the life of the option. In that case, the holder will not require the writer to sell the asset. (Why buy from the writer for a strike price that is higher than the current value of the asset?) Thus, the net gain to the writer (and the net loss to the holder) is the fee paid by the holder. Alternatively, if that asset value were to rise substantially relative to the strike price during the life of the option, the holder may require the writer to sell the asset for the strike price. After purchase, the holder can immediately sell the asset for a profit at the higher market value. The net gain for the holder will be the current value of the asset minus the sum of the option fee and the strike price. Similarly, the net loss to the writer will be the difference between the value of the asset plus the fee, minus the strike price.

In a similar manner, put options lead to speculative trading. The holder of a put option (which would force the writer to buy) is guarding against the value of the underlying asset falling. If that happens, the holder is able to sell the asset for the (higher) strike price—thus minimizing potential losses. Conversely, the writer in this scenario is anticipating an increase in the asset value. Both cannot be right, and a similar zero-sum calculation, as in the call option scenario, pertains.

As a simple example, consider the following. On November 30, 2007 an investor decides to buy 1000 IBM options to purchase stock with the expiration date of July 18, 2008 for the strike price of $120/share (the investor thus becomes a holder). At the time of purchase, the closing price of this stock is $105.18/share. The fee for this option, at $4.40/share, is 1000 × $4.40/share = $4400. This outlay compares favorably with 1000 shares × $105.18/share = $105,180, which would be the cost of buying 1000 shares outright on November 30, 2007.

Now, assume that on March 4, 2008 the IBM stock trades at $143/share and the investor (holder) decides to exercise the option and pays the strike price ($120,000) for the 1000 IBM shares (1000 shares × $120/share). These shares could be resold immediately at market value to yield $143,000 (1000 shares × $120/share). The investor's (holder's) profit, and indeed the writer's loss, is thus 143,000 – (120,000 + 4400) = $18,600.

Instead of selling, suppose that the investor (holder) expects the stock to rise further and does not exercise the option on March 4, 2008 and the next day the stock plunges and trades at $110, remaining there until the option expires. In this case it makes no sense for the investor to exercise the option at the strike price of $120 and then loose the $4400 option fee.

The writer of an option is a financial institution; underwriting options involves risks due to market volatility. In our example, assume that a financial institution underwrites 1000 call options with the strike price $120/share when the call option fee is $4.50/share and 1000 put options with the same strike price and a fee of $16.35/share. Thus, the writer collects $20,850 (4500 + 16,350) at the time when it underwrites the two batches of options. If, at the exercise date, the market is down and the price of a share is $100, then the call option will not be exercised, but the put option will be. Thus, the writer has to buy the 1000 shares from the holder of the put option and pay $120,000 for them. The writer can then resell the 1000 shares for only $100,000; as a result of these transactions, the writer makes a profit of $850 (20,850 – (120,000 – 100,00)). If the market goes up and the price at the exercise date is $145/share, then the holder of the put option has no reason to sell, but the holder of the call option will exercise her/his option and pay the writer $120,000. The writer will get the 1000 shares at the current market price and pay for them $145,000. This time the writer will have a loss of $4,150 [20,850 – (145,000 – 120,000)]. Recall that the bid price is the highest price an investor is willing to pay to buy an option; the ask price is the lowest price a trader will accept to sell an options. In our calculations we used an average of the bid and strike prices.

Table 5.2 presents the information regarding the price of options as it appears in newspapers, or is provided by financial institutions. Specifically, it shows the *call* and *put* option prices in US dollars as a function of the strike price for IBM options for July 18, 2008 as of December 1, 2007. As we can see, for the call option the lower the strike price, the larger the option price; indeed, when the current price is around $105, the option to buy the stock for $65/share on, or before July 18, 2008 should cost more. The situation is reversed for the put options. If you want to sell of an IBM share at the strike price of $65/share or before July 18, 2008 then the option should cost you next to

TABLE 5.2 "Call" and "Put" Option Prices in US$ as Functions of Strike Price for IBM Options for July 18, 2008 as of December 1, 2007[a]

Strike Price	Bid Price (Call Option)	Ask Price (Call Option)	Bid Price (Put Option)	Ask Price (Put Option)
65	42.40	43.00	0.45	055
70	37.80	38.30	0.70	0.85
75	33.50	33.70	1.05	1.20
80	29.10	29.30	1.55	1.65
85	24.90	25.20	2.20	2.30
90	20.90	21.10	3.10	3.20
95	17.20	17.40	4.20	4.40
100	13.80	14.10	5.80	6.00
105	10.90	11.10	7.70	7.90
110	8.30	8.50	10.10	10.30
115	6.20	6.30	12.90	13.10
120	4.40	4.60	16.20	16.50
125	3.10	3.30	20.00	20.20
130	2.15	2.30	24.10	24.40
135	1.45	1.55	28.60	29.90
140	0.95	1.05	33.30	33.90
145	0.60	0.70	38.30	38.90

[a] The expiration date is the third Friday of the month, in this case, Friday July 18, 2008. The closing price on November 30, 2007 was $105.18/share. The strike prices are listed in increments of $5 and range from ~65% to ~160% of the closing price. The bid and ask prices for call options are on the left, and for put options on the right. The information is from Wachovia.

nothing. Such tables for different exercise dates show that the price of an option increases with the duration of the contract, due to market volatility; it is harder to predict the range of the price of a stock a year from now than the next day's price.

This section gave an overview of the options terminology and mechanism for financial markets. In the next section, we will examine this more rigorously.

5.5 OPTION PRICING ON FINANCIAL MARKETS AND THE BLACK–SCHOLES MODEL

The prices of assets are governed by the *efficient market hypothesis*, which states that (1) the current price reflects the history and does not provide any additional information, and (2) markets respond immediately to new information about an asset [11,14]. The asset price obeys the stochastic differential equation:

$$\frac{dS}{S} = \sigma(dX) + \mu(dt) \tag{5.1}$$

Here, S is the price of the asset at time t; dS is the change in price in a short interval of time dt; dX is a sample from a normal distribution; σ is the *volatility*, which reflects the standard deviation of the return; and μ is the *drift*, an average rate of growth of the asset price. We assume that the asset volatility is a known function of time. This equation describes a stochastic process called a *random walk*. The solutions of this equation fit well with the time series for equities and indices gathered from observations of the markets, while the data regarding currency do not. In addition, the model does not predict large variations of the asset prices experienced sometimes by real markets.

Before proceeding, we introduce the lognormal distribution used to model variables that are multiplicative products of a large number of independent factors, each one with a small contribution. A random variable whose logarithm is normally distributed is said to have a lognormal distribution; if Y is a random variable with a normal distribution, then $X = \exp(Y)$ has a lognormal distribution.

The probability density function (pdf) and the cumulative distribution function (cdf) of a lognormal distribution with μ and σ the mean and the standard deviation of the logarithm of the random variable are displayed in Figure 5.5 for a range of values of the mean and standard deviations; their analytical expressions are respectively

$$f(x;\mu,\sigma) = \frac{e^{-(\ln x-\mu)}2/2\sigma^2}{x\sigma\sqrt{2\pi}} \quad \text{and} \quad F(x;\mu,\sigma) = \frac{1}{2} + \frac{1}{2}\mathrm{erf}\left[\frac{\ln(x)-\mu}{\sigma\sqrt{2}}\right] \tag{5.2}$$

Equation (5.1) describes a Markov process, where the asset price depends solely on the current price and not on the past history. When μ is constant, and the price at time t_0 is S_0, then

$$S = S_0 e^{\mu(t-t_0)} \tag{5.3}$$

The probability density function of S follows the lognormal distribution

$$\frac{1}{\sigma S\sqrt{2\pi t}} e^{-(\log(S/S_0)-(\mu-1/2\sigma^2)t)^2/2\sigma^2 t} \tag{5.4}$$

and the stochastic process is called a *lognormal random walk*.

Equation (5.1) formalizes a basic tenet of financial theories, namely, that there are never opportunities to make an *instantaneous* and *risk-free* profit. Virtually all financial models assume the existence of risk-free investments with a guaranteed return, such as a sound bank, or a government issued bond; an investor could make a risk profit over time by depositing the cash in a bank, or by investing in bonds, but we should emphasize that this profit can only be made over time, it is not instantaneous. One can probably beat the risk-free investment by investing in equities but, a greater return, implies a greater risk. There is no free “lunch”; instantaneous and risk-free profits are not possible. This brings us to the concept of *arbitrage*, the practice of taking advantage of a price differential between two or more markets. An arbitrager is

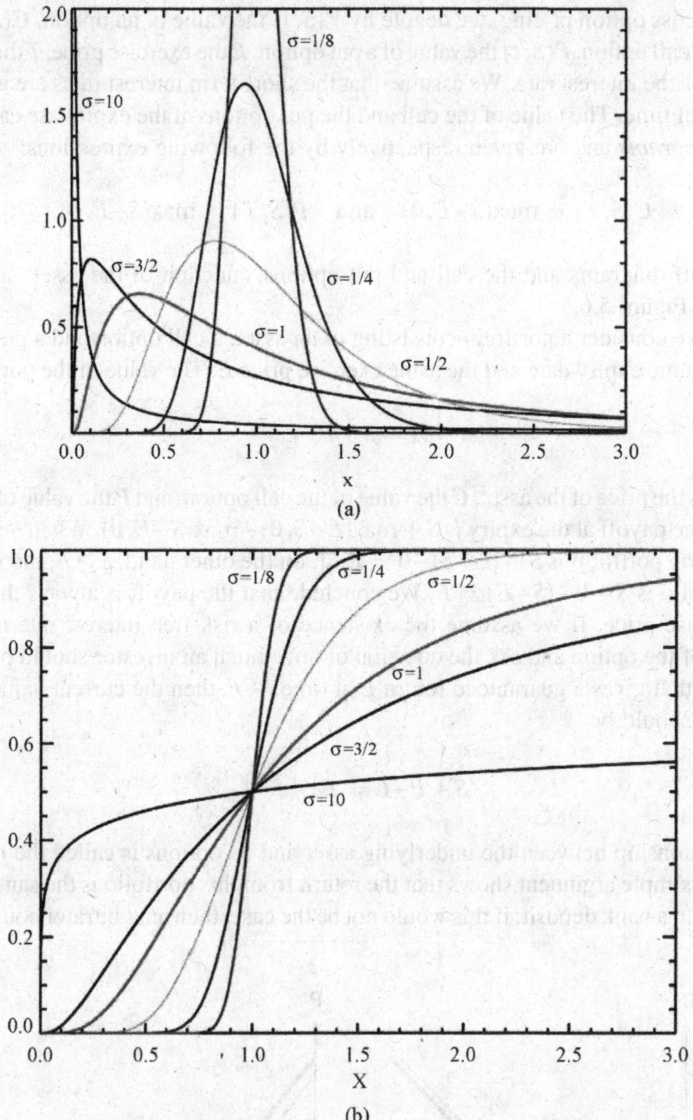

Figure 5.5 (a) The probability density function of a lognormal distribution with the mean and the standard deviation of the logarithm of the random variables μ and σ (in the range $\frac{1}{8} - 10$); (b) The cumulative distribution function.

an individual who seeks out and takes advantage of mispricing. If market prices do not allow for profitable arbitrage, prices are said to constitute an *arbitrage equilibrium* or *arbitrage-free* market. An *arbitrage equilibrium* is a precondition for a general economic equilibrium. The assumption that there is no arbitrage is used to calculate a unique risk-neutral price for derivatives.

To discuss option pricing, we denote by $V(S,t)$ the value of an option, $C(S,t)$ the value of a call option, $P(S,t)$ the value of a put option, E the exercise price, T the expiry date, and r the interest rate. We assume that the short-term interest rates are a known function of time. The value of the call and the put options at the expiry are called the *payoff diagrams* and are given respectively by the following expressions:

$$C(S,T) = \max(S{-}E,0) \quad \text{and} \quad P(S,T) = \max(S{-}E,0) \tag{5.5}$$

The payoff diagrams and the call and put options, function of the asset value, are shown in Figure 5.6.

Now we consider a portfolio consisting of an asset, a call option and a put option with the same expiry date and the same exercise price E. The value of the portfolio is

$$\Pi = S + P - C \tag{5.6}$$

where S is the price of the asset, C the value of the call option, and P the value of the put option. The payoff at the expiry is $S + \max(E{-}S,0) - \max(S{-}E,0)$. When $S \leq E$, the value of the portfolio is $S + (E{-}S) - 0 = E$; if, on the other hand, $S \geq E$, the value of the portfolio is $S + 0 - (S{-}E) = E$. We conclude that the payoff is always the same, the exercise price. If we assume the existence of a risk-free interest rate over the lifetime of the option and ask the question of how much an investor should pay for a portfolio that gives a guaranteed return E at time $t{-}T$, then the current value of the portfolio should be

$$S + P - C = Ee^{-r(T-t)} \tag{5.7}$$

This relationship between the underlying asset and its options is called the *put–call parity*. A simple argument shows that the return from this portfolio is the same as the return from a bank deposit; if this would not be the case, then an arbitrator could make

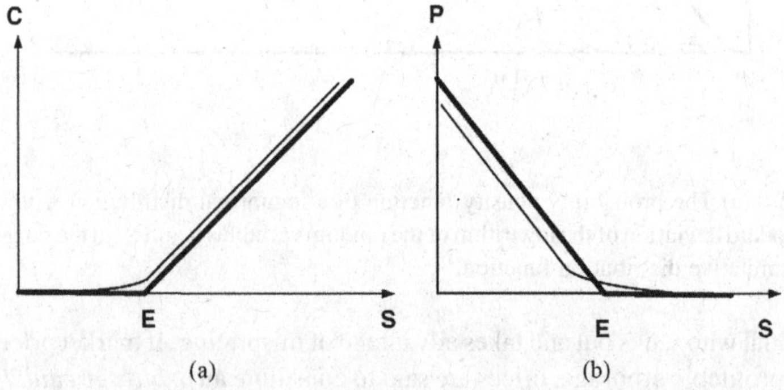

Figure 5.6 (a) The payoff diagram (thick line) for a call option and the option value prior to expiry (thin line) function of the asset value S; (b) the payoff diagram (thick line) for a put option and the option value prior to expiry (thin line) function of S. The exercise price is E.

an instantaneous profit by buying and selling options and shares, while borrowing and lending money from the bank.

The Black–Scholes partial differential equation is a fundamental result in computational financing [28]; it interrelates the value of an option, the price of the asset, the volatility, and the risk-free interest rate

$$\frac{\partial V}{\partial t} + \frac{1}{2}\sigma^2 S^2 \frac{\partial^2 V}{\partial S^2} + rS\frac{\partial V}{\partial S} - rV = 0 \tag{5.8}$$

where $V(S, t)$ is either a call or a put option. Several assumptions are necessary to derive this equation:

1. The value of an option $V(S, t)$ is only a function of the price of the asset S and the time t.
2. The price S of the asset is based on a lognormal random walk.
3. The assets are divisible.
4. The assets do not pay any dividends during the lifetime of the option.
5. The risk-free interest rate r and the volatility σ are known functions of time over the lifetime of the option.
6. There are no transaction fees for hedging a portfolio.
7. Selling short is permissible.
8. Trading the underlying asset is continuous.

The Black–Scholes equation is based on Itô's lemma [28]; if S is described by a logonormal random walk thus, it satisfies Equation (5.1), and if $f(S)$ is a smooth function of S, then

$$df = \frac{df}{dS}(\sigma S\, dX + \mu S\, dt) + \frac{1}{2}\sigma^2 S^2 \frac{d^2 f}{dS^2} dt = \sigma S \frac{df}{dS} dX + \left(\mu S \frac{df}{dS} + \frac{1}{2}\sigma^2 S^2 \frac{d^2 f}{dS^2}\right) dt \tag{5.9}$$

Itô's lemma allows us to write

$$dV = \sigma S \frac{\partial V}{\partial S} dX + \left(\mu S \frac{\partial V}{\partial S} + \frac{1}{2}\sigma^2 S^2 \frac{\partial^2 V}{\partial S^2} + \frac{\partial V}{\partial t}\right) dt \tag{5.10}$$

It is easy to determine the boundary conditions for solving this partial differential equation for European options [27]. But we are interested primarily in American options; in this case we have a *free-boundary* problem. At time t there is a particular value of the asset value S, called the *optimal exercise price* and denoted as $S_f(t)$, which delineates the boundary between two regions; in one region we should hold the option, and in the other region we should exercise the option. The valuation of American options demands several constraints:

- The option value must be greater than or equal to the payoff function.
- The option value must be a continuous function of S.
- The first derivative (the slope) of the option value must be continuous.
- The Black–Scholes equation should be replaced by an inequality.

When we assume that the return from the portfolio cannot be greater than the return from a bank deposit, then we can show that for an American put option the following inequality should hold [28]:

$$\frac{\partial P}{\partial t} + \frac{1}{2}\sigma^2 S^2 \frac{\partial^2 P}{\partial S^2} + rS\frac{\partial P}{\partial S} - rP \leq 0 \tag{5.11}$$

This section explored some of the mathematics underlying the financial commodity market. In the next section we discuss commodity markets for computing resources.

5.6 OPTION PRICING IN COMMODITY MARKETS FOR COMPUTER RESOURCES

As mentioned earlier, options are critical for a commodity market of computing resources, but striking a price for options poses many challenges. Moreover, traditional concepts from financial markets cannot be directly applied to determining prices for computing assets or associated options.

Options in a commodity market for computing resources are likely to play a more intricate role than they have in financial markets for a variety of reasons. Options are likely to be a critical component of such a commodity market because we cannot possibly ensure critical attributes of the system such as quality of service (QoS), fault tolerance, or security, when all resources are traded on the spot market (i.e., the cash market or physical market). Long-term contracts and overprovisioning are necessary, but not sufficient; service providers should have the flexibility offered by *the right, but not the obligation*, to acquire resources when they are certain that those resources will be needed. Another major difference between the financial markets with a few, well-established exchanges, and computer resource commodity markets is due to the need for self-organization; quality of service, fault tolerance, and security considerations will favor the formation of *virtual organizations* that will develop their own internal commodity markets for computing resources to satisfy the majority of contracts within each organization. Striking a price for options also can be more objective when the utility–pricing strategies discussed in Section 5.7 are considered.

Service request rates and, consequently, the amount of resources needed by service providers obey *heavy-tailed distributions*: stochastic distributions with large coefficients of variation (the coefficient of variation is a dimensionless number formed from the ratio of the standard deviation to the mean of a distribution). *Overprovisioning,* the strategy that makes worst-case assumptions about the amount of resources needed, used alone would be very costly and socially wasteful. Last, but not least, the commodities in the subject of this chapter are perishable—one cannot store CPU cycles, or communication bandwidth; hence, such resources are either used or lost. Moreover, there is an inherent time lapse associated with any transaction; options could partially hide this interval and provide immediate access to resources when needed. Neither the suppliers, nor the consumers of resources of the system discussed in Section 5.2, know ahead of time the precise amounts of resources that they can offer or require. As service providers build their reputations, they will likely experience heavier loads and so need more resources. Service providers should secure excess capacity to cope with the uncertainties pertaining to resource consumption for individual requests, excess load, or other unforeseen events; they should also have the ability, offered by options, to get additional resources, or to sell excess capacity based on the dynamics of the system. In turn, the market authority should have the ability to respond to catastrophic events, communication failures, and so on.

In summary, a mix of options and overprovisioning could prove to be an optimal solution for a service-based computing economy; options not only offer the ability to speculate and hedge but also are a critical element of the computer economy.

5.7 A MACROECONOMIC MODEL BASED ON PRICE–UTILITY FUNCTIONS

Bai et al. [5] introduced a macroeconomic economic model that captures traditional concepts such as consumer satisfaction and provider revenues for resource sharing. This model enables us to analyze the effect of different pricing strategies on measures of performance important for consumers and providers alike. Economic models are usually very complex and require a significant number of parameters, and the model discussed in this section is no exception.

Given a particular set of model parameters satisfaction reaches an optimum [5]; this value represents the perfect balance between the utility and the price paid for resources. Simulations confirmed that brokers play a very important role and can positively influence the market. From these studies, we learned that consumer satisfaction does not track consumer utility; these two important consumer performance metrics behave differently under different pricing strategies. Pricing strategies affect the revenues obtained by providers, as well as the ability to satisfy a larger population of users.

5.7.1 Pricing Functions

We consider three pricing functions in Figure 5.7a. Given the constant ξ, the three particular pricing functions we choose are

1. The price per unit is constant regardless of the amount of resources consumed (linear pricing):

$$p(r) = \xi \cdot r \tag{5.12}$$

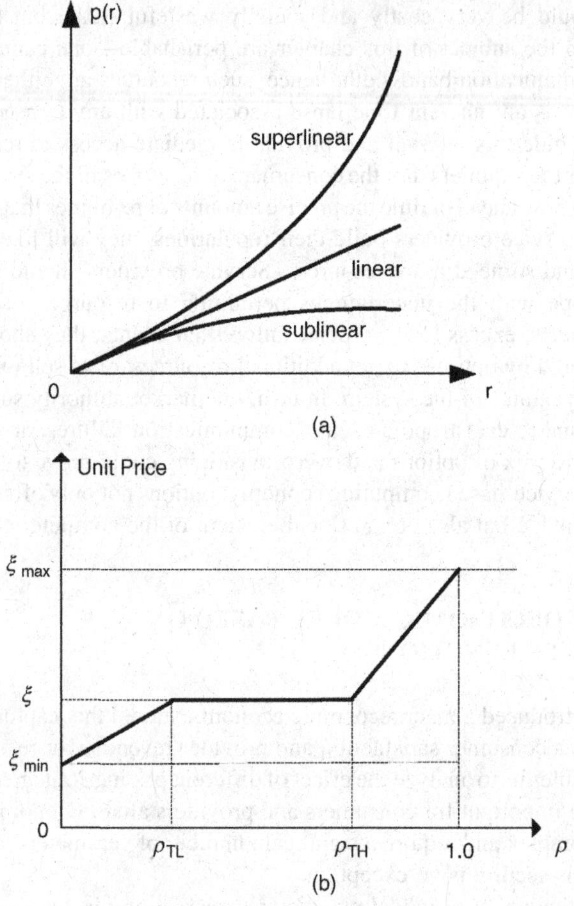

Figure 5.7 (a) Sublinear, linear, and superlinear price functions; (b) the unit price varies with ρ, the load index of the provider.

2. Discourage consumption—the more resources are used, the higher the average unit price (superlinear pricing)

$$p(r) = \xi \cdot r^d \tag{5.13}$$

where $d > 1$, (e.g., $d = 1.5$).

3. Encourage consumption—the more resources are used, the lower the average unit price (sublinear pricing)

$$p(r) = \xi \cdot r^e \tag{5.14}$$

where $e > 1$ (e.g., $e = 0.5$).

In Figure 5.7b we analyze the effect of resource abundance; in that case we define the load index ρ as the ratio of total amount of allocated resources to the capacity of the provider and consider three regions: low, medium, and high load indices. The pricing strategy for each region is different. We consider two models: EDL - encourage/ discourage linear (EDL) and encourage/discourage nonlinear (EDN).

5.7.2 Utility Function

The utility function should be a nondecreasing function of r, the amount of resources; thus, we assume that the more resources are allocated to the consumer, the higher the consumer utility. However, when enough resources have been allocated to the consumer, that is, when some threshold is reached, an increase of allocated resources would bring no improvement of the utility. On the other hand, if the amount of resources is below some threshold, the utility is disproportionately low. Thus, we expect the utility to be a concave function that reaches saturation as the consumer gets all the resources it can effectively use. These conditions are reflected by the following equations:

$$\frac{du(r)}{dr} \geq 0 \quad \text{and} \quad \lim_{r\to\infty}\frac{du(r)}{dr} = 0 \tag{5.15}$$

For example, if a parallel application could use at most 100 nodes of a cluster, its utility, reflected by a utility function, will not increase if its allocation increases from 100 to 110 nodes. If we allocate less than 10 nodes then the system may spend most of its time paging and experiencing cache misses and the execution time would be prohibitively high. Different functions can be used to model this behavior, and we choose to use a sigmoid

$$u(r) = \frac{(r/\omega)^{\varsigma}}{1+(r/\omega)^{\varsigma}} \tag{5.16}$$

where $\zeta \geq 2$ and $\omega > 0$ are constants provided by the customer. Clearly, $u(\omega) = \frac{1}{2}$, and the utility function is a real number between 0 and 1, specifically, $0 \leq u(r) \leq 1$. A sigmoid is a tilted S-shaped curve (Fig. 5.8a) that could be used to represent the lifecycles relating to living, as well as many anthropogenic (human-made), social, or economical systems. It has three distinct phases: a starting phase, a maturing phase, and a declining, or aging, phase.

5.7.3 Satisfaction Function

A consumer satisfaction function takes into account both the utility provided to the consumer and the price paid for resources. For a given utility $u(r)$, the satisfaction function $s(u(r),p(r))$ should increase when the price decreases and, for a given price, the satisfaction function should increase when the utility $u(r)$ increases.

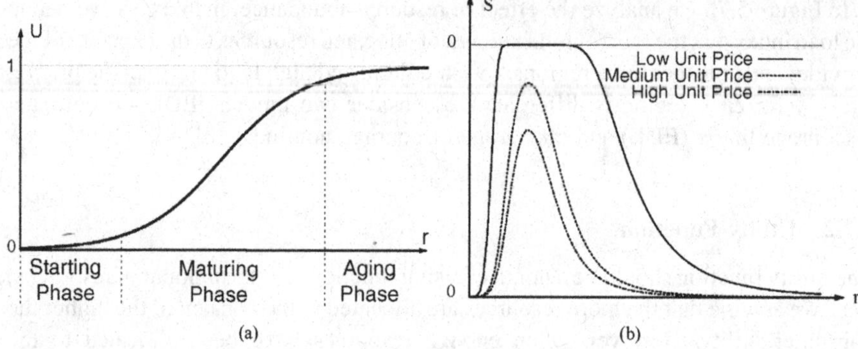

Figure 5.8 (a) A sigmoid is used to model the utility function (a sigmoid includes three phases: the starting phase, the maturing phase, and the aging phase); (b) the satisfaction function for a sigmoid utility function and three linear price functions with low, medium, and high unit prices.

These requirements are reflected by the following equations:

$$\frac{\partial s}{\partial p} \leq 0 \quad \text{and} \quad \frac{\partial s}{\partial u} \geq 0 \tag{5.17}$$

Furthermore, a normalized satisfaction function should satisfy the conditions:

- Given the price $p(r)$, the satisfaction function $s(u(r),p(r))$ should approach the minimum (0) when the utility $u(r)$, approaches 0 and should approach the maximum (1) when the utility $u(r)$ approaches infinity:

$$\forall p > 0, \lim_{u \to 0} s(u,p) = 0 \quad \text{and} \quad \lim_{u \to \infty} s(u,p) = 1 \tag{5.18}$$

- Given the utility $u(r)$, the satisfaction function $s(u(r),p(r))$ should approach the maximum (1) when the price $p(r)$ approaches 0 and should approach the minimum (0) when the price $p(r)$ approaches infinity:

$$\forall u > 0, \lim_{p \to 0} s(u,p) = 1 \quad \text{and} \quad \lim_{p \to \infty} s(u,p) = 0 \tag{5.19}$$

A candidate satisfaction function is

$$s(u,p) = 1 - e^{\kappa u^{\mu} p^{-\varepsilon}} \tag{5.20}$$

where κ, μ, and ε are appropriate positive constants. The satisfaction function based on the utility function in Equation (5.16) is normalized; given a reference price ϕ, we consider also a normalized price function and arrive at a satisfaction function given by

$$s(u,p) = 1 - e^{\kappa u^{\mu} (p/\phi)^{-\varepsilon}}$$

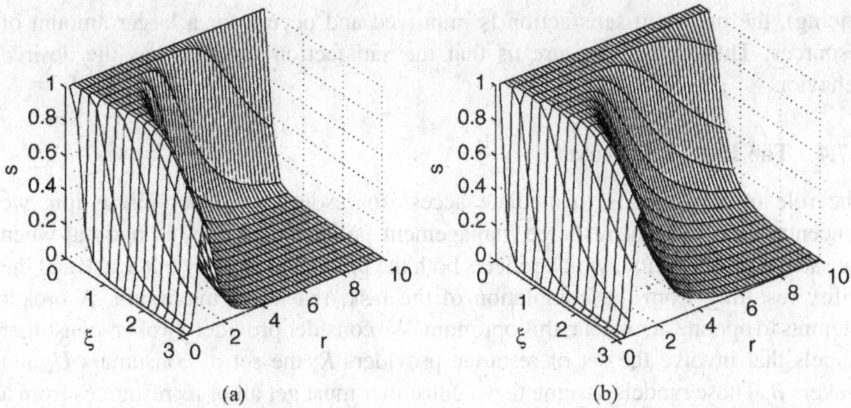

Figure 5.9 The Relationships between satisfaction $s = s(r, \xi)$ and satisfaction s and the unit price ξ and amount of resources r. The satisfaction function is based on a sigmoid utility function and two price functions: (a) discourage consumption (superlinear); (b) linear.

Because u and p are functions of r, satisfaction increases as more resources are allocated, reaches an optimum, and then declines, as shown in Figure 5.8b. The optimum satisfaction depends on the pricing strategy; not unexpectedly, the higher the unit price, the lower the satisfaction.

The three-dimensional (3D) surfaces representing the relationship $s = s(r, \xi)$ between satisfaction s and the unit price ξ and the amount of resources r for several pricing functions (superlinear and linear) are presented in Figure 5.9; the surfaces for sublinear pricing and a cut through the surfaces $s = s(r, \xi)$ at the constant ξ are shown in Figure 5.10. As we can see from the cut through the surfaces $s = s(r, \xi)$, at constant ξ, when we discourage consumption (superlinear pricing), the optimum satisfaction is lower and occurs for fewer resources; when we encourage consumption (sublinear

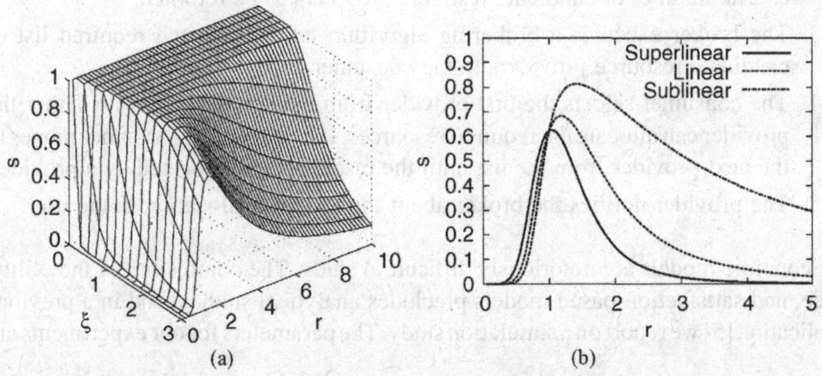

Figure 5.10 Relationships between satisfaction $s = s(r, \xi)$ and satisfaction s and the unit price ξ and amount of resources r: (a) encourage consumption (sublinear); (b) a cut through the three surfaces at a constant ξ.

pricing), the optimum satisfaction is improved and occurs for a larger amount of resources. These plots reassure us that the satisfaction function has the desired behavior.

5.7.4 The Role of a Broker

The role of a broker is to mediate access to resources. In our discussion, we concentrate on optimal resource management policies. A policy is optimal when the satisfaction function, which reflects both the price paid to carry out a task and the utility resulting from the completion of the task, reaches a maximum. A broker attempts to operate at, or near, this optimum. We consider provider–broker–consumer models that involve the set of resource providers R, the set of consumers U, and brokers B. These models assume that a consumer must get all of its resources from a single provider. Brokers have "societal goals" and attempt to maximize the average utility and revenue; in contrast, providers and consumers that have individualistic goals—each provider wishes to maximize its revenue, while each consumer wishes to maximize its utility for the lowest possible cost.

To reconcile the requirements of consumers and candidate providers, a broker chooses a subset of providers offering satisfaction above a given threshold; all providers in this subset have an equal chance of being chosen by a given consumer. We call the size of this subset the *satisficing size*, and denote it by κ; the word "satisfice" was coined by Nobel Prize winner Herbert Simon in 1957 to describe the desire to achieve a minimal value of a variable instead of its maximum [22]. The resource negotiation protocol consists of the following steps:

1. All providers reveal their capacity and pricing parameters to the broker.
2. A consumer sends, to the broker, a request with the following information:
   a. The parameters of its utility function
   b. The parameters of its satisfaction function
   c. The number of candidate resource providers to be returned
3. The broker executes a brokering algorithm and returns the required list of candidate resource providers to the consumer.
4. The consumer selects the first provider from the list and verifies whether the provider can allocate the required resources. If it cannot, the consumer moves to the next provider from the list until the resources are allocated by a provider.
5. The provider notifies the broker about the resource allocation to the user.

Economic models are notoriously difficult to study. The complexity of the utility, price, and satisfaction-based models precludes analytical studies, and in a previous publication [5] we report on a simulation study. The parameters for our experiments are

- The target utility for consumers τ
- The satisficing size κ, which reflects the extent of the choices given to the consumer by the broker

- The demand-to-capacity ratio, which measures the commitment and, thus, the load placed on providers

We study the evolution in time of (1) the average hourly revenue, (2) the request acceptance ratio (the ratio of resource requests granted to the total number of requests), (3) the average consumer satisfaction, and (4) the average consumer utility. We investigate the performance of the model for different target utilities, satisficing sizes, and demand to capacity ratios. We study several scenarios, for the linear, EDN, and EDL pricing strategies.

The goal of our simulation study is to validate our choice of utility, price, and satisfaction function, to study the effect of the many parameters that characterize our model, and to gain some intuition regarding the transient and the steady-state behavior of our models. We are interested primarily in qualitative rather than quantitative results; specifically, we are interested in trends, rather than actual numbers.

In our model, the actual shape of the utility function is controlled by the parameters dictated primarily by the application. On the other hand, the satisfaction function mostly reflects the user's constraints. The model inhibits selfish behavior: greedy consumers pay a hefty price, and greedy providers who insist on high prices are bypassed. The satisfaction function ensures a balance between the amount of resources consumed and the price paid for them.

The function of a broker is to monitor the system and to tune τ and κ for optimal performance. For example, if the broker perceives that the average consumer utility is too low, it has two choices: increase τ, or increasee κ. At the same time, the system experiences an increase in the average hourly revenue and a decrease of the average consumer satisfaction. The fact that increasing utility could result in lower satisfaction seems counterintuitive, but reflects the consequences of allocating more resources; we increase the total cost possibly beyond the optimum predicated by the satisfaction function. The simulation results shown here are consistent with those when we use linear pricing and simpler models based on a synthetic quantity to represent a vector of resources.

The EDL pricing strategy leads to the highest average consumer utility and the highest average hourly revenue, while it gives the lowest request acceptance ratio and the lowest average consumer satisfaction. The EDN pricing strategy allows the highest request acceptance ratio and the highest average consumer satisfaction, while it leads to lower average consumer utility and average hourly revenue than EDL. It is also remarkable that the average consumer satisfaction does not track the average consumer utility. This reflects the importance of the satisfaction function. One could argue that in practice it would be rather difficult for users to specify the parameters of their utility and satisfaction functions. Of course, this is true in today's environments, but entirely feasible in intelligent environments where such information could be provided by societal services. The advantages of elastic requests for the computational economy of the future are likely to motivate the creation of services that could provide the synthetic parameters required to compute the satisfaction and utility functions.

Even though we limit our analysis to a single-broker system, we are confident that the most important conclusions we are able to draw from our model will still be valid for multibroker systems. These conclusions can be summarized as follows:

- Given a particular set of model parameters, the satisfaction reaches an optimum; this value represents the perfect balance between the utility and the price paid for resources
- The satisfaction does not track the utility
- Differentiated pricing perform better than linear pricing
- Brokers can effectively control the computing economy

In an environment with multiple brokers, individual brokers could apply different policies; providers and consumers could join with the one that best matches with their individual goals. The other simplifying assumptions for our analysis; for example, the uniformity of the demand to capacity ratio for all resources available at a consumer's site, will most likely have second order effects. The restriction that we impose by requiring a consumer to obtain all necessary resources from a single broker is also unlikely to significantly affect our findings.

It is very difficult to make a direct comparison between systems based on different models with different objective functions. The results discussed in the paper by Bai et al. [5] are qualitative rather than quantitative; the goal of our work is to show that our formal mathematical model captures and predicts performance trends.

5.8 CONCLUSIONS

A service-oriented computing economy based on resource virtualization has the potential to stimulate the further growth of Web-based service delivery. Here we have described our plans for the Pleiades system that will allow excess computing resources to be bought and sold as in a commodities market. Options enable a service provider in a service-oriented computing economy to minimize its costs while being able to adapt to sudden change of demand for services. Our future work involves developing the implementation of the Pleiades system (please see http://condgraf.ucc.ie/Pleiades/).

ACKNOWLEDGMENTS

The research reported in this chapter was partially supported by the Ernest T. S. Walton award from the Science Foundation of Ireland to Dan C. Marinescu. John P. Morrison gratefully acknowledges the support of the Science Foundation Ireland under the Principal Investigator award scheme. The work by H. J. Siegel was supported by the US National Science Foundation Grant CNS-061570 and the Colorado State University Abell Endowment Fund.

REFERENCES

1. S. Ali, A. A. Maciejewski, H. J. Siegel, and J.-K. Kim, Measuring the robustness of a resource allocation, *IEEE Transactions on Parallel and Distributed Systems* **15**(7): 630–641 (2004).
2. A.-L. Barabàsi, R. Albert, and H. Jeong, Mean-field theory for scale-free random networks, *Physica A* **272**(1–2):173–187 (1999).
3. A.-L. Barabàsi, R. Albert, and H. Jeong, Scale-free theory of random networks; the topology of World Wide Web, *Physica A* **281**(1–4):69–77 (2000).
4. A.-L. Barabàsi and R. Albert, Emergence of scaling in random networks, *Science* **286** (5439):509–512 (1999).
5. X. Bai, D. C. Marinescu, L. Bölöni, H. J. Siegel, R. E. Daley, and I.-J. Wang, A macroeconomic model for resource allocation in large scale distributed systems, *Journal of Parallel and Distributed Computing (JPDC)* **68**(2):182–199 (2008).
6. B. Bolobàsi, *Random Graphs*, Academic Press, London, 1985.
7. L. Bölöni and D. C. Marinescu, Robust scheduling of metaprograms, *Journal of Scheduling* **5**(5):395–412 (2002).
8. L. Bölöni, D. Turgut, and D. C. Marinescu, Task distribution with a random overlay network, *Future Generation Computer Systems* **22**(6):676–687 (2006).
9. X. Bai, H. Yu, G. Wang, Y. Ji, G. M. Marinescu, D. C. Marinescu, and L. Bölöni, Coordination in intelligent grid environments, *Proceedings of the IEEE* **93**(3):613–630 (2005).
10. C. Gershenson and F. Heylighen, When can we call a system self-organizing, *Advances in Artificial Life* **2801**:606–614 (2003).
11. G. Gemmill, *Option Pricing*, McGraw Hill, New York, 1992.
12. C. Gershenson, *Designing and Control of Self-Organizing Systems*, PhD thesis, Vrjie Univ., 2007, http://cogprints.org/5442/.
13. F. Heylighen and C. Gershenson, The meaning of self-organization in computing, *IEEE Intelligent Systems* **18**(4):72–75 (2003).
14. J. Hull, *Options, Futures and Other Derivative Securities*, Prentice-Hall, 1993.
15. J. Kephart and D. Chess, The vision of autonomic computing, *IEEE Computer Magazine* **36**(1):41–50 (2003).
16. C. Lin and D. C. Marinescu, Temporal logic workflow models, in *Process Coordination and Ubiquitous Computing*, D. C. Marinescu and C. Lee, eds., CRC Press, London, 2002.
17. D. C. Marinescu, *Internet-Based Workflow Management; Towards a Semantic Web*, Wiley, Hoboken, NJ, 2002.
18. D. C. Marinescu, Y. Ji, and G. M. Marinescu, The complexity of scheduling and coordination in computational grids, in *Process Coordination and Ubiquitous Computing*, D. C. Marinescu and C. Lee, eds., CRC Press, London, 2002.
19. L. W. McKnight and J. Boroumand, Pricing Internet services: Approaches and challenges, *IEEE Computer* **33**(2):128–129 (2000).
20. J. P. Morrison, C. Norwik, D. C. Marinescu, G. M. Marinescu, and H. J. Siegel, Managing contracts in Pleiades using trust management, submitted 2008.
21. J. P. Morrison, D. A. Power, and J. J. Kennedy, An evolution of the WebCom metacomputer, *Journal of Mathematical Modeling and Algorithms* (special issue on computational science and applications) **2**(3):263–276 (2003).

22. H. A. Simon, *Models of Man–Social and Rational*, Wiley, New York, 1957.
23. M. Stonebraker, R. Devine, M. Kornacker, W. Litwin, A. Pfeffer, A. Sah, and C. Staelin, An economic paradigm for query processing and data migration in Mariposa, *Proc. 3rd International Conf. Parallel and Distributed Information Systems*, Austin, TX, Sept. 28–30, 1994.
24. R. G. Smith, The contract net protocol: High-level communication and control in a distributed problem solver, *IEEE Transactions on Computers* **C-29**(12):1104–1113 (1980).
25. B. Snowdown and H. R. Vane, *Modern Macroeconomic: Its Origin, Development and Current Status*, Edward Elgar Publishing, London, 2005.
26. V. Shestak, J. Smith, A. A. Maciejewski, and H. J. Siegel, Stochastic robustness metric and its use for static resource allocations, *Journal of Parallel and Distributed Computing*.
27. P. Wilmot, J. N. Dewynne, and S. D. Howison, *Option Pricing: Mathematical Models and Computations*, Oxford Univ. Press, 1985.
28. P. Wilmot, S. D. Howison, and J. N. Dewynne, *The Mathematics of Financial Derivatives*, Cambridge Univ. Press, 1995.
29. R. Wolski, J. S. Plank, J. Brevik, and T. Bryan, G-commerce: Market formulations controlling resource allocation on the computational grid, *Proc. 15th International Parallel and Distributed Processing Symposium (IPDPS-01)*, San Francisco, CA, April 23–27, 2001.
30. C. S. Yeo and R. Buyya, Integrated risk analysis for a commercial computing service, *Proc. 21st IEEE International Parallel and Distributed Processing Symp.* (*IPDPS-07*), Long Beach, CA, March 26–30, 2007.
31. H. Yu, X. Bai, and D. C. Marinescu, Workflow management and resource discovery for an intelligent grid, *Parallel Computing* **31**(7):797–811 (2005).
32. C. Yu, D. C. Marinescu, G. M. Marinescu, J. P. Morrison, and C. Norvik, A reputation algorithm for a self-organizing system based upon resource virtualization, *Proc. 22nd IEEE International Parallel and Distributed Processing Symp. (IPDPS-08), Heterogeneity in Computing Workshop 2008* (*HCW-08*), Miami, FL, April 14 – 18, 2008.

PART II

BUSINESS MODELS

6

GRID BUSINESS MODELS, EVALUATION, AND PRINCIPLES

STEVE TAYLOR AND PAUL MCKEE

6.1 INTRODUCTION

It is easy to imagine a list of Grid business models that sound as if they will be viable, but it is not easy to confirm this rigorously without the dangerous step of operating them. For this reason we believe that it is important to provide analytical methods that can be used by a prospective adopter, who alone has the market and financial data needed to perform an analysis. This will allow business models to be evaluated using the methods that we have provided to determine which are viable in that situation, and which are not.

We begin by discussing background and related work, with the aim of providing a working definition of the term "business model" as applied to Grid to be used throughout this chapter. We need to clearly determine what we mean when we use the term. This may sound obvious, but it is difficult to find a consistent definition the term. Our definition basically asks the following question: "How does what you are proposing make money sustainably?"

We next propose a questionnaire containing questions regarding the viability of the business proposition. The questions highlight important issues that a prospective operator of a business model needs to consider, especially when applied to the Grid. We have identified these issues on the basis of research, discussion, and experience.

Next, a number of candidate business models are analyzed with respect to the questionnaire. The candidate business models covered have been chosen partly to illustrate commonly occurring Grid situations and business actors (participants). This analysis indicates how the questionnaire can be applied in practice, focusing attention

Market-Oriented Grid and Utility Computing Edited by Rajkumar Buyya and Kris Bubendorfer

on the important issues that arise for each business model. The aim of the analysis is to show that each business model has different pros and cons associated with it. These are highlighted by applying our approach through use of the questionnaire, which also brings out the significant (and sometimes unique) features each business model illustrates.

After this, a number of principles arising from the analysis are presented and discussed, with the aim of providing guidelines to a potential practitioner of a Grid business. These principles give rise to research challenges, where elements have not been sufficiently addressed, and these are also discussed. We conclude with a brief summary.

6.2 BACKGROUND AND RELATED WORK

The term "business model" gained significant popularity during the Internet bubble when every successful business needed a good business model, but was somewhat discredited when the bubble burst. Any discussion about business models is immediately complicated by the lack of a common definition and understanding of the meaning of the phrase "business model" [1]. In addition, Linder and Cantrell [2] assert that "Executives can't even articulate their business models. Everyone talks about business models but 99 percent have no clear framework for describing their model."

A Google search for the term currently returns 253 million references, very few of which share a common definition or structure for the concept. Hence there is a need to determine a common understanding of the term, and this must be based on well-accepted wisdom.

The most commonly used minimal description of the term is simply that the business model articulates how the business makes money. This sounds obvious, but there are many aspects to the description, and these are not always obvious and are certainly not easily answered. The slightest difference in one small element in two business models can mean the success of one and the failure of another. The elements are discussed below, drawing from a number of frequently cited sources.

One of the more frequently cited references is the report by Timmers [3], who describes a business model as follows:

- An architecture for the product, service, and information flows, including a description of the various business actors and their roles
- A description of the potential benefits for the various business actors
- A description of the sources of revenue.

Chesborough and Rosenbloom [4] specify that the six functions of a business model are to

- Articulate the value proposition, that is, the value created for users by the offering

- Identify a market segment, that is, the users to whom the offering is useful and for what purpose, and specify the revenue generation mechanism for the firm
- Define the structure of the value chain within the firm to create and distribute the offering and determine the complementary assets needed to support the firm's assets in this chain
- Examine the cost structure and profit potential of producing the offering given the value proposition and value chain structure chosen
- Describe the position of the firm within the value network linking suppliers and customers, including identification of potential complementors and competitors
- Formulate the competitive strategy by which the innovating firm will gain and hold advantage over rivals.

Magretta [5] provides a complementary analysis of what is important in a business model. Broadly, the important factors can be broken down into two categories, the *story* and the *numbers*, both of which must be carefully considered if a candidate business model stands any chance of success.

The story is a narrative that describes the business model. It must provide a convincing argument for the business model in a number of areas, some of which are listed briefly below:

- The actors—who are the participants in the model, and why should they participate? What is in it for them? There must be clear motivations for all actors in the model. What are the risks to the actors in the business model? How are these risks counteracted?
- The offering to the customers—what exactly is the thing the customers will be buying? Why is it attractive to customers? Is the value obvious and clear in the mind of the customer? This is most important—there must be clear and obvious value to the target customers—if it is not already there, how will it be introduced?
- Who are the customers? Define the target market. Is the value in the offering obvious and clear to this market? What is the competition? How will the market change over time? How does the benefit offered to the customers differ from that competition? How is it better? What is the "unique selling point" (USP)?
- How is the offering produced? What are the "raw materials" (which must be bought in)? How are these transformed into the offering to the customers (what is the added value)?

The numbers deals with a financial analysis of whether the offering can be produced and sold cost-effectively, and generate the required profit for the organization selling it. This typically involves a detailed analysis of *all* the costs that are faced by the organization in order to create the offering. The list of costs must be exhaustive; otherwise the analysis is falsely optimistic. The price at which the offering is sold at is determined by the costs analysis together with the desired profit, which is then tested using market analyses to determine whether the market will stand the price charged.

Both the story and the numbers must make sense. Quoting Magretta [5]: "When business models don't work, it's because they fail either the narrative test (the story doesn't make sense) or the numbers test (the P&L [profit and loss] doesn't add up)."

Often there is iteration or adaptation of the model as market conditions change, as discussed by Voelpel et al. [6]. For example, the model may be refined over time on the basis of experience in operating it, there may be a new entrant into the market, and the competition must react; or interest rates may rise, giving customers less disposable income. This may cause situations that result in changes to the business model. Adaptation of a business model is a common occurrence as market conditions change, and in contemporary markets the situation can change rapidly.

There are no agreed-on formats for the presentation of business models, and the most accepted format is a single-page simple narrative statement that addresses the abovementioned topics. It should be noted that the business model *does not explicitly include implementation technologies*. It is driven by business requirements and simply enabled by technology. It is also worth noting that articulation of a business model is no guarantee of its success; only implementation will tell if the model actually works.

One final complication is that new business models are increasingly viewed as key intellectual property (e.g., Amazon.com's attempt to patent its one-click shopping model [7]). Often attempts are made to protect them by patent, and at the very least they are viewed as trade secrets.

6.3 BUSINESS MODEL EVALUATION QUESTIONNAIRE

6.3.1 Introduction

We now describe a questionnaire (or checklist) that contains questions that must be answered to initially test the viability a business model candidate. The questionnaire directly addresses the prospective operator of the business model under test, and hence there are direct first-person references. The aim of the questionnaire is to direct thinking and ensure that critical areas are considered, and to weed out unprofitable or unworkable business models at an early stage of analysis, or to determine the areas that need further investigation.

6.3.2 The Questionnaire

1. *What is the offering to the customer?* This is what the customer will pay for. Here there must be enough value in the eyes of the customer that they will be prepared to pay for it. The business model must provide a description of what the offering is to the customers, in terms that they will understand and be interested in. Why should customers be interested? There must be a convincing justification of why the customers will want your offering. Any guarantees offered to a customer will be

represented in an SLA with that customer. This describes the obligations on both the service provider and customer side of the relationship. What guarantees are offered in the service? This is likely to be linked to the price of the service, since a service with very strict QoS guarantees will be more costly to you (and hence the customer) than one provided on a best efforts basis. Are there market segments that will be interested in different combinations of price/guarantee?

2. *What value do you add?* What is the value proposition of the business model? What extra value is added to bought-in "raw materials" to make products or services that your customers want? Why should customers come to you and not your competitors? What is your unique selling point? Is the added value you provide clear to your customers? If not, how will you make this clear? How will you use this added value to attract customers?

3. *What internal motivations for being in business are there?* Why do you want to operate this business model—for example, you may have spare computational or storage capacity that you wish to make money on. List these internal motivations and identify if and where they conflict with or support the delivery of the service. For example, are you interested only in selling spare capacity and when you are busy with your own work, will you neglect your customers?

4. *What are the costs of the service offering?* These costs are many and varied, and may not all be financial. Some examples are listed below:

- Costs of purchasing raw materials (e.g., software licenses).
- Staff costs that both directly and indirectly affect creation of the product or service (e.g., maintenance and customer support staff).
- Overheads, such as office rental, electricity, water, and support staff.
- Cost of purchasing services from suppliers (e.g., outsourced computation, any network transmission costs, support services such as credit checking, payment, archiving, or raw data).
- Hardware maintenance costs (e.g., computing, storage, network equipment).
- Costs of annoying a customer (e.g., when refusing them service when another customer deemed more important comes along). This may be financial, in that a penalty may be paid, or not directly financial, as in the case that annoying the customer results in them going elsewhere and there is a loss of business and possible damage to reputation, if the customer is able to pass on his/her dissatisfaction to other customers. Word of mouth can be powerful, as discussed by Kumar et al. [8].
- Advertising, marketing, and sales costs.
- Transport costs. In the case of a service-oriented architecture (SOA)-type service, this is most likely to be network bandwidth/leased lines, and so on.
- Asset purchase. The purchase of assets is the eventual reduction of a cash asset (with the corresponding increase in the asset's value).
- Asset depreciation. This is represented on the balance sheet as a reduction in the value of assets.

It is critical to ensure that *all* costs contributing to the production and selling of the offering are considered. Otherwise, the total will be unrealistically optimistic, and any profit resulting from sales will also be unrealistically optimistic. To neglect or underestimate a cost can be a fatal error to the business. For example, academic users often consider their use of network bandwidth to be essentially free, as it is not paid for at the point of use.

5. *What must be bought in so as to deliver the offering?* What are your raw materials (computer hardware, software licenses, other services, etc.)? Who are the suppliers? What do you purchase from them? How much raw materials are required? What is your sensitivity to supply disruption? What happens if the raw materials are delivered early or late? How much does it cost you (financially or otherwise)? Are you dependent on one or a small group of suppliers? For example, if your business is dependent on the licensing of a particular third-party application code, then your business is dependent on its supplier—if they choose not to supply you any more, you are out of business. This is a highly undesirable situation as it indicates an imbalance of power not in your favor, and the more this is reduced, the greater the chances of success. A simple question to ask here is whether there are alternative suppliers for the same item.

6. *How are prices set?* The first question to answer here is: What are your costs? Then you need to determine how much profit do you want to make, and this is determined to a large part by what price you think the market will withstand. You must analyze the market and provide a convincing justification for the price you are targeting. The price level may be obvious if you are entering a crowded marketplace, as the price is likely to be set by the competition between offerings already there. Here your problem is more likely to be determining and advertising the difference in your offering, which can be down to price—if you can sell a similar product more cheaply than the competition; this is your differentiating factor.) For a new product or service, market research and understanding are required to set the price, but as the product or service matures in its lifecycle (assuming that it is successful), there will be competition that will likely drive the price down until it settles at a market average. Some specific questions are

- Are there other similar products or services in the market place?
- How do your prices compare to these?
- How can you justify any significant differences in your prices when compared to competitors' prices for similar products?
- Do you have favored customers to whom you want to offer preferential rates? Do you want to offer volume discounts?

7. *How will customers pay for the service?* How is the service priced? A tariff is a common means of describing the payment models and plans, but what are the "units of consumption" that measure the capacity of the service offered and the customer pays for? Two popular payment models at the moment are utility computing (where customers pay for what they use—also applicable to software as a service) and subscription (where customers pay a fixed amount regularly, e.g., a month) for a set amount of capacity. In particular, "mobile phone" payment models seem to fit well

here, and may offer benefits for the provider as well as the customer. Any subscription payment model with "free minutes" is useful to the provider because it provides a capacity limit and thus can offer considerable assistance in capacity planning and a useful benefit for the provider; there is also the possibility that customers do not use all they have paid for (unused minutes often expire after a time). Prepaid models (e.g., mobile phone prepay models) are also useful to the provider, in that the customers are effectively giving the provider an interest-free loan (when they pay upfront), which may (or may not) be used in the form of consumption of the service at a later date (paraphrased from Magretta [5]). The grain size of the prepay amounts is also significant—the customers can be encouraged to pay in large chunks (by discount perhaps), and the larger the chunk ("loan"), the better for the provider.

8. *How is a service provisioned for?* If you operate finite resources, how can you be sure that you can answer the requests made on your service? How can you determine which of your customers gets to use them and when? Use of a cluster is consumable—the opportunity to access it perishes with time, and thus there is a considerable desire to get maximum usage out of it. There is usually a great deal of tension between the provider's desire to get maximum utility out of a resource, while also wanting to keep it highly available so as to service users' requests. This has been addressed in a number of ways; for example, the service provider can take advantage of regular heterogeneous demand—that different customers have different patterns, and given enough customers, demand peaks should become more uniform. Monitoring the usage generated by a particular offering over time may elicit management information that may permit heuristic mappings based on experience to be generated. Monitoring the usage of the service is important also for determining whether if a user has used up or is near any quota limits.

9. *In what way are relationships important to you?* Where are you in the value chain? Who are the suppliers? Who are the customers? What are your relationships with all the actors to deal with?

- Relationships with suppliers. You are most likely to want to keep suppliers on their toes by negotiating the lowest price while keeping them reliable suppliers. How can you negotiate cheap deals? Can you offer suppliers repeating orders of a reasonable size, for example? How dependent are you on individual suppliers? A significant supplier here is a software vendor, with potentially a great deal of power. Can you insulate yourself from being dependent in this way?
- Relationships with customers. How important is your reputation? What is your desired image to your customers? Ultrareliable? Expensive (what is the reason for customers to pay your prices)? Cheap (what sacrifice will customers make to get the cheap prices)? High-performance? What sort of customer relationship do you want? Do you want to cultivate long-term relationships for a (perhaps) high-price bespoke (custom-made) service that makes the effort in building the relationship worthwhile, or are you more interested in a commoditized service that needs little in the way of customer relationship or service management?

10. *What are the market characteristics?*

- What is the market sector? Is there a specific good or service type that the market you are targeting is concerned with? How big is the market? Who is in it? What characterizes them? Are there segments? How mature is the market? How can this determine the prices you can set?
- Analyze the competition. Who are they? What is their offering? Are there comparable products or services in the marketplace? Why is yours better? In what way are you different? It is vitally important for a successful business model to have a way of being different (the so-called "unique selling point" or "competitive advantage"). What is yours?
- Are you creating a market? If so, how are you sure that there is a market? Are you the first mover? Can you protect a first-mover advantage? What will happen if others come into the marketplace to compete? How will you protect yourself from erosion of your market position in the (inevitable, if the market is successful) event of competition? Beware of second-mover advantages. These are organizations that observe emerging markets and learn from the mistakes of the first movers. Only then do they enter the marketplace, and are typically in a stronger position than a mistakemaking first mover. Traditionally, the leading (or bleeding) edge is a dangerous place to be as it is largely untested.

11. *How will you make customers aware of and want your offering?*

- What users are you targeting? How will you communicate with them? Are you going to advertise? If so, where will you advertise? Are there communities already out there that you could target? Do they have any forums that they use?
- What do you want to tell the potential customers? Have you a clear message that the customers will understand? What is that message? How can you be certain that your message is clear to customers?
- How will you make the customers want the offering? What is important to your customers? How do you address this in your marketing communication? What sets your offering apart from others in the marketplace?

12. *What are the risks in this business model?* Describe the risks that face this business model. For example, do you have a lot of machines that could potentially be unutilized? Are you dependent on one supplier? Are there elements of QoS in an SLA beyond your control? How will you offset these risks? In short, perform a detailed and comprehensive risk analysis—for each risk identified, list its severity and measures to reduce the chances of it occurring or its severity.

6.4 CANDIDATE BUSINESS MODEL ANALYSIS

This section presents a number of candidate business models, which are discussed with reference to the questionnaire presented above. The aim here is not to answer all the questions in the questionnaire, but to illustrate the important and characteristic features of the business model with reference to the questionnaire and its questions.

6.4.1 Basic Compute Resources

1. *What is the offering to the customer?* The offering is basic: rental of compute resources. The model offers no application-level guarantees and cannot be tied to the customer's business objectives. Little in the way of QoS is offered—there may be some statement of best efforts regarding availability or reliability, but the aim is to make this model as cheap as possible, and since any guarantees on QoS will make it more expensive, they have been removed. In addition, because of the cheapness of the pricing, management of the service by the provider is kept at a minimum.

2. *What value do you add?* The value is in the ability to access computational power greater than most customers can afford, without the need to purchase hardware. Today, with reasonable outlay, an organization can purchase a reasonable amount of computing power. The customers' main costs are likely to be in peripheral expenses, for example, space, cooling, and electricity. These can be significant operational expenditure, and can soon exceed the purchase price of a machine. Electricity is a significant, often ignored cost; Laudon [9] indicates that the new focus of server total cost of ownership (TCO) is the relationship of performance to watt (the unit of electrical power), and the US Environmental Protection Agency states that national energy consumption in 2006 by servers and data centers is over twice that in 2000, and could nearly double again by 2011 [10]. The ability to rent compute resources, and thus save these significant costs, may be valued by the customer. However, given that there are little guarantees of QoS, this value is limited to the reduction of these costs.

3. *What internal motivations for being in business are there?* The service provider may have a resource cluster on which they want to increase utilization, or in which to maximize their return on investment (ROI). In this case selling off the spare CPU cycles may assist. Alternatively, the service provider might have a dedicated cluster and they hope to make profits by renting the resources out to customers.

4. *What are the costs for delivering the offering to the customer?* There is capital expenditure in the ownership and depreciation of hardware. In addition, there are real estate, utility, and staff costs directly related to the offering. The electrical costs discussed previously are as significant here as for anyone else owning servers, but here the costs should be amortized over many customers (if the provider is successful). There are also software costs, in the form of operating systems and any virtualization technology, such as sandboxes and virtual machines required for adequate user segregation.

5. *What must be bought in so as to deliver the offering?* The primary raw material is the hardware required to build the resource pool that will be rented out to customers. Other items could include any operating system software, together with any virtualization technology.

6. *How are prices set?* Prices are set following the costs plus the profit margin desired. The price the market will stand is a major factor (see the article by Bala and Green [11], which discusses value in the eyes of the customer relative to the price charged), and may be the main problem with this business model, as the costs of hardware are reducing all the time. Because of the continuous reduction in hardware

costs, the significant contribution to this cost in the future could come from the operational costs mentioned above. In addition, the market is mature, with suppliers like Amazon [12,13] and Sun [14], and these have already set prices.

7. *How will customers pay for the service?* There are many ways of charging and billing for this type of offering. There are many methods of charging and units of consumption for Grid services, discussed in many publications (e.g., see Ref. 15). As an example, customers can either

- Pay for what they use (e.g., usage is monitored and the customer receives a bill at the end of the month)
- Subscribe to a service with fixed limits (*X* CPU hours per month rolled into the price)
- Reserve machines, and pay on a time basis (i.e., one machine of *X* specification for a week—real "rental")

8. *How is a service provisioned for?* Since little QoS is offered in this model, provisioning is less important in this model. It is essentially a case of "best efforts."

9. *In what way are relationships important to you?* In this model, the relationships to the customers are more important than the relationship with suppliers. If the service provider is managing their own resources, the suppliers are typically contacted when hardware purchases need to occur.

10. *What are the market characteristics?* Because of the commodity nature of the low-level resources on offer, the target market is unclear as it is potentially diverse. The offering does not solve specific customers' problems; rather it provides a platform for the customers to solve their own problems. The competition however is clear. There are a few embryonic commercial services available today offering this sort of business proposition, notably Sun Grid [14] and Amazon Elastic Compute Cloud (Amazon EC2) [12]. Both organizations are capable of using massive purchasing power to keep costs to their absolute minimum. This is the competition in the marketplace, and it is tough competition, indeed. It is asserted that leveraging the economies of scale and buying power to which these organizations have access is one of the few ways of offering a service such as this, as any value-added benefit to the customer is low, and thus the price must be correspondingly low.

11. *How will you make customers aware of and want your offering?* Since the market is highly diverse and unfocused, few options exist apart from blanket advertising in general computer or high-performance computing media, which is likely to be expensive and offer an unsatisfactory return on the investment.

12. *What are the risks in this business model?* The risks are many and varied. They have been discussed in previous sections, and are summarized here:

- The cost to supply the offering is greater than the price the market is willing to accept.
- The value proposition to the market is low.
- The target market is ill-defined.
- The investment required to set up in business is great, with no guarantee of a return.

6.4.2 Hosting

1. *What is the offering to the customer?* The basic type of offering to the customer is access to a high-quality managed infrastructure at an agreed price. Security, privacy, and reliability are key parts of this offering. All are specified as QoS with penalties for failure. The key difference between this business model and that of Section 6.4.1 is that this business model offers a managed service, with QoS guarantees on the security, reliability, network connectivity, and availability of the service. This business model is based on the premise of a long-term relationship with the customer, where the service provider takes the responsibility of resource management away from the customer.

2. *What value do you add?* The hosting provider adds value by delivering a reliable QoS managed service to the end user, without the end user having to grow or purchase the expertise necessary to do this in-house, which reduces their costs. The added value is in the management aspect. This business model represents outsourcing to an organization whose core business it is, and is therefore most efficient and expert in its execution. It is an implementation of one of the fundamental principles of economics, that of specialization.

3. *What internal motivations for being in business are there?* The companies most likely to adopt the role of hosting providers are those who already have data centers, and want to increase their utilization. These organizations typically have the skills required to manage the resources, and this model enables them to sell the skills and resources.

4. *What are the costs for delivering the offering to the customer?* For a provider starting from scratch in this business there is a huge upfront cost involved in construction of the data center. However, given a preexisting infrastructure (the more likely scenario), the costs of adding new, hosted applications are those associated with hardware and software. Other costs are associated with the efficient running of the data center and will include management costs, power for equipment, cooling facilities, and so on together with any costs associated with network connectivity.

5. *What must be bought in so as to deliver the offering?* The major purchase is the hardware and software necessary to support the service (this may include supporting hardware such as firewall appliances and other networking infrastructure).

6. *How are prices set?* There is wide variation in the quality of hosting that could be provided, and the price will be determined by these quality levels and the amount of compensation that the provider is prepared to commit to for underdelivery.

7. *How will customers pay for the service?* This is a service based on a long-term relationship—many hosting contracts last for multiple years, and the payments are likely to be made on a periodic subscription basis.

8. *How is a service provisioned for?* The provisioning is mostly hardware/ management-related: machines for hosting and firewalls. The resources are commissioned with respect the users' needs, and since the agreement is long-term, real, rather than virtual, machines may be used.

9. *In what way are relationships important to you?* The suppliers are hardware providers of all types, such as computers, storage, and networking. Much of this is commoditized, and thus the hosted service provider is in a relatively strong position. The customers are users of hosted services who lack either the skills or motivation to provide the services in-house. It is important that the end users view the hosting supplier as both reliable and reasonably priced, and hence the provider needs to offer QoS with guarantees.

10. *What are the market characteristics?* The potential market is heavily segmented and highly competitive, particularly at the lower end. Providers in this space may choose to adopt a range of strategies to position themselves in the market; they may focus on the high-end market offering utmost reliability and resilience, or they may take a much more low-cost approach and target basic hosting at the most competitive price. They might also align themselves with one type of software for a specific industry segment. All of these potential strategies (and others) serve to create a highly fragmented marketplace where price and capability comparisons may be difficult, throwing emphasis onto reputation.

11. *How will you make customers aware of and want your offering?* This is a very broad market, and there will be a number of channels to market at different levels within the range of product offerings. At the highest level where major corporations seek to outsource all or some of their internal computing estate, any supplier of hosting services at the appropriate scale will engage in an individual dialog with the potential customer. As we move lower down the price–capability scale, there are trade journals in which hosting services are advertised. At the lowest end of the market many of the Internet service provider (ISP) connectivity packages sold in this market offer some low level of Web-based hosting that may act as a lead to further business.

12. *What are the risks in this business model?* The major risk in this business model is that the investment made in the resources required to run the service is not returned in the form of service contracts. This problem is, however, alleviated by the long-term nature of the contracts offered by the service provider. Given their long-term status, the problem of provisioning and planning for capacity to service the contracts is simplified as the forward demand to largely known as the contracts are in place for a set amount of resource and time period. There are other operational risks, concerning what happens if the service provider fails in some way to deliver on an aspect of a contract.

6.4.3 Software License Reseller/Broker

1. *What is the offering to the customer?* The end user is offered the option of purchasing software licenses for use on either their own machines or the machines of a third-party service provider with a lower cost than that of an annual license. There exists a large body of commercial software that is licensed and maintained by the software providers on an annual (or other long-term) basis at high cost to the software user. This high cost naturally acts as a barrier to the use of the software by many small- and medium-sized enterprises that cannot afford the costs. In this model, the end user

is offered the option of purchasing software licenses for use either on their own machines or on the machines of a third-party service provider with a finer granularity, and hence lower cost, than that of an annual license.

2. *What value do you add?* For the software vendor the purchase of blocks of annual licenses and service contracts offers a stable financial planning regime without the added overhead of license management for a finer granularity offering. The end user gains the use of high-value software, only when required, at a much lower cost than an annual license.

3. *What internal motivations for being in business are there?* The broker represents a classic middleperson role, exploiting relationships and economies of scale to deliver value to its business partners. The profit made from the difference between bulk purchases of long-term licenses and the sale of multiple short-term licenses is the major motivation.

4. *What are the costs for delivering the offering to the customer?* The main cost to the reseller is the purchase costs of the licenses they wish to resell, and sometimes this will involve a long-term commitment of funds. The broker will require a fairly minimal infrastructure to manage the licenses and a low staff overhead; it is essentially a middleperson role.

5. *What must be bought in so as to deliver the offering?* In order to deliver the service, the reseller has to have access to software licenses. In the simplest case these will be owned by other parties with the reseller just managing the reselling process. The reseller may also purchase licenses for resale, in which case they may attempt to get volume discounts from the software suppliers.

6. *How are prices set?* We can assume that the ceiling price for licenses from the original software vendors is known to those people who would make use of such software, and this will be a contributing factor to the price the market can stand. There will need to be some markup, but this knowledge obviously limits the scaling factor that can be applied. The situation is similar to a "rent versus buy" situation in other areas, and the differences between the prices in these areas may be worth considering. However, the operating costs of this business role are typically low, and thus the broker can be reasonably competitive.

7. *How will customers pay for the service?* This is essentially a utility-based offering of licenses, and customers would be able to pay in advance for a fixed amount of quota, or the usage of the software may be measured with the customers paying in arrears.

8. *How is a service provisioned for?* The resource in this model is the software license, which the reseller partitions and sells in smaller proportions. The bought-in software license determines the limit of capacity, and once this is reached, the reseller has a choice of whether to invest in a new license, or to reject customers' requests. There may be agreements with software vendors that commit the reseller to regular license purchases, and in this case the provisioning is a question of the mapping between the supply and demand rates.

9. *In what way are relationships important to you?* The relationship with the software vendors is key to the success of this model, as they have the ability to render

the model impractical by simply changing the license details for their software, or impossible by refusing to supply more licenses. The benefits to the software vendors are that the reseller buys blocks of long-term licenses and stabilizes the cash flow of the software vendor. It is important that the end users view the reseller as both reliable and reasonably priced. As purely an intermediary, there is potentially a lot of competition in the license reseller space, and the reputation of the reseller may be the key differentiation in the marketplace.

10. *What are the market characteristics?* The potential market is heavily segmented, and currently there are few, if any, competitors in this space. There will be a considerable first-mover advantage as many of the specialist market segments will be too small to support too many competitors. A key differentiator is price—the product is the same for different resellers' access to the application. Reliability is another differentiator—if the reseller cannot supply a license on demand, this will be significantly detrimental to their competitiveness. Differentiation may also be achieved by differentiating the product—offering bundles of licenses for all of the specialist software associated with complex tasks, for example, including analysis and visualization software in the same bundle as design software.

11. *How will you make customers aware of and want your offering?* The value proposition to the target market is clear—access expensive, high-end software at a fraction of the cost of a perpetual license. Software of this type tends to have user groups, discussion groups, and even trade shows and conferences devoted to the use of the product where end users can be made aware of the offering. To attract new users, sector-specific publications may be used to target advertising at potential customers who are aware of the product but have been discouraged from using it by the high costs associated with licenses.

12. *What are the risks in this business model?* The major risk to this business model is the clear and severe dependence that the broker has on the suppliers of the software licenses. If the license supplier chooses to stop supplying licenses or prevents the broker from reselling the licenses, this business model cannot be operated. This business model is also vulnerable to attack by the software vendors themselves if the potential profits are high enough, and by service companies who can potentially negotiate lower license purchase costs. The vendor will be keen to ensure that the use of licenses is adequately policed and auditable, and this is the responsibility of the reseller. If the license supplier gets any hint that license policing technology is cracked, they will terminate any agreements forthwith, thus shutting down this business model.

6.4.4 Flexible Licensing—Application Provider's Business Model

1. *What is the offering to the customer?* The offering to the customer is more choice in licensing for high-value, high-cost software. Customers have an additional option—rather than pay for a traditional long-term and expensive license, they can instead purchase much more affordable short-term (or otherwise limited) licenses, as

and when they need them. This model is important as it explores whether flexible licensing is realistic in terms of the application provider, as they have the power to stop all related flexible licensing business models for their software.

2. *What value do you add?* The value is in the use the customer can put the software to, and this is the same regardless of whether the software is available on a long-term license (the traditional situation) or a shorter-term license (the new situation). This business model is all about reaching new customer segments.

3. *What internal motivations for being in business are there?* The primary motivation is to widen the customer base—to reach customers not previously accessible. The targeted segment is the population who want the software but cannot afford a long-term license. They can purchase the right to use the software in smaller quantities.

4. *What are the costs for delivering the offering to the customer?* The costs to develop, maintain, support, and sell the software are the same regardless of the licensing or delivery strategy. These costs should already be well known and understood, as the software is already developed and in the marketplace. On top of these, the costs are reasonably small and are concerned mainly with automated payment processing and the granting and enforcement of the licenses. For this the main costs are computer hardware to act as license servers and software for creating, granting, managing, and enforcing licenses.

5. *What must be bought in so as to deliver the offering?* License enforcement technology is the main requirement from outside. This is much more likely to be bought in rather than developed in-house, as it is complex and not the application provider's core business.

6. *How are prices set?* The price will be constrained by the existing price of the perpetual or annual licenses for the code. In addition, prices are in part set by the costs incurred in delivering the service. For the short-term licensed software, prices are likely to be set on a pro rata basis compared to the price of the long-term license, and how the smaller licenses are related to it. A sliding scale of unit price that decreases with the increase of the units purchased may be a good idea—even though the plan is to attract new customers by offering smaller licenses, appealing to their sense of value for money if they were to buy a little more than they need. There is some crossover point, where it becomes sensible to purchase the long-term license, and this must be carefully considered, as there is a considerable danger of undermining the long-term license business with this new venture.

7. *How will customers pay for the service?* The unit of consumption here can be either time-limited (e.g., a license for a limited period of time), or work-based licenses (e.g., a license for a fixed amount of "work"—resource-based consumption defined in any number of ways). Each type of unit has its own pros and cons. Time-limited licenses are easier to implement than work-based licenses as the only monitoring required is the wall clock time, and this is a universal unit. However, customers will get better value out of the software if they have a powerful machine, as they can perform more work than if they had a less powerful machine. Work-based licenses are

more difficult to implement, as the definition of "work" can be application-agnostic (e.g., in CPU-seconds), or application-specific (e.g., number of frames of a specific complexity rendered to a specified resolution). However, work-based licenses give the application provider a means of influencing the value customers get out of their software.

8. *How is a service provisioned for?* No provisioning is required; as many license tokens that the customers can pay for can be created with ease.

9. *In what way are relationships important to you?* In production of the goods that the end user wants, there are no direct suppliers, as the software has been written in-house. However, enforcement of the license tokens may be provided by an external supplier as a technology or service (e.g., Macrovision's FlexNet licensing technology [16]). The relationship with a provider of such technology is likely to be very important as they have the power to prevent unauthorized use of the software.

10. *What are the market characteristics?* The target market is an expansion of the existing market to capture customers for whom the cost of long-term licenses is prohibitive. Its population is specialized and usually highly trained—in short, prospective users of the software. This could be occasional users of the software, for whom the long-term license is not cost-effective, potential users of the software who want to test it before committing to a long-term license, users who cannot afford the high cost of a long-term license, and existing users of the software who think they are paying too much for it. Competition arises from other organizations in the same sector—those producing software or services in the same or similar application areas. This business model is an attempt at securing a larger proportion of the potential user base by attracting more occasional users of the software. If this organization is the first mover, there may be an advantage, but if successful, this advantage is likely to be shortlived, as there are few entry costs for other application code suppliers entering this market.

11. *How will you make customers aware of and want your offering?* The target market is slightly different from that of the existing user base, and thus there must be a means of identifying and reaching them. The message is an extension to an existing message—the existing message is that the application code is good and can provide useful results, and the extension is that users can now access it much more cheaply than before. Some members of the target market need the whole message—what the software is and why it is good, and that they can now get it cheaper. Others that know what the software is and want it just need to know that it is more affordable now. The channels to reach these customers are typically those in use already—specialist journals, conferences, and trade publications.

12. *What are the risks in this business model?* A major risk is that license enforcement technology does not enforce the license terms (i.e., the duration or quotas), or is cracked. This issue must be addressed. Another risk is that existing customers that can afford the long-term license might switch to the short-term license, especially if they were not using the software much. This is a considerable potential loss of revenue, and analysis must be undertaken to determine whether the new venture will offset this risk and improve profitability overall.

6.4.5 Applications and Computation

1. *What is the offering to the customer?* The offering is a complete software solution for the customer from licensed application code down to the optimum hardware for its execution, all wrapped as a service. The user only has to pay one price for the bundle of hardware and software.

2. *What value do you add?* The value added is in the aggregation of compute resources and licensed software, thus providing a "total solution"—the customers get both the hardware and the software, wrapped into a service that may be delivered on a paid-per-use basis. Offering a high-value, high-cost application code is the key to success of this model.

3. *What internal motivations for being in business are there?* The primary motivation here is to generate demand for the service—an application code contains much value for customers, as it is a tool that they can put to direct business use. Offering this extra significant value as a service constitutes a competitive advantage. Alternatively, an organization may have expertise in operating an application code and wish to sell their expertise bundled as a service running on their hardware.

4. *What are the costs for delivering the offering to the customer?* Costs fall into two categories: hardware and software. Hardware costs are the same as those discussed in the previous hardware-based models. The software cost is the license with the application providers for the rights to use their software and sell it as a service. The terms of the deal will determine exactly what the costs are, but a likely model is that the application provider will want to monitor the usage of their software, and be paid pro rata for its use, or so that usage limits can be enforced.

5. *What must be bought in so as to deliver the offering?* Here there are two main categories: hardware and software. Each has been discussed in the section on costs.

6. *How are prices set?* In addition to the costs incurred by the service provider, the price will depend on a number of issues. First, there is the market's value of the software and hardware combined into a service. The customer's desired QoS will also affect the price. There is also the issue of grain size. It is likely to be cheaper per unit the more the customer signs up for (i.e., commits to). In addition, there is the required profit margin.

7. *How will customers pay for the service?* A pay-per-use model is possible, where the customer uses the combined hardware and software service on an ad hoc basis and is billed for the usage. Subscriptions are also possible. This implies a longer-term commitment (e.g., there may be minimum contract periods of a year), and this gives the service provider a guaranteed revenue stream and assists them in capacity planning, but this obviously only makes sense for regular or higher usage customers.

8. *How is a service provisioned for?* The compute resources are provisioned using the techniques described in the models described in Sections 6.4.1 and 6.4.2. How the software licenses are provisioned for depends on the agreement with the application provider. Software licenses are finite resources, as if they run out, the customer will need to purchase more, or wait until one becomes free. Licenses are also possibly perishable in the sense that a ROI needs to be generated as soon as possible on the

investment in a license, especially for time-limited (e.g., annual) licenses. The converse is also true; bought-in but unused licenses are dead stock, just as is unused hardware. Hence, for the service provider, the provisioning considerations of hardware and software are similar. Both demand maximum utilization if the ROI is to be maximized.

9. *In what way are relationships important to you?* Here the value chain is fairly clear. The main suppliers are the application providers, the suppliers of the licenses. There are other actors in the value chain, such as hardware suppliers, but these are much less important to the service provider than are application providers, as hardware is a commodity, whereas the software is typically bespoke and available from one supplier, the owner of the IP in the software. The customers are also important for more obvious reasons—they are the ones who provide the income for the service provider.

10. *What are the market characteristics?* The target audience is made up of users who want to solve high-performance computing (HPC)-type problems (e.g., heat transfer simulations) using application codes, and will know the code they want (most likely)—if a service provider supports the application, this is the deciding factor (alongside other terms such as nondisclosure). Competition could come from the application provider itself! Competition is also from other service providers offering the same or similar software or owners of similar software.

11. *How will you make customers aware of and want your offering?* This might include advertising in the press or other media associated with the application's target audience (e.g., if the application is a rendering code, advertising in the video sector's trade press is possible). The main selling point is what differentiates this service from the competition—this service is a simple-to-use rental of an in-demand application at a fraction of the cost of purchasing a long-term license, on demand and with no licensing or management worries for the customer. This service has low entry and exit costs, is simple to use, and is available when the customers want it.

12. *What are the risks in this business model?* The major risk to this business model is the service provider is dependence on the suppliers of the software licenses (whether they are the actual author of the software, or a middleperson license provider). If the license supplier chooses to stop supplying licenses or prevents the service provider from hosting their application, then the service provider cannot operate this business model. Hence, if the service provider wants to operate this business model, they must insulate themselves from this risk, and the major option is to diversify. The service provider should offer more than one application code (possibly in related areas). This will not only insulate them if one application provider chooses to stop supplying licenses but also widen the potential audience for the service provider's offerings. The second insulation option is applicable if the service provider is dealing with a middleperson independent software vendor (ISV), selling the licenses. If this is the case, the service provider should create relationships with other ISVs so as to reduce their reliance on the ISV they are dealing with. Finally, it may be the case that the license supplier *is* the service provider. For example, the

author of the application code wants to attract new users through selling smaller license units (see Section 6.4.4), and they decide to do this by hosting a service that runs the application code. Hence they are *both* the license suppler and the service provider. Given this, they avoid the dependence on the license supplier.

6.5 VISIONARY THOUGHTS FOR PRACTITIONERS

From the analyses of the candidate business models, a number of common patterns emerged. These have been elaborated on the basis of further research and discussion and are presented in this section in the form of guidelines and important issues that can assist a potential practitioner of a Grid business.

6.5.1 Service Specification and Quality

The service offering usually consists of two elements: a specification of what the service offers and the quality at which it is offered. The specification is considered fixed for the lifetime of the service, while the quality is specified in the SLA and may be offered at varying levels (usually in relation to the price of the service offering).

It is important to describe a service offering in terms that the users understand and can demonstrate clear value to them. There is no point in offering CPU cycles when the users want frames of video rendered. The basic lesson to learn here is to target the audience market and communicate with them on their own terms.

A significant element of the QoS in the service offering is the management of the customers' expectations. The consumers of the service form their own impressions of the service based on their experience of the service as received by them, which is distinct from the QoS delivered by the provider. This is termed *quality of experience* (QoE). A classic example of the difference between QoS and QoE concerns response time. The provider offers a guarantee concerning the response time of the service measured at the provider's boundary. However, the service consumer sees a response time that includes the propagation delay of the transmission network in addition to the service provider's turnaround time, and bases their QoE judgment on this.

6.5.2 Pricing

Pricing is interdependent with a great many factors of service provision and consumption. Both the customer and the provider have factors that affect what they think the price should be, and these are kept strictly private. On the provider's side the factors influencing the price are the costs that they have incurred in providing the service, and how much they think the customers will value the service. Here, "value" means economic utility—how much the provision of the service will enhance the customer's business or lifestyle. On the customer's side their utility is the primary factor that will affect the price they are prepared to pay for the service. Some examples of the types of factors that affect the price are listed below:

- QoS and price are tightly linked. The value to the customer is reflected in the quality parameters of the service. The level of guarantee is directly proportional to the price of the service—if the customer wants a "guaranteed" service (possibly backed up with compensation for underdelivery), then this is obviously more costly and risky to provide and hence will be more expensive to the customer. This reliability is valuable to a customer, and hence a customer will be prepared to pay more for it than a service with lower levels of guarantee.
- The price is obviously affected by the resource costs that the provider faces, for example, the resource costs of providing the service—machines, software, or human. Whether the service is a commodity that is inexpensive to produce or a costly-to-provide (high-end) bespoke service will also affect the price.
- The reputation of the provider in the eyes of the customers affects the price. A provider who is consistently reliable will be able to use this as a bargaining point to maximize the prices that they can charge their customers.
- The level of risk that the provider aggregates will affect the price. A provider who is a prime contractor, managing subcontractors and responsible to one customer, is responsible for all subcontractors and must take the risk that any of the subcontractors may underdeliver. This is a significant risk that will increase the prime contractor's costs, and hence the price to the customer will increase.
- The amount of trade that a customer commits to give the provider affects the unit price. This can be in many forms, such as a bulk purchase in advance or a subscription with a minimum term of a year and a set amount of "free minutes" each month. The customer has made a fixed commitment for the term of the agreement.

6.5.3 Flexible Software Licensing

Flexible software licensing that permits application codes to be offered as services is critical to the success of the Grid in the future, as the application code provides the means to solve the customers' problems, and hence customers see clear value in it. Fortunately, there is a major trend toward more flexible software licensing. More recently, the landscape has changed from the bulk of providers preferring perpetual licenses to providers determining that there is a realistic revenue stream in offering more flexible licensing terms. The major focus has been on pay-per-use licensing models, such as software as a service (SaaS) and floating licenses (as exemplified by Macrovision's FlexNet, described along with other license strategies in Ref. 16), and the major challenge is ensuring that the amount of "use" is correctly enforced or recorded so that it may be billed for. The benefit to the application provider is that new markets are opened up featuring casual users that cannot justify the expense of a perpetual license, but are would be prepared to rent the software for specific purposes.

The ability to use commercial software should be regarded as a resource available to a service provider or a consumer, and that licensing terms should be able to accommodate this. The licensing terms may be such that the provider is able to purchase a perpetual license from the software owner, which includes the right to use the software as a component part of a service created by the provider. Here is the concept of the supply chain—the provider buys in the software as a raw material, adds value to it, and sells the resultant service onto its customers. This type of license is likely to be more expensive than a traditional perpetual license, as it includes an extra right that may be potentially lucrative to the service provider.

6.5.4 Payment and Consumption Models

It is important to consider how the service offerings are measured and paid for. What is the "unit of consumption"—the measurable quantity that the customers are paying for? The unit of consumption is important because all prices will be based on it. In electrical utility provision, the standard unit of consumption is a kilowatt-hour (kWh)—the consumption of a kilowatt of electrical power for an hour. This is a well-known and understood measurement, as the measurement of electrical power and time have both been standardized. With the Grid, things are more complex, as not all machines are created equal, and other elements such as the use of software codes and transmission channel usage need to be measured. With the increasing popularity of SaaS, the application codes and their metered usage are increasingly becoming units of consumption and a component of the price the customer pays.

A number of payment models from more traditional businesses are directly applicable to Grid computing. Utility computing came directly from borrowing ideas from utility supply models, such as the electricity example described above. Here the user pays for what they have used on a metered basis, and after the point of use. Typically, the amount of usage is measured and the user is billed at the end of the month.

Payment models can also be borrowed from mobile phone payment models. Some models use a subscription-based agreement, where the customer agrees a minimum term contract with a monthly payment. For this they get the line rental together with some "free minutes" of calls (note here that the unit of consumption is the minutes). Any consumption above the free limit is charged at a tariff rate per minute. This gives us a composite model—a fixed amount of capacity requirement every month for the provider (which is easy to provision for since it is known in advance), with overflow calls on a pay-per-use basis.

6.6 FUTURE RESEARCH DIRECTIONS

The business model analysis and the major principles discussed in the previous sections give rise to certain research challenges, where the current state of the art is not yet sufficient, and these research challenges are discussed in this section.

Since a large amount of customer value resides in applications, the application providers need a convincing argument to enable their application to be hosted as a service (SaaS), and the research challenge here is to provide them with the means of analyzing the financial impact to them of hosting applications on the Grid or service-oriented architecture (SOA). Research projects cannot provide this argument, as this will involve confidential information that is only known to the individual companies, but providing means for the application providers to evaluate the pros and cons of SaaS licensing pattern is a research challenge. Most of the time this means demonstrating clear revenue streams for software hosted as a service, and the application providers need to be shown that the returns will be greater when hosting the software as a service is permitted. This includes migration issues from traditional to new licensing models; there may be a loss of perpetual license customers that migrate to cheaper SaaS. The providers need to be convinced that new business from new customers more than offsets any reduction in revenue from perpetual licenses, in other words, a win–win situation for customers and providers.

In addition to the financial analysis of the previous point, the application providers also need to be convinced that the license terms will still be respected if their applications are hosted by third-party providers in these new software service models. Application providers must be convinced that there is strong license enforcement, that any third party (provider or user) cannot abuse the terms of the license, and the application provider will be correctly recompensed for use of the application when hosted remotely. Solutions here include automatic usage monitoring, auditing of the service providers, license terms accommodating SaaS, and cryptographic token-based right-of-use enforcement.

Provisioning policies and the demands made on them need to be investigated. For example, there is a tradeoff to be made by the service provider regarding keeping resources available to ensure a responsive service, and keeping them highly utilized to ensure reasonable ROI on them. Demand prediction is a valuable provisioning aid. Experience in the particular market sector (e.g., typical usage patterns) is a likely method for determining demand, and thus how to provision. It is almost certain that management information should be automatically gathered, so that lessons on the demand and its patterns can be learned. Detailed monitoring and recording of all the factors that contribute to the provisioning for a service—elements such as the provisioning requirements, usage patterns, and amount of underdelivery for a particular service type is strongly recommended. Techniques such as data analysis and mining can then be utilized to determine a highly tuned relationship between the service offered and the resources required for it.

Pricing is a complex issue—it is interdependent with many other aspects of producing and selling the service. There exists much research on pricing policies and techniques, but these need to be applied to Grid situations, for example, the relationship between the "unit of consumption" that the user consumes and pays for, the costs to provide it, and business relationships.

6.7 CONCLUSIONS

In this chapter, we have aimed to address the task of evaluation of business models applied to the Grid, and to draw principles from analysis. First, we have addressed the complication that business models themselves are complex and not well understood—they lack any formal basis that would facilitate both description and comparison.

We have addressed this issue by providing a working definition of a business model and a detailed analysis in the form of a questionnaire. We next proposed some candidate business models and analyzed them using the questionnaire, in order to illustrate the important points that arise from each business model in line with our goal of acquiring principles that may be of use to a prospective operator of a Grid business, rather than to justify each business model. Some common themes have emerged, and these have been discussed, as they represent important issues that can affect a practitioner of a potential Grid business. These issues also present some research challenges, which are also discussed.

ACKNOWLEDGMENTS

The authors acknowledge the funding of the European Commission, and the work reported here was conducted within the NextGRID (the next-generation Grid) Integrated Project [17], Contract 511563. This chapter expresses the opinions of the authors and not necessarily those of the European Commission. The European Commission is not liable for any use that may be made of the information contained in this chapter.

REFERENCES

1. M. Morris, M. Schindehutte, J. Richardson, and J. Allen, Is the business model a useful strategic concept? Conceptual, theoretical, and empirical insights, *Journal of Small Business Strategy* **17**(1):27–50 (2006).
2. J. C. Linder and S. Cantrell, *Changing Business Models: Surveying the Landscape*, White Paper, Institute for Strategic Change, Accenture, 2000.
3. P. Timmers, *Business Models for Electronic Markets*, European Commission, DG III April 1998.
4. H. Chesborough and R. Rosenbloom, The role of the business model in capturing value from innovation: Evidence from Xerox Corporation's technology spin-off companies, *Industrial and Corporate Change* **11**(3):529–555 (2002).
5. J. Magretta, Why business models matter, *Harvard Business Review* **80**(5):86–93 (2002).
6. S. Voelpel, M. Leibold, and E. B. Tekie, The wheel of business model reinvention: How to reshape your model to leapfrog competitors, *Journal of Change Management* **4**(3): 259–276 (2004).
7. J. C. Lang, Management of intellectual proprty rights, *Journal of Intellectual Capital* **2**(1):8–26 (2001).
8. V. Kumar, J. A. Petersen, and R. P. Leone, How valuable is word of mouth? *Harvard Business Review* **85**(10):139–144 (2007).
9. J. Laudon, Performance/watt: The new server focus, *ACM SIGARCH Computer Architecture News* **33**(4):5–13 (Nov. 2005).

10. *Report to Congress on Server and Data Center Energy Efficiency*, Public Law 109-431, US Environmental Protection Agency ENERGY STAR Program, http://www.energystar.gov/ia/partners/prod_development/downloads/EPA_Datacenter_Report_Congress_Final1.pdf, Aug. 2, 2007.
11. V. Bala and J. Green, Charge what your products are worth, *Harvard Business Review* (Sept. 1, 2007).
12. Amazon EC2, http://aws.amazon.com/ec2.
13. Amazon S3, http://aws.amazon.com/s3.
14. Sun Grid, http://www.network.com/.
15. C. Da Rold and G. Tramacere,*Pricing Poses a Major Challenge for Infrastructure Utility*, Gartner Report ID: G00139283.
16. S. Manoharan and J. Wu, Software licensing: A classification and case study, *Proc. Digital Society, 1st International Conf. Digital Society (ICDS'07), Gosier, Guadeloupe, Jan.* 2007.
17. NextGRID (The Next Generation Grid) EC IST Framework 6 Integrated Project, Contract 511563, www.nextgrid.org.

7

GRID BUSINESS MODELS FOR BROKERS EXECUTING SLA-BASED WORKFLOWS

Dang Minh Quan and Jörn Altman

7.1 INTRODUCTION

In the Grid computing environment, many users need the results of their calculations within a specific period of time. Examples of those users are meteorologists running weather forecasting workflows and automobile producers running dynamic fluid simulation workflow [7]. Those users are willing to pay for getting their work completed on time. However, this requirement must be agreed on by both the users and the Grid provider before the application is executed. This agreement is called the *service-level agreement* (SLA). In general, SLAs are defined as an explicit statement of expectations and obligations in a business relationship between service providers and customers. SLAs specify the a priori negotiated resource requirements, the quality of service (QoS), and costs. The application of such an SLA represents a legally binding contract. This is a mandatory prerequisite for next-generation Grids.

In order to finish the workflow on time, subjobs of the workflow must be distributed to Grid resources. Assigning subjobs of the workflow to resources requires consideration of many constraints such as workflow integrity, on-time conditions, and optimality conditions. To free users from those tedious tasks, it is necessary to have a SLA workflow broker performing the cooperation task of many entities in the Grid.

Market-Oriented Grid and Utility Computing Edited by Rajkumar Buyya and Kris Bubendorfer

The business relationship of the SLA workflow broker with the users and the Grid service providers will determine the working mechanism of the broker.

In this chapter, we introduce a set of business models that are based on incentive structure for users to consume high-performance computing center (HPCC) services, and for brokers to perform efficiently. The business model also leads to several economic issues.

A challenge for the contractual relationships between users and brokers is that users have less information about the Grid system than a broker does. The broker knows all aspects of all service providers such as resource configurations, pricing schemes, and past performance. This means that there is asymmetric information regarding the execution environment, and this may adversely affect the business relationships between the broker and the user. We will analyze the effect of asymmetric information with several scenarios and show how it can be negative. We also propose some possible solutions for the asymmetric information issue, such as increased pricing or a fining policy imposed by the broker and the negotiation strategy between users and brokers.

From the business model, we can see that the user and the broker are business entities. With a workflow, the user is willing to pay up to C_h (denoting a high or maximum cost) and the broker will not accept anything below C_l, $C_l < C_h$. The user wants to have a price as low as possible while the broker wants to maximize its profit. There is a bilateral negotiation between the user and the broker to find the appropriate price. Thus, the central problem is how to set an appropriate price that both user and broker can accept. We present a mechanism using fuzzy logic to determine that price.

7.2 RELATED WORK

The literature records many efforts supporting QoS for workflow. AgFlow is a middleware platform that enables the quality-driven composition of Web services [13]. QoS-aware "Grid workflow" is a project that aims at extending the basic QoS support to Grid workflow applications [2]. Other work [12] focuses on mapping the sweep task workflow to Grid resources with deadline and budget constraints. However, none of these studies defines a business model for the system. More recent Grid projects have addressed the SLA issue [5,11], Focusing mostly on single-job applications, and thus only direct relationships between user and service provider have been considered. The business role of the broker in such systems has not been fully evaluated. Moreover, the asymmetric information issue and bargaining are not considered in all the studies cited above.

On the topic of bargaining, Sim developed a market-driven bargaining strategy for G-Commerce negotiation agents [9]. Sim describes the price setting and adjusting along multiple negotiation steps among agents representing the customers and providers. The key difference between our work and Sim's work. is that our work attempts to determine a suitable price at the first negotiation round while Sim tries to reach the suitable price after many negotiation rounds.

7.3 BUSINESS MODEL

7.3.1 Grid-Based Workflow Model

Workflows received enormous attention in the database and information system research and development (R&D) community [6]. According to the definition from the Workflow Management Coalition (WfMC) [4], a workflow is "The automation of a business process, in whole or parts, where documents, information or tasks are passed from one participant to another to be processed, according to a set of procedural rules." Although business workflows have great influence on research, another class of workflows emerged in sophisticated scientific problem-solving environments, called *Grid-based workflows* [1,7]. A Grid-based workflow differs slightly from the WfMC definition as it concentrates on intensive computation and data analysis but not the business process. A Grid-based workflow has following characteristic [10]:

- A Grid-based workflow usually includes many subjobs (i.e., applications), which perform data analysis tasks. However, those subjobs are not executed freely but in a strict sequence.
- A subjob in a Grid-based workflow depends closely on the output data from previous subjobs. With incorrect input data, a subjob will produce erroneous results and damage the result of the whole workflow.
- Subjobs in the Grid-based workflow are usually computationally intensive. They can be sequential or parallel programs and require a long runtime.
- Grid-based workflows usually require powerful computing facilities (e.g., supercomputers or clusters) to run on.

Like many popular systems handling Grid-based workflows [3,7], our system is of the directed acyclic graph (DAG) form. The user specifies the required resources needed to run each subjob, the data transfer between subjobs, the estimated runtime of each subjob, and the expected runtime of the whole workflow.

7.3.2 Grid Service Model

The computational Grid includes many high-performance computing centers (HPCCs). Sub-jobs of the workflow will be executed in HPCCs as it brings many important advantages for this task:

- Only these HPCCs can handle the high-computing demand of scientific applications.
- The cluster or supercomputer in a HPCC is relatively stable and well maintained. This is an important feature to ensure finishing the subjob within a specific period of time.
- The HPCCs usually connect to the worldwide network by high-speed links, whose broad bandwidth makes the data transfer among subjobs easier and faster.

The resources of each HPCC are managed by a type of software called a *local resource management system* (RMS). In this chapter, RMS is used to represent the cluster/supercomputer as well as the Grid service provided by the HPCC. Each RMS has its own unique resource configuration. A resource configuration comprises the number of CPUs, the amount of memory, the storage capacity, the software, the number of experts, and the service price. To ensure that the subjob can be executed within a dedicated time period, the RMS must support advance resource reservation such as a command–control subsystem (CCS) [5].

7.3.3 Business Model

In order to finish the workflow on time, subjobs of the workflow must be distributed to Grid resources. Figure 7.1 depicts a sample scenario of running a workflow in the Grid environment. Letting users work directly with resource providers has two main disadvantages:

- The user needs sophisticated resource discovery–mapping tools in order to find the appropriate resource providers.
- The user has to manage the workflow, ranging from monitoring the running process to handling error events.

Thus, it is necessary to have a SLA workflow broker performing the task of integrating many entities in the Grid. The business relationship between entities in the system running the SLA-based workflow is depicted in Figure 7.2. There are three main types of entities: end-user, SLA workflow broker, and service provider:

- The end user wants to run a workflow within a specific period of time. The user asks the broker to execute the workflow for him/her and pays the broker for the workflow execution service. The user does not need to know the details of how much is to be paid to each service provider, only the total amount. This amount depends on the urgency of the workflow and the budget of the user. If there is a

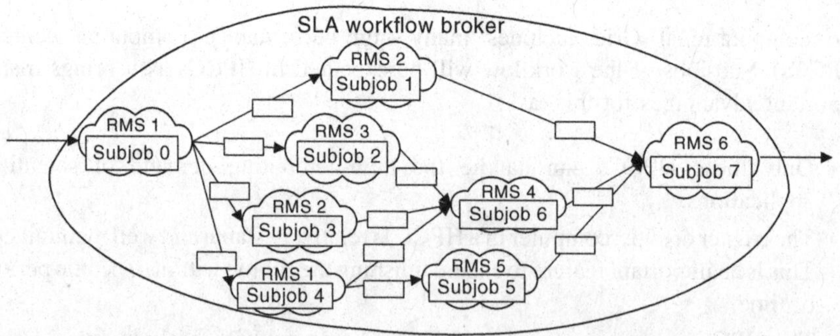

Figure 7.1 A sample running Grid-based workflow scenario.

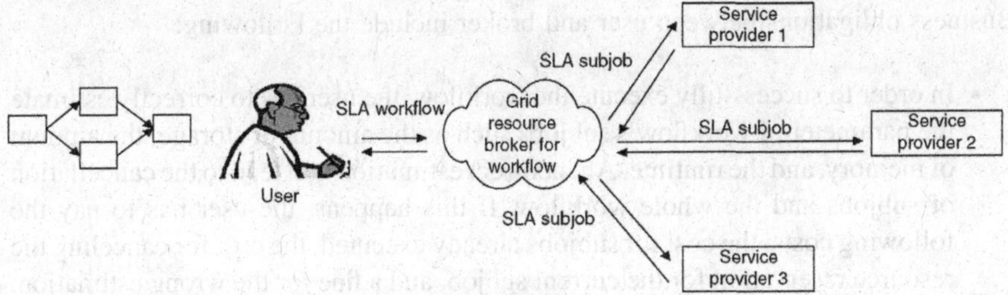

Figure 7.2 Stakeholders and their business relationship.

SLA violation, for example, if the runtime deadline has not been met, the user will ask the broker for compensation. This compensation is clearly defined in the service-level objectives (SLOs) of the SLA. In addition

- The SLA workflow broker represents the user as specified in the SLA with the user. It controls the workflow execution. This includes mapping of subjobs to resources, signing SLAs with the service providers, monitoring, and error recovery. When the workflow execution has finished, it settles the accounts. It pays the service providers and charges (bills) the end user. The profit of the broker is the difference. The value-added benefit that the broker provides is the handling of all tasks for the end user.
- The service providers execute the subjobs of the workflow. In our business model, we assume that each service provider fixes the price for its resources at the time of the SLA negotiation. As the resources of a HPCC usually have the same configuration and quality, each service provider has a fixed policy for compensation if its resources fail. For example, such a policy could be that *n*% of the cost will be compensated if the subjob is delayed by one timeslot.

Business obligations between broker and service providers include

- The broker asks a service provider to execute a subjob of the workflow. If parameters such as amount of storage, amount of memory, and runtime are not correct, the provider has to cancel the subjob. Otherwise, other subjobs would be affected through less available resources. In this case, the broker has to pay the fee for using the resource.
- If the subjob cannot be finished because of serious computing system failure, the subjob will be canceled and the provider will be fined. This case arises when the whole system is down, for example, when the electric power or the network link to the Internet is broken.
- If the runtime of the subjob exceeds the limit because of computing system failure, the subjob can continue running and the provider has to pay a fine for late timeslots. This happens when there are some small errors inside the computing system, such as when some nodes executing the subjob are down. To recover from the error, the provider restarts the subjob from the checkpoint image leading to the small lateness.

Business obligations between user and broker include the Following:

- In order to successfully execute the workflow, the user has to correctly estimate the parameter of workflow's subjobs such as the amount of storage, the amount of memory, and the runtime. An incorrect estimation will lead to the cancellation of subjobs and the whole workflow. If this happens, the user has to pay the following costs: the cost for subjobs already executed, the cost for canceling the resource reservation for the current subjob, and a fine for the wrong estimation.
- If the workflow cannot be finished because of computing system failure, it will be canceled and the broker is fined. If this case happens, the broker has to pay the following cost: the cost for already executed subjobs, the cost for canceling resource reservation of the waiting subjob, and the fine for not finishing the workflow.
- If the runtime of the workflow exceeds the limit within an acceptable period because of computing system failure, the broker has to pay a fine of k\$ for each additional timeslot.

To distinguish between cases of subjob delay due to wrong estimation or computing system failure, we have to monitor the system status. If there is a failure in the computing system and the subjob cannot finish on time, we can deduce that any delay detected is caused by the failure. However, if the runtime of the subjob exceeds a certain threshold (which includes the extra time for error recovery), we can say that the user had an incorrect estimation and the subjob is canceled.

All activities between end users, SLA workflow broker, and service providers are specified in legally binding contracts (SLAs). We believe that the consideration of business models is important in order to establish incentive structures for users to consume HPCC services at low risk, and for brokers to perform efficiently. This means that

- If the broker does not receive any monetary compensation for managing the workflow, there is little incentive for the broker to find a high-quality mapping solution. On the contrary, it will encourage the broker to find some unreliable solutions, increasing its income.
- With the proposed business model, the broker takes responsibility for the mapping solution. When a failure occurs and the workflow does not finish within the desired period, the user can fine the broker and the broker will not be compensated. This method allows the user to obtain a guaranteed service.
- The business model described above frees the user from the hard work of managing the workflow execution. The user signs an SLA only with the SLA workflow broker and then waits for the result.

7.4 ASYMMETRIC INFORMATION AND NEGOTIATION

From the business model, we can see that the broker has more information about the Grid than the user does. The broker is aware of all aspects of all service providers such as resource configurations, pricing scheme, and past performance. It is difficult for user to have all this information. This situation leads to the asymmetric information issue.

7.4.1 Asymmetric Information Issue

In the contractual context between user and broker, asymmetric information could bring negative effects. We look at the following scenarios.

7.4.1.1 Scenario 1: Asymmetric about Grid State. We assume that the provider's price is fixed at the time of mapping. This assumption is suitable as many present resource providers such as Sun, Amazon, and the Distributed European Infrastructure for Supercomputing Appications (DEISA) use this model. The cost of running a workflow depends mainly on the cost of the mapping solution. The cost of a workflow mapping solution depends on the Grid state. When the Grid is free, many free resources are available and the broker could have ample chance to assign many subjobs of the workflow to less expensive providers. Moreover, when the resource in each provider is free, dependent subjobs of the workflow will likely be executed on the same RMS, thus providing a solution to the information asymmetry. Thus, the cost of data transfer among those subjobs is neglected. This leads to a low-cost mapping solution. In contrast, when the Grid is busy, there are few free resources and the broker may have to assign many subjobs of the workflow to expensive providers. The busy state of the Grid also leads to the significant chance that subjobs of the workflow must be executed in different RMSs. In this case, the cost of data transfer could represent a significant part of the total workflow running cost. Therefore, the cost of running the workflow could be high.

The user does not know beforehand whether the Grid is free or busy. Therefore, the user's best guess for a mapping solution is that the mapping is done in the average state of the Grid. The user is willing to pay a cost correlated with the average state. Thus, when the Grid state is busy, the high cost of the mapping solution may annoy the user.

7.4.1.2 Scenario 2: Asymmetric about Quality of Mapping Solution. The deadline of the workflow has different meanings for different people. The importance of a deadline depends on the urgency of the workflow. For example, the result of the weather forecasting workflow is very important, especially in storm prediction. Tardiness of the weather forecasting workflow in this case may lead to the deaths of many people. Thus, the urgency is very high. In contrast, a minor delay of a dynamic fluid workflow in a scientific research project does not significantly affect the overall progress of the project. In this case, the urgency is very low.

With different urgency levels, the user requires different levels of ensuring the deadline. This requirement is equivalent to running the workflow with different risk levels. The risk is defined here as the ability of not finishing the workflow on time. Among many factors affecting the risk level of a workflow mapping solution, the probability of failure is the most important. This probability includes small-scale failure and large-scale failure. Small-scale system failure is caused mainly by failure of computing nodes. Large-scale system failures could affect the whole computing system of the provider. These failures can include large hardware failure, network connection failure, and security holes.

With the workflow with a high urgency level, workflow subjobs should be assigned to RMSs having low failure probability. For the workflow with a low urgency level, the demand for mapping subjobs with high reliability is not so high. In general, the price for an RMS having a higher reliable level is higher than that for an RMS having a lower reliable level. Thus, the cost of running a high-urgency workflow could be higher than that for running a lower-urgency one.

However, the user does not know beforehand about the failure probability of RMSs and how to evaluate the risk of the mapping solution. A user who requires a high degree of certainty in ensuring the deadline and is asked to pay a high price may suspect that the broker found an unreliable mapping solution to get a higher revenue.

In both scenarios described, above, if the broker does not have suitable ways to resolve the asymmetric information problem, the broker may loose customers.

7.4.2 Possible Solutions for the Asymmetric Information Issue

7.4.2.1 Pricing and Guarantee as the Signal. From the obligation description between user and broker, we referred to the fine. A broker who cannot finish the workflow execution on schedule will be fined. There is a the issue of determining a suitable fining rate. We now present a way to address.

The user and the broker form a contract to execute the Grid-based workflow. The workflow can be finished on time or late. If the workflow finishes on time, its monetary value to the user is b_1. If the workflow is late, its monetary value to the user is b_2. Assume that the late probability of the workflow mapping solution is q. We can also assume that the broker is risk-neutral and the user is risk-averse. The broker proposes a contract that the cost to execute the workflow is p with a guarantee g. If the workflow is late, the broker has to pay the user g. The utility of the buyer is $u(b_1 - p)$ if the workflow is not late and $u(b_2 - p + g)$ if it is. As the user is risk-averse, $u'' < 0$. The user will accept the contract when his expected utility is greater than or equal to $u(0) = 0$. The utility of the broker is formulated as follows:

$$B(p, g) = (1 - q)^{*}p + q^{*}(p - g) \tag{7.1}$$

The utility of the user is

$$U = q^{*}u(b_2 - p + g) + (1 - q)^{*}u(b_1 - p) \tag{7.2}$$

The optimal contract must satisfy the following conditions:

$$\max\{B(p, g)\}\text{subject to } U >= u(0).$$

Using Lagrange multipliers, we have the following results:

$$g = b_1 - b_2 \tag{7.3}$$

$$p = b_1 - u^{-1}(u(0)) = b_1 \tag{7.4}$$

$$\frac{g}{p} = 1 - \frac{b_2}{b_1} \tag{7.5}$$

It is possible to say that with a low urgency level, the monetary difference between late and on-time results is not significant. For example, if dynamic fluid workflow in a scientific research project is late by only 1 or 2 h, this has little effect on the overall progress of the project. This means that the b_2/b_1 value is high. Thus, from Equation (7.5), the g/p value would be low. In contrast, with the high urgency level, for example, with the weather forecasting workflow, if the result is 1 h late, many ships may not be able to return the harbor to avoid the storm. Thus, the monetary difference will be great. This means that the b_2/b_1 value is low and the g/p value will be high. From Equation (7.5) and the analytical aspect of price and guarantee, we apply following conditions to our case:

- The broker provides a menu of contract. Each contract contains urgency level and the appropriate guarantee. The guarantee is computed in percent of the total cost. The guarantee is higher when the urgency level is higher.
- The user chooses a contract from the menu. On the basis of this requirement, the broker will perform the mapping solution and negotiate the SLA.

The higher guarantee rate with higher price will persuade the user to believe in the quality of the service provided by the broker.

7.4.2.2 Signaling during the SLA Negotiation. From the business mode, there are three different types of sub-SLA negotiation using three different types of SLA text: (1) user–broker negotiation, which focuses on the definition of the submitted SLA; (2) broker–provider negotiation, which considers the workflow subjobs and analyses the subjob SLAs; and (3) provider–provider negotiation, which deals with the data transfer between subjobs (and also between providers) so that the SLA portion of the data transfer is utilized.

Although there are three types of SLA negotiation, the negotiation procedure remains the same; only the service attributes differ. In a first step, the client creates a template SLA with some preliminary service attributes and sends these to the server. The server parses the text and checks the client requirements. In case of conflict, a new SLA version is compiled and sent back. Here, we focus on the negotiation process between user and broker. When receiving an SLA from the customer, the broker parses it to obtain all the information about the general SLA, subjobs, SLO, data transmission, interdependence among subjobs, and structure of the workflow. From the information on subjobs and the workflow structure, the broker does the mapping to determine the appropriate provider and the time period for running each subjob. During the negotiation process, the broker could provide the user the following information to avoid the asymmetric information issue:

- The number of feasible solutions in the reference set created by the H-Map algorithm [8].
- Mapping information, which includes the start and stop times of the workflow and the RMS for each subjob. Depending on the state of the Grid, a mapping module can or cannot find a feasible solution in the expected time period. If not, it will find the earliest solution and ask for the consumer's approval.

This information contains many signals for the user:

1. The number of feasible solutions in the reference set created by the H-Map algorithm can say much about the Grid state. The H-Map algorithm creates a reference set that distributed over the search space. If the number of feasible solutions is low, this means the Grid is busy and vice versa.
2. The start and stop times of the workflow. If these are not within the preferred period from the user, then the Grid is very busy and the user should prepare for a high execution cost.
3. The RMS for the subjobs of the workflow. By providing this information, the broker signals the user about the cost of the mapping solution. With this information, the user can estimate the price from each provider and can then evaluate the cost of the mapping solution.

It is noted that the broker should not provide detailed information about subjob start and stop times or data transfer, because this information does not signal the user about the mapping solution. It may help user to bypass the broker to work directly with providers.

7.5 BARGAINING GAME IN NEGOTIATION

One workflow has many parameters such as the number of input/output data, required CPU speed, required amounts of memory and storage, QoS, and execution duration. With each user, one or some of those parameters are modified to fit with the specific requirement. As far as we know, no two users have identical workflows.

In the early phase of the business Grid, the scale of the Grid is small and the number of SLA workflow brokers is also small. Even when the Grid is large-scale, some local Grid organizations such as the Distributed European Infrastructure for Supercomputing Appications (DEISA) still exist. When the local Grid organization establishes an SLA workflow broker service, this broker could have many recommendations and support on techniques and pricing policies from experts in the local Grid community. It is obvious that those users of this Grid should choose this broker as default.

The analytical situation described above applies for a workflow market with one user and one broker. This is the ideal most conducive condition for bilateral bargaining to occur. The user wants to have a price as low as possible while the broker wants to maximize its profit. Thus, the central problem is how to set the appropriate price that both user and broker can accept.

7.5.1 Bilateral Bargaining Game

Assume that after many times running the same workflow, the user knows the highest cost C_h of running the workflow. Thus, C_h is the highest price that the user can pay for the workflow execution. The broker performs mapping to determine the base price C_l of running the workflow. C_l includes the cost incurred for service providers and the cost for the broker service. The broker will not agree to run the workflow if the price is less than C_l. If $C_l > C_h$, the trading will not occur. Assuming that $C_l < C_h$, the price scenario is as presented in Figure 7.3. As the broker is a business entity, she/he also wants to gain profit. Thus, the actual price of the service C will satisfy $C_l < C < C_h$. As presented discussion in mentioned in Section 7.4, it is noted that the broker signals the user about the base cost C_l and the Grid state.

During the negotiation phase, the broker and the user will bargain over the division of the surplus $C_h - C_l$ using alternate offers. The negotiation process cannot take place forever. There is a defined start time for workflow execution, while each negotiation round needs about one timeslot for the user to recognize the change in the SLA content or for the broker to find a mapping solution. With this feature, we say that both broker and user are impatient. The level of user's impatience is different from that of the broker's impatience. This is discussed in more detail in the next section. With this feature, we can say that this is a bargaining game with asymmetric impatience. The participants will accept the offer when they are completely indifferent about accepting or rejecting it.

We assume that the cost of delaying agreement by one round reduces the gains from trade by s_u% with the user and s_b% with the broker. This cost relates to the missed opportunity when the negotiation time is extended. s_u and s_b are common knowledge of both user and broker because all related information is revealed. The $1 - s$% is defined as the discount factor. We denote d_u% ($d_u = 1 - s_u$), d_b% ($d_b = 1 - s_b$) as the discount factor of the user and the broker, respectively.

Assume that the game can take place in N rounds. Considering the subgame beginning with the final round N, the broker offers a price C_h and the user accepts it. The reason is that if the user does not accept it, her/his utility will be seriously reduced because of the delay. Thus, at this subgame, the share surplus of the broker $Sb_N = 100\%$ and the share surplus of the user $Su_N = 0\%$. Now, we move back the

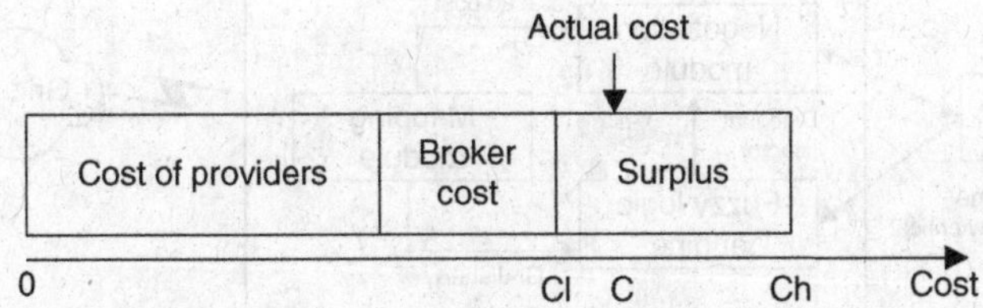

Figure 7.3 Pricing schema of the bargaining game.

subgame at round $(N-1)$ beginning with the user's offer. As the user knows that delaying the negotiation one more round can waste the broker s_b% of the share surplus, the user offers the broker a share surplus as in Equation (7.6), and the broker should accept it:

$$Sb_{N-1} = Sb_N * d_b \tag{7.6}$$

The share surplus of the user is

$$Su_{N-1} = 100(\%) - Sb_{N-1} \tag{7.7}$$

At the subgame at round $(N-2)$ beginning with the broker's offer, the broker also knows that delaying the negotiation one more round can waste the user s_u% of the share surplus, the broker offers the user a share surplus as in Equation (7.8) and the user should accept it:

$$Su_{N-2} = Su_{N-1} * d_u \tag{7.8}$$

The share surplus of the broker is

$$Sb_{N-2} = 100(\%) - Su_{N-1} \tag{7.9}$$

Using the backward deduction as above, we can compute the price at the first round and conclude that it is the ideal proposed price for both user and broker. From the analysis, we can see that the discount factor is the key issue in the price determination process. The discount factor depends on many variables: the remaining time period, the urgency of the workflow, and the Grid state. We will apply fuzzy logic to determine the discount factor as described in the following section.

7.5.2 Using Fuzzy Logic to Determine the Discount Factor

The overall architecture for using fuzzy logic in the price negotiation process is presented in Figure 7.4.

As can be seen in Figure 7.4, the fuzzy-logic engine receives the remaining time period and the workflow urgency level from the user and the Grid state, from the mapping module. On the basis of these input parameters, the fuzzy-logic engine will compute the discount factors d_u and d_b and will provides them to the negotiation module. The negotiation module uses d_u, d_b, C_l, C_h to compute the cost of execution the workflow and then proposes it to the user.

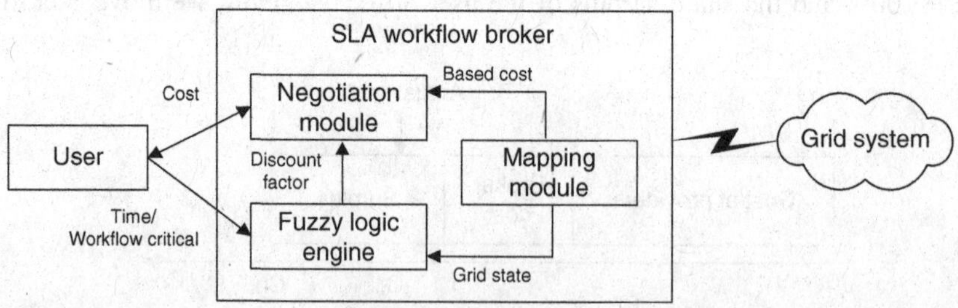

Figure 7.4 The architecture for using fuzzy logic in the price negotiation process.

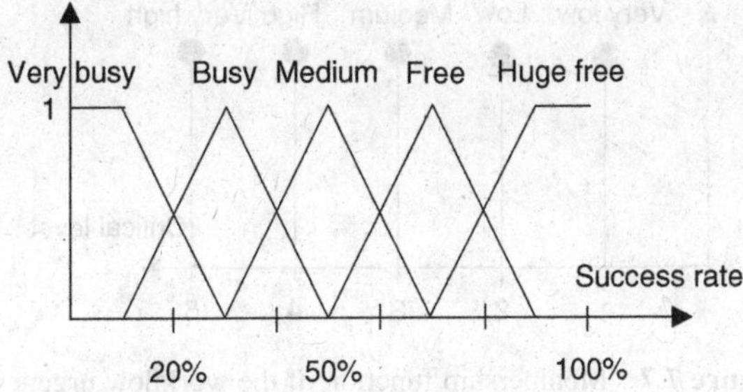

Figure 7.5 Membership function of the Grid state.

7.5.2.1 Membership Function of the Input Parameters

7.5.2.1.1 The Grid State. The Grid state has five levels: very busy (VB), busy (B), medium (M), free (F), and very free ["huge" Free (HF) in Fig. 7.5]. The level is determined by the number of feasible solutions that the Grid can propose to the workflow. This number is reflected through the number of feasible solutions in the reference set created by the H-Map algorithm [8]. H-Map algorithm created a reference set that distributed over the search space. If the number of feasible solutions is low, this means that the Grid is busy and vice versa. Call n_f the number of feasible solutions and n_t the total number of reference set members. The Grid state level is mapped to the rate n_f/n_t as presented in Figure 7.5.

7.5.2.1.2 The Time-Remaining Period. The time-remaining period has five levels: very short (VS), short (S), medium (M), long (L), and very long (VL). The level is determined according to the ability to renegotiate with the broker. As each negotiation round needs about one timeslot, nine timeslots is a safe period for the user to change a lot of things. Thus, if the time-remaining period is greater than or equal to 9, it is considered very high (VH). In contrast, if the time-remaining period is one timeslot, the user has one timeslot to recognize what should be changed and zero timeslots to negotiate with the broker. Thus, the period of one timeslot is quite dangerous for the user and is considered to be very low (VL). The level of the time-remaining factor is mapped to the real value as presented in Figure 7.6.

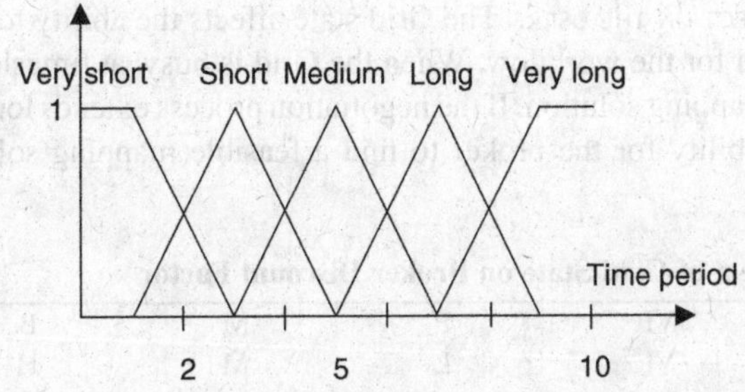

Figure 7.6 Membership function of the time-remaining period.

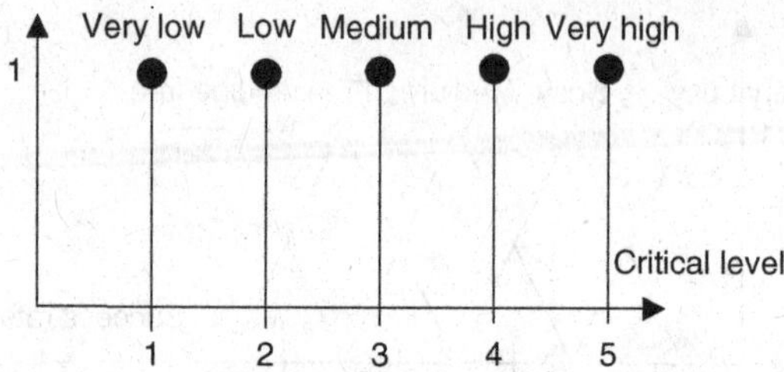

Figure 7.7 Membership function of the workflow urgency.

7.5.2.1.3 Urgency of the Workflow. The urgency of the workflow has five levels: very low (VL), low (L), medium (M), high (H), and very high (VH). As the user selects the discrete value for the urgency of the workflow, the membership function is as presented in Figure 7.7.

7.5.2.2 Effect of Input Parameters on the Discount Factor. In this section we will analyze the effect of input parameters on the user discount factor and the broker discount factor. These effects are then expressed as fuzzy inference rules. With the broker, the discount factor is determined according to the ability of encouraging the user to use the service. If the ability of attracting user is significant, the discount factor is low and vice versa. With the user, the discount factor is determined mainly according to the utility of ensuring the deadline for the workflow. If the probability of delaying the deadline is high, the discount factor is low and vice versa.

7.5.2.2.1 State of the Grid

7.5.2.2.1.1 EFFECT ON THE BROKER. The Grid state affects the policy of encouraging the user to use the Grid. When the Grid is free, this means that only a small number of customers use the Grid at that time. Thus, the broker wants to attract more users to using the Grid. If the negotiation takes a long time, the negotiation could annoy the user and, therefore, could negatively affect the success of attracting users. Thus, the discount factor of the broker is low. The discount factor is high when the Grid is busy and low when the Grid is free. The assumption about effect of the Grid state on the broker discount factor is shown in Table 7.1.

7.5.2.2.1.2 EFFECT ON THE USER. The Grid state affects the ability to find a feasible mapping solution for the workflow. When the Grid is busy, at timeslot t, the broker finds a feasible mapping solution. If the negotiation process extends longer to timeslot $t + 1$, the probability for the broker to find a feasible mapping solution is small.

TABLE 7.1 Effect of Grid State on Broker Discount Factor

Grid state	VF	F	M	B	VB
Discount	VL	L	M	H	VH

TABLE 7.2 Effect of Grid State on the User Discount Factor

Grid state	VF	F	M	B	VB
Discount	VH	H	M	L	VL

Because the number of free resources is small, just another resource demand within $[t, t+1]$ can greatly eliminate the available resource space of the workflow. The situation is reversed when the Grid is free. The effect of the Grid state on the user discount factor is summarized in Table 7.2.

7.5.2.2.2 Urgency of the Workflow

7.5.2.2.2.1 EFFECT ON THE BROKER. High or low workflow urgency does not affect the broker's ability to attract users.

7.5.2.2.2.2 EFFECT ON THE USER. The urgency of the workflow affects the ability to find a feasible mapping solution for the workflow. When the urgency of the workflow is high, high-quality resources will be required. If the negotiation process is lengthened, the probability of loosing the feasible solution that has been found is very high. Because the space of suitable Grid resources is small, just one additional resource demand can greatly eliminate the feasible resource space of the workflow. The situation is reversed when the urgency level is low. Therefore, the discount factor is low when the urgency of the workflow is high and vice versa, as summarized in Table 7.3.

7.5.2.2.3 Time-Remaining Period

7.5.2.2.3.1 EFFECT ON THE BROKER. Length of the time-remaining period does not affect the broker's ability to attract users.

7.5.2.2.3.2 EFFECT ON THE USER. The time-remaining period will affect the utility of the user through the probability of ensuring the deadline for the workflow. When the time-remaining period is short and the negotiation time is extended, the user will face a high probability of not starting the workflow on time. The situation is reversed when the period is long. The effect of the time-remaining period on the user's discount factor is summarized in Table 7.4.

TABLE 7.3 Effect of Urgency on User Discount Factor

Urgency	VL	L	M	H	VH
Discount	VH	H	M	L	VL

TABLE 7.4 Effect of Time-remaining Period on User Discount Factor

Time	VS	S	M	L	VL
Discount	VL	L	M	H	VH

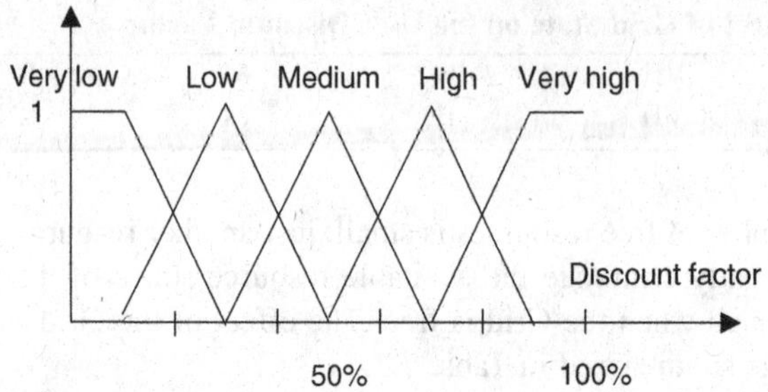

Figure 7.8 Membership function of the output.

7.5.2.3 ***Membership Function of the Output.*** The output of the fuzzy-logic system is the discount factor for either the user or the broker. With both discount factors, we use the membership function as illustrated in Figure 7.8. To determine the crisp value of the discount factor, we use the popular root-mean-square (rms) and centroid methods.

7.5.3 Algorithm to Determine the Price

The algorithm for calculating the proposed price includes the following steps:

- *Step 1.* Gets the urgency level of the workflow from user, computes the remaining time period, determines the highest cost of executing the workflow C_h.
- *Step 2.* Uses the H-Map algorithm to calculate the Grid state and the cost for providers.
- *Step 3.* Computes the broker service cost. This cost could be computed in a simple way for example $k\%$ of the cost for providers.
- *Step 4.* Computes the surplus share between broker and provider with procedure presented in Figure 7.9. At each remaining time period value, we compute the discount factor and then determine the share. As the Grid state could only remain busy or become busier during the time period, the broker discount factor increases and the user discount factor decreases. Thus, the user's share will be slightly greater than the equilibrium. However, in the procedure, we use the Grid state determined at the time of negotiation for all remaining time period values. It is an incentive for the user to accept the proposed price.
- *Step 5.* Computes the final cost and propose to the user.

7.5.4 Validation

The goal of this task is to validate and visualize the impact of the input parameters on the discount factor and the surplus share. First, we set all the parameters to medium values. Then, we change each input parameter from a very low value to a very

```
Share_broker=1
Share_user=0
For l=1 To (time Remaining/2)
{
Compute The Disc_brk, Disc_user Using Fuzzy
With Remaining Time=2*i-1 And Grid State In Step 2
Share_broker=Share_broker* Disc_brk
Share_user=1-Share_broker
Compute The Disc_brk, Disc_user Using Fuzzy
With Remaining Time = 2*i And Grid State In Step 2
Share_user= Share_broker* Disc_user
Share_broker=1-Share_user
}
```

Figure 7.9 Computing the surplus share procedure.

high value. The discount factor and the surplus share of both user and broker are recorded.

7.5.4.1 Grid State. From Figure 7.10, we can see that the user's discount factor does not start from 0 and does not reach 1 because beside the Grid state, it also depends on the urgency of the workflow and the time-remaining period. The discount factor and the surplus share of the user increases while the broker's discount factor, and surplus share decreases with the increase in the Grid state. In practical business applications, when the good is sold slowly, the seller usually reduces the price to motivate the trade. Here, we can see the same picture. This means that if the Grid is free, the broker reduces its share surplus to attract more users.

7.5.4.2 Time-Remaining Period. From Figure 7.11, we can see that the broker's discount factor does not depend on the time-remaining period while the user's discount factor increases when this period is increased. The user's surplus share increases while the broker's surplus share decreases along with increase in the time-remaining period. In practical business applications, we usually see a technique of negotiation where the seller tries to postpone the negotiation until the deadline comes

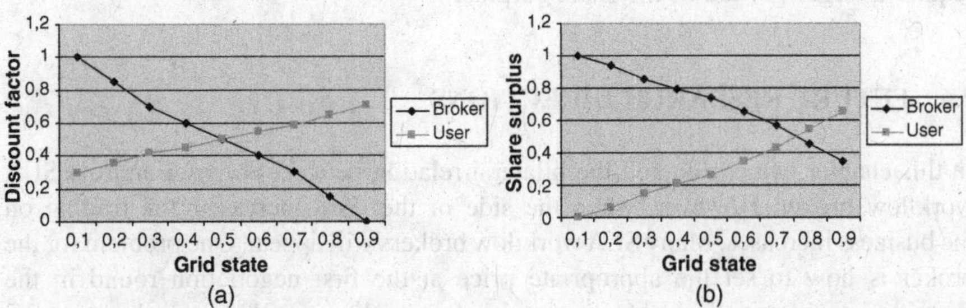

Figure 7.10 Effect of the Grid state on the discount factor and the surplus share.

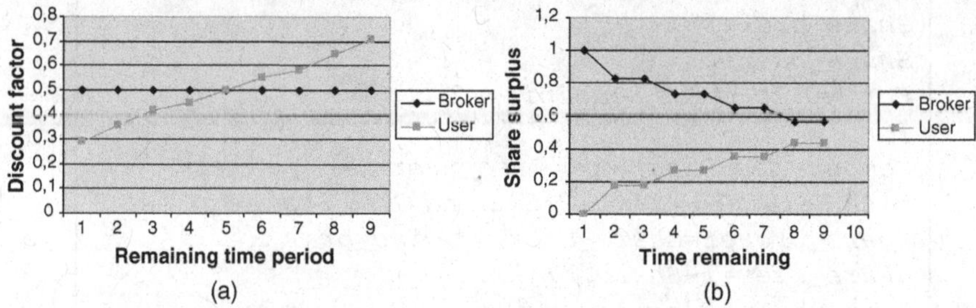

Figure 7.11 Effect of time-remaining period on the discount factor and the surplus share.

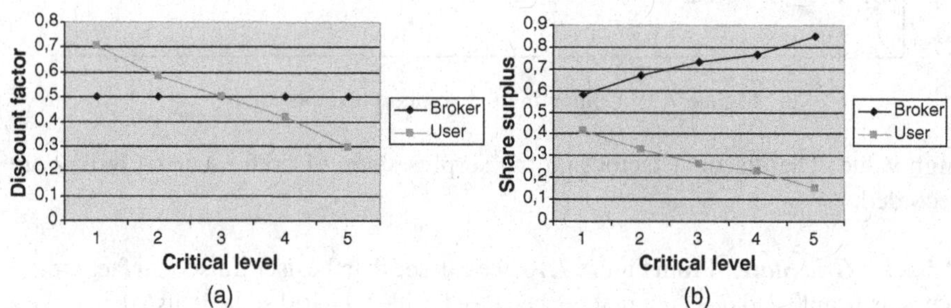

Figure 7.12 Effect of urgency level on discount factor and surplus share.

very close. Then, the seller imposes a high price on the customer. We can also see the same situation with the case of the broker and the user. The broker receives a larger part of the surplus when the time-remaining period is short.

7.5.4.3 Workflow Urgency. Figure 7.12 shows that the broker's discount factor does not depend on the urgency of the workflow. The user's discount factor decreases with increase in the urgency level. Thus, its share surplus also decreases. In real life, a seller who knows that a customer really wants or needs a particular good will impose a high price on that customer. The result shown in Figure 7.12 reflects clearly this behavior. This means that if the urgency of the workflow is high, the broker will require a larger portion of the share surplus.

7.6 FUTURE RESEARCH DIRECTIONS

In this chapter, we considered the bilateral relation between the user and the SLA workflow broker. However, when the side of the Grid increases, the trading on the business increases. Many SLA workflow brokers will appear. One problem for the broker is how to set the appropriate price at the first negotiation round in the competitive context. With the competitive factor, the game between the user and the broker becomes more complicated and needs to be approached carefully.

When the Grid market becomes larger, many new business components may appear such as insurance broker or risk broker. The functionalities as well as the business roles of these new components are still unclear at present. The answers for those questions could enrich the business Grid structure and motivate further development of the Grid.

7.7 CONCLUSION

This chapter presents a business model and related economic issues for the SLA-based workflow broker. In the business model, the user, the broker, and the provider are business entities. In particular, we consider the broker also as a service provider that provides workflow execution service. A set of business obligations among the user, the broker, and the provider is defined to ensure a clear and legal relationship. The business model leads to asymmetric information issues between the user and the broker. The user has less information about the cost of executing the workflow and the quality of mapping solution than does the broker. The user may suspect that the broker benefits from this information. To avoid the negative effects, the broker should have suitable guarantee policy and signal information. Another issue derived from the business model is the bargaining game between user and broker. We proposed a method using fuzzy logic to determine the price that both user and broker can accept at the first negotiation round. The validation results show that the solution reflects correctly the behavior of the practical business.

REFERENCES

1. G. B. Berriman, J. C. Good, and A. C. Laity, Montage: A Grid enabled image mosaic service for the National Virtual Observatory, *Proceedings of the Astronomical Data Analysis Software and Systems XIII* **13**:145–167 (2003).
2. I. Brandic, S. Benkner, G. Engelbrecht, and R. Schmidt, QoS support for time-critical Grid workflow applications, *Proc. 1st IEEE International Conf. e-Science and Grid Computing* (*e-Science 2005*), Melbourne, Australia, Dec. 5–8, 2005.
3. E. Deelman, J. Blythe, Y. Gil, C. Kesselman, G. Mehta, S. Patil, M. Su, K. Vahi, and M. Livny, Pegasus: Mapping scientific workflows onto the Grid, *Proc. 2nd European across Grids Conf.*, Nicosia, Cyprus, Jan. 28–30, 2004.
4. L. Fischer, *Workflow Handbook 2004*, Future Strategies Inc., Lighthouse Point, FL, 2004.
5. M. Hovestadt, Scheduling in HPC resource management systems: Queuing vs. planning, *Proc. 9th Workshop on Job Scheduling Strategies for Parallel Processing at GGF8*, Washington, DC, June 24, 2003.
6. M. Hsu, ed., (Special issue on workflow and extended transaction systems) *IEEE Data Engineering*, **16**(2) (1993).
7. R. Lovas, G. Dózsa, P. Kacsuk, N. Podhorszki, and D. Drótos, Workflow support for complex Grid applications: Integrated and portal solutions, *Proc. 2nd European Across Grids Conf., Nicosia, Cyprus, Jan. 28–30*, 2004.

8. D. M. Quan, Mapping heavy communication workflows onto grid resources within SLA context, *Proc. 2nd International Conf. High Performance Computing and Communication* (*HPCC06*), Munich, Germany, Sept. 12–14, 2006.
9. K. M. Sim, G-Commerce, market-driven G-negotiation agents and Grid resource management, *IEEE Transactions on Systems, Man and Cybernetics, Part B* **36**(6): 1381–1394 (2006).
10. M. P. Singh and M. A. Vouk, Scientific workflows: Scientific computing meets transactional workflows, *Proc. NSF Workshop on Workflow and Process Automation in Information Systems: State of the Art and Future Directions*, Athens, GA, 1996.
11. M. Surridge, S. Taylor, D. De Roure, and E. Zaluska, Experiences with GRIA, *Proc. 1st IEEE International Conf. e-Science and Grid Computing* (*e-Science 2005*), Melbourne, Australia, Dec. 5–8, 2005.
12. J. Yu and R. Buyya, Scheduling scientific workflow applications with deadline and budget constraints using genetic algorithms, *Scientific Programming Journal* **14**(3–4):217–230 (2006).
13. L. Zeng, B. Benatallah, A. Ngu, M. Dumas, J. Kalagnanam, and H. Chang, QoS-aware middleware for Web services composition, *IEEE Transactions on Software Engineering* **30**(5):311–327 (2004).

8

A BUSINESS-RULES-BASED MODEL TO MANAGE VIRTUAL ORGANIZATIONS IN COLLABORATIVE GRID ENVIRONMENTS

Pilar Herrero, José Luis Bosque, and María S. Pérez

8.1 MOTIVATION

The concept of Grid computing came into existence primarily as a manner of sharing computational loads among multiple heterogeneous resources, and across administrative boundaries, with the ability to afford high-performance computing problems using virtual computer architecture. However, most of the complex requirements imposed on Grid environments are behavioral and functional, and can be associated with formal requirements that could be realized as part of a gathering process during the initial stages of a project.

Grid computing intends "to provide flexible, secure and coordinated resource sharing among dynamic collections of individuals, institutions and resources" [13], in a dynamic, stable, flexible, and scalable network without geographic, political, or cultural boundaries, offering real-time access to heterogeneous resources and still offering the same characteristics of the traditional distributed networks.

Sharing is a very broad concept that could be used in different applications with very different meanings. In this research we understand sharing as "access to resources, as is required by a range of collaborative problem-solving and resource brokering strategies" and, according to Ian Foster [13], the set of individuals and/or institutions defined by such sharing rules form is called *virtual organization* (VO) in Grids.

Market-Oriented Grid and Utility Computing Edited by Rajkumar Buyya and Kris Bubendorfer

However, which kind of "sharing" rules should be applied? When and why? Which will be the conditions for sharing theses resources? In short, something that is still missing but needed in this kind of systems is how to manage resources according to a set of rules. These rules, defined by each component of this dynamic infrastructure, will allow having "management policies" for open distributed systems.

Business rules or business rulesets could be defined as a set of "operations, definitions and constraints that apply to an organization in achieving its goal*s*" [3]. Business rules produce knowledge. They can detect whether a situation has occurred and raise a business event or even create higher-level business knowledge.

Business rule engines helps manage and automate business rules, registering and classifying all of them; verifying their consistency; and even inferring new rules. There are mainly two different types of rule engines: *production/inference* and *reactive* rule engines. The major difference between these types is that rule engines with production rules infer knowledge while the reactive rule engine only reacts, automatically, when a certain rule is called. From all the possible rule engines, such as Haley, Oracle rule engine, Common Knowledge, OpenRules, business rules management system (BRMS), JBoss Rules, and so on [3], we have selected JBoss Rules (Drools) for achiving our prurposes. Drools is a rule engine but is more correctly classified as a production rule system. The term "production rule" refers to a type of rule engine and also an expert system [23].

The brain of a production rules system is an inference engine that is able to scale to a large number of rules and facts; the engine is able to schedule hundreds of thousands of facts that are eligible for execution at the same time through the use of a "conflict resolution" strategy, making decisions, quickly, reliably, and repeatedly.

Drools implements the Rete algorithm and its descendants, such as Drools' ReteOO. The Rete algorithm, an efficient pattern-matching algorithm for implementing production rule systems, was designed by Dr. Charles L. Forgy in 1974 [9], and later elaborated in 1979 [10] and 1982 [11]. Because of this algorithm, Drools provides speed and scalability beyond what is practical to achieve and maintain manually.

Considering all these questions, the key issue to be addressed is management of collaborative dynamic virtual organizations by means of a business rules engine. This chapter focuses on the management of resources by means of the collaborative/cooperative awareness management (CAM) model, based on agent-based theories, techniques, and principles, and its implementation (WS-CAM). WS-CAM has been made as generic, open, easily extended, adaptable to new modifications in the model, scalable, and free of bottlenecks as possible.

The CAM model has been designed from the beginning as a parametric, generic, open model that could be extended and adapted easily to new ideas and purposes. This model deals with resource sharing and resource dispatching within the environment by applying a set of business rules based on information regarding the immediate environment. More specifically, CAM allows (1) control of the user interaction, (2) guiding awareness toward specific users and resources, and (3) scaling interaction through the awareness concept.

This chapter first reviews the CAM model and then describes rules-based management, analyzing the key functionalities of autonomic computing and how these functionalities are carried out by means of WS-CAM. The next section describes how the WS-CAM rules-based management application works when it is applied to different scenarios to conclude with the CAM user-based validation.

8.2 RELATED WORK

Resource management is one of the most critical aspects of a Grid because of the importance of efficiently sharing resources in this kind of environment. Indeed, Grid resource management has been widely studied [22], offering different techniques that include economic and prediction-based approaches.

Many researchers have developed resource management systems and schedulers oriented to Grid environments. Condor [20], Legion [8], GridWay [21], AppLeS [2], and NetSolve [7] are some of the best known proposals.

Among several different alternative ways to address the issue of resource management, market-based approaches have been found to be very appropriate for modeling Grids and the "utility" of scheduling specific jobs over resources [4]. Several market-based approaches have emerged in the distributed systems field.

Spawn [24] is a market-based system for harnessing idle computational resources in a network of heterogeneous workstations. This system allows for the execution of both concurrent application and independent tasks.

G-Commerce [25] aims to develop economics-based systems for allocating resources on Grids. This research is based on economic concepts, such as commodities markets and auctions. Four criteria are evaluated in order to provide G-commerce resource allocation strategies: (1) price stability at Grid level, (2) market equilibrium, (3) application efficiency, and (4) resource efficiency.

GRACE (G*r*id *a*rchitecture for *c*omputational *e*conomy) [6] is a generic infrastructure that provides the functionality needed in the known "economy Grid." This framework is compatible with Grid middleware such as Globus and Legion. GRACE uses Nimrod/G [5] as a scheduler, providing the possibility of negotiating access to resources. GRACE is extensible, offering generic protocols and APIs to applications in order to develop new software.

The Gridbus project [16] provides cluster and Grid tools and middleware for the creation of distributed applications. Within this project, Libra, an economy-based scheduler for clusters, is included. This scheduler manages sequential and parallel jobs over homogeneous Linux clusters, trying to maximize user satisfaction. Two important parameters are added: the allocated budget and the deadline for the job.

Tycoon [12] has as its main goal the allocation of resources in large clusters or Grids by means of market-based schemes. Tycoon is composed of parent and child agents, which are responsible for implementing the strategy corresponding to user preferences. One of the most innovative aspects of this architecture is the separation between allocation mechanisms and the agent strategy. Tycoon also provides fault tolerance. The local scheduler of Tycoon is called *auction share*.

Although all these systems are widely kwon in the resource allocation community, the CAM model promotes collaboration, cooperation, and interaction among resources geographically distributed without depending on any specific middleware or toolkit. The CAM key concepts have been implemented by means of a multiagent architecture that uses a load-balancing algorithm for dynamically dispatching processes among resources, taking into account changes in the system as well as possible modifications in the administrative rules that this model uses for managing purposes. CAM also makes use of the autonomic computing key concepts in order to configure and optimize collaboration/cooperation in the environment.

8.3 WS-CAM: COLLABORATIVE AWARENESS MANAGEMENT

The design principles of WS-CAM, which allows managing awareness in collaborative Grid environments, are based on the extension and reinterpretation of the spatial model of interaction (SMI) [1], an awareness model designed for computer–supported cooperative work (CSCW) (see Fig. 8.1). This reinterpretation, open and flexible enough, merges all the open Grid services architecture (OGSA) [14] features with theoretical principles and theories of multiagent systems, to create a collaborative and cooperative Grid environment within which it is possible to manage different levels of awareness. WS-CAM extends and reinterprets the SMI key concepts, to solve a task *T*—consisting of a set of processes—in a collaborative and, if possible, cooperative way, by means of a set of key concepts, shown in Figure 8.1.

Given an distributed environment *E* containing a set of resources $E = \{R_i\}$, and a task *T* that needs to be solved in this environment, if this task consists of a set of processes such as power, disk space, data, and/or applications, CAM attempts to solve

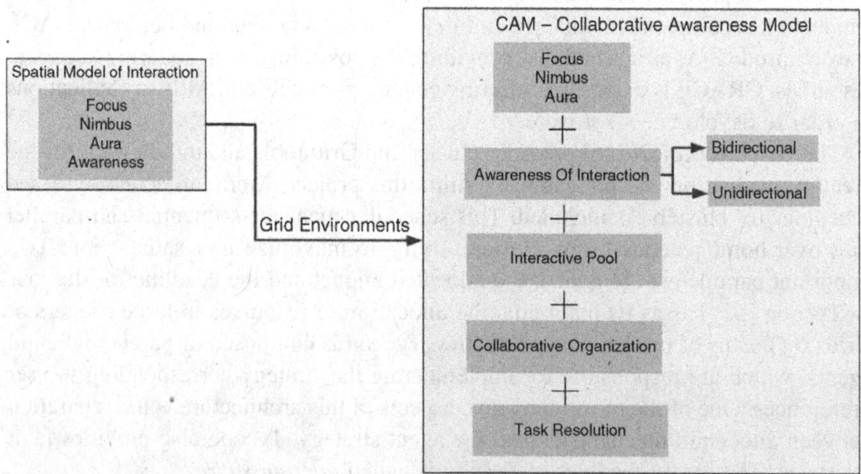

Figure 8.1 CAM's key concepts: extension of the SMI key concepts.

the task *T* in a collaborative and, if possible, cooperative way, by extending and reinterpreting the key SMI concepts in the context of the Grid environment [18]:

Focus. This can be interpreted as a subset of the space on which the user focuses and interacts with. This selection will be based on different parameters and characteristics, such as power, disk space, data, and/or applications.

Nimbus. This is defined as a tuple `(Nimbus = (NimbusState, NimbusSpace))` containing information about the state of the system in a given time `(NimbusState)`; the subset of the space in which a given resource projects its presence `(NimbusSpace)`.

- *Awareness of Interaction* $(AwareInt_{Ri\text{->}Rj}(R_i, R_j))$. This is based on Dourish and Bellotti definition "an understanding of the activities of others which provides a context for your own activity." This concept will quantify the degree, nature, or quality of asynchronous unidirectional interaction between a pair of distributed resources in the environment (*E*). This awareness could be full, peripheral, or null.
- *Awareness of Interaction* $(AwareInt(R_i, R_j)$. This concept will quantify the degree, nature, or quality of asynchronous bidirectional interaction between a pair of distributed resources. This awareness could also be full, peripheral, or null.

Aura. This is a subspace that effectively bounds the presence of a resource within a given medium and acts as an enabler of potential interaction. It can delimit and/or modify the focus, the nimbus `(NimbusSpace)`, and therefore the awareness.

Interactive Pool. This function returns the set of resources interacting with a given resource in a given moment.

Task Resolution. This function determines whether there is a service in the resource *R*, namely, `NimbusState(R) /= Null`, which could be useful for executing task *T* (or at least a part of this task).

Virtual Organization. This function will factor in the set of resources determined by the interactive pool function and will return only those that are more suitable for executing task *T* (or at least one of its processes p_i). This selection will be made by means of the `TaskResolution` function. Resources belonging to this virtual organization (VO) could provide access to additional resources, as they are aware of them, to solve specific problems, and they could collaborate with each other, thus providing a virtual organization (VO) [15]. *Collaboration* is broadly defined as the interaction among two or more individuals and can encompass a variety of behaviors, including communication, information sharing, coordination, cooperation, problem solving, and negotiation.

The CAM model also attempts to determine whether there is cooperation among resources in the context of Grid environments by means of the following concepts:

- *Cooperative awareness of interaction* $(CoopAwareInt_{Ri \rightarrow Rj \rightarrow Rk}(R_i, R_j, R_k))$. This concept quantifies the degree, nature, or quality of asynchronous

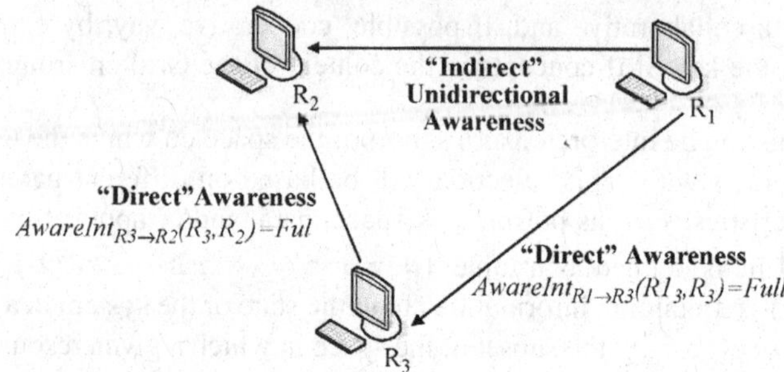

Figure 8.2 Scheme of unidirectional ("indirect") awareness in CSCW.

cooperative interaction between distributed resources. In computer-supported cooperative work (CSCW), this awareness could be due to the direct or indirect interaction between resources [17]. In fact, the awareness that one resource (R_i) has of another resource (R_j) could be classified as "indirect" when it is associated to the presence of a third resource (R_k) in the environment. This "indirect" awareness could also be unidirectional (Fig. 8.2) or bidirectional (Fig. 8.3). `Cooperative_Awareness_of_Interaction` provides information about cooperation among resources in the environment by means of the three functions: `TypeAwareness,` `TypeInteraccion`, and `StateAwareness`, where `TypeAwareness` could be direct or indirect; `TypeInteraccion` could be unidirectional or bidirectional; and `StateAwareness` could be full, peripheral, or null.

- *Cooperative Directional Pool.* This function returns the set of resources cooperating unidirectionally (`StateAwarenes = Full`).
- *Cooperative Pool.* This function returns the set of resources cooperating bidirectionally, in a given moment (`StateAwarenes = Full`).
- *Cooperative Directional Organization.* This organization consists of a set of resources cooperating unidirectionally in the environment, owing to the cooperation of their cooperative directional pools.

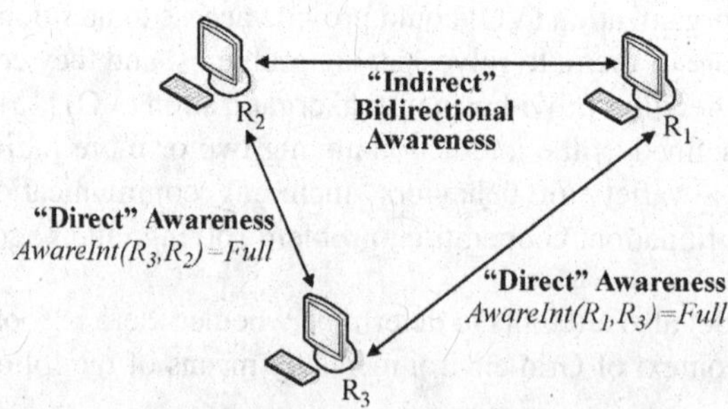

Figure 8.3 Scheme of unidirectional ("indirect") awareness in CSCW.

- *Cooperative Organization*. This organization consists of a set of resources cooperating bidirectionally in the environment, due to the cooperation of their cooperative pools.

As far as we know, none of the latter Web services (WS) specifications offers functionalities sufficiently useful to create awareness models in an environment or offers specific functionalities to manage different levels of awareness in cooperative environments.

8.4 WS-CAM RULES-BASED MANAGEMENT ARCHITECTURE

As was described in Section 8.3, this model makes use of a rule engine. This rule engine interacts with both configuration and optimization agents (see Fig. 8.4) to respond to the demands related to the specific circumstances. The CAM model relies on a set of rules defined in a set of predicates and functions that describe the resources' properties in a given environment. These rules help optimize interaction in the environment as well as collaboration/cooperation among resources allocated in that environment. Each resource publishes its computational (CPU, memory, programs, or services) and administrative (department or category) properties and attributes (`WS-DataExtension`).

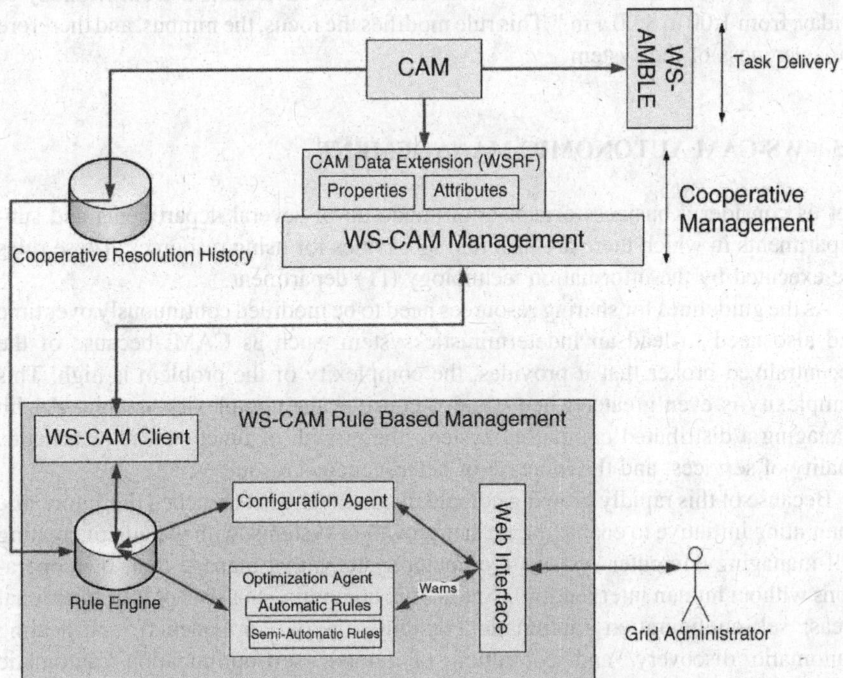

Figure 8.4 WS-CAM management architecture.

The resources involved in this management will be able to receive information on how these parameters (properties and attributes) have been defined once they have been published. In the same way, they will receive information about their corresponding modifications.

The CAM model records a history of all collaborations that were successfully carried out in the environment for future reference in performance of collaborative/cooperative tasks, automatically selecting the most suitable resource to carry out a single task and/or the most suitable resource for a collaborative/cooperative task (i.e., the more effective), as well as for optimization (using the optimization agent).

The *optimization agent* will check the information stored in the "history" of the system, analyzing the role of each resource involved in a collaborative task during the performance of that task. An example of this optimization could be, "if $B \in$ focus (A) but A did not use B's services in the past 80% collaborative tasks, then remove B from the A's focus." This optimization could be automatic (executed automatically) or semiautomatic (where a warning message is sent but the control is transferred to the system administrator).

The *configuration agent* will be endowed with a set of rules to trigger the corresponding modifications in the system. These rules could be classified as configuration and optimization rules. An example of configuration rules could be "All the resources belonging to the manufacturing department with at least 2 GB of memory will be available for the whole distributed environment from Monday to Friday, from 1:00 to 8:00 a.m." This rule modifies the focus, the nimbus, and therefore the awareness of the system.

8.5 WS-CAM AUTONOMIC MANAGEMENT

Let us consider a business organization made up of several departments and subdepartments in which there are different local rules for using resources. These rules are executed by the information technology (IT) department.

As the guidelines for sharing resources need to be modified continuously over time and also need to lead an indeterministic system, such as CAM; because of the decentralized broker that it provides, the complexity of the problem is high. This complexity is even greater when we also consider the complexity associated with managing a distributed computing system, the growth of functional requirements, quality of services, and the increase of heterogeneous resources.

Because of this rapidly growing complexity, in 2001 IBM launched the autonomic computing initiative to enable the further growth of systems, with the aim of creating self-managing computer systems (computer systems that manage their own operations without human intervention). Autonomic computing consists of four functional areas: self-configuration (automatic configuration of components), self-healing (automatic discovery, and correction of faults); self-optimization (automatic monitoring and control of resources to ensure optimal functioning with respect to the defined requirements), and self-protection (proactive identification and protection from arbitrary attacks) [19]. WS-CAM (CAM's implementation) endows collaborative/cooperative environments with three of these functionalities: self-configuration, self-optimization, and self-healing ensure to proper operation without human intervention.

8.5.1 WS-CAM Self-Configuration

To provide the autonomous configuration of its components, CAM offers three different services: self-deployment of services, self-awareness, and self-parameter configuration. As the characteristic of self-deployment of services is inherent to the CAM model, before describing self-configuration, it is important to introduce a few more details about how services are deployed in CAM.

8.5.1.1 Self-Deployment of Services. From all the resources available in the environment, one can determine which resources can offer specific services as well as the services' autodeployment, if necessary. If these services have not been deployed in the destination resource in advance, they will be propagated in the environment toward its final destination.

If the service is not compatible with the resource in which a process has to be executed, that process will never be assigned to that resource for execution purposes. The CAM model assigns processes to resources only if these processes can be executed in those resources (this compatibility is controlled by means of the `TaskResolution` function) It is also possible to include temporal advantages on the basis of certain planning rules to deploy and remove specific services. For example, the same resource can offer the service "salary calculation" for batch systems at night and offer the service "risk variable" during the day. WS-CAM is able to update, in real time, this temporal self-deployment.

8.5.1.2 Self-Awareness. A resource can be aware of those resources in its surroundings that could be useful in carrying out a specific task, and vice versa; it can also be aware of those resources for which it could be useful.

The self-awareness will manage the CAM key concepts in order to achieve the most suitable interaction in the environment. Let us imagine, for example, a given resource (*R*) having a number (*N*) of resources belonging to its focus such that each of them is able to execute a specific process (*p*):

```
Focus(R) ={Ri / IsPossibleToExecute(p)}
```

Let us also assume that the work load of these resources is high and therefore none of their `NimbusSpace` functions is null. If this is the case, the CAM self-configuration will extend its aura to extend *R*'s focus, catching new resources in the environment with the aim of ensuring effective awareness of interaction among resources in the environment.

8.5.1.3 Self-Parameter Configuration. A resource can modify any of its parameters (focus, nimbus, aura, etc.) by means of a set of rules or by making use of this service. In this way, in the previous example the self-parameter configuration would be responsible for increasing the aura with the aim of increasing the interaction potential in the environment.

8.5.2 WS-CAM Self-Optimization

To provide the best quality of service and control of resources, ensuring the optimal function with respect to the defined requirements, WS-CAM offers self-parameter optimization. As the collaborative resolution history (CRH) registers all the collaborations carried out among resources in the environment, this service is in charge of optimizing the value of the parameters to assure an optimal interaction.

If a given resource (R_1) has to extend its aura from a value of 1 to a value of 2 in order to ensure effective interaction with R_2 and its services (`aura(R1, R2)` $=2$), the next time R_1 requires the execution of a similar task, it will adapt its aura (by means of the self-parameter configuration) to `aura(R1, R2)` $=1$, including R_2 inside its nimbus from the beginning. This logic optimizes the CAM load-balancing algorithm, bringing auras closer if the information stored in the CRH (regarding previous interactions between resources) is favorable. This logic also must be extended to a higher level; if both resources (R_1 and R_2) have cooperated successfully during the last 3 h, then the `Coop_R1_R2` attribute will have a `HIGH` value (`Coop_R1_R2` $=$ `HIGH`), and the `aura(R1,R2)` will decrease to a lower value (`aura(R1, R2)` $=1$). Once the resource has been identified, it will also deploy the corresponding service.

8.5.3 WS-CAM Self-Healing

To complement the WS-CAM self-optimization, WS-CAM also offers self-proactive discovery. If several resources are collaborating/cooperating and the "self-parameter optimization" service detects that a resource (A) is becoming overloaded, the "self-proactive discovery" service will determine, from all the resources available in the collaborative organization, which of them would be most suitable to execute, if possible, some of the processes that A is running, automatically deploying the corresponding services, reducing A's, load and ensuring the optimal function of the system.

8.5.4 Discussion

The three functionalities of WS-CAM described in Sections 8.5.1–8.5.3 attempt to reduce the effort associated with the complexity of the system, reducing responding/recovery time in very dynamic environments and scenarios, as discussed in this chapter.

As for the evaluation of the model according to its autonomous computing properties, it has been based on the model's flexibility to create a set of rules for managing the configuration of the environment according to three fundamental components of the model (see Fig. 8.6): the configuration agent, the CAM data extension (CDE), properties and attributes and the collaborative resolution history (CRH). The combination of these three components allows CAM to manage an open distributed environment by means of the autonomic computing directresses.

As it can be appreciated in Figure 8.6, the CRH registers all the collaborations that are carried out among resources in the environment. The configuration agent will factor in this information in order to establish the most suitable set of administrative rules, allowing the environment's autooptimization and autoconfiguration.

These rules can access the properties and attributes of each resource via the configuration agent by means of the CDE interface, which has been specifically designed for this purpose in the CAM data extension (CDE). The CDE properties are inherent to the resources themselves, as they refer to issues specific to each resource, such as operating system and disk space, and they are accessible only for reading purposes. On thé other hand, the CDE attributes are logic elements that are determined by means of administrative rules, such as `Department = Mathematics`.

8.6 WS-CAM RULES-BASED MANAGEMENT APPLICATION

WS-CAM provides a highly configurable environment for managing resource sharing rules through its key concepts. These rules will allow the automatic configuration of the key concepts—*focus*, *nimbus,* and *awareness*—in order to enable the appropriate collaborative organization to solve task T in a given moment.

This section first describes how WS-CAM rules-based management handles awareness in the scenario described in Section 8.4, which also describes how the WS-CAM rules-based management application (Fig. 8.4) implements all the WS-CAM functionalities to optimize a collaborative/cooperative management.

Given an environment with eight resources, $E_{a1} = \{R_1,R_2,R_3,R_4,R_5,R_6,R_7,R_8\}$ (see Table 8.1), if one of these resources, R_5, intends to solve the following task: $T = \{p_1, p_2, p_3, p_4,\}$.

TABLE 8.1 CAM Key Concepts

	R_1	R_2	R_3	R_4	R_5	R_6	R_7	R_8
`Focus`	R_8,R_5,R_7	R_1	R_7	R_1,R_7	$R_2,R_3,$ R_4,R_6,R_7	R_8	$R_5,R_8,$ R_1	$R_1,R_7,$ R_5
`Nimbus-State`	Null	Medium	Medium	Maximum	Null	Medium	Null	Medium
`Nimbus-Space`	R_8,R_5,R_7	$R_1,R_2,$ R_3,R_5	$R_3,R_8,$ R_5	$R_1,R_2,$ R_3,R_4,R_5	$R_1,R_2,$ $R_3,R_4,$ $R_5,R_6,$ R_7,R_8	$R_4,R_5,$ R_6	$R_5,R_8,$ R_1	$R_1,R_4,$ R_5,R_6,R_7

The CAM model selects the more suitable resources to establish a future interaction with R_5:

$AwareInt_{R5\text{->}R2}(R_5, R_2) = AwareInt_{R5\text{->}R3}(R_5, R_3) =$
$AwareInt_{R5\text{->}R4}(R_5, R_4) = AwareInt_{R5\text{->}R6}(R_5, R_6) =$
$AwareInt_{R5\text{->}R7}(R_5, R_7) = Full$
$InteractivePool(R_5) = \{R_2, R_3, R_4, R_6, R_7\}$

In the next step, CAM considers those resources such as `NimbusState≠Null` as possible candidates to solve task T:

$TaskResolution(R_2, T) = \{ (p1,1), (p2,0.8) \}$
$TaskResolution(R_3, T) = \{ \}$
$TaskResolution(R_4, T) = \{ (p2,0.8), (p3,1), (p4,0.5) \}$
$TaskResolution(R_6, T) = \{ (p1,1) \}$

Therefore:

$VirtualOrganization_{Ea1}(R_5, T) = \{R_2, R_4, R_6\}$

Among all the possible interactions, we select only those that can help explain in more detail how resources will cooperate with in the environment:

$AwareInt_{R7\text{->}R5}(R_7, R_5) = AwareInt_{R5\text{->}R6}(R_5, R_6) = Full$
$CoopAwareInt_{R7\text{->}R5\text{->}R6}(R_7, R_5, R_6) = (Indirect, Unidirectional, Full)$
$AwareInt_{R6\text{->}R8}(R_6, R_8) = AwareInt_{R8\text{->}R1}(R_8, R_1) = Full$
$CoopAwareInt_{R6\text{->}R8\text{->}R1}(R_6, R_8, R_1) = (Indirect, Unidirectional, Full)$

On one hand

$CooperativePool_{R7 \rightarrow R6}(R_7, R_6) = \{ R_7, R_5, R_6 \}$
$CooperativePool_{R6\text{->}R1}(R_6, R_1) = \{ R_6, R_8, R_1 \}$
$CooperativeOrganization_{R7\text{->}R1}(R_7, R_1) = \{ R_7, R_5, R_6, R_8, R_1 \}$

On the other hand

$AwareInt_{R5\text{->}R7}(R_5, R_7) = AwareInt_{R7\text{->}R5}(R_7, R_5) = Full$
$AwareInt(R_5, R_7) = Full$
$AwareInt_{R7\text{->}R8}(R_7, R_8) = AwareInt_{R8\text{->}R7}(R_8, R_7) = Full$
$AwareInt(R_7, R_8) = Full$
$CoopAwareInt_{R5\text{->}R7\text{->}R8}(R_5, R_7, R_8) = (Indirect, Bidirectional, Full)$
$CooperativePool(E_{a1}) = \{ R_5, R_7, R_8 \}$
$AwareInt_{R1\text{->}R8}(R_1, R_8) = AwareInt_{R8\text{->}R1}(R_8, R_1) = Full$
$AwareInt(R_1, R_8) = Full$
$CoopAwareInt_{R7\text{->}R8\text{->}R1}(R_7, R_8, R_1) = (Indirect, Bidirectional, Full)$
$CooperativePool(E_{a1}) = \{ R_7, R_8, R_1 \}$

$$CooperativeOrganization(E_{a1}) = \{ R_5, R_7, R_8, R_1 \}$$

In the following scenario CAM will be applied to a new environment:

$$E_{b1} = \{R_2, R_3, R_5\}$$

Then R_5 tries to solve the task $T = \{p_1, p_2, p_3, p_4,\}$ by making use of the following rule:

```
{Name: Focus Biological Department, Type: addFocus, Operation:
 SO= Linux & RAM=2GB}
```

Focus $(R_5) = \{R_2, R_3\}$
Nimbus $(R_2) = (Medium, \{R_1, R_2, R_3, R_5\})$
Nimbus $(R_2) = (Medium, \{R_2, R_3, R_5\})$
Nimbus $(R_3) = (Null, \{R_3\})$ *Nimbus* $(R_5, T) = (Null, \{R_2, R_3, R_5\})$

$AwareInt_{R5\to R2}(R_5, R_2) = Full$	$InteractivePool(R_5) = \{R_2\}$
$AwareInt_{R5\to R3}(R_5, R_3) = Peripheral$	

$TaskResolution(R_2, T) = \{(p_1, 1), (p_2, 0.8)\}$

$VirtualOrganization_{Eb1}(R_5, T) = \{R_2\}$

As R_2 cannot solve task T, the aura will increase ($b_1 \to b_2$), modifying the focus and the nimbus (`NimbusSpace`):

$Eb2 = \{R_2, R_3, R_5, R_8, R_9, R_{10}\}$
$Focus(R_5) = \{R_2, R_3, R_9, R_{10}\}$

Then R_9 and R_{10} have to follow a new rule:

```
{Name: "PowerProjection: 15 processors, 7GB with Time
Constraint"; Type: "Nimbus"; Operation: "Project its
characteristics from Monday to Friday, from 1 to 8 am"}
```

If $((1{:}00 \le time \le 8{:}00) \wedge (Monday \le day \le Friday))$
$\{NimbusSpace(R_9) = NimbusSpace(R_{10}) = \{R_2, R_3, R_5, R_9, R_{10}\}\}$
Then
$\{NimbusSpace(R_9) = NimbusSpace(R_{10}) = \{\}\}$
Moreover
$NimbusState(R_9) = NimbusSpace(R_{10}) = Maximum$

$AwareInt_{R5\to R2}(R_5, R_2) = Full$	
$AwareInt_{R5\to R9}(R_5, R_9) = Full$	$InteractivePool(R_5) = \{R_2, R_9, R_{10}\}$
$AwareInt_{R5\to R10}(R_5, R_{10}) = Full$	

$TaskResolution(R_2, T) = \{(p_1, 1), (p_2, 0.8)\}$
$TaskResolution(R_{10}, T) = \{(p_1, 1)\}$
$TaskResolution(R_9, T) = \{(p_2, 0.8), (p_3, 1), (p_4, 0.5)\}$

$VirtualOrganization_{Eb2}(R_5, T) = \{R_2, R_9, R_{10}\}$

Then R_2 follows the rule

{Name: "Disk Space Selection", Type: "Focus"; Operation: "Disk Space ≥ 10GB"}

Focus(R_2) ={ R_{10} }	AwareInt$_{R2\text{->}R10}$(R_2, R_{10})= Full
NimbusSpace(R_{10})={ R_2, R_3, R_5, R_9, R_{10}}	

Taking into account

AwareInt$_{R5\text{->}R2}$(R_5, R_2)= Full

CAM would obtain

CoopAwareInt$_{R5\text{->}R2\text{->}R10}$($R_5$, R_2 , R_{10}) = (Indirect, Unidirectional, Full)

CooperativePool $_{R5\text{->}R10}$ (R_5, R_{10})={ R_5, R_2, R_{10}}

Then R_{10} follows the rule

{Name: "CPU-Power Selection", Type: "Focus", Operation: "CPU-Power ≥ 2GHz"}

Focus(R_{10}) ={ R_8 }	AwareInt$_{R_{10}\text{->}R8}$(R_{10}, R_8)= Full
NimbusSpace(R_8)={ R_1, R_{10}}	

and R_8 follows the rule

{Name: "CPU-Power Selection y Disk Space Selection", Type: "Focus", Operation: "CPU-Power ≥2GHz y Disk Space ≥ 10GB"}

Focus(R_8) ={ R_1 }	AwareInt$_{R8\text{->}R1}$(R_{10}, R_8)= Full
NimbusSpace(R_1)={ R_8}	

CoopAwareInt $_{R10\text{->}R8\text{->}R1}$ (R_{10}, R_8, R_1)=(Indirect, Uni directional, Full)

CooperativePool $_{R10\text{->}R1}$ (R_{21}, R_8)={ R_{10}, R_8, R_1}

8.7 USER-BASED VALIDATION

This part of the validation process consists of a scenario consisting in a number of tasks that users need to complete to approach the system usage (usability).

Usability can be defined in many ways. We see usability broadly according to the ISO (International Standards Organization) 9241 definition: "the effectiveness, efficiency and satisfaction with which specified users achieve specified goals in particular environments," where effectiveness, efficiency, and satisfaction are defined as

- *Effectiveness*—the accuracy and completeness with which specified users can achieve specified goals in particular environments
- *Efficiency*—the resources expended in relation to the accuracy and completeness of goals achieved
- *Satisfaction*—the comfort and acceptability of the working system to its users and other people affected by its use

We selected 30 people with the aim of carrying out the scenario's tasks in the WS-CAM application. The users collected were students in the Faculty of Computer Science at the Universidad Politécnica de Madrid (UPM), distributed as shown in Figure 8.5. In this Faculty, the degree in computer science is a 5-year course plus a final-year project.

The scenario selected for this purpose was described in a previous section. It is a very simple, but complete, scenario as we did not want to confuse users with too many concepts or tasks. In fact, the scenario included only five resources with the following attributes:

- *First resource*: `Memory = 3GB; Department = StudyBiological; SO = Windows; Unit = Proteins_Deisgn_Unit`
- *Second resource*: `NumberProc = 2; Department = SupportBioinformatic; Unit = Proteins_Design_Unit`
- *Third resource*: `Memory = 3GB; Unit = Biocomputation_Unit; Department = 2`
- *Fourth resource*: `Center = Nuclear_Center; location = bcn; software = MATLAB; processor = 64bits`
- *Fifth resource*: `Center = Medical_Investigation; location = bcn; SO = Linux`

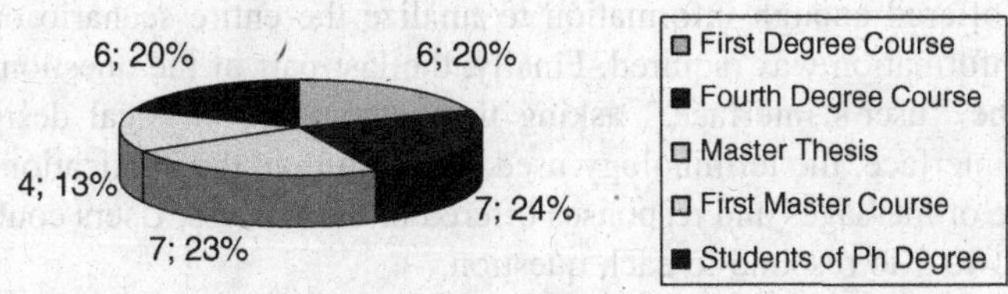

Figure 8.5 Distribution of population for user-based validation.

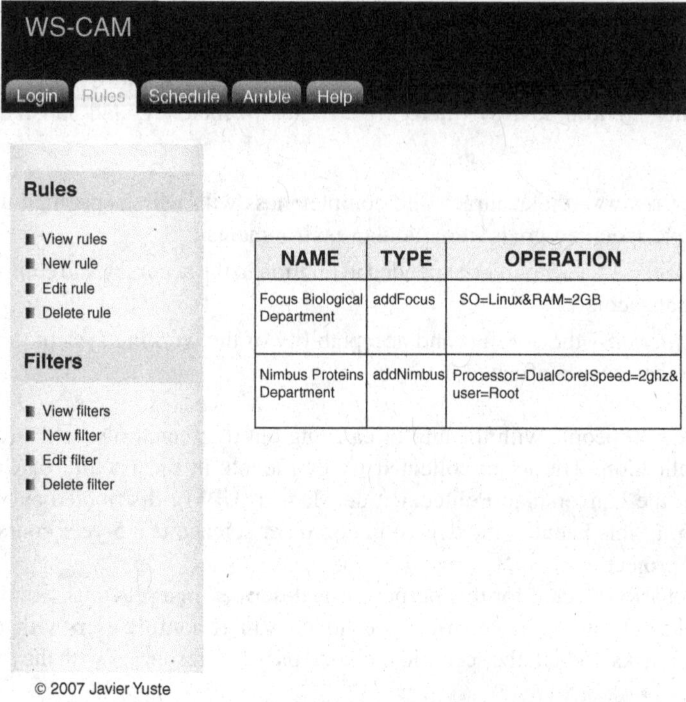

Figure 8.6 Some *focus* and *nimbus* rules.

Before starting the experiment, all of the students received the same information as well as a document briefly describing the set of tasks, rules, and schedules to be introduced in the application (Fig. 8.6). Users cannot see this document until the beginning of the experiment.

This experiment was carried out in two different steps. First, they had to complete the entire scenario in a time $(t) \leq t_{max}$ (where t_{max} was the maximum time established). The second step consisted of responding to a questionnaire to study the application's usability.

This questionnaire was divided into three parts. The first part was related to the "user's overall impression," asking users about their level of satisfaction, the application efficiency and effectiveness from the user's perspective, and the overall complexity of the application. The second part was related to the "ease in managing the application," asking users how easy it was to manage the application at first, whether the sequence of steps seemed to be natural or logical, and whether the application offered enough information to finalize the entire scenario or whether additional information was required. Finally, the last part of the questionnaire was related to the "user's interface," asking them about the physical design of the application interface, the terminology used, how intuitive the application was, and the sequence of messages and responses offered in the process. Users could select a value from 1 to 5 to respond to each question.

The results produced in this experiment were very significant because 90% of the users selected the values ranging from 4 to 5 in the overall impression. More specifically, 60% chose 4 and 30% chose 5 to score their satisfaction—where 5 meants very satisfactory; 80% opted for 4 and 10% opted for 5 to count the application efficiency and effectiveness from the user's perspective. Here, 5 signifies a high efficiency and effectiveness, and almost 100% decided on 1 to grade the application's complexity, in general—where 1 represents noncomplex. As for the second questionnaire, 90% of the users chose 5 to score the application management at first, therefore considering the application very easy to manage even the first time; 70% opted for 4 to reflect the naturalness of the sequence of steps. Here, 5 means a natural sequence of steps, and almost 100% of the students decided on 5 to grade the application's ability to help them finalize the entire scenario, where 5 indicates that no additional information is required. Finally, 100% of the students opted for 5 to score the suitability of the application's interface, where 5 denotes a suitable interface for the designed application. Then 90% selected 2 to grade possible improvements, where 1 means no improvement and 2 denotes minor improvements; 100% agreed on the terminology used, as they selected 5, and 80% judged the application as quite intuitive, selecting 4 or 5 to respond to the corresponding questions.

In short, we can conclude that, it was generally very easy to run the experiment. None of the participants encountered any problems in completing the scenario. Even though the CAM model was a bit more difficult to understand for the undergraduate students, the WS-CAM application was still fairly natural and intuitive, as its usability and suitability were evaluated quite satisfactorily.

8.8 CONCLUSION AND ONGOING WORK

This chapter has described how virtual organizations can be managed using a collaborative/cooperative awareness management (CAM) model and a business engine for computer-supported cooperative work (CSCW). The output of this integration is strongly needed: an efficient, flexible, and dynamic resource-sharing infrastructure, endorsing interaction by means of a set of rules. CAM manages awareness of interaction by means of a set of rules, optimizing the resources' collaboration, promoting the resources' cooperation in the environment, and responding to the specific-circumstance-related demands at a given moment. This chapter also describes how CAM works in some specific examples and scenarios, also explaining how the WS-CAM rules-based management application has been designed, implemented, and validated to tackle virtual organization (VO) management in collaborative Grid environments.

The CAM model described throughout this chapter has been evaluated in different steps: following a scenario-based validation to confirm that the model is working properly, as well as a user-based validation to check user preferences, obtaining satisfactory results in each and every evaluation step.

REFERENCES

1. S. D. Benford and L. E. Fahlén, A spatial model of interaction in large virtual environments, *Proc. 3rd European Conf. Computer Supported Cooperative Work*, Milano, Italy, 1993.
2. F. Berman and R. Wolski, The AppLeS project: A status report, *Proc. 8th NEC Research Symp.*, Berlin, Germany, May 1997.
3. I. Graham, *Business Rules Management and Service Oriented Architecture: A Pattern Language*, Wiley, Chichester, UK, 2007.
4. J. Broberg, S. Venugopal, and R. Buyya, Market-oriented Grids and utility computing: The state-of-the-art and future directions, *Journal of Grid Computing* **6**(3):255–276 (2008).
5. R. Buyya, D. Abramson, and J. Giddy, Nimrod/G: An architecture for a resource management and scheduling system in a global computational Grid, *Proc. 4th International Conf. High-Performance Computing in the Asia-Pacific Region (HPC Asia 2000)*, Beijing, China, 2000.
6. R. Buyya, D. Abramson, and S. Venugopal, The Grid economy, *Proceedings of the IEEE* **93**(3):698–714 (March 2005).
7. H. Casanova and J. Dongarra, NetSolve: A network server for solving computational science problems, *International Journal of High-Performance Computing and Applications* **11**(3):212–223 (1997).
8. S. J. Chapin, D. Katramatos, J. F. Karpovich, and A. S. Grimshaw, The legion resource management system, *Proc. 5th Job Scheduling Strategies for Parallel Processing*, Springer-Verlag, San Juan, Puerto Rico, April 1999.
9. C. Forgy, A Network Match Routine for Production Systems, Working Paper, Dept. Computer Science, Carnegie-Mellon Univ., 1974.
10. C. Forgy, *On the Efficient Implementation of Production Systems*, PhD thesis, Carnegie-Mellon Univ., 1979.
11. C. Forgy, Rete: A fast algorithm for the many pattern/many object pattern match problem, *Artificial Intelligence* **19**(1):17–37 (1982).
12. M. Feldman, K. Lai, and L. Zhang, A price-anticipating resource allocation mechanism for distributed shared clusters, *Proc. 6th ACM Conf. Electronic Commerce*, Vancouver, BC, Canada, 2005.
13. I. Foster, C. Kesselman, and S. Tuecke, The anatomy of the Grid: Enabling scalable virtual organizations, *International Journal of High-Performance Computing and Applications* **15**(3):200–222 (2001).
14. I. Foster, C. Kesselman, J. Nick, and S. Tuecke, *The Physiology of the Grid: An Open Grid Services Architecture for Distributed Systems Integration*, Open Grid Service Infrastructure WG, Global Grid Forum, June 2002.
15. I. Foster and C. Kesselman, *The Grid 2: Blueprint for a New Computing Infrastructure*, Elsevier, 2004.
16. R. Buyya and S. Venugopal, The Gridbus toolkit for service oriented Grid and utility computing: An overview and status report, *Proc. 1st IEEE International Workshop on Grid Economics and Business Models (GECON 2004)*, Seoul, South Korea, April 23, 2004.
17. P. Herrero, Covering your back: Intelligent virtual agents in humanitarian missions providing mutual support, *Lecture Notes in Computer Science* **3290**:391–407 (2004).

18. P. Herrero, J. L. Bosque, M. Salvadores, and M. S. Pérez, Managing dynamic virtual organizations to get effective cooperation in collaborative Grid environments, *Proc. 2nd International Conf. Grid Computing, High-Performance and Distributed Applications*, Vilamoura, Portugal, 2007.
19. X. Jin and J. Liu, From individual based modeling to autonomy oriented computation, *Agents and Computational Autonomy: Potential, Risks, and Solutions; Lecture Notes in Computer Science*, **2969**:151–169 (2004).
20. M. Litzkow, M. Livny, and M. Mutka, Condor—a hunter of idle workstations by, *Proc. 8th International Conf. Distributed Computing Systems*, San Jose, CA, June 1988.
21. R. S. Montero, E. Huedo, and I. M. Llorente, Grid scheduling infrastructures based on the GridWay meta-scheduler, *IEEE Technical Committee on Scalable Computing (TCSC)* **8**(2) (2006).
22. J. Nabrzyski, J. M. Schopf, and J. Weglarz, eds., *Grid Resource Management: State of the Art and Future Trends*, Springer, Sept. 2003.
23. J. M. Schopf, M. D'Arcy, N. Miller, L. Pearlman, I. Foster, and C. Kesselman, *Monitoring and Discovery in a Web Services Framework: Functionality and Performance of the Globus Toolkit's MDS4*, Argonne National Laboratory Technical Report ANL/MCS-P1248-0405, 2004.
24. C. A. Waldspurger, T. Hogg, B. A. Huberman, J. O. Kephart, and W. S. Stornetta, Spawn: A distributed computational economy, *IEEE Transactions on Software Engineering* **18**(2):103–117 (Feb. 1992).
25. R. Wolski, J. S. Plank, J. Brevik, and T. Bryan, Analyzing market-based resource allocation strategies for the computational Grid, *International Journal of High-Performance Computing Applications* **15**(3):258–281 (2001).

9

ACCOUNTING AS A REQUIREMENT FOR MARKET-ORIENTED GRID COMPUTING

ANDREA GUARISE AND ROSARIO M. PIRO

This chapter explores important aspects of resource usage accounting—intended as the metering, collection, processing, and reporting of resource usage information to keep track of computational resources consumed by Grid users—and its importance for market-oriented Grid computing. We discuss theoretical and practical issues such as different accounting architectures, the essential requirements that a Grid accounting system should address, current accounting practices, the normalization of usage information, and the standardization of accounting interfaces.

9.1 INTRODUCTION

Computational Grids are evolving from collaborative, application-domain-specific distributed systems for research and academia [e.g., the US TeraGrid[1] or the Large Hadron Collider (LHC) Computing Grid[2]] to general-purpose service-oriented computing platforms of commercial interest. Whether being of collaborative or commercial nature, Grid infrastructures require a timely and thorough accounting of the resources consumed by the users' service requests. Providing accurate and reliable usage information from many geographically distributed and heterogeneous service

[1]See http://www.teragrid.org.
[2]See http://lcg.web.cern.ch/LCG/.

Market-Oriented Grid and Utility Computing Edited by Rajkumar Buyya and Kris Bubendorfer

instances is a difficult and error-prone task, but of fundamental importance for establishing computational economies.[3]

9.1.1 The Importance of Resource Usage Accounting for Computational Economies

The application of market principles to the exchange of computational services (including but not limited to processing power) in computational Grids is aimed mostly at an efficient and fair allocation of available resources to the Grid's user community, but may also provide strong financial incentives for resource owners to contribute an increasing number of services to the system.

The most important objective associated with resource allocation in Grids is a balance between the overall throughput of the system and the quality of service (QoS) for single applications, thus seeking high utilization, but not at the expense of QoS and vice versa, while guaranteeing fairness among Grid users. This is particularly difficult when resource demand exceeds resource supply and when producers (resource owners) and consumers (resource users) have different goals, objectives, and strategies. Computational economies, namely, economic approaches to the problem of resource allocation, are widely believed to offer natural and decentralized self-regulating mechanisms that help in balancing demand and supply [1–7]. The adoption of a computational economy model, given an appropriate resource pricing scheme to attract or deter users according to the current workload of the single services, can aid not only in balancing demand and supply but also in efficiently assigning the incoming service requests to different service providers on the Grid (workload balancing by means of economic scheduling; see, e.g., Refs. 8 and 9).

In a commercial context, accurate resource usage information is essential to allow for billing and charging for the services rendered to remote users. The cost of executing an application, for example, might depend on its runtime, the number of processors or nodes it occupied, the memory it used (especially when it exceeded the available physical memory), and its input/output (I/O) operations. But even multi-organizational noncommercial environments with stringent funding policies, such as collaborative Grid infrastructures used by research and academia in which users are seldom charged for their resource consumption, are interested in tracing the resource usage by single users as well as entire virtual organizations (VOs) in order to guarantee a fair sharing of available resources, allow for a balanced cost allocation among the participating organizations, and evaluate whether Grid service providers fulfill the established service-level agreements (SLAs).

The historical resource usage information provided by a Grid accounting system could also be used to predict the resource consumption of Grid jobs, or more generally service requests, before scheduling, and hence to estimate the total cost associated with their execution. Research on predicting job runtimes has, for example, been done by Downey [10] and Smith, et al. [11]. Such resource usage predictions and cost

[3]We use the more generic term "computational economy" for what often is also called a "Grid economy" in the context of Grid computing [1].

estimations may be of importance in computational economies [4], since they could significantly influence scheduling decisions to be taken under budget constraints.

Apart from providing the basis for billing and charging mechanisms, resource usage information could also be exploited by an automated policy management system to ensure Gridwide quota enforcement [12] or simply for the analysis of usage statistics and summaries for single users or entire organizations.

Moreover, the collection of usage data can help in identifying resources that are highly requested as well as in predicting future demand for specific services and hence in improving the Grid infrastructure for the benefit of both its users and the service providers.

Whether considering a commercial or a noncommercial Grid infrastructure, resource usage accounting is one of the key middleware tasks in Grid computing, but while noncommercial computing environments can theoretically function correctly without a thorough accounting, market-oriented Grid and utility computing cannot.

9.1.2 What Is Grid Accounting?

The need for an accurate usage accounting exists also in traditional multiuser systems. The geographic distribution, the dynamic nature, the high degree of heterogeneity (e.g., different batch systems on computational resources), and the division into different administrative domains of Grid infrastructures, however, pose additional challenges to Grid accounting systems, in terms of decentralization, scalability, and flexibility [5]. In turn, they can benefit from the Grid's underlying authentication and authorization mechanisms to establish the identity and credentials of Grid users that request the accounted services [5].

Generally, accounting in multiuser computational environments is intended as the metering, collection, processing, and reporting of resource usage information for the purpose of keeping track of the resources consumed by the single users. Because of their distributed nature and the existence of multiple administrative domains, the accounting of resource usage in computational Grids is closely related to the authentication of Grid users on remote resources and the authorization mechanisms that determine whether they have the permission to use these resources. Therefore, accounting is often considered as an important part of the Grid's authentication, authorization, and accounting (AAA) infrastructure.

Resource types that should be accounted and eventually charged for may include, but are not limited to, computing power, memory usage, storage space, network activity, and access to particular software libraries and data repositories. In a commercial, service-oriented Grid infrastructure, so-called value-added (composed) services may be of particular importance. A Web service, for example, that, given a specific DNA sequence, searches related sequences in multiple large databases, can require a considerable amount of processing power as well as access to possibly proprietary databases (most likely also causing network traffic).

Although—especially in commercial computing environments—mechanisms for cost computation and payment may be fundamental and are closely related to the accounting task (relying on accurate resource usage information), neither the pricing

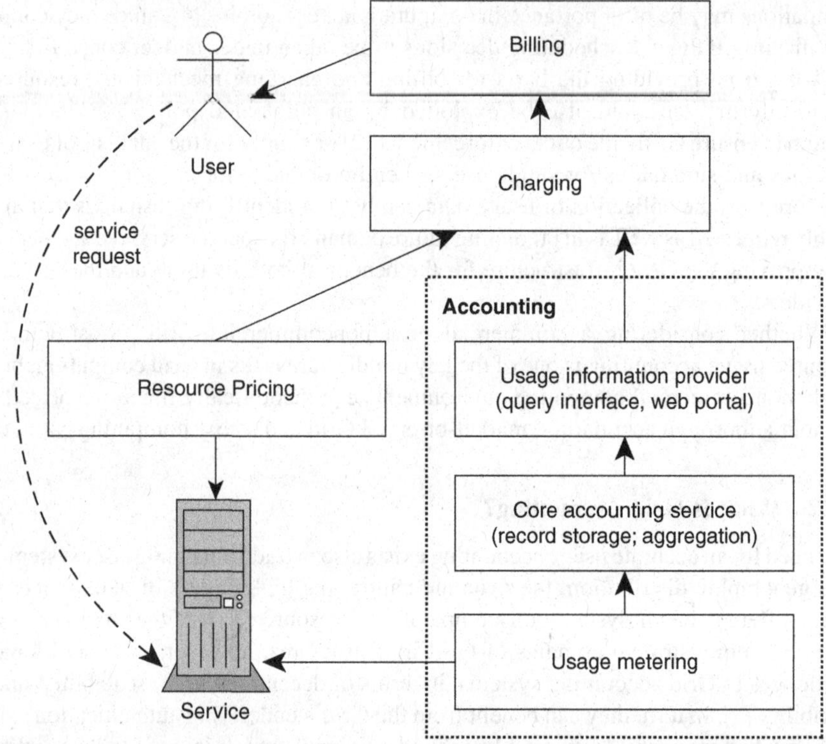

Figure 9.1 Simplified layered model of accounting, pricing, charging, and billing.

of nor billing and charging for services rendered are strictly required for Grid accounting, intended as the tracking of resource consumption by Grid users [13,14]. Because of this close relationship, the meaning of the terms *accounting, charging*, and *billing* are often not sufficiently delimited, but they can be defined according to the simple layered model depicted in Figure 9.1 [13]:

- *Accounting* is the gathering (metering and collection), processing (e.g., aggregation), and reporting of resource usage information. This does not necessarily (but may) include cost and payment information.
- *Resource pricing* is the dynamic or manual assignment of a price to an offered resource or service. Note that the price of a resource, if expressed as a price per unit, may be very different from the cost for using it, since the latter often depends also on the amount of resources consumed (see *Charging*, below).
- *Charging* is the assignment of a cost to a resource or service consumption. This cost may be determined from the prices per unit (see *Resource pricing*, above) and the actual amount of consumed resources. Charging is logically located on top of metering and accounting, but does not include *billing* [15]. Service cost and charging information can (and should) be fed back into the accounting system to complement the resource usage information.

- *Billing* is the collection and processing of charging information, its delivery to the user, or its (virtual) bank, and the processing of the payment. Payments can also regard virtual credits rather than true currencies. For an example of a billing–payment system for Grid services that does not provide but instead is build on top of *accounting* and *charging* mechanisms, see the paper by Nissi and Silander [16].

An accounting system requires more than just accounting servers that store usage records and associate them with service instances and the users that requested them. Resource usage has to be metered, and the resulting records have to be collected from the service instances. This is usually accomplished by dedicated accounting sensors installed on the service hosts (see also Section 9.2.1). For the purpose of usage data analysis, an interface to the accounting system must be provided, such that the accounting data (for single requests or statistics) can be communicated to authorized clients (see Section 9.2.3.2).

Different billing and charging concepts may be based on accounting information (pay-per-use model, prepay model, pay-per-access/fixed-cost model, subscription/flatrate model, etc.), and in general the purpose of a Grid accounting system should not be to define (and hence limit) the economic interactions between users and resource owners, but to provide the necessary information to enable them.

The differences between accounting, billing, and charging, however, are of a conceptual nature, and implementations of accounting and/or charging and billing systems may combine the different concepts in a single framework, as is done, for example, by GridBank [17]. In this chapter we focus on accurate and reliable resource usage accounting as a fundamental requirement for applying market principles to Grid computing environments and implementing billing and charging systems.

9.1.3 Accounting versus Monitoring

Although there is some overlap between the accounting of resource usage and the monitoring of services and service requests, the final purpose of these two important middleware tasks is substantially different since they have to fulfill the requirements of mostly distinct use cases, as exemplified by the following (nonexhaustive) list:

1. Monitoring use cases:
   a. Infrastructure monitoring (availability and load):
      (1) Is a specific service currently available?
      (2) What is the current CPU load on a computational resource?
      (3) What is the number of free CPUs?
      (4) What is the remaining capacity of a storage service?
   b. Service provision monitoring:
      (1) Is a job still being executed?
      (2) What is the status of a file up-/download?

2. Accounting use cases:
   a. Storage of detailed usage information:
      (1) What and how much resources did a particular service request or job consume?
      (2) (In case of economic accounting.) What did a request/job execution cost?
   b. Request mapping:
      (1) To what services or computational resources did a user submit requests/jobs?
      (2) Which users did submit requests to a specific service instance?
   c. Aggregation/usage statistics:
      (1) How many requests/jobs did a given user submit?
      (2) What amount of resources did a given VO consume at a specific site or over the entire Grid during the last day, month, or year?
3. Overlapping use cases:
   a. Detailed usage information and service provision monitoring:
      (1) For how long has a service already been occupied by a specific request (e.g., a job being executed)?
   b. Aggregation/usage statistics and service provision monitoring:
      (1) How many requests/jobs have been submitted per organization, per service, or per site?
      (2) Does a VO consume a higher share of the Grid resources than it has been assigned?

The monitoring activity can roughly be classified as infrastructure monitoring and application monitoring [18]. Application monitoring, or more generally service provision monitoring, aims at observing the status of the execution of service requests (e.g., the status of a job execution or a file upload), allowing users to keep track of their single requests and to identify reasons for job failures [19]. This may involve the determination of some usage information (hence the overlap with accounting).

Many existing monitoring tools instead focus on infrastructure monitoring [19], to provide information on services and sites, such as the status of a service (whether it is up and running), the CPU load of a computational resource and its number of available CPUs, the number of queued requests, the remaining space on a storage resource, and the available bandwidth. An accounting system, as described above, is usually concerned with accurately and reliably measuring and reporting the amount of resources consumed, not the status of the services that provide the resources.

9.2 BACKGROUND: ACCOUNTING APPROACHES, REQUIREMENTS, AND CURRENT PRACTICES

As is true for most Grid middleware tasks, accounting can be done in widely differing ways. Before describing some of the current practices in Section 9.2.6, the following sections discuss several important issues regarding accounting approaches, requirements of market-oriented Grid computing, the normalization of usage information, and the standardization of accounting interfaces from a theoretical perspective.

The most relevant differences regarding procedural and architectural approaches to Grid accounting mostly concern the frequency of usage metering and the distribution of accounting servers and repositories.

9.2.1 Frequency of Usage Metering and Accounting

Usage metering can be defined as the measuring of the service request's resource consumption on the service host and the generation of the corresponding accounting record [13]. After usage metering, accounting records are collected and forwarded to the accounting servers that manage the usage information repositories. Both the metering and the collection of usage data are usually accomplished by dedicated accounting sensors that may come in different flavors, since they have to be capable of extracting the required usage information from heterogeneous service instance implementations (e.g., from widely differing local resource management systems, or batch systems, used for computational resources).

Depending on the exact purposes for which usage information is gathered, the usage metering and the collection of accounting records can be done in different frequencies:

- *Periodic* accounting—the usage metering and forwarding of usage records to the accounting repositories are done in defined time intervals (e.g., once per day).
- *Immediate* accounting—usage metering and record forwarding are done for single requests on (or shortly after) service/job completion.
- *Real-time* accounting—usage metering is done incrementally while furnishing a service, and records in the accounting repositories are frequently updated until final versions after service/job completion can be built.

Most systems implement either periodic or immediate accounting, since real-time accounting is difficult to realize because it requires in-depth instrumentation of the computing service, with greater overhead than in periodic or immediate metering. Moreover, real-time accounting is rarely required. A possible application is the adoption of dynamic resource access policies based on up-to-date accounting information [12], but immediate accounting combined with resource usage estimation of currently executed jobs could probably be similarly efficient and less difficult to implement. However, so far no studies to confirm or reject this hypothesis have appeared in the literature.

9.2.2 Accounting Architectures

Several conceptually different architectures for the deployment of an accounting infrastructure can be, and have been, adopted by different Grid projects and

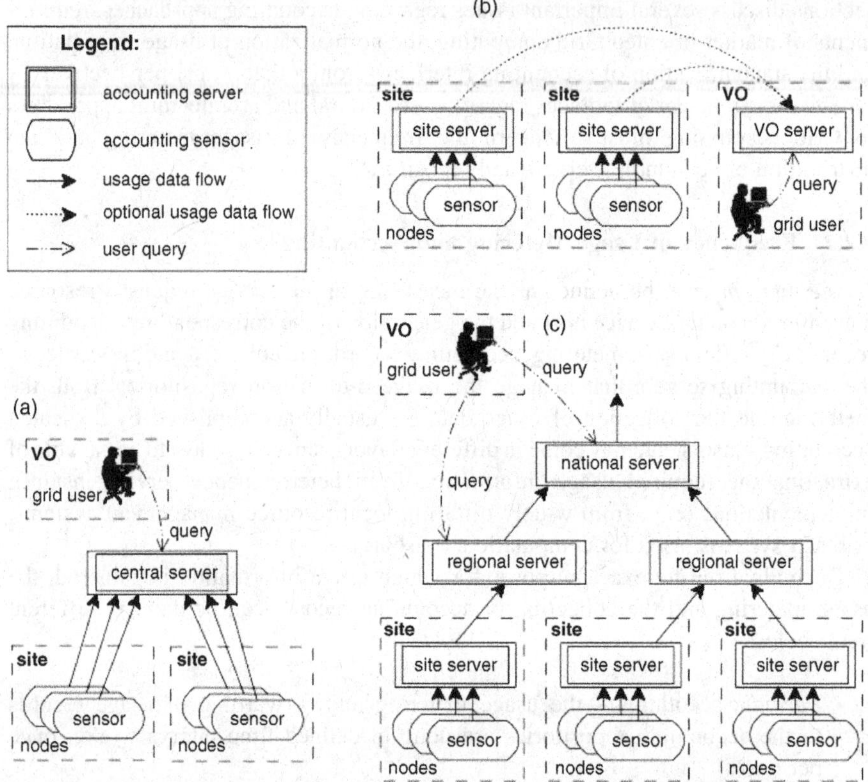

Figure 9.2 Schematic examples of possible accounting architectures: (a) centralized, (b) distributed, and (c) hierarchical. Note that the optional forwarding of accounting information to user- or VO-level accounting servers [exemplified in (b), but possible also in (c)] is not supported by all accounting systems.

accounting systems. These architectures, schematically depicted in Figure 9.2, can roughly be divided into *centralized, distributed,* and *hierarchical* approaches. We briefly discuss their advantages and limitations in the following sections.

9.2.2.1 Centralized Architecture. A centralized approach, such as that taken by the Accounting Processor for Event Logs (APEL) [20], foresees the deployment of only one central accounting repository, as the only distributed components of the system are the accounting sensors installed on the different sites or service hosts. The central accounting server or accounting portal is usually the only component that can be queried for usage information.

The advantages of such an approach are straightforward:

- A centralized approach demands less deployment and maintenance effort from the sites or service providers, since only the sensors have to be installed and configured.

- A central database is usually easier to maintain and configure than a distributed set of accounting servers. It can be maintained and operated by a small group of trained system administrators. The service can be improved more easily, since server-side upgrades are limited to a single central computing center.
- The management and control of authentication, authorization, and security issues (e.g., access control to private usage information; see Section 9.2.3.2) is reduced to a minimum, since there is a single "entry point" for both the upload of usage information and the user queries.[4]

Unfortunately, there are also significant disadvantages, and these, too, are straightforward:

- A central service naturally imposes scalability limitations. The amount of sites or service instances and user queries that a central accounting server can handle depends on the capability of both the hardware and the software to sustain the corresponding load. Increasing the number of sites that publish usage records to a centralized database, or the number of users that need to access it, may have a strong impact on the performance of the central database and require the capability to tempestively upgrade the hardware or the software in order to cope with the increasing demands, if possible at all. Some systems, in order to avoid performance problems, allow access only to aggregated usage statistics instead of detailed information about single service requests or job executions (e.g., the accounting Web portal that displays accounting information collected by APEL; see Section 9.2.6.1).
- A single central accounting server is also a single point of failure. This may be problematic, particularly for Grid middleware components that rely on accounting information in order to function properly, such as for the purpose of billing and charging.

An entirely centralized accounting architecture should thus be used mainly in small to medium-scale Grids with a limited growth, where scalability problems are more likely to play a marginal role.

9.2.2.2 Distributed Architecture. A completely distributed approach to Grid accounting, instead, has no central repositories for usage records. Each site or service provider might, for example, have its own accounting server and make the records in its accounting repository available to authorized users. In such a scenario the accounting information is stored for each service provider on site-level accounting servers, but might additionally be forwarded to user-level accounting servers that are managed by the users' home organizations, as it is for example, possible (although not mandatory) with the Distributed Grid Accounting System (DGAS) [21].

[4]Of course, each centralized service is also more vulnerable to cyber attacks (a successful attack exposes the entire service), but we do not consider such security problems here.

This approach has clear advantages:

- It is extremely scalable, since the size of the database of a site-level accounting server will never grow beyond the needs of a single site, which is seldom a problem with current hardware and software performances.
- Having multiple accounting servers increases the robustness of the entire system by avoiding single points of failure, since a failure in one of the distributed accounting servers would affect only a fraction of the Grid resources or users. If the service is carefully designed and deployed (given appropriate backup mechanisms), the negative effects of such a failure can in principle be avoided.

Nonetheless, the disadvantages due to information partitioning, that is, the distribution of accounting data over multiple databases, should not be ignored:

- If no user-level accounting servers are available, it is most difficult for a single Grid user, requesting services of tens or hundreds of service providers (e.g., submitting jobs to hundreds of sites), to have an exhaustive view of the resource consumption of his/her service requests or job submissions (e.g., usage statistics), even if the user should have access rights on hundreds of site-level accounting servers.
- For specific use cases, Gridwide usage statistics, such as for comparing the resource usage of all participating VOs, may be more difficult to obtain. Such Gridwide usage statistics may require queries to all distributed accounting servers (apart from access rights on all of them), causing a considerable amount of network traffic if executed frequently.

A distributed accounting approach as implemented, for example, by the SweGrid Accounting System (SGAS) [22], GridBank [17], Resource Usage Data management and Accounting (RUDA) [23], and DGAS [21], is particularly suitable for reliable low-level accounting, for example, for the purpose of quota enforcement [12] or for providing detailed usage information for billing and charging.

9.2.2.3 ***Hierarchical Architecture.*** Some of the distributed accounting systems (e.g., DGAS and RUDA) try to overcome the limitations of a completely distributed accounting architecture by allowing a usually optional hierarchical deployment of higher-level accounting servers on top of the distributed infrastructure of primary accounting servers.

In a hierarchical accounting infrastructure, each accounting server can receive or collect information from a lower-level accounting server and in turn forward or provide such information to a higher-level sever. Thus accounting information becomes more complete, the higher the level of a node in the hierarchy is.

Many different implementations and deployments are possible, depending on the use cases that the infrastructure has to fulfill. For example, higher-level servers in the hierarchy might collect only aggregated usage statistics, letting only the lower-level nodes retain detailed information. Alternatively, it may be possible to have all the nodes retain detailed information and implement appropriate mechanisms to keep the load on higher-level servers under control, for example, by replicating the usage data to multiple equipollent nodes and sharing the load due to user queries among such data replicas.

9.2.3 Requirements for Grid Accounting

Market-oriented Grid computing and billing and charging systems have strict requirements in terms of reliability and completeness of accounting information, robustness and fault tolerance of the information gathering process, and confidentiality of private information with proper access control mechanisms. The following discussion examines the most important requirements, which often distinguish the accounting task in a Grid environment from local site accounting, and describes how they are generally addressed.

9.2.3.1 Association of Accounting Information with Grid Entities. For a reliable accounting of resource usage in Grid infrastructures, especially when considering its importance for market-oriented systems, it is fundamental that the collected usage data be unequivocally associated with all involved Grid entities. This usually means that each accounting record, apart from the actual usage data, must contain

- The unambiguously defined and Gridwide unique identifier of the user (e.g., certificate subject or "distinguished name") that requested the service.
- The user's affiliation or home organization (if the service is requested, e.g., on behalf of a virtual organization that, in a commercial context, may provide payment guarantees for the user). This information is of particular importance, if users, as happens in practice, may be affiliated to multiple VOs on behalf of which they can request services.
- The user's group or role within the VO, if, for example, defined by the fully qualified attribute name (FQAN) of a VOMS certificate [24]. The group/role of the user might have a significant impact on the billing process. Job submissions for the purpose of administration, maintenance, or monitoring, for example, might be free of charge.
- The unambiguously defined and Gridwide unique identifier of the service instance or resource that fulfilled the request (e.g., the Globus contact string in a Grid infrastructure based on the Globus toolkit[5]).
- The service request's or job's unique Grid ID (if present), indicating with which specific service request the resource usage information is associated.

In practice, however, the assignment of resource consumption data to Grid entities is not trivial (and in some cases even impossible). Computational resources, for example, are often managed by local batch systems, most of which record only local

[5]See http://www.globus.org.

information for single jobs and are not aware that a job has entered their queues through a Grid middleware component/gatekeeper. Moreover, some Grid sites allow jobs to be submitted also through non-Grid interfaces to the same computing resources. On the LHC Computing Grid (LCG), for example, a considerable amount of "out-of-band" work is being done through non-Grid interfaces, notwithstanding the fact that most of it is being performed on behalf of the LCG VOs and hence consumes the Grid resources assigned to them. Consequently, a Grid accounting system should not ignore local service requests; and users (or at least their home organizations) should be accounted for the resource consumption caused by both remote (Grid) and local submissions. Whether or not to charge users for local submission must be determined by agreements on billing and charging policies.

9.2.3.2 Granularity, Availability, and Privacy of Accounting Information. One obvious purpose of a Grid accounting system is to make the gathered usage information available. A less obvious question is how to make it available and above all, to whom. Many use cases for accounting information can be identified. We omit details in this discussion and summarize only the most important use cases, concentrating on those related to market-oriented Grid computing and their implications to Grid accounting.

Generally, accounting information should be gathered and reported at multiple levels. In many cases, detailed information for single service requests is required, such as CPU time, runtime, memory usage, and start and end times in case of execution of a "job" on a remote computational resource. Detailed usage information for each resource request is essential above all in an economic context, where charging and billing require a nonrepudiable proof of resource consumption. Other use cases, however, involve the aggregation of accounting information, for example, to determine the total resources requested on behalf of a VO at a specific site or over the entire Grid for the purpose of quota enforcement. To satisfy such diverse use cases, a Grid accounting system should be able to report usage data from fine granularity (for single service requests/job submissions) to coarse granularity (usage statistics). In other words, a Grid accounting system, in order to be as generic as possible, should not make limiting assumptions about whether accounting information is gathered and reported for single service requests, per user, per group, per project, or per site [5].

Accounting information should be made available to the sites that provide the services accounted for (resource-level accounting), to the users that request the services (user-level accounting), to the VO managers that supervise the work done by the users, and to Grid operations managers (VO and Grid-level accounting) and, of course, to billing and charging mechanisms in order to allow for cost computation and the processing of payment transactions. Other Grid middleware components as well might require access to accounting information, for example, for the purpose of quota enforcement or workload prediction.

However, accounting information is mostly confidential and must be handled with care in order not to compromise the users' privacy. This implies that such information must be made available only through strict access control mechanisms (e.g., by means of access control lists based on x509 certificates) guaranteeing that only authorized persons can consult usage data that are associated with a specific Grid user. Information confidentiality can be guaranteed by the use of different authorization levels. In most cases, a Grid user (or a middleware component on the user's behalf) can be granted access only to accounting records regarding the user's own service requests, while administrators or managers may have access to the accounting information regarding the group of users and/or services that they are responsible for. A payment procedure implemented by a billing/charging mechanism would most likely be initiated by the resource owner that, of course, has access to accounting information regarding the provided service.

Aggregated and anonymized usage statistics that cannot be attributed to a single person can often be made public. In any case, when deciding on access rights, the applicable national and international legislation for data privacy has to be considered.

9.2.3.3 Scalability of the Accounting Process. A requirement that is seldom properly addressed during the design, implementation, and deployment of accounting solutions for large-scale Grid infrastructures, although it regards not only accounting systems but also most Grid middleware components, is the need for scalability without a significant loss of performance. Especially in future commercial, service-oriented environments, a Grid accounting system, given its importance for the market-oriented approach, will have to cope with a continuously growing number of Grid participants, both service providers and users.

This requirement can best be met through a decentralized accounting architecture that, as described is Section 9.2.2, allows the distribution of accounting data over multiple databases. For smaller infrastructures with a limited growth, such as many enterprise Grids for industry or campus Grids for academia, a centralized approach may be sufficient as well. Hence, the ideal accounting solution would be a middleware flexible enough to be deployed in both a centralized or distributed (or hierarchical if more appropriate) fashion.

9.2.3.4 Reliability and Consistency of Accounting Information. The usage information provided by a Grid accounting system must, of course, be reliable in order to guarantee a successful implementation of market-oriented infrastructures, but even in collaborative Grid environments the reliability and consistency of usage data are often considered essential. This requirement implies the following:

- The *accuracy* of accounting information—the process of metering, gathering, and reporting resource consumption must not alter or falsify usage values (this does not exclude a normalization of the gathered information; see Section 9.2.4).
- The *completeness* of accounting information—no usage data that are important for obtaining an exhaustive picture of the resource consumption of users and/or VOs should be omitted (e.g., the out-of-band work mentioned in Section 9.2.3.1).
- The *integrity* of accounting information—all steps in the accounting process, from metering to reporting, should be robust and fault-tolerant, such that the

probability of data loss is reduced to a minimum. A decentralized accounting infrastructure may help in avoiding single points of failure. Communication failures between the components of an accounting system should be recognized and handled appropriately (e.g., by retrying the communication at a later point in time or providing automatic alternative mechanisms for delivery).

- The *authenticity* of accounting information—the nonrepudiation of payment requests through a charging/billing mechanism requires the authenticity of the underlying accounting information to be guaranteed. The accounting information originates from the very same site that is eventually charging the user for the provided service. This implies the existence of a trust relationship between the consumer (the user or the corresponding VO) and the supplier (the resource or service provider) in order to guarantee a fair charging process. But even such a trust relationship is still not sufficient to guarantee the authenticity of accounting information, since the information travels across the internet and can be stored in multiple hosts (e.g., accounting servers) that are possibly out of control of both the users and the resource providers. Consequently, there is also a stringent need for a data transport through secure and authenticated communication channels between the components of a Grid accounting system, such that accounting information cannot be compromised or falsified by a third party. We may also speak of a trust relationship between the accounting layer and both users and service providers.

Our experience with the Distributed Grid Accounting System (DGAS) on the production Grid of the Italian National Institute of Nuclear Physics (INFN)[6] demonstrated that, at least in the development or prototype phase, it is crucial to pedantically cross-check the information available in the accounting databases with the raw source for this information (batch system and gatekeeper logs). This allows for the discovery of configuration problems, bugs, or undesired behaviors that otherwise might be completely ignored, leading to errors in the billing/charging process.

9.2.4 Normalization

One of the most underestimated difficulties regarding Grid accounting is the normalization of accounting data originating from heterogeneous resources and service implementations or configurations. However, normalizing the usage information can be very important for comparing resource usage across heterogeneous services and hence for obtaining meaningful aggregated usage statistics that span multiple resources (e.g., the total resource consumption of a specific user or VO over the entire Grid or over all sites located in a given country). Service cost computations as well should take the innate heterogeneity of computational Grids into account.

9.2.4.1 Usage Metrics and Benchmarks. The core of the problem is that simply measuring the raw usage metrics associated with a service request is seldom sufficient

[6]See http://grid.infn.it.

to ensure good comprehension of the actual amount of resources consumed by that request. For example, a part of the measured resource usage of an application (e.g., CPU time) can depend significantly on the processor performance (and other characteristics) of the executing resource. It is clear that a given CPU consumption on an aged computing resource does not have the same weight or value as an equal consumption (in terms of metrics, i.e., CPU time) on an up-to-date computing farm.

The differences in usage metrics on heterogeneous resources for providing the same (or at least comparable) services must, of course, also be taken into account when considering the billing and charging of users for the resources that they consume. Service cost computations should be based not only on raw usage metrics (e.g., CPU time) but also on the "value" of a resource (e.g., its processing power). In other words, the service cost, in order to be fair, should be based on the *computational energy* consumed by a service request, which we have defined as "the product of a performance factor or power p (e.g., a benchmark of CPU speed) and the amount of usage u (e.g. the CPU time), which ideally should be independent of the resource's characteristics" [21].

Thus, it is obvious that additional information on resource characteristics should be associated with each accounting record. In general, an accounting system needs to record the raw resource consumption as reported from the underlying operating system or batch scheduler plus additional characteristics regarding the service provider that allow for normalization, instead of storing already normalized usage values. This is necessary to guarantee that usage data remain valid in case normalization procedures should change.

The problem of comparing usage metrics of service requests fulfilled by different service providers (e.g., jobs executed on different machines) is of great relevance for market-oriented Grid computing. Unfortunately, there is no common agreement on normalization procedures, and the problem is still a matter of investigation.

One hurdle toward well-defined and widely accepted normalization procedures is the benchmarking of Grid resources that is still an open research issue. Since many years, the SPEC (Standard Performance Evaluation Corporation)[7] suite of benchmarks is the de facto standard for CPU-related computing benchmarks, providing a meaningful evaluation of the real processing power of a computing platform while accounting for the different application areas (e.g., CPU-intensive applications, I/O-intensive applications) in which such a platform is used.

Since each single benchmark evaluates a specific aspect of system performance, a meaningful description of the performance of Grid resources requires an entire set of benchmarks. Current practice in Grid computing, however, is to limit the measured benchmarks to those related to processing power (mostly SPECint2000 for integer-based computation and SPECfp2000 for floating-point computation). Even regarding this limited use of benchmark metrics some problems can arise, if normalization of usage information, as often happens in practice, is done only according to a single benchmark (SPECint2000). It is clear, however, that on the same Grid resources,

[7]See http://www.spec.org.

different user communities could be running both integer-based computations and floating-point computations. Hence, whether to normalize the CPU usage according to integer-based or floating-point benchmarks for comparing different resources or service providers depends mostly on the type of computation that has been, or is supposed to be, executed. This is another strong argument for storing benchmark metrics and raw usage metrics separately, instead of already normalized usage values.

Another issue is that benchmark suites evolve with time. During the lifetime of a Grid infrastructure, it is possible, and most likely, that new benchmark suites will replace older ones. The implemented procedures for resource usage accounting should be flexible enough to face such changes.

9.2.4.2 Usage Metrics and Site Policies/Configurations. Apart from performance benchmarks, other more or less subtle aspects related to the site or service provider can influence the effective performances delivered to the users' payload. Different computing sites, for example, can have different policies regarding the number of concurrent jobs or applications that can be executed on a single CPU core, often referred to as the number of "job slots." While this seldom affects the CPU time consumed by an application, it clearly alters its runtime or "wall clock time"—the perceived processing time that depends on how many user processes a single processor core has to execute contemporaneously (time sharing). Therefore, when normalizing the affected usage metrics, such as the runtimes of different jobs, especially if they have an impact on the service cost, it is essential to consider the number of job slots. It should be noted that this regards the number of *occupied* job slots, that only on computational resources with a high throughput, is approximately equal to the maximum number of job slots allowed by the system. Such information, however, is very difficult to obtain for a Grid accounting system and is therefore currently, to our best knowledge, not considered by any Grid project for the normalization of usage metrics.

9.2.4.3 Usage Metrics and Application Characteristics. The characteristics of an application or service request itself can affect some of its usage metrics and should therefore not be ignored when normalizing these metrics. The number of processors, or processor cores, used by a parallel application that allows for a variable degree of parallelism, for example, can significantly alter its runtime. In some cases it can therefore be important to normalize these runtimes according to the number of cores utilized, in order to compare the performance of the application over different service providers.

9.2.5 Standardization

Distributed Grid computing infrastructures are not only composed of several administrative domains, but may also consist of multiple interconnected Grid systems based on different middleware stacks. The Worldwide LHC Computing Grid (WLCG), for example, is a collaboration of the EGEE/LCG (Enabling Grids for

E-sciencE)[8] infrastructure, the Open Science Grid (OSG),[9] and several national and regional Grids such as NorduGrid[10] and GridPP,[11] all set up with at least partly different middleware implementations (and different accounting systems in particular). This illustrates the need to address the problem of ensuring "Grid interoperability"—the seamless and transparent interoperation of middleware components that have been implemented for different Grid environments.

An accurate and reliable accounting of resource usage should, of course, also be guaranteed across different collaborating Grid systems in order to accommodate VOs and users that utilize multiple Grid platforms [25]. Especially in a commercial context, service providers will be eager to account and charge not only for resources consumed by remote users of the same Grid project/environment but also for those consumed by external users that can access their services. The adoption of standard interfaces for accounting tools allows Grids to exchange usage information, such that all involved Grid entities (the user or Grid components on its behalf, its home organization, the service provider, etc.) may access their respective accounting information, even if they are part of different Grid infrastructures. Moreover, such standard interfaces may allow service providers to contribute their resources to multiple infrastructures by ensuring the resource usage to be traceable across different Grid middleware implementations.

Since accounting information may be of interest also for other components of the Grid middleware (e.g., for policy management systems to enforce quotas or resource brokers to estimate service costs), the adoption of standard interfaces would also allow to query such information over heterogeneous middleware implementations. Two emerging Open Grid Forum (OGF)[12] recommendations in particular are related to Grid accounting and are briefly introduced here.

9.2.5.1 The OGF Usage Record. The Usage Record (UR) Working Group[13] defined an XML-based accounting record format for the exchange of "atomic" (i.e., for single application runs/jobs) usage information. The current specification of the OGF UR [26], however, is very batch-job-specific and is therefore not suitable for the accounting of storage and other services.

An OGF UR document can contain various usage data, such as `CpuDuration`, `WallDuration`, `Memory`, `Swap`, `Disk`, and `NodeCount`, allowing the specification of usage metrics for the consumption of computational resources. These metrics can be associated with a specific computational resource (`MachineName`, `Queue`, and `Host`), user (`UserIdentity`), and job (`JobIdentity` and `JobName`).

Although the UR format is syntactically well defined, it is semantically unclear in some of its data fields. The `ProjectName`, for example, may be the user's VO, or

[8]See http://www.eu-egee.org.
[9]See http://www.opensciencegrid.org.
[10]See http://www.nordugrid.org.
[11]See http://www.gridpp.ac.uk.
[12]See http://www.ogf.org.
[13]See https://forge.gridforum.org/sf/projects/ur-wg/.

alternatively the specific Grid project with which the user is associated (e.g., the Grid projects that collaborate in WLCG, as described above); and the `MachineName` may be the site's name, the cluster's name, or the name of the host that executed a job. The UR format also misses, among its explicitly defined data fields, some important information required for many large-scale Grid environments/projects (EGEE, OSG, LCG, etc.), such as the virtual organization (and the role therein) of the user that submitted a job. To address usage properties that are not explicitly covered by the OGF specification, the UR format provides an extension framework. An extensive and abusive use of this framework, however, may lead to incompatible although valid OGF UR documents [25].

The risk of having incompatible usage records can in most cases be neglected when considering the exchange of accounting information *within* a single Grid environment that uses a specific accounting tool or has agreed on a precise form of UR documents, but it may undermine interoperability when exchanging accounting information *across* different Grids or accounting systems, especially if the extension framework has to be used to specify properties that are essential for the correct functioning of the accounting procedures [25]. This leads to the concrete risk of having a "standard" that, although properly implemented, does not provide real interoperability between different Grid infrastructures.

9.2.5.2 The OGF Resource Usage Service. The OGF Resource Usage Service (RUS) Working Group[14] defines a Web services–based interface to accounting systems for a standardized upload and retrieval of resource usage information in the form of OGF UR documents [27]. Such an interface can enable different implementations of accounting services to exchange resource usage information and is therefore important for the interoperability of different Grid infrastructures.

The current draft specification of the RUS interface covers the basic functionalities that should be provided by a storage service for usage information. The most important ones are:

- `insertUsageRecords`
- `extractRUSUsageRecords`
- `modifyUsageRecordPart`
- `deleteUsageRecords`

They are invoked by means of Simple Object Access Protocol (SOAP) messages. User queries are specified as input parameters to the SOAP messages. The XML query languages XPath/XQuery can be used to extract stored URs or to select them for deletion, while XUpdate allows their modification.

The OGF UR specification, and consequently also the RUS interface, regard only "atomic" usage records (i.e., for single application runs/jobs). Therefore, the RUS interface currently cannot be used to obtain aggregated/summarized usage statistics

[14]See https://forge.gridforum.org/sf/projects/rus-wg/.

from a Grid accounting system. The functionalities provided by a RUS interface focus on a storage service for usage records, and less on an information service.

9.2.6 Current Practices

To our best knowledge there is currently no Grid accounting system suitable for accounting generic service requests (computational resources, storage resources, value-added Web services, etc.). Almost all efforts have so far regarded computational or CPU resources, but some interesting research on storage accounting has recently been initiated. The following are a few representative approaches to CPU and storage accounting.

9.2.6.1 Accounting of CPU Resources. Although the CPU-related accounting tools used by the major Grid projects differ widely, their accounting practices mostly reflect the simplified model depicted in Figure 9.1.

Most sites of the EGEE/LCG infrastructure, for example, use the APEL accounting sensors to periodically meter resource usage (except local or out-of-band submissions; see Section 9.2.3.1) and forward accounting records to a database located at the central Grid operations center (GOC) where usage statistics (but no detailed job information) are available through a Web portal. Usage information is transmitted from the APEL sensors to the GOC database using the Relational Grid Monitoring Architecture (R-GMA) [20], which offers no strict authorization mechanism for data insertion (i.e., no guarantee for authenticity) or retrieval. Therefore APEL encrypts the unique Grid user identifier for the sake of privacy. A notable exception is the INFN Production Grid, a national Grid initiative that groups the Italian EGEE/LCG sites and uses DGAS for immediate usage metering (including local submissions) and accounting (via secure and authenticated channels) on a distributed, hierarchical network of accounting servers. Usage information is available in the form of usage statistics as well as for single jobs. Accounting records are periodically converted to the format used by APEL to be forwarded to the GOC portal.

On the TeraGrid resource consumption is metered by local, site-specific accounting systems. Local usage information is then converted into a shared format and forwarded to a central database [28].

Gratia,[15] the hierarchically organized accounting tool of the Open Science Grid, implements periodic metering and inserts records into distributed accounting servers from where they are fetched for storage in a central repository. Both detailed job-level and summary accounting information is available through Web portals and Web services interfaces.

GridBank [17] implements the Grid accounting services architecture (GASA) as developed by the Gridbus project,[16] closely integrating the authorization to access computational resources, the accounting of resource usage, and the charging and (virtual) billing for it into a single framework. Although GridBank was originally designed as a

[15]See http://gratia-osg.fnal.gov:8880/gratia-reporting/.

[16]See http://www.gridbus.org.

TABLE 9.1 Features of Accounting Systems

Tool/Project	APEL[a]	DGAS	Gratia	GridBank	NGS	RUDA	SGAS	TeraGrid
Basic architecture	C	C,D,H	H	C,D	C	D,H	C,D	C
Metering frequency	P	I	P	I	P	P	I/P[b]	P
Detailed job information	No[f]	Yes	Yes	Yes	Yes	Yes	Yes	Yes
Accounting of local or out-of-band jobs	No	Yes	Yes[c]	No	Yes	Yes	No[d]	Yes
RUS interface	No	Yes[c,e]	No	Yes	Partly	No	Yes[c,e]	No
Charging	No	Limited[c]	No	Yes	No	No	Limited	No
Resource pricing	No	Yes[c]	No	No	No	No	Limited	No

Legend: C = centralized; D = distributed; H = hierarchical; P = periodic; I = immediate.
[a] Including the EGEE accounting Web portal (APEL is an accounting sensor, not a complete system).
[b] Immediate usage metering, but periodic upload of usage data to accounting servers.
[c] Optional.
[d] Technically possible with appropriate ad hoc site configurations.
[e] Prototype RUS interfaces.
[f] Recorded but not accessible by users.

centralized service, it can be organized in distributed branches (bank servers) that keep usage information and manage accounts and funds of users and service providers.

Other Grid infrastructures/projects have adopted comparable solutions, such as the Resource Usage Service of the UK National Grid Service (NGS)[17] or SGAS used by NorduGrid, but a detailed review of the different accounting solutions is beyond the scope of this chapter.

Few of the accounting services mentioned above provide an OGF RUS interface, with the exceptions of DGAS and SGAS, which have developed prototypes within the OMII-Europe project,[18] and NGS-RUS, whose OGF RUS compliance, however, regards only the insertion of records, not their extraction (user queries).

Table 9.1 summarizes the most important features of some representative Grid accounting systems and projects, describing their basic architecture, the frequency with which usage information is metered and collected, whether detailed job information is available on queries, whether local and/or out-of-band work is accounted for (see Section 9.2.3.1), and whether the systems provide a RUS interface or components for charging and resource pricing[19].

9.2.6.2 Accounting of Storage Resources. Most of the research effort in the field of Grid accounting in this early stage of Grid development and deployment focused on

[17] See http://www.grid-support.ac.uk.
[18] See http://www.omii-europe.com.
[19] These features result from a survey made early 2008.

CPU-related accounting, given the fact that it was perceived as contemporaneously being the most urgent and the easiest to implement, due to the innate capabilities of the available middleware and batch systems.

However, in data Grid environments, which are conceived for the processing of huge amounts of information such as experimental data from high-energy physics, the accounting of storage occupation and eventually data access is paramount to both Grid users and resource providers.

Storage accounting is still mostly a research and development issue and the underlying Grid middleware, responsible for the storage facilities, didn't focus so far on providing reliable usage information to the accounting middleware. This however is rapidly going to change as, for example, recent versions of data management middleware components and standards, such as storage resource management (SRM), provide native support for accounting. For these reasons few storage accounting solutions are currently available, and their capabilities are still limited.

One example is the storage accounting solution provided by the EGEE GOC Web portal[20] that simply reports usage statistics, taken as periodic snapshots of the storage space occupied by the single VOs (hence being closely related to monitoring). The solution is based on ad hoc configurations of the operating system of the Grid storage elements (the Grid nodes used to archive huge amounts of data), without the aim of greater flexibility (no user-level storage accounting) and deployability beyond the scope of EGEE.

A more general approach is followed by the Storage Accounting for Grid Environments (SAGE) project,[21] whose aim is to implement an accounting system, with an architecture inspired by DGAS, to collect storage accounting information with a granularity of single files stored on storage elements, and with enough information to assign storage usage to specific Grid users.

Both projects, however, are still in the prototype phase and not yet ready for a production use.

9.3 FUTURE RESEARCH DIRECTIONS

Although the accounting of resource usage, at least regarding CPU resources, has made significant progress, there are still some open issues that may pose problems in market-oriented Grid and utility computing.

In a commercial Grid environment, it may be necessary, or at least desired, to charge users not only for consumed, but also for requested and reserved resources. Current Grid accounting systems, however, have focused only on keeping track of resource consumption and offer no possibility to do so for resource reservation. In the future, when advance reservation of resources will be extensively used in production Grids, the accounting and ultimately charging of reserved resources will likely become a major topic.

[20] See http://goc02.grid-support.ac.uk/storage-accounting/.

[21] See http://gilda-forge.ct.infn.it/projects/sage/.

Apart from resource reservation accounting, a more generic framework for resource usage accounting will have to be developed as well, since it is likely that future service-oriented infrastructures will provide more and more value-added services instead of only "raw" resources such as computational power and storage space. Service-oriented computing not only will be of importance in a commercial context but may also have a significant impact on scientific research [29].

In principle, even the utilization of high-level Grid middleware services required in complex, geographically distributed computational Grids—such as resource brokers (metaschedulers), interactive Web portals, and user interfaces—could be accounted and charged for. However, up to now the tracing of provided Grid middleware services is not covered by the available Grid accounting systems.

The standardization of interfaces to Grid accounting systems will require further research work to extend the already existing OGF specifications (UR and RUS) to non-CPU resources and beyond single atomic usage records toward a proper handling of aggregated information. Moreover, standard interfaces for billing/charging and payment mechanisms will be required for future market-oriented Grid computing environments, but have so far not been addressed by the Grid standardization bodies.

Meaningful normalization procedures for usage data originating from heterogeneous resources and service instances will have to be defined for the purpose of aggregating accounting information to accurate usage statistics. For this purpose the research on appropriate benchmarks for Grid computing resources, although currently often considered secondary, will be of particular importance.

A more acute issue is related to so-called pilot jobs that are being submitted by many VOs of large-scale Grid infrastructures (e.g., EGEE/LCG and OSG) more recently. These jobs are placeholders that, when running on a worker node of a Grid site, exploit as much runtime as they can by fetching one "true" job after the other from a remote task queue owned by the VO. This poses a particular problem to resource usage accounting, since an accounting system recognizes only the initial pilot job and associates it with the user certificate subject with which the pilot was submitted. The accounting procedure is not aware that the pilot executes several other jobs (most probably even from different users) and hardly can obtain detailed usage information. The site (and hence the Grid accounting system) has only the summary information for the entire pilot job with all its user tasks, but no detailed information on how much resources have been consumed by each single task. Many VOs have therefore agreed to provide the sites with information on whose jobs are being executed by a pilot job and how long these jobs run. Such an approach, however, seems to contradict the very meaning of accounting on a computing platform, since the resource provider no longer tells the user what has been consumed; rather, the user (or the VO) tells the resource provider; thus, the roles have been reversed.

9.4 CONCLUSIONS

In this chapter we presented issues related to Grid accounting, intended as the tracking of resource usage by Grid users, and explained its fundamental importance for successfully establishing computational economies and accurate billing and charging mechanisms. We have described different architectural approaches to Grid accounting, the frequencies at which usage information can be metered and collected, as well as the most important requirements that market-oriented Grid computing poses on accounting systems.

Particular emphasis was placed on issues that are often overlooked by current research on Grid accounting, namely, the normalization of usage data and the standardization of accounting interfaces. In a heterogeneous distributed computing environment, and even more so between collaborating Grid infrastructures based on different middleware stacks, however, the importance of these issues must not be underestimated.

Most current practices regard the accounting of computational jobs, that is, the usage of processing power and related resources (such as the memory occupied by a job). Only first, preliminary steps toward storage accounting have been taken. Nonetheless, a more generic approach will be necessary for service-oriented infrastructures that offer a growing number of value-added computational services.

Although Grid accounting has come far, it has not yet come far enough to accommodate all future use cases, and much more effort in research, standardization and implementation will be necessary before it can fulfill all requirements of general-purpose market-oriented Grid computing.

REFERENCES

1. R. Buyya, D. Abramson, and S. Venugopal, The Grid economy, *Proceedings of the IEEE* **93**(3):698–714 (2005).
2. C. Ernemann, V. Hamscher, and R. Yahyapour, Economic scheduling in Grid computing, *Lecture Notes in Computer Science* **2537**:128–152 (2002).
3. T. Eymann et al., Catallaxy-based Grid markets, *Multiagent and Grid Systems* **1**(4): 297–307 (2005).
4. J. Shneidman et al., Why markets could (but don't currently) solve resource allocation problems in systems, *Proc. 10th Conf. Hot Topics in Operating Systems* (*HotOS X*), Santa Fe, NM, June 2005.
5. W. Thigpen, T. J. Hacker, L. F. McGinnis, and B. D. Athey, Distributed accounting on the Grid, *Proc. 6th Joint Conf. Information Sciences*, Durham, NC, March 2002.
6. R. Wolski, J. S. Plank, J. Brevik, and T. Bryan, Analyzing market-based resource allocation strategies for the computational Grid, *International Journal of High Performance Computing Applications* **15**(3):258–281 (2001).
7. R. Woslki, J. Brevik, J. S. Plank, and T. Bryan, Grid resource allocation and control using computational economies, in *Grid Computing: Making the Global Infrastructure a Reality*, F. Berman, G. Fox, and A. Hey, eds., Wiley, 2003.
8. R. M. Piro, A. Guarise, and A. Werbrouck, Simulation of price-sensitive resource brokering and the hybrid pricing model with DGAS-Sim, *Proc. 13th International Workshops on Enabling Technologies: Infrastructures for Collaborative Enterprises* (*WETICE 2004*), Modena, Italy, June 2004.

9. R. M. Piro, A. Guarise, and A. Werbrouck, Price-sensitive resource brokering with the hybrid pricing model and widely overlapping price domains, *Concurrency and Computation: Practice and Experience* **18**(8):837–850 (2006).
10. A. B. Downey, Predicting queue times on space-sharing parallel computers, *Proc. 11th International Parallel Processing Symp.*, Geneva, Switzerland, April 1997.
11. W. Smith, I. Foster, and V. Taylor, Predicting application run times using historical information, *Lecture Notes in Computer Science* **1459**:122–142 (1998).
12. V. Ciaschini et al., An integrated framework for VO-oriented authorization, policy-based management and accounting, *Proc. Conf. Computing in High Energy and Nuclear Physics* (*CHEP'06*), TIFR, Mumbai, India, Feb. 2006.
13. R. M. Piro, Resource usage accounting in Grid computing, in *Handbook of Research on Grid Technologies and Utility Computing: Concepts for Managing Large-Scale Applications*, E. Udoh and F. Wang, eds., Information Science Reference (Idea Group Publishing), Hershey, PA, 2009.
14. P. Schnellmann and A. Redard, *Accounting for the Authentication and Authorization Infrastructure (AAI)—Pilot Study*, Technical Report, SWITCH (The Swiss Education & Research Network), Zurich, Switzerland, 2006.
15. C. Morariu, M. Waldburger, and B. Stille, *An Accounting and Charging Architecture for Mobile Grids*, Technical Report 2006.06, Dept. Informatics (IFI), Univ. Zurich, Switzerland, 2006.
16. T. Nissi and M. Silander, Electronic payment system for Grid services, *Proceedings 25th IASTED International Multi-Conf., Track on Parallel and Distributed Computing and Networks*, Innsbruck, Austria, Feb. 2006.
17. A. Barmouta and R. Buyya, GridBank: A Grid accounting service architecture (GASA) for distributed systems sharing and integration, *Proc. 17th Annual International Parallel and Distributed Processing Symp.*, Nice, France, April 2003.
18. C. Aiftimiei et al., Recent evolutions of GridICE: A monitoring tool for Grid systems, *Proc. 2007 Workshop on Grid Monitoring*, Monterey, CA, June 2007.
19. R. Müller-Pfefferkorn et al., Monitoring of jobs and their execution for the LHC computing Grid, *Proc. Cracow Grid Workshop (CGW 06)*, Cracow, Poland, Oct. 2006.
20. Byrom et al., APEL: An implementation of Grid accounting using R-GMA, *Proc. UK e-Science All Hands Conf.*, Nottingham, UK, Sept. 2005.
21. R. M. Piro, A. Guarise, and A. Werbrouck, An economy-based accounting infrastructure for the DataGrid, *Proc. 4th International Workshop on Grid Computing* Phoenix, AZ, Nov. 2003, pp. 202–204.
22. T. Sandholm et al., An OGSA-based accounting system for allocation enforcement across HPC centers, *Proc. 2nd International Conf. Service Oriented Computing*, New York, Nov. 2004.
23. M. L. Chen et al., The design and prototype of RUDA, a distributed Grid accounting system, *Lecture Notes in Computer Science* **3482**:29–38 (2005).
24. R. Alfieri et al., From gridmap-file to VOMS: Managing authorization in a Grid environment, *Future Generation Computer Systems* **21**(4):549–558 (2005).
25. R. M. Piro et al., Tracing resource usage over heterogeneous Grid platforms: A prototype RUS interface for DGAS, *Proc. 3rd IEEE International Conf. e-Science and Grid Computing 2007, Bangalore*, India, Dec. 2007.

26. R. Mach et al., *Usage Record—Format Recommendation*, version 1, GDF.98, Open Grid Forum, 2006, (available from http://www.ogf.org/documents/GFD.98.pdf).

27. J. Ainsworth, S. Newhouse, and J. MacLaren, *Resource Usage Service* (*RUS*) *based on WS-I Basic Profile 1.0*, Open Grid Forum, 2006 (available from http://forge.ogf.org/sf/go/doc7965?nav=1).

28. P. H. Beckman, Building the TeraGrid, *Philosophical Transactions of the Royal Society A* **363**:1715–1728 (2005).

29. I. Foster, Service-oriented science, *Science* **308**:814–817 (2005).

PART III

POLICIES AND AGREEMENTS

10

SERVICE-LEVEL AGREEMENTS (SLAs) IN THE GRID ENVIRONMENT

BASTIAN KOLLER, EDUARDO OLIVEROS, AND ALFONSO SÁNCHEZ-MACIAN

10.1 INTRODUCTION

With the advent of electronic business (e-business), service-level agreements (SLAs) become an essential tool for entities doing their business in an electronic environment.

Service-level agreements have already been used in business, but usually in another context. Usually these SLAs are simple documents (parts of contracts) and handled manually.

The direction of research in the SLA area has brought change to the Field of electronics with a focus on the automation of usage in a Grid environment. Basic research has focused on academic Grids, which severely limit the available technological implementation of SLAs. In contrast to the academic Grid, business Grids need stronger control mechanisms to maintain control over the states of services and the environments in which they are executed.

The usage of SLAs in e-business would be a valuable basis for service providers to offer and sell their services and to manage their resources. On the other hand, service consumers would be able to use SLAs to formalize guarantees on service quality properties and to have support mechanisms pursuing their business goals.

As mentioned before, the e-business movement implies a departure from the manual handling of the SLA lifecycle. Contracts, and with them, SLAs, currently not only are written and agreed on by humans (and thus involve human interaction) but also have to be translated into technical terms to produce SLAs for managing the system. In the future, SLAs are expected to be commonplace in all business

Market-Oriented Grid and Utility Computing Edited by Rajkumar Buyya and Kris Bubendorfer

transactions, and thus it will be impossible to still handle everything manually in the Grid environment. Many research activities in the Grid environment are currently concentrating on automation of the SLA lifecycle, and while this research continues, a set of issues have been identified that have to be overcome before automated service-level agreement management is possible.

This chapter concentrates on the overall SLA lifecycle and a set of side issues with respect to the usage of service-level agreements in e-business that have already been identified and are of great importance. Starting with a short section on the background and related work with respect to SLAs, a walk through the SLA lifecycle follows preparing the basis for a set of thoughts with respect to single aspects of SLA usage and management in Grid environments. The chapter concludes with an outlook for future research directions for SLAs and then a summary is given before the concluding section gives a topics of the addressed in this chapter.

10.2 BACKGROUND AND RELATED WORK

Before we start our excursion into the life of a service-level agreement, we should have a look at the current developments in the SLA research area. There are two (more or less) competing specifications: The WS-agreement [26] and the Web Service-Level Agreement Language (WSLA) [27].

The Web Services Agreement Specification (WS-agreement) is a Web services protocol for publishing and establishing quality-of-service (Qos) agreements between two parties in a provider–consumer relationship. WS-Agreement focuses more on protocols and extending Web services with the according functionalities than on provisioning of a SLA language. It is developed by the Grid Resource Allocation Agreement Protocol (GRAAP)-WG [22] at OGF [22], which is attempting to make it a standard.

The main objective of the WSLA [27] is to provide a framework and a technology for monitoring and evaluation of SLAs. It is based on a language schema that was developed to enable the parties involved to define service parameters and statements about the QoS, as well as terms of contracts such as penalties and benefits.

On the basis of the usability of the both WS-agreement and WSLA specifications, IBM made an initial attempt to combine them into one specification. However, these activities seem discontinued, and WSLA has not been updated for a long time. Thus it seems that WS-agreement is the only one currently alive.

Having this small amount of specifications available, a set of research projects are dealing or have dealt with enhancements of the current state of the art of service-level agreements. These projects focus on either developments of single components of the lifecycle of an SLA or the overall lifecycle itself. Examples of these projects are BREIN [21], NextGRID [28], GRIA [29], TrustCoM [29], or AssessGrid [].

Providing comprehensive insight into all these projects (those mentioned above are only a subset of all projects dealing with SLAs) would exceed the scope of this chapter. We restrict ourselves here to describing in detail only those projects that are closely related to the topics discussed in this chapter.

10.3 THE LIFECYCLE OF A SERVICE-LEVEL AGREEMENT

As mentioned in previous sections, a service-level agreement is a document that specifies components of an electronic contract. It can be represented in different ways, some of which facilitate its management, storage, and use in automated and (in best-case scenarios) autonomous systems.

To understand the implications of using SLAs in a Grid environment, and also to select the appropriate format, it is crucially important to know its lifecycle, including the different functions where it is used and the different operations in which it is involved. Thus, the SLA lifecycle is discussed extensively in the following text.

10.3.1 A Scenario

Understanding the SLA lifecycle is much easier, when relating it to specific a scenario.

Jim is leading a small company that is responsible for designing parts of airplane seats (e.g., armrests). After some time spent collaborating with other seat designers, Jim gets the offer to take over the design and construction of the entire airplane seats. This means an important extension of Jim's business field, and at the same time a major responsibility because agreeing on this offer means a guarantee that this task will be fulfilled. Accepting this would imply that Jim's company needs many more resources to do computing calculations (e.g., ergonomic concerns such as the shape of seats, comfort, electronic equipment in the seats, and related costs) than needed before, exceeding the capabilities of Jim's existing infrastructure. Therefore Jim has two options:

- Invest more money to extend the infrastructure.
- Search for a service provider offering available capacities to outsource tasks.

As this is the first time that Jińs company receives such an offer and he has no knowledge about the exact complexity as well as the future possibilities (benefit) to provide such a service, he chooses the second option and searches for a service provider offering the required service.

10.3.2 The Different Phases of the SLA Lifecycle

The complete lifecycle of an SLA for BREIN foresees the following phases:

- Development of service and SLA templates
- Discovery and negotiation of an SLA
- Service provisioning and deployment
- Execution of the service
- Assessment and corrective actions during execution (a phase parallel to execution of the service)
- Termination and decommission of the service

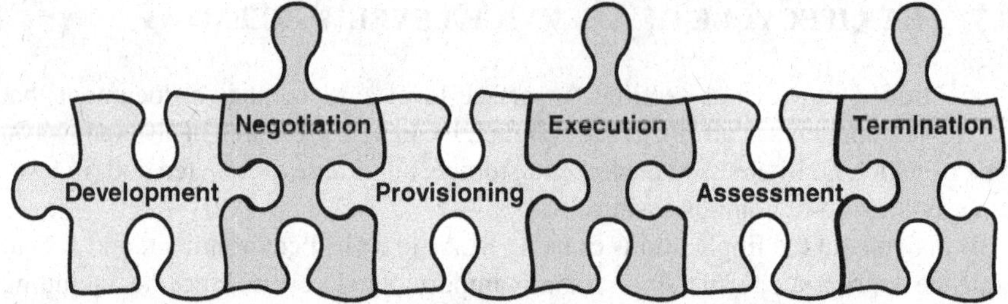

Figure 10.1 The SLA lifecycle in puzzle format.

There is still ongoing discussion as to whether the creation of a service and SLA template that identifies and defines the nonfunctional QoS attributes and the price (having a strong impact on all later stages of the SLA lifecycle, including negotiation, monitoring, and service provisioning) should be part of the lifecycle or whether is it a predecessor of the lifecycle. We see it as a part of the lifecycle as depicted in Figure 10.1.

The main capabilities pursued by the SLA management layer are

- Publication of services and their capabilities
- Establishing contractual bindings—service-level agreements
- Provisioning of the service
- Supervision, monitoring, and evaluation of the SLA parameters

10.3.3 A Walk through the Life of an SLA

It all starts with a service provider offering a service. In our case, the service provider is Bob, who is the boss of a high-performance computing center that is offering calculation power to external customers. As Bob wants to make moneys, he decides to enter the world of electronic business, which provides him better and more optimal sells of his capacities.

10.3.3.1 Development of Service and SLA Templates. To enter this world, the service provider (Bob) has to represent his service by a corresponding service-level agreement template (SLA template), containing the properties (parameters) of his offered service. By using that, he is able to give a first impression on his capabilities and business fields to the potential customers.

In general, it is worth mentioning that the numbers of SLA templates created and published are not automatically the same. As in real-life business, the business entity providing a service may decide to offer special variations of a service (special parameters, price, etc.) to a group of "special" customers only. This means that templates are created in advance, with special terms (e.g., the price could be lower for best customers) and published only inside the service provider domain.

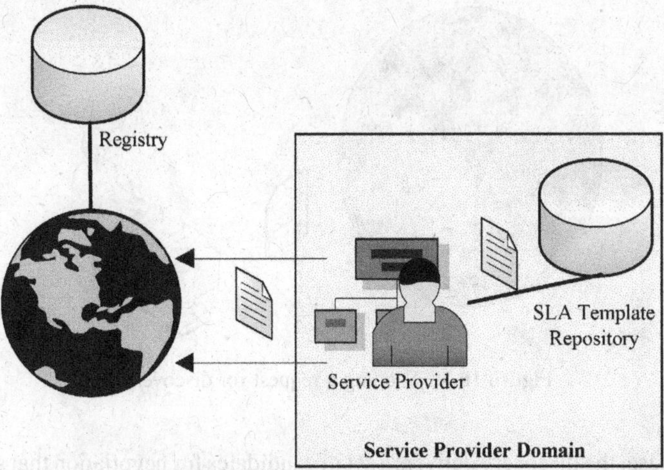

Figure 10.2 Publication of a service.

A complementary approach is based on the customer publishing requirements to a set of trusted providers and those providers receiving the request and publishing their SLA templates in the customer domain.

So, the first phase of the SLA lifecycle, "development of service and SLA templates," is based on marketing the service.

Figure 10.2 shows the publication process for a service developed by a service provider. For that purpose the SLA template is stored in an external database acting as a service registry for the outside world. This approach is similar to the "yellow pages" approach. All SLA templates are also stored in the service provider's domain SLA template repository. Additionally or alternatively, the service provider can publish those SLA templates in a place with access restricted to specific customers, such as the customer domain or a special area in the service provider domain.

10.3.3.2 Discovery and Negotiation of an SLA. The second phase of the SLA lifecycle covers the creation of an agreement, starting from the discovery of matching business partners to the negotiation about detailed terms of the SLA and the signature of the binding document at the end.

10.3.3.2.1 Discovery. Our company owner Jim is searching for a possibility to outsource his calculations. Having in mind his companies' capabilities, Jim can easily define what he needs from a service provider. By defining this request in a document format, he can use discovery services to search for the respective matching service providers (Fig. 10.3). In this chapter we do not the format of this request in great detail, as several projects such as NextGRID and TrustCoM have addressed this issue in documents available to the public (see also Ref. 31).

The search for matching service providers can be performed by a discovery service that is either sitting on the side of the customer (which again means an investment for installing and maintaining this service) or is offered by a third party.

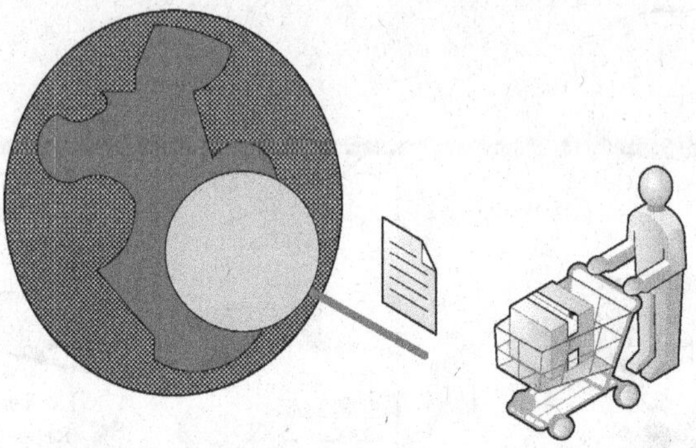

Figure 10.3 Sending a request for discovery.

In our case, the discovery delivers a set of candidates for negotiation that should be able (according to their SLA templates) to fulfill Jim's request. Among others, Bob is one of these candidates and (by surprise) he has the best-fitting service, so Jim decides to start negotiating with him.

10.3.3.2.2 Negotiation. Currently the negotiation of a service-level agreement is a widely discussed topic in several communities. At first, measures were taken to specify a protocol for SLA negotiation (e.g., WS-Agreement Negotiation) but were never released and accepted as a complete specification as there is still ongoing discussion about the flexibility of the protocol.

Two different main approaches are currently competing with each other:

- *The Discrete-Offer Protocol.* This "take it or leave it" approach represents a rather limited approach to negotiation as it consists of one offer to the customer and its decision as to whether to accept it (it's up to discussion as to whether this is in fact a negotiation). This is the approach of fixed prices for fixed quality of services; for example, a phone card for 25 euros is worth 25 euros and is sold for 25 euros. There is no negotiation possible. The positive aspect of this protocol is that the service provider quickly knows whether the business will be done. Imagine Bob offering Jim the service. To guarantee that Jim can use the service offered, Bob has to reserve his resources for him until he gets an accept/decline message. If in this case negotiation would take long, this could have an implication on the availability of resources for parallel negotiations with other customers, as surely Jim is not the only customer who wants something from Bob.
- *Multiphase (n-Phase) Negotiation.* In contrast to the discrete-offer protocol, the multiphase (n-phase, where n denotes the number of rounds) protocol assumes that there could be several rounds of negotiation. A customer asking for a service with special properties receives gets an offer from a service provider with different term values (parameters) and changes them again in order to send another request for an offer. Theoretically, this could last for an infinite duration,

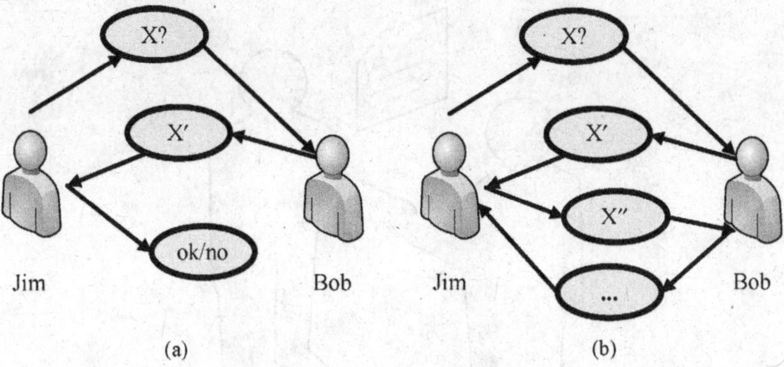

Figure 10.4 Discrete offer (a) versus multiphase negotiation (b).

which is the chief concern of those opposed to this approach. On the other side, it gives both business entities the chance to get to their best solution (compare this with the Turkish bazaar). Of course, the implication of this model is that if the service provider decides to reserve resources for the customer, he runs into danger of blocking his resources until the end of negotiation. But this is a decision that is up to the provider himself (if he takes the risk to block resources or if he takes the risk to offer resources without blocking them) and depending on his business model.

Nevertheless, initiatives are also on their way to assuming that both cases are special instances of one more widespread protocol (imagine a discrete offer being an n-phase negotiation protocol where $n = 0$). As mentioned before, in some cases one or the other approach would be helpful or simply not sensible to use for creation of an agreement. Imagine Jim needing the service immediately, which means that he surely does not want to discuss hours or days with Bob about this. However, if Jim needs the service in 5 h from now, he would be more relaxed and open to spend some time finding a good and cheap solution.

This shows that the best solution would be to give the parties a certain degree of freedom to decide whether they want one more round of negotiations.

It is very important to mention that during the SLAs negotiations all parties involved in the business have obligations to reach an agreement; this includes the service provider and also the customer. These obligations are represented, of course, in terms of payment and penalties but also in other aspects such as licensing, where a service provider provides software but the customer has to have the license to use it.

Each of these obligations can be represented in multiple versions; for instance, payment could be on a lump-sum basis or split up into monthly or weekly installments, with bonuses awarded for completion ahead of schedule or for quality exceeding the level of QoS expected. Besides penalty clauses, there could also possibly be "benefit" clauses, for higher Qos and faster turnaround; these terms have to be considered carefully. Stating and agreeing on these terms requires complex calculations but at the same time allows for fine-tuning of the agreement to gain the

Figure 10.5 An agreement has been reached.

best benefit for both. A complete excursus of this topic would be beyond the limits of this chapter; however, raising this topic should indicate that the topic of SLA has now reached a level of maturity (at least on the theoretical layer), which more closely approaches real-life business—and that real-life business is, indeed, a complex area.

Independent of the approach taken, this negotiation phase ends with either an agreement or a negotiation stop. In the latter case, negotiation with other service providers continues until an agreement is reached. But in our case, Jim and Bob found a consensus and now sign the contract to make it valid. Note that usually the term *service-level agreement* formally applies only after both parties have signed it.

In our case we assumed that only Bob and Jim are represented when the agreement is negotiated and signed. Previously finalized project such as TrustCoM have dealt with real-world approaches allowing for the involvement of a trusted third party acting in an optional role of a notary. This suggestion has been raised with respect to the trustworthiness of partners in a business relationship.

Other factors to keep in mind are legal and validity issues, discussed in Section 10.4.1. The legal validity of SLAs is still a research topic, and it is not yet completely clear when an SLA is legally valid (e.g., this depends on the negotiation protocol involved). This means that SLAs currently might not have attained the status of being valid contracts in a law court, depending on the procedure followed and the legislation of the particular country.

This concludes the second phase of the SLA lifecycle; a contract has been created containing boundaries for both service provider and service customer. But what happens now at Bob's company, in his domain? This directly leads to the third phase of the lifecycle.

10.3.3.3 Service Provisioning and Deployment. Jim has agreed to a SLA with Bob. From Bob's perspective, this implies that he can use the service with the conditions stated in the document. On the other side, Bob has to ensure that Jim can use the service as agreed, meaning that he has to prepare his system until it is ready for use.

This implies the configuration and reservation of resources as well as the configuration of internal mechanisms, which is helpful to control the execution of the service and to support the service provider and customer to optimize the benefits from this business. This is done mainly by close monitoring during the execution time and the evaluation of the respective monitored data.

More theoretical background on these mechanisms is presented below, describing execution, assessment, and the corrective-action phase in the SLA lifecycle.

10.3.3.4 Execution of the Service. The execution of the service is the phase that decides the success or failure of an SLA. It is now time to deliver this service and to provide anything that is necessary to satisfy the users needs to finally achieve the common goal of keeping within the agreed-on terms. So the most important action for Bob here is to provide and execute Jim's services, but Jim must also fulfill his obligations as stated in the agreement (if any are stated).

Therefore, both service provider and customer must always be aware of what is happening during execution of the service. Thus, the approaches of monitoring and evaluation of the service (with respect to the SLA) are essential mechanisms that are needed in an electronic environment to ensure the success of the business performed. These are assessment methods, which are executed in a parallel running lifecycle phase.

10.3.3.5 Assessment and Corrective Actions during Execution. During the runtime of a service, it is crucially important for the service provider to maintain control over what is happening inside his/her domain and it is equally important for the customer to obtain knowledge about the status of the service, when needed (usually within the SLA defined time intervals, milestones, etc.). This means that activities that are parallel to the execution of the service are needed to ensure support for both business entities.

10.3.3.5.1 Monitoring. Monitoring is an important action, which is needed to control the status and the performance during execution of the service. It is necessary for providing at any time, data related to the service-level agreement that can be evaluated to gain insight into service-specific information such as whether

- The service status is in line with the agreed-on values (e.g., at halfway through the runtime, whether the progress level is also around 50%, etc.)
- All required resources are working

At this point it is important to distinguish monitoring from evaluation of the data. The monitoring task itself does *not* evaluate the data. This means that it is configured according to the SLA but does not know what the monitored data means with respect to the accepted terms and the system/service status.

10.3.3.5.2 Evaluation. Evaluation is the process where the monitored data are reviewed with respect to the SLA and the results are rated. In theory, there are two different types of evaluation possible depending on the business entity that wants to evaluate: internal evaluation and external evaluation.

With *internal evaluation* is the service provider internally watches what is happening in the system and with the service. With respect to the SLA, Bob in our case can define metrics on the basis of plain monitored data, which are retrieved by the SLA monitor. Inside the service provider this is no problem, because Bob is allowed to access the plain system data without any limitation due to confidentiality issues (this is discussed further in Example 10.1). Whenever the evaluator detects unfavorable behavior of the system (which is not necessarily limited to a violation of the contract that has already occurred), measures have to be taken to adapt the system in such a way that will still meet the terms of the SLA (if possible; see also Section 10.3.3.5.3).

A special case of internal evaluation is the evaluation with respect to a so-called preventive SLA. The difference between the original SLA and the preventive SLA is that the latter one has adjusted values of the terms, which are used to evaluate the status for potential future violations of the SLA. Using thresholds for the terms, Bob could specify critical values that, when reached, create events inside the system that prevent the contract violation by adjusting the system accordingly to meet the requirements (if possible).

On the other hand, *external evaluation* takes place outside (as the term implies) of the domain of the service provider and raises with it some issues with respect to confidentiality issues. This evaluation can be performed by the customer (Jim) itself or by a trusted third-party evaluator, which is then bound with another contract to Jim.

In principle, this kind of evaluation is similar to the normal case of internal evaluation, with one major difference—the monitored data. In the case of external evaluation, it has to be clear that no service provider wants a customer to gain access to the plain system data or the detailed metrics that are used inside. This means that an external evaluation process has to obtain the data in a format where the plain data are rendered anonymous and are represented in a usable form to relate them to the SLA.

Figure 10.6 shows examples for the different but parallel viewpoints evaluated internally and externally. In this case for Jim everything seems to be quite OK, while Bob is aware of upcoming problems and now has to take care to prevent it.

This is where the concept of corrective action during the service runtime comes into play.

10.3.3.5.3 Corrective Action. Whenever the service or the system environment is malfunctioning or misbehaving, anything should be changed in the domain (unless the customer has misbehaved, which rarely is the case). This means that a clear analysis has to be performed to determine what has happened and countermeasures have to be created and executed to bring the system or service back on track.

Such countermeasures could be manifold. Two examples are presented here.

Figure 10.6 Examples of external evaluation and internal evaluation.

Example 10.1: Replacement of a Misbehaving Resource by Another One from the Service Provider's System. This can take place, for instance when Bob has other resources left that could salvage the task from failure. For example, imagine a simple requirements statement in the SLA such as "I want four CPUs during the whole service execution." This is a clear statement, and when Bob fails to provide all four assigned CPUs because one fails, it's a problem. A corrective action here would be to add another CPU from Bob's system. If this is not possible, another countermeasure could be possible (Example 10.2).

Example 10.2: Replacement of a Misbehaving Resource by One from Another Service Provider. This can happen if Bob's system is fully used (exhausted) and there is no alternative resource left. This would mean a new SLA between Bob and another service provider, but this would also depend on a cost calculation of the penalties for failure to fulfill the SLA with costs for buying in an additional resource.

It is worth mentioning that all these corrective actions used in realizations need human interactions for decisionmaking. Retrieving, calculating, and/or creating these actions requires in-depth knowledge of the business background (business-level objectives) of the provider, the system status, and so on.

Currently running projects in the European Community (EC) are dealing with the automation of these internal corrective actions, e.g. the Framework Program 6 IST (Information Society Technologies) project BREIN (business-objective-driven reliable and intelligent Grids for real business). BREIN plans to enhance the Grid as it exists today with concepts from the semantic Web and multiagent domain. By combining the flexibility and stability of Grid technologies with the intelligence and adaptability of artificial-intelligence (AI) systems (as developed for multiagents) and with knowledge technologies from the semantic Web area, BREIN will enable individuals and business entities to provide and handle their services in a controlled and "easy to handle" environment that allows intelligent and optimal management of the respective resources according to the individual business goals/constraints and to react intelligently to changes in the service environments.

One issue with respect to violations, which is seldom really addressed by adequate systems or theoretical studies, is the intentional violation of an SLA, if it is in the interest of a provider. Suppose that Bob is doing business with Jim, and everything is working well. During the execution of Jim's service Bob gets an interesting offer from a huge company that offers to pay generously, but he now faces the problem that this job could not be fulfilled with the remaining available resources. But looking at his system, Bob sees that with some of the resources used by Jim he could manage to do the job for the big player. So, what are Bob's options? These might include

- Rejecting the request from the big company and losing the opportunity to enter business dealings with them.
- Renegotiating an agreement with Jim that covers fewer resources or other changes in the SLA terms.
- Accepting the request and intentionally taking the risk (if it is only a risk) of violating the SLA with Jim (or maybe others as well). This implies a good calculation on the service providers' side taking into account benefits and penalties for actions that will be taken.

During the whole execution process, a close linkage to accounting and billing processes is necessary, supported by logging functions to enable execution of the business also in a cash-flow-related manner. This implies that all events occurring, that could trigger monetary actions (e.g., charging penalties for the number of violations that have occurred), which has to be factored in at the end of the SLA lifecycle:

10.3.3.6 Termination and Decommission of the Service. The last phase of the SLA lifecycle is the termination and decommission of the service. The termination could occur at two points:

- The service ends "normally," which implies that it has satisfied the SLA, with tasks performed on schedule and delivered with the required quality of service. Usually an SLA has a validity duration, which could be also an exit condition, when no explicit target outcome of the service was defined.
- The service ends during its execution because of a violation of the SLA when reaching a terminating condition.

In both cases, a wrapup has to take place that activates final accounting and billing mechanisms, determining which party has to pay/charge and executing the payment processes. Additionally, the system configuration has to be reverted and Bob can free his resources from the boundaries to the SLA with Jim.

However, termination and decommission do *not* implicitly mean deletion of that SLA from the list of SLAs. These documents are usually stored for a while to provide a basis for future discussions, for statistical purposes, and for auditing (when audits occur).

10.4 VISIONARY THOUGHTS FOR PRACTITIONERS

10.4.1 Service-Level Agreements and Legal Implications

A service-level agreement (SLA) is part of the contract between a service provider and a customer. It includes the identification of the services being delivered, together with the agreed-on performance (quality) levels and other important clauses such as the obligations, duties, and responsibilities; the liability in terms of penalties; compensation; termination; and legal compliance. Considering the contract nature of an SLA, this implies that contract laws need to be considered when working with this type of agreement. Consequently, when moving to an electronic environment, such as Grid communication through computer networks, the generation of an SLA is covered by the regulation on electronic contracts.

The Internet allows service providers and customers from different countries to conduct business. As in any other international transaction, the commerce laws to be applied in this circumstance need to be clear. Different countries have different laws in relation to electronic contracts. Two sample cases are the European Union (EU) and the United States.

The EU have several directives that have been transposed to national legislation; especially noteworthy are the Electronic Commerce Directive and the Community Framework for Electronic Signatures Directive. In the United States, the Uniform Electronic Transaction Act (UETA) has been adopted by most of the states, the Uniform Computer Information Transaction Act (UCITA) is used by the other states, and the Electronic Signatures in Global and National Commerce Act (E-Sign) is a federal statute.

Having many divergent laws adds an extra barrier to the already complex electronic market. In this context, the United Nations Commission on International Trade Law (UNCITRAL) is trying to promote the United Nations Convention on the Use of Electronic Communications in International Contracts (already signed by a small number of countries) to remove obstacles to the use of electronic communications in international contracting. Previous documents published by this organization include the *Model Law on Electronic Commerce* and the *Model Law on Electronic Signatures*.

Thus, e-contracts are covered by legislation in many countries by giving validity to the use of electronic records in the contract formation and application of the electronic signature during this process. The electronic signature is accepted with differences between countries, as some of them (e.g., the EU) require the application of specific technologies in order to satisfy the same legal requirements as a handwritten signature. To enable the business entities to conduct transactions by electronic means, laws expect the different actors (contract participants) to follow a consent process that can be an electronic well-defined procedure (e.g., the EU) or a simple agreement between parties (e.g., the United States).

The approach for the formalization of an SLA in a Grid environment can involve a negotiation between two humans, human–software communication, or interactions between software agents. Additionally, contracts are usually studied from business–consumer (B2C) and business–business (B2B) perspectives. Each possible combination has unique legal implications, and the legislation does not always clearly cover all these cases. The focus of some laws is mainly on B2C transactions, but the law could be applied to B2B if the right of representation is considered when e-signatures are used.

The process for the formation of an electronic contract needs to be examined. The traditional phases in the creation of a contract are offer and acceptance. First, there is an unequivocal offer from an offeror to an offeree, and then the offeree communicates the acceptance to the offeror. When moving to electronic contracts, including SLAs in a Grid environment, there is a requirement in some legislation (e.g., in the EU) for including an additional step consisting in the acknowledgment of receipt by the offeror. It is also important to distinguish between "binding offers" and "invitations to deal," as, for instance, an SLA template published by a service provider in a public registry could be seen as a binding offer under Spanish or Danish laws, while it could be an invitation to offer under US law. This means that it must be clear which law would determine the nature of these communications (law from the service provider or consumer residence country). This would be done using the "choice of law" clause. Some supplementary requirements in terms of providing information to the customer before placing an order might need to be fulfilled when considering EU laws. This information relates to technical information to conclude contracts or amend errors or the storage and accessibility of the contract.

The most complex situation in negotiating SLA agreements occurs when this negotiation is done between two electronic agents. It is not clearly accepted in all the e-commerce laws. The UNCITRAL has stated that "A contract may be formed by the interaction of electronic agents of the parties, even if no individual was aware of or reviewed the electronic agents' actions or the resulting terms and agreements." A similar approach is followed in the US legislation. The European directives do not comment on this aspect; rather, they discuss it only if the agents are implicitly excluded or included and make this clear in the transposition (application) to each country (e.g., in Polish or Spanish laws). Usually, these electronic contracts are based on existing relationships between the different actors, which could have agreed on a framework specifying the format of the data exchange, inherently accepting the use of these agents.

An agent who is acting in these environments needs to identify the person who is liable for the offer, with the appropriate signature to indicate an intention to be bound to the contract terms and conditions. An additional problem for the agents is the "battle of forms" where the customer and provider suggest different terms for the contract. Negotiation is not easy in this case, and some laws (e.g., the US Uniform Commercial Code) allow participants to incorporate only those terms agreed to by both parties.

10.4.1.1 Addressing Legal Implications in Grid Projects. There have been several efforts to address these legal implications for the SLAs in Grid projects. Some of them are discussed in the following paragraphs.

Parkin et al. [5] present some suggestions to manage these legal issues in a European marketplace with an approach that tries to solve the problems from a service provider's perspective. The main ideas are based on considering the service provider as the offeree. This is not always possible, as stated before, because of the difference between laws when talking about binding offers and invitations to deal. To solve the battle-of-forms problem they suggest that the service provider publish different sets of boilerplate terms and conditions. The customer would choose one and would not have option of including any additional term or removing an existing one. One of the terms included in these sets would be the "choice of law" clause, which would be set by the service provider. To avoid any discrepancies between B2B and B2C scenarios, the service provider would consider that the European e-commerce directive could cover all of these interactions even if the businesses and professional bodies acting as consumers are not covered by the particular directive. The conclusion is that this proposal is oriented to satisfy the needs and solve any concerns of the service provider.

Mahler et al. [3] use a different method in the European-funded project TrustCoM. The focus of their work is in e-business collaboration in a virtual organization (VO). The contract model presented in TrustCoM is based on a preexisting relationship between the participants through an enterprise network (EN). All the businesses taking part in this network need to sign a contract establishing the basic rules of collaboration (virtual organizations). This contract can follow the traditional flow as it is signed only once for all the collaborations between partners in the network. The proposed contracts cover most of the legal issues presented such as the choice of law, liability, intellectual property rights (IPRs), or dispute settlement. A second level of contract is the VO level designed to agree on the Qos requirements and the access control to shared resources. To manage this second level of contracts automatically, a set of templates can be defined in the EN to ensure that every partner in the network has already read and accepted the general terms of the contract. The SLA agreement reached during the creation of a VO would be related to the previous existing EN contract and the VO contract templates.

GRIA [1] considers the preexistence of a bipartite relationship between the customer and the service provider as a trade account needs to be approved before signing any SLA. This means that all the legal terms have been already agreed to and signed before any SLA is created. This umbrella agreement must cover the transactions between both actors, including things such as liability, choice-of-law clauses, or IPRs. The approach would be similar to the one of TrustCoM, but considering one-to-one relationships instead of enterprise networks or VO contracts. GRIA does not constrain the nature of this framework agreement, allowing e-commerce operators to use the more appropriate mechanism in every case.

10.4.2 SLAs and Quality Perspectives: The Tower of Babel

When selecting the Qos parameters and defining the service-level objectives to include in an SLA, it is important to understand the meaning of the term *quality* according to the different perspectives of the different stakeholders and actors (see Fig. 10.7).

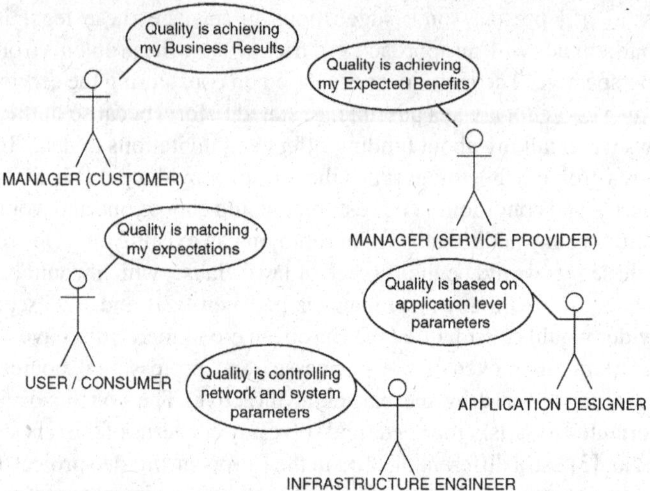

Figure 10.7 Quality and the Tower of Babel.

Imagine an animation studio that wants to use the resources of a service provider to render the new sequel of a famous movie. The following is an analysis of some of the different ideas of quality:

- *Customer Quality of Business.* The customer-side project manager states that the Qos depends on how it contributes to get the film produced in a particular deadline and meeting the goals specified in the business case (e.g., increase the number of people attending the cinema to watch this film while comparing it to the previous one).
- *Service Provider Quality of Business.* A manager working for a service provider organization will evaluate the quality of the service in terms of how that service helps in achieving their business objectives, which could be related to maximizing the benefits (e.g., giving priority to customers who spend more money), enhancing one's reputation, or attracting new customers.
- *Application-Level Technical Quality of Service.* From an application designer's perspective, the quality should be measured on the basis of the application-specific parameters such as the number of frames processed per second.
- *Low-Level Technical Quality of Service.* The infrastructure engineer at the service provider's side is convinced about the quality of service being a set of low-level parameters to be monitored and kept between certain thresholds, such as CPU time and memory consumption.
- *Quality of Experience.* A user evaluates the service as a combination of the objective and subjective (expectations) components. Quality includes the response time, but also factors such as ease of use. Economic models based on surveys have been adapted or created to study user expectations and perception in information systems.

All these perspectives turn the whole picture into a Tower of Babel that needs to be sorted out. The parameters and objectives included in the Grid SLAs should address all these approaches to quality in different ways, by mapping between different levels of quality, adding clauses to the SLA related to the user experience (such as time taken to solve a support request) or connecting the business rule engines to the policy-based management systems.

10.5 FUTURE RESEARCH DIRECTIONS

The SLA has been identified as a fundamental component for adoption of the Grid in the enterprise. It is an essential for creating confidence between customers and service providers. However, SLAs still show some downsides that can slow down adoption of the Grid. Current implementations of SLA management and negotiation are very static in several aspects: (1) the process of finding a suitable service provider is based on syntactical matching of strings (operation, SLO parameters, warranties, and penalties); and (2) during the service discovery process the client does not have information about the nonfunctional characteristics of the service until the negotiation starts, which means that the QoS of the service is discovered during the negotiation. Furthermore, the current implementations lack for a major automation in the process, human intervention is usually required at certain points of the negotiation process.

In addition, GRAAP-WG is working on WS-Agreement negotiation but, at the moment, there is no establish/standardize negotiation protocol (WS-agreement has been designed independently of any negotiation model and does not define concrete negotiation protocols). This affects the availability of interoperable solutions that can be broadly used by companies in an open marketplace to negotiate SLAs.

All these negative aspects can be further improved owing to the utilization of semantic Web and multiagent systems.

10.5.1 Use of the Semantic Web in SLA

The value of applying semantic Web technologies to the information and knowledge in Grid applications was immediately apparent [13]. This close relationship between the semantic Web and Grid has led to the definition of the semantic Grid, which uses the semantic Web to improve several aspects of the Grid such as workflow creation, service discovery, and SLA management.

The basic idea behind the use of the semantic Web is to provide meaningful concepts that permit a common understanding of the various aspects of SLA to the different parties (computers and humans) participating in the process; in this way programs can automatically reason over SLAs.

In that sense, in order to achieve efficient semantic matches, Oldham et al. [14] have extended the original WS-Agreement schema with several additional tags. The new tags allow for the incorporation of semantics into the WS-Agreement and add additional structure for clarity during parsing and matching and also apply rules to define the policies for the selection of the service providers on the basis of the information in the SLA. This permits a major capacity to understand, automate, and improve the negotiation of SLAs.

Another approach, followed by Frankova et al. [23], consists in converting the WS-Agreement in an ontology and using agents for the automatic negotiation that allows (1) early warnings before agreement violation and (2) negotiation and possibly renegotiation of running agreements.

We need to consider that to be effective in a global B2B scenario, there are two prerequisites:

1. The SLA should contain terms that are related only to business-level objectives (BLOs) to ensure that deployment and management details of a service are hidden by virtualization in the provider's domain and therefore should not be expressed in the SLA [15]. Current SLAs are too focused on the low-level infrastructure values, but companies are interested in high-level business objectives that are difficult to map with these low-level values.
2. For the semantic Web to succeed, a common and generic ontology for SLA and particular ontologies for specific industrial sectors are required to be publicly available; some efforts have begun in that direction [16].

10.5.2 Multiagent System for SLA Negotiation and Monitoring

Multiagent systems have two main characteristics than are interesting to SLA management and negotiation process: the capacity to reach agreements on complex agent communities and the ability to react to unexpected changes.

The use of the negotiation capabilities has been studies in several projects as a way to improve the SLA negotiation process. In OntoGrid [17], a combination of semantic Web and multiagent systems has been used for task/resource allocation and coordination, which will enable processes to reason about these activities in a meaningful way.

In terms of the agent's protocols employed for negotiation, the contract-net protocol has been used in several initiatives [17–20] to perform the negotiation of SLA. The contract-net protocol resembles protocols that companies usually follow to reach an agreement. Instead of using the traditional Web services schema (where the service provider publishes its offer in a repository and the customer searches for possible service providers that match its needs), in the contract-net protocol is the customer, who publishes its need or problem and the service providers, who provide bids to the customers. This protocol allows service providers to adapt their bids to the current state of the infrastructure [18]. The iterated contract-net interaction protocol (ICNIP) is another FIPA protocol that can be considered. This protocol supports recursive negotiation and allows for multiround iterative negotiation to find an outcome.

The advantages of the contract-net protocol include the following: dynamic task allocation via self-bidding, which leads to better agreements; natural load balancing, as busy agents need not bid; flexibility, as agents can be introduced and removed dynamically; and reliability, since it provides a robust mechanism for distributed scheduling and failure recovery [20].

The capacities of agents to react to changes can also be used in monitoring of the SLA. Agents can detect the possibility of a future SLA violation and act on the infrastructure to try to avoid the infringement of the agreement. Initial work has been done in the project BREIN [21] in the rescheduling of tasks based on information already gathered that could lead to a SLA violation.

10.5.3 Other SLA Challenges

Besides the use of the semantic Web and the multiagent system, there other open issues that should be further investigated.

There is an open debate about the need of renegotiating the SLA during the duration of the agreement. It has been understood that the SLA cannot be changed by definition, but in certain situations, changing the SLA during the service execution could be beneficial to the service provider and the customer [18]. These situations include extending the runtime of an increasingly interesting simulation and increasing the computational resources dedicated to either the simulation, thereby accelerating the experiment, or to the visualization, in order to improve the resolution of a rendering. Also, more generally, resources may fail unpredictably, high-priority jobs may be submitted, and so on.

Moreover, for a company to rely on other companies to perform its activity, it is important to possess a high degree of confidence in your service providers. There is a real problem in identifying the more suitable provider. The AssessGrid project introduces risk analysis in the selection of the service providers, so the selection is based not only on the information supplied by the service provider in their SLA but also on past references and the risk analysis performed (on the basis of previous experience and knowledge of this service provider). These strategies can help to reduce the risk involved in selecting a concrete service provider.

NextGRID provided the concept of a QoS history log, where both provider and consumer are able to store and retrieve information about past experience with services (and providers), in particular enabling especially providers to optimize their service offers (Tserpes et al. [32]. Also, TrustCoM has done research on the integration of a reputation system for enabling a trusted environment.

Finally, it is not a simple task the definition of your own SLA when your application is based on the composition of several services in a workflow. There are already methods that help to define the final QoS on the basis of each QoS of the component services, but the QoS values of the internal infrastructure do not have a direct translation on the business-level objectives present in the SLA. This QoS needs to be transduced to your own SLA that will be negotiated with your customer. As this translation is not direct, uncertainty in user requirements such as time and cost constraints could be represented by fuzzy numbers [18]. Further work needs to be done in this area of SLA composition.

10.6 CONCLUSIONS

During reading of this chapter it should have become clear that the topic of service-level agreements, especially their usage in Grid environments for e-business, is currently the focus of many research activities and is also widely discussed among groups not directly involved in those activities. The lifecycle of an SLA consists of many phases, each of which has special requirements to fulfill if there should be uptake of the SLA technology in real business. With the limited length of this chapter, it was possible to give only a brief snapshot of what is happening in this domain, but the aim was to provide enough information about what is currently possible, what the theoretical concepts are, and where research should focus on to act as a sound basis for further discussion.

From the viewpoint of the authors of this chapter, the fundamental research in the SLA area has been done and it is now time to extend the results obtained so far. This means as well a departure from the limited focus only on Grid technology to realize working implementations for SLA management. There are several research areas, including those in the semantic Web domain or the multiagent domain, whose results could be partially integrated in Grid technology to extend its capabilities.

However, it is also clear that all implications of the usage of service-level agreements, especially from a legal viewpoint, have to be exactly identified and clarified to ensure the usability in e-business.

REFERENCES

1. M. J. Boniface, S. C. Phillips, and M. Surridge, Grid-based business partnerships using service-level agreements, *Proc. Cracow Grid Workshop 2006*, Cracow, Poland, Oct. 16–18, 2006.
2. A. M. Jurewicz, *Contracts Concluded by Electronic Agents—Comparative Analysis of American and Polish Legal Systems*, Working Paper 714, bepress Legal Series, 2005.
3. T. Mahler, A. Arenas, and L. Schubert, Contractual frameworks for enterprise networks and virtual organisations in e-learning, in *Exploiting the Knowledge Economy—Issues, Applications, Case Studies*, Vol. 3, P. Cunningham and M. Cunningham, eds., IOS Press, The Netherlands, 2006.
4. S. Mercado Kierkegaard, E-contract formation: U.S. and EU perspectives, *Shidler Journal of Law, Commerce and Technology*, **3**: art. 12 (2007).
5. M. Parkin, D. Kuo, J. Brooke, and A. Macculloch, Challenges in EU Grid contracts, in *Exploiting the Knowledge Economy—Issues, Applications, Case Studies*, Vol. 3, P. Cunningham and M. Cunningham, eds., IOS Press, The Netherlands, 2006.
6. A. Villecco Bettelli, The trustworthiness in software agents' electronic signatures, in A. Oskamp and E. M. Weitzenböck, eds., *Proceedings of the Law and Electronic Agents Workshop (LEA'03)*, 2003, pp. 81–95.
7. *Electronic Signatures in Global and National Commerce Act*, Public Law 106–229. US Congress, 2000.

8. *Uniform Commercial Code,* The American Law Institute and the National Conference of Commissioners on Uniform State Laws, Philadelphia, PA, 1977 (several articles amended later).
9. *Uniform Computer Information Transaction Act,* National Conference of Commissioners on Uniform State Laws, Chicago, IL, 2002.
10. *Uniform Electronic Transaction Act,* National Conference of Commissioners on Uniform State Laws, Chicago, IL, 1999.
11. *Electronic Commerce Directive,* European Parliament and European Council, Brussels, Belgium, European Union, 2000.
12. *Community Framework for Electronic Signatures,* European Parliament and European Council, Brussels, Belgium, European Union, 1999.
13. C. Goble and D. De Roure, The semantic Grid: Myth busting and bridge building, *Proc. 16th European Conf. Artificial Intelligence* (*ECAI-2004*), Valencia, Spain, 2004.
14. N. Oldham, K. Verma, A. Sheth, and F. Hakimpour, Semantic WS-Agreement partner selection, *Proc. 15th International WWW Conf.*, Edinburgh, UK, 2006.
15. P. Masche, P. Mckee, and B. Mitchell, The increasing role of service level agreements in B2B systems, *Proc. 2nd International Conf. on Web Information Systems and Technologies*, Setubal, Portugal, April 2006.
16. G. Dobson and A. Sanchez-Macian, Towards unified QoS/SLA ontologies, *Proc. 3rd International Workshop on Semantic and Dynamic Web Processes* (*SDWP 2006*), Chicago, IL, 2006.
17. M. Wooldridge, V. Tamma, and M. Koubarakis, D2.1 *A Framework for Multi-Agent Support to the Semantic Grid*, OntoGrid Project, Feb. 2005.
18. D. Ouelhadj, J. Garibaldi, J. MacLaren, R. Sakellariou, and K. Krishnakumar, A multi-agent infrastructure and a service level agreement negotiation protocol for robust scheduling in grid computing, *Proc. European Grid Conf.; Lecture Notes in Computer Science* (2005).
19. M. Baruwal, S. Goh, J. Lin, J. Brzostowski, and R. Kowalczyk, Agent-based negotiation of service level agreements for Web service compositions, *Proc. Joint Conf. INFORMS Section on Group Decision and Negotiation, the EURO Working Group on Decision and Negotiation Support, and the EURO Working Group on Decision Support Systems*, Montreal, Canada, May 14–17, 2007.
20. J. MacLaren, R. Sakellariou, K. T. Krishnakumar, J. Garibaldi, and D. Ouelhadj, Towards service level agreement based scheduling on the Grid, *Workshop on Planning and Scheduling for Web and Grid Services* (*in conjunction with ICAPS-04*), Whistler, BC, Canada, June 3–7, 2004.
21. G. Laria et al., *BREIN—The Initial Overall Architecture*, public deliverable, BREIN Project, EU, Oct. 2007.
22. GRAAP-WG, OGF, http://forge.ogf.org/sf/projects/graap-wg.
23. G. Frankova, D. Malfatti, and M. Aiello, Semantics and extensions of WS-Agreement, *Journal of Software* **1**:23–31 (2006).
24. G. Birkenheuer, K. Djemame, I. Gourlay, O. Kao, J. Padgett, and K. Voss, Introducing Risk Management into the Grid, *Proc. 2nd IEEE International Conf. e-Science and Grid Computing* (*e-Science'06*), Amsterdam, the Netherlands, Dec. 4–6, 2006.
25. A. van Moorsel, *Metrics for the Internet Age: Quality of Experience and Quality of Business*, HP Labs Technical Report HPL-2001-179, 2001.

26. A. Andrieux, K. Czajkowski, A. Dan, K. Keahey, H. Ludwig, T. Kakata, J. Pruyne, J. Rofrano, S. Tuecke, and M. Xu, *GFD.107 Web Services Agreement Specification (WS-Agreement)*, GRAAP-WG, OGF, May 2007.
27. H. Ludwig, A. Keller, A. Dan, R. P. King, and R. Franck, *Web Service Level Agreemente (WSLA) Language Specification, Version 1.0*, IBM Corporation, Jan. 2003.
28. *NextGRID Vision and Architecture White Paper v5*, D. Snelling, M. Fisher, A. Basermann, F. Wray, P. Wieder, and M. Surridge, eds., NextGRID Project, EU, May 2007.
29. M. D. Wilson, D. Chadwick, T. Dimitrakos, J. Döser, P. Giambiagi, D. Golby, C. Geuer-Pollman, J. Haller, S. Ketil, T. Mahler, L. Martino, X. Parent, S. Ristol, J. Sairamesh, L. Schubert, and N. Tuptuk, The TrustCoM approach to enforcing agreements between interoperating enterprises, *Proc. Interoperability for Enterprise Software and Applications conf.* (*I-ESA'06*), Bordeaux, France, March 22–24, 2006.
30. M. Surridge, S. Taylor, D. De Roure, and E. Zaluska, Experiences with GRIA—industrial applications on a Web Services Grid, *Proc. 1st IEEE International Conf. e-Science and Grid Computing* (*e-Science'05*), Melbourne, Australia, Dec. 5–8, 2005.
31. P. Hasselmeyer, H. Mersch, B. Koller, H.-N. Quyen, L. Schubert, and P. Wieder, Implementing an SLA negotiation framework, in *Exploiting the Knowledge Economy: Issues, Applications, Case Studies*, Vol. 4, P. Cunningham and M. Cunningham, eds., IOS Press, 2007, pp. 154–161.
32. K. Tserpes, L. Schubert, B. Koller, D. Kyriazis, and T. Varvarigou, Learning from the past—SLA Composition using QoS history, in *Exploiting the Knowledge Economy: Issues, Applications, Case Studies*, Vol. 4, P. Cunningham and M. Cunningham, eds., IOS Press, The Netherlands, 2007.

11

SLAs, NEGOTIATION, AND CHALLENGES

PAUL MCKEE, STEVE TAYLOR, MIKE SURRIDGE, AND RICHARD LOWE

11.1 INTRODUCTION: THE FUTURE SERVICE MARKETPLACE

The global IT industry is facing a number of major challenges—industry growth is slowing, and for existing market leaders there are growing numbers of competitors. The rapid pace and scale of globalization is associated with rapid spread of ICT, which fragments value chains and results in geographically distributed production in order to minimize costs. Businesses are faced with increasing pressure to introduce products and services in increasingly shorter timescales and at reducing costs. Traditional IT departments have experienced difficulties in coping with the levels of agility required. Increasingly, the successful companies are the fastest, as they trade off risk against speed of product introduction and are comfortable with products that are only "good enough." The first-mover advantage is once again relevant in such markets as agile businesses move to take advantage of new opportunities. They may even make use of user communities to define and develop new products, and they are driven by financial performance to demonstrate their value in the latest high-tech solutions.

This has led to great interest in technologies such as service-oriented architectures (SOA) and its supporting service-oriented infrastructure (SOI), Grid computing, and the new range of software as a service (SaaS) offerings. We also see a high level of activity in virtualization that decouples the software from the underlying hardware, and more recently infrastructure as a service (IaaS). Using such technologies it is hoped that businesses will be able to rapidly create new applications, either for use internally or for sale, from services that may be assembled and executed rapidly and

Market-Oriented Grid and Utility Computing Edited by Rajkumar Buyya and Kris Bubendorfer

economically. A report prepared by Gartner [1] identifies 14 new delivery models that may be used in a future IT marketplace, many of them service-based. To achieve maximum economic benefit, it is essential that the services be reused and that as the technology matures fewer be developed from scratch. This all leads to the supposition that there will be a marketplace for applications and services that will have a global reach and potential consumers of services will be able to choose from such a global marketplace. This marketplace would be analogous to a number of existing global e-marketplaces such as Bizipoint [2] for electronics and IntercontinentalExchange (ICE) [3] for energy. One of the key challenges faced by consumers in such a global and dynamic marketplace will be making the correct choice of component services to meet their functional and nonfunctional requirements. We feel that in order for this to be successful, there is a strong requirement for the use of well-specified and appropriate service-level agreements together with precise business-domain-specific descriptions of the offered services.

11.2 BACKGROUND AND RELATED WORK: SERVICES AND THE ROLE OF SLAs

In a traditional marketplace where goods are sold, the customer is able to make an informed choice of product on the basis of a number of criteria that filter the array of available products down to a preferred option. Initially this may be based on the function of the product—does it do what the customer wants? This choice may then be further refined by considerations of cost—is it available within the budget that the customer has allocated? This will eventually produce a shortlist of suitable products that the customer is then able to assess using less functional and more quality-based assessment methods: the customer may handle the product to gauge its quality of construction and ease of use, they may take into account the prosperity of the shop, the attitude of the staff, and other less tangible features before making their choice. Even with the rise of online shopping for goods, attempts are made to mimic the real-world purchasing experience through the use of videos and three-dimensional (3D) views together with third-party reviews that assist the customer in the assessment of the product. The traditional model for services was very similar—a customer for a service such as household repair, for instance, would meet potential suppliers, thus obtaining an impression of their character and making a judgment as to the degree of trust placed in the trader. Previous users of the service would often be contacted for recommendations and the result of the service examined. Only then would a choice be made, often between tenders from a small number of candidate suppliers.

The situation with services in a modern high-speed electronic marketplace is, of course, quite different. The marketplace is global, and the rate of change within the marketplace is fast, and the decisionmaking process needs to be lighter and faster. In this chapter we focus on services offered by providers to consumers. For this purposes, we define a service as "the undertaking of work for the benefit of others." We use this generic definition because we want to concentrate on the business aspects of the provision of service rather than the technical definition (e.g., a Web service), which constrains the structure and use of the term. We also want to address a wider range of potential offerings than just software services, as the future IT landscape will include services that range from those provided by the infrastructure such as storage or networking on demand, right up to complete business processes. By definition, services are intangible, and may not even exist before they are required; they may be instantiated on demand by the supplier. This means that the potential purchaser has limited potential to assess the quality of a service before use, and a reduced level of useful information from previous users of the service, which will have been functionally equivalent but may have been executed on different infrastructure and possibly at a different physical locations. Hence there is a need for consumers to determine the nature of a service and whether it will live up to their expectations in a way that does not depend on physical examination. This may be achieved through the use of service-level agreements (SLAs).

The SLA is essentially a business tool used to describe and advertise services, by way of specification of the service, the level of quality that they offer and the price. They also allow the provider to manage the customers' expectations by explicitly listing the service characteristics and any expectations that the provider has of the consumer that might limit successful delivery of the service. We believe that the service description and performance guarantees offered within an SLA should link to specific business requirements of the customer and have a clear impact on the financial bottom line.

There has been considerable interest in the application of market-based approaches to computational system design since the 1990s. The paper by Buyya et al. [4] describes the issues and contains a useful summary of previous activities including systems such as Popcorn [5]. In our opinion, many of the previous efforts focus at too low a level and concentrate on technical objectives such as processor cycles and network bandwidth. In a future service marketplace, this leaves a gap in understanding between customers and suppliers. Real business end users will not be computer experts and will not necessarily understand the relationship between their applications performance and its hardware requirements. There is also a drive from customers to consolidate services into larger more easily managed bundles. Matzke [6] et al. highlight the desire of customers to be able to purchase bundles of services to reduce the complexity of SLA management and operational costs. We believe it is essential that the SLA have a strong end-user benefit component, and that services being offered should be described in terms of their impact at the business level of the potential consumer, and not in terms of the technology supplied. This approach is discussed by Hiles and Villabona [7], who identify the translation from critical success factors (CSFs) through key performance indicators (KPIs) and finally down to the technical performance measurements. The marketing benefits of this should be obvious—it is much easier to convince a financial decisionmaker of the benefits of a service that guarantees to process 10,000 online shopping transactions per hour rather than one that guarantees the availability of three servers.

We believe that the value to a market customer lies at a higher level than resources—the customers need solutions to their problems, rather than the resources required. This is consistent with our definition of a service, which is focused on the benefit to the customer. We believe that the resources should be the domain of the provider and the customer need not be concerned with them. SLA management for utility computing based on business objectives has previously been discussed by Buco et al. [8] together with the design of an SLA management system called *SLA action manager* (SAM). The conclusions of their paper include the observation that evaluations of this approach using event-driven techniques have shown a significantly reduced financial risk of service-level violations, which suggests that business-oriented process-centric management of utility computing contracts is both practical and useful.

This approach, of course, raises a number of significant challenges but also a number of advantages. By presenting services in a business-relevant context and by being able to link successful delivery directly to a measurable business objective, the services should be easier to market. Because the price directly relates to the benefit, it will be easier to maintain prices rather than be forced into an ever-reducing commodity pricing regime, for basic hardware services and usage-based pricing become easier to both implement and justify. Customer satisfaction should be higher and more easily maintained. There are significant challenges for the service provider, who has to provide the translation between service-level guarantees and the hardware requirements necessary to meet those goals. The technical performance measurements derived from the high-level business objectives will have a distribution; as discussed earlier, what constitutes an online shopping transaction, and how long does a single transaction last? The service provider will need to use some load characterization to provide a meaningful SLA and will to some extent be managing risk, which again produces revenue. By decoupling service guarantees from resource requirements we also allow the service provider some flexibility in resource management and hopefully cost reduction. It is the choice of service providers how to provision resources to satisfy the quality of service specified in an SLA—for example, if they spot that the customer demand for transaction processing rarely reaches that specified in the SLA, they can make a business decision to scale back the provision and use the freed resources for other jobs. This will also have an impact on energy usage and the carbon footprint of the activity, something of increasing concern in an era of rising energy prices and global warming.

We have proposed the use of bipartite (i.e., two-party) SLAs to describe both the functional and nonfunctional aspects of a service to allow consumers to make informed choices. An SLA is an agreement (as denoted by its name), and a contract for service is likely to be based on it, so the SLA has to describe to what each of its signatories is obliged in order to be compliant with the agreement [9]. The SLAs being developed using this approach are significantly different from what could be regarded as conventional SLAs in two main ways:

1. We believe that the strong linkage to business impact benefits both the customer and the provider; customers can assign costs within their businesses and the service provider retains the flexibility in operations to strive to reduce cost of

delivery and ultimately the price paid by the customer. This view contrasts with the use of SLAs in the more established academic Grid community where the SLAs described in the literature [10–12] focus on resources rather than services. This is, of course, appropriate for a community of experienced users running frequently experimental codes. For a market to address the needs of business users, the value of the service must be articulated at the business level rather than the resource level—the provision of a service (in a way consistent with our definition), rather than provision of raw resources. Management of resources should remain the domain of the service provider, with the customer reaping the benefits of reduced costs and guaranteed qualities if service. For example, the costs of computational hardware are in general low compared to the cost of an application code that runs on it, and customers usually want access to applications, as they will solve their problems rather than the raw hardware. Our position is that the value to the customer is at a higher level, and that the application code contains much more customer value.

2. The second major characteristic of a future SLA for services is that it recognizes the fact that in a future service-oriented marketplace, application delivery will be collaborative and that SLAs need to recognize the impact of this collaboration. We have introduced the notion of obligations on both parties in the agreement that describe necessary commitments in order for the SLA to be valid, and their relationships. The WSLA specification [13] also denotes the use of obligations, but does not determine that they may be dependent relationships, and how these relationships are dependent. We propose that there may also be a dependence in the obligations, where necessary. For example, if a customer wishes to outsource payroll processing and asks a service provider to guarantee that the payroll processing will always be completed by the 28th of any month except April, and by April 27, it is entirely reasonable for the service provider to place a precondition on the customer requiring that data be available 24 h before the delivery deadline. Through the use of obligations, the SLA clearly sets out the expectations and obligations of both parties involved, which we believe is an essential component of a future electronic marketplace for services.

11.3 VISIONARY THOUGHTS FOR PRACTITIONERS

11.3.1 The Challenge of Choice

It has always been assumed by those that, in terms of market products and services, the more choices offered to customers, the more likely they are to find something that completely satisfies their requirements. This is particularly true in the world of electronically delivered services where we see increasing efforts devoted to personalization or customization of product to meet each end users' specific requirements. If we consider a future view of electronic service-based marketplaces where services are fully described using SLAs and may then be instantiated on demand on a flexible infrastructure such as a Grid, it is tempting to suggest that this vision could be realized to meet the specified customer requirements. We believe, however, that such a goal may turn out to be less successful than expected for a number of reasons.

Services need to be particularly robust because they may be used with any number of other services to deliver a wide range of final applications. Increasing the range of options available to personalize a service will need extensive thought to avoid complications arising from interactions with other services. When offered against an SLA, the service provider will have had to develop and test a comprehensive management system to handle the full SLA lifecycle for the service. This will be expensive and slow, and as the number of possible variations in the service increases will become ever more expensive. These costs will be passed to end users in the form of higher subscription or usage charges. Because of these costs there will be a significant cost barrier to entry to the marketplace and a reduction in the number of new and innovative services that will be developed.

Although limiting the number of available products may seem counterintuitive, the impact on costs may be significant. Gottfredson and Aspinall [14] discuss the notion of the "innovation fulcrum" and its impact on a number of manufacturing activities. They describe how careful selection of options and minimization of complexity leads to a more efficient business and that each business has an optimal number of products. Too few products mean that they are missing out on customers, whole too many products causes complexity to rise and become difficult to manage. They feel that managers overestimate the value that customers place on choice and discuss a number of industry examples that highlight the innovation fulcrum in a number of industry sectors. A particular example notes that H. J. Heinz, after reducing the number of distinct products from 30,000 to around 20,000, added a full percentage point to the gross profit margin. Each potential new option should be scrutinized for its potential impact on the profit margins of the company before the costs of introduction are incurred. We believe that the use of SLAs that focus clearly on business benefits contribute to this reduction in potential complexity.

For the service consumer, the problems associated with too much choice may be equally severe. Faced with an SLA for a service that contains a large number of potentially variable terms, the end user is unlikely to be aware of the tradeoffs associated with combinations of the various settings and may unwittingly specify a set of parameters that significantly increase the cost of the service without increasing its quality. Indeed, the availability of a large number of parameters may, in fact, obscure which parameters are in fact important to the end user—as discussed by Twing [15] it is essential that SLA focus on critical service items that drive the business, and have clear financial implications. We regard this as further support for high-level business SLAs. As the end user is a person, other less technical problems may be observed. Iyengar and Lepper [16] have shown that a customer who has too much choice does not always see this as a benefit; in three separate experiments those authors found that limited choice led to greater satisfaction being reported by participants, and higher-quality output in the case of academic essays. There appears to be a choice paralysis that occurs when one is faced with too many options—the customers may be overwhelmed and make no purchase at all or will be uncertain if the choice they made was actually the best for them and have a lingering sense of dissatisfaction with the process. These early studies have been confirmed in other areas as diverse as convenience-store sales and retirement investment options, as the choice increases; customer satisfaction falls, as do sales. The conclusion offered is that choice is no longer sufficient motivation for introducing new product variants—more isn't always better, and getting the balance right is a considerable challenge. Customers often resort to very simple and nonoptimal strategies to choose in such conditions, and this raises the interesting question for automated systems in that if customers are unable to make the choice effectively in person: how do they program an automated system to achieve the best result for them?

11.3.2 Complexity Reduction: The Discrete-Offer Approach

If we consider the twentieth-century approach to shopping, with the advent of the supermarket, much of the complexity has been removed from commodity purchases by some degree of standardization. Many household purchases have standard pack sizes that facilitate both automated production (thereby reducing costs) and efficient comparison between products by the consumer. It is fairly easy for the customer to make a value judgment between two packets of different-branded soap powder, for example. In addition, the prices of the goods would greatly increase if the customer had total freedom to specify their features. For these reasons, we have advocated the use of a "discrete offer" system for services. It should be noted that by "discrete offer" we do not mean one single offer per service, but rather that every service provider should have commodity services with fixed quantized service levels, each constituting a separate, "discrete" offering of their service. Customers may then have the confidence that the combination of quality parameters offered will at least work, and the service provider has created a suitable management infrastructure for each level of the service, hopefully leading to reduced costs. Buco et al. [8] discuss the strategy of offering a few standardized, customer-neutral service functions on a utility platform to better exploit the economies of scale rather than pursuing customized contracts per customer. They report a study that has shown that several million dollars could be saved annually by reducing the costs of generating monthly reports for 100 customer-specific SLA contracts by no more than 20%. We recognize the fact that the commoditized approach will not be suitable for every situation and that there will be a continuum stretching from the simple purchasing of commodity services through to more complex fully negotiated contracts. The deciding factor governing which strategy is appropriate will be the cost incurred in the negotiation process versus the cost of the delivered service, and this is discussed in the next section.

11.3.3 The Cost of Negotiation and Yield Management Challenges

The costs of service discovery and negotiation form part of what have been termed "transaction costs." These were first proposed by Nobel laureate Ronald Coase in 1937 [17] in discussions surrounding the topic of why firms exist, and taken up in the Internet era by authors such as Tapscott et al. [18]. Coase blames transaction costs for the contradiction between the theoretical agility of the marketplace and the durability of the firm. Transaction costs are incurred when a firm goes out to the open market for a product or service rather than produce it in-house, and are discussed in detail by Benham and Benham [19]. In order for a market to exist and thrive, the transaction costs plus the product or service costs must be lower than the cost of producing the equivalent product or service in-house. In the nascent market for services based on service-oriented architectures or Grid computing, reduction of transaction costs will be an important driving force. We believe that certain pragmatic choices related to SLAs will help reduce these costs and enable the market.

Negotiation (e.g., of SLAs) is a transaction cost, and may be significant. It is worth spending much time, money, and effort negotiating only when the cost, value, and risk associated with the item being negotiated for are significant. In line with the discussion earlier, the supermarket approach has no negotiation. The customer chooses from a set of discrete offers and pays the labeled price. This is appropriate because the vast majority of real-world supermarket items are low-cost and commoditized. Conversely, a high-value, high-cost, complex service contract will have a great deal of negotiation, as the end item is extremely expensive and the risks of not carefully working out the contact between customer and provider are significant. In the real world, a contract for the construction of a new motorway would not go ahead without careful negotiation from all parties concerned. The costs, value, and risks are too great to leave negotiation to chance.

Applied to the Grid, there are a number of automated "discover, find and bind" protocols and demonstration systems (e.g., those described by Czajkowski et al. [20] and Shen et al. [21]), some of which use software agents to perform the negotiation to gain access to the services being negotiated for. While these are certainly useful, we assert that there must be a limit on the cost, risk, and value of the negotiated item, above which humans will get involved. An organization may be perfectly happy for software systems to take responsibility for low-value agreements, but humans must get involved when the stakes get higher, so that they can make more advanced decisions and take responsibility for their actions on behalf of their organization. The greater the level of risk and investment, the greater the need there is for human decision making and responsibility. The legal position regarding automated promises made by software that the organization then fails to deliver is unclear. You cannot sue a computer because it made a promise that your organization cannot deliver! There are a number of factors that determine the total cost of negotiation; the following is a checklist of some these factors:

1. There is a significant time–cost factor for the customer in searching for suppliers. The customer may already have preferred (i.e., prediscovered and preapproved suppliers) and will be likely to use these if they are available, but if suppliers need to be discovered (and possibly approved), there will be a significant overhead for the customer. This also allows for the existence of brokers in the electronic marketplace who may have lists of "guaranteed" suppliers for which the broker assumes the risk of supplier selection and offers a form of insurance in return for a fee.

2. Many negotiation protocols use an "invite tender" approach. This is where an invitation to tender is issued by a customer that providers respond to. Thus there are significant costs in the form of preparation and issuance of the invitation, the preparation, and delivery of tenders, and evaluation of the tenders. This is generally used only for high-cost, high-value bespoke (custom-tailored) services, where the focus is on building long-term supply relationships.

3. The customer will have difficulty in comparing the value from offers from different providers—these are not likely to be directly comparable, and thus the customers have to compare apples and oranges and determine which suits their needs best. This is a risk that the supermarket approach aims to address—if the offers are discrete and to some extent standardized, the task of comparing them is greatly simplified. Within a single commercial domain it is highly likely for a common well-understood vocabulary to be used (the "shop talk" of that domain), and this greatly enables easier comparison of services, as the nomenclature is well known. When the comparison is between industrial sectors, some form of semantic equivalence will have to be established for effective cost–value comparison.

4. There is a considerable time and risk cost to both customer and provider of iterative negotiation. Offers and counteroffers need to be computed and responded to, and there is the significant risk of no guarantee that iterative negotiation will converge. There is thus a potential for a significant amount of effort for no reward.

5. There is a major risk to the provider of reserving resources at offer time. The provider would do this to guarantee availability to the clients, and hence the service offered would be of high quality. This high quality would be reflected in the SLA and the price of the service. The price must offset the risk of the offers not being accepted. The corollary is that there is a risk to the customer that the provider will offer the same resources to another customer during the negotiation period.

6. As discussed earlier, there is a significant risk to customer and provider of giving the customer too much freedom in choosing the service profile—what the customer chooses may not be workable or be too costly to provide.

7. There is a considerable financial cost of any human interaction (decisionmaking, responsibility, etc.). Humans are much more costly than computers. In addition, this does not scale well—if there are many negotiations, the need for human interaction may be prohibitive. Even the requirement for automated agreements validated by a human before they become valid will add considerable delays in a commodity marketplace.

In conclusion, providers and customers need to analyze the costs and potential risks of any negotiation that they enter into and appropriately target resources. Depending on the situation, too much or too little attention to negotiation can be costly or dangerous.

11.3.4 Management Challenges

To manage an application against an SLA, the high-level business goals need to be decomposed into appropriate goals for subcomponents and SLAs for those services and components that are bought in from third parties. Hiles and Villabona [7] discuss critical success factors, key performance indicators, and their role in establishing the technical parameters measured to maintain SLA performance. If we include the possibility for subcontracting, information needs to move between a number of different parts of the management chain, each with a different idea of what constitutes success in order for the overall management process to be successful. This whole management chain needs to be orchestrated by a management function that understands the relationships between component parts and is able to act to ensure that overall performance is maintained. This will require context mapping as messages transit the various levels in the architecture between low-level fabric providers and end users at the business level.

The management system has to consider management not only of applications to meet SLAs but also of all SLAs involving the service provider to meet their business goals. One of the main rationales behind service-oriented architectures and flexible infrastructure is increasing the utilization of resources and hence the profitability. This means that from time to time the service provider will be operating in a resource-constrained regime and will need to make decisions about which SLAs to break to maintain service on others. Similar decisions may need to be taken in balancing the payment of performance penalties against increased costs, such as purchasing or subcontracting extra resources.

Finally, to return to the collaborative nature of future SLAs, customers may have similar management functionality running on their sites to ensure that their resources are efficiently supplied. This means that the customer may also breach an SLA and the SLA must now identify any penalties that may be placed on the customer, while at the same time removing penalties accrued by the service provider, further reinforcing the symmetric nature of SLAs in the new environment.

Of course, the flexibility and reuse touted as major benefits of service-oriented architectures and flexible infrastructures present their own significant management challenges. It is highly likely that a future market ecosystem will contain services that are shared between numbers of customers, possibly with different SLAs in place. Each application may be managed individually, and each manger will receive performance metrics. The problem arises when one application sees a fall in performance due to the actions of another application (such as massive demand increases)—at what level are actions taken and by whom? The manager of the application noting poor performance may want to collect a penalty payment from the service provider, or even switch providers because of the influence of the third party, and this raises interesting challenges in the areas of payment and management. The same effect can be observed at the infrastructure level, where it is possibly even harder to resolve with the increasing use of virtualization to maximize hardware utilization by running multiple virtual machines on a single physical machine. The performance of a service running in one environment may be affected by the resource demands of another virtual machine. It is undoubtedly true that the agility and flexibility promised by the service-oriented approach can easily lead to massive increases in system complexity, further reinforcing the need for pragmatic simplification of the system to make management a tractable problem.

The question of resource reservation to meet performance guarantees being negotiated will be discussed in the next section, together with results that show that given a poor choice of reservation strategy, an economic self-denial of service can occur. The potential tradeoffs between scale of supplier and reservation strategy and its impact on the number of customers will be discussed in detail, and the results of simulations presented to confirm the conclusions.

11.3.5 Self-Denial of Service

In this section we briefly describe simulation results of an initial investigation into the behavior of a "Grid marketplace." The overall aim of this work was to arrive at a means of simulating or modeling a Grid marketplace. The reason for this was that at the time there did not exist enough real-world information regarding how different actors operated in such a situation. This is still largely true, but the trend toward SOA and SaaS is likely to change this in the near to medium term. We first briefly describe the simulator code itself, and then discuss the experiment conducted, and the results, analysis, and conclusions drawn.

11.3.5.1 Simulation. We chose a simulation-based approach, as it was deemed to be the most flexible—the other alternatives considered were analytical modeling and measurement. Measurement was obviously not possible, and it was deemed that simulation allowed more "what if" types of analysis to be performed than did modeling.

We based the simulator code on the GridSim toolkit [22], with appropriate extensions. There are two main actors in the simulation—users and service providers. For the service provider we added two major extensions: (1) we added the capability to negotiate with users—the providers would receive requests and make offers, which are valid for a specific time (the validity period), and users may accept them within this time; and (2) we removed the "status disclosure." In GridSim as it was delivered, the users could see the internal resource utilization of the service providers, and in a market situation, this is clearly not desirable for the service provider, as it gives the user an unfair bargaining advantage. It is also consistent with the notion that a service provider should be free to make resourcing decisions to provide for a service offered to a customer, rather than provide the resources directly. For the users we added a complementary negotiation capability with service providers. The users issue requests for work, evaluate responses from providers, and select the most appropriate ones on the basis of a utility function.

11.3.5.2 Scenario. First, we had to choose the actors in our marketplace. We chose a population for our scenario of 80 users and 20 service providers. The ratio between the number of clients and service providers is based on the assumption that in a marketplace of this type (small to medium-sized enterprise (SME) clients and larger service providers) there will be significantly more clients than service providers. Here we have set it at four to one.

The users submit job requests to the Grid marketplace, and receive offers from providers able and willing to do the work. The users pick one of the offers, confirm it, and proceed with the provider to run the job. All offers have validity periods, after which they are invalid, and the unaccepted offers expire. The users differentiate between the offers using a cost–time selection strategy. This is where the benefit to the user is determined by both the financial cost to perform the job and the time taken. The cost–time algorithm aims to optimize the processing time for jobs that cost the same. Hence price is the major governing factor—offers are considered first on price, then on runtime to distinguish between jobs that cost the same. The service provider population comprises different types of service providers. We determined that the service providers in our scenario can be categorized in terms of

- *Size*—large, medium, small
- *Price*—low, high
- *Speed*—slow, fast

The *size* is in terms of number of processing units (i.e., machines), while the *speed* refers to the speed of an individual processing unit. In order to create service providers' profiles, combinations of these three categories were created. We used an incremental approach where we considered subsets of categories and eliminated the nonrealistic ones—for example a small, low-priced service provider is not realistic because it will not create enough revenue to survive. We also excluded slow, low-capacity, expensive service providers, since they are very unlikely to succeed in a competitive market. We then decided which percentage of the total number of service providers had each profile. The service providers' distribution was chosen to reflect a marketplace in which large service providers exploit the economies of scale to reduce their costs and therefore attract the majority of the business. However, we have included some medium and small providers as well to study their impact on the market. Service providers' size is in terms of number of processing units (machines). We assumed that size classes differ by an order of 3. Therefore, choosing the small service provider with one machine leads to the medium one with three machines and the large one with nine machines.

Processor rate is expressed in standard machine units, based on an arbitrarily defined standard machine. The actual performance of the standard machine is not important as all performance figures and measurements are relative to it—the standard machine effectively defines the "1" point.

We assumed that speed classes differ by an order of 2. Thus, we have chosen the slow service provider to have a CPU with a rate of 10 standard machines, while the fast one has a CPU a rate of 20 standard machines. Price is given per hour and per processor used. The values chosen are in the range of \$0.25–\$1 per hour. The prices are indicative of a reasonable charge for computation today, but the exact values are not intended to be representative of a real-world market price. What is important in the prices is their relative values, so that expensive and cheap providers can be identified and simulated. The final service providers' profiles are shown in Table 11.1.

TABLE 11.1 Service Provider Profile Parameters

Size–Price–Speed	Number of Service Providers	Number of Processors	Processor Rate (Standard Processor Unit)	Price per Hour per Processor (euros)	Equivalent Standard Processor—Hour Price (euros)
Large–low–slow	3	9	10	0.25	0.03
Large–low–fast	2	9	20	0.50	0.03
Medium–low–slow	3	3	10	0.25	0.03
Medium–low–fast	1	3	20	0.50	0.03
Large–high–slow	1	9	10	0.75	0.08
Large–high–fast	2	9	20	1.00	0.05
Medium–high–fast	3	3	20	1.00	0.05
Small–high–fast	5	1	20	1.00	0.05

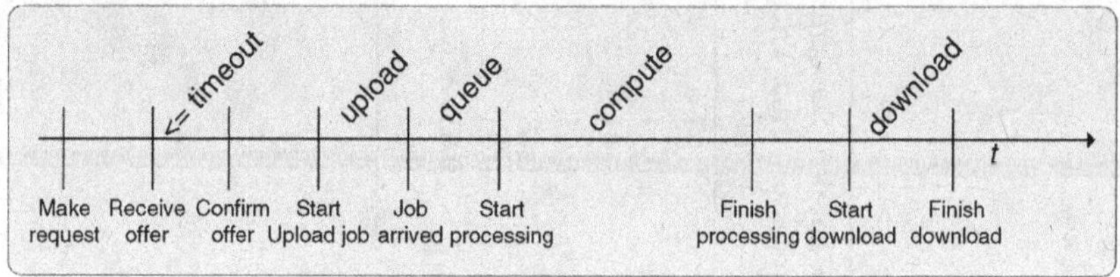

Figure 11.1 Job lifecycle.

Finally, Figure 11.1 shows the job lifetime from the request to the job completion, intended as download of completed job. The time ranges do not reflect any particular case (i.e., ranges are not at all proportional), but merely show the sequence of the events in the lifecycle of a job.

In our case, "confirm offer" and "start upload job" happen at the same time and the job deadline is considered the final processing event and does not take into account upload and download time. In future development service providers could consider those events as well.

The simulations we ran were designed to investigate the effect of the offer validity period, that is, the time for which service providers' offers are valid. The experiments used different durations of offer validity period, and here we present a number of graphs based on simulation runs to show the distribution of work across different providers on the basis of different offer validity periods.

We use one key principle for service providers' operation: that the service providers commit resources at offer time, and that the commitment of the resources is valid for the duration of the offer validity period. After this time, any resources committed for offers that are not accepted are released, and can be offered again. The reason for this is so that the providers do not overcommit their resources when making offers. Hence, the service providers cannot overoffer their resources (even though this is a valid business strategy).

11.3.5.3 Simulation Results and Analysis. This section shows a number of results based on different simulation runs with different values of *offer validity period,* namely, the length of time for which the offers made by providers remain valid, and hence the duration of commitment of resources that potentially may not result in work. Figure 11.2 shows the situation where the offer validity period is 3456 s. The figure shows the amount of outsourced work processed by each of our population of 20 service providers, as described in Table 11.1. The notation for the *X* axis is the number of the service provider (SP01 to SP20), followed by the following code:

`SIZE{Big|Medium|Small}PRICE{Low|High}Speed{Slow|Fast}`

So, BLS, for example, is a `Big` service provider who charges `Low` prices and has `Slow` machines. The ordering of the service providers on the *X* axis is important so that patterns can be discerned. For example, there is a clear breakpoint in the *X* axis of

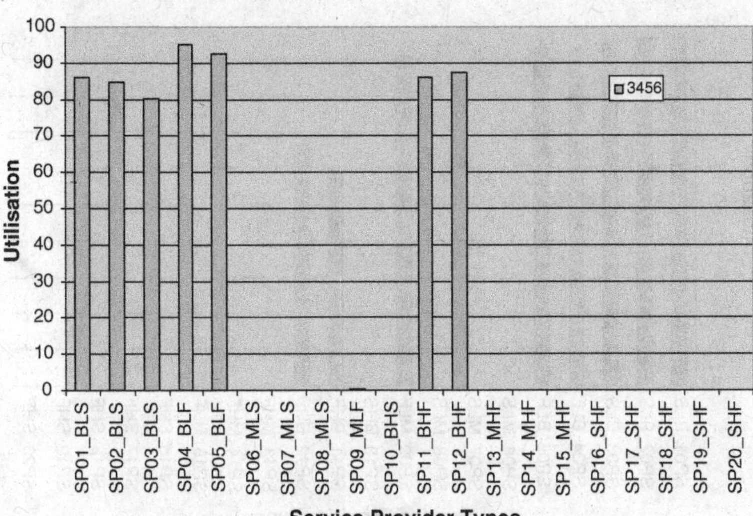

Figure 11.2 Utilization for different service provider types for an offer validity period of 3456 s.

the graph, between SP9 and SP10, where the service providers' price changes from `Low` to `High`.

Because of the users' cost–time minimization strategy, we expect the cheapest and fastest service providers to get the most work; we can see this in the graph. SP01 to SP05 inclusive are almost 100% utilized. We also see SP11 and SP12 highly loaded. Although they are expensive, they are preferred to SP06 to SP10, who are lower-capacity. (Note that SP10 is unlikely ever to get work—they are high-cost and have low-speed resources. SP10 is the "big–high–slow" provider in Table 11.1, and has a considerably higher price/performance ratio, as denoted by the "Equivalent Standard Processor-Hour Price" column.) It can also be seen that SP09 gets a tiny amount of work. This is because it is cheap and has moderate capacity, but nowhere near that of "big" service providers.

If we reduce the validity period for offers, we get a significant change in the work distribution. This is shown in Figure 11.3. Here the validity period is less than half what it was in Figure 11.2, at 1440 s.

The major change is that now SP09 (medium size, cheap, and fast) is winning work—to the detriment of SP11 and SP12. SP09, previously able to win very little work (see the small amount it won in Fig. 11.2 when the offer validity period was 3456 s) is now able to win a great deal of work with the reduction of the offer validity period, and is just over 90% utilized in Figure 11.3.

So, why is SP09 now winning work when the offer validity period reduces? The reason is down to the agility caused by providers' capacity and the commitment of resources at offer time correlated with the length of the offer validity period. When providers make offers, they must commit their resources for the duration of the

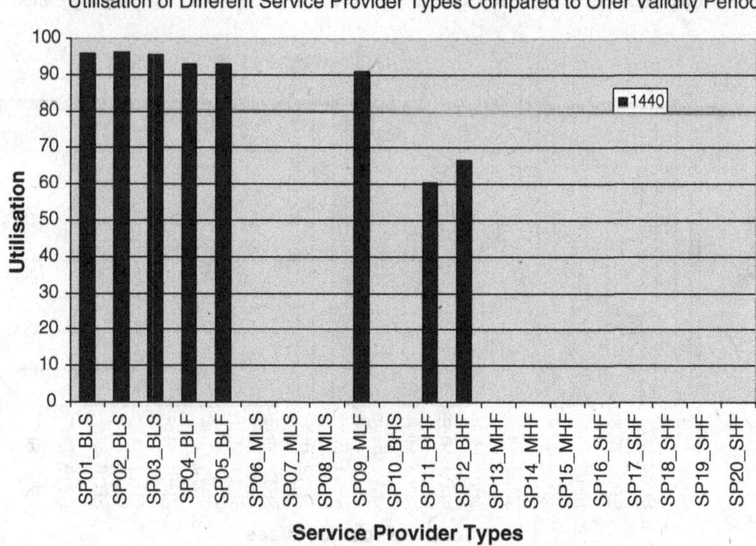

Figure 11.3 Utilization for different service provider types for an offer validity period of 1440 s.

validity period of the offers, and hence the low-capacity service providers commit all their resources much sooner than do the larger ones and as a consequence cannot make offers for some users as they are fully committed until the offers they have made expire. Thus the lower-capacity providers considerably less agile and highly sensitive to the validity period of the offers that they make.

In this example, the cheap and low-capacity providers have made offers that they must commit resources for, and keep valid for the entire validity period, and as a result, they fill up quickly, not with real work but offers of work. In Figure 11.3, where the offer validity period is 1440 s, the fastest of the lower capacity providers, SP09, is able to make more offers because the validity period is shorter, and they are denying themselves work to a far less extent than in Figure 11.2 (where the offer validity period was 3456 s), as in Figure 11.3 (where the offer validity period is 1440 s), the period they must commit their resources for is much less.

In Figure 11.4, the offer validity period is further reduced, this time to 720 s, and we see another shift in the work distribution following the trend of the lower-capacity workers winning work. However, this time the difference is much less extreme.

What we see is that SP06–SP08 are now winning work, again to the cost of SP11 and SP12. SP06–SP08 are all medium-size and cheap, and the further reduction of the offer validity period means that they can make enough offers in order to stand a good chance of some getting accepted.

11.3.5.4 Simulation Conclusions. Cases were run covering a cross section of offer validity period (the time that the providers were committing resources

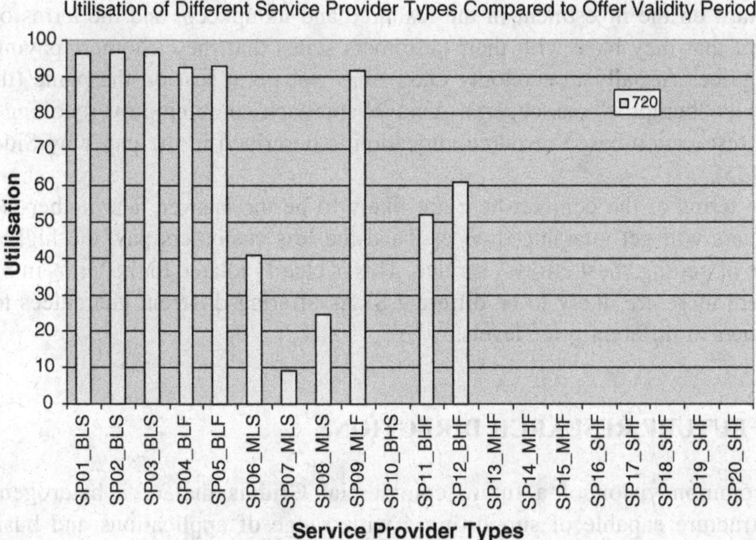

Figure 11.4 Utilization for different service provider types for an offer validity period of 720 s.

regardless of whether they were accepted by the clients). The main conclusions are as follows:

- When the offer validity period is long, the large, low-price, fast service providers get the bulk of the work. However, there is a significant proportion of large, high-cost, fast service providers also doing well. This is due to their high capacity and means that they are in a good position to make offers when other lower-capacity service providers are fully committed. The lengthy offer period (during which the providers commit resources regardless of whether they are used by the clients) of this case incapacitates the lower-capacity service providers, allowing the higher-capacity service providers (whether they are cheap or expensive) to win work.
- As the offer validity period reduces, the agility of the slower, lower-capacity service providers increases and they are able to compete with the faster ones. The observable effect is that the cheaper, lower-capacity providers are "stealing" work from the higher-capacity, high-price providers.

We thus conclude that there is a significant business risk to the commitment of resources when making offers, as it makes a provider highly sensitive to the duration of the validity of the offer. The problem for the service providers is in provisioning—do they overbook their resources in the hope that some of their offers get turned down, or do they only make enough offers that they know they can service?

This is common in resource-intensive real business. It is well known that airlines routinely overbook their planes to account for "no shows," and thus increase the return on the investment in the resource and its upkeep, and the terms of the contract that they have with their customers states that the customers paying the lower prices (usually in economy class) may not get a seat on the plane (this is known as "bumping" passengers). A novel approach combining overbooking with actual reservation-based resource allocation is described in the paper by Siddiqui et al. [25].

The terms of the contract here are likely to be the answer. The higher-paying customers will get guaranteed access, and the less customers pay, the higher the chance of getting "best efforts" service. This is clearly related to the terms in SLAs, and here there are likely to be different SLAs offering different guarantees to the customers at different price levels.

11.4 FUTURE RESEARCH DIRECTIONS

The common vision of a future commercial Grid is that of a heterogeneous infrastructure capable of supporting a wide range of applications and business processes throughout the lifecycle. There will be a wide range of resources such as hardware, software, and data made available from competing suppliers in a self-sustaining commercial market. In order to achieve this vision, there needs to be a transition of Grid technology from the existing academic and research environment through to the commercial world. Given the interest and existing work undertaken in the established academic Grid community, it is easy to imagine a seamless transition to a global Grid marketplace trading computing resources and services at will. This is a high-level goal that has yet to be realized; in practice, where industrial users have adopted the Grid, it has usually been at the level of a single organization and motivated largely by cost savings. This is because the issues of risk and reward in cross-organizational applications are different from those in existing academic Grids. The lack of explicit business models makes this difficult to assess; conventional business relationships are usually governed by contracts that make all aspects of the interaction explicit. It is for this reason that this chapter has focused on the use of the service-level agreement. Almost independently of the ongoing Grid developments, there has been increasing industrial activity in the area of SLAs, driven by the adoption of service orientation and business models such as software as a service (SaaS), which rely on service-based contracts. Currently the major trend is for the use of service-oriented computing within the enterprise, but the familiarity and expertise gained in such internal deployments will ease the transition to the use of external third-party services that we expect to be available in a future market-oriented Grid environment. In order to fully realize the goals of SLA-based management, a number of significant research challenges must be addressed. As our proposed SLAs are described in high-level business terms, there is a requirement that these goals be mapped to lower-level technical goals and the required management and monitoring infrastructure. Initially domain experts who are fully conversant with the business vocabulary will carry this out manually, but eventually this needs to become an automated process, for both the translation and the creation of automated management systems. The overhead introduced by this manual input will, of course, be amortized across the number of times that the service is reused, so we expect that a virtuous circle will exist in which high-quality services benefit from the most development effort.

The early stages of Grid development focused on computationally intensive high-performance computing tasks from the academic domain, where the expertise of the end users made the operation of Grid technologies straightforward and the benefits obtained obvious. Business services are more diverse in nature than the typical academic applications addressed thus far, and the benefits obtained may be less easy to quantify in an environment with diverse requirements that are peaky in demand. The tying of service guarantees specified in SLAs to relevant business goals makes this relationship more obvious and increases the likelihood of industrial takeup of Grid technologies.

Tying the service guarantees to qualities of service is a significant departure from the situation observed by early academic Grid users and may have significant impact on the ability of service providers to operate at a profit. Early users of the Grid had significant expertise and were accustomed to requesting resources at a low level, such as storage volume or number of processors, and because much of the software was experimental, it was accepted that not every execution was a success. Moving to service guarantees means that the end user can focus on results and does not need as much experience of resource usage and the service provider can have greater flexibility in use of the resources. This trend is reinforced by the increasing use of virtualization that breaks the link between services and an exact hardware allocation. This is an important psychological hindrance to successful takeup of Grid technologies that needs to be removed.

Of course, a necessary prerequisite in a system that offers service delivery against SLA is the ability to provide predictable and manageable qualities of service to end users and operators. Again, traditional academic, Grids have the advantage of an expert user base well used to working with prototype software and a large supply of relatively cheap labor to ensure that systems operate. Indeed, the original motivation for the Grid was the sharing of scarce high-cost infrastructure. In industry, the situation is a little different—there has been continual erosion in the cost of hardware, and the major costs of data center operations are now energy and management. In addition, skilled operatives are expensive and the management of QoS to meet SLA-based guarantees needs to be automated as much as possible. Businesses today are constantly trying to reduce operating costs to remain competitive or to retain their margin; it will therefore be necessary to demonstrate efficient operation of future Grids to speed acceptance of the technology.

The move to guaranteed levels of service maintained by automated management systems increase resource allocations in response to real-world demands, and that breaks the link between services and resources, and places increased emphasis on software licensing. Most of the commercial value in a business-oriented Grid lies in the intellectual property embodied in the application codes, but traditional software licensing has taken a number of less than flexible approaches such as user locking, node locking, processor locking, and even location locking of applications in order to maintain income from software licensing and maintenance contracts. The current interest in software as a service is eroding this a little, but fully flexible Grid marketplaces will require more flexible software licenses, and work needs to be undertaken to demonstrate to software vendors that their intellectual property and revenue streams will be protected.

There also needs to be more economic research related to the impacts of pricing and reservation in a dynamic service marketplace, together with approaches to the management of collections of SLAs and services with a view to maximizing economic benefit to both the end user and service provider. The problem faced is that computation is a perishable asset; compute cycles cannot be stored and used later. With multiple customer classes and potentially multiple prices (if dynamic pricing is available), the challenge faced by the service provider is to determine which customers should be served and at what price. The problem may be further complicated by customers having bundles of services and longstanding relationships that shift the priorities of even their smaller jobs, so the economic benefit has a weighting related to the volume of current and future business anticipated from that customer.

11.5 CONCLUSIONS

In this chapter, we have considered strategies for service-oriented future markets. This work has come out of discussion, research, and thinking into what is currently called the "Grid," and it seems that it will evolve into a service-oriented market, and hence the emphasis on services.

We have discussed the differences between products and services, and the difficulty that consumers have in judging the quality of an unexperienced service, compared with the relative ease of judging the quality of a product. The well-known answer to this problem is the service-level agreement (SLA), and we describe the SLA's role within the service framework. Our chief findings are as follows:

- An SLA must be focused on the user's requirements, and service providers' offerings must "talk the user's language" and clearly illustrate the *business* benefit to the user; otherwise the user is unlikely to be interested or even understand the offerings.
- A contract for delivery of the service is likely to be based on the SLA, and hence the SLA must denote what *all* its signatories (not just the service provider) agree to. The simplest example of this is that the service provider agrees to provide service and the customer agrees to pay, although we have investigated more complex dependent relationships between the obligations where delivery of the service may depend on input provided by the consumer.
- The SLA must denote what will happen if one of the obligations is not met. This may be the invalidation of another dependent obligation, the suspension of a guarantee, a penalty payment, or the termination of the entire agreement for example.

For this approach to be manageable, we propose a number of pragmatic simplifications to the specification and negotiation of SLAs. The aim of this pragmatism is the reduction of complexity that will, if allowed, derail the commercial adoption of Grid technologies.

We have advocated a "discrete offer" approach for service providers. This simplifies the providers' resourcing as their offerings are in standardized discrete portions, increasing efficiency and driving down costs for both the provider and the customer. We argue that if customers are given too much choice, they are likely to get overwhelmed by the permutations available to them, and may produce unworkable combinations of service factors. In addition, it has been argued that there is an "innovation fulcrum" describing the number and complexity of offerings from a provider. If a provider has too few offerings, there will be gaps in the market that could be filled by them and hence business opportunities missed, but too many offerings will introduce costly complexity and management problems. The fulcrum is where there is balance achieved through the combination of adequate market coverage and enough simplicity and manageability. We have discussed the cost of negotiation and argue that it must be carefully balanced with the cost, value, and risk of the offering being negotiated for. For example, it is not sensible to negotiate extensively for a low-value service, as the cost of the negotiation becomes a significant component of the overall cost (financial and otherwise) of the service. Conversely, a high-cost, bespoke high-value service should have extensive negotiation as the value and risks to all parties are magnified, and each party will want to ensure that its position is secure.

We add to the negotiation analysis with presentation of some simulation results showing a simulated Grid marketplace and show that it is possible for service providers to deny themselves work through attempting to offer a high-quality guaranteed service and conclude by determining that there should be levels of service related to its price. Finally we discuss a number of key areas for future research that would contribute to the realization of the ultimate vision of a global flexible reliable market-driven Grid for services.

ACKNOWLEDGMENTS

The authors acknowledge the funding of the European Commission, and the work reported here was conducted within the NextGRID (next-generation Grid) Integrated Project. This chapter expresses the opinions of the authors and not necessarily those of the European Commission. The European Commission is not liable for any use that may be made of the information contained in this chapter.

REFERENCES

1. C. Da Rold, M. A. Margevicius, L. R. Cohen, and T. J. Bittman, *Alternative Delivery Models: A sea of New Opportunities and Threats*, Gartner, October 2007.
2. Bizipoint: www.bizipoint.com.

3. IntercontinentalExchange: www.theice.com.
4. R. Buyya, D. Abramson, and J. Giddy, A case for economy grid Architecture for service oriented Grid computing, *Proc. 10th IEEE International Heterogeneous Computing Workshop (HCW 2001)*, in conjunction with IPDPS 2001, San Francisco, CA, April 2001.
5. O. Regev and N. Nisan, The Popcorn market—online markets for computational resources, *Proc. 1st International Conf. Information and Computation Economies*, Charleston, SC, 1998.
6. P. Matzke, T. Mendel, and D. Krauss, *Service Provider Strategists: Take Converged Service Delivery to the Next Level!*, Forrester Research, July 2007.
7. A. Hiles and R. Villabona, *Effective Strategies for Service Management*, Vol. **2**, SLM e-Book, nextslm.org.
8. M. J. Buco et al., Utility computing based upon business objectives, *IBM Systems Journal* **43**(1):159–178 (2004).
9. T. Davis Jr. and P. Fitzgerald, Deconstructing service level agreements, *New York Law Journal* (March 4, 2002), http://www.clm.com/pubs/pub-1166910_1.html.
10. R. Buyya, D. Abramson, and S. Venugopal, The Grid economy, *Proceedings of the IEEE* **93**(3):698–714 (2005).
11. K. Czajkowski, I. Foster, and C. Kesselman, Agreement-based resource management, *Proceedings of the IEEE* **93**(3):631–643, (2005).
12. C. S. Yeo and R. Buyya, Service level agreement based allocation of cluster resources: Handling penalty to enhance utility, *Proc. 7th IEEE International Conf. Cluster Computing (Cluster 2005)*, IEEE Computer Society, Los Alamitos, CA, 2005.
13. A. Keller and H. Ludwig, The WSLA framework: Specifying and monitoring service level agreements for Web services, *Journal of Network and Systems Management*, **11**(1): 57–81, (2004).
14. M. Gottfredson and K. Aspinall, Innovation versus complexity: What IS too much of a good thing, *Harvard Business Review*, **83**(11):62–71 (Nov. 2005).
15. D. Twing, Are you savvy about SLA negotiations?, *Network World* (Oct. 5, 2005).
16. S. Iyengar and M. Lepper, When choice is demotivating: Can one desire too much of a good thing, *Journal of Personality and Social Psychology* **79**(6):995–1006 (2000).
17. R. Coase, The nature of the firm, *Economica* **4**(16):386–405 (Nov. 1937).
18. D. Tapscott, D. Ticoll, and A. Lowy, *Digital Capital Harnessing the Power of Business Webs*, Nicholas Beasley, London, 2000.
19. A. Benham and L. Benham, *The Costs of Exchange*, Ronald Coase Institute Working Paper 1, July 2001, http://www.coase.org/workingpapers/wp-1.pdf.
20. K. Czajkowski, I. Foster, C. Kesselman, C. Sander, and S. Tuecke, SNAP: A protocol for negotiating service level agreements and coordinating resource management in distributed systems, *Proc. Job Scheduling Strategies for Parallel Processing: 8th International Workshop (JSSPP 2002), Edinburgh*, UK, July 24, 2002.
21. W. Shen, Y. Li, H. Ghenniwa, and C. Wang, Adaptive negotiation for agent-based Grid computing, *Proc. AAMAS2002 Workshop on Agentcities: Challenges in Open Agent Environments*, Bologna, Italy, 2002, pp. 32–36.
22. R. Buyya and M. Murshed, GridSim: A toolkit for the modeling and simulation of distributed resource management and scheduling for Grid computing, *Concurrency and Computation: Practice and Experience* **14**(13–15):1175–1220 (2002).

23. A. Sulistio, G. Poduvaly, R. Buyya, and C. Tham, Constructing a Grid simulation with differentiated network service using GridSim, *Proc. 6th International Conf. Internet Computing*, Las Vegas, NV, June 27–30, 2005.
24. R. Buyya, M. Murshed, D. Abramson, and S. Venugopal, Scheduling parameter sweep applications on global Grids: A deadline and budget constrained cost-time optimisation algorithm, *Software: Practice and Experience* **35**(5):491–512 (April 2005).
25. M. Siddiqui, A. Villazon, and T. Fahringer, Grid capacity planning with negotiation-based advance reservation for optimized QoS, *Proc. International Conf. High Performance Computing, Networking and Storage (SC06), Tampa, FL*, 2006.
26. NextGRID (next-generation Grid) EC IST Framework 6 Integrated Project, Contract 511563, www.nextgrid.org.

12

SLA-BASED RESOURCE MANAGEMENT AND ALLOCATION

JORDI GUITART, MARIO MACÍAS, OMER RANA, PHILIPP WIEDER, RAMIN YAHYAPOUR, AND WOLFGANG ZIEGLER

12.1 INTRODUCTION

The aim of the chapter is to describe how service-level agreements (SLAs) could be utilized to provide the basis for resource trading based on economic models. SLAs enable a service user to identify their requirements, and a provider to identify their capabilities. Subsequently, the terms in an SLA are necessary to ensure that mutually agreeable quality is being delivered by the provider according to the agreement. The use of service-level agreements (SLAs) in a resource management system to support Grid computing applications is described. To this end, we provide an architecture that supports the creation and management of SLAs. The architecture of the system, in terms of the components and their interactions, is first presented, followed by a description of the specific requirements for a market-oriented Grid economy. We use SLAs as a means to support reliable quality of service for Grid jobs. The creation of such an SLA requires planning and orchestration mechanisms. We will discuss these functionalities and also consider the economic aspects such as dynamic pricing and negotiation mechanisms. These mechanisms are necessary to enable SLA formation and use, and to ensure that an SLA is being adhered to during service provision.

Market-Oriented Grid and Utility Computing Edited by Rajkumar Buyya and Kris Bubendorfer

12.2 BACKGROUND AND RELATED WORK

An SLA represents an agreement between a service user and a provider in the context of a particular service provision. An SLA may exist between two parties, for instance, a single user and a single provider, or between multiple parties, for example, a single user and multiple providers. SLAs contain certain quality-of-service (QoS) properties that must be maintained by a provider during service provision—generally defined as a set of service-level objectives (SLOs). These properties need to be measurable and must be monitored during the provision of the service that has been agreed in the SLA. The particular QoS attributes that are used must be preagreed to between the user and provider(s), before service provision begins, and also they define the obligations of the user/client when the provider meets the quality specified in the SLA. The SLA must also contain a set of penalty clauses when service providers fail to deliver the preagreed- to quality. Although significant work exists on how SLOs may be specified and monitored, not much work has focused on actually identifying how SLOs may be impacted by the choice of specific penalty clauses. The participation of a trusted mediator may be necessary in order to resolve conflicts between involved parties. Automating this conflict resolution process clearly provides substantial benefits. Different outcomes from such a process are possible. These include monetary penalties, impact on potential future agreements between the parties and the enforced rerunning of the agreed service. Market mechanisms provide an important basis for attributing the cost of meeting/violating an SLA. While it may seem reasonable to penalize SLA noncompliance, there are a number of concerns when issuing such penalties. For example, determining whether the service provider is the only party that should be penalized, or determining the type of penalty that must be applied to each party becomes a concern that needs to be considered.

12.3 SLA LIFECYLCE

As outlined in Chapter 10 of this book, an SLA goes through various stages within its lifecycle. Assuming that an SLA is initiated by a client application, these stages include the following:

- *Identifying the Provider.* This could either be "hardwired" (i.e., predetermined) or obtained through the use of a discovery (registry) service. Provider selection is an activity often outside the scope of the SLA lifecycle, but nevertheless an important stage to be executed.
- *Defining the SLA.* This stage involves identifying the particular terms that should be included in the SLA. These terms may relate to QoS issues that must subsequently be monitored, and also form the basis for penalty clauses. The definition also includes the period during which the SLA is valid.
- *Agreeing on the Terms of the SLA.* This stage involves identifying the constraints that must be met by a provider during service provisioning. A negotiation

process may be used to converge on such constraints. This stage would also involve identifying penalty clauses.

- *Provisioning and Execution.* This stage is responsible to use the previously agreed-on SLA and facilitate the practical provisioning. This stage involves the interaction with execution management services to setup resources and services accordingly.
- *Monitoring SLA Violations.* This stage involves monitoring the agreed-to terms and ensuring that they are not being violated. Who does the monitoring and how often is an aspect that needs to be considered at this stage.
- *Destroying SLAs.* Once a service provision has completed, the SLA must be destroyed.
- *Penalties for SLA Violation.* Once a service provision has completed, the monitoring data may be used to determine whether any penalties need to be imposed on the service provider.

12.3.1 Provider Identification Phase

The provider identification phase involves choosing possible partners to interact with. This may consist of a discovery phase, which involves searching a known registry (or a number of distributed registries) for providers that match some profile—generally using predefined metadata. The outcome of this stage is a list of providers (which may comprise only one provider) that offer the capability a client needs. Once a service provider (or multiple service providers) has been identified, the next stage involves defining the SLA between the client and the provider. The SLA may be between a single client and provider, or it may be between one client and multiple providers. In the subsequent analysis, we assume a two-party SLA (i.e., one involving a single client and a single provider).

12.3.2 Definition Phase

The definition of the SLA impacts the other stages in the SLA lifecycle—as the mechanisms used to identify particular service-level objectives (SLOs) will determine how violations will be identified in the future. Hence, an SLA may be defined using (name, value) pairs—where "name" refers to a particular SLO and "value" represents the requested quality/service level. An alternative is to use constraints that are more loosely defined—such as the use of (name, relationship, value) triples. In this context, provided the "relationship" between the "name" and "value" holds, the provider would have fulfilled the SLA requirements. Examples of relationships include "less than," "greater than," or a user-defined relationship function that needs to be executed by both the client and the provider. Other representation schemes have included the use of server-side functions—whereby an SLA is defined as a function $f(x_1, x_2, \ldots, x_n)$, where each (x_i) corresponds to a metric that is managed by the service provider. Using this approach, a client requests some capability from the service provider that is a function of what is available at the service provider. For instance, if the service provider has 512 GB of available memory at a particular point in time, the client requests 50% of this. In this context, $f(x)$ is evaluated according to the currently available capacity at the service provider [1]. An SLA must also be valid within some time period, a parameter that also needs to be agreed upon by the client and the provider.

12.3.3 Negotiation–Agreement Phase

Agreeing on SLA terms takes place once a description scheme has been identified. The next step is to identify the particular SLOs and their associated constraints. There needs to be some shared agreement on term semantics between the client and the provider. There is, however, no way to guarantee this, unless both the client and the provider use a common namespace (or term ontology), and therefore rely on the semantic definitions provided within this namespace. For example, the job submission description language (JSDL) [2] a proposed recommendation of the Open Grid Forum is often used to express SLOs related to computational resources.

Agreeing on SLO terms may be a multishot process between the two parties. This process can therefore be expressed through a "negotiation" protocol (a process requiring a provider to make an "offer" to the client, and the client then making a "counter offer"). The intention is to either reach convergence/agreement on SLOs—generally within some time bounds (or number of messages)—or indicate that the SLOs cannot be met. Also associated with an SLA must be the "penalty" terms that specify the compensation for the client if the SLA was not observed by the service provider. These penalty terms may also be negotiated between a client and a provider—or a fixed set of penalty terms may be used.

12.3.4 Provisioning and Execution Phase

The actual provisioning of services and resources on the basis of previously agreed-on SLAs is typically part of the underlying resource management systems. This part can be abstracted from the SLA management. The enablement can utilize existing systems like OGSA-Basic Execution Service (OGSA-BES) or Globus Resource Allocation Manager (GRAM) to facilitate the execution. This may require additional features to ensure that particular SLOs can be guaranteed.

12.3.5 Monitoring Phase

Once a service is executed according to an SLA, the compliance of the service provision with the SLA is monitored. A copy of the SLA must be maintained by both the client and the provider. It is necessary to distinguish between agreeing an SLA, and subsequently providing a service on the basis of the SLOs that have been agreed. A request to invoke a service based on the SLOs, for instance, may be undertaken at a time much later than when the SLOs were agreed. During provision it is necessary to determine whether the terms agreed in the SLA have been adhered to. In this context, the monitoring infrastructure is used to identify the difference between the agreed-on SLO and the value that was actually delivered during service provisioning—which is *trusted* by both the client and the provider. It is necessary to also define what constitutes a violation.

12.3.6 Termination Phase

An SLA may be destroyed/deleted in two situations: (1) when the service being defined in the SLA has completed and (2) when the time period over which the SLA has been agreed on has expired. In both cases, it is necessary for the SLA to be removed from both the client and the provider. Determining penalties for any SLA violation takes place after provisioning. Where an SLA was actually used to provision a service, it is necessary to determine whether any violations had occurred during provisioning. As indicated above, penalty clauses are also part of the SLA, and need to be negotiated between the client and the provider.

These stages demonstrate one cycle through the creation, use, and deletion of an SLA. Any violations detected in the SLA may be used in future cycles to choose between service providers. Clearly, the main parts of such a lifecycle need direct interaction with resource management functions. For instance, agreement and negotiation requires knowledge about the resource allocation plans in many application scenarios. The agreement might also require advance reservation of resources, which requires such capability to exist in resource management systems (RMSs) to establish an agreement. Similarly, the provisioning and termination needs enactment on the level of the resources. Considering the execution of a computational application as subject of the SLA, the SLA management needs some linkage to the underlying job management systems. In the following sections, we provide more details about the practical aspects of SLA-based resource management, and offer an architectural vision and methodology.

12.4 AN SLA-BASED RESOURCE MANAGEMENT–ALLOCATION ARCHITECTURE

12.4.1 Architectural Overview

As described above, a consumer and a provider use a predefined SLA to agree on certain QoS metrics. To achieve this, and then execute, monitor, and finalize any activity according to the SLA, a number of additional services are necessary. To ensure generality, we consider that several parties may be involved in the process of providing an SLA. This may include, besides consumers and providers, also brokers and intermediary SLA providers. In the following we consider a simplified model with only consumer and provider. Figure 12.1 shows a general SLA-based architecture with the necessary services. We use a classification in the following main areas:

- Consumer (or application)
- SLA negotiation and supervision
- Middleware services
- Provider
- Supporting services, which may be SLA-specific or more general in scope

We will discuss the individual entities in more detail in the subsequent paragraphs.

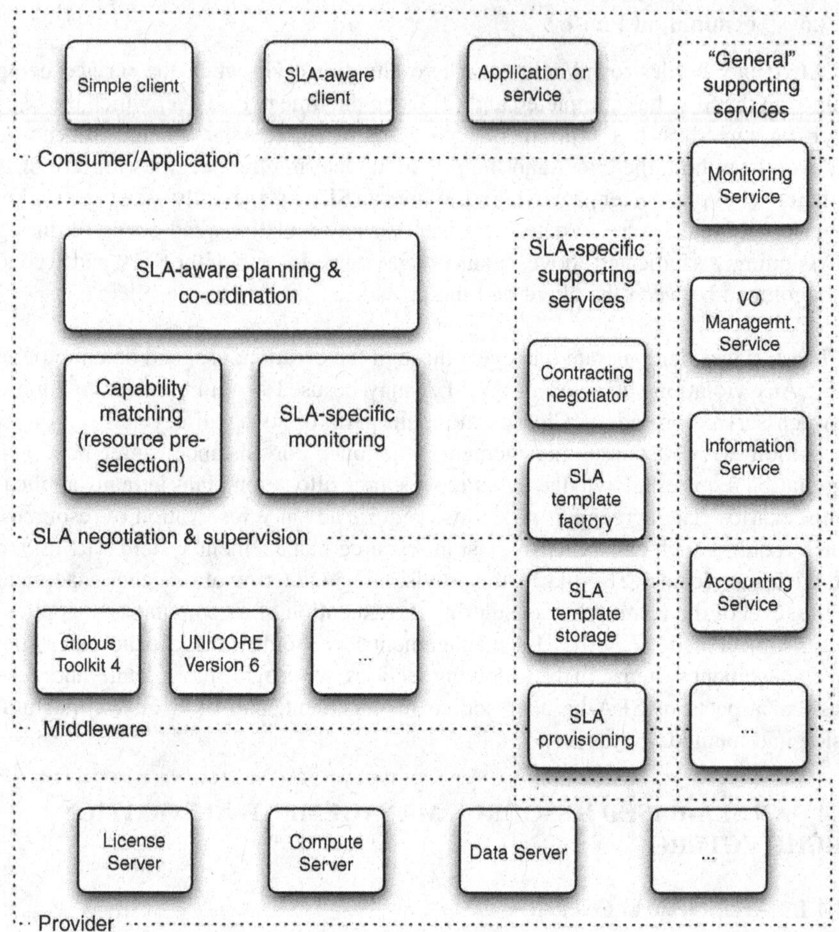

Figure 12.1 SLA-based resource management–allocation architecture.

12.4.2 Stakeholders and Services

12.4.2.1 Consumer View. Figure 12.1 shows different ways in which the client can interact with an SLA-based Grid: (1) SLA-aware services can access the SLA service layer directly through service calls, (2) customer services or applications can implement "SLA-specific" APIs to exploit the functionality of the SLA service layer, and (3) "simple" clients can be used without any SLA functionality in cases where it is not required. In general it cannot be expected that consumers directly deal with SLAs. Instead, they specify their requirements according to their business-level objectives. Those requirements are then included into an SLA for further processing, where characteristics and level of detail are dependent on the domain or the application respectively. Mapping such business-level objectives into SLAs remain a difficult and time-consuming process.

12.4.2.2 Provider View. The core business of a provider in a Grid is the provisioning of resources or services. In the context we consider here, this is achieved according to one or more SLOs which, a priori, have been agreed upon and captured in an SLA. In contrast to the consumer, who normally wants to deal mainly with application-specific requirements and not with SLAs, the provider has to "translate" the low-level technical details of what can be provided into SLA templates. That is, the user is interested in the high-level fulfillment of certain quality features, but may not necessarily know how these will be achieved. However, to achieve this goal, specific technical information may need to be included in the SLA. It is useful to note that both the providers and consumer operate according to their business-level objectives, which may differ substantially [3].

12.4.2.3 SLA Service Layer: Negotiation and Supervision. This layer covers the functionalities of finding suitable service providers (capability matching) and negotiating with them to establish usable SLA. On the basis of the requirements provided by the SLA consumers, the SLA service layer can automatically select SLA offers and plan the service allocation. These services include some limited scheduling functionality to coordinate the SLA. Different resource types can be considered in a similar fashion. Within this layer, the use of resources is considered in only a generic fashion, where different resource types can be modeled with different SLA templates. The selection is based on the information given in the SLA request to optimize a given preference. More sophisticated strategies are necessary to plan workflow-like SLA requests in which several different resources/services may be required. Such requirements may require combining several SLAs. This layer also includes SLA monitoring facilities in which the current SLAs are checked for fulfillment. This includes the timely identification of current and potential future SLA violations. According to data obtained from a monitoring service, the SLA service layer may optionally deploy automatic recovery mechanisms.

12.4.2.4 Middleware Layer. Although support for SLAs is provided in some existing middleware, such as GRIA [4], our architecture assumes "classical," non-SLA-enabled middleware, which is used mainly to submit, monitor, and control workflows or jobs. Such middleware is deployed at a majority of sites, with gLite [5], Globus [6], and UNICORE [7] as three of the more popular representatives, and it also provides the basis for a number of SLA-related developments such as the VIOLA metascheduling service [8] or ASKALON [9]. From the architecture in Figure 12.1, the middleware is the entity that executes the workflow or job once the consumer and provider have agreed on an SLA. The middleware provides command-line tools, Web service interfaces or APIs that enable services from the SLA service layer or the supporting services to access middleware functions. Additional services are needed for a real-life deployment of an SLA. This includes security-related services but also accounting functions. Such account and billing services are necessary for market-oriented Grids in which resource consumption is subject to cost.

12.4.2.4.1 SLA-Specific Supporting Services. This category includes services that provide support for SLA template repositories, such as factories for creation of new templates and services for storing templates. In addition, there is a need for initiating the provisioning of resources on the basis of constraints defined in the SLA.

12.4.2.4.2 General Supporting Services. This category of services comprises those that are often deployed in Grid infrastructures independent of the use of SLAs. This includes information and monitoring services about resources and jobs. In addition, there is need for security management and authorization support for virtual organizations, and support for accounting and billing.

12.4.3 Web Services Agreement

The Web Services Agreement (WS-Agreement) specification [10] from the Open Grid Forum (OGF) describes a protocol for establishing an agreement on the usage of services between a service provider and a consumer. Although other similar specifications exist (e.g., the Web Services Agreement Language [11]), one can observe that the use of WS-Agreement prevails in the Grid community [12].The specification defines a language and a protocol to represent the services of providers, create agreements based on offers, and monitor agreement compliance at runtime. An agreement defines a relationship between two parties that is dynamically established and dynamically managed. The objective of this relationship is to deliver a service by one of the parties. In the agreement each party agrees on the respective roles, rights, and obligations. A provider in an agreement offers a service according to conditions described in the agreement. A consumer enters into an agreement with the intent of obtaining guarantees on the availability of one or more services from the provider. Agreements can also be negotiated by entities acting on behalf of the provider and/or the consumer. An agreement creation process usually consists of three steps: (1) the initiator retrieves a template from the responder, who advertises the types of offers the responder is willing to accept; (2) the initiator then makes an offer, which is either accepted or rejected by the responder; and then (3) WS-Agreement–Negotiation, which sits on top of WS-Agreement, furthermore describes the re/negotiation of agreements. An agreement consists of the agreement name, its context, and the agreement terms. The context contains information about the involved parties and metadata such as the duration of the agreement. Agreement terms define the content of an agreement—service description terms (SDTs) define the functionality that is delivered under an agreement. A SDT includes a domain-specific description of the offered or required functionality (the service itself). *Guarantee terms* define assurance on service quality of the service described by the SDTs. They define SLOs, which describe the quality of service aspects of the service that have to be fulfilled by the provider. WS-Agreement allows the usage of any domain specific or standard condition expression language to define SLOs. The specification of domain-specific term languages is explicitly left open and subject to domain-specific standardization.

12.5 INTERACTION WITH GRID RESOURCE MANAGEMENT AND SCHEDULING

The use of SLAs is typically part of the Grid resource management and scheduling. In other words, if a Grid scheduling instance needs to select suitable resources for a Grid job, SLAs can be used for establishing well-defined quality of service. This happens on the higher level between a service provider and a service consumer and on the lower level between the Grid scheduler and a component of the respective local resource management system. The roles of service provider and service consumer may range from individuals to institutions, software agents, or other systems acting on behalf of physical entities. The "upper level" SLA (primarily focusing on business policy) often are based on general agreements, such as framework contracts that govern the relationship between the parties. These general agreements may include legal aspects and may set boundaries for SLAs, which have to be respected in the agreement templates. Today, the technology most frequently used is the aforementioned WS-Agreement [12].

12.5.1 Deducing SLA-Relevant Information from Provider Layer

Information from the provider layer is needed

- Before starting the dynamic creation of an SLA using a WS-Agreement factory, the provider has to be selected that is expected to have the capacity for the job.
- After the creation of the SLA both parties need information to verify whether the SLA is fulfilled or violated.

Moreover, with a large number of providers, the manual selection of resources is no longer feasible and will be delegated to a resource selection service (RSS) [13,14]. The RSS creates a shortlist of potentially appropriate resources and respective providers that the Grid-level scheduler then uses for SLA negotiation; naturally, this shortlist will be based on the information about the requirements of the application and information from the provider.

12.5.2 Retrieving Templates from a Template Storage

In our architecture, we consider SLA templates as a starting point for establishing an SLA. Providing templates for SLAs in template storage is a convenient approach for a service provider minimizing the overhead and complexity of negotiating individual SLAs on the fly. The approach using templates from template storage is similar to shopping in supermarkets where the goods tailored in advance to suit the expected demand of the customers—either the packaging unit does or does not meet the demand. Retrieving preconfigured templates from storage offers both the provider and the customer a simple way to create SLAs for frequently recurring patterns of resource usage. The customer selects a template appropriate for the task to be executed and sends the template to the provider as an agreement offer. The provider either rejects the offer or agrees and sends an endpoint reference (EPR) back to the customer. Depending on the template, the provider may additionally allow limited modifications of the template before the customer sends it to the provider as an offer. In this case the template also contains constraints on the types of modification that can be made, and allows the provider to easily check the validity of the customer's offer.

12.5.3 Accessing a Factory to Create a New Template

Creating templates on the fly using a factory increases the flexibility of both parties. For the consumer the template created dynamically may better reflect the actual resource requirements, the QoS, and the acceptable policy for a task. The service provider, on the other hand, has the possibility to react dynamically if important properties and conditions of the resource pool change. For example, more resources may have to be allocated to particular types of customers; furthermore, resources with new characteristics may enter the pool or may drop out of the pool because of failure.

The factory is maintained by the service provider and may be accessed via an EPR. In case consumers are allowed to access the factory to create templates, the EPR has to be published beforehand. The major drawback of using dynamically created templates is the additional effort for validating the SLOs defined in the templates "guarantee terms and penalties."

12.6 ADVANCE RESERVATION OF RESOURCES

12.6.1 Advance Reservation for Better Planning of Resource Usage

Submitting a job to a Grid resource usually results in inserting the job into a queue of the local resource management system for execution. This kind of service level is called *best effort*, indicating that there are no guarantees associated with the requested service. However, this mode of operation is not sufficient for many application scenarios. The benefit of advance reservation for the customer is the guarantee associated with the SLA that the required resources would be available for the execution of a job while the provider may better plan resource utilization.

12.6.2 Increasing Reliability

However, results of an application are often required at a certain time requiring resources to be made available at a fixed time, for example

- Because results of an application need to be available by a deadline
- To limit waiting time between the different tasks of a workflow
- To support interactive and collaborative applications

Advance reservation is just another QoS requirement and must be supported by the local resource management system(s). Providing guarantees with respect to availability of resources through advance reservation has proved to be an approach offering both the customer and the provider a number of advantages.

Until now the advance reservation of the required resources often was negotiated with the provider by mail or telephone. As the number of providers and resources in the Grid increases, doing this negotiation manually becomes tedious or unfeasible. The growing use of SLAs for expressing and negotiating SLOs gives new opportunities, and indeed SLAs play an important role for reserving resources in advance. Negotiating the availability of appropriate resources during a given timeslot is usually the task of a Grid scheduler—as this scheduler may connect to a number of local and remote resource management systems for the negotiation.

12.6.3 Enabling Resource Orchestration and Coallocation

Using advance reservation, more complex tasks may be performed efficiently:

- Coallocation of distributed applications that need multiple resources at the same time, for example, for multiple physics simulations such as fluid dynamics or structural mechanics [15].
- Orchestration of workflows with dependencies between the tasks distributed across multiple resources; for example, workflow tasks depending on results of the preceding tasks may be executed with smaller gaps between the individual tasks, resulting in smaller makespans [16], as depicted in Figure 12.2.
- Reserving additional types of resources like storage, network, and software licenses along with computational resources may further increase the efficiency and reliability of complex task execution in both coallocation and orchestration scenarios [17].

In addition to specifying the normal job requirements, a user now additionally specifies the date and time when the resources are needed and the duration of the usage.

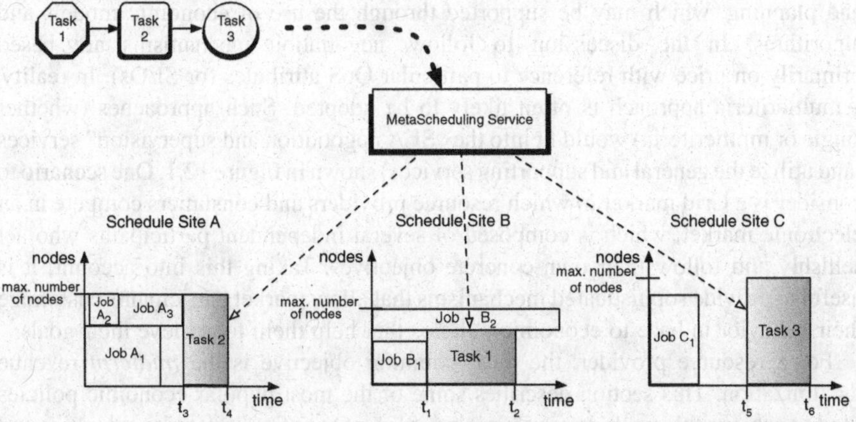

Figure 12.2 A Grid scheduler reserving slots for components of a workflow across three sites.

On receiving a request, the Grid scheduler begins negotiation for the availability of resources offering the required properties with the local resource management systems. Depending on whether the application is a single job requiring only one resource or a workflow-like application where multiple resources are needed, the negotiation process may need multiple iterations until all required resources are reserved [18].

12.6.4 Renegotiation of SLAs

Currently, SLAs once negotiated are static and may not be altered; canceling an SLA and negotiating a new one is the only way to modify an existing SLA. However, in many situations one of the parties may wish to modify an agreement, for example

- The provider has a higher interest in using assigned resources for another job.
- The user detects that the job will run longer than expected.
- The user needs the results earlier and needs more resources than initially planned.

Renegotiation of existing SLAs is studied in a number of projects [19–21] and in the GRAAP (Grid Resource Allocation Agreement Protocol) working group of the Open Grid Forum [22]. Besides the open questions of the renegotiation itself, such as how to create a completely new SLA or an extension to the existing one, or how to constrain the SLA to speed up the negotiation process by reducing the complexity, there are a number of issues with the local resource management systems; however currently only very few of these support dynamic changes to the resource allocation for an application or a user. If there are not enough resources available, other jobs must be migrated or terminated.

12.7 MARKET MODELS FOR RESOURCE ALLOCATION SUPPORT

The practical application of some of the concepts outlined above requires negotiation and planning, which may be supported through the use of economic models and algorithms. In the discussion to follow, negotiation mechanisms are based primarily on price with reference to particular QoS attributes (or SLOs). In reality, a multicriteria approach is often likely to be adopted. Such approaches (whether single or multicriteria) would fit into the "SLA negotiation and supervision" services (and utilize the general and supporting services) shown in Figure 12.1. One scenario to consider is a Grid market in which resource providers and consumers compete in an electronic market, which is composed of several independent participants who act selfishly and follow their own concrete objectives. Taking this into account, it is useful to provide sophisticated mechanisms that allow market participants customize their behavior in base to economic policies that help them to achieve their goals.

For a resource provider, the most common objective is the *midterm* revenue maximization. This section describes some of the most popular economic policies used to achieve this goal: dynamic pricing, SLA negotiation strategies, penalties and rewards, and selective SLA fulfillment.

12.7.1 Dynamic Pricing

Economic markets are composed of a set of tradable goods (*supply*) offered by the market, and a set of buyers (*demand*) who ask for a subset of the supplied goods. In a Grid market the *supply* consists of computer resources, such as storage systems, or clusters, and the *demand* are the users and applications that are willing to pay for accessing these resources. The goal of dynamic pricing is to find an efficient allocation of the supply among the demand.

The *law of demand* states that the higher the price of a good, the lesser the demand for this good; the *law of supply* states that the higher the price of a good, the higher the quantity that will be supplied, because selling higher amounts of goods at higher prices will increase the revenue. Thus, both supply and demand can be controlled by changing the prices of goods; at lower prices, supply is low and demand is high, and at higher prices, supply is high and demand is low. This leads to the market being in disequilibrium.

In a market in disequilibrium, if the prices are too low, the demand cannot be satisfied because the supply is too scarce, and if the prices are too high, the supply cannot be sold completely because demand is too low. The efficient allocation that dynamic pricing pursues is achieved when it reaches the *equilibrium* point, and both demand and supply are satisfied. Two approaches to finding the optimal pricing within such a market will be explained: tâtonnement and auctioning [23].

12.7.1.1 Tâtonnement. *Tâtonnement* (literally meaning "groping about" in French) is an iterative method used to progressively adapt the prices to the current market status. Ferguson et al. [24] propose the following algorithm for this process:

1. Choose an initial price vector $\rightarrow \vec{p} = \{p_1, p_2, \ldots, p_n\}$, where $p_1, p_2, \ldots, p_n$ are the prices for the resources numbered between 1 and n, respectively, and a minimum price vector $\vec{m} = \{m_1, m_2, \ldots, m_n\}$, which is the price below which the provider will not sell the resource.
2. For each resource, find the *excess demand function*$Z_i(\vec{p})$, which is the demand for a resource i at a given price p_i minus the supply of it.
3. If for each resource i, $Z_i(\vec{p}) = 0$ or $Z_i(\vec{p}) \leq 0$ and $p_i = m_i$, equilibrium has been reached, then the iteration stops.
4. Otherwise, for all the resources update the price vector $\vec{p}$ following the next formula:

$$p_i = \max\left[p_i + p_i \frac{Z_i(\vec{p})}{S_i}, m_i\right]$$

   where S_i is the supply for resource i.
5. Go to step 2.

The formula in step 4 can be replaced by another that the provider considers better for its requirements. Using this approach (step 4), the market evolves to equilibrium quickly in the first few iterations, with an increase in accuracy in the next ones. If the number of resources is high, the prices will be always low and the market will not be profitable. In this case, the provider should consider applying a *quantity tâtonnement* process [25], where the supply is adapted to the demand by altering the prices.

12.7.1.2 ***Auctions.*** In *auctions*, the price can be initially established by the seller, but the final price is determined by the customer who wins the auction based on specific rules (determined by the type of auction being considered):

- *English auction*—seller gives a start price, and buyers who are interested in acquiring the resource increment the price in their bids. The highest bidder obtains the resource.
- *Dutch auction*—seller gives the highest price, and it is gradually lowered by the seller until one of the buyers claims the resource.
- *Hybrid auction*—asking price of a resource is increased if a bid is submitted, and decreased if no bid is submitted.
- *Sealed-bid auction*—each customer submits a sealed bid, without knowing the bids from other customers and vice versa. When all the bids are received, the seller gives access to the resource to the highest bidder.

12.7.2 SLA Negotiation Strategies

Negotiation is the process toward creating suitable agreements between different parties in a Grid. The whole task of negotiation is challenging, as the resources are heterogeneous and the service provisioning is not a standardized good (as, e.g., in stockmarkets) but depends on the individual requirements and preferences of the user for a particular task. During the negotiation process, the conflicts between the different objectives and policies of the negotiating parties must be reconciled.

Strategic negotiation models are introduced in the paper by Li and Yahyapour [26], where bilateral negotiation models consist of (1) the negotiation protocol, (2) utility functions or preference relationships for the negotiating parties, and (3) the negotiation strategy that is applied during the negotiation process. In the negotiation model described, the negotiation parties do not know the opponents' private reservation information and their preferences/utility functions. The utility function of the customer and the preference relationship of the seller are given for their respective automated negotiation agents. Typically, objectives of customers are related to specifications such as response time, CPU (number, speed, architecture), and amount of memory; such specifications may also include business requirements such as "best price" or "maximize efficiency." The main objective of resource/service providers usually is to maximize the economic profit. All the different objectives are independent and should be dealt with simultaneously, taking into account the multiple criteria [29].

Li and Yahyapour [26] propose to divide the different criteria in subutility functions and express the user preferences by assigning different weights to them. For example

$$U_{\text{price}} = \frac{P_c^{\max} - P_c^t}{P_c^{\max} - P_c^{\min}}, \qquad U_{\text{time}} = \frac{T_c^{\max} - T_c^t}{T_c^{\max} - T_c^{\min}}$$

where U_{price} is the subutility function for the price of a Grid job and U_{time} is the subutility function for the job's waiting time; $P_c^{\max}$ is the maximum acceptable price for the user, and $P_c^{\min}$ is the minimum offered price from the user. The user weighs his/her preferences with W_{price} and W_{time} to obtain the following aggregate utility function:

$$U_{\text{job}} = W_{\text{price}} U_{\text{price}} + W_{\text{time}} U_{\text{time}}, \qquad W_{\text{price}} + W_{\text{time}} = 1$$

In the negotiation process, an agent may change its preference by changing the weight associated to that issue.

12.7.3 Penalties and Rewards

The *reward* can be defined as the amount of money that a client must pay to a Grid provider when it finishes a task or service correctly. If the provider does not fulfill one of the SLA terms, the *penalty amount* must be paid to the client. Both reward and penalty must be agreed at negotiation time and must be defined specified in the SLA.

Penalty can be specified in SLA as a *penalty function* [27], which not only penalizes the provider for service failures but also compensates the users for them. An example of a reward and the penalty function is as follows:

$$\texttt{reward} = \texttt{price} - (\texttt{delay} \times \texttt{penalty\_rate}),$$

$$\texttt{where delay} = \begin{cases} 0,\ \textit{if finish\_time} \le \textit{deadline} \\ (\textit{finish\_time} - \textit{submit\_time}) - \textit{deadline}\ \texttt{otherwise} \end{cases}$$

Figure 12.3 illustrates the reward/penalty function; the provider earns the agreed- to price if it completes the job before the established deadline. The value decreases linearly with the delay until the reward is negative, which represents a penalty. The penalty could be bounded to avoid excessive penalties.

Reward/penalty functions can be improved with additional parameters; for instance, they may contain not only the finish time but also additional parameters such as disk speed or number of CPUs. Also, the SLA can specify in more precise terms what constitutes an SLA violation—to violate a single SLA term, a particular number of terms, violate the SLA terms during a time interval, or over repeated intervals.

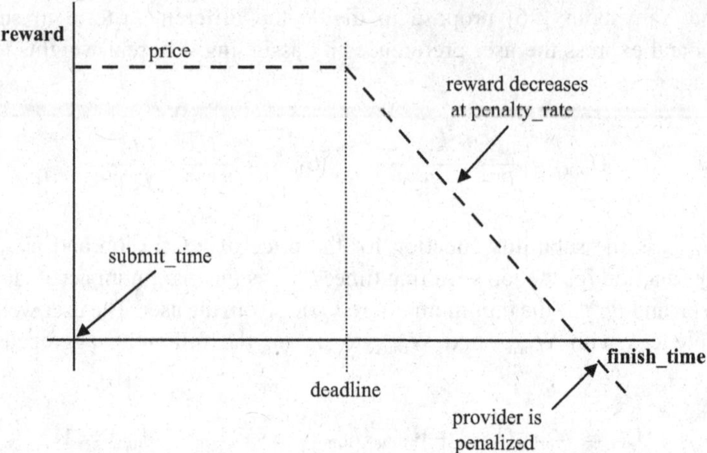

Figure 12.3 Example of reward/penalty defining function.

The reward/penalty function can be used by the resource provider to perform more accurate scheduling for its incoming jobs, by considering reward, penalty rates, deadlines, and managing the risk of paying any penalties. Macias et al. [28] performed some experiments that demonstrated the economic benefit of taking into account penalties and rewards in system overloading scenarios: if not all the SLAs can be agreed to, it is possible to combine selective SLA violations and task reallocations to minimize the economic loss. Figure 12.4 shows that using selective SLA fulfillment will allow providers have up to 60% of higher economic revenue when the resource pool is heavily overloaded: in a farm of 75 resources, if part of the resource pool

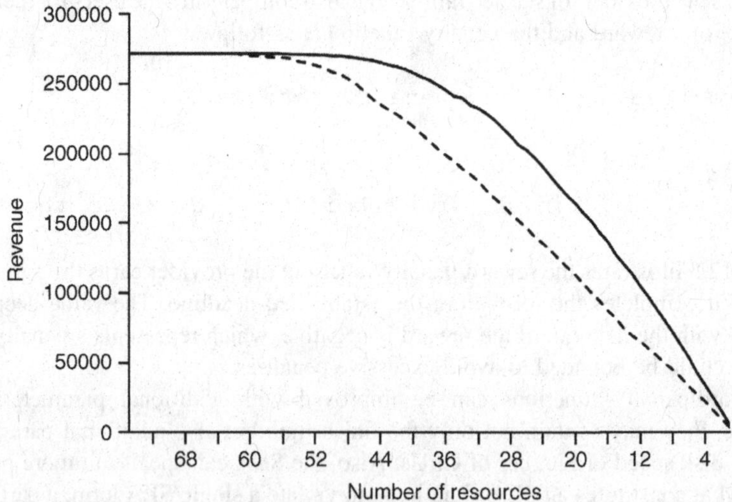

Figure 12.4 Comparison of revenue between policies usage (continuous line) and no policy (dashed line).

crashes, a portion of the previously accepted SLAs will be violated. Figure 12.4 also shows how the maximum revenue is maintained with fewer resources if economic policies are applied.

12.8 CASE STUDY

Various applications could benefit from the use of SLA-based electronic market mechanisms within a Grid computing infrastructure. Let us consider one application scenario that requires a highly specialized service, such as, a specific data-mining service, with several suppliers offering this service. An application example is the *ca*tallactic *co*llaborative *vi*rtual *te*ams (Cat-COVITE) [30,31] prototype application consisting of three main elements: (1) one or more user services; (2) a "master Grid service" (MGS), responsible for interacting with a Grid market manager (GMM) to find an EPR of a service instance; and (3) one or more service instances that are being hosted on a particular resource. The Cat-COVITE application involves searching through distributed product catalogs—modeled as a Web services–enabled database, and using a distributed search strategy. The particular approach adopted in the Cat-COVITE application is also employable in other industrial applications that make use of distributed databases.

The interaction between the application prototype and the GMM is based on the WS-Agreement. When a client issues a request, the application determines which services are required to fulfill it. These services represent either software executables (e.g. a mathematical algorithm) or computational resources. The application service translates these requirements to a WS-Agreement template, which is submitted to the GMM. The middleware searches among the available service providers, which have registered their particular service specifications, such as contractual conditions, policies, and QoS levels. When a suitable service provider is found, the application requirements are negotiated by agents implemented in the middleware who act on behalf of the service providers as sellers, and the applications as buyers. Once an agreement is reached between trading agents, a service instance is created for the application, and a reference is returned to the application (which can subsequently be used to invoke it).

In the COVITE prototype, suppliers, and purchasers collaborate to procure supplies for a particular construction project by using the COVITE application. These projects are usually unique, very complex, and involve many participants from a number of organizations. These participants need to work concurrently, thus requiring real-time collaboration between geographically remote participants. Each consortium is in effect a virtual organization (VO). The application requires the search to take place across a large number of supplier databases to retrieve products matching a criteria set by the purchasers or contractors. The application enables a search to be performed using a cluster of machines in a Grid network.

The COVITE prototype application is divided into two functional services: (1) security service and (2) multiple database search services (DSSs). Each DSS enables searching across a large number of supplier databases (SDs) using a MGS

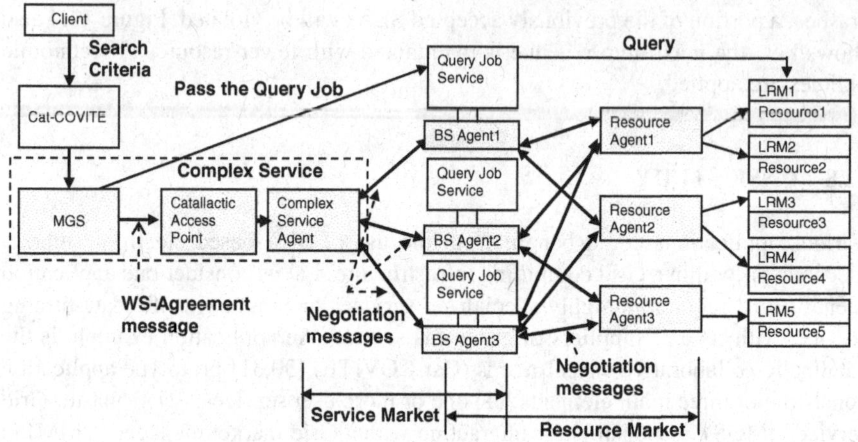

Figure 12.5 Cat-COVITE prototype and catallactic agents.

instance via a cluster. In this instance, the query is defined according to a data model that is specific to a given application domain. Arbitrary text queries (e.g., as in the Google search engine) are not allowed. The COVITE application allows VOs to plan, schedule, coordinate, and share components between designs, and from different suppliers. The ability of a free-market economy to adjudicate and satisfy the needs of VOs, in terms of services and resources, represents an important feature of the catallaxy mechanism. There are also possibilities for each of these VOs to try maximizing their own utility on the market.

12.8.1 Cat-COVITE Prototype and the Catallactic Grid Markets

Figure 12.5 shows the Cat-COVITE components and related catallactic agents as buyers and seller in a service and a resource market. The complex service, which is an abstract component consisting of the MGS, the catallactic access point (CAP)—the access point between the application and the market, and the complex service agent; the query job service—a type of basic service; and the resource where the query service is executed—as a type of computational resource. We do not consider any service composition mechanisms and concentrate on the allocation process for each basic service.

'The complex service agent is the buyer entity in the service market, and the query job service, via the basic service agent, is the seller entity on the service market. complex service agent starts parallel negotiation with a number of agents representing query job services (basic services) and choses one of them on the basis of negotiation on price, while the complex service, via MGS, translates a request to a basic service, of query job service type. The complex service includes the following activities:

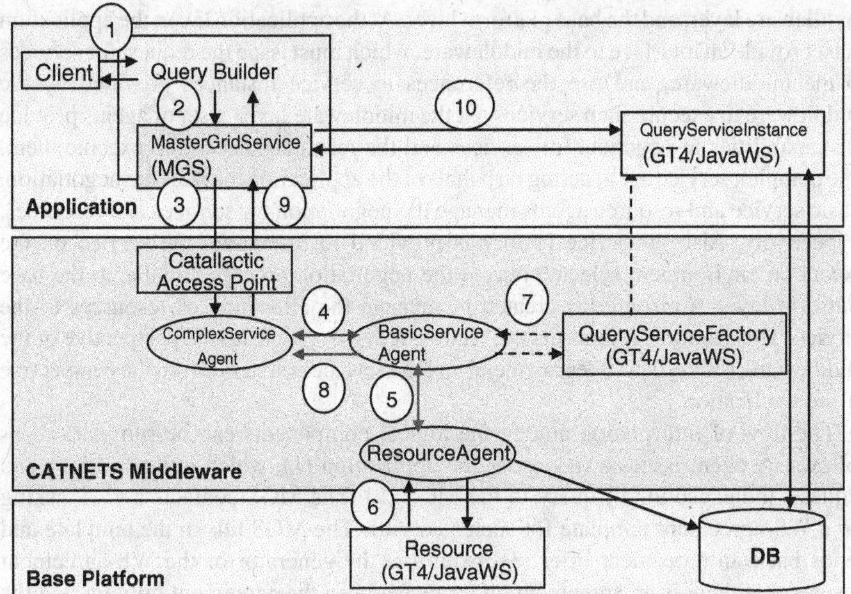

Figure 12.6 Integration of Cat-COVITE and catallactic middleware.

- Translates a request to a basic service—of query job service type
- Starts parallel negotiation with a number of agents representing query job services (basic services)
- Sends a query to a list of query job services (basic services)

The query job service is the buyer entity in the resource market, and the local resource managers (LRMs) are the seller entities in the resource market. The main function of a basic service agent within the resource market is coallocation of resources (resource bundles) by parallel negotiation with different resource providers (LRM entities). The query job service, which is a type of basic service, involves query execution on a particular database and consists of

- Query job execution environment (offers the deployment of "slaves," which are able to execute the query)
- Translation of query to resource requirements

Within the Cat-COVITE application, the query job service needs to support response time as the main QoS metric. With this goal the query job service buys resources in the resource market. Resource seller entities are able to provide a set of resources via the LRM. The resource agents act on behalf of these LRMs, which hide the physical resources behind them.

Figure 12.6 shows a detailed view of the architecture, identifying the placement of logical components along the three layers: the application layer, the catallactic middleware layer, and the base platform layer. At the application layer, the application must provide an interface to the middleware, which must issue the request for services to the middleware, and use the references to service instances provided by the middleware to execute such services. At the middleware layer, a set of agents provide the capabilities to negotiate for services and the resources needed to execute them. The complex service agent acting on behalf of the application initiates the negotiation. Basic service and resource agents manage the negotiation for services and resources, respectively. Also, a service factory is provided to instantiate the service on the execution environment selected during the negotiation process. Finally, at the base platform layer, a resource is created to manage the allocation of resources to the service. This resource represents the "state" of the service from the perspective of the middleware. (*Note:* This does not mean that the service is stateful from the perspective of the application.)

The flow of information among the logical components can be summarized as follows: A client issues a request to the application (1), which builds a query and requests the execution of query to the MGS (2). The MGS contacts a CAP asking for a WS-agreement template for such a service. The MGS fills in the template and sends back an agreement offer (3). Note that the generator of the WS-agreement ensures that there is an agreement on terms between the agreement initiator and the agreement offer provider. The creation of the agreement template in this way ensures that there is some consensus on the use of particular terms between the application and the CAP. The complex service agent initiates catallactic mechanisms to find the appropriate basic services and resources. The complex service agent uses discovery mechanisms implemented in the middleware to locate basic service agents providing a query service. When a number of basic service agents are discovered, it starts negotiations with one of them (4). In turn, such basic service agent must discover and negotiate with a resource agent for query execution resources in the resource market (5). Negotiations are implemented by the economic framework layer, where different protocols can be used depending on the agent's strategy. When an agreement with a basic service agent is reached, the resource agent instantiate a Resource to keep track of the allocated resources and provides to the basic service agent a handle for this resource (6). Subsequently, a basic service agents use the query service factory to instantiate the query service on the selected GT4 container (7). A basic service agent returns to the complex service agent the reference of the newly instantiated query service and the related resource(s) (8). The reference to the query service is returned to the MGS (9), which uses it to invoke the service, passing the query to be executed (10).

The example scenario in terms of the Cat-COVITE application in the prototype interacting with the middleware is as follows. An MGS needs to run a search request. The MGS sends an agreement offer (AO), based on the agreement template (AT) (see Listing 12.1) downloaded from the CAP, to find a query job service. The complex service agent, acting on behalf of the complex service (in this case represented by the MGS) negotiates with the basic service agent for query services to fulfil the job. The AT specifies the service description elements that are allowed by the factory that advertises it.

```
<?xml version="1.0" encoding="UTF-8"?>
<wsag:AgreementTemplate AgreementID="QueryTemplate-v001"
xmlns:wsag="http://schemas.ggf.org/graap/2005/09/ws-
agreement">
<wsag:Name>QueryComplexService</wsag:Name>
<wsag:Context>
  <wsag:AgreementInitiator> <! - can be a URI or a security
identity of the initiator -> NameOfTheInitiator
</wsag:AgreementInitiator>
  <wsag:ExpirationTime>DateTime</wsag:ExpirationTime>
  <wsag:TemplateID>QueryTemplate-001</wsag:TemplateID>
  <wsag:TemplateName>QueryComplexService </wsag:Template
  Name>
</wsag:Context>
<wsag:Terms>
  <BasicServiceType>QueryBasicService </BasicServiceType>
  <NumberOfBasicServiceNodes> <!- between 1 to 10 ->
  </NumberOfBasicServiceNodes>
  <BasicServiceConstraints>
    <ResponseTimePerRequest>10
    <!- maximum milliseconds ->
    </ResponseTimePerRequest>
  </BasicServiceConstraints>
  <Price> </Price>
</wsag:Terms>
</wsag:AgreementTemplate>
```

Listing 12.1 Agreement template.

The agreement offer is initiated by the agreement initiator, in this case the MGS and presented in Listing 12.2. If the agreement provider does not accept the offer, the agreement initiator has to send another agreement offer. The negotiation between the agreement provider and initiator, in this scenario, is based on price.

12.9 CONCLUSIONS

An overview of current efforts making use of service-level agreements for resource management and allocation has been provided. The emergence of service-oriented Architectures provide new approaches for increasing the pool of available resources beyond local ones for executing distributed applications. Adding resources provided by collaborating institutions or from a commercial service provider to satisfy resource demand exceeding the locally available capacity is close to becoming a common operation rather than a proof of concept deployed in a limited context within a project environment. However, distributed environments crossing administrative boundaries have no centralized coordinators, and need new mechanisms to ensure a level of reliability similar to that in the local environment. The use of SLAs to specify and

```
<?xml version="1.0" encoding="UTF-8"?>
<wsag:AgreementTemplate AgreementID="QueryTemplate-v001"
xmlns:wsag="http://schemas.ggf.org/graap/2005/09/ws-
agreement">
<wsag:Name>QueryComplexService</wsag:Name>
<wsag:Context>
  <wsag:AgreementInitiator> <! - can be a URI or a security
identity of the initiator -> NameOfTheInitiator </wsag:
AgreementInitiator>
  <wsag:ExpirationTime>DateTime</wsag:ExpirationTime>
  <wsag:TemplateID>QueryTemplate-001</wsag:TemplateID>
  <wsag:TemplateName>QueryComplexService </wsag:Template
  Name>
</wsag:Context>
<wsag:Terms>
  <BasicServiceType>QueryBasicService </BasicServiceType>
  <NumberOfBasicServiceNodes>1 <!- between 1 to 10 ->
  </NumberOfBasicServiceNodes>
  <BasicServiceConstraints>
    <ResponseTimePerRequest>10
    <!- maximum milliseconds ->
    </ResponseTimePerRequest>
  </BasicServiceConstraints>
  <Price>100</Price>
</wsag:Terms>
</wsag:AgreementTemplate>
```

Listing 12.2 Agreement offer.

provision access to resources on the basis of QoS properties, even where the service level cannot be enforced because of to the autonomy of the different domains, has become an important new research objective recently.

With the proposed OGF recommendation WS-Agreement the technology is now available to define and implement SLAs in an interoperable way. Over the last year a number of resource management systems and Grid schedulers have been adopting SLAs as a means for reliable allocation. Applying SLAs for resource management and allocation allows one to consider computational and data resources as tradable goods. This broadens the traditional approach of resource management towards implementation of economic models. As shown in section 12.7, this facilitates the establishment of sophisticated methods for resource selection, dynamic pricing, and allocation. Finally, we presented a case study highlighting the use of SLAs in an auction-based economic model for allocating jobs to resources in an environment for the architecture/engineering/construction industry (COVITE). The next step involves making the management of SLAs more dynamic. To that end, the possibility of negotiating agreements needs to be extended. Providing mechanisms to securely renegotiate existing agreements will provide additional flexibility in supporting highly dynamic service provisioning environments in the future.

REFERENCES

1. V. Yarmolenko and R. Sakellariou, An evaluation of heuristics for SLA based parallel job scheduling, *Proc. 3rd High Performance Grid Computing Workshop* (in conjunction with IPDPS 2006), Rhodes, Greece, 2006.
2. *Job Submission Description Language (JSDL) Specification v1.0*, Grid Forum Document, GFD.56, Open Grid Forum, 2005.
3. P. Masche, B. Mitchell, and P. Mckee, The increasing role of SLAs in B2B, *Proc. 2nd International Conf. Web Information Systems and Technologies,* Setubal, Portugal, April 2006.
4. M. Surridge, S. Taylor, D. de Roure, and E. Zaluska, Experiences with GRIA: Industrial applications on a Web services Grid, *Proc. 1st IEEE International Conf. e-Science and Grid Computing,* Melbourne, Australia, 2005.
5. *gLite—Lightweight Middleware for Grid Computing*, http://glite.web.cern.ch/glite/, last accessed June 2008).
6. I. Foster, Globus toolkit version 4: Software for service-oriented systems, *Proc. IFIP International Conf. Network and Parallel Computing,* LNCS, Vol. 3779, Springer, 2006.
7. M. Riedel et al., Web services interfaces and open standards integration into the European UNICORE 6 Grid middleware, *Proc. 2007 Middleware for Web Services (MWS 2007) Workshop at 11th International IEEE EDOC Conf. "The Enterprise Computing Conference,"* Annapolis, MD, 2007.
8. H. Ludwig, T. Nakata, O. Wäldrich, P. Wieder, and W. Ziegler, Reliable orchestration of resources using WS-Agreement, *Proc. 2006 International Conf. High Performance Computing and Communications (HPCC06)*, Munich, Germany, Sept. 2006.
9. T. Fahringer, R. Prodan, R. Duan, F. Nerieri, S. Podlipnig, J. Qin, M. Siddiqui, H. L. Truong, A. Villazón, and M. Wieczorek, ASKALON: A Grid application development and computing environment, *Proc. 6th IEEE IEEE International Workshop on Grid Computing (Grid 2005)*, Seattle, WA, 2005.
10. *Web Services Agreement Specification (WS-Agreement)*, Grid Forum Document, GFD.107, Open Grid Forum, 2007.
11. A. Keller and H. Ludwig, The WSLA framework: Specifying and monitoring service level agreements for Web services, *Journal of Network and Systems Management* (special issue on e-business management) **11**(1):57–81 (March 2003).
12. J. Seidel, O. Wäldrich, P. Wieder, R. Yahyapour, and W. Ziegler, Using SLA for resource management and scheduling—a survey, *Proc. Workshop on Using Service Level Agreements in Grids* (in conjunction with Grid 2007), Austin, TX, Sept. 2007.
13. OGSA Resource Selection Services WG (OGSA-RSS-WG), http://www.ogf.org/gf/group_info/view.php?group=ogsa-rss-wg (last accessed June 2008).
14. R. Gruber, V. Keller, P. Manneback, M. Thiémard, O. Wäldrich, P. Wieder, and W. Ziegler, Integration of Grid cost model into ISS/VIOLA meta-scheduler environment, *Proc. UNICORE Summit 2006* (in conjunction with Euro-Par 2006), Dresden, Germany, 2006.
15. T. Eickermann, W. Frings, O. Wäldrich, P. Wieder, and W. Ziegler, Co-allocation of MPI jobs with the VIOLA Grid metascheduling framework, *Proc. German eScience Conf. GES2007,* Baden-Baden, Germany, 2007.

16. P. Wieder, O. Wäldrich, R. Yahyapour, and W. Ziegler, Improving workflow execution through SLA-based advance reservation, In *Achievements in European Research on Grid System*, CoreGRID Integration Workshop 2006 (selected papers), October 19–20, Krakow, Poland. S. Gorlatch, M. Bubak, T. Priol (eds.), Springer Science + Business Media, New York, 2008, pp. 207–222.
17. C. Barz, T. Eickermann, M. Pilz, O. Wäldrich, L. Westphal, and W. Ziegler, Co-allocating compute and network resources—bandwidth on demand in the VIOLA testbed, *Proc. CoreGRID Symp.*, Rennes, France, Aug. 2007.
18. P. Wieder, O. Wäldrich, and W. Ziegler, A meta-scheduling service for co-allocating arbitrary types of resources, *Proc. 6th International Conf. Parallel Processing and Applied Mathematics* (*PPAM 2005*), Poznan, Poland, 2005.
19. NextGRID: Architecture for next generation Grids, http://www.nextgrid.org/ (last accessed June 2008).
20. CoreGRID—European Research Network on Foundations, software infrastructures and applications for large-scale distributed, GRID and peer-to-peer technologies, http://www.coregrid.net/ (last accessed July 2009).
21. BREIN—Business objective driven Reliable and Intelligent Grids for Real BussiNess, http://www.eu-brein.com/ (last accessed June 2008).
22. Grid Resource Allocation Agreement WG (GRAAP-WG), http://www.ogf.org/gf/group_info/view.php?group=graap-wg (last accessed July 2009).
23. D. F. Ferguson, *The Application of Microeconomics to the Design of Resource Allocation and Control Algorithms*, PhD thesis, Columbia Univ., New York, 1989.
24. D. F. Ferguson, C. Nikolaou, J. Sairamesh, and Y. Yemini, Economic models for allocating resources in computer systems, in *Market-Based Control: A Paradigm for Distributed Resource Allocation*, S. Clearwater, ed., World Scientific, Hong Kong, 1996.
25. A. Mas-Colell, M. D. Whinston, and J. R. Green, *Microeconomic Theory*, Oxford Univ. Press, UK, 1995.
26. J. Li and R. Yahyapour, Learning-based negotiation strategies for Grid Scheduling, *Proc. 6th IEEE International Symp. Cluster Computing and the Grid,* Singapore, May 16–19, 2006.
27. C. S. Yeo and R. Buyya, Service level agreement based allocation of cluster resources: Handling penalty to enhance utility, *Proc. 7th International Conf. Cluster Computing,* Boston, MA, Sept. 26–30, 2005.
28. M. Macias, O. Rana, G. Smith, J. Guitart, and J. Torres, Maximising revenue in Grid markets using an economically enhanced resource manager, *Concurrency and Computation: Practice and Experience*, DOI 10.1002/cpe.1370.
29. B. Schnizler, D. Neumann, D. Veit, and C. Weinhardt, Trading Grid services—a multi-attribute combinatorial approach, *European Journal of Operational Research* **187**(3): 943–961 (2006).
30. L. Joita, J. S. Pahwa, P. Burnap, A. Gray, O. Rana, and J. Miles, Supporting collaborative virtual organisations in the construction industry via the Grid, *Proc. UK e-Science All Hands Meeting 2004,* Nottingham, UK, Aug. 31–Sept. 3, 2004.
31. L. Joita, O. Rana, P. Chacin, I. Chao, F. Freitag, L. Navarro, and O. Ardaiz, Application deployment using catallactic Grid middleware, *Proc. 3rd International Workshop on Middleware for Grid Computing* (*MGC 2005*), co-located with ACM/USENIX/IFIP Middleware 2005, Grenoble, France, Nov. 28–Dec. 2, 2005.

13

MARKET-BASED RESOURCE ALLOCATION FOR DIFFERENTIATED QUALITY SERVICE LEVELS

H. Howie Huang and Andrew S. Grimshaw

13.1 INTRODUCTION

The emergence of the Grid makes it possible for researchers and scientists to access and share computation and storage resources across the organization boundaries. In a Grid environment, individual users have their own service requirements; that is, they may demand different levels of quality of service (QoS) in terms of availability, reliability, capacity, performance, security, and so on. Each QoS property imposes various constraints and performance tradeoffs. Because of the complexity of managing client-specific QoS requirements and the dynamism inherent in supply and demand for resources, even highly experienced system administrators find it difficult to manage the resource allocation process. In the real world, markets are used to allocate resources when there are competing interests, with a common currency used as the means to place a well-understood and comparable value on items. Given the nature of distributed resource management, it is natural to combine economic methods and resource management in Grid computing to provide differentiated quality service levels. A market-based model is appealing in Grids because it matches the reality of the situation where clients are in competition for scarce resources. It holds the hope that it will provide a simple, robust mechanism for determining

Market-Oriented Grid and Utility Computing Edited by Rajkumar Buyya and Kris Bubendorfer

resource allocations. However, before we can apply a market model to a Grid, we must address two challenges:

1. The model should be able to scale to a large number of machines and clients. Traditional economic models have been studied for distributed resource brokering, and these approaches usually focus on optimizing some global systemwide metric such as performance. In order to compute the market clear price, these approaches need to poll or estimate the global demand and supply from providers and consumers, which inevitably incur high communication and computation overheads, and are inherently nonscalable.
2. It is crucial that the model has the capability of supporting many points in the QoS space simultaneously. The model must not be one size fits all, because a particular client will likely value one QoS property more than others. For example, a client who analyses data or runs data-mining tasks may wish to have high-performance data access to cache space of temporary data, but may not care whether data are secured or permanently lost once the application completes. In another example, a client who archives critical data may desire a highly reliable storage at the cost of a degraded performance. The presence of this variety in QoS should allow the model to evaluate the tradeoffs and provide differentiated Grid services at a level that satisfies the QoS properties for each client with a specific budget.

In this chapter, we will present two models, an auction market model, where the providers offer resources and bid for consumers, and a posted-price market model, where providers periodically adjust the price of resources that are available for purchase. Note that we use providers and sellers, consumers and buyers, interchangeably in this chapter. In a Grid system the resource providers typically possess dynamic characteristics such as workload and connectivity. For example, two machines may be able to supply the same amount of storage resources; however, the machine with higher availability and reliability will likely charge more for the better service. Our models distinguish producers by the resource quality that they provide. Furthermore, our models deal with various QoS aspects of storage services. This leads to a more complex cost function that can determine the cost of a storage service from its QoS guarantees. To demonstrate the effectiveness of the models, we present a storage Grid called Storage@desk (SD) and demonstrate how they work in SD. Storage@desk is a new virtual storage Grid that can aggregate free storage resource on distributed machines and turn it into virtual storage pool transparently accessible by a large number of clients. We evaluate our models using a real-world trace and present the results.

The rest of the chapter is organized as follows. First, we discuss the background in Section 13.2. Next, we present Storage@desk and its market models in Sections 13.3 and 13.4. The evaluation results are presented in Section 13.5. Finally, we give some future research directions in Section 13.6 and conclude in Section 13.7.

13.2 BACKGROUND

A trade involves the exchange of goods, services, or both. The invention of money allows the indirect exchange in the markets where prices can be determined in many forms. Bargaining market was a dominating business practice for thousands of years, where the buyer and seller continue to improvise their offers during a trading time window and accept or reject each other's offer at the end of the negotiation. Both parties favor an agreement that maximizes their own utility. In this case, the buyer and seller are in direct communication and their offers are not extended to all possibly interested parties. Although bargaining is not disappearing, this ancient practice has given ways to auction market and posted-price market, especially with the advance of the Internet and electronic commerce that shares an environment similar to our storage market. This can be attributed to a few limitations:

1. Bargaining involves a time-cost factor as the buyer and seller negotiate for a final price to be agreed on. In cases where time is critical, it would be difficult for both sides to reach a consensus within a short time window. They may have to make a compromised decision because of the time pressure.
2. As each side deals with only one other party, the information gathered by each side could be very limited that may also lead to a compromised decision. As a result, in both situations even if a consensus can be made, either side may possibly dissatisfy with the result because the utility is not maximized because of lack of time or information.
3. Bargaining often needs human involvements in each stage of the negotiation process and autonomic bargaining remains an open research question. Therefore, with a few exceptions such as priceline.com (where a customer can name a price), the Internet marketplace has adopted auction and posted price as dominant forms of practice.

The auction market [1–4] has many variations depending on participants, bids, and time limits. For example, buyers bid for goods or services in a demand auction, sellers offer them in a supply auction, or both can participate in a double auction. For another example, participants may reveal their bids in an open-bid auction and repeatedly bid in a continuous auction, whereas bids are kept secret in a closed auction. In this chapter, we choose to focus our attention on sealed-bid first-place auction for the following reasons:

1. The sealed-bid auction inherently prevents the buyers from knowing each other's bids; thus each buyer can evaluate the utility individually and make a quick decision on bids. It simplifies the bidding process and facilities the exchange of money and services. This is a highly desirable property in electronic commerce where minimum human intervene is needed.
2. Because the winner is required to pay the highest price, it encourages the participants to reveal their true valuations. However, the auction market also has

> some limitations. From the perspective of a buyer, she can deal with only one seller at one time and is uncertain about the result. The buyer having to commit to a resource quantity and price without knowing whether they will receive the resource makes it difficult to reason about how to accomplish a resource allocation. Also, the opportunity cost is quite high when a buyer has to go through several auctions before wining one. From the perspective of a seller, she may be forced to sell at an undesirable price when there is lack of competitions, or unable to sell the desired quantity when there is lack of bids.

The posted-price market in electronic commerce is a natural extension from our daily experience; that is, we pay goods or services for the specified price in supermarkets, gas stations, restaurants, and so on. The most significant advantage is that posted prices facilitate quick transactions. This enables sellers to publicly announce their prices. Knowing the price, the buyer can reach a decision locally and the other buyer's decision has no adverse effect if the seller has unlimited quantity of goods to offer. Furthermore, a buyer can potentially collect the prices from many sellers and make "smart" decisions. In the meantime, a seller can be certain about the profit when a transaction occurs. Compared to the auction market, where the buyers have to decide whether to bid, to whom, and at which price, the posted-price market requires the sellers to decide at which price to sell, for how many, and for how long. The burden is now on the sellers' shoulders.

In addition to bid-based models, previous research on applying market methods on distributed resource management has focused on commodity market models, where a resource is viewed as an interchangeable commodity in a commodity market, in which the consumers buy the resource from the providers at a publicly agreed-on market price. G-Commerce [5] is an example of this commodity market model. In the G-commerce model, the key is to determine the price of a resource at which supply equals demand, namely, market equilibrium. Therefore, G-commerce adopts a specific scheme of pricing adjustments based on the estimated demand functions. Commodities markets assume that all resources are identical within the market and that a market-wide price can be established that reflects the natural equilibrium between supply and demand. Some systems, such as G-commerce, have used such an approach to resource allocation—in their case CPU and disk for jobs. Unfortunately, as different providers naturally provide various levels of services, the assumption of equivalent resources is not a good fit for Storage@desk. Further, as Storage@desk exists in a dynamic environment that consists of a large number of distributed machines, it is difficult to adopt the G-commerce approach to analytically determine equilibrium based on supply and demand formulas. The storage exchange [6] mimics the stock exchange model and builds a double-auction model, in which providers and consumers submit their bids to buy and sell storage service. As the clearing algorithm is crucial in terms of utilization and profit, different algorithms have been investigated in storage exchange to meet various goals. In this chapter, we will focus on both the auction and posted-price market models where prices or bids can be determined on the basis of local information. The goal is to reduce the computation and communication cost, as well as to create a scalable algorithm in a distributed environment that consists of a large number of service providers and consumers.

13.3 Storage@desk

Before we present our storage market model, let us introduce Storage@desk [9] from two aspects, specifically the architecture and QoS model. Since the mid-1990s, scientific advances have enabled applications, sensors, and instruments to generate a vast amount of information, which, in turn, creates an enormous demand for storage. We believe that desktop PCs represent a tremendous potential in the form of available storage space that can be utilized to relieve the increasing storage demand. To this end, we are developing Storage@desk to harness the vast amount of unused storage available on a large number of desktop machines and turn it into a useful resource for clients within a large organization. Storage@desk aggregates unused storage (disk) resources in an organization to provide virtual volumes accessible via a standard interface. The disk resources reside in a large number of hosts with different QoS properties, such as availability, reliability, performance, and security. SD clients can specify their QoS requirements (including size), and SD provides them with a volume that meets their requirements. The goal is to enable clients or client agents (storage consumers) to create virtual storage volumes with well-defined QoS requirement, accessible via the ubiquitous Internet small-computer systems interface (iSCSI) standard [10] on top of storage resources on distributed machines (storage providers).

13.3.1 Architecture

Storage@desk, shown in Figure 13.1, has five "actors" in the architecture: clients that consume the virtual storage resources provided by Storage@desk, iSCSI servers that serve the clients' requests, volume controllers that monitor and manage virtual volumes, storage machines (including pricing agents on them) that provide the physical storage resources, and one or more backend databases that store the system metadata. Clients interact with iSCSI servers via the iSCSI protocol, reading and writing blocks. Thus, client interaction is legacy based, requiring no code changes. The iSCSI layer is the main interface between the clients and administrators on the outside, and the Storage@desk services inside the system. It is a standards-based rendering of the SCSI protocol, but is implemented over standard Transmission Control Protocol/Internet Protocol (TCP/IP) channels rather than a traditional SCSI bus. iSCSI servers implement the iSCSI protocol and interact with the database to acquire the block to storage machine mappings, with storage machines to read and write blocks, and with volume controllers to notify them of QoS warnings and errors. As client agents, volume controllers manage volumes on behalf of clients, mapping and remapping blocks to storage machines, ensuring proper replication, enforcing QoS characteristics, and responding to client hints about future-use patterns. Storage machines interact with the database, keeping it updated with current QoS properties and available storage, with volume controllers that request block allocations, and with iSCSI servers that read and write blocks. On each storage machine, there exists a pricing agent that makes periodic adjustments to the local storage price. This agent will become the auctioning agent that holds the auction for the storage machine in the

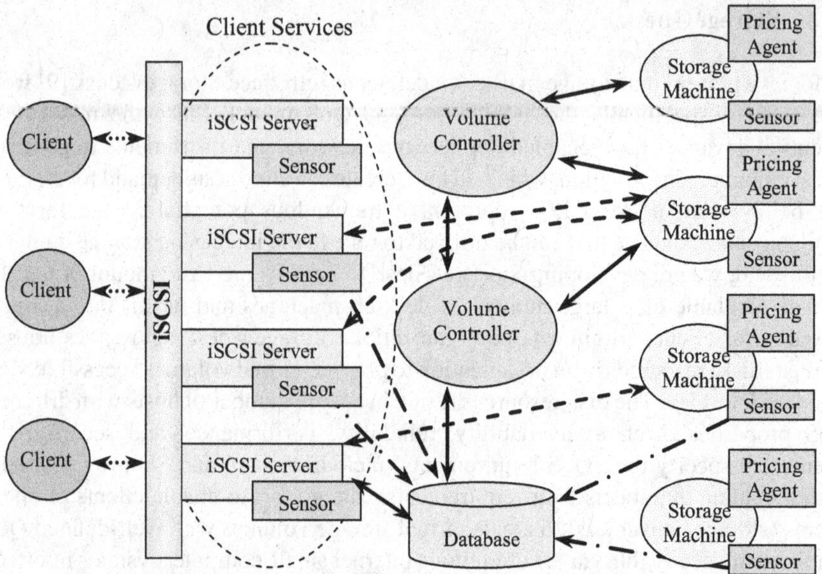

Figure 13.1 Architecture of the Storage@desk system. Clients interact with the system via an iSCSI interface (thus isolating them from the distributed nature of the resources behind the scenes). Arrows → indicate internal, Storage@desk volume control channels; arrows ····➤ indicate the iSCSI operations from clients; arrows --➤ indicate data interactions between iSCSI servers and machines; arrows –·➤ indicate sensors pushing QoS data to the storage database.

auction market model. Further, storage machines and iSCSI servers act as sensors that feed vital QoS information to both the volume controllers and the database. Finally, the database stores the information needed in the implementation. The database can be replicated and distributed to avoid becoming a hotspot.

13.3.2 QoS Model

Quality of service (QoS) is at the heart of Storage@desk. Storage@desk attempts to address the individual needs of its clients on a volume-by-volume basis. QoS is specified at volume creation and can also be updated throughout the volume's lifetime. For example, QoS may be changed to relax constraints that can no longer be met, or to change budget or lifetime. A client is free to change the QoS, which may become necessary when a client loses to others in a competition to a particular resource. We use a QoS vector $Q = [A, B, C, D, R, S, W]$ to represent seven QoS attributes, although we expect additions as work progresses:

- *Availability* (A). We define availability as the percentage of time that all bytes of a volume are accessible to the client. This value is calculated by dividing mean time to failure (MTTF) by the sum of MTTF and mean time to repair (MTTR).

The specified value marks the minimum availability the client is willing to accept. Since this is from the client's perspective, volume controllers can create replicas, use erasure codes, and/or dynamically migrate blocks in order to mask failures from less available resources.

- *Budget* (*B*). We define budget as the virtual concurrency a client has to purchase raw storage resources for each budget period. This budget will be used over a period time of the storage volume. When a budget is exceeded, a client will have to drop the request and release the resource.
- *Capacity* (*C*). We define capacity as the total amount of storage that the client desires in blocks. SD models raw storage as a number of blocks, whose sizes are fixed at the volume creation time.
- *Duration* (*D*). Duration defines the lifetime of a volume.
- *Reliability* (*R*). We define reliability as the probability that no data within a volume will be permanently lost. This value defines the minimum reliability rate the client is willing to accept.
- *Security* (*S*). Security is another QoS issue, and comes in many flavors and forms and various clients require differing levels of security. Some clients may require wire-level and storage-level data integrity guarantees, while others may additionally require various privacy guarantees as well. Sometimes a volume may wish to prevent certain users from adding and removing blocks of data, while other scenarios may allow for arbitrary addition of blocks of data, but limited deletion or replacement. Security can be addressed in all forms and at all stages in the Storage@desk system. Everything from storage level security, to wire-level security; from block level to volume level must be addressed. At a minimum Storage@desk will support specification of the level of privacy and data integrity required on target storage machines, the level of privacy and data integrity on the wire, and the acceptable methods for authenticating clients to storage machines for access.
- *Write Semantics* (*W*). We define write semantics as either write once–read many (WORM) or write many. These semantics can be important clues for efficiently implementing other QoS metrics. For example, by specifying that a volume is WORM, caching can be aggressively used for blocks already written.

Each QoS property defines the minimum level of service required by a client. In Storage@desk, it is the volume controller that will attempt to find resources to meet the client's minimum requirements subject to the budget of the client. The client can also specify a different QoS property to optimize—for example, maximizing availability. Clients will configure Storage@desk volumes with QoS policy documents and may submit similar documents at various stages during a volume's lifetime for the purposes of providing hints to the system about more immediate scheduling decisions (how much data to prefetch into a block, etc.). Example 13.1 shows a sample of such a document. Note that the end client may not ever see a document of this form if proper user interface (UI) tools are developed that translate more natural client requirements into requirements the system understands

```
<volume id="672362D1-06A6-45db-B4E1-A77D0B3AB4E5">
    <name>UVa Volume</name>
    <owner>CN=Thomas  Jefferson  1,E=jefferson@virginia.edu,
     OU=UVA  Standard
PKI User,O=University of Virginia, C=US</owner>
    <availability>99%</availability>
    <budget>1000</budget>
    <capacity>524288000 bytes</capacity>
    <duration>infinite</duration>
    <reliability>99.9%</reliability>
    <security>
           <storage>
           <privacy-level>encrypted</privacy-level>
           <integrity-level>checksum</integrity-level>
           </storage>
           <on-wire>
                <privacy-level>encrypted</privacy-level>
                <integrity-level>checksum</integrity-level>
           </on-wire>
           <authentication-mechanism>X.509
             </authentication-mechanism>
    </security>
    <performance allocation="50">
      <read-write-ratio>2.5</read-write-ratio>
      <coherence-window>5 minutes</coherence-window>
    </performance>
    <optimize>cost</optimize>
</volume>
```

Example 13.1: Illustrative Document Describing Some QoS Properties that a Volume of Storage Might Have. We have shown several different QoS properties: persistence, performance, availability, and integrity. Also included is an optional "allocation" for each. This indicates the relative importance the user attaches to different QoS elements.

13.4 STORAGE MARKET MODEL

In Storage@desk, competing independent clients or applications "purchase" storage resources from competing independent machines. In the auction market, storage machines hold auctions and solicit bids from a number of interested clients. At the beginning of the auction, each machine will announce the quantity of storage resources and history data on QoS properties. Because each client may receive bidding invitations from multiple storage machines, she will independently evaluate them and make a sealed bid to one machine. A bid includes quantity, and the price. On receiving bids, a storage machine will try to select a client that is willing to offer the highest price.

In the posted-price market, competing independent clients or applications purchase storage resources from competing independent machines. The model utilizes pricing agents to help storage providers determine the price for local resources. With the help of local search algorithms, pricing agents require no direct information of providers and consumers, which makes this approach very suitable for a Grid environment. Thus, pricing agents only need to adjust resource prices periodically in response to locally observed consumer demand.

In both market models, the consumers are free to use their own strategies to choose from which provider to purchase. However, they can't always get what they want because of the budget constraints. When two clients have the identical QoS requirement, the one with the larger budget should have a better chance to meet the QoS. The use of a budget-based system provides a mechanism to arbitrate between competing and likely conflicting clients and also provides a mechanism for system administrators to assign relative priorities between clients (or at least their purchasing power). We will use this market approach to produce a storage Grid that can (1) achieve a relatively stable state, (2) fulfill client QoS when adequate budgets are available, and (3) degrades in accordance with relative budget amounts.

13.4.1 Assumptions

In the Storage@desk market model, we assume that the value, or relative worth, of a storage resource is ultimately determined by supply and demand. Traditionally, a market is said to be in equilibrium state when there is a perfect balance of supply and demand. In the Grid environment, as is often the case in real life, the balance is difficult to achieve and maintain because of the existence of unpredictable system dynamics. Therefore we choose to measure market dynamics by the degree to which the utilizations on storage machines fluctuate. The utilization of a storage machine is defined as the percentage of used resources. As we will see, when the utilization does not change widely, neither does the price. Thus, if few changes to resource allocation are needed, we say the system is in a stable state.

We assume that the storage consumers and providers are self-interested "individuals" driven by personal goals. Obviously, a storage consumer aims to purchase storage resources that are affordable within the budget and satisfy the QoS.

13.4.2 Virtual Volumes

Clients create virtual volumes, each of which has a particular size and consists of a number of blocks. A client will need to buy a number of blocks in the market. Each block represents the capability of storing a fixed amount of data on a specific machine. It is important to emphasize that we differentiate the blocks in terms of quality. For instance, some blocks are considered to have better QoS because the underlying machines are highly available and reliable. While the same quantity of disk storage is provided, the blocks with better QoS properties should become more expensive for two reasons: (1) it is fair to reward a provider for a better services rendered, and (2) it will help the clients to tell a "good" block from a "bad" one and thus spend the budget efficiently and have better chance to achieve QoS goals.

For simplicity, we say that the market consists of a finite number S of blocks, distinguishable in terms of quality, from which a consumer may choose to create a virtual volume. We use R^S to denote the resource space. As a volume consists of a number of blocks, an allocation vector $x = [x_1, \ldots, x_S]$ can represent the blocks purchased by a consumer, where x is in R^S and a nonnegative number x_i denotes the amount of the ith blocks.

13.4.3 Storage Providers

A storage provider, as a storage machine, sells a number of blocks out of the available free disk space that it has via some allocation policy, such as a fixed amount of dedicated storage, some percentage of currently unused storage, and so on. Each storage machine is responsible for determining how many raw storage blocks it has to offer, for how long, and at what price (with the help of a pricing agent). All of the storage managed by a single storage machine is equivalent so that a storage machine simply has to determine and advertise the number of blocks available and a single price point for any of them. However, as we pointed out before, storage resources on two machines are not necessarily equivalent. For each storage machine, the revenue is calculated as the product of the price and the number of used blocks. There exists a software agent on each machine, which is called the *auctioning agent* in the auction market and the *pricing agent* in the posted-price market, respectively.

In the auction market, the auctioning agent will hold the auction for the resources on the storage machines. When the auction starts, the agent on the ith machine sends the invitations to the potential interested buyers in the form of (y_i, q_i), where y_i represents the number of the blocks and q_i, the history data on the QoS properties. A bid from the jth machine can be represented as (x_j, p_j), where x_j represents the number of the blocks that the machine needs and p_i, the price that the buyer is willing to pay. It is important to note that x_j is less than or equal to y_i. When the auction ends, the agent will select the machine with the highest price and award the requested resources. In case there is a tie, the earliest bid wins. If there are more resources than what the machine needs, for instance, $y_i > x_j$ if the jth machine wins, the agent will go through the buyer list in the descending order of their bidding price and repeat the selection process.

In the posted-price market, as each machine wants to maximize the revenue, the pricing agent will leverage the pricing power to affect the utilization and, in turn, the revenue. We will discuss the pricing algorithm in detail in Section 13.4.5. We define a price vector $p = [p_1, \ldots, p_S]$ to represent the prices of the blocks, where p_i is the price of the ith blocks. Once a client makes a purchase, this storage service will be rendered by the storage provider for a predefined period of time. It is the machine's job to make sure the blocks solely available to the client.

13.4.4 Storage Consumers

Storage consumers are volume controllers that clients use as their agents. Clients express their needs to volume controllers in the form of virtual volumes. Each volume

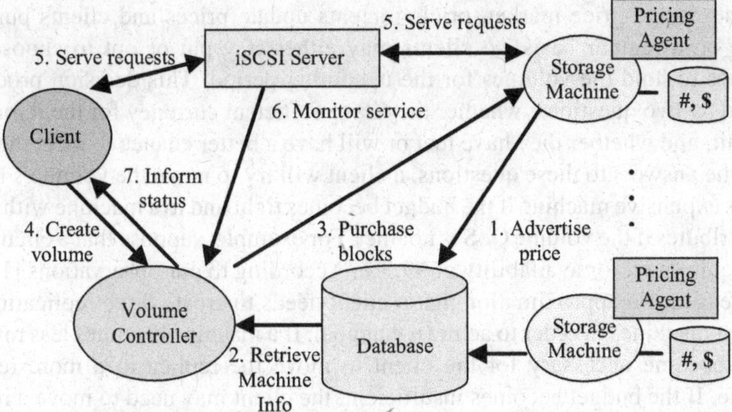

Figure 13.2 Logical resource allocation process.

is specified in the form of a QoS vector $q = [A, B, C, D, R]$. Clients allocate portions of their overall budget to each of their volumes, and the volume controllers use this budget to purchase resources from storage machines. Acting on behalf of clients, volume controllers agree to buy blocks from storage machines to construct virtual volumes. Figure 13.2 shows the steps of resource allocation when clients want to create a volume: (1) storage machines advertise their current price and QoS attributes, (2) clients specify QoS and budget constraints, (3) volume controllers retrieve machine information, (4) volume controllers purchase blocks from a number of storage machines and (5) construct a storage solution to meet the client-specific QoS criteria, (6) iSCSI servers serve client requests via iSCSI protocol, and (7) volume controllers monitor service and (8) update clients on the current status of resource prices and the QoS properties.

The allocation problem can be formalized as follows. Given the resource space R^S and the price vector $p = [p_1, \ldots, p_S]$, a consumer would seek an allocation vector $x = [x_1, \ldots, x_S]$ for a volume with a QoS vector $q = [A, B, C, D, R]$, which can

1. Meet the budget constraint: $x * p <= B$
2. Satisfy the QoS requirements: $q' >= q$, where q' is the vector of measured values

It is up to volume controllers to choose simple or complex strategies to solve this problem. In this chapter, a volume controller follows a simple strategy in both the auction and posted-price markets.

In the auction market, the controller can only submit a bid once in each bidding time period. In this research, we assume that the clients have high valuations, that is, that they are willing to spend their entire budgets to secure the needed resources. It is never desirable for these clients to have nothing, because they need storage resources to hold their data. Thus, the clients will bid with the maximum prices within their budgets.

In the posted-price market, pricing agents update prices and clients purchase storage on a regular basis, so clients may either stay put or opt to choose new machines to hold the volumes for the upcoming period. This decision process is affected by two questions: whether they have sufficient currency for the remaining time unit, and whether they have met or will have a better chance to meet the QoS. Given the answers to these questions, a client will try to move the volume's blocks to a less expensive machine if the budget becomes tight and to a machine with better QoS attributes if the volume QoS is not met. For example, suppose that a client has a QoS requirement for availability of 99.9%. According to our observations [11,12], it is a reasonable approximation that a client needs to create three replications on different machines in order to achieve that goal. If a machine becomes less reliable, it may become necessary for the client to move the replica to a more reliable machine. If the budget becomes insufficient, the client may need to move a replica to a less expensive machine or reduce the number of replicas. It is possible that a client does not have sufficient budget to compete for "good" resources. As a result, the client has to make the tradeoffs between various QoS criteria—including tradeoffs between the amount of space one can get and the quality of the service one receives.

13.4.5 Storage Resource Pricing

At its heart, Storage@desk is a storage scavenging system that must deal with machines that are typically under the direct control of desktop users. Those machines often exist in an environment that is highly unstable and dynamic. This implies that those machines experience dramatic changes in load, disk usage, connectivity, uptime, and so on, depending on the whims of the user sitting at the console. Additionally, administrative domains may enforce policy leading to large, coordinated downtimes and periods of unavailability. However, the chaotic nature of this environment should not prevent us from delivering a reasonable level of QoS. Indeed, we believe that local search pricing agents will hold the most promise for Storage@desk. A local search pricing agent requires no assumption or knowledge of other providers and of the consumer population. Such an agent utilizes a local search algorithm that periodically adjusts the resource price according to the demands observed in the previous and current time windows.

We choose to employ two classes of local search algorithms: the greedy algorithm and derivative-following (DF) algorithms. A greedy pricing agent starts with a predefined price and makes small changes (increase or decrease) as long as the demand increases. Such an agent stops changing the price when it cannot see any improvement in demand. At this point, it is considered that a good price is found. Ideally, the price is close to the optimal value. The price moves in a small step δ, which is chosen randomly from a specified range; in the simulation we use a uniformly random distribution between 10% and 30%. We have found a random increment helps reduce the negative impacts from unpredicted dynamics in a distributed environment. Algorithm 13.1 lists the pseudocode of the greedy algorithm.

```
Set direction as UP or DOWN based on initial observations
FOR each time interval, t_i (i >=2) DO
  IF d_i >= d_i-1 THEN
          IF direction == UP THEN
                    p_i = p_i-1 * (1 + δ)
          ELSE
                    p_i = p_i-1 * (1 - δ)
          END IF
  ELSE
          RETURN the price p_i
  END IF
END FOR
```

Algorithm 13.1 Greedy pricing algorithm.

In contrast, a DF pricing agent will not terminate the search when there is no increase in demand. Rather, a DF agent will reverse the search direction at that point. A DF agent starts with a predefined price and changes the price in the same direction at each observation window until the most recent demand is observed to decrease from the demand in the previous window. In that case, the agent reverses the search direction and begins to make price changes in the other direction. When the demand again decreases, the price movement will be reversed again. Therefore, the agent is able to track the changes in the observed demand and react fairly quickly to reverse the undesirable trend. In addition, it is very intuitive and requires only local knowledge. The latter makes it possible to develop a highly efficient solution in a Grid, which involves a large number of distributed machines. Algorithm 13.2 lists the pseudocode of the DF algorithm.

In conclusion, our market-based model has three advantages:

1. A storage machine is only required to know the local demand. There is no need for a storage machine to know prices from others, although they may compete for consumers; nor does a storage machine need to know demands from all consumers.
2. A storage machine is allowed to leverage independent pricing power to compete for positions in the market. Thus, rather than one price fits all, the market

```
FOR each time interval, t_i DO
  IF d_i > d_i-1 THEN
     p_i = p_i-1 * (1 + δ)
  ELSE IF d_i < d_i-1 THEN
     p_i = p_i-1 * (1 – δ)
  ELSE
     p_i = p_i-1
  END IF
END FOR
```

Algorithm 13.2 DF pricing algorithm.

recognizes the quality differences between storage resources and enables prices to reflect those differences.

3. With the feedback price signals, a client is encouraged to make tradeoffs among many QoS attributes and compose a service that maximizes QoS under a specific budget.

13.5 EVALUATIONS

Using our market model, we want to provide two things with respect to availability and resource allocation: (1) the overall resource allocation system and pricing performance in the system can be stable; and (2) when resources are available, the resource allocation mechanism must perform efficiently and effectively—meaning that volume controllers make the proper decisions and can purchase the proper resources to meet their availability goals. Additionally, the resource allocation process should degrade such that it favors those who have allocated higher budgets to their storage when all other things are equal.

To evaluate our model, we construct a trace-driven simulation. In this simulation, we choose to study volume availability to demonstrate the effectiveness of our market model. We simulate our model using trace data, which we collected from 729 public machines in the classrooms, libraries, and laboratories at the University of Virginia. An analysis of this data has been published as a feasibility study of Storage@desk [9]. During a time period of 3 months in 2005, these public machines send to a central database a snapshot for each 5-min interval that contains statistics such as free disk space, CPU utilization, and memory usage. Figure 13.3 shows the number of available machines for each 5-min interval. Around 700 machines were reachable most of the time. There were several events where large number of machines went down because of problems such as network partition, power outage, and scheduled maintenance, which are displayed as the downward spikes in the figure.

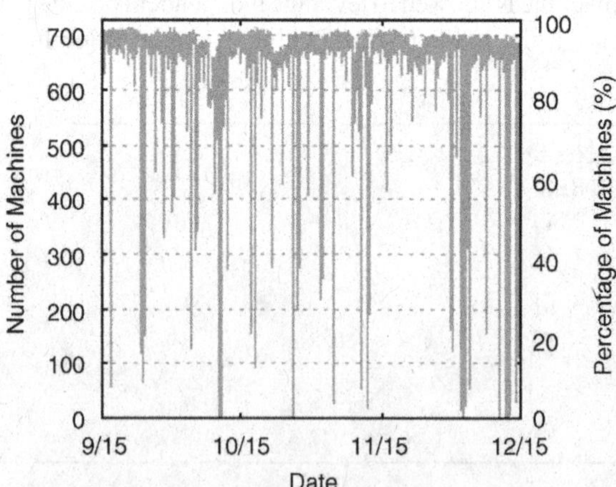

Figure 13.3 Number of available machines.

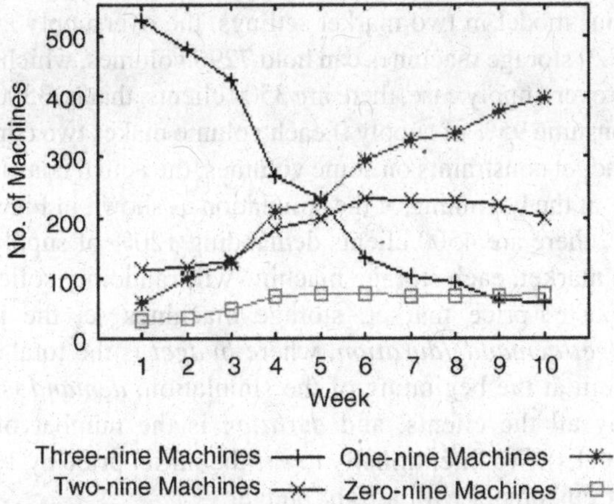

Figure 13.4 Machine counts by availability.

Figure 13.4 shows the number of machines categorized by their availabilities in terms of nines over the 10-week span. We use three–nine machines to represent the machine group whose availability is greater than 99.9%, two–nine machines for availability greater than 99%, and one–nine machines for availability greater than 90%. The majority of the machines had an availability of 2 nines or 3 nines. Although more than 500 machines started with 3 nines at the first week, their availabilities gradually decreased as time went by. This was expected given the unreliable nature of machine usage on these desktops. At the same time, the number of one–nine and two–nine machines increased significantly. The population of zero–nine machines remained steady for 10 weeks. In the end, there were about 60 three–nine machines, 200 two–nine machines, 400 one–nine machines, and 75 zero–nine machines.

Each volume is assigned with a budget of 100 (low budget), 200 (medium budget) and 300 (high budget), in a random, uniform distributed fashion. Also, a volume is randomly given an availability requirement of 1 nine, 2 nines, and 3 nines. This assignment creates a good mix of various budgets and availabilities among the volumes. In our simulation, we assume that each volume consists of one block, and each machine has 10 blocks available for Storage@desk, so each machine can hold up to 10 volumes.

Under a predefined budget and availability requirement, each client creates one volume by purchasing blocks and makes a number of replicas for the volume in order to satisfy the availability requirement. The number of replicas that a client tries to make is determined by how many nines the client desires. For example, a client with a requirement of 3 nines will make three replicas of the volume. As we pointed out earlier, this is a reasonable choice given the fact that the majority of the machines have an availability of 90% or higher. We make sure that one machine will not hold two replicas of the same volume, so a client will distribute three copies on three different machines.

From the trace, we know the status of each machine, in other words, whether the machine is available, at every 5-min interval. A volume is available as long as there is at least one replica accessible; otherwise it is unavailable. Thus, we can easily obtain MTTF and MTTR for each volume, and compute its availability.

We simulate our model in two market settings, the oversupply and undersupply cases. Note that 729 storage machines can hold 7290 volumes, which is the supply in the market. In the over-supply case, there are 3500 clients, that is, 3500 volumes in the system, which consume 95% of supply if each volume makes two copies on average. Because of the budget constraints on some volumes, the actual consumption is much lower, about 76% at the beginning of the simulation as shown in Figure 13.7a. In the undersupply case, there are 4500 clients demanding 120% of supply.

In the auction market, each storage machine will randomly solicit bids from 60 clients. In the posted-price market, storage machines set the initial price as $price_{\text{initial}} = (budget/demand)/duration$, where *budget* is the total amount of currency in the system at the beginning of the simulation, *demand* is the number of blocks needed by all the clients, and *duration* is the number of weeks in the simulation (10 weeks). We intentionally lower the initial price by 10% to create an initial leeway for customers with a tight budget.

13.5.1 Price and Allocation Stability

In this section we study the mean price and mean utilization distributions under two demand scenarios. Figure 13.5 shows the mean price distribution in the auction market model for the oversupply case (a) and the undersupply case (b). In both cases, while the prices increase slowly from week 2 to week 9 for machines that have less than 3 nines, they jump in the end of the simulation. The weekly increase is significantly larger for three–nine machines. This is caused by the fact that the low-budget clients who do not have sufficient funds to win bids in the beginning of the simulation are able to afford good-quality machines later on. As we will see later, the posted-price market model can avoid this problem, as low-budget clients manages to purchase "cheap" resources from low-quality machines.

Now we will first look at how greedy pricing affects the price for the time period of 10 weeks. For the over-supply case (Fig. 13.6a), all machines start with the same initial price of 9.17, but begin to diverge in week 3. As the simulation continues, the clients begin to assess their volumes and resource allocations, and take appropriate

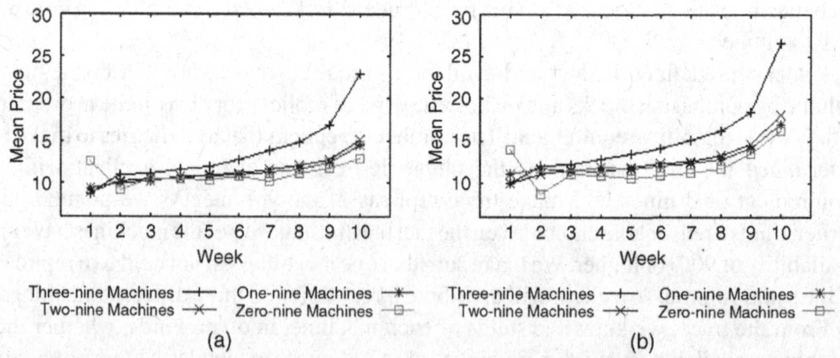

Figure 13.5 Auction—mean price distribution for 10 weeks: (a) oversupply case; (b) undersupply case.

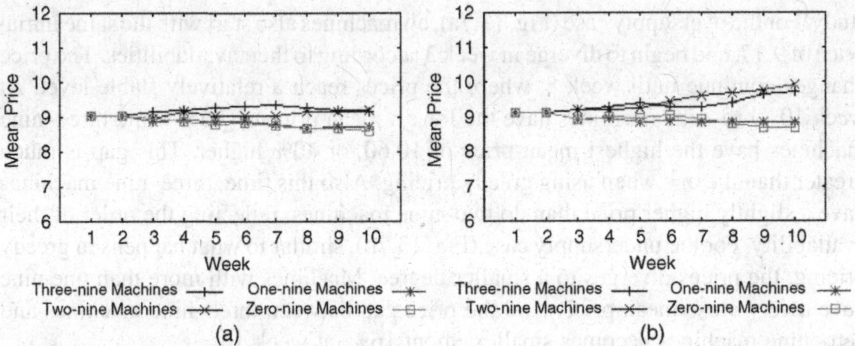

Figure 13.6 Greedy pricing—mean price distribution for 10 weeks: (a) oversupply case; (b) undersupply case.

actions on the basis of perceived availabilities and the remaining budget. Subsequently, the machines with higher number of nines will see more demand from clients, while those with lower nines experience diminishing demands. So, machines with 2 or 3 nines begin to ask a higher price for its storage resources, while machines with 0 or 1 nine begin to ask for a lower price. As a result, two–nine machines have a price of about 7% higher than do zero–nine machines. Since there are more two–nine machines, they have a better chance of seeing higher demand than three–nine machines and thus have a higher price in the end of the simulation. For the undersupply case (Fig. 13.6b), the prices also diverge, but to a much smaller degree. The machine groups with lower nines will not experience a significant drop of client demands, since the demand exceeds the total supply in the system. The clients become less quality-sensitive, and pay more attention to the quantity. As a result, machines with more than 2 nines have a very close mean price, so do machines with zero or one nine. And the price gap between two–nine machines and zero–nine machines becomes larger, about 15%, at week 10.

Figure 13.7 illustrates the mean price distribution for derivative-following pricing for each of the four availability classes (base on the number of nines) over the 10-week

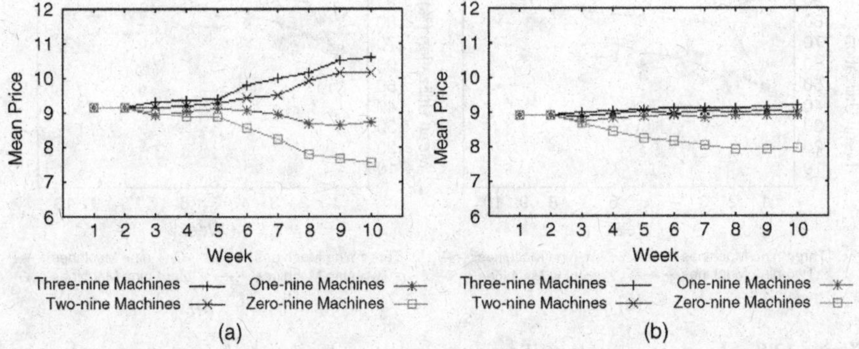

Figure 13.7 Derivative-following pricing—mean price distribution for 10 weeks: (a) oversupply case; (b) undersupply case.

study. For the oversupply case (Fig. 13.7a), all machines also start with the same initial price of 9.17, and begin to diverge in week 3 according to their availabilities. The price changes continue until week 8, where the prices reach a relatively stable level. At week 10, zero–nine machines have the lowest mean price of 7.55, while three–nine machines have the highest mean price of 10.60, or 40% higher. This gap is much greater than the one when using greedy pricing. Also this time, three–nine machines have a slightly higher price than do two–nine machines, reflecting the order of their availability. For the undersupply case (Fig. 13.7b), similar to what happens in greedy pricing, the prices diverges to a smaller degree. Machines with more than one nine have a very close mean price. And the price gap between three–nine machines and zero–nine machines becomes smaller, about 16%, at week 10.

The clients try to shy away from low-availability machines and pursue machines with high availability if the budget allows. Figure 13.8 show the mean utilizations in the auction market. In the auction market, the three–nine machines at week 10 have a mean utilization of 86% and 97% in the oversupply and undersupply cases, respectively. In contrast, the zero–nine machines at week 10 have a mean utilization of 50% and 58% in the oversupply and undersupply cases, respectively. The utilization in the posted-price market is higher as shown in Figure 13.9, because in this case clients can always get what they intend to purchase. In contrast, the clients who do not win bids in the auction market will not get another chance to purchase resources until next week. As both pricing algorithms have similar effects on resource utilization, we choose to only present derivative-following pricing here. For the over-supply case (Fig. 13.9a), three–nine machines start with 76% utilization and become close to fully utilized at week 8; on the other hand, zero–nine machines see the utilization decreases gradually until ~40% at week 7. For the undersupply case (Fig. 13.9b), machines with 2 or 3 nines quickly become fully utilized. The utilization on zero–nine machines and one–nine machines remains 82% and 94%, respectively, due to the overwhelming demand in the system.

Figures 13.10 and 13.11 present volume migration rates in 10 weeks for greedy pricing and derivative-following pricing, respectively. We can see that, for both

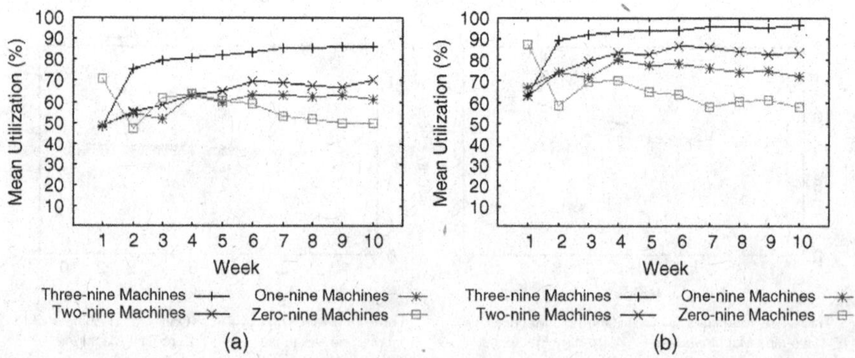

Figure 13.8 Auction — mean utilization distribution for 10 weeks: (a) oversupply case; (b) undersupply case.

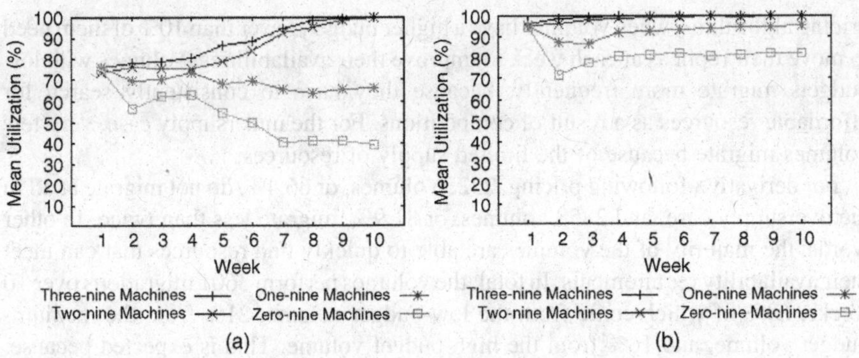

Figure 13.9 Derivative-following pricing—mean utilization distribution for 10 weeks: (a) oversupply case; (b) undersupply case.

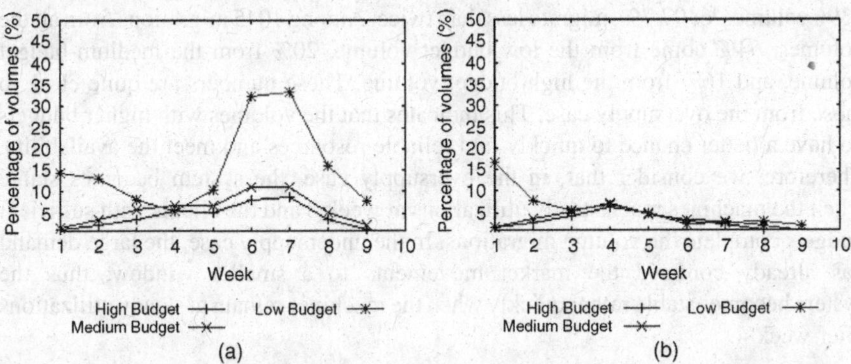

Figure 13.10 Greedy pricing—volume migration rates for 10 weeks: (a) oversupply case; (b) undersupply case.

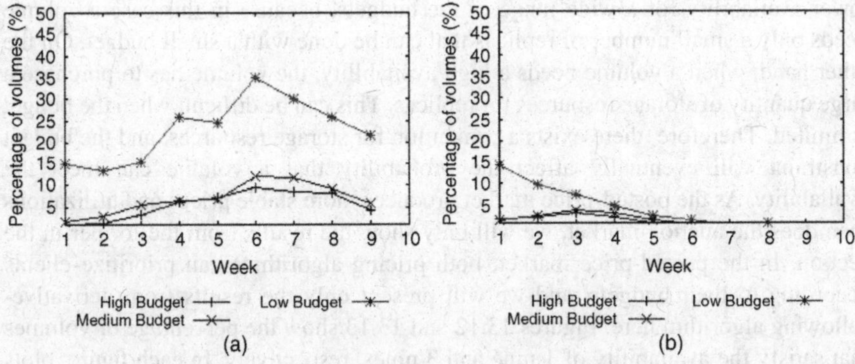

Figure 13.11 Derivative-following pricing—volume migration rates for 10 weeks: (a) oversupply case; (b) undersupply case.

pricing algorithms, when volumes have a higher budget, fewer than 10% of them need to move their replicas at each week to improve their availabilities. Volumes with low budgets migrate more frequently, because they have to consistently search for affordable resources as a result of competitions. For the undersupply case, very few volumes migrate because of the limited supply of resources.

For derivative-following pricing, 2325 volumes, or 66.4%, do not migrate at all in the oversupply case, and 2858 volumes, or 81.9%, migrate less than twice. In other words, the majority of the volumes are able to quickly find resources that can meet their availability requirements. In total, the volumes perform 3601 migrations over 10 weeks, 63% of which come from the low-budget volume, 21% from the medium-budget volume, and 16% from the high-budget volume. This is expected because, while the high-budget volumes can still afford good resources, some low-budget volumes are forced to move as the price pressure increases. In the undersupply case, with limited supply, the market does not have much room for the volumes to move around. As a result, 3896 volumes, or 86.6%, do not migrate once, while 4396 volumes, or 97.7%, migrate less than twice. Among 1045 migrations from all the volumes, 64% come from the low-budget volume, 20% from the medium-budget volume, and 16% from the high-budget volume. These numbers are quite close to those from the oversupply case. This indicates that the volumes with higher budgets do have a better chance to quickly find reliable resources and meet the availability. Therefore, we consider that, in the oversupply case, the system becomes stable when the machines reach steady utilizations at week 8 and the clients with sufficient budgets complete the volume migrations. In the undersupply case, the large demand has already confined the market movements to a smaller window; thus the system becomes stable rather quickly when the machines remain at steady utilizations after week 4.

13.5.2 Meet Availability Goals and Adherence to Budgeted Priorities

For each client, the key is to meet the availability goal under the budget constraint. It is expected that, to a high probability, a volume should be able to meet a relatively lower availability for a wide range of the budgets, because in this case a volume needs only a small number of replicas that can be done with a small budget. On the other hand, when a volume needs a high availability, the volume has to purchase a large quantity of storage resources for replicas. This can be difficult when the budget is limited. Therefore, there exists a contention for storage resources, and the budget constraint will eventually affect the probability that a volume can meet the availability. As the posted-price market produces more stable prices and utilizations than does the auction market, we will only show the results from the former in the section. In the posted-price market, both pricing algorithms can prioritize clients according to their budgets, and we will present only the results from derivative-following algorithm here. Figures 13.12 and 13.13 show the percentage of volumes that satisfy the availability of 1 nine and 3 nines, respectively. In each figure, plots (a) illustrate the oversupply case and plots (b) present the undersupply case. From Figure 13.12, we can see that the budget plays a small role for one–nine volumes.

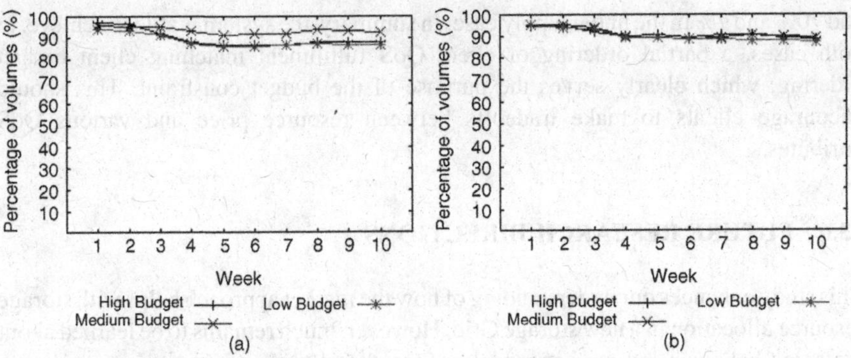

Figure 13.12 Percentage of one–nine volumes that satisfy the availability: (a) oversupply case; (b) undersupply case.

In the oversupply case, 88% of high-budget volumes meet the 1 nine availability at week 10, while 87% of low-budget volumes do. This small difference becomes even smaller in the undersupply case. It indicates that low budget is sufficient for a volume that needs a low availability.

The situation changes when a volume has an availability of 2 nines. The chance for a low-budget volume having 2 nines availability decreases from 87% at week 1 to 36% at week 10 in the oversupply case and from 87% to 33% in the undersupply case. In comparison, > 90% of the medium- and high-budget volumes still have a good chance of meeting the availability requirements. In this case, the budget draws a clear distinction between low-budget volumes and higher-budget volumes, while medium- and high-budget volumes still can be considered equivalent. The latter can no longer hold true as shown in Figure 13.13 when the volumes demands an availability of 3 nines, where each volume needs to purchase storage for three replicas. While about 92% of high-budget volumes meet the goal at week 10, the percentage for medium-budget volumes and low-budget volumes drop to 70% and 8% in the oversupply case,

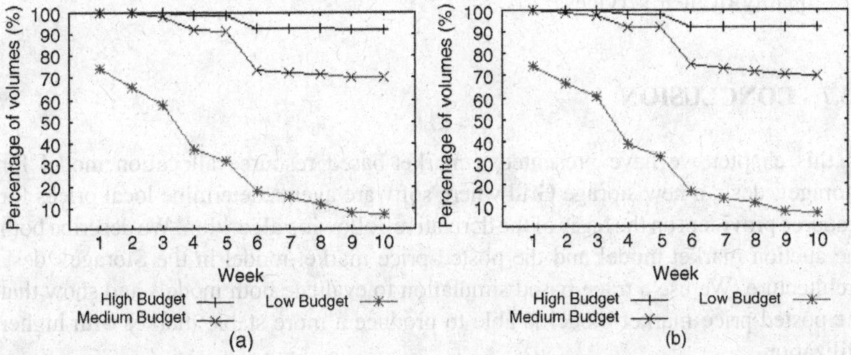

Figure 13.13 Percentage of three–nine volumes that satisfy the availability: (a) oversupply case: (b) undersupply case.

and 70% and 7% in the undersupply case. In summary, the system is able to achieve, in both cases, a partial ordering of client QoS fulfillment matching client budget ordering, which clearly serves the purpose of the budget constraint. This should encourage clients to make tradeoffs between resource price and various QoS attributes.

13.6 FUTURE RESEARCH DIRECTIONS

This study enhances our understanding of how the market approach helps with storage resource allocation in a new storage Grid. However, much remains to be learned about the agent behavior and market model in Storage@desk:

- We will study the utilization of computing and network resources to give our model a higher level of realism. This will inevitably introduce new research challenges. When a client purchases various resources from multiple providers, it needs to carefully make a purchase plan ahead of time in order to coordinate the consumption of different resources at the desirable time.
- We will explore new QoS properties, such as security and performance, and support them in our market model. Their impacts on resource management can be twofold. First, as in the previous problem of multi resource purchase, a client needs to have a good plan in order to simultaneously achieve multiple QoS properties. There may come a time when it is not possible to achieve all desired QoS properties. At that time the client has to prioritize one or more most important properties. We also plan to research other possible pricing algorithms, such as, those based on the genetic algorithm or ant colony algorithm.
- We will introduce the concept of penalty to the market. A penalty will be assessed when a resource provider cannot meet its prespecified QoS level. For example, a resource provider advertising an availability of 99.9% needs to pay a certain amount of penalty for the time periods that it did not provide a three–nine service. This will provide an incentive for providers to honestly announce the quality of their services.

13.7 CONCLUSION

In this chapter we have presented a market-based resource allocation model for Storage@desk, a new storage Grid where software agents determine local prices for resource providers on the basis of the derivative-following algorithm. We describe both the auction market model and the posted-price market model in the Storage@desk architecture. We use a trace-based simulation to evaluate both models and show that the posted-price market model is able to produce a more stable market with higher utilization.

In the posted-price market, once the price, quantity, and quality of storage resources are advertised, storage consumers can choose from which providers, and how many, to buy. With the help of the volume controller, a client can make tradeoffs among many QoS attributes and compose a service that achieves the desirable QoS under a specific budget. A good resource allocation can be achieved by the cooperation from two sides: (1) providers adjust prices for their resources in accordance with the demand that they experience, while (2) consumers adjust their allocation in response to the QoS experienced and the price changes according to the amount of currency left in the budget.

ACKNOWLEDGMENT

This chapter is a substantial extension of a paper published in *IEEE/WIC/ACM International Conference on Web Intelligence (WI)* in November 2007.

REFERENCES

1. C. A. Waldspurger, T. Hogg, B. A. Huberman, J. O. Kephart, and W. S. Stornetta, Spawn: A distributed computational economy, *IEEE Transaction on Software Engineering* **18**(2): 103–117 (1992).
2. K. Lai, L. Rasmusson, E. Adar, S. Sorkin, L. Zhang, and B. A. Huberman, Tycoon: An implementation of a distributed market-based resource allocation system, *Multiagen Grid System* **1**(3):169–182 (2005).
3. A. AuYoung, B. Chun, A. Snoeren, and A. Vahdat, Resource allocation in federated distributed computing infrastructures, *Proc. 1st Workshop on Operating System and Architectural Support for the Ondemand IT InfraStructure*, 2004.
4. B. Chun and D. Culler, *Market-Based Proportional Resource Sharing for Clusters*, Technical Report CSD-1092, Univ. California Berkeley, Computer Science Div., Jan. 2000.
5. R. Wolski, J. Plank, J. Brevik, and T. Bryan, G-commerce: Market formulations controlling resource allocation on the computational Grid, *Proc. International Parallel and Distributed Processing Symp.,* San Francisco, CA, April 23–27, 2001.
6. M. Placek and R. Buyya, Storage exchange: A global trading platform for storage services, *Proc. 12th International European Parallel Computing Conf.,* Dresden, Germany, Aug. 29–Sept. 1, 2006.
7. T. Eymann, M. Reinicke, O. Ardaiz, P. Artigas, F. Freitag, and L. Navarro, Decentralized resource allocation in application layer networks, *Proc. 3rd International Symp. Cluster Computing and the Grid,* Tokyo, May 12–15, 2003.
8. P. Padala, C. Harrison, N. Pelfort, E. Jansen, M. P. Frank, and C. Chokkareddy, OCEAN: The open computation exchange and arbitration network, a market approach to meta computing, *Proc. International Symp. Parallel and Distributed Computing,* Ljubljana, Slovenia, 2003.
9. H. H. Huang, J. F. Karpovic, and A. S. Grimshaw, A feasibility study of a virtual storage system for large organizations, *Proc. 1st IEEE/ACM International Workshop on Virtualization Technologies in Distributed Computing (held in conjunction with SC06),* Tampa, FL, Nov. 17, 2006.

10. IETF. *Internet Small Computer Systems Interface (iSCSI)*, http://www.ietf.org/rfc/rfc3720.txt, April 2004.

11. J. Sairamesh and J. O. Kephart, Price dynamics of vertically differentiated information markets, *Proc. 1st International Conf. Information and Computation Economies, Charleston,* SC, 1998.

12. J. O. Kephart, J. E. Hanson, and A. R. Greenwald, Dynamic pricing by software agents, *Computer Networks* **32**(6):731–752 (2000).

14

SPECIFICATION, PLANNING, AND EXECUTION OF QoS-AWARE GRID WORKFLOWS

IVONA BRANDIC, SABRI PLLANA, AND SIEGFRIED BENKNER

14.1 INTRODUCTION

The emergence of Grid technology is strongly affecting the way in which information-processing tasks are performed. Grid computing is considered as a promising solution for relevant problems in various domains such as life sciences, financial services, and high-performance computing [1,2]. Commonly, the user defines the process needed for the problem solution as a flow of activities, each capable of solving a part of the problem. This form of specification of activities that should be performed on the Grid is referred to as *Grid workflow*. Resources that perform these activities are not necessarily located in the user's vicinity; rather, they are geographically distributed. This may enable the use of unique resources such as expensive measurement instruments or powerful computer systems. In our opinion, for the wide acceptance of Grid technology, two aspects are particularly relevant: (1) the process of specification of Grid activities should be further streamlined, and (2) the execution of Grid activities should meet user's requirements regarding the *quality of service* (QoS). In this chapter we address *application-level* QoS for applications that are expressed as workflows, where a set of nonfunctional requirements (such as execution *time*, *price*, or *location affinity*) should be met during the application execution.

Resource sharing business models are typical for collaborations among academic institutions in which each partner provides parts of required resources. In return, they can use their partner's resources. In such resource-sharing models the participants

Market-Oriented Grid and Utility Computing Edited by Rajkumar Buyya and Kris Bubendorfer

seldom pay for the resource usage. In this chapter we address scientific computing in the business context. Thus, we address resource sharing models where the participants pay for the usage of resources and are not obliged to provide any resources to the community. However, participants expect that non-functional requirements specified by means of *quality of service* (QoS) are satisfied.

This chapter addresses various domains of Grid workflows [3] such as the development of planning strategies for the execution of large-scale Grid workflows [4] or cost-based scheduling of scientific workflows [5]. However, there is a lack of a holistic environment for Grid workflows that supports QoS in all phases of the workflow lifecycle from specification to execution. Existing Grid workflow systems either support the whole workflow lifecycle but lack QoS support, or provide only partial QoS support for certain phases of the workflow lifecycle.

In this chapter we present *Amadeus*, which is a novel service-oriented environment for QoS-aware Grid workflows [29]. A distinguishing feature of Amadeus is the holistic approach to QoS support during all stages of the workflow lifecycle. At specification time Amadeus provides an adequate tool-support for a high-level graphical specification of QoS-aware workflows, which allows the association of a comprehensive set of QoS constraints to any activity or to the whole workflow. Commonly, complex scientific problems are defined as a flow of activities or tasks, where each activity solves a part of the scientific problem. During the planning phase Amadeus provides a set of QoS-aware service-oriented components that support automatic constraint-based service negotiation and workflow optimization. During the execution phase, using the information from the planning phase, Amadeus executes the workflow activities in the manner that the specified requirements in terms of QoS constraints are met. As resources invoked by the QoS-aware workflow we use QoS-aware services that are able to give QoS guarantees. A QoS-aware service enables clients to negotiate about its QoS properties. This kind of support is provided by the Vienna Grid Environment (VGE) [6]. VGE provides application-level QoS support [25], for example, with respect to execution time or price. VGE has been successfully used for the development of a Grid testbed for medical simulation services [28] in the context of the European Commission (EC)-funded GEMSS project [27].

There are a large number of application domains for Grid workflows, such as life sciences (e.g., medical simulation services) and engineering (e.g., vehicle development support) demanding a guarantee that workflow activities are performed within the specified *time*, *cost*, *security*, and *legal* constraints. Therefore, we are developing an XML-based language for QoS-aware Grid workflows (QoWLs), by extending the business process execution language (BPEL) [17] with language constructs for specification of QoS constraints [7,32]. A distinctive feature of QoWL is the ability to account for the user's preferences regarding the execution time and price of the activities as well as the execution *location affinity* for activities with specific security and legal constraints. The concept of *location affinity*, introduced in this chapter, facilitates the realization of *virtual organizations* [31]. Furthermore, *location affinity* enables the accounting of security and legal QoS aspects at workflow specification time.

The main contributions of this book chapter include (1) description of a holistic service-oriented environment for Grid workflows and its experimental evaluation, (2) description of the concept of location affinity, (3) discussion of strategies for workflow annotation with QoS information, (4) explanation of an approach for QoS-aware workflow reduction that simplifies the planning phase, and (5) description of the workflow execution models for static and dynamic planning.

The remainder of this chapter is organized as follows: We present the related work in Section 14.2. Section 14.3 describes a set of workflow-related concepts and terminology, introduces the concept of location affinity, and briefly describes the purpose and the relationship of the main components of the Amadeus environment. Furthermore, it introduces a sample workflow that is used for illustration and evaluation of the main Amadeus components. Section 14.4 describes how the Amadeus environment supports all phases of the QoS-aware Grid workflow lifecycle. A set of experiments that demonstrates the feasibility of QoS-aware planning and execution of Grid workflows is presented in Section 14.5. Section 14.6 describes how the work presented in this chapter can positively influence and simplify the work of practitioners in the future. Section 14.7 briefly describes future work, whereas Section 14.8 concludes the chapter.

14.2 BACKGROUND AND RELATED WORK

Most of the existing work on workflow systems may be grouped in three categories: (1) systems that are tailored for *scientific workflows* based on Globus [12] Grid infrastructure [4,14,34], (2) systems for *business workflows* that are based on Web services–related technologies (such as SOAP, WSDL, and BPEL) [15–17], and (3) systems for scientific workflows that use and further extend the standard Web services technologies developed for business workflows [9,14,18]. In comparison to business workflows, the distinguishing features of Grid workflows are the long execution time of compute-intensive activities and the large data transfer between activities (typically the data exchange is performed via large files). As identified by Taylor et al. [38] business workflows usually address production workflows accessed by a large number of clients. Scientific workflows are mostly used in explorative and experimental way.

Triana [16], ASKALON [34], and JOpera [36] projects are developing tools and languages for graphical workflow composition. Pegasus [4] and LEAD [35] projects are focused on the development of workflow support for large-scale Grid applications (such as galaxy morphology, tomography, and mesoscale meteorology). The aspects of semantic Grid workflows are investigated within the Taverna [37] project.

Cardoso et al. elaborate theoretical concepts of a QoS-aware workflow defining QoS workflow metrics [19]. Zeng et al. investigate QoS-aware composition of Web services using the IP method [11]. The services are scheduled using local and global planning approaches. The prediction of the invocation time of a Web service is calculated using an arithmetic mean of historical invocations. Canfora et al. [20] compare the usage of genetic algorithms and IP approaches for the selection of the appropriate Web services in the context of a Web service workflow by specified global constraints. Similar to the study by Zeng et al. [11], neither application-based performance models nor performance prediction of data transfer are considered. Al-Ali et al. [21] analyze QoS for distributed Grid applications. Work presented by Liang et al. [22] deals with adaptive multiresource prediction for distributed resource sharing. Menasce and Casalicchio [23] give an overview of QoS mechanisms used in the context of Grid computing.

However, there is a lack of a holistic environment for Grid workflows supporting QoS in all phases of the workflow lifecycle. Existing Grid workflow systems either support the whole workflow lifecycle but lack QoS support, or provide only partial QoS support for certain phases of the workflow lifecycle. The Gridbus project [24] addresses QoS-aware Grid workflows. While time and cost constraints are considered, there is no support for security and legal constraints [7]. In contrast, the Amadeus framework provides QoS support during the whole workflow lifecycle, from specification to execution, considering a rich set of QoS constraints. Besides performance (i.e., activity execution time) and economical aspects of QoS, Amadeus considers the user's preferences regarding execution *location affinity* for activities with specific security and legal constraints [7]. A distinguishing feature of Amadeus is the support for QoS-aware services that are able to negotiate regarding their QoS properties. This kind of services is provided by VGE [6].

14.3 OVERVIEW OF AMADEUS ENVIRONMENT

In this section we describe the preliminaries and give an overview of the Amadeus architecture.

14.3.1 Preliminaries

A *Grid workflow* is a flow of a finite set of *activities*. An *activity* is a unit of work. We distinguish two kinds of activities, *basic* and *complex*. A *basic activity* is an activity that is not decomposed into smaller units of work. Commonly, in the context of scientific workflows, activities represent CPU-intensive computation or data transfer. A *complex activity* may comprise a set of basic and/or complex activities.

A Grid workflow W is a pair (A,D), where A is a finite set of activities and D is a finite set of activity dependencies. Each activity dependency D_i, $D_i \in D$, is associated with an ordered pair of activities (A_m,A_n), where A_m, $A_n \in$ A.

A *service* is a software entity that performs the work specified by an activity. A *registry* comprises information (e.g., location, semantic description and keywords) about a set of services. In the context of Grid workflows, *quality of service* (QoS) refers to a set of properties that specify requirements regarding a specific activity or the whole workflow. A *QoS-aware service* is a service that enables clients to negotiate about its QoS properties. The *requested QoS* indicates requirements of the user (e.g., maximum price and execution time) for a specific activity. The *offered QoS* indicates the constraints within which a service can perform a specific activity. *Metadata*

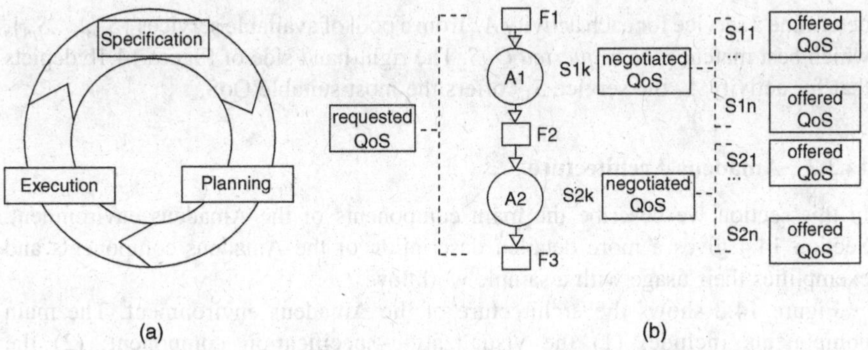

Figure 14.1 (a) Workflow lifecycle; (b) sample workflow.

indicate the information that describes the input data of a service (e.g., the size of input file). Commonly, *metadata* are used for the performance evaluation of a service during the estimation of the *offered QoS*. The *negotiated QoS* is the *offered QoS*, selected from a pool of available services, that best matches the *requested QoS*.

Quality of service is an *n*-tuple $Q = \{Q_i: 1 \leq i \leq n, n \in N\}$, where Q_i is a constraint and N is the set of positive integers. At present, within the Amadeus framework, QoS is specified as a six-tuple $\{BT, ET, PR, SA, OA, GA\}$, where BT is the begin time, ET is the end time, PR is the price, SA is the site affinity, OA the organization affinity, and GA is the geographic affinity. For security or legal reasons the user may express the *location affinity* regarding Grid resources on which certain workflow tasks may be executed [7]. Location affinity is expressed by *SA*, *OA*, and *GA* constraints. QoS of the complex activities is calculated using the *aggregation functions*. In this chapter we use aggregation functions described by Brandic et al. [7] for the recursive computation of the QoS constraints of the overall workflow and of the complex activities.

An *abstract Grid workflow* specifies the types of activities, their execution order, and the *requested QoS*. *Planning* is the process of mapping workflow activities to available services based on the *requested QoS*. The outcome of the *planning* process is a concrete *Grid workflow*, which is a ready to execute workflow that comprises information about the *negotiated QoS*.

Figure 14.1a depicts the main phases of a workflow lifecycle: *specification*, *planning*, and *execution*. We describe how the corresponding Amadeus components support each phase of the workflow cycle in Section 14.4. In this chapter, we use a sample workflow that is depicted in Figure 14.1b for the illustration and evaluation of Amadeus framework. Our sample workflow consists of two complex activities (A_1 and A_2 in the Figure), each comprising a sequence of basic activities.[1] The workflow details are shown in Figure 14.9. F_1 represents the input file for activity A_1, F_2 is the output file of activity A_1 and the input file of A_2, and F_3 is the output file of activity A_2. The left-hand side of Figure 14.1b depicts the requested QoS, which is specified during the workflow *specification* phase. The aim of the *planning* phase is to

[1]Basic activities are not shown for the sake of simplicity.

determine a service for each activity A_j, from a pool of available services $\{S_{j1},\ldots,S_{jn}\}$, which best matches the *requested QoS*. The right-hand side of Figure 14.1b depicts that for activity A_1 the service S_{1k} offers the most suitable QoS.

14.3.2 Amadeus Architecture

In this section we describe the main components of the Amadeus environment. Section 14.4 gives a more detailed description of the Amadeus components and exemplifies their usage with a sample workflow.

Figure 14.2 shows the architecture of the Amadeus environment. The main components include: (1) the visualization–specification component; (2) the planning–negotiation–execution component, called the *QoS-aware Grid workflow engine* (QWE); and (3) a set of Grid resources.

The specification–visualization component comprises Teuta [8], a tool for UML-based Grid workflow modeling and visualization. A user may specify the workflow with Teuta by composing predefined workflow elements. For each workflow element different properties (e.g., execution time, price and location affinity) may be specified that indicate the user's QoS requirements. After validation of the specified workflow, Teuta generates the corresponding XML representation following the syntax of QoWL [9]. The QWE engine interprets the QoWL workflow, applies the selected optimization strategy, negotiates with services, selects appropriate services, and finally executes the workflow. The *requested QoS* and the *negotiated QoS* may be expressed using a language for the specification of electronic contracts, as, for example, the Web Service Level Agreement (WSLA). For the activities annotated with QoS constraints, we use VGE services, which are able to provide certain QoS guarantees. For other activities non-VGE services may be used.

The implementation of the QoS-aware planning for workflows in arbitrary form is a complex task. Therefore, the current implementation of the Amadeus framework is applicable only to the workflows that have the form of acyclic graphs. Workflows that comprise loops (i.e., cycles) pose specific challenges for QoS-aware planning. For instance, for the `while` loop it is not possible to determine exactly the number of iterations in advance. Therefore, the performance-related QoS constraints for the `while` loop cannot be guaranteed in the general case.

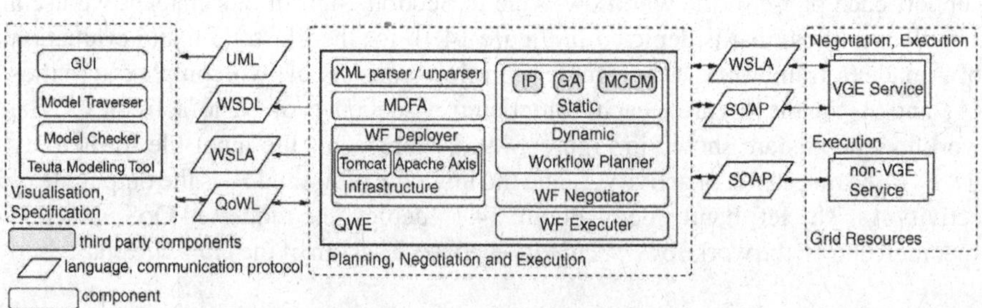

Figure 14.2 Amadeus architecture.

14.4 AMADEUS' SUPPORT FOR GRID WORKFLOW LIFECYCLE

In this section we explain how the Amadeus environment supports all phases of a QoS-aware Grid workflow lifecycle. For each phase we describe the responsible Amadeus components and evaluate these components using the sample workflow introduced in Section 14.3.1.

14.4.1 Specification

The required QoS constraints of a certain workflow may be specified in different ways. As shown in Figure 14.7, we distinguish between *local* and *global* constraints of a Grid workflow. Those constraints marked with question marks have to be calculated by the QoS-aware engine.

Local constraints usually address QoS constraints of single activities invoking external services. As shown on the left side of Figure 14.7, QoS constraints of the basic activities A_1, A_2, and A_3 are specified by the user. The QoS constraints of the overall workflow are calculated in a *bottom–up* way approach by considering aggregation functions of the particular activities.

Global constraints address the QoS of the overall workflow or of complex activities. The middle part of Figure 14.7 depicts an approach where the QoS constraints of the overall workflow are specified by the user. The appropriate services for the underlying tasks (A_1, A_2, A_3) are selected using a heuristic or analytical solver, where the global constraints of the workflow correspond to the constraints of the solver (e.g., maximum execution time or budget for the overall workflow). Global constraints may be used to annotate complex activities, for example, if the complex activity in question encompasses some critical basic activities (the right side of Fig. 14.9). If we assume that the activity A_2 shown on the right side of Figure 14.7 is a complex activity, we may apply a global constraint approach in order to bind the underlying basic activity. Constraints of the remaining workflow are computed in a *bottom–up* approach considering the aggregation functions of the corresponding workflow elements [33].

14.4.1.1 XML-Based Specification of QoS-Aware Workflows. In this section we describe the QoWL language, which is an XML-based language for QoS-aware Grid workflows.

The QoWL language comprises a subset of the business process execution language (BPEL) [18] and a set of QoS extensions that is used for specification of the QoS requirements of Grid workflows considering begin time, response time, price, and location affinity. The elements of our BPEL subset include `process`, `invoke`, `copy`, `sequence`, flow, `receive`, `reply`, *`Switch`*, and *`while`*. QoWL elements are used for the specification of QoS before QoS negotiation and for the expression of QoS after negotiation.

Figure 14.3 depicts the structure of a QoWL element. A QoWL element is defined as a BPEL element extended with a set of QoS constraints. The attributes of the `qowl-element`, such as `name` and `portType`, are used as defined in the BPEL specification [18]. The `<qos-constraints>` element specifies the QoS

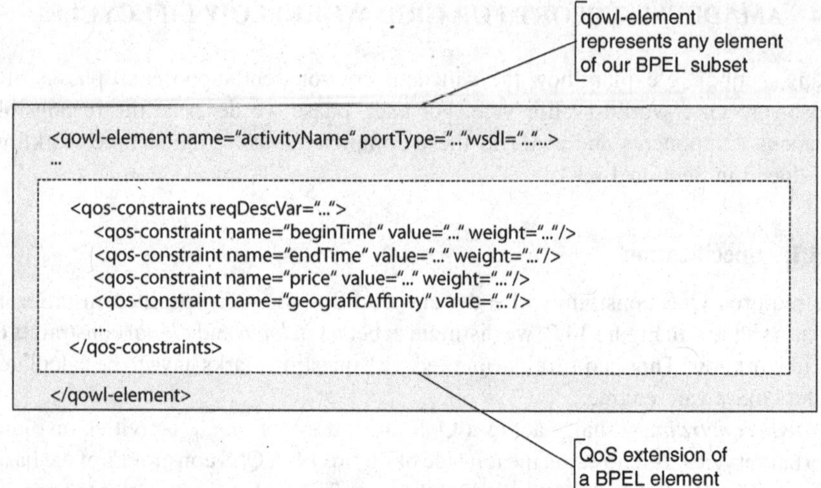

Figure 14.3 The structure of a QoWL element.

constraints of a specific workflow element. The attribute reqDescVar defines the variable that specifies the input metadata. Each <qos-constraints> element may contain several <qos-constraint> elements. Each element of type <qos-constraint> specifies a QoS constraint as a tuple (name, value, weight).

Quality-of-service extensions are used to express both the *requested* QoS constraints of a workflow before the QoS negotiation (see Fig. 14.4) and the *offered* QoS

```
...
<invoke name=''start'' portType=''appex''
  operation=''start'' inputVar=''startRequest''>
  <qos-constraints reqDescVar=''startReqDesc''>
     <candidate-registry inputVar=''queryRequest''
        ...
        wsdl= ''http://kim:9357/registry/reg?wsdl''/>
    <qos-constraint name=''beginTime'' weight=''0.3''
       value=''18-08-2005 12:00,0 MET'' />
     <qos-constraint name=''endTime'' weight=''0.2''
        value=''18-08-2005 14:00,0 MET'' />
     <qos-constraint name=''price'' weight=''0.5''
        value=''20.00'' />
     <qos-constraint name=''geographicAffinity''
        value=''at'' />
  </qos-constraints>
</invoke>
...
```

Figure 14.4 An excerpt of an abstract QoWL.

of a workflow after the negotiation with the services (see Fig. 14.4). Please note that the offered QoS may differ from the requested one.

Figure 14.4 depicts a fragment of an *abstract* workflow that represents an `<invoke>` activity. The `<qos-constraint>` element named `beginTime` specifies the earliest begin time of the workflow execution. The budget for the activity execution is specified by defining the `price<qos-constraint>` element. The `weight` attribute may be used to balance the effect of different QoS constraints on the service selection process. The weight attribute is specified for the `beginTime`, `endTime`, and the `price` elements. The `<candidate-registry>` element specifies where potential services may be found. The `<candidate-registry>` element may be specified by the user or automatically mapped from the workflow engine as predefined option. Generally, candidate registries comprise a number of dynamically registered services. Keywords may be used in order to find matching services.

The `<invoke>` element `start` depicted in Figure 14.4 comprises the set of constraints defined within the `<qos-constraints>` element (see lines 4–16 in Fig. 14.4). The `<qos-constraints>` element contains one `<candidate-registry>` element (see line 5 in Fig. 14.4). The metadata necessary for QoS negotiation of that activity is specified using the `startReqDesc` variable. The payload data is set using the `startRequest` variable.

Additionally, the user may express preferences regarding the location of Grid resources where an activity should be executed, by specifying the Grid site or organizational or geographic affinity. For instance, the QoS constraint `geographicAffinity` with value `at` specifies that the activity should be executed on Grid resources that are geographically located in Austria (see lines 14–15 in Fig. 14.4).

Figure 14.5 depicts a corresponding *concrete workflow*. Now, in the concrete workflow, the `<invoke>` element `start` contains instead of the `<candidate-registry>` element a `wsdl` attribute with the endpoint of the selected service (see line 3 in Fig. 14.4). The `<qos-constraints>` element now also contains the `wslaVar` variable specifying the service-level agreement between the engine and the particular service. The `<qos-constraints>` element of the `invoke` activity considers the offered QoS of a VGE service.

14.4.1.2 Specification of Location Affinity with QoWL. Most of the existing related work focuses on performance (i.e., activity execution time) and economic aspects (i.e., activity price) of QoS [5,11]. We believe that while performance is of paramount importance for time-critical applications, the wide acceptance of Grid technology strongly depends on security and legal aspects. We have experienced that many potential users from industry hesitate to use Grid technology even if the performance and economic benefits are clear because of security and legal concerns [26]. Therefore, we consider that it would be useful for the user to have the possibility to restrict the location of Grid resources on which certain activities may be executed. For instance, for security or legal reasons the user may specify that an activity should be executed only on Grid resources that belong to the user's organization.

```
...
<invoke name= ''start'' portType=''appex''
  wsdl=''http://bridge:9355/SPECT/appex?wsdl''
  operation=''start'' inputVar=''startRequest''>
 <qos-constraints reqDescVar=''startReqDesc''
   wslVar=''wslaStart''>
   <qos-constraint name=''beginTime'' weight=''0.3''
     value=''18-08-2005 12:13:06,0 MET'' />
   <qos-constraint name=''endTime'' weight=''0.2''
     value=''18-08-2005 13:45:04,0 MET'' />
   <qos-constraint name=''price'' weight=''0.5''
     value=''16.00'' />
   <qos-constraint name=''geographicAffinity''
     value=''at'' />
 </qos-constraints>
</invoke>
...
```

Figure 14.5 An excerpt of a concrete QoWL.

Figure 14.6 depicts how location affinity can be expressed with QoWL. The user may specify that a certain workflow activity should be executed on a specific *Grid site*, on the Grid resources of a specific *organization*, or on the Grid resources of a specific *geographic region*.

Commonly, *Grid site affinity* is not specified by the user, but the Grid environment automatically maps workflow activities to Grid resources according to the availability and performance of resources [7]. Usually, the goal is to minimize workflow execution time. However, a user who has information (related to security or law) that cannot be automatically obtained by the Grid environment can then manually map the activity to a specific Grid site. Such examples are medical applications with legal restriction considering electronic transfer of patient specific data [26]. Grid-site preference is specified by using the QoS constraint named *gridSiteAffinity*. Figure 14.6 shows that activities A_3 and A_5 encompassed by group G_1 should be on the same Grid site. The reason could be the large data transfer between the activities A_3 and A_5 or some security reasons. The QoWL code of A_3, A_7, A_{11} depicts the specification of the affinity on the language level (see Fig. 14.6).

Organization affinity indicates the preference of the user regarding the location where an activity should be executed considering resources that belong to a specific organization. These resources can be geographically distributed. The user's preferences may be based on established trust relationships with other companies. For instance, a vehicle manufacturing company may wish to execute certain critical activities on a subset of the Grid in order to ensure that any relevant information is not visible for competitors. Organization preference is specified by using the QoS constraint named `organizationAffinity`. Figure 14.6 depicts that activities A_7, A_8, A_{10}, and A_{11} encompassed by group G_2 should be executed on resources that belong to the same organization.

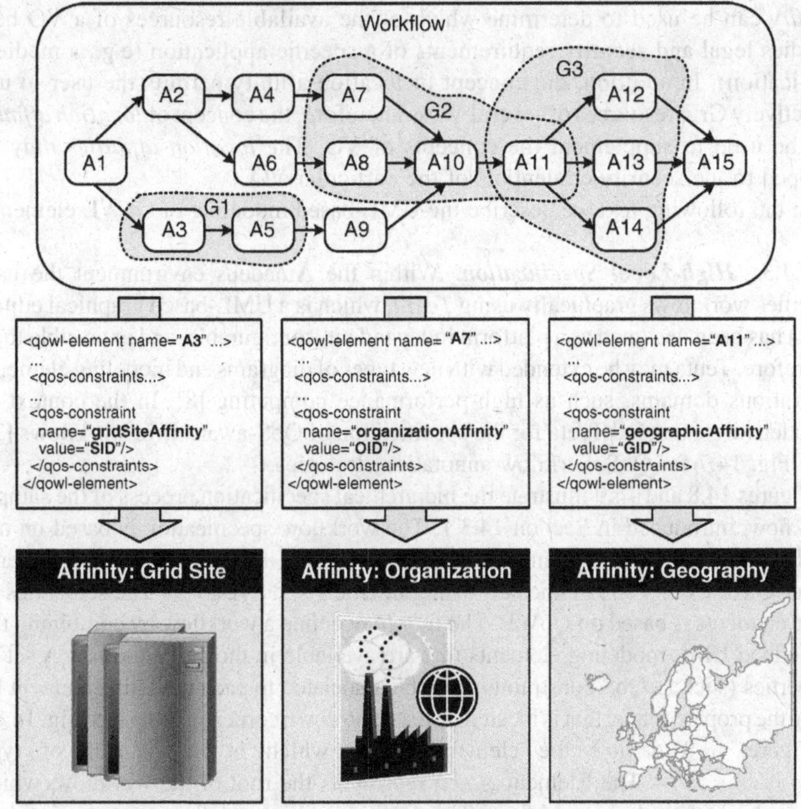

Figure 14.6 Specification of location affinity.

Geographic affinity indicates the preference of the user regarding the location of activity execution on Grid resources that belong to a specific geographic region. Examples of geographic region include country, state, or set of states. For instance, several countries that have the same legal conditions for the electronic transfer of medical data may be eligible for execution of certain activities. Geographic preference is specified by using the QoS constraint named `geographicAffinity`. Figure 14.6 shows that activities A_{11}, A_{12}, A_{13}, and A_{14} encompassed by group G_3 should be executed on resources that belong to the same geographic region.

The agreement on *time* and *cost* constraints as well as *location affinity* constraints requires a negotiation process with the candidate services as described in Section 14.4.2.3. The specified location affinity may be integrated with the available security infrastructure, such as *Web services policy* [30]. The security and legal related QoS can be used to support the concept of the *virtual organization* (VO). The VO concept defines policies governing access to resources of the organizations (e.g., unique authentication, authorization) which form a specific VO [31]. *Location affinity* can be used to determine which of the available resources of a VO best satisfies legal and security requirements of a specific application (e.g., a medical application). In addition, the concept of location affinity permits the user to use selectively Grid resources of several VOs. Therefore, the concept of *location affinity* can be used to supplement the concepts of VO. The *location affinities may* be mapped to the security credentials of the particular VO.

In the following text we describe the UML-based modeling of QoWL elements.

14.4.1.3 High-Level Specification. Within the Amadeus environment the user specifies workflows graphically using *Teuta*, which is a UML-based graphical editor. Teuta has been designed as a platform independent, configurable, and extensible tool. Therefore, Teuta may be extended with new types of diagrams and modeling elements for various domains, such as high-performance computing [8]. In the context of Amadeus we extended Teuta for the specification of QoS-aware Grid workflows [7]. (See Fig. 14.7 for QoS workflow annotation strategies.)

Figures 14.8 and 14.9 illustrate the hierarchical specification process of the sample workflow, introduced in Section 14.3.1. The workflow specification is based on our UML extension for the domain of Grid workflows [7]. The type of modeling elements of our UML extension is indicated with guillemets <<type>>. The semantics of these elements is based on QoWL. The user may define a workflow by combining the predefined UML modeling elements that are available in the Teuta toolbar. A set of properties (such as QoS constraints) may be associated to each modeling element by using the property panel that is located on the right-down corner of Teuta (see Fig. 14.8).

Figure 14.8 depicts the element *Main*, which is an instance of type <<process>>. The Element *Main* represents the root of the workflow, which encapsulates the whole workflow. The QoS constraints of the <<process>> element are shown in the bottom right corner of Figure 14.8. For instance, the user may define the earliest possible time of the workflow execution *beginTime* = *01-05-2006 10:00*, and the latest possible time of the workflow completion *endTime* = *01-05-2006 10:06*. The maximum *price* for the workflow

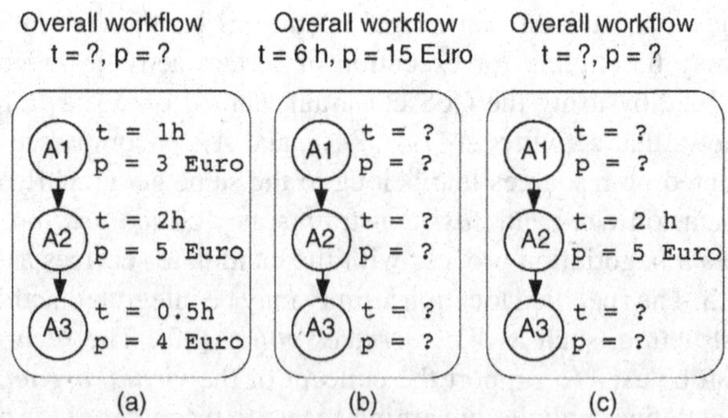

Figure 14.7 QoS workflow annotation strategies: (a) specification of local constraints; (b) specification of global constraints; (c) specification of local constraints for critical activities.

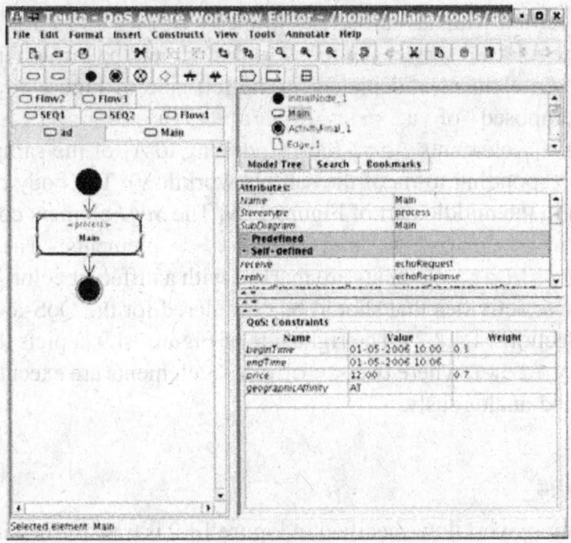

Figure 14.8 Annotation of a sample workflow with global constraints.

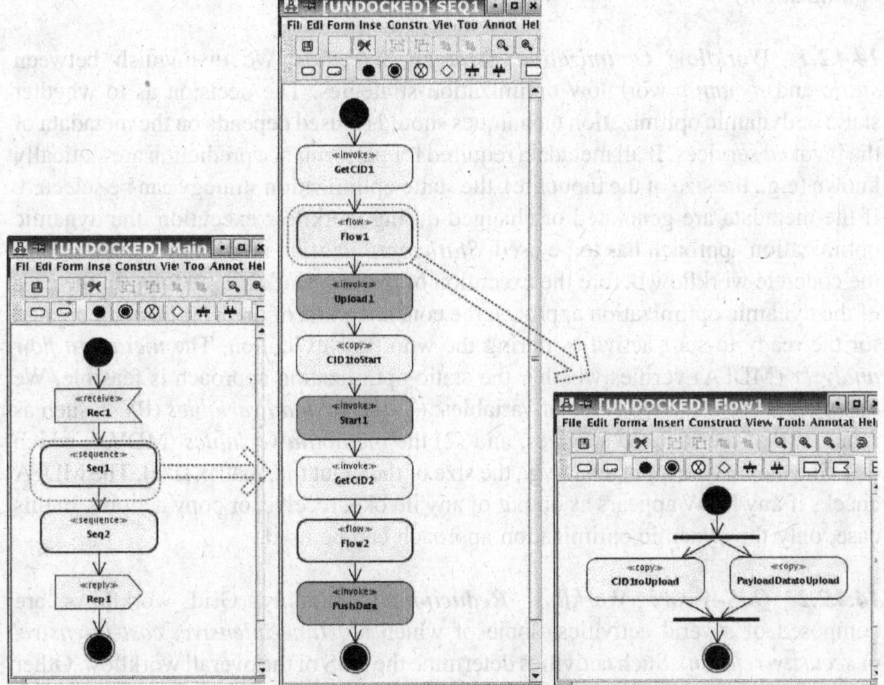

Figure 14.9 Hierarchical workflow specification.

execution is specified with 12 euros. The property `geographicAffinity` $=$ `AT` indicates that the selected services of the workflow should be located in Austria. The body of the `Main` element is depicted on the left side of Figure 14.9. The `Main` element is composed of a `<<receive>>`, a `<<reply>>`, and two `<<sequence>>` elements `Seq1` (corresponding to A_1 of the sample workflow) and `Seq2` (corresponding to A_2 of the sample workflow). The body of the element `Seq1` is shown in the middle part of Figure 14.9. The *Seq1* element contains several `<<invoke>>`, `<<copy>>`, and <<flow>> elements. The `Upload1`, `Start1`, and `PushData` elements are marked with a different color. This indicates compute-intensive activities that should be considered for the QoS-aware workflow planning (see Section 14.4.2.2). The right side of Figure 14.9 depicts the body of the complex activity `Flow1`, where two `<<copy>>` elements are executed in parallel. `Seq2` is specified analogously.

14.4.2 Planning

The sample abstract workflow specified in Figure 14.9 is transformed into a concrete workflow using the *workflow planner* component. The aim of this component is to automate the selection of services in accordance with the *requested QoS*. Workflow planning comprises the following phases: (1) selection of the workflow optimization strategy, (2) QoS-aware workflow reduction, (3) negotiation, and (4) the workflow optimization.

14.4.2.1 Workflow Optimization Strategy Selection. We distinguish between *static* and *dynamic* workflow optimization strategies. The decision as to whether static or dynamic optimization techniques should be used depends on the metadata of the invoked services. If all metadata required for performance prediction are statically known (e.g., the size of the input file), the static optimization strategy can be selected. If the metadata are generated or changed during workflow execution, the dynamic optimization approach has to be used. *Static optimization* implies the generation of the concrete workflow before the execution of the first workflow activity. In the case of the dynamic optimization approach the concrete parts of the workflow are created for the ready-to-start activities during the workflow execution. The *metadata flow analyzer* (MDFA) verifies whether the static optimization approach is feasible. We distinguish between two types of variables: (1) *the payload variables* (PVs), such as input data of the invoked services; and (2) the *metadata variables* (MDVs), which describe the service input data (e.g., the size of the input file, matrix size). The MDFA checks if any MDV appears as output of any invoke, receive, or copy activity. In this case, only the dynamic optimization approach can be used.

14.4.2.2 QoS-Aware Workflow Reduction. Commonly, Grid workflows are composed of several activities, some of which are *time-intensive*, *cost-intensive*, or *security-relevant*. Such activities determine the QoS of the overall workflow. Other kinds of activities (e.g., control tasks) that do not significantly affect the overall QoS may be neglected during the optimization phase of the workflow planning. Workflow reduction can be done either manually, semiautomatically, or automatically. In the first case the user can manually select activities, which should be considered for the workflow planning. In the second case the resource-consuming activities may be detected by considering all activities having associated QoS. In the third case, if, for example, QoS is assigned only on the global level, a trial workflow run may be done to figure out which of the specified resources offer or demand QoS. Thus, resource-intensive activities may be detected.

The process of eliminating activities without QoS constraints is called *QoS-aware workflow reduction.* In the simplest case workflow reduction is performed by eliminating all activities, which do not have specified QoS constraints. Figure 14.10a, shows the reduced workflow model of the sample workflow. The reduced workflow includes the following activities: `Upload1`, `Start1`, and `PushData`, which belong to the complex activity `Seq1` (i.e., A_1); `Start2` and `Download2` activities, which belong to the complex activity `Seq2` (i.e., A_2). The next section describes the negotiation process within the Amadeus environment.

14.4.2.3 Negotiation. On the basis of the selected *optimization strategy*, the *WF negotiator* queries all specified registries, generates the necessary *requested QoS*, and receives *offered QoS* from services. Figure 14.10b depicts the negotiation process and participating components. The *WF planner* starts the negotiation by initializing one or more instances of the *WF negotiator*. Each instance is responsible for the negotiation process of one activity. If the static planning approach is used, the negotiation starts concurrently for all activities of the reduced QoS-aware model.

After the initialization of the *WF Negotiators*, each WF negotiator supplies each candidate service with a `QoSRequest (QoSReq)` and a `RequestDescriptor (ReqDesc)`. A `QoSReq` contains the requested QoS, whereas a `ReqDesc` contains metadata about the input data necessary for the evaluation of QoS constraints. If the `QoSReq` is specified, each service tries to meet the specified constraints. For instance, if a low price is requested, a service may run the application on fewer nodes to meet

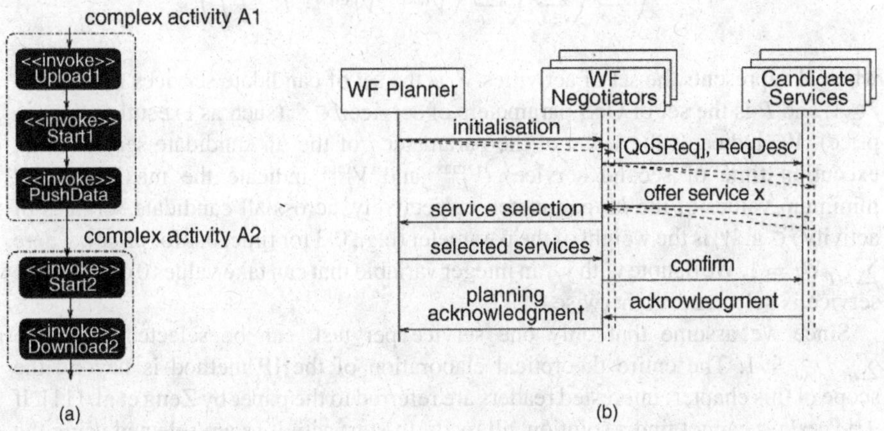

Figure 14.10 (a) Reduced form of the sample workflow; (b) WF negotiation process.

the price constraint. After collecting all offers, each WF negotiator notifies the WF planner about the received offers. Thereafter, the WF planner selects appropriate services, which fit into global or local constraints by applying the selected optimization strategy. The selected services are confirmed and the WSLA is generated between services and the QWE. If no suitable service is found, the user has either to change the candidate registries or to modify the constraints.

14.4.2.4 Optimization

14.4.2.4.1 Static Optimization. If the user specifies his/her requirements in form of *global* QoS constraints, analytical or heuristic solvers are needed in order to find services that satisfy the QoS constraints. We apply the integer programming (IP) method for selecting services, if the global constraints are specified. The implementation of the optimization component of Amadeus is based on the `lp_solve` package [10]. Please note that before the optimization procedure is performed, it is ensured that services considered for the workflow optimization match user requirements regarding location affinity (e.g., only services located in European Union are considered). Each QoS constraint (e.g., maximum time, maximum price) of an activity represents an (IP) constraint. The outcome of the optimization process with `lp_solve` is an array that contains the IDs of the selected services. The order of service IDs within this array corresponds to the execution order of activities of the reduced workflow. Since most of our reduced workflows have the form of a simple straight-line code, IP is a more appropriate approach than complex heuristic techniques (e.g., genetic algorithms). Since finding such a solution is an NP-hard problem, there is no guarantee that the best and the most efficient solution can be found. However, by applying this approach, near-optimal solutions may be found.

We consider the *objective function*, defined as

$$\max\left(\sum_{j\in A}\left(\sum_{i\in S_J}\left(\sum_{l\in p}\left(\frac{V_l^{\max}-V_{l,i}}{V_l^{\max}-V_i^{\min}}W_i\right)y_{ij}\right)\right)\right) \tag{14.1}$$

where A represents the set of activities, S_j is the set of candidate services for activity $j\in A$, and P is the set of QoS parameters of service $j\in S_j$ (such as execution time or price). $V_{t,l}$ indicates the value of the parameter l of the lth candidate service (e.g., execution time of second service). $V_l^{\max}$ and $V_l^{\min}$ indicate the maximum and minimum values of the lth parameter, respectively, across all candidate services of activity $j\in A$. W_l is the weight of the parameter (e.g., 0.3 for time, 0.4 for price), where $\sum_{l\in P} W_l = 1$. We denote with $y_{i,j}$ an integer variable that can take values 0 or 1; 1 if the service is selected; 0 otherwise.

Since we assume that only one service per task can be selected, we have $\sum_{i\in S_j} y_{i,j} = 1$. The entire theoretical elaboration of the IP method is beyond the scope of this chapter; interested readers are referred to the paper by Zeng et al. [11]. If `lp_solve` cannot find a solution, all ready-to-start activities are selected using the local optima. Then `lp_solve` is invoked for all remaining activities, for which no solution is found, and the global constraints are adapted considering the QoS constraints of the already selected services. This procedure is repeated until all activities have assigned services.

14.4.2.4.2 Dynamic Optimization. The dynamic optimization strategy starts the workflow planning for ready-to-start activities only. For each activity $j \in A$ the negotiation and optimization is performed individually before the execution. The services are selected using the multicriteria decisionmaking (MCDM) mechanisms [11]. After the execution of activity *j*, the next activity $j + 1$ is considered for optimization and so on until all activities of the workflow are executed.

14.4.3 Execution

The outcome of the workflow planning phase is a concrete workflow, which is ready for execution. In the case of the static planning approach the workflow execution phase is started after the completion of the workflow planning phase. However, in the case of dynamic planning the execution and planning phases are performed for each activity of the workflow in an alternate fashion.

Figure 14.11a depicts the relationship between static workflow planning and workflow execution. *Static workflow planning* involves the following steps: strategy selection, WF reduction, WF negotiation, and WF optimization. As we described in Section 14.4.2 for the static planning approach, global constraints (GCs) (such as maximum price of the workflow) are specified for the whole workflow. If the GCs cannot be satisfied after WF negotiation and WF optimization, the workflow is reduced by excluding the first activity of the workflow. The excluded activity is optimized separately from the rest of the workflow by searching for the candidate service that offers the best QoS. In the next iteration only the reduced workflow is considered. However, the user may annotate each activity with the expected average

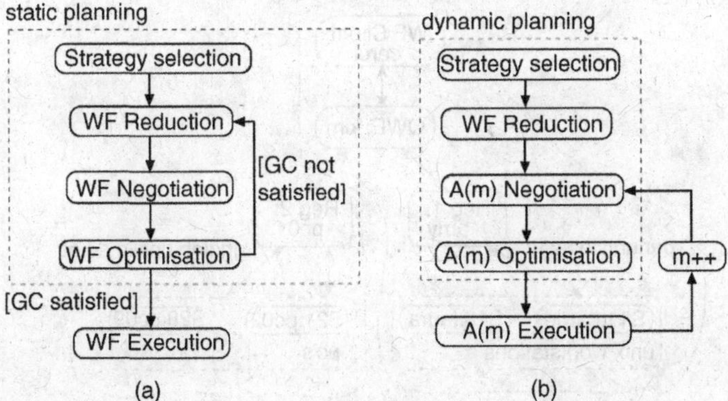

Figure 14.11 (a) Workflow execution with static planning; (b) workflow execution with dynamic planning.

runtime in order to increase the chance to find a solution with fewer iterations. If the GCs are satisfied, the WF execution may start.

If the execution of certain activities modifies the metadata, the dynamic workflow planning is applied (see Fig. 14.11b). For each activity $A(m)$ the negotiation and optimization is performed individually before the execution. After the execution of activity $A(m)$, the next activity, $A(m+1)$, is considered. This iterative process of dynamic planning is completed after all activities of the workflow are executed.

14.4.3.1 WF Deployer. The purpose of the WF deployer is to publish the workflow as a Grid service. On the basis of the XML representation of the concrete workflow, the corresponding WSDL file is generated, which serves as the input for the WF deployer. The WF deployer parses the WSDL file using `wsdl4j`, which is an IBM reference implementation of Java APIs for WSDL. Thereafter, the WF deployer generates Java code for a Grid service that represents the workflow. Finally, the WF deployer deploys the generated Grid service using Apache Axis and Tomcat to the location specified by the user.

In the case of static workflow planning, the WSLA may be provided to the consumer of the workflow. The WSLA includes the information on the negotiated QoS for the whole workflow. For the dynamic workflow planning, the WSLA is not provided.

14.5 EXPERIMENTAL RESULTS

Figure 14.12 depicts the experimentation platform used for the execution of the sample workflow. The *Amadeus* components (e.g., QWE and the WF client) and the required Grid software infrastructure are deployed on the depicted experimentation platform. The candidate services for the complex activity A_1 of the sample workflow (see Fig. 14.1b), namely, $\{S1x: 1 \leq x \leq 8\}$, are deployed on eight UNIX

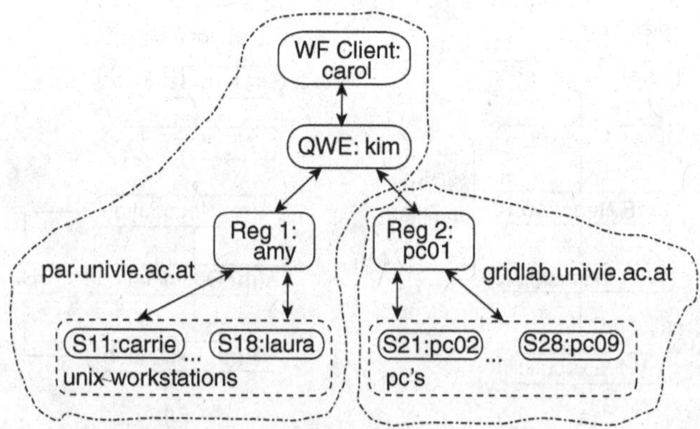

Figure 14.12 Experimentation platform.

workstations. The registry `Reg1` containing the information about `S1x` services, the QWE, and the WF client are deployed each on a different UNIX workstation. The workflow client, the QWE, and the candidate services of activity A_2 are deployed in the domain `par.univie.ac.at`. The candidate services for the complex activity A_2 (see Fig. 14.1b), namely { $S2x$: $1 \leq x \leq 8$}, are deployed on eight PCs. Registry `Reg2` is deployed on a separate PC. The registry and the candidate services of A_2 are deployed in the domain `gridlab.univie.ac.at`.

Table 14.1 depicts the experimental results for the static planning approach. In this experiment the solution (i.e., services that satisfy the GCs) was found already in the first iteration of planning (i.e., `lp_solve` was called only once) because we used a rather simple sample workflow. For real-world workflows more than one iteration of the planning phase may be necessary to find a solution.

The time to *upload* the file from the client to service `S1x` is 27.676 s, whereas the time to *push* the file from service `S1x` to `S2x` is 18.086 seconds. This difference in data transfer time may be due to the fact that service `S1x` is deployed on a machine with a shared file system and intensive read/write activity. The invocation of operation `Start1` starts a Java application, which simulates the invocation of a native application spending 2 min and 10.066 s for data processing. The total workflow completion time is defined as $T_{\text{total}} = T_{\text{planning}} + T_{\text{execution}}$. T_{planning} denotes the time needed for the negotiation with the candidate services and optimization with `lp_solve`. The execution time is defined as $T_{\text{execution}} = T_{\text{reduced}} + T_{\text{remained}}$. T_{reduced} denotes the time for the execution of the activities of the reduced workflow as depicted in Figure 14.10a. T_{remained} indicates the time for the execution of the remaining activities that are not included in the reduced workflow. As assumed, T_{total} is dominated by T_{reduced}, which is 98.16% of the overall workflow execution time (see the rightmost column of the Table 14.1).

TABLE 14.1 Experimental Results for Static Workflow Planning and Execution

Workflow Phase	Activity	Time	Time (%)
Planning	UML2QoWL	0.095 s	0.03
	QoS negotiation `S1x, S2x`	3.319 s	1.01
	`lp_solve optimization`	0.553 s	0.17
	T_{planning}	3.967 s	1.21
Execution	`<<invoke>>` *Upload* `(S1x)`	27.676 s	8.41
	`<<invoke>>` *Start1* `(S1x)`	2 min 10.066 s	39.53
	`<<invoke>>` *PushData* `(S1x)`	18.086 s	5.50
	`<<invoke>>` *Start2* `(S2x)`	2 min 10.039 s	39.53
	`<<invoke>>` *Download2* `(S2x)`	17.078 s	5.19
	T_{reduced}	5 min 22.950 s	98.16
	T_{remained}	2.088 s	0.63
	$T_{\text{execution}} = T_{\text{reduced}} + T_{\text{remained}}$	5 min 25.033 s	98.79
	$T_{\text{total}} = T_{\text{planning}} + T_{\text{execution}}$	5 min 29 s	100.00

TABLE 14.2 Experimental Results for Dynamic Workflow Planning and Execution

Workflow Phase	Activity	Time	Time (%)
Planning 1	UML2QoWL	0.095 s	0.03
	QoS negotiation `S1x`	4.544 s	1.36
	$T_{\text{planning 1}}$	4.639 s	1.39
Execution 1	<<invoke>> *`Upload1 S1x`*	28.567 s	8.55
	<<invoke>> *`Start1 S1x`*	2 min 10.081 s	38.95
	<<invoke>> *`PushData S1x`*	18.081 s	5.46
	$T_{\text{reduced 1}}$	2 min 56.882 s	52.96
Planning 2	QoS negotiation `S2x`	2.621 s	0.78
	$T_{\text{planning 2}}$	2.621 s	0.78
Execution 2	<<invoke>> *`Start2 (S2x)`*	2 min 10.094 s	38.95
	<<invoke>> *`Download2 (S2x)`*	10.031 s	5.40
	$T_{\text{reduced 2}}$	2 min 28.125 s	44.35
	$T_{\text{planning}} + T_{\text{planning 1}} + \mathrm{T}_{\text{planning 2}}$	7.260 s	2.17
	$T_{\text{reduced}} + T_{\text{reduced 1}} + T_{\text{reduced 2}}$	5 min 25.007 s	97.31
	T_{remained}	1.733 s	0.52
	$T_{\text{execution}} = T_{\text{reduced}} + T_{\text{remained}}$	5 min 26.740 s	97.83
	$T_{\text{total}} = T_{\text{planning}} + T_{\text{execution}}$	5 min 34 s	100.00

Table 14.2 depicts the experimental results for the dynamic planning approach. Planning is performed for each activity individually before execution. This involves multiple negotiations with candidate services, which results in an increase of the total planning time for the complete workflow. For the static planning approach we obtained $T_{\text{planning}} = 3.967$ s (see Table 14.1), whereas for the dynamic planning approach the total planning time was $T_{\text{planning}} = 7.26$ s (see Table 14.2). Therefore, the total workflow completion time for the dynamic approach ($T_{\text{total}} = 5$ min 34 s) is larger than in the static case ($T_{\text{total}} = 5$ min 29 s). The workflow completion time T_{total} is dominated by T_{reduced}, which is 97.31% of the total workflow completion time (see the rightmost column of Table 14.2). This demonstrates that the subset of activities in the reduced workflow (see Fig. 14.10a) determines the completion time of the whole workflow.

14.6 VISIONARY THOUGHTS FOR PRACTITIONERS

Despite considerable effort invested in the development of QoS support for standalone Grid services and for business workflows, QoS support for Grid workflows is still an open issue. In this chapter we present a holistic service-oriented environment for QoS-aware Grid workflows. A distinguishing feature of our system is the support of a comprehensive set of QoS requirements that in addition to performance and economic aspects also consider legal and security aspects.

We present two application scenarios of our approach: (1) a scenario that demonstrates the usage of the application-level QoS to meet security and legal requirements of the practitioners and (2) a scenario that exemplifies QoS with respect to application execution time and price:

- *Security/Law-Related QoS.* Organization affinity indicates the preference of the user regarding the location where an activity should be executed on the Grid. These resources can be geographically distributed. For instance, a vehicle manufacturing company may wish to execute certain critical activities on a subset of the Grid in order to ensure that any relevant information is not visible for competitors. Another examples are Grid-based life science applications, where legal conditions for electronic transfer of medical data may vary between different countries.
- *Performance/Economy-Related QoS.* For instance, time and price constraints are necessary for medical practitioners. Usually, medical practitioners need to execute computation-intensive simulations as a means of decision support during medical surgery. It is important that simulations be executed in near-real time and that the resources necessary for the execution of the simulation be available during the specific timeframe (i.e., during surgery). Moreover, the expected price for the usage of the simulation service should comply with the agreed-on constraints (i.e., should not cost more than a certain amount, e.g., 100 euros).

In the following example with maxillofacial surgery simulation (MFSS), we emphasize the relevance of *location affinity*, *time,* and *price constraints*. MFSS is one of the six medical applications that we have used within the framework of GEMSS project [27]. The application facilitates the work of medical practitioners and provides the preoperative virtual planning of maxillofacial surgery. The application consists of a set of components that can run on a local machine or on different remote machines. These components may be organized as a Grid workflow in order to simplify the work of the end users. MFSS is used for patients with inborn deformations of the midface [39]. The MFSS simulation predicts the results of the surgery by putting the bone into a new position using the finite-element method. The goal of the surgery is to achieve pleasant medical and cosmetic results. We use the Amadeus system in order to automate the execution of the MFSS application. The user may combine the predefined UML modeling elements, which are available in the Teuta toolbar, to specify the flow of workflow activities and to assign various QoS constraints. Figure 14.13 depicts a fragment of the MFSS workflow, namely the body of the `FEMSequence` activity.

An `invoke` element, which is indicated by the stereotype `<<invoke>>`, specifies the invocation of a remote or local service operation. For instance, the activity `UploadOperation` invokes the `upload` operation of the remote service. With each workflow element we have associated a set of properties by using the property panel, which is located on the right-hand side of the Teuta GUI. The lower right corner of Figure 14.13 shows the properties of the invoke element `StartOperation`, which starts the MFFS application running on a cluster. The top compartment of the property panel allows the association of attributes such

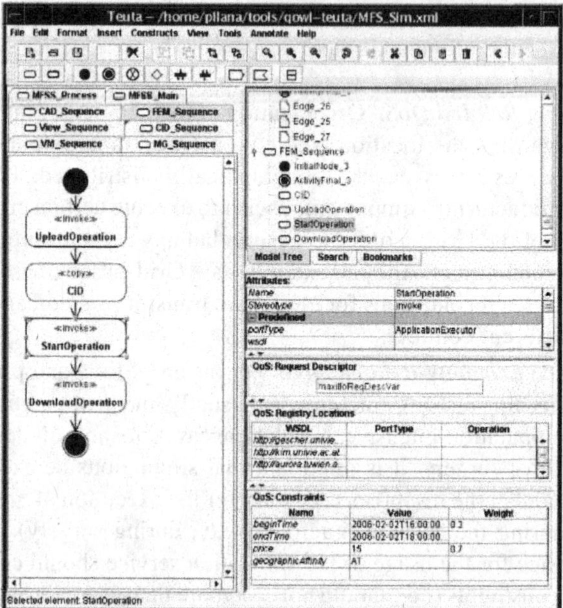

Figure 14.13 Maxillofacial surgery simulation.

as `name`, `portType`, and `operation`. We use the lower three compartments to specify QoS constraints such as `beginTime`, `endTime`, `price`, and `geographicAffinity`.

Thus, as shown in the lower right corner of Figure 14.13, using the Amadeus system we can ensure that

- The MFSS simulation will start after `2-2-2006 16:00` by specifying the QoS constraints `beginTime`.
- The results of the MFFS sumulation will be available before `2-2-2006 18:00` by specifying the QoS constraints `endTime`.
- The simulation will cost less than 15 euros by specifying the QoS constraints `price`.
- The sensitive patient data will not be transferred out of Austria by specifying the QoS constraints `geographicAffinity`.

14.7 FUTURE RESEARCH DIRECTIONS

Scientists using Grid workflow technologies seldom know the exact outcome of their experiments. Often they have to replan the experiments on demand depending on the produced intermediary experiment data. Grid workflow systems should enable a dynamic and adaptive workflow execution, where the end user can steer the execution of a workflow in an interactive and adaptive way considering the intermediary data products and QoS of the already executed activities. Thus, user-driven steering of the workflow execution, monitoring features, and dynamic workflow replanning are gaining importance and represent challenging future research directions.

The initiative work on QoS-aware Grid workflows presented in this chapter covers the high-level specification and planning of Grid workflows with multiple constraints by applying linear integer programming methods. However, owing to the explorative nature of scientific Grid workflows, advanced QoS negotiation strategies are required to gather information about the services on demand. Thus, another challenging research direction is development of the generic concepts to obtain QoS information of the services on demand, such as a sequence of messages, which has to be invoked to accomplish the QoS negotiation and to generate a valid contract between the workflow engine and the service.

14.8 CONCLUSION

In this chapter we have presented a holistic service-oriented environment that supports the whole lifecycle of QoS-aware Grid workflows. Our system allows the specification of a comprehensive set of QoS requirements that consider performance, economic, legal and security aspects. For each phase of the workflow lifecycle we have used a sample workflow to illustrate and experimentally validate the usefulness of the Amadeus environment. By applying our technique of QoS-aware workflow reduction, we have obtained a reduced workflow suitable for optimization using linear programming. The reduced workflow involves fewer activities with a simple control flow, which reduces the complexity of planning. We have observed that the time spent for optimization based on linear programming represents only a small percentage (~0.17%) of the total workflow completion time. Furthermore, in our experiments we have observed that ~98% of the workflow completion time is spent for the execution of activities involved in the reduced workflow. By optimizing the execution of activities of the reduced workflow, the total workflow completion time may be improved.

ACKNOWLEDGMENTS

The work described in this chapter was supported by the Austrian Science Fund as part of the Aurora Project under Contract SFBF1102 and by the European Union's GEMSS Project under Contract IST 2001-37153.

REFERENCES

1. W. Gentzsch, Grid computing, vision, strategy, and technology, *Proc. 2nd International Workshop on Grid and Cooperative Computing* (*GCC 2003*), Shanghai, China, 2003.
2. F. Berman, G. Fox, and A. J. G. Hey, *Grid Computing: Making The Global Infrastructure a Reality*, Wiley, Hoboken, NJ, 2003.

3. J. Yu and R. Buyya, *A Taxonomy of Workflow Management Systems for Grid Computing*, Journal of Grid Computing, **3**(3–4):171–200, 2005.
4. J. Blythe, E. Deelman, Y. Gil, Automatically composed workflows for Grid environments, *IEEE Intelligent Systems* **19**(4):16–23 (2004).
5. J. Yu, R. Buyya, and C. K. Tham, QoS-based scheduling of workflow applications on service Grids, *Proc. 1st IEEE International Conf. e-Science and Grid Computing* (*eScience05*), Melbourne, Australia, Dec. 5–8, 2005.
6. S. Benkner, I. Brandic, G. Engelbrecht, and R. Schmidt, VGE—a service-oriented Grid environment for on-demand supercomputing, *Proc. 5th IEEE/ACM International Workshop on Grid Computing* (*Grid 2004*), Pittsburgh, PA, Nov. 2004.
7. I. Brandic, S. Pllana, and S. Benkner, An approach for the high-level specification of QoS-aware Grid workflows considering location affinity, *Scientific Programming Journal* **14**(3–4):231–250 (2006).
8. S. Pllana and T. Fahringer, Performance prophet: A performance modeling and prediction tool for parallel and distributed programs, *Proc. IEEE 2005 International Conf. Parallel Processing; Performance Evaluation of Networks for Parallel, Cluster and Grid Computing Systems*, Oslo, Norway, June 2005.
9. I. Brandic, S. Benkner, G. Engelbrecht, and R. Schmidt, QoS support for time-critical Grid workflow applications, *Proc. 1st IEEE International Conf. eScience and Grid Computing*, Melbourne, Australia, Dec. 5–8, 2005.
10. The lp_solve Project, http://lpsolve.sourceforge.net/5.1, 2008.
11. L. Zeng, B. Benatallah, A. H. H. Ngu, M. Dumas, J. Kalagnanam, and H. Chang, QoS-aware middleware for Web services composition, *IEEE Transactions on Software Engineering* **30**(5):311–327 (2004).
12. The Globus Toolkit, http://www.globus.org, 2008.
13. Askalon Project, http://dps.uibk.ac.at/projects/askalon, 2008.
14. B. Plale, D. Gannon, D. A. Reed, S. J. Graves, K. Droegemeier, B. Wilhelmson, and M. Ramamurthy, Towards dynamically adaptive weather analysis and forecasting in LEAD, *Proc. 5th International Conf. Computational Science*, Atlanta, GA, May 22–25, 2005.
15. Y. Wang, M. Li, J. Cao, F. Tang, L. Chen, and L. Cao, An ECA-rule-based workflow management approach for Web services composition, *Proc. 4th International Conf. Grid and Cooperative Computing* (*GCC05*), Beijing, China, Nov. 30–Dec. 3, 2005.
16. S. Majithia, M. S. Shields, I. J. Taylor, and I. Wang, Triana: A graphical Web service composition and execution toolkit, *Proc. International Conf. Web Services*, San Diego, CA, July 6–9, 2004.
17. OASIS, Web Services Business Process Execution Language (WSBPEL) 2.0, 2006.
18. P. M. Kelly, P. D. Coddington, and A. L. Wendelborn, Distributed, parallel Web service orchestration using XSLT, *Proc. 1st International Conf. e-Science and Grid Computing* (*eScience05*), Melbourne, Australia, Dec. 5–8, 2005.
19. J. Cardoso, *Quality of Service and Semantic Composition of Workflows*, PhD dissertation, Dept. Computer Science, Univ. Georgia, Athens, 2002.
20. G. Canfora, M. Di Penta, R. Esposito, and M. L. Villani, An approach for QoS-aware service composition based on genetic algorithms, *Proc. Genetic and Computation Conf.* (*GECCO 2005*), Washington, DC, ACM Press, June 25–29, 2005.

21. R. Al-Ali, K. Amin, G. von Laszewski, O. Rana, D. Walker, M. Hategan, and N. Zaluzec, Analysis and provision of QoS for distributed Grid applications, *Journal of Grid Computing* **2**(2):163–182 (2004).
22. J. Liang, K. Nahrstedt, and Y. Zhou, Adaptive multi-resource prediction in a distributed resource sharing environment, *Proc. 4th IEEE/ACM Symp. Cluster Computing and the Grid* (*CCGrid'04*), Chicago, IL, April 19–22, 2004.
23. D. A. Menasce and E. Casalicchio, QoS in Grid computing, *IEEE Internet Computing* **8**(4):85–87 (2004).
24. R. Buyya and S. Venugopal, The Gridbus Toolkit for Service Oriented Grid and Utility Computing: An Overview and Status Report, *Proceedings of the First IEEE International Workshop on Grid Economics and Business Models* (GECON 2004), Seoul, Korea, April 2004.
25. S. Benkner and G. Engelbrecht, A generic QoS infrastructure for Grid Web services, *Proc. International Conf. Internet and Web Applications and Services*, Guadeloupe, French Caribbean, Feb. 19–25, 2006.
26. The GEMSS Project: Grid-Enabled Medical Simulation Services, EU IST Project, IST-2001-37153, http://www.gemss.de, 2008.
27. GEMSS Consortium, *Report on COTS Security Technologies and Authorisation Services*, Deliverable D2.2c. GEMSS project, European Commission Framework V Project No. IST-2001-37153, 2004.
28. D. M. Jones, J. W. Fenner, G. Berti, F. Kruggel, R. A. Mehrem, W. Backfrieder, R. Moore, and A. Geltmeier, The GEMSS Grid: An evolving HPC environment for medical applications, *Proc. HealthGrid 2004,* Clermont-Ferrand, France, Jan. 29–30, 2004.
29. I. Brandic, S. Pllana, and S. Benkner, Specification, planning, and execution of QoS-aware Grid workflows within the Amadeus environment, *Concurrency and Computation: Practice and Experience* **20**(4):331–345 (2008).
30. Web Services Policy (WS-Policy), http://ifr.sap.com/ws-policy/index.html, 2008.
31. I. Foster, C. Kesselman, and S. Tuecke, The anatomy of the Grid-enabling scalable virtual organizations, *International Journal of High-Performance Computing Applications* **15**(3):200–222 (2001).
32. I. Brandic, S. Benkner, G. Engelbrecht, and R. Schmidt, Towards quality of service support for Grid workflows, *Proc. European Grid Conf. 2005* (*EGC2005*), Amsterdam, The Netherlands, Feb. 2005.
33. I. Brandic, S. Pllana, and S. Benkner, High-level composition of QoS-aware Grid workflows: An approach that considers location affinity, *Proc. Workshop on Workflows in Support of Large-Scale Science* (*in conjunction with the 15th IEEE International Symp. on High Performance Distributed Computing*), Paris, June 2006.
34. T. Fahringer, A. Jugravu, S. Pllana, R. Prodan, C. Seragiotto, and H.-L. Truong, ASKALON: A tool set for cluster and Grid computing, *Concurrency and Computation: Practice and Experience* **17**(2–4):143–169 (2005).
35. K. K. Droegemeier, V. Chandrasekar, R. Clark, D. Gannon, S. Graves, E. Joseph, M. Ramamurthy, R. Wilhelmson, K. Brewster, B. Domenico, T. Leyton, V. R. Morris, D. Murray, B. Plale, R. Ramachandran, D. Reed, J. Rushing, D. Weber, A. Wilson, M. Xue, and S. Yalda, Linked environments for atmospheric discovery (LEAD): Architecture, technology roadmap and deployment strategy, *Proc. 21st Conf. Interactive Information*

Processing Systems for Meteorology, Oceanography, and Hydrology, San Diego, CA, 2005.

36. C. Pautasso, JOpera: Visual composition of Grid services, *ERCIM News* no. 59 (Oct. 2004).
37. T. Oinn, M. J. Addis, J. Ferris, D. J. Marvin, M. Senger, T. Carver, M. Greenwood, K. Glover, M. R. Pocock, A. Wipat, and P. Li, Taverna: A tool for the composition and enactment of bioinformatics workflows, *Bioinformatics* **20**(17):3045–3054 (2004).
38. I. J. Taylor, E. Deelman, D. B. Gannon, and M. Shields, *Workflows for e-Science*, Springer-Verlag, New York, 2007.
39. J. Cao, G. Berti, J. Fingberg, and J. G. Schmidt, Implementation of Grid-enabled medical simulation applications using workflow techniques, *Proc. 2nd International Workshop on Grid and Cooperative Computing* (*GCC 2003*), Shanghai, China, 2003.

15

RISK MANAGEMENT IN GRIDS

Karim Djemame, James Padgett, Iain Gourlay,
Kerstin Voss, and Odej Kao

15.1 INTRODUCTION

Advances in Grid computing research have resulted in considerable commercial interest in utilizing Grid infrastructures to support commercial applications and services [1–3]. However, significant developments in the areas of risk and dependability are necessary before widespread commercial adoption can become a reality. Specifically, risk management mechanisms need to be incorporated into Grid infrastructures, in order to move beyond the best-effort approach to the service provision that current Grid infrastructures follow.

Consider a scenario in which an end user is willing to pay a Grid resource provider for use of their resources to execute a task or process. The end user may want to associate quality-of-service (QoS) requirements with such a request. For example, one such requirement might specify that the task be completed by a specified deadline with a penalty clause to cover financial losses if the requirement is not met. Alternatively, such tasks may generate large amounts of data, which, if lost or corrupted, will also result in financial loss for the end user's organization. Consequently, end users (or their organisations) may wish to negotiate service-level agreements (SLAs) that define all aspects of the relationship between themselves and a Grid resource provider(s) and specify all contractual obligations and liability limits. In particular, such SLAs need to specify the performance guarantees of the resource provider in addition to penalty fees for both end users and providers, if either fails to deliver what is guaranteed.

Market-Oriented Grid and Utility Computing Edited by Rajkumar Buyya and Kris Bubendorfer

Hence, an infrastructure that supports SLA negotiation is clearly desirable. The importance of SLAs to Grid commercialization has stimulated a drive to standardize automated SLA negotiation/agreement process within the Grid research community [4]. However, both providers and end users are cautious on adopting such an approach since agreeing to an SLA represents a business risk for both parties. From the provider's perspective, an SLA represents a commitment to meet the objectives specified therein and to pay a penalty if it fails to provide the guaranteed service. SLA violation can be caused by many events, such as resource or network failures, operator unavailability, or even a power cut. Without a means of formally evaluating the likelihood and expected impact of such negative events, a provider faces serious difficulties and potential risk in deciding to which SLAs it will commit. Similarly, end users need to know the likelihood of an SLA violation in order to accurately compare SLA quotes and take appropriate decisions in relation to acceptable costs and penalty fees, since these, too, have a potential impact on their business.

These issues are addressed through risk management, a discipline that takes account of the possibility that future events may cause adverse effects. Risk management is important in a diverse range of fields, including statistics, economics, biology, engineering, systems analysis, and operations research. Risk management has been extensively used in IT technologies [5], but applying the concept to Grid infrastructures is still in its infancy. While risk is traditionally seen as a negative force, modern risk management recognizes its positive aspects and that, in contrast to risk avoidance strategies, accepting certain risks can be beneficial. A typical modern-day example is that of the insurance industry. For example, if a customer takes out insurance, then the risk of potential financial loss due to theft is transferred from the customer to the insurance company at the cost of a premium.

In the scenario mentioned earlier, risk management and assessment mechanisms are of value to resource providers, enabling them to make informed decisions regarding which SLA requests they wish to commit to, as well as building a resource management schedule through consideration of risk assessment information. Additionally, risk assessment and management enable a provider to identify infrastructure bottlenecks and mitigate potential risk, in some cases by initiating fault tolerance mechanisms to prevent SLA violations. An end user also benefits, since risk assessments can be used to determine whether an SLA request will be made after an SLA quote has been analyzed on the basis of its price, penalty, and probability of failure (PoF). Further, an end user may make use of a broker, and its reliability and risk assessment mechisms, to identify and negotiate with suitable providers. Risk assessment enables the broker to evaluate the risk involved in mapping a workflow consisting of a number of subjobs onto more than one resource provider on the basis of the providers' published PoFs. In addition, the functionality to evaluate the reliability of a provider's risk assessment, on the basis of historical data, is useful and significantly enhances the service of a broker.

This chapter is outlined as follows: Section 15.2 discusses background issues such as Grid SLAs, risk management, and trust. Section 15.3 describes the integration of risk awareness within a Grid computing architecture. The AssessGrid project addresses the problem of risk management in Grid computing and forms the basis of Section 15.3. Section 15.4 examines potential economic issues in relation the AssessGrid architecture and its actors—end user, broker, and provider.

15.2 BACKGROUND

Service-level agreements specify contractual obligations between end users and resource providers. However, there is a gap between SLAs as a concept and as an usable tool to drive Grid commercialization. If their widespread acceptance is to become a reality, a number of issues need to be addressed that are important to the two main Grid actors: the resource providers and the end users. Resource providers may be unwilling to agree on an SLA since they are aware of the possibility of resource failure and the subsequent SLA violation and penalty fees. To establish SLAs as a tool for commercial utilization, integrating a risk-aware SLA model into current Grid technology is desirable. However, end users are unlikely to place complete trust in a broker or resource provider since they are also aware of the possibility of resource failure and the knowledge that a 100% guarantee that they will not occur is impossible. This uncertainty places great importance on the trustworthiness of providers to deliver on the guarantees they make to end users. The remainder of this section examines the issues of SLAs, risk management, and trust.

15.2.1 Grid Service-Level Agreements

An SLA represents an explicit statement of expectations and obligations that exist in a relationship between the parties of the agreement. Within the Grid research community attempts have been made to specify SLAs; however, no single specification is likely to address the full requirements of usage within a specific domain discipline attempting to use the Grid for tasks or processes. As a result, a large body of literature exists on the subject but approaching the topic from differing perspectives.

For example, contract negotiation within distributed systems have been the subject of research for the specific needs of business–business [business-to-business (B2B)] service guarantees [6], whereas Leff et al. [7] concentrate on the effect of SLAs on commercial Grid infrastructures. The work recognizes SLAs as a method of controlling resource provision in the context of overall system utilization. Architectures from Sahai et al. [8] view the primary goal of SLAs as formal statements describing the type and frequency with which Grid resources are monitored. The WSLA specification [9] defines an SLA language to support dynamic electronic services implementing QoS guarantees.

The Grid Resource Allocation Agreement Protocol (GRAAP) group, a working group of the Open Grid Forum (OGF), have published a specification for agreement between two parties including all required description terms: the WS-Agreement specification [10]. The specification consists of three main elements: (1) a description format for agreement templates and agreements, (2) a basic protocol for establishing agreements, and (3) an interface specification to monitor agreements at runtime. Attempts toward dynamic creation of SLAs based on negotiation between service providers and consumers by extending WS-Agreement are found in the literature [11–13].

15.2.2 Risk Management

In professional risk assessment, risk combines the probability of an event with its impact, and computes their average effect under all possible (and conceivable) circumstances. In the case where assets are priced by markets, all probabilities and impacts are reflected in the market price, and therefore risk comes only from the *variance* of the outcomes. Risk management (RM) is the process of measuring or assessing risk and of developing strategies on the basis of the results in order to manage that risk. Managing a risk includes determining whether an action—or a set of actions—is required, and then finding the optimal action program to deal with the risk. The strategies employed in an optimal action program can include (1) *transferring* the risk to another party, (2) *avoiding* the risk, (3) *reducing* the negative effects of the risk, and (4) *accepting* or *absorbing* some or all of the consequences of a particular risk.

In the risk assessment (RA) process we have to deal with uncertainty in reference to both the *rate of occurrence* of an event and the *impact* or *consequences* of the event. Moreover, we formally have to accept the fact of working with imprecise categories and events. The classification of risk with linguistic categories (e.g., *unlikely*, *low*, *medium*, *high*) and that of the impact or consequences with corresponding imprecise categories (e.g., *negligible*, *low*, *medium*, *high*) indicates that we essentially have to combine two types of modeling tools for risk assessment and risk management: (1) *probabilistic* modeling tools that characterize and manipulate *systematic uncertainties*, for which we have sufficient statistics available; and (2) *possibilistic* modeling systems that describe and process *nonsystematic* uncertainties, for which we have only imprecise and uncertain (i.e., vague) data available.

In a Grid context, RM is tasked with formulating processes for (1) identifying, evaluating, and classifying risks (systematic, nonsystematic); (2) analyzing exposures to risks and the impact or consequences of the risks; and (3) determining the best possible (yet workable) practices to handle exposures to risks, and the impact or consequences of risks in the Grid context. The resulting RM process must consider the full spectrum of risk: financial, strategic, operational, and other risks that are facets of a Grid computing business. Thus, the success of RM depends on finding a balance between enhancing profits and managing risk. The risk assessment process, which is part of RM, determines risk relationships between (1) the assets of the business (Grid computing resources), (2) the external threats (e.g., power failures and natural disasters, malicious attacks), and (3) internal vulnerabilities (intangible risks).

15.2.3 Trust

Trust is defined as the confidence in or reliance on some quality or attribute of a person or thing, or the truth of a statement. Trust is generally classified into two categories: identity trust and behavior trust [14]. *Identity trust* is concerned with verifying the authenticity of an entity and determining the authorizations to which the entity is entitled using cryptographic techniques such as encryption and digital signatures. *Behavior trust* deals with a wider notion of an entity's "trustworthiness" and focuses more on the behavior of that entity. The lack of trust mechanisms within Grid infrastructures has been cited as responsible for stifling Grid commercialization [15]. The complex nature of trust and trust relationships within Grid infrastructures is a likely cause of this problem, despite attempts by many within the Grid research community to address the issue. For example, its integration through a resource management model, such that the allocation process is aware of certain security implications, is discussed by Azzedin and Maheswaran [16]. Basney et al. [17] extend the Grid security infrastructure to provide better support for dynamic and cross-organizational Grid activities, by adding facilities for dynamic establishment of trust between parties. A trust model for Grid environments based on a recommendation method, a fair-trading scheme, and an access control model, is proposed by Tran et al. [18]. The approach preserves the Grid's decentralized structure and participant's autonomy, but also enables secure service exchange. Access control solutions for large-scale Grid computing environments are investigated by Dillaway [19]. The Conoise-G infrastructure, which supports robust and resilient virtual organization (VO) formation and operation, integrates a component within the architecture to monitor the performance of the members of a VO in terms of their trustworthiness, QoS, and conformance to contract, and to restructure the VO in light of perturbations so that the integrity and usefulness of the VO are maintained [20].

The TrustCoM framework [21] ensures secure collaborative business processing in self-managed and highly dynamic VOs created on demand. The TrustCoM approach to legal risk analysis as described by Mahler [22], provides the legal basis for an overall risk analysis required for partner selection [23], coalition formation [24], and the negotiation of individual SLAs [25] as parts of contracts between coalitions of self-interested parties. The TrustCoM approach to cooperation risks based on reputation measures [26] also contributes to the overall risk analysis.

GridTrust [27] aims to develop methods for reasoning about trust along the VO lifecycle, with particular attention to autonomic properties such as self-organization, self-management, and self-healing. Attempts to quantify the trustworthiness of a provider, using a broker-based reputation model utilizing end-user feedback, is found in a paper by Silaghi et al. [28].

15.3 RISK-AWARE ARCHITECTURE TO SUPPORT SLAs: AssessGrid

AssessGrid (based on the concept of advanced risk assessment and management for trustable Grids) focuses on the integration of risk management functionality within Grid middleware. It does this by addressing the concerns of end users and providers through encouraging greater commercial interest in Grid usage through incorporation of risk assessment mechanisms into Grid infrastructures as well as automated SLA agreement processes utilizing risk information. Incorporation of risk-aware components within the SLA negotiation process as an additional decision support parameter for the end user is of primary importance. Risk is an ideal decision support parameter within the AssessGrid scenario since it combines both the quantifiable probability of SLA failure with the nondeterministic expected loss, a parameter known only to the beneficiary of the services stated in the SLA. The usage scenarios addressed by the AssessGrid architecture consider three principal actors: end user, broker, and provider.

An *end user* is a participant from a broad public approaching the Grid in order to perform a specific task that consists of one or more services. To request such services, the end user must indicate the task and associated requirements formally within an SLA template. The information contained within the template is used to negotiate access for the end user with providers offering these services, such that the task may be completed. The inclusion of risk information within the SLA negotiation process allows the end user to make informed, risk-aware decisions on the SLA offers received so that any decision is acceptable and balances cost, time, and risk.

A *broker* acts as matchmaker between an end user and provider, furnishing a risk optimized assignment of SLA requests to SLA offers. It is responsible for matching SLA requests to resources and services, which may be operated by an arbitrary number of providers. The broker's goal is to drive this matchmaking process to a conclusion, when the provider will propose an SLA offer. Beside resources and services for single tasks, the end user may also ask the broker to find resources for a workflow. Here, the broker has to decompose the workflow, finding suitable resources and services for each subtask, while respecting the end user's requirements. For the end user, a major service of the broker is the preselection of Grid providers, comparable with an independent insurance agent that is supporting its customers by preselecting insurance policies from a number of insurance companies.

A *provider* offers access to resources and services through formal SLA offers specifying risk, price, and penalty. Providers need well-balanced infrastructures, so they can maximize the quality of service (QoS) and minimize the number of SLA violations. Such an approach increases the economic benefit and motivation of end users to outsource their business processes and IT tasks. A prerequisite to this is a providers' trustworthiness and ability to deliver an agreed-on SLA offer. Assessments of risk allow the provider to selectively choose which SLA requests result in offers.

15.3.1 Architectural Overview

The AssessGrid architecture consists of three layers, one for each of the actors: end user, broker, and provider. Figure 15.1 illustrates the main components within each layer and the interfaces through which they interact.

The end user layer includes a Web browser that is responsible for authenticating users, invoking broker and provider services, capturing business process or IT task requirements, and displaying SLA offers. This layer also contains a portal entity that provides the end user with a number of abstract applications making use of Grid services deployed within the broker and Grid fabric layers. Principally, SLA requests and offers are exchanged between end users, brokers, and providers, until agreement is reached and an SLA is created between the parties. Policy statements may exist

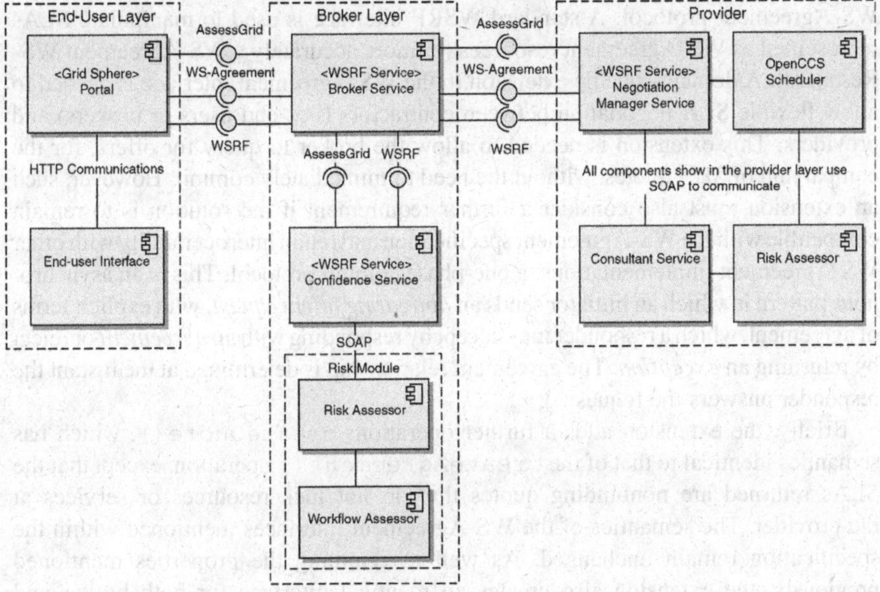

Figure 15.1 AssessGrid architecture overview.

within the end user's organization that place restrictions on the metrics open for negotiation as well as acceptable thresholds (e.g., maximum price). Such policies may also exist within the broker and provider's organization for similar reasons.

The broker layer consists of two principal components: a broker service and a confidence service. The *broker service* receives SLA requests from end users for the purpose of negotiating with providers, as well as ranking offers according to price, penalty, and risk. The *confidence service* provides an interface to methods that enable an evaluation of the reliability of providers' risk assessments. This is based on historical data from past SLAs offered by that provider. In addition, the confidence service allows the historical data to be updated with new records.

The Grid fabric layer is based on the OpenCCS resource management system [29] and is extended by the addition of a negotiation manager, a consultant service, and a risk assessor. The negotiation manager is responsible for receiving SLA requests and returning SLAs to either broker or end user. In order to determine its own risk assessment, the risk assessor utilizes a consultant service that provides access to statistics relating to the provider's infrastructure, and metrics such as current workload, system outages, temporary performance shortages, monitored network traffic, experts' availability, or general information regarding number of incoming jobs may all be considered. The risk assessment is returned within the SLA.

15.3.2 Component Interaction

The core of the communications between end user, broker, and provider layers is accomplished using WSRF (Web services resource framework) and the

WS-Agreement protocol. A standard WSRF interface is used to manipulate SLAs represented as WS-Agreement resources (or more accurately a WS-Agreement WS-Resource). A domain-specific extension to the WS-Agreement interface is needed to allow flexible SLA negotiation between contractors (i.e., end users or brokers) and providers. This extension is needed to allow the broker to query for offers, for the comparison of SLA quotes, without the need to immediately commit. However, such an extension must also consider a further requirement if the solution is to remain compatible with the WS-Agreement specification and retain interoperability with other WS-Agreement implementations: a one-phase commit protocol. This is an asynchronous pattern in which an initiator sends an *obligating offer request,* with explicit terms of agreement, which a responder may accept by responding with an *agreement* or reject by returning an *exception*. The agreement relationship is determined at the instant the responder answers the request.

Briefly, the extension adds a further operation: `createOuote()`, which has semantics identical to that of the `createAgreement()` operation, except that the SLAs returned are nonbinding quotes that do not lock resources or services at the provider. The semantics of the WS-Agreement interfaces mentioned within the specification remain unchanged. As well as retaining the properties mentioned previously, the extension also creates an identical interface for both broker and provider. An end user can interface seamlessly with either using the same mechanisms to retrieve an SLA template, receive SLA quotes, and create SLAs.

The semantics of the SLA agreement process within AssessGrid involve an end user or broker assuming the role of `agreement initiator` while the providers assume the role of `agreement responder`. The `agreement initiator` requests an SLA template from the `agreement responder` by querying a property of the `AgreementFactory` WS-Resource using the `getResourceProperty()` method. The `agreement initiator` completes the template with respect to any creational constraints within the template and can either request an onbinding SLA quote using `createQuote()` or a binding SLA using `createAgreement()`.

15.3.3 Risk Awareness Integrated in the Grid Fabric Layer

Integration of risk management functionality in the Grid fabric layer is realized through extension of a planning-based resource management system (RMS): Open CCS [29]. From a commercial perspective a planning-based system is preferable for agreeing risk-aware SLAs, since the alternative (queuing-based systems) provide insufficient estimations about job execution time and available resources.

Figure 15.1 shows the components of the architecture within the Grid fabric layer. The architecture integrates risk awareness into an RMS by extending existing modules (negotiation manager and scheduler) to handle information about probabilities of SLA failures (PoFs) and incorporating new components: a risk assessor and a consultant service with associated database. The *consultant service* uses monitoring information from the historical database in order to generate statistical data required by the risk assessor as input. The *risk assessor* is responsible for estimating the probability of an SLA failure (PoF), for each SLA, in order to determine whether an SLA should be agreed to. The probability of an SLA violation is influenced by the availability of spare resources, which can be used in the case of a resource outage, as well as the provider's fault tolerance capabilities. Checkpointing and migration are available, having previously been integrated in the RMS during the HPC4U (highly predictable cluster for Internet Grids) project [30].

An SLA request typically contains a maximum tolerable probability of failure (PoF), specified by the end user (see discussion below). When a provider receives an SLA request, it performs the following activities:

- Searches for resources for the job execution and makes an advance reservation.
- Estimates the SLAs PoF when using resources selected.
- If the PoF estimated is higher than the maximum tolerable PoF specified within the SLA request, the RMS evaluates whether the upper bound can be fulfilled by reserving additional dedicated spare resources.
- If the provider is unable to satisfy the request, then an exception is returned, corresponding to a rejection.
- If the provider is able to satisfy the request, including the PoF, then the SLA is returned to the initiator (end user or broker). The PoF estimate, price and penalty are published in the SLA.

The aim is to combine risk management with standard RMS processes rather than replacing them. The scheduling policy used in step 1 above does not consider risk information and doesn't need to be altered in order to integrate risk awareness.

Resource failures are the main cause of SLA violations. The risk assessor initially computes the PoF under the assumption that the reserved resources are to be used, without fault tolerance mechanisms. The data considered to date indicate that the failure process can be accurately modeled as a memoryless process. Consequently, the risk assessor does not currently consider failures caused by deterioration of components due to age, or account for hardware behavior such as memory load, or CPU temperature. Rather, failure rates are derived from data relating to job arrival rates and resource failure rates. The provider has a pool of spare resources, which are used for SLA jobs in case of resource failures. The size of the pool is fixed and it is envisioned that best-effort jobs are executed on those resources when sufficient resources are online and no SLA jobs need them.

In addition, it is possible to reserve dedicated spare resources. As indicated, when the PoF is initially estimated, it is compared with the maximum PoF accepted from the contractor. If the PoF estimate is higher than the upper bound, the RMS can reserve dedicated spare resources for the job. These dedicated spare resources, are then added to the advance reservation and are usable only for the specific job in question. On the basis of the maximum tolerable PoF, the number of dedicated spare resources that have to be reserved can be computed. Before sending the SLA request to the scheduler, the negotiation manager sets the maximum number of dedicated spare resources to be reserved. This maximum value is determined according to policies as well as the minimum profit that the provider wants to make.

We initiate checkpointing for all SLA-bound jobs in order to avoid restarting the job from the beginning in the event of a resource failure. The affected (sub)job can then be resumed on a spare resource. If dedicated spare resources had been reserved, the job uses one of these. If the job has no (or not enough) dedicated spare resources to cope with the resource failures that have occurred, the scheduler assigns resources from the general spare pool. However, if too many resources have crashed, the usage of spare resources would not prevent all SLA violations; in other words, not all SLA-bound jobs could be executed without an SLA violation. This is the trigger for initiating the risk management process in order to generate a new schedule:

- Sort SLA-bound jobs according to expected profit and expected loss by taking into account the effort already spent for the job execution.
- Add jobs according to this sorting into the schedule S', adding them in order of priority (highest to lowest).
- Initiate SLA negotiation with other providers/brokers for outsourcing SLA jobs that cannot be inserted in the schedule S' without resulting in a violation.

Since the job priority is defined according to the expected profits and expected losses, the risk management policy is commercially driven, with the objective of reducing the amount of money lost. In addition, the consequence of the sorting process is that jobs that would result in the least losses are outsourced. This implies that either the profit or penalty are (in comparison to the other jobs) low and that the provider has to pay less to other providers than for the job execution of more highly prioritized jobs.

Finally, it is important to note that, while the price and penalty are included as SLA guarantee terms, the PoF estimate is included as a service description term. It cannot be a guarantee term, since it is not possible to verify or falsify. As a consequence, it is possible for the provider to be dishonest and claim to be able to satisfy the requested PoF even if it is unable to do so. The only protection against this is to ensure that the penalty fee is adequate. The provider's reputation is likely to become damaged if end users become aware that their PoF estimates do not correspond to observed failure rates. A broker can be helpful in this respect, as discussed in the following sub-section.

15.3.4 Risk Awareness Integrated in the Broker Layer

In the AssessGrid project, the broker layer is responsible for supporting risk-aware negotiations with resource providers on behalf of end users. It is currently assumed that, when making an SLA offer, a provider also presents an associated PoF to the entity (end user or broker) it is negotiating with. When a broker receives this information, it is responsible for the following:

- Evaluate the reliability of the provider's PoF estimate
- If a provider is unreliable, provide its own estimate on the basis of historical data
- Rank SLA offers and present them to end users on the basis of PoF assessments
- If the request is a workflow, combine providers' offers into a single package

- Compute an overall PoF for workflow mappings
- Agree on SLAs with both end users and resource providers
- Where the broker is acting as a "virtual" provider, submit jobs to providers

The broker layer includes a number of components (see Fig. 15.1) that support this functionality: a broker, a confidence service, a risk module (consisting of a risk assessor and a workflow assessor), and a historical database.

The confidence service uses statistical data relating to previous SLAs to estimate the reliability of resource providers' PoF assessments. In order to compute the reliability, the confidence service calls a method in the risk assessor, which takes historical data and the SLA offer as input. The confidence service uses a "traffic light" system, identifying providers as green (reliable), amber (unreliable), or red (very unreliable) depending on the correlation between their previous PoF assessments and the frequency of failures to honor previous SLAs. This information can be requested by external entities that may contact the broker's confidence service, such as end users who do not wish to use the full functionality of the broker.

The risk module consists of a risk assessor and a workflow assessor. The former contains functionality to compute, its own PoF estimate, for example, if the provider's published PoF is considered unreliable. It also provides methods to compute a reliability measure for providers' PoF assessments. Both operations make use of statistical data relating to previous SLA executions stored in the historical database. The role of the workflow assessor is to provide risk assessments for entire workflows consisting of a number of (possibly interdependent) subtasks.

Since a provider may not share detailed data about their infrastructure or their risk assessment methods, it is difficult for end users to verify the reliability of provider's risk assessments. This problem is exacerbated in a Grid environment, since end users wish to choose the best (according to their own criteria) provider for their task and may have little or no past dealings with many providers.

On the basis of the above mentioned points, a question arises: Why should an end-user trust a provider's PoF estimate? Even if a provider utilizes sophisticated and accurate risk assessment techniques, it might wish to convince end users that the PoF is lower than it is in reality, for instance, to increase the likelihood that the SLA negotiation is successful. If a provider's offered PoFs are consistently considerably lower than the actual PoF, then its reputation may be damaged and an end user may become aware of this. If the difference isn't large (while still being statistically significant and therefore potentially having an impact on the end user's average profit), it may require large volumes of historical data to enable the provider's inaccuracy or dishonesty to be identified. Hence it would clearly be of value if the end user could obtain additional information to provide some indication of the reliability of a provider's risk assessment prior to requesting a an SLA. A number of issues arise in relation to this approach.

First, if the end-user does not trust the provider, is it reasonable to assume that the broker is to be trusted? For example, the broker could have a private agreement with a particular provider, whereby it accepts a portion of the provider's profits if it evaluates that provider as being reliable. While this is possible, it is undoubtedly better to have a second opinion than none at all. Just as with other reputation and ranking systems (e.g., the star ratings that are prevalent in hotel review Websites), it is up to the end user to decide how much trust to place in the reliability measure. Further, steps could be taken such as requiring brokers to sign up to a governing body that has sufficient access to check brokers for breaches of regulations. Detailed discussion of these issues is beyond the scope of this chapter. A further issue is how to evaluate the reliability, based only on historical data on SLAs relating to previously executed data and how to estimate an adjusted PoF. Specifically, it is assumed that the broker has access to a historical database containing (for each provider) a record of the offered PoF and the final SLA status.

Three approaches to reliability estimation have been considered, and a detailed discussion can be found in a paper by Gourlay et al. [31]. The first approach considers all SLAs for previously executed applications with the same provider, stored in the historical database. Compute the expectation (mean) for the number of SLA failures and the standard deviation, on the assumption that the provider's offered PoFs were all accurate. Compare the number of SLAs that actually failed with the expectation, using the standard deviation computed in step 1 for normalization. This gives a measure of how may standard deviations the number of fails observed is from the number predicted by the provider's offered PoFs. While this measure is likely to identify cases where a provider is consistently underestimating (or overestimating) the PoF, there are cases where this algorithm would not identify a problem. An extreme example would be if a provider offered a PoF of 0.001 (the measure presented here breaks down if all the PoFs are 1 or 0 since the standard deviation is then 0) for half the SLAs, all of which failed, and a PoF of 0.999 for the other half, none of which failed. In this case, the confidence value would be 0, indicating that the provider is very reliable when in fact the offered PoFs were completely inaccurate. This is, of course, a somewhat artificial example, since offered PoFs would typically be considerably less than 0.5. However, it is perfectly possible for the average failure rate be close to the predicted failure rate while the individual PoFs are inaccurate. Two alternative approaches have been considered in order to address this problem. Both are based on considering the effect of betting on the SLA outcomes, applied to the SLAs in the historical database. The first considers the effect of betting an amount linearly proportional to the probability of success (i.e., one offered PoF). The second considers the effect of using an odds-based betting scheme as discussed in detail by Gourlay et al. [31].

If a provider is deemed to be unreliable, then the broker makes its own estimate of the PoF for the SLA offer. Preliminary investigations into this problem are underway. One method is to simply take the observed failure rate as a more accurate measure than the provider's PoF estimate (since they have not been reliable in the past). This is, of course, a pretty rough estimate. A better method is to consider only past SLAs that had an offered PoF that is close in value to the current SLA offer; "close" obviously needs to be defined. Numerous approaches have been considered but this is beyond the scope of this chapter—the idea is to choose an interval around the offered PoF in the current SLA offer to ensure that there are enough SLAs in the sample to make a meaningful estimate but the interval is small enough that all the offered PoFs in the sample are approximately the same as the offered PoF in the current SLA offer. The failure rate in the past SLAs in this sample is used as the confidence service's PoF estimate. Initial simulations indicate that, with this method, the performance is sensitive to the threshold value chosen for the confidence value, beyond which the provider is deemed to be unreliable. Investigation of risk estimation methods therefore includes consideration of the threshold value used.

15.3.5 Risk Awareness Integrated in the End-User Layer

As discussed above, the end user can either negotiate directly with a provider or make use of the added functionality provided by a broker. Two issues need to be considered: (1) what risk information is made available to the end-user and (2) how this information is presented to the end user.

Regarding issue 1, if negotiation takes place directly with a provider and an SLA offer is made, the provider's estimate of the PoF is made available. In this case, the end user can still make use of the broker to obtain a reliability measure object, which contains both the reliability measure and the broker's own PoF estimation, discussed in Section 15.3.4. If an end user negotiates using the broker, then the reliability object is returned with each SLA offer, so that the end user has access to both the provider's PoF estimate and the broker's estimate. Regarding issue 2, the information is accessed by the end user via the portal, enabling them to view the SLA offer and associated risk information within a Web browser. The end user may want only a rough estimate of the risk associated with a particular SLA offer ("high risk," "medium risk," "low risk"). Consequently, the PoF is displayed using a traffic-light system with green, amber, and red corresponding to low, medium, and high PoF, respectively.

15.4 ECONOMY ASPECTS IN AssessGrid

A number of projects have started to develop basic Grid components and architectural support for building economy-aware Grid middleware [32,33]. The potential economic issues underlying risk management in the AssessGrid architecture and the obstacles that may be faced if similar economic aware components were to be integrated are discussed below, in Section 15.4.1.

15.4.1 End-User Layer

The end user is provided with a number of abstract applications that make use of Grid services deployed within the Grid fabric layer. SLA requests and offers are exchanged between end user and broker or provider, in order to agree on an SLA that grants permission to invoke a Grid service in the fabric layer. Within each layer, the organization performing the role of each actor must define a policy statement governing the acceptable bounds of negotiation. This restricts end users and contractors to request or offer SLAs that fall outside the organization's acceptable limits. For example, in addition to specifying budget constraints, there may be a restriction on a provider's penalty conditions to limit the financial loss incurred because of an SLA violation. Taking these policy limits into consideration, an end user can negotiate an SLA to run a Grid service by defining requirements as well as the requested QoS in an SLA request. During the definition process the end user evaluates the importance of the job in terms of its urgency and the consequences of delayed results or failure. A further validation of the policy limits must be made against the SLA offers received from the broker or providers.

Where several SLA offers have been negotiated on behalf of the end user, the broker can return a ranked list—according to price, penalty, and PoF. The challenge for the end user is to find an SLA offer that offers the best service in terms of price, penalty, and PoF. Here we can apply a mathematical model to help the end user make the *best* offer selection on the basis of quality criteria. The end user defines a ranking of the quality criteria (e.g., PoF is more important than price) in order to measure each offer according to its closeness to the criteria. A possible approach is the application of an analytic hierarchy process that is based on criteria weights specified by the end user [34].

15.4.2 Broker Layer

Within the AssessGrid architecture the broker role facilitates SLA negotiation between entities fulfilling the end-user and resource provider roles. After the negotiation has returned an SLA offer, the broker is responsible for performing reliability checks on the PoFs contained in the SLA offers. Without this check, the end user has no independent views on the provider's assessment, which cannot be assumed to be impartial. SLA offers that are deemed unreliable are subjected to an additional risk assessment by the broker using historical data related to the provider making the offer. Where multiple SLA offers are returned by the SLA negotiation process, the broker can rank these according to a price–penalty–PoF matrix depending on the priorities of the end user.

The economic benefit of using a broker within the SLA negotiation process affects all three Grid actors and provides the opportunity for an economy model where SLAs for software services are bought and sold on the basis of differentiated classes of service. In the provision of SLA negotiation, the broker offers two classes of service: mediator and runtime-responsible. In the case of *mediator* service, the broker provides a marketplace for providers to advertise their SLA templates to a wider number of end users; for end users it allows selecting a provider and their services from a larger set.

Use of the broker as a runtime-responsible service offers the greatest scope for Grid economy research. In this scenario the broker has the ability to buy SLA offers from providers and resell them to end users transparently using its own SLA offer. In this way a broker becomes a virtual provider and can offer price–penalty–PoF combinations unavailable from a single provider. In addition, the broker can orchestrate workflows, which combine multiple single SLA offers and combine them into SLA offers for an entire workflow. The broker can make tradeoffs against price, penalty, and PoF between providers in order to maximize the economic benefit for itself. Where a task is executed redundantly, such as to reduce the PoF, or where it forms part of a workflow, the broker has additional responsibilities during runtime. Should an SLA governing one of these tasks be violated, the broker must determine whether it is more economical to pay its own penalty fee or negotiate a new SLA with a different provider at a price that minimizes its losses. During postruntime, the broker is responsible for updating the historical data it holds on each registered provider's. When offering it's runtime-responsible service, the broker can easily access the final status of SLA offers as they are agreed between itself and the provider. When acting as a mediator, the broker must persuade the end user to pass on the same information about the SLA final status. A rebate or bonus payment may be built into the economy model to encourage end users to give SLA offer feedback to the broker. As well as the financial benefit, end users will benefit through up-to-date historical data and greater confidence in the reliability checks.

15.4.3 Grid Fabric Layer

A provider offers access to resources and services through formal SLA offers specifying the requirements as well as PoF, price, and penalty. Providers need well-balanced infrastructures, so that they can maximize the offerable QoS and minimize the number of SLA violations. Such an approach increases the economic benefit and motivation of end users to outsource their IT tasks. A number of economic issues have been identified that affect the provider. These issues can be categorized as belonging to the preruntime (i.e., during SLA negotiation), runtime, and postruntime phases.

In the preruntime phase a risk-aware negotiation requires that a provider place an advance reservation for the SLA and calculates the PoF [35]. A provider then determines the price and penalty fee that will be offered to an end user. To ensure that an unsuitable SLA is not agreed to, end users define minimum and maximum limits for price, penalty, and PoF within the SLA request. A provider's decision to agree or reject an SLA depends on the fees and requested PoF in comparison with the current status of its infrastructure. The publication of the SLA PoF opens further research fields. A provider must not offer the PoF it had assessed during the reservation process since no mechanism can be developed that can coerce it into telling the truth. However, the broker's confidence service is designed to ensure that providers do not lie about published PoFs. Therefore it is the ability of the provider to fulfill SLA offers that identifies it as being reliable, rather than its ability to offer SLAs with a low PoF.

For contractors (end users or brokers), an important provider selection criterion is the price. The SLA template contains pricing information for actions such as data transfer, CPU usage, and storage. Within the AssessGrid model these prices are variable since the price depends on the PoF value specified within the SLA.

The market mechanism will influence the pricing since each provider has only a limited resource set with variable utilization. Consequently, prices for resource usage will not be fixed but will depend on the economics of supply and demand. Reservations, which were made well in advance, will usually result in a reduced price since there will be access to a greater number of free reservation slots. Immediate resource usage may also result in reduced prices, as providers try to increase their utilization if demand is low. End users risk resource unavailability if they wait too long before reserving resources. These pricing dynamics are valid only in the scope of resource costs and do not consider PoF. After an SLA has been agreed to by the provider and the end user, the provider has to ensure during runtime that the SLA will not be violated. The provider's risk management activities are controlled by estimating the penalty payments in the case of an SLA violation. AssessGrid components initiate precautionary fault tolerance mechanisms in order to prevent SLA violations. The penalty fees, as well as the PoF (i.e., risk), are decisive factors determining which fault tolerance mechanisms to initiate.

In the postruntime phase the provider has to evaluate the final SLA status to determine whether a penalty fee has to be paid. Even in the case where the SLA had been fulfilled, the costs for the fulfillment have to be checked since the initiation of a fault tolerance mechanism also consumes resources and therewith results in additional costs. The results of the evaluation process will point out on one hand whether adjustments in the offermaking policies are necessary in order to increase the provider's profit. On the other hand, statistics can be generated to show whether initiated fault tolerance mechanisms had been able to prevent an SLA violation.

15.5 FUTURE RESEARCH DIRECTIONS

Enhancing the broker to function as a virtual provider is identified as the next stage in the AssessGrid development process. An agreement service will be implemented to allow the broker to offer its own SLAs. This will enable the end user to submit workflow requests to the broker, which will agree one SLA for the whole workflow. The broker will provide a higher class of service to the end user by searching for appropriate providers and computing the associated risk (PoF) for the entire workflow. In particular, the broker will consider workflow mappings where a provider may be responsible for executing one or many subtasks from within the workflow. Mapping policy will be highly dependent on an end user's requirements, such as the fastest, cheapest, or most trustworthy provider. This scenario will necessitate refinements to the confidence service, which will need to consider reliability estimation and risk assessment methods to support such workflow requests. From the provider's perspective, investigations are underway to determine a suitable mechanism to determine which control actions to initiate in situations when the PoF increases significantly while an SLA is active. Future work will include implementation of self-adaptive fault tolerance mechanisms based on risk assessment, possibilistic risk, and end-user trust as well as outsourcing mechanisms.

15.6 CONCLUSIONS

This chapter has addressed important issues in relation to risk management within Grid middleware, and has described an architecture that provides a framework for supporting risk assessment and management throughout the Grid infrastructure for three Grid actors: the end user, the broker, and the resource provider.

The end user is able to interact with a broker and providers via a Grid portal interface that presents SLA quotes and associated risk information in a user-friendly way. Transparent access to resources is provided by a broker that queries resource providers on behalf of end users. The broker relies on a confidence service to assess the reliability of risk assessments received by providers on the basis of historical data relating to previous SLAs. A risk assessor enables the broker to make its own risk assessments, while a workflow assessor supports the broker by providing a risk assessment for entire workflows consisting of multiple subtasks.

Providers are able to assess the SLA's PoF before committing to it, through a consultant service that utilizes statistical information. This can also be used to identify bottlenecks in the provider's infrastructure. The ability to assess the risk associated with an SLA request before it commits, enables a resource provider to build a planning-based RMS schedule using the computed PoF values.

The architecture developed within the AssessGrid project is expected to increase demand for Grid services and resources through heightened end-user confidence and more stable business/market models resulting from the introduction of risk management and SLAs.

REFERENCES

1. F. Berman, G. Fox, and A. Hey, *Grid Computing: Making the Global Infrastructure a Reality*, Wiley, Chichester, UK, 2003.
2. G.A. Thanos, C. Courcoubetis, and G. D. Stamoulis, Adopting the Grid for business purposes: The main objectives and the associated economic issues, *Lecture Notes in Computer Science* 1–15 (2007).
3. K. Stanoevska-Slabeva, C. F. Talamanca, G. A. Thanos, and C. Zsigri, Development of a generic value chain for the Grid industry, *Lecture Notes in Computer Science* 44–57 (2007).
4. A. Andrieux, K. Czajkowski, A. Dan, K. Keahey, H. Ludwig, J. Pruyne, J. Rofrano, S. Tuecke, and M. Xu, *Web Services Agreement Specification (WS-Agreement)*, Global Grid Forum, 2004.
5. G. Stoneburner, A. Goguen, and A. Feringa, Risk management guide for information technology systems recommendations of the National Institute of Standards and Technology, *Nist Special Publication Sp* (800; Part 30), 2002.
6. A. Goodchild, C. Herring, and Z. Milodevic, *Business Contracts for B2B*, Distributed Systems Technology Center (DSTC), Queensland, Australia, 2000.
7. A. Leff, J. T. Rayfield, and D. M. Dias, Service-level agreements and commercial Grids, *IEEE Internet Computing* 7(4):44–50 (2003).

8. A. Sahai, A. Graupner, V. Machiraju, and A. van Moorsel, Specifying and monitoring guarantees in commercial Grids through SLA, *Proc. 3rd IEEE/ACM International Symp. Cluster Computing and the Grid*, Tokyo, 2003.
9. H. Ludwig, A. Keller, A. Dan, and R. King, A service level agreement language for dynamic electronic services, in *Advanced Issues of E-Commerce and Web-Based Information Systems*, Newport Beach, CA, June 2002.
10. A. Andrieux, K. Czajkowski, A. Dan, K. Keahey, H. Ludwig, J. Pruyne, J. Rofrano, S. Tuecke, and M. Xu, *Web Services Agreement Specification (WS-Agreement)*, Global Grid Forum, 2007.
11. A. Ludwig, P. Braun, R. Kowalczyk, and B. Franczyk, A framework for automated negotiation of service level agreements in services Grids, *Lecture Notes in Computer Science* 89–101 (2006).
12. G. Di Modica, V. Regalbuto, O. Tomarchio, and L. Vita, Enabling re-negotiations of SLA by extending the WS-Agreement specification, *Proc. 2007 IEEE International Conf. on Services Computing (SCC 2007)*, 2007.
13. A. Pichot, P. Wieder, O. Wäldrich, and W. Ziegler, *Dynamic SLA-Negotiation Based on WS-Agreement*, Institute on Resource Management and Scheduling, 2007.
14. L. Woodas, K.-W. Ng, and M. Lyu, Integrating trust in Grid computing systems, *Lecture Notes in Computer Science* **3251**:887–890 (2004).
15. W. Johnston, Implementing production Grids, in *Grid Computing: Making the Global Infrastructure a Reality*, F. Berman, G. Fox, and A. Hey, eds., Wiley, Chichester, UK, 2003.
16. F. Azzedin, and M. Maheswaran, Towards trust-aware resource management in Grid computing systems, in *Cluster Computing and the Grid*, Berlin, May 2002.
17. J. Basney, W. Nejdl, D. Olmedilla, V. Welch, and M. Winslett, Negotiating trust on the Grid, *Proc. 2nd Workshop in P2P and Grid Computing, New York, May* 2004.
18. H. Tran, P. Watters, M. Hitchens, and V. Varadharajan, Trust and authorization in the grid: A recommendation model, *Proc. IEEE International Conf. Pervasive Services (ICPS'2005)*, Santorini, Greece, 2005.
19. B. Dillaway, *A Unified Approach to Trust, Delegation, and Authorization in Large-Scale Grids*, Microsoft, 2006.
20. J. Patel, W. T. L. Teacy, N. R. Jennings, M. Luck, S. Chalmers, N. Oren, T. J. Norman, A. Preece, P. M. D. Gray, and G. Shercliff, Agent-based virtual organisations for the Grid, *AAMAS Workshop on Agent-Mediated Electronic Commerce; Agent-Mediated Electronic Commerce: Designing Trading Agents and Mechanisms; AAMAS 2005 Workshop, AMEC 2005, IJCAI 2005 Workshop, TADA 2005*, Utrecht, The Netherlands, July 2005.
21. T. Dimitrakos, D. Golby, and P. Kearney, Towards a trust and contract management framework for dynamic virtual organizations, *Proc. eAdoption and the Knowledge Economy Conf. (eChallenges'2004)*, Vienna, Austria, Oct. 27–29, 2004.
22. T. Mahler, Utilizing legal risk management to secure ICT outsourcing, *Proc. Commercial Contracting for Strategic Advantage Potentials and Prospects*, Turku, Finland, June 2007.
23. W.H. Ip, M. Huang, K. L. Yung, and D. Wang, Genetic algorithm solution for a risk-based partner selection problem in a virtual enterprise, *Computers and Operations Research* **30**(2):213–231 (2003).

24. C. Merida-Campos, and S. Willmott, The effect of heterogeneity on coalition formation in iterated request for proposal scenarios, *Proc. European Workshop of Multi-Agent Systems*, Lisbon, Portugal, Dec. 2006.

25. H. Demirkhan, M. Goul, and D. S. Soper, Service level agreement negotiation: A theory-based exploratory study as a starting point for identifying negotiation support system requirements, *Proc. Annual Hawaii International Conf. System Sciences*, 2005, p. 37.

26. A. Josang, C. Keser, and T. Dimitrakos, Can we manage trust?, *Lecture Notes in Computer Science* **3477**:93–107 (2005).

27. GridTrust, Trust and Security for Next Generation Grids. Available from http://www.gridtrust.eu (accessed Nov. 8, 2007).

28. G. Silaghi, A. Arenas, and L. Silva, A utility-based reputation model for service-oriented computing, *Proc. CoreGRID Symp.* Rennes, France, Aug. 2007.

29. Open Computing Center Software (OpenCCS), available from https://www.openccs.eu/ (accessed Nov. 8, 2007).

30. Highly Predictable Cluster for Internet-Grids (HPC4U), available from http://www.hpc4u.org (accessed Nov. 8, 2007).

31. I. Gourlay, K. Djemame, and J. Padgett, Reliability and risk in Grid resource brokering, *Proc. IEEE International Conf. Digital Ecosystems and Technologies 2008 (DEST 2008)*, Phitsanulok, Thailand, Feb. 2008.

32. NextGRID: Architecture for Next Generation Grids, available from http://www.nextgrid.org (accessed Nov. 8, 2007).

33. Grid Economics and Business Models (GridEcon), available from http://www.gridecon.eu (accessed Nov. 8, 2007).

34. T. L. Saaty, How to make a decision: The analytic hierarchy process, *European Journal of Operational Research* **48**:9–26 (1990).

35. M. Hovestadt, O. Kao, and K. Voss, The first step of introducing risk management for prepossessing SLAs, *Proc. IEEE International Conf. Services Computing (SCC)*, IEEE Computer Society, Chicago, IL, 2006.

PART IV

RESOURCE ALLOCATION AND SCHEDULING MECHANISMS

16

A RECIPROCATION-BASED ECONOMY FOR MULTIPLE SERVICES IN A COMPUTATIONAL GRID

NAZARENO ANDRADE, FRANCISCO BRASILEIRO,
MIRANDA MOWBRAY, AND WALFREDO CIRNE

16.1 INTRODUCTION

Economic production can be organized in different ways, such as markets, centrally by a state entity, or through various forms of sharing [5], such as reciprocation [18] and gift economies [23]. When the sharing approach is used, resource owners contribute to a common resource pool that provides a service of economic value to requesters.

For different goods, the different organizational models will have different efficiencies and will likely coexist in different proportions. For example, in the economy that allocates books, bookstores, state-owned public libraries and the widely popular habit of sharing books with friends all coexist.

In a Grid, resource providers use privately owned resources to provide valuable services for consumers. As in other economies, different models can be used for organizing the production and consumption of such services. In this chapter, we are concerned with the use of sharing for resource allocation in Grids. We are motivated by the fact that, for several scenarios, sharing systems have efficiencies that are at least comparable to and sometimes even outperform their market counterparts. Examples of such scenarios are the car-pooling system in parts of the United States [27], *Wikipedia*, and, more closely related to our discussion, voluntary computing systems like SETI@Home and peer-to-peer systems for file sharing (e.g. Kazaa, Gnutella). All of these examples are sharing systems that operate very efficiently compared to their market equivalents.

Market-Oriented Grid and Utility Computing Edited by Rajkumar Buyya and Kris Bubendorfer

This phenomenon happens because markets rely on the existence and efficiency of contract negotiation, norm enforcement, banking and accounting mechanisms. For several scenarios in distributed computing (and also outside computing), it is complex, costly, or inefficient to implement such mechanisms. On the other hand, in these situations, sharing systems may be efficient. This is so because they (1) can use information that is loosely structured and therefore easier to obtain, (2) can also make use of social mechanisms for monitoring and enforcement, and (3) have lower marginal transaction costs [5].

Our target systems are large-scale, open peer-to-peer (P2P) computational Grids, in which a peer donates its local resources when they are idle in exchange for using idle resources from other peers when its local demand cannot be fulfilled by its local resources alone. Such systems have the potential to serve, for example, the computing needs of thousands of small and medium-sized research laboratories around the world, and to coexist with a global market for computing services [8].

A fundamental issue in such systems is how to organize the provision and consumption of services in such a way that it is in each participant's own interest to contribute as much as possible to the system as a whole. Because of the large scale envisioned for these systems and the potential anonymity of its users, social relations have limited efficiency in encouraging sharing. If sharing is to occur, there must be incentives for peers to contribute resources to the Grid. Otherwise, peers have an economic incentive to become *free riders*, that is, only consuming resources and not donating back to the P2P Grid, reducing the resources available in the system and diminishing the Grid's utility.

We will present an incentive mechanism termed the *network of favors*, which builds on sharing to encourage contributions to the system. The network of favors uses pairwise reciprocation between peers [3,24]. A peer decides to whom to donate a spare resource based on *local history*, that is, information gathered from its past direct interactions with other peers. Using only local history obviates the need to ensure the integrity of secondhand information.

In this chapter, we describe the network of favors and discuss why it is efficient in encouraging contributions in a computational Grid where peers share multiple services. Explicitly supporting multiple services is important as computer applications typically demand a set of noninterchangeable requirements, varying from low-level resources (such as CPU, disk, and bandwidth) to high-level ones (such as specialized datasets and libraries). Throughout the chapter we will provide evidence that the sharing-based approach can be used efficiently to allocate multiple services in a large-scale, open Grid while keeping transaction costs low and encouraging contributions. We also discuss the implementation of the network of favors in the OurGrid middleware. We start with a brief overview of related work.

16.2 BACKGROUND AND RELATED WORK

Incentive mechanisms have been proposed for conventional Grids and also for other types of P2P systems. They can be broadly classified into market-based and reciprocation mechanisms.

Markets are a well-known mechanism for regulating access to resources by selfish agents. Therefore, applying this mechanism is a natural way of addressing the resource allocation problem in Grids [1,21] and P2P systems [7]. However, a computational market presumes the existence of a currency distribution system, banking services, and norm enforcement, which inherently require trusted institutions. Furthermore, they require very precise and crisp information to be available in the form of prices. All these characteristics increase the transaction costs of participating in such economy. Our approach is to seek an alternative that is able to rely on less costly information and mechanisms and that might still serve for a broad audience of Grid users.

In a system where resource allocation is based on sharing, incentive mechanisms other than markets must play the role of encouraging agents to contribute resources. One way to provide such incentives is to make the system reward peers according to their past contributions to the system. Naturally, for the system to reciprocate the past contributions of peers, it needs a way to store information about peers' past behavior.

Under reputation-based incentive mechanisms, peers decide how to allocate their resources according to the reputations of the requesting peers [11,19,32]. To aggregate this information in a way that is robust to malicious peers and collusions, these mechanisms rely on polling protocols and on specialized secure score management systems.

The network of favors differs from these as it does not use any aggregation, relying instead only on the local information available to each peer. Thus, it can be particularly lightweight, and operate securely in the absence of advanced infrastructure. For example, it does not need certified identities, trusted third parties, or score management systems.

The idea of using pairwise reciprocation has been explored in other P2P systems [10,14,17]. However, although these mechanisms are similar to the network of favors, they deal only with the simpler case in which a single service is shared, rather than an arbitrary number of them. Introducing multiple services in a reciprocation economy for a P2P network complicates matters because, in such a setting, a peer should be able to reciprocate a favor of one type of service by a different type of service, and different peers may value services differently. Thus, it is in the interest of peers to choose trading partners based not only on the likelihood that they will reciprocate but also on an estimate of how profitable it will be to maintain a long-term reciprocation relationship with a trading partner, bearing in mind the services that the trading partner is likely to request and provide.

Finally, although several P2P grids have been proposed, apart from OurGrid [2], no other P2P grid addresses the issue of providing incentives for the contribution of resources. Nevertheless, the network of favors, as we will discuss shortly, is independent of the architecture of the OurGrid system and, therefore, can be adapted for use in other P2P systems such as the "self-organizing flock of condors" proposed by Butt et al. [6], XtremWeb [15], "cluster computing on the fly" [22], and P3 (parallel peer-to-peer) [25], to name only a few.

16.3 THE NETWORK OF FAVORS

The basic idea of the network of favors is that peers prioritize the requests they receive solely on the basis of the record of their past interactions with the requesters. As a result, there is no need to trust other peers or a central entity in order to assess the global reputation of each requester.

We consider a system of peers in which each peer owns a set of resources and can provide multiple services with them. All peers alternate independently between periods where they have spare resources and periods where they have demand for services that cannot be entirely met by their resources. We call a peer that currently has a spare resource a *provider*, and the work done by a provider for another peer is called a *favor*, which in the general case may be any combination of the services available in the system.

16.3.1 Notation and Assumptions

Here are our general assumptions about the system:

A1. The system is a peer-to-peer system in which peers independently decide whether to perform favors requested by other peers. Peers are content to participate in the system if their expected future net utility gain as a result of being in the system (i.e., utility gain from being donated favors minus utility loss from the cost of donating favors to others) is positive.

A2. Each peer A can accurately estimate the utility cost $v_A(f)$ that it would incur if it provided favor f for another peer. Costs are additive, that is, the cost of providing favor f_1 and then favor f_2 is $v_A(f_1) + v_A(f_2)$. For all non-zero favors f, the utility cost $v_A(f)$ is positive.

A3. The utility to a peer A of receiving a favor f, written $u_A(f)$, may vary over time, but always satisfies $u_A(f) > v_A(f)$; that is, the utility to A of receiving a favor that it requests is greater than the cost to A of donating the same favor to another peer. A way to make this assumption very likely in practice is to donate favors only when the underlying services are not being locally used.

A4. If a peer A tries to pay back a favor to peer B, it will eventually succeed in doing so. This implies that eventually A will be able to provide a service at a time that it is requested by B, and that the granularity of requests for services by B can be made small enough that a request is eventually not too large for A to satisfy.

A5. Some peers in the system are *collaborative*, and follow the algorithm specified. However, some are *noncollaborative*, and choose alternative behavioral strategies in order to maximize their expected net utility gain. In particular, one strategy that they may consider is *free riding*, that is, requesting and consuming favors from the system but donating no favors to the system. They may spread false information about other peers, or about themselves, and may conspire with other noncollaborative peers to make their falsehoods more plausible. Moreover, a noncollaborative peer can "whitewash" its identity, using a different identity for every interaction with other peers. Thus, there may be a very high churn of noncollaborative peers.

A6. There is low churn of collaborative peers in the system. (Note that without this assumption, the network of favors would not work. By "churn" here we mean the rate at which peers join the system for the first time and leave it for the last time. We do not mind if peers have frequent temporary disconnections.)

16.3.2 Selecting and Prioritizing Partners

When there are multiple services, a favor of one type of service may be repaid with another type of service, and peers may value services differently. The main design challenge this imposes for the mechanism is the need for peers to choose with which other peers they should interact. Providers need to decide both with which other peers it is worthwhile to interact in the long run, and which of the current requests for their services they should prioritize. Ideally, they would do so by using selection and prioritization policies, respectively.

The selection policy allows peers to protect their overall utility, by not donating to another peer if they assess that the expected effect on their overall utility resulting from a long-term interaction with this peer is unsatisfactory. The prioritization policy governs to whom a provider decides to donate a favor, when there are several other peers that are not excluded by the selection policy and that are currently requesting favors. This decision is based on information from interactions with these peers in the past. When an available resource is not requested by any peer with whom the provider has interacted in the past, the provider donates it to any peer requesting it that is not excluded by the selection policy.

We will now describe a pair of accurate selection and prioritization policies, which we refer to as *positive interactions* (or *PosInt* for short) selection and prioritization policies. Unfortunately, the PosInt policies require knowledge of information that is not necessarily available in practice, but these policies provide us with a useful reference for the comparison of other policies.

16.3.2.1 PosInt Selection Policy. Let f_A be the average favor that a peer A requests from the other peers. This represents a probability distribution of the types of favors requested by A over the long term. For instance, if in a typical time interval A requests on average one unit of basic service s_1 and three units of basic service s_2, then f_A will be $(s_1 + 3s_2)/4$.

Now, suppose that peer A is deciding whether to interact with B. For a long-term interaction in which A donates $n \times f_B$ to B and B donates $m \times f_A$ to A for some m,n to be beneficial to both A and B, both $m \times u_A(f_A) - n \times v_A(f_B)$ and $n \times u_B(f_B) - m \times v_B(f_A)$ need to be positive. Such $m, n > 0$ exist if and only if

$$u_A(f_A) \times u_B(f_B) > v_A(f_B) \times v_B(f_A) \tag{16.1}$$

If A does not know the value of f_B a priori, A can estimate it by recording B's requests to the system and calculating the average favor that B has requested so far. It is difficult for A to estimate the functions $u_A(f)$ or $u_B(f)$, but by assumption A2, A knows the function $v_A(f)$; if A also knew $v_B(f)$ and taking into account assumption A3, A could check whether the following more stringent inequality holds:

$$v_A(f_A) \times v_B(f_B) \geq v_A(f_B) \times v_B(f_A) \tag{16.2}$$

Roughly speaking, this inequality means that the cost to the pair of peers A and B of producing the average favors that they request themselves is greater than that of producing the requested favors for each other. Note that if $f_A = f_B$, the inequality is automatically satisfied. In particular, in the special case that all requested favors are multiples of a single service, then all pairs of peers can gain by interacting.

For pairs of peers A,B for which inequality (16.2) holds, both peers know that they can benefit from a long-term exchange of favors, and so both have an incentive to initiate such an exchange of favors. When A has spare resources it will look for peers B requesting favors for which this inequality is satisfied, and use the spare resources to grant favors to one of these peers.

Pairs of peers for which (16.2) does not hold cannot tell whether it is possible for them both to benefit from a long-term exchange of favors. Conservatively, they do not interact, so as to avoid being drawn into an interaction that decreases their utility.

At first glance, it might appear that A would only be interested in whether A itself can gain from a long-term interaction with B, not in whether B can gain from this interaction. However, if B knows that it is likely to lose out from a long-term interaction with A, B's best strategy is not to return any favor that A donates to it, so as to retain the utility received from this favor; and therefore A's best strategy is not to donate anything to B in the first place.

16.3.2.2 PosInt Prioritization Policy. Now suppose that there is more than one peer B requesting favors with which the selection policy of a provider A does not prevent interactions. How does A decide which of these peers to donate to? The answer is that A donates to whichever of these peers it expects to gain most from interacting with; A calculates this using its prioritization policy.

The *PosInt* prioritization policy uses the *cost balance* from the previous interactions between peers. For each other peer with which it interacts, each peer keeps a record of this number, which is calculated as follows. Before the two peers have ever interacted, the cost balance is equal to zero (this value does not need be explicitly recorded). If peer A donates a favor f to peer B, then A decreases its cost balance for interactions with B by the cost $v_A(f)$ of producing this favor – or, if the original cost balance was less than $v_A(f)$, peer A sets its cost balance for B to zero. Meanwhile, B increases its cost balance for A by $v_A(f)$. Note that different peers will in general record different cost balances for the same peer A. Also, scores are always greater than or equal to zero. This renders innocuous whitewashing attacks in which a free rider keeps presenting itself to the system as a new peer with a brand-new identity. Since zero is the worst score that any peer can have, and newcomers have zero scores, a peer cannot gain by leaving the system and reentering with a new identity. This use of nonnegative scores is inspired by Yamagishi and Matsuda's reputation experiments [33].

When choosing which peer to donate a favor to, provider *A* donates the favor to the candidate peer with the highest cost balance, where the candidate peers are the peers requesting the favor for which inequality (16.2) holds. If all candidates have cost balances equal to zero, the peer chooses one of the candidates randomly.

16.3.2.3 Policies for the Network of Favors. As mentioned before, an obvious caveat of the way the PosInt policies are calculated is that they require knowledge of the costs that other peers would incur when donating a favor. Other peers are not necessarily trustworthy, and may be able to increase their expected utilities by giving false information about these costs. In the absence of reliable information on other peers' costs, it is not feasible to use a selection policy that distinguishes profitable collaborative peers from unprofitable ones. The alternative used by the network of favors is to remove this check, or equivalently to use a trivial selection policy that never prevents two peers from interacting, and rely simply on the prioritization policy to marginalize both free riders and unprofitable collaborative peers.

In addition, the way the cost balance accounts for favors received needs to be changed. The approach used by the network of favors is instead of a peer using the unknown cost function of a favor's provider to calculate the cost balance, it uses its own cost function. Thus, the prioritization policy for the network of favors differs from that of PosInt in that when *B* receives favor *f* from *A*, *B* increases its cost balance for *A* by $v_B(f)$ rather than by $v_A(f)$.

We have simulated the effects of the network-of-favors policies and the PosInt policies on the allocation of resources for services that are a combination of two basic services (e.g., CPU and disk), for a variety of different values of consumption frequency, service availability, and donation costs [24]. We found that although the network-of-favors policies do not require as much knowledge about other peers as the PosInt policies do, in our simulations the effectiveness of the network of favors at marginalizing free riders was very close to that of PosInt, and that the network of favors can effectively provide incentives for peers to collaborate even when the cost of donating a service is nearly as large as the utility gained by receiving it.

For any pairwise reciprocation mechanism to work, peers that have interacted once must have a high probability of interacting again, which requires frequent interactions, symmetry of interests, and low churn. Feldman et al. [16] and Lai et al. [20] have shown that when interactions between peers are infrequent (e.g., because of asymmetry of interest or rapid population turnover), then incentive mechanisms for sharing based on local history do not scale well beyond 1000 peers. Asymmetry of interest occurs when peer *A* is interested in the resources of a peer *B*, but *B* is not interested in *A*'s resources. A large peer population with rapid turnover makes repeated interactions between pairs of peers less likely, and therefore makes it harder for collaborators to be rewarded.

However, the network of favors is effective in P2P Grids of the scale that we consider because in these systems, compared to the file-sharing systems considered by Feldman et al. [16] and Lai et al. [20] (1) there is much more symmetry of interest, (2) interactions among peers follow a many-to-many pattern, (3) there is a relatively slow-changing population of collaborators, and (4) the calculation of local scores encourages repeated interactions.

Interest is much more symmetric in P2P Grids than in file-sharing systems. A file-sharing system may share many thousands of files, only a few of which will be interesting to a peer, but there are not too many different services that are provided in a Grid.

The many-to-many interactions in P2P Grids make it more likely that two peers interact frequently than is the case in systems with one-to-one interactions, such as most file-sharing systems. A peer in a P2P Grid running high-performance computational Grid applications likely interacts with a large number of other peers each time it requests resources, due to the large demand for resources that is a characteristic of these applications. Moreover, a peer providing resources does not need to allocate all its resources to a single consumer and can utilize the fact that it has several resources to signal to several peers at once that it is collaborative.

We believe it is reasonable to assume a relatively slow-changing population of collaborative peers (assumption A6). This is because each peer of the Grid is a service that will be managed by system administrators for one or more users in an organization. The rate at which new collaborative peers join the Grid will be slow compared to the frequency of peer interactions.

Finally, the way the local scores are calculated has the effect of encouraging repeated interactions between collaborative peers. Let $s_A(B)$ be the cost balance that *A* records for its interactions with *B*. If collaborative peers *A* and *B* have ever interacted, it is guaranteed that $s_A(B) + s_B(A) > 0$. This implies that at least one of them will prioritize the other over free riders and peers with which it has not interacted.

16.3.3 Consequences of the Policies

Whether the cost balance is calculated in the way specified by the prioritization policy for PosInt or the one used in the network of favors, the cost balance that *A* records for *B* decreases when *A* donates favors to *B* (provided that it was not zero to start with) and increases when *B* donates favors to *A*. It can therefore be regarded as an indication of the net benefit that *A* has gained so far by interacting with *B*. By donating the favor to the candidate peer with the highest value of the cost balance, provider *A* is choosing to interact with a peer with whom it expects to have beneficial interactions in the future, based on its past experience.[1] Since donating a favor to a collaborative peer increases the expected amount of favors received from that peer in the future, over the long run the more a peer donates to the system the more it can expect to receive back.

The cost balance is greater than or equal to zero for all peers. If it is zero for all candidate peers, *A* still donates the service to one of the candidate peers. This allows newcomers to the system to have a chance of donating and receiving favors. It also serves as a bootstrap mechanism.

[1]A similar way of selecting peers to interact with is described (for a different context) by Banerjee et al. [4].

Free riders will sometimes be donated favors, and *A* will lose utility as a result of any donations that it makes to a free rider. However, *A* will not donate a favor to a free rider unless all the candidate peers have zero cost balance. As a consequence, free riders receive services with low priority. Thus the expected long-term utility gain for free riders should be lower than that for peers that do not free ride, and so noncollaborative peers will choose not to free-ride.

Since we do not assume that there is a limit on the number of different IDs that a peer can use in the system, free riders can whitewash their identities, and thus become indistinguishable from collaborative newcomers. However, they cannot increase their chances of obtaining services from any peer *A* by doing so, because *A*'s cost balance for their new identity will be zero, the minimum value. Peers can only increase their priority for donations from others by making donations to others themselves. As soon as a peer makes a donation, it becomes distinguishable from a free rider, so collaborative peers should not remain isolated indefinitely. Note, however, that if a collaborative peer changes strategy and becomes a free rider, eventually its cost balance will be zero for all other peers and it will end up with the same priority as free riders and collaborative newcomers.

Another consequence of peers' potential ability to use multiple identities is that it is particularly difficult to design a reliable global reputation system, because a non-collaborative peer has the possibility of creating very many clones of itself that propagate false reputations [13]. The network of favors provides incentive for donation without the need to rely on a global reputation system.

16.4 THE OurGrid SYSTEM

We have implemented and evaluated the network of favors in a real scenario using OurGrid, a P2P Grid middleware that aims to support the execution of bag-of-tasks (BoT) applications, namely, those parallel applications whose tasks are independent [9,31]. OurGrid considers CPU and disk as the good being shared, as these are the critical resources for most BoT applications.

A characteristic of BoT applications is that their users are often eager consumers; if they are in consuming mode and are offered additional computing power, they are likely to find profitable ways to use it. Two types of applications that exemplify this usage pattern are simulations of the effectiveness of pharmaceutical drugs and computer animation rendering. Moreover, Paranhos et al. [26] and Santos-Neto et al. [29] have shown that replication of tasks among the available resources improves the completion time (makespan) of BoT applications running on Grids. These arguments suggest that contention for resources is very likely in a Grid used to run BoT applications.

To implement the incentive mechanism of the network of favors, the following is needed: (1) a way of calculating what the utility cost is to the local peer of providing a particular favor, taking into account both cost of provision of CPU power and cost of provision of storage; and (2) a way of calculating what the utility cost would have been to the local peer of providing a favor that is actually provided for the local peer by a remote peer.

Since we assume that costs are additive, we can estimate the utility cost of providing a favor by adding together the costs of providing the CPU power and of providing the storage necessary to carry out the favor. The costs to the local peer of providing a unit of CPU power and a unit of storage are locally configured by each peer. Note that service in OurGrid is provided using the idle computing power that a user already owns. In practice, it may be difficult to estimate precisely the cost of providing service using such resources, as this includes, for example, the maintenance costs of keeping the OurGrid software in operation, and the cost of mitigating security risks associated with OurGrid. One practical way of estimating the cost function, however, is to estimate the operational costs of all local resources that are made available to the Grid. The costs of operating OurGrid and of having the resources turned on in order to be available to OurGrid are likely to be a fraction of this total cost.

Once a peer can estimate the utility costs of providing specified amounts of CPU power and storage, in order to calculate the cost of carrying out a particular favor, the peer needs to calculate the amount of CPU power and storage used to do this.

The cost function that we have implemented works as follows. For the storage part of a favor, it simply records the number of bytes stored, regardless of whether the favor is provided or received. On the other hand, the CPU power part of favors received is accounted on a per-application basis. We make use of the fact that applications in OurGrid consist of a large number of independent tasks. For a given application, some tasks are scheduled to execute locally and others, at remote machines.

The consumer peer then values the work done by a provider by averaging the time it took to run the application's tasks on its local resources and dividing this value by the average time it took to run tasks of the same application on the resources of the remote peer. It then multiplies this relative power by the CPU power used in a local calculation of the length of time that the tasks took to execute remotely, to give an estimation of the amount of CPU power provided by the remote peer, and hence the cost of providing this amount of CPU power locally. We have shown [28] that this idea can be used to implement an accounting scheme that is accurate even when both the CPU power of the resources of a peer and the size of the tasks of an application vary.

16.5 VISIONARY THOUGHTS FOR PRACTITIONERS

One of the main implications of the work we present in this chapter is the recognition that sharing can be considered as a first-class citizen in the organization of Grids.

It has been previously discussed in the literature that market mechanisms might be costly to implement and complex to use in large-scale distributed computing [30]. This discussion fits well with the more general analysis of Benkler about markets and sharing economies [5], and we argue therefore that the conclusions of Benkler for the wider context should be taken into account by the distributed computing community.

Distributed computing poses challenges in implementing mechanisms for auditing, banking, and norm enforcement. In a sharing economy, the use of social relations, intrinsic motivations, and low-cost incentive mechanisms to regulate the transactions considerably lower the transaction costs incurred by participants and may therefore give rise to a highly efficient system by encouraging the participation of a large number of contributors.

Several of the use cases that motivate Grid computing are related to a group of research labs that have resources they sometimes do not need to use locally. Although prices and markets might be the information and mechanisms more adequate for commercial use cases, where providers sell their resources to consumers, their transaction costs might be too high for the research labs use case. We therefore believe that both sharing and other methods for resource allocation that incur lower transaction costs should gain more attention from the Grid research community.

16.6 FUTURE RESEARCH DIRECTIONS

Our results have shown the viability of applying a reciprocation-based approach to enable the creation of P2P Grids based on a sharing economy. The natural next step in this research is to evaluate empirically the efficiency of this approach in practice. To enable such analysis we are currently collecting data from the OurGrid community, an open peer-to-peer Grid that uses the OurGrid middleware and that has been in production since December 2004; however, the study of other Grids is still necessary to assess the generality of the approach.

Because of their budget limits, it is likely that peers will need to choose only a subset of services to offer to the system from the set of all services that they can provide. Since different services will yield different utilities, in such a scenario it becomes necessary to answer the question of how peers should choose among services to maximize their utility from participating in the system.

Finally, as in other economies, it is very likely that sharing-based Grids will coexist with market-based ones. Considering this scenario, how should users of applications that demand large amounts of computational plan their computing infrastructures? Some initial steps in the direction of answering this question have already been taken [12].

16.7 CONCLUSION

In this chapter we have described the network of favors, a reciprocation-based economy for resource allocation in P2P grids that can share multiple services. We have discussed its behavior and its implementation in a real Grid infrastructure.

Compared to alternative solutions for the problem considered, the network of favors is much simpler and less costly, allowing systems that use it to depend on much less infrastructure than would be necessary for more sophisticated mechanisms. The drawback is that by choosing this simple reciprocation-based mechanism, one loses the greater flexibility provided by market-based incentive mechanisms.

REFERENCES

1. D. Abramson, R. Buyya, and J. Giddy, A computational economy for grid computing and its implementation in the Nimrod-G resource broker, *Future Generation Computer Systems Journal* **18**(8):1061–1074 (2002).
2. N. Andrade, W. Cirne, F. V. Brasileiro, and P. Roisenberg, OurGrid: An approach to easily assemble grids with equitable resource sharing, *Proc. 9th Workshop on Job Scheduling Strategies for Parallel Processing*, Seattle, WA, June 24, 2003.
3. N. Andrade, F. Brasileiro, W. Cirne, and M. Mowbray, Automatic grid assembly by promoting collaboration in peer-to-peer grids, *Journal of Parallel and Distributed Computing* **67**(8):957–966 (2007).
4. D. Banerjee, S. Saha, S. Sen, and P. Dasgupta, Reciprocal resource sharing in P2P environments, *Proc. 4th International Joint Conf. Autonomous Agents and Multiagent Systems*, Utrecht, The Netherlands, July 25–29, 2005.
5. Y. Benkler, Sharing nicely: On shareable goods and the emergence of sharing as a modality of economic production, *The Yale Law Journal* **114**:273–358 (2004).
6. A. Butt, R. Zhang, and Y. C. Hu, A self-organizing flock of condors, *Journal of Parallel and Distributed Computing* **66**(1):145–161 (2006).
7. R. Buyya and S. Vazhkudai, Compute power market: Towards a market-oriented grid, *Proc. 1st IEEE/ACM International Symp. Cluster Computing and the Grid*, Brisbane, Australia, May 15–18, 2001.
8. W. Cirne, F. Brasileiro, N. Andrade, L. Costa, A. Andrade, R. Novaes, and M. Mowbray, Labs of the world, unite!!!, *Journal of Grid Computing* **4**(3):225–246 (2006).
9. W. Cirne, F. V. Brasileiro, J. Sauvé, N. Andrade, D. Paranhos, E. L. Santos-Neto, R. Medeiros, and F. Silva, Grid computing for bag-of-tasks applications, *Proc. 3rd IFIP Conf. E-Commerce, E-Business and E-Government*, São Paolo, Brazil, Sept. 21–24, 2003.
10. B. Cohen, Incentives build robustness in BitTorrent, *Proc. 1st Workshop on Economics of Peer-to-Peer Systems*, Berkeley, CA, June 5–6, 2003.
11. E. Damiani, S. De Capitani di Vimercati, S. Paraboschi, and P. Samaranti, Managing and sharing servents' reputations in P2P systems, *IEEE Transactions on Data and Knowledge Engineering* **15**(4):840–854 (2003).
12. P. Ditarso, F. Figueiredo, D. Candeia, F. V. Brasileiro, and A. V. de Souza Côelho, On the planning of a hybrid IT infrastructure, *Proc. 21st IEEE/IFIP Network Operations and Management Symp.*, Salvador, Brazil, April 7–11, 2008.
13. J. R. Douceur, The Sybil attack, *Proc. International Workshop on Peer-to-Peer Systems*, Cambridge, MA, March 7–8, 2002.
14. eMule, http://www.emule-project.net/, 2002–2008.
15. G. Fedak, C. Germain, V. Neri, and F. Cappello, XtremWeb: A generic global computing system, *Proc. 1st IEEE/ACM International Symp. on Cluster Computing and the Grid*, Brisbane, Australia, May 15–18, 2001.
16. M. Feldman, K. Lai, I. Stoica, and J. Chuang, Robust incentive techniques for peer-to-peer networks, *Proc. 5th ACM Conf. Electronic Commerce (EC 2004), New York, May 17–20*, 2004.
17. C. Grothoff, An excess-based economic model for resource allocation in peer-to-peer networks, *Wirtschaftsinformatik* **44**(3):285–292 (June 2003).

18. D. M. Kahan, *The Logic of Reciprocity: Trust, Collective Action, and Law*, Yale Law & Economics Research Paper 281, Yale Law School, New Haven, CT, 2002.
19. S. D. Kamvar, M. T. Schlosser, and H. Garcia-Molina, The EigenTrust algorithm for reputation management in P2P networks, *Proc. 12th International World Wide Web Conf. (WWW 2003)*, Budapest, Hungary, May 20–24, 2003.
20. K. Lai, M. Feldman, I. Stoica, and J. Chuang, Incentives for cooperation in peer-to-peer networks, *Proc. 1st Workshop on Economics of Peer-to-Peer Systems*, Berkeley, CA, June 5–6, 2003.
21. K. Lai, B. A. Huberman, and L. Fine, *Tycoon: A Distributed Market-Based Resource Allocation System*, Technical Report, arXiv:cs/0404013, HP Labs, 2004.
22. V. M. Lo, D. Zappala, D. Zhou, Y. Liu, and S. Zhao, Cluster computing on the fly: P2P scheduling of idle cycles in the internet, *Proc. 3rd International Workshop on Peer-to-Peer Systems (IPTPS' 04)*, La Jolla, CA, Feb. 26–27, 2004.
23. K. McGee and J. Skågeby, Gifting technologies, *First Monday* **9**(12) (2004).
24. M. Mowbray, F. V. Brasileiro, N. Andrade, J. Santana, and W. Cirne, A reciprocation-based economy for multiple services in peer-to-peer grids, *Proc. 6th IEEE International Conf. Peer-to-Peer Computing (P2P 2006)*, Cambridge, UK, Sept. 6–8, 2006.
25. L. Oliveira, L. Lopes, and F. Silva, P3 (parallel peer to peer): An Internet parallel programming environment, *Proc. Web Engineering and Peer-to-Peer Computing Workshop*, Pisa, Italy, May 19–24, 2002.
26. D. Paranhos, W. Cirne, and F. V. Brasileiro, Trading cycles for information: Using replication to schedule bag-of-tasks applications on computational grids, *Proc. 9th International Conf. Parallel and Distributed Computing (Euro-Par 2003)*, Klagenfurt, Austria, Aug. 26–29, 2003.
27. J. Pucher and J. Renne, Socioeconomics of urban travel: Evidence from the 2001 national household travel survey, *Transportation Quarterly* **57**(3):49–78 (2003).
28. R. Santos, A. Andrade, W. Cirne, F. V. Brasileiro, and N. Andrade, Accurate autonomous accounting in peer-to-peer grids, *Proc. 3rd International Workshop on Middleware for Grid Computing (MGC '05)*, Grenoble, France, Nov. 28–29, 2005.
29. E. L. Santos-Neto, W. Cirne, F. V. Brasileiro, and A. Lima, Exploiting replication and data reuse to efficiently schedule data-intensive applications on grids, *Proc. 10th Workshop on Job Scheduling Strategies for Parallel Processing*, New York, June 13, 2004.
30. J. Schneidman, C. Ng, D. Parkes, A. AuYoung, A. C. Snoeren, A. Vahdat, and B. N. Chun, Why markets could (but don't currently) solve resource allocation problems in systems, *Proc. 10th USENIX Workshop on Hot Topics in Operating Systems*, Santa Fe, NM, June 12–15, 2005.
31. J. A. Smith and S. K. Shrivastava, A system for fault-tolerant execution of data and compute intensive programs over a network of workstations, *Proc. 2nd International Euro-Par Conf.*, Lyons, France, Aug. 26–29, 1996.
32. V. Vishnumurthy, S. Chandrakumar, and E. Sirer, KARMA: A secure economic framework for peer-to-peer resource sharing, *Proc. 1st Workshop on Economics of Peer-to-Peer Systems*, Berkeley, CA, June 5–6, 2003.
33. T. Yamagishi and M. Matsuda, *The Role of Reputation in Open and Closed Societies: An Experimental Study of Online Trading*, Working Paper 8, Center for the Study of Cultural and Ecological Foundations of the Mind, http://joi.ito.com/archives/papers/Yamagishi_ASQ1.pdf, Hokkaido Univ., Japan, 2003.

17

THE NIMROD/G GRID RESOURCE BROKER FOR ECONOMICS-BASED SCHEDULING

Rajkumar Buyya and David Abramson

17.1 INTRODUCTION

Computational Grids enable the coordinated and aggregated use of geographically distributed resources, often owned by autonomous organizations, for solving large-scale problems in science, engineering, and commerce. However, application composition, resource management, and scheduling in these environments are complex undertakings [18,30]. This is due to the geographic distribution of resources that are often owned by different organizations having different usage policies and cost models, and varying loads and availability patterns. To address these resource management challenges, we have developed a distributed computational economy framework for quality-of-service (Qos)-driven resource allocation and regulation of supply and demand for resources. The new framework offers incentive to resource owners to participate in the Grid and motivates resource users to trade off between time for results delivery and economic cost, namely, deadline and budget [19].

Resource management systems need to provide mechanisms and tools that realize the goals of both service providers and consumers. Resource consumers need a utility model, representing their resource demand and preferences, and brokers that automatically generate strategies for choosing providers on the basis of this model. Further, the brokers need to manage as many issues associated with the execution of the underlying application as possible.

Market-Oriented Grid and Utility Computing Edited by Rajkumar Buyya and Kris Bubendorfer

TABLE 17.1 Economics Models and Their Use in Some Distributed Computing Scheduling Systems

Economic Model	Adopted by
Commodity market	Mungi [9], MOSIX [29], Nimrod/G [20]
Posted price	Nimrod/G
Bargaining	Mariposa [15], Nimrod/G
Tendering or contract-net model	Mariposa
Auction model	Spawn [2], Popcorn [17]
Bid-based proportional resource sharing	Rexec and Anemone [1]
Community and coalition	Condor and SETI@Home [28]
Cooperative bartering	MojoNation [16]
Monopoly and oligopoly	Nimrod/G broker can be used to choose between resources offered at different quality and prices

A computational economy offers many advantages in this environment, because it allows producers and consumers to dynamically negotiate a level of service quality that suits them both. Moreover, when there are multiple users with conflicting demands, they can negotiate access to resources (and thus response time) by "trading" units of currency. A computational economy gives clients a common currency in an otherwise totally distributed system. Service providers benefit from price generation schemes that increase system utilization, as well as economic protocols that help them offer competitive services. For the market to be competitive and efficient, coordination mechanisms that help the market reach an equilibrium price are required; that is, the market price at which the supply of a service equals the quantity demanded [8]. Numerous economic theories have been proposed in the literature, and many commonly used economic models for selling goods and services can be employed as negotiation protocols in Grid computing. Some of these market or social driven economic models are shown in Table 17.1 along with the identity of the distributed system that adopted the approach [21].

These economic models regulate the supply and demand for resources in Grid-based virtual enterprises. We demonstrate the power of these models in scheduling computations using the Nimrod/G resource broker on a large global Grid testbed, called the World Wide Grid (WWG). While it is not the goal of the system to earn revenue for the resource providers, this approach does provide an economic incentive for resource owners to share their resources on the Grid. Further, it encourages the emergence of a new service-oriented computing industry. Importantly, it provides mechanisms to trade off QoS parameters, deadline, and computational cost, and offers incentive for users to relax their requirements. For example, a user may be prepared to accept a later deadline if the computation can be performed at a lower cost.

The rest of this chapter explores the use of an economic paradigm for Grid computing with particular emphasis on providing the tools and mechanisms that support economics-based scheduling. The emphasis will be placed on the Nimrod/G resource broker that supports soft-deadline and budget-based scheduling of parameter sweep applications [18,32]. Depending on the users' quality-of-service (QoS) requirements, the resource broker dynamically leases Grid services at runtime depending on their cost, quality, and availability. The broker supports the optimization of time or cost within specified deadline and budget constraints. The results of a series of scheduling experiments that we conducted on the WWG testbed using the Nimrod broker will be reported.

17.2 THE NIMROD/G GRID RESOURCE BROKER

17.2.1 Objectives and Goals

Nimrod/G [20,31] is a tool for automated modeling and execution of parameter sweep applications (parameter studies) over global computational Grids [3–7]. It provides a simple declarative parametric modeling language for expressing parametric experiments. A domain expert can easily create a plan for a parametric experiment and use the Nimrod/G system to deploy jobs on distributed resources for execution. It has been used for a very wide range of applications over the years, ranging from quantum chemistry [32] to policy and environmental impact [33]. Moreover, it uses novel resource management and scheduling algorithms based on economic principles. Specifically, it supports user-defined deadline and budget constraints for schedule optimisations and manages supply and demand of resources in the Grid using a set of resource-trading services [19].

Nimrod/G provides a persistent and programmable task-farming engine (TFE) that enables "plugging" of user-defined schedulers and customized applications or problem-solving environments (e.g., ActiveSheets) in place of default components. The task-farming engine is a coordination point for processes performing resource trading, scheduling, data and executable staging, remote execution, and result collation. The Nimrod/G project builds on the early work [5,7] that focused on creating tools that help domain experts compose their legacy serial applications for parameter studies and run them on computational clusters and manually managed Grids. The Nimrod/G system automates the allocation of resources and application scheduling on the Grid using economic principles in order to provide some measurable quality of service (QoS) to the end user. Thus, the focus of this work is within an intersection area of Grid architectures, economic principles, and scheduling optimizations (see Fig. 17.1), which is essential for pushing the Grid into the mainstream computing.

17.2.2 Services and End Users

The Nimrod/G system provides tools for creating parameter sweep applications and services for management of resources and scheduling applications on the Grid. It supports a simple declarative programming language and associated portal and GUI tools for creating scripts and parameterization of application input data files, and a Grid resource broker with programmable entities for scheduling and deploying

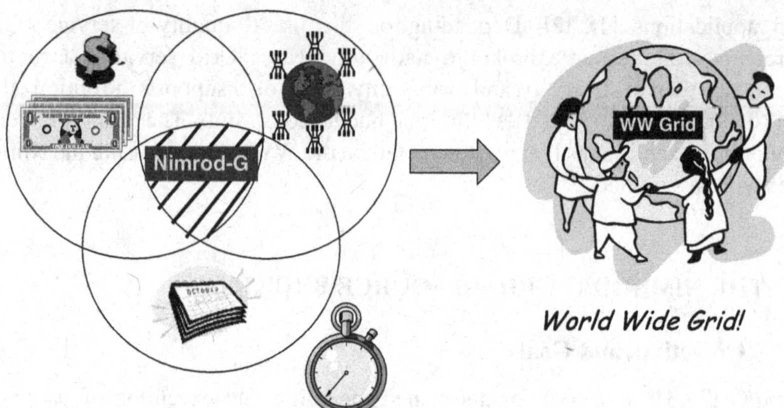

Figure 17.1 QoS-based resource management: intersection of economic, scheduling, and Grid worlds.

jobs on distributed resources. The Nimrod/G resource broker is made up of a number of components—namely, a persistent and programmable task farming engine, a schedule advisor, and a dispatcher—whose functionalities are discussed later. It also provides job management services that can be used for creating user-defined schedulers, steering and monitoring tools, and customized applications. Therefore, the end users that benefit from Nimrod/G tools, protocols, and services are

- *Domain Experts.* This group includes scientific, engineering, and commercial users with large-scale dataset processing requirements. Parameter applications can use Nimrod/G tools to compose them as coarse-grained data-parallel, parameter sweep applications for executing on distributed resources. They can also take advantage of the Nimrod/G broker features to trade off between a deadline and the cost of computation while scheduling application execution on the Grid. This quality of service aspect is important to end users, because the results are useful only if they are returned in a timely manner.
- *Problem-Solving Environments Developers.* Application developers can Grid-enable their applications with their own mechanisms to submit jobs to the Nimrod/G resource broker at runtime depending on user requirements for processing on the Grid. This gives them the ability to create applications capable of directly using Nimrod/G tools and job management services, which, in turn, enables their applications for Grid execution.
- *Task Farming or Master-Worker Programming Environments Designers.* These users can focus on designing and developing easy-to-use and powerful application creation primitives for task farming and master-work style programming model, developing translators and application execution environments by taking advantage of Nimrod/G runtime machinery for executing jobs on distributed Grid resources. Other tools, like Nimrod/O [3,4] use the services of Nimrod/G, for example, to launch jobs on Grid resources.

- *Scheduling Researchers.* The scheduling policy developers generally use simulation techniques and tools such as GridSim [14] for evaluating performance of their algorithms. In simulation, it is very difficult to capture the complete property and behavior of a real-world system; hence, evaluation results may be inaccurate. Accordingly, to prove the usefulness of scheduling algorithms on actual systems, researchers need to develop runtime machinery, which is a resource-intensive and time-consuming task. This can be overcome by using Nimrod/G broker programmable capability. Researchers can use Nimrod/G job management protocols and services to develop their own scheduler and associated scheduling algorithms. The new scheduler can be used to run actual applications on distributed resources and then evaluate the ability of scheduling algorithms in optimally mapping jobs to resources.

17.2.3 Architecture

Nimrod/G leverages services provided by Grid middleware systems such as Globus and Legion. The middleware systems provide a set of low-level protocols for secure and uniform access to remote resources, and services for accessing resources information and storage management. The modular and layered architecture of Nimrod/G is shown in Figure 17.2. The Nimrod/G architecture follows an hourglass

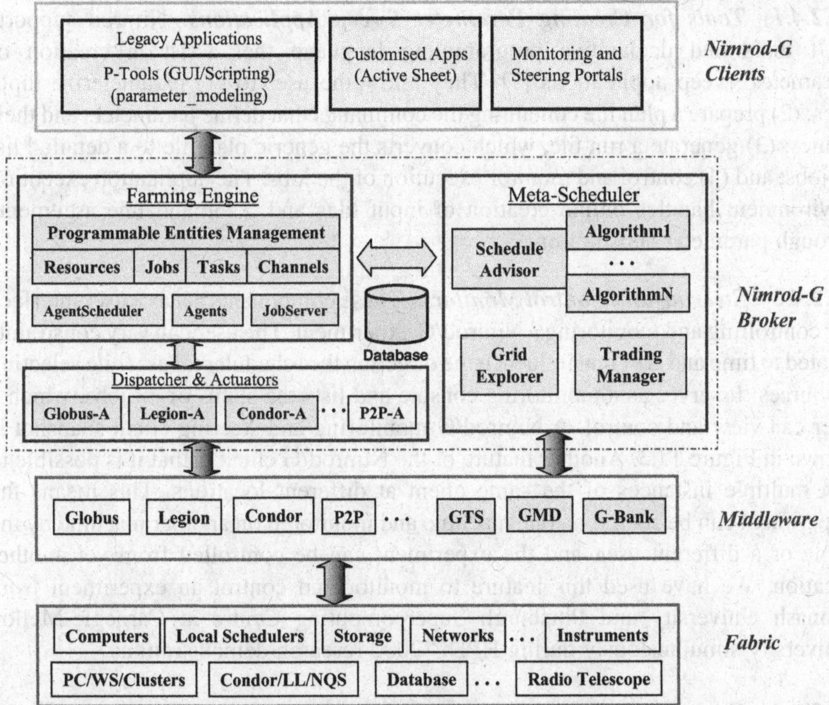

Figure 17.2 A layered architecture of the Nimrod/G system.

design model that allows its implementation on top of different middleware systems and enables the usage of its services by multiple clients and applications.

The key components of Nimrod/G resource broker are:

- Nimrod/G clients, which can be
  - Tools for creating parameter sweep applications
  - Steering and control monitors
  - Customized end-user applications (e.g., ActiveSheets [6])
- The Nimrod/G resource broker, which consists of
  - A task-farming engine (TFE)
  - A scheduler that performs resource discovery, trading, and scheduling
  - A dispatcher and actuator
  - Agents for managing the execution of jobs on resources

The Nimrod/G broker architecture leverages services provided by lower-level different Grid middleware solutions to perform resource discovery, trading, and deployment of jobs on Grid resources.

17.2.4 Nimrod/G Clients

17.2.4.1 Tools for Creating Parameter Sweep Applications. Nimrod supports GUI tools and declarative programming language that assist in creation of parameter sweep applications [7]. They allow the user to (1) parameterize input files; (2) prepare a plan file containing the commands that define parameters and their values; (3) generate a run file, which converts the generic plan file to a detailed list of jobs; and (4) control and monitor execution of the jobs. The application execution environment handles online creation of input files and command line arguments through parameter substitution.

17.2.4.2 Steering and Control Monitors. These components act as a user interface for controlling and monitoring a Nimrod/G experiment. The user can vary constraints related to time and cost that influence the direction the scheduler takes while selecting resources. It serves as a monitoring console and lists the status of all jobs, which a user can view and control. A Nimrod/G monitoring and steering client snapshot is shown in Figure 17.3. Another feature of the Nimrod/G client is that it is possible to run multiple instances of the same client at different locations. This means the experiment can be started on one machine and monitored on another machine by the same or a different user, and the experiment can be controlled from yet another location. We have used this feature to monitor and control an experiment from Monash University and Pittsburgh Supercomputing Centre at Carnegie-Mellon University simultaneously during HPDC-2000 research demonstrations.

17.2.4.3 Customized End-User Applications. Specialized applications can be developed to create jobs at runtime and add jobs to the Nimrod/G engine for

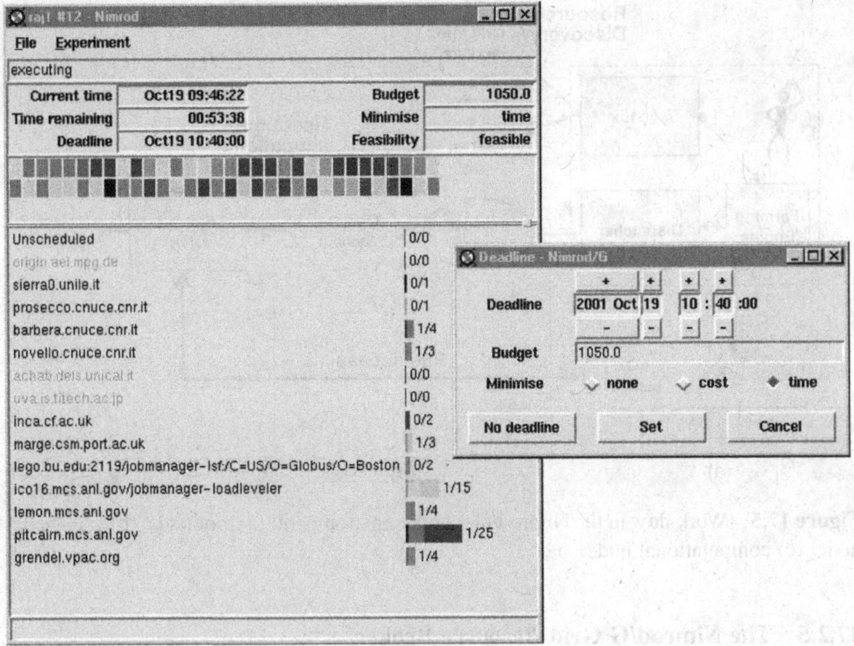

Figure 17.3 A snapshot of Nimrod/G execution monitoring–steering client.

processing on the Grid. These applications can use the Nimrod/G job management services (APIs and protocols described in Ref. 27) for adding and managing jobs. One such application is ActiveSheets [6], an extended Microsoft Excel spreadsheet that submits cell functions as jobs to the Nimrod/G broker for parallel execution on the Grid (see Fig. 17.4). Another example is the Nimrod/O system, a tool that uses nonlinear optimization algorithms to facilitate automatic optimal design [3,4]. This tool has been used on a variety of case studies, including antenna design, smog modeling, durability optimization, airfoil design, and computational fluid dynamics [4].

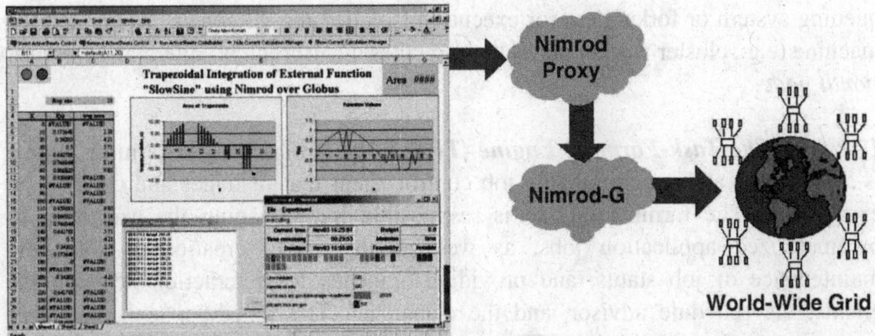

Figure 17.4 ActiveSheet: spreadsheet processing on the Grid using the Nimrod/G broker.

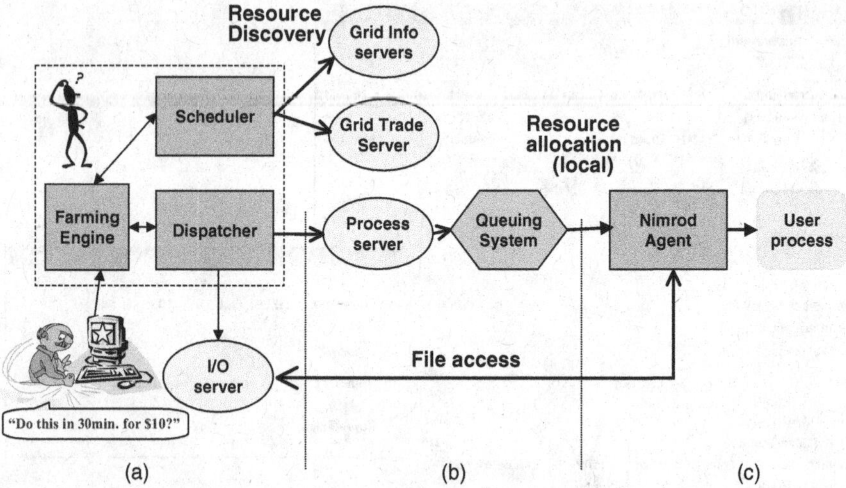

Figure 17.5 Work flow in the Nimrod/G runtime environment: (a) root node; (b) gatekeeper node; (c) computational node.

17.2.5 The Nimrod/G Grid Resource Broker

The Nimrod/G resource broker is responsible for determining the specific requirements that an experiment places on the Grid and performing resource discovery, scheduling, dispatching jobs to remote Grid nodes, starting and managing job execution, and gathering results back to the home node. The submodules of our resource broker are the task-farming engine, the scheduler that consists of a Grid explorer for resource discovery, a schedule advisor backed with scheduling algorithms and a resource trading manager, a dispatcher and an actuator for deploying agents on Grid resources, and agents for managing execution of Nimrod/G jobs on Grid resources. The interaction between components of the Nimrod/G runtime machinery and Grid services during runtime is shown in Figure 17.5. The machine on which the broker runs is called the *root node*, the machine (e.g., a cluster master node) that acts as a front end to a Grid resource and forwards the user jobs to a queuing system or forks them for execution is called the *gatekeeper node*, and the machine (e.g., cluster worker node) that executes the user job is called the *computational node*.

17.2.5.1 The Task-Farming Engine (TFE). The Nimrod/G task-farming engine is a persistent and programmable job control agent that manages and controls an experiment. The farming engine is responsible for managing the execution of parameterized application jobs, as well as the actual creation of jobs, the maintenance of job status, and providing a means for interaction between the clients, the schedule advisor, and the dispatcher. The scheduler and dispatcher respectively interact with the TFE to map jobs to resources and deploy on them; that is, the TFE manages the experiment under the direction of schedule advisors, and then instructs the dispatcher to deploy an application job for execution on the selected resource.

The TFE maintains the state of an entire experiment and ensures that it is recorded in persistent storage. This helps in keeping track of the experiment progress (e.g., status of jobs execution and resources status) and allows the experiment to be restarted if the root node fails without the need for execution of jobs that are already executed. The TFE exposes interfaces for job, resource, and task management along with the job-to-resource mapping APIs and protocols [27]. The developers of scheduling algorithms can use these interfaces to implement their own schedulers rapidly by taking advantage of Nimrod/G TFE and dispatcher capability without concern for the complexity of low-level remote execution mechanisms.

The programmable capability of the task-farming engine enables "plugging" of user-defined schedulers and customized clients or problem-solving environments (e.g., ActiveSheets [6]) in place of the default components. The task-farming engine is a coordination point for processes performing resource trading, scheduling, data and executable staging, remote execution, and result collation.

17.2.5.2 The Scheduler. The scheduler is responsible for resource discovery, resource trading, resource selection, and job assignment. The resource discovery algorithm interacts with an information service [the metacomputing directory service (MDS) in Globus], identifies the list of authorized and available machines, trades for resource access cost, and keeps track of resource status information. The resource selection algorithm is responsible for selecting those resources that meet the deadline and budget constraints along with optimization requirements. Nimrod/G incorporates three different algorithms (discussed in Section 17.4 for deadline/budget-constrained scheduling [22]).

17.2.5.3 The Dispatcher and Actuators. The dispatcher triggers appropriate actuators—depending on the type of middleware running on resources—to deploy agents on Grid resources and assign one of the resource-mapped jobs for execution. Even though the schedule advisor creates a schedule for the entire duration according to user requirements, the dispatcher deploys jobs on resources periodically, depending on the load and the number of free CPUs available. When the dispatcher decides to deploy computation, it triggers the appropriate actuator depending on middleware service. For example, a Globus-specific actuator is required for Globus resources, and a Legion-specific actuator is required for Legion resources.

17.2.5.4 Agents. Nimrod/G agents are deployed on Grid resources dynamically at runtime depending on the scheduler's instructions. The agent is submitted as a job to the resource process server (e.g., GRAM gatekeeper for a resource running Globus), which then submits to the local resource manager (fork manager in case of time-share resources and queuing system in case of space-shared resource) for starting its execution. The agent is responsible for setting up the execution environment on a given resource for a user job. It is responsible for transporting the code and data to the machine, starting the execution of the task on the assigned resource and sending results back to the TFE. Since the agent operates on the "far side" of the middleware resource management components, it needs to provide error detection for the user's job, sending the job termination status information back to the TFE.

The Nimrod/G agent also records the amount of resource consumed during job execution, such as the CPU time and wall clock time. The online measurement of the amount of resource consumed by the job during its execution helps the scheduler evaluate resource performance and change the schedule accordingly. Typically, there is only one type of agent for all mechanisms, irrespective of whether they are fork or queue nodes. However, different agents are required for different middleware systems.

17.3 SCHEDULING AND COMPUTATIONAL ECONOMY

The integration of computational economy as part of a scheduling system greatly influences the way computational resources are selected to meet the user requirements. The users should be able to submit their applications along with their requirements to a scheduling system such as Nimrod/G, which can process the application on the Grid on the user's behalf and try to complete the assigned work within a given deadline and cost. The deadline represents a time by which the user requires the result, and is often imposed by external factors such as production schedules or research deadlines.

To arrive at a scheduling decision, the scheduling system needs to take various parameters into consideration, including the following

- Resource architecture and configuration
- Resource capability (clock speed, memory size)
- Resource state (such as CPU load, memory available, disk storage free)
- Resource requirements of an application
- Access speed (such as disk access speed)
- Free or available nodes
- Priority (that the user has)
- Queue type and length
- Network bandwidth, load, and latency (if jobs need to communicate)
- Reliability of resource and connection
- User preference
- Application deadline
- User capacity/willingness to pay for resource usage
- Resource cost (in terms of dollars that the user need to pay to the resource owner)
- Resource cost variation in terms of timescale (e.g., high at daytime and low at night)
- Historical information, including job consumption rate

The important parameters of computational economy that can influence the way resource scheduling is done are

- Resource cost (set by its owner)
- Price (that the user is willing to pay)
- Deadline (the period by which an application execution needs to be completed)

The scheduler can use the information gathered by a resource discoverer and also negotiate with resource owners to establish service price. The resource that offers the best price and meets resource requirements can eventually be selected. This can be achieved by resource reservation and bidding. If the user deadline is relaxed, the chances of obtaining low-cost access to resources are high. The cost of resources can vary with time, and the resource owner will have the full control over deciding access cost. Further, the cost can vary from one user to another. The scheduler can even solicit bids from resource providers in an open market, and select the feasible service provider(s). To accomplish this, we need scheduling algorithms that take the application processing requirements, Grid resource dynamics, and the user quality-of-service (QoS) requirements such as the deadline, budget, and their optimization preference into consideration. In the next section, we discuss deadline/budget-constrained (DBC) algorithms that we developed for scheduling parameter sweep applications on globally distributed Grid resources.

17.4 SCHEDULING ALGORITHMS

The parameter sweep applications, created using a combination of task and data-parallel models, contain a large number of independent jobs operating different datasets. A range of scenarios and parameters to be explored are applied to the program input values to generate different datasets. The programming and execution model of such applications resemble the single-program multiple-data (SPMD) model. The execution model essentially involves processing N independent jobs (each with the same task specification, but a different dataset) on M distributed computers, where N is, typically, much larger than M.

When the user submits a parameter sweep application containing N tasks along with QoS requirements, the broker performs the following activities:

1. Resource discovery—identifying resources and their properties and then selecting resources capable of executing user jobs.
2. Resource trading—negotiating and establishing service access cost using a suitable economic model.
3. Scheduling—select resources that fit user requirements using *scheduling heuristic/algorithm* and map jobs to them.
4. Deploy jobs on resources (dispatcher).
5. Monitor and steer computations.

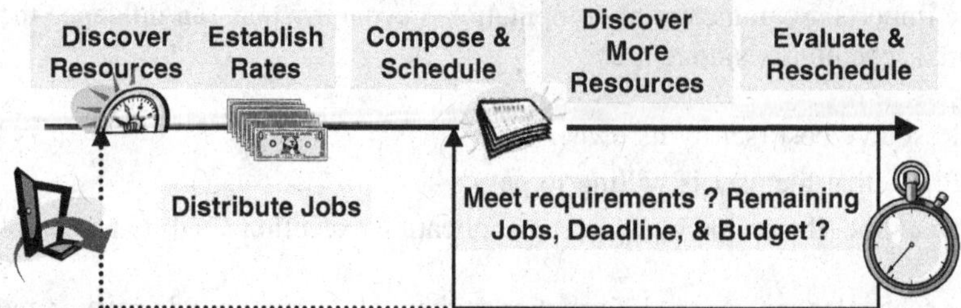

Figure 17.6 High-level steps for adaptive scheduling used in the Nimrod/G broker.

6. Perform load profiling for future usage.
7. When the job execution is finished, gather results back to the user home machine (dispatcher).
8. Record all resource usage details for payment processing purpose.
9. Perform rescheduling—repeat steps 3–8 until all jobs are processed and the experiment is within the deadline and budget limit.
10. Perform cleanup and postprocessing, if required.

The high-level steps for scheduling with deadline and budget constraints are shown in Figure 17.6.

The scheduling and orchestration of the execution of parameter sweep applications on worldwide distributed computers appear simple, but complexity arises when users place QoS constraints such as deadline (execution completion time) and computation cost (budget) limitations. Such a guarantee of service is difficult to provide in a Grid environment since its resources are shared, heterogeneous, distributed in nature, and owned by different organizations having their own policies and charging mechanisms. In addition, scheduling algorithms need to adapt to the changing load and resource availability conditions in the Grid in order to achieve performance and at the same time meet the deadline and budget constraints. In our Nimrod/G application-level resource broker (also called an *application-level scheduler*) for the Grid, we have incorporated three adaptive algorithms for deadline and budget constrained scheduling:

- Cost optimization, within time and budget constraints
- Time optimization, within time and budget constraints
- Conservative time optimization, within time and budget constraints

The role of deadline and budget constraints in scheduling and the objectives of different scheduling algorithms are listed in Table 17.2.

We have developed another new algorithm, called *cost–time optimization scheduling*, which extends the first two (cost–time optimization) scheduling algorithms. This new algorithm and the performance evaluation results are discussed in Section 17.6.

TABLE 17.2 Deadline/Budget-Constrained Scheduling Algorithms and Objectives

Scheduling Algorithm Strategies	Execution Time (Not beyond the Deadline)	Execution Cost (Not beyond the Budget)
Cost optimization	Limited by deadline	Minimize
Time optimization	Minimize	Limited by budget
Conservative time optimization	Limited by deadline	Limited by budget

The *time optimization scheduling* algorithm attempts to complete the experiment as quickly as possible, within the budget available. A description of the core of the algorithm is as follows:

1. For each resource, calculate the next completion time for an assigned job, taking into account previously assigned jobs and job consumption rate.
2. Sort resources by next completion time.
3. Assign one job to the first resource for which the cost per job is less than or equal to the remaining budget per job.
4. Repeat steps 1–3 until all jobs are assigned.

The *cost optimization scheduling* algorithm attempts to complete the experiment as economically as possible within the deadline:

1. Sort resources by increasing cost.
2. For each resource in order, assign as many jobs as possible to the resource, without exceeding the deadline.

The *conservative time optimization* scheduling algorithm attempts to complete the experiment within the deadline and cost constraints, minimising the time when higher budget is available. It spends the budget cautiously and ensures that a minimum of "the budget per job" from the total budget is available for each unprocessed job:

1. Split resources as to whether cost per job is less than or equal to the budget per job.
2. For the cheaper resources, assign jobs in inverse proportion to the job completion time (e.g., a resource with completion time = 5 gets twice as many jobs as a resource with completion time = 10).
3. For the more expensive resources, repeat all steps (with a recalculated budget per job) until all jobs are assigned.

Note that the implementations of all the algorithms described above contain extra steps for dealing with the initial startup (when the average completion times are unknown), and for when all jobs cannot be assigned to resources (infeasible schedules). Detailed steps of the above mentioned scheduling heuristics are described in Section 17.6.

17.5 IMPLEMENTATION ISSUES AND TECHNOLOGIES USED

The Nimrod/G resource broker follows a modular, extensible, and layered architecture with an "hourglass" principle as applied in the Internet Protocol suite [11]. This architecture enables separation of different Grid middleware systems *mechanisms* for accessing remote resources from the end-user applications. The broker provides uniform access to diverse implementations of low-level Grid services. The key components of Nimrod/G, the task-farming engine, the scheduler, and the dispatcher are loosely coupled. To support the interaction between them, the job management protocols described in Reference 27 have been implemented. Apart from the dispatcher and the Grid Explorer, the Nimrod/G components are independent of low-level middleware used. The modular and extensible architecture of Nimrod/G facilitates a rapid implementation of Nimrod/G support for upcoming peer-to-peer computing infrastructures such as Jxta [12] and Web services [24]. To achieve this, it is necessary to implement only two new components, a dispatcher and an enhanced Grid Explorer. The current implementation of Nimrod/G broker uses low-level Grid services provided by Globus [10] and Legion [25] systems. The Globus toolkit components used in the implementation of Nimrod/G are GRAM (Globus resource allocation manager), MDS (metacomputing directory service), GSI (Globus security infrastructure), and GASS (global access to secondary storage). We also support Nimrod/G dispatcher implementation for Condor [13] resource management system. The use of various Grid and commodity technologies in implementing Nimrod/G components and functionality are listed in Table 17.3.

TABLE 17.3 Nimrod/G Resource Broker Modules Functionality and Role of Grid Services

Nimrod/G Module	Implementation and Grid Technologies Used
Application model	Coarse-grained task farming, master worker, and data parallelism
Application composition	We support mechanism for application parameterization through parameterization of input files and command-line inputs for coarse-grained data parallelism; Nimrod/G basically supports coarse-grain, data-parallel, task farming application model, which can be expressed using our declarative programming language or GUI tools
Application interface	The Nimrod/G broker supports protocols and interfaces [27] for job management; Nimrod/G clients or problem-solving environments can add, remove, and enquire about job status and can set user requirements such as deadline and budget; start/stop application execution at both job and entire-application levels
Scheduling interface	The Nimrod/G broker supports protocols and interfaces [27] for mapping jobs to resources; schedulers can interact with TFE to access user constraints and application jobs details to develop a schedule that maps jobs to resources appropriately
Security	Secure access to resources and computations (identification, authentication, computational delegation) is provided by low-level middleware systems (Globus GSI infrastructure)

TABLE 17.3 *(Continued)*

Nimrod/G Module	Implementation and Grid Technologies Used
Resource discovery	Resource discovery involves discovering appropriate resources and their properties that match the user's requirements; we maintain resource listings for Globus, Legion, and Condor and their static and dynamic properties are discovered using Grid information services; for example, in case of Globus resources, we query Globus LDAP-based GRIS server for resource information
Resource trading and market models	Nimrod/G broker architecture is generic enough to support various economic models for price negotiation and using the same in developing application schedules
Performance prediction	Nimrod/G scheduler performs user-level resource capability measurement and load profiling by measuring and establishing the job consumption rate
Scheduling algorithms	Deadline/budget-based constraint (DBC) scheduling performed by Nimrod/G schedule advisor; Along with DBC scheduling, we support further optimization of time-, cost-, or surplus-driven divide-and-conquer in scheduling
Remote job submission	The Nimrod/G dispatcher performs deployment of Nimrod/G agents using Globus GRAM, Legion, or Condor commands; the agents are responsible for managing all aspects of job execution
Staging programs and data on remote resources	In the case of Legion and Condor, it is handled by their I/O management systems; on Globus resources, we use http protocols for fetching required files
Accounting (broker level)	Nimrod/G agents perform accounting tasks such as measuring resource consumption, and the scheduler performs the entire application-level accounting
Monitoring and steering	Nimrod/G monitoring and steering client
Problem-solving environments	ActiveSheets and Nimrod-O are Grid-enabled using the Nimrod/G broker job management services
Execution testbed	The World Wide Grid (WWG) having resources distributed across five continents

While submitting applications to the broker, user requirements such as deadline and budget constraints need to be set and start application execution. These constraints can be changed at any time during execution. The complete details on application parameterization and jobs management are maintained in the database. In the past the database was implemented as a file-based hierarchical database. In the latest version of Nimrod/G, the TFE database is implemented using a standard "relational" database management system.

The commodity technologies and software tools used in the Nimrod/G implementation include the C and Python programming languages, the Perl scripting language, SQL, and Embedded C for database management. The PostgreSQL database system is used for management of the TFE database and its interaction with other components.

17.6 SCHEDULING EVALUATION ON NIMROD/G SIMULATED TEST QUEUES

In addition to accessing real computational resources, Nimrod can also simulate the execution of jobs on a test queue. These simulated queues are useful for testing the scheduling algorithms, since their behavior can be controlled very precisely. A test queue runs each submitted job in succession, and the apparent wall clock time and reported CPU usage can be controlled exactly. It simulates job execution by waiting for a job length period in "real time," and it is assumed that each test queue has a single CPU. This feature is meant for a simple testing of scheduling algorithms incorporated into the Nimrod/G broker. For a detailed performance evaluation, discrete-event simulation tools such GridSim are used (discussed in the next two sections).

For this simulation, we created experiments containing 100 jobs, each with a 90 s runtime, giving a total computation time of 9000 s. For each experiment, we created 10 test queues with different (but fixed) access costs of 10, 12, 14, 16, 18, 20, 22, 24, 26, and 28 G$/(CPU·s). The optimal deadline for this experiment is achieved when each queue runs 10 jobs in sequence, giving a runtime of 900 s for the 100 jobs.

We selected three deadlines: 990 s (the optimal deadline plus 10%), 1980 s (990 × 2), and 2970 s (990 × 3). The 10% allowance allows for the fact that although the queues are simulated, and behave perfectly, the standard scheduler has some delays built in.

We selected three values for the budget. The highest is 252,000 units, which is the amount required to run all jobs on the most expensive queue. Effectively, this allows the scheduler full freedom to schedule over the queues with no consideration for the cost. An amount 171,000 G$ is the budget required to execute 10 jobs on each of the queues. Finally, the lowest budget of 126,000 G$ is the budget required to execute 20 jobs on each of the five cheapest queues. Note that for this value, the deadline of 990 s is infeasible, and the deadline of 1980 s is the optimal deadline plus 10%.

Table 17.4 summarizes results for each combination of scheduling algorithm, deadline and budget, and the resulting percentage of completed jobs, the total runtime, and the final cost. The jobs marked "infeasible" have no scheduling solution that enables 100% completion of jobs. The jobs marked "hard" have only one scheduling solution.

Queue behavior is analyzed by examining queue usage over the period of the experiment. For the cost optimization algorithm, Figure 17.7 shows the node usage for a deadline of 1980s. After an initial spike, during which the scheduler gathers information about the queues, the scheduler calculates that it needs to use the four or five cheapest queues only in order to satisfy the deadline. (Actually, it requires exactly five, but the initial spike reduces the requirements a little.) Note that the schedule is similar, no matter what the allowed budget is. Since we are minimizing cost, the budget plays little part in the scheduling, unless the limit is reached. This appears to have happened for the lowest budget, where the completion rate was 97%. The budget of 126,000 units is only enough to complete the experiment if the five cheapest nodes are used. Because of the initial spike, this experiment appears to have run out of money. The other experiments also did not complete 100% of the jobs, but

TABLE 17.4 Behavior of Scheduling Algorithms for Various Scenarios on Grid

Algorithm	Deadline	Budget ($)	Completed (%)	Time(s)	Cost (G$)	Remarks
Cost optimization	990	126,000	85	946	125,820	Infeasible
	990	171,000	84	942	139,500	Hard
	990	252,000	94	928	156,420	Hard
	1980	126,000	97	1927	124,740	Hard
	1980	171,000	99	1918	128,520	–
	1980	252,000	98	1931	127,620	–
	2970	126,000	98	2931	116,820	–
	2970	171,000	98	2925	116,820	–
	2970	252,000	100	2918	118,800	–
Time optimization	990	126,000	36	955	50,040	Infeasible
	990	171,000	100	913	171,000	Hard
	990	252,000	100	930	171,000	Hard
	1980	126,000	80	1968	101,340	Hard
	1980	171,000	100	909	171,000	–
	1980	252,000	100	949	171,000	–
	2970	126,000	100	2193	126,000	–
	2970	171,000	100	928	171,000	–
	2970	252,000	100	922	171,000	–
Conservative time optimization	990	126,000	78	919	120,060	Infeasible
	990	171,000	99	930	168,480	Hard
	990	252,000	100	941	171,000	Hard
	1980	126,000	97	1902	125,100	Hard
	1980	171,000	100	1376	160,740	–
	1980	252,000	100	908	171,000	–
	2970	126,000	99	2928	125,100	–
	2970	171,000	100	1320	161,460	–
	2970	252,000	100	952	171,000	–

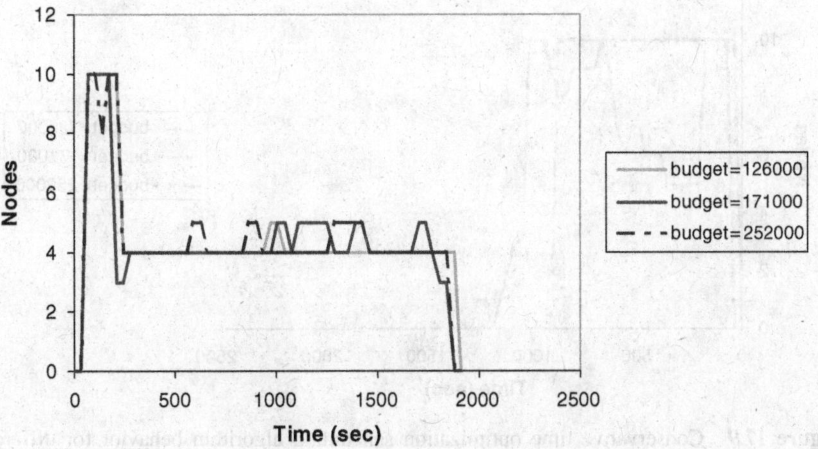

Figure 17.7 DBC cost optimization scheduling algorithm behavior for various budgets.

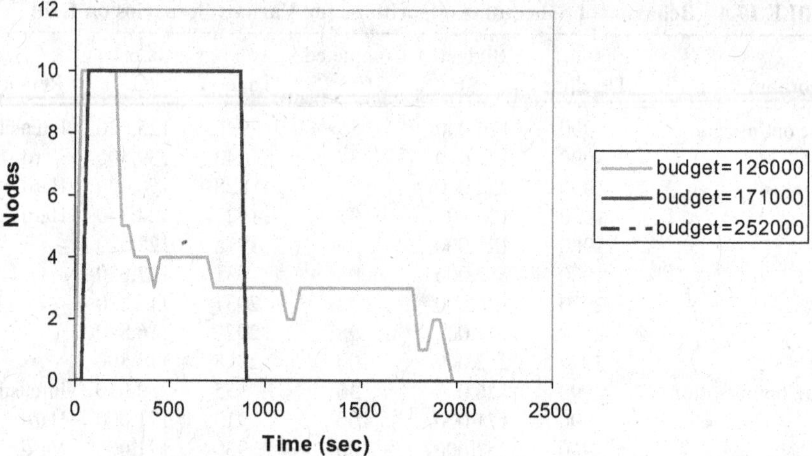

Figure 17.8 Time optimization scheduling algorithm behavior for various budgets.

this is mainly because, in seeking to minimize cost, the algorithm stretches jobs out to the deadline. This indicates the need for a small margin to allow the few remaining jobs to complete close to the deadline.

The equivalent graph for the time optimization algorithm is shown in Figure 17.8. Here we see that, except for the case of a limited budget, we get a rectangular shape, indicating the equal mapping of jobs to each resource. Only the experiment with a very limited budget follows the pattern experienced above.

Looking at the equivalent graph for the conservative time optimization algorithm shown in Figure 17.9, we see much more variation in the schedules chosen for

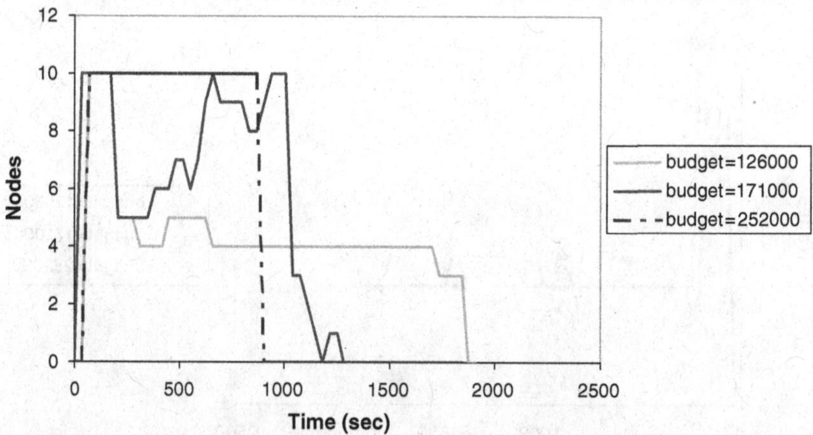

Figure 17.9 Conservative time optimization scheduling algorithm behavior for different budgets.

different budgets. The schedule with a very large budget is equivalent to the time optimization algorithm. The schedule with the low budget is almost the same as the cost optimization algorithm.

17.7 SCHEDULING EXPERIMENTS ON THE WORLDWIDE GRID

We have performed a number of deadline- and budget-constrained scheduling experiments with different requirements at different times by selecting different sets of resources available in the WWG [23] testbed during each experiment. They can be categorized into the following scenarios:

- Cost optimization scheduling during Australian peak and off-peak times
- Cost and time optimization scheduling using cheap local and expensive remote resources

We briefly discuss the WWG testbed followed by a detailed discussion of these scheduling experiments.

17.7.1 The WWG Testbed

To enable our empirical research and experimentations in distributed computational economy and Grid computing, we created and expanded a testbed called the *World Wide Grid* (WWG) in collaboration with colleagues from numerous organizations around the globe. A pictorial view of the WWG testbed depicted in Figure 17.10 shows the name of the organization followed by type of computational resource they have shared. Interestingly, the contributing organizations and the WWG resources themselves are located in five continents: Asia, Australia, Europe, North America, and South America. The organizations whose resources we have used in scheduling experiments reported in this chapter are Monash University (Melbourne, Australia), Victorian Partnership for Advanced Computing (Melbourne, Australia), Argonne National Laboratories (Chicago, USA), University of Southern California's Information Sciences Institute (Los Angeles, USA), Tokyo Institute of Technology (Tokyo, Japan), National Institute of Advanced Industrial Science and Technology (Tsukuba, Japan), University of Lecce (Italy), and CNUCE—Institute of the Italian National Research Council (Pisa, Italy), Zuse Institute Berlin (Berlin, Germany), Charles University, (Prague, Czech Republic), University of Portsmouth (UK), and University of Manchester (UK). In Nimrod/G, these resources are represented using their Internet hostnames.

The WWG testbed contains numerous computers with different architectures, capabilities, and configurations. They include PCs, workstations, SMPs, clusters, and vector supercomputers running operating systems such as Linux, Sun Solaris, IBM AIX (Advanced IBM Unix), SGI IRIX (Silicon Graphics UNIX-like Operating System), and Compaq Tru64. Further, the systems use a variety of job management systems such as OS-Fork, NQS (Network Queueing System),

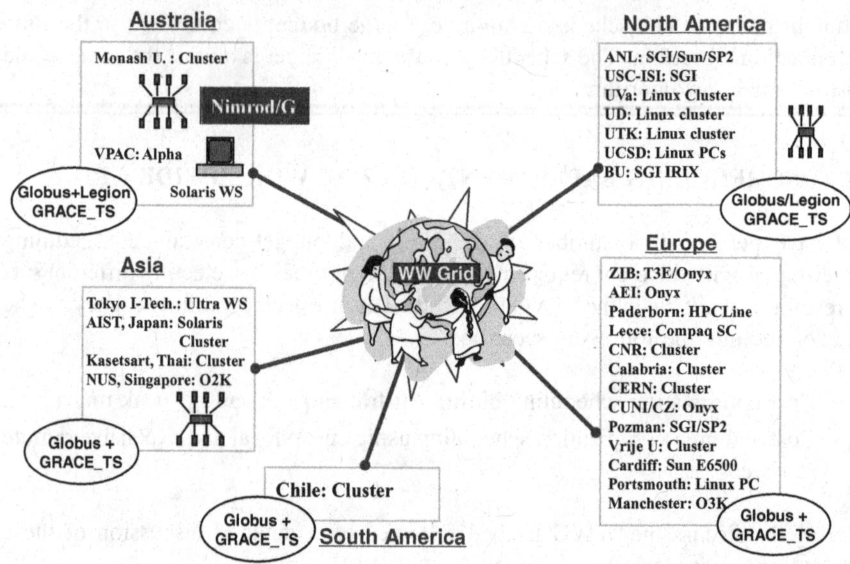

Figure 17.10 The WWG testbed.

Condor, RMS, PBS (Portable Batch System), and LSF (Load Sharing Facility). These system characteristics can be identified by accessing the Grid Information Service (GIS) provided by middleware systems such as Globus running on each resource.

Most of the resources in the WWG testbed support secure remote access through the Globus system and a Linux cluster at Virginia (USA) is managed using the Legion system. The Solaris workstation from where this scheduling experiment is performed runs Globus, Legion, and Condor systems along with the Nimrod/G resource broker. At runtime, the Nimrod/G agents are deployed on resources for managing the execution of jobs.

The properties of WWG testbed resources selected for use in scheduling experiments are discussed in the respective sections. To deploy applications on the Grid using the Nimrod/G broker, the users need to supply the plan that defines application paramterization and task specification, the list of resources that can possibly be utilized, and their QoS requirements such as the deadline, budget, and optimization strategy. The broker discovers the properties of resources using the GIS (e.g., GRIS in the case of Globus) running on them and selects the resources that meet various constraints such as the cost and performance. It also ensures that the application code is available for the target resource architecture. After the selection of resources, the broker maps application jobs to resources using suitable scheduling algorithms. The jobs are then deployed on the Grid by the Nimrod/G dispatcher. To facilitate the tracing of experiments for performance evaluation, the Nimrod/G scheduler records the mapping of jobs and their status at every scheduling event.

Given that the WWG testbed has been used in numerous scheduling experiments with computational economy and real applications (like molecular modeling for drug design), we believe that it truly represents a blueprint of an emerging scalable Grid computing infrastructure for integrating and aggregating dispersed heterogeneous resources.

17.7.2 Cost Optimization Scheduling—Australian Peak and Off-Peak Times

In a competitive commodity market economy, the resources are priced differently at different times according to the supply and demand. For example, they are priced higher during peak hours and lower during off-peak hours. In this experiment we explore their impact on the processing cost, by scheduling a resource-intensive parameter sweep application containing a large number of jobs on the WWG resources, during Australian peak and off-peak hours.

17.7.2.1 WWG Computational Resources. The WWG testbed resources selected for use in this experiment and their properties are shown in Table 17.5. To test the trading services provided by GTS (Grid trade server), we ran an experiment entirely during peak time and the same experiment entirely during off-peak time. It is important to note access price variations during peak and off-peak times and also time difference between Australia and the United States. The access price is expressed in Grid units (G$) per CPU second.

We selected five resources (see Table 17.5) from the testbed, each effectively having 10 nodes available for our experiment. Monash University has a 60-processor Linux cluster running Condor, which was reduced to 10 available processors for the experiment. Similarly, a 96-node SGI at Argonne National Laboratory (ANL) was made to provide 10 nodes by using *Condor glidein* to add 10 processors to the Condor pool. An 8-node Sun at Argonne and a 10-node SGI at the Information Sciences Institute (ISI) of the University of Southern California were accessed using Globus directly. Argonne's 80-node SP2 was also accessed directly through Globus. We relied on its high workload to limit the number of nodes available to us. We assigned artificial cost (access price per second) for each of those resources depending on their relative capability. This is achieved by setting a resource cost database, which is

TABLE 17.5 Worldwide Grid Testbed Resources Used in the Experiment[a]

Resource Type and Size (Nr. of Nodes)	Organization and Location	Grid Services and Fabric	Price at AU Peak Time	Price at AU Off-Peak Time
Linux cluster (60 nodes)	Monash, Australia	Globus/Condor	20	5
IBM SP2 (80 nodes)	ANL, Chicago, USA	Globus/LL	5	10
Sun (8 nodes)	ANL, Chicago, USA	Globus/Fork	5	10
SGI (96 nodes)	ANL, Chicago, USA	Globus/Condor-G	15	15
SGI (10 nodes)	ISI, Los Angeles, USA	Globus/Fork	10	20

[a] Prices are given in Grid units (G$) and CPU per second.

maintained on each resource by its owner. The resource cost database contains access cost (price) that resource owners like to charge to all their Grid users at different times of the day. The access price generally differs from user to user and time to time.

17.7.2.2 Parameter Sweep Application. We have created a hypothetical parameter sweep application (PSA) that executes a CPU-intensive program with 165 different parameter scenarios or values. The program `calc` takes two input parameters and saves results into a file named "output." The first input parameter `angle_degree` represents the value of angle in degree for processing trigonometric functions. The program `calc` needs to be explored for angular values from 1 to 165°. The second parameter `time_base_value` indicates the expected calculation complexity in minutes plus 0–60 s positive deviation. That means that the program `calc` is expected to run for anywhere between 5 and 6 min on resources with some variation depending on resource capability. A plan file modeling this application as a parameter sweep application using the Nimrod/G parameter specification language is shown in Figure 17.11. The first part defines parameters, and the second part defines the task that needs to be performed for each job. As the parameter `angle_degree` is defined as a range parameter type with values varying from 1 to 165 in step 1, it leads to the creation of 165 jobs with 165 different input parameter values. To execute each job on a Grid resource, the Nimrod/G resource broker, depending on its scheduling strategy, first copies the program executable(s) and necessary data to a Grid node, then executes the program, and finally copies results back to the user home node and stores output with job number as file extension.

17.7.2.3 Scheduling Experiments. The experiments were run twice, once during the Australian peak time, when the US machines were in their off-peak times, and again during the US peak, when the Australian machine was off-peak. The experiments were configured to *minimize the cost*, within a *one-hour deadline*. This requirement instructs the Nimrod/G broker to use the *cost optimization scheduling* algorithm in scheduling jobs for processing on the Grid.

```
#Parameters Declaration
parameter angle_degree integer range from 1 to 165 step 1;
parameter time_base_value integer default 5;

#Task Definition
task main
    #Copy necessary executables depending on node type
    copy calc.$OS node:calc
    #Execute program with parameter values on remote node
    node:execute ./calc $angle_degree $time_base_value
    #Copy results file to use home node with jobname as extension
    copy node:output ./output.$jobname
endtask
```

Figure 17.11 Nimrod/G parameter sweep processing specification.

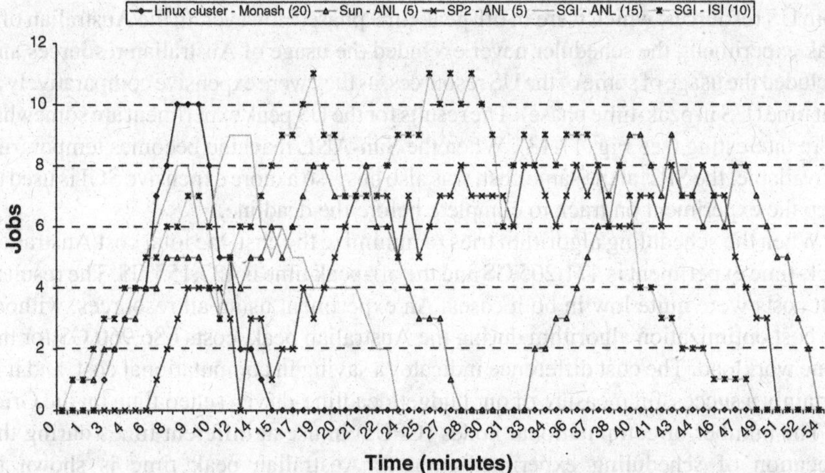

Figure 17.12 Computational scheduling during Australian peak time (US off-peak time).

The number of jobs in execution or queued on resources during the Australian peak and off-peak time scheduling experimentations is shown in Figures 17.12 and 17.13, respectively. The results for the Australian peak experiment show the expected typical results. After an initial calibration phase, the jobs were distributed to the cheapest machines for the remainder of the experiment. This characteristic of the scheduler is clearly visible in both experiments. In the Australian peak experiment, after calibration period, the scheduler excluded the usage of Australian resources as they were expensive and the scheduler predicted that it could still meet the deadline using cheaper resources

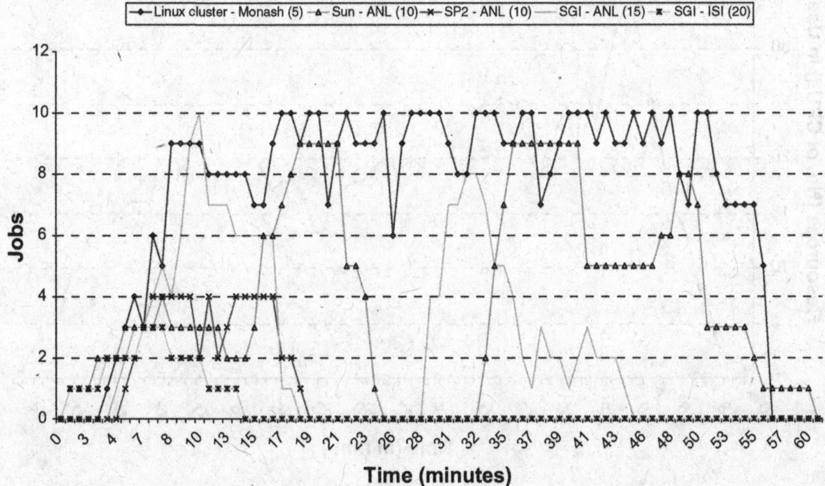

Figure 17.13 Computational scheduling during Australian off-peak time (US peak time).

from US resources, which were in off-peak time phase. However, in the Australian off-peak experiment, the scheduler never excluded the usage of Australian resources and excluded the usage of some of the US resources, as they were expensive comparatively at that time (US in peak-time phase). The results for the US peak experiment are somewhat more interesting (see Fig. 17.13). When the Sun-ANL machine becomes temporarily unavailable, the SP2, at the same cost, was also busy, so a more expensive SGI is used to keep the experiment on track to complete before the deadline.

When the scheduling algorithm tries to minimize the cost, the total cost Australian peak-time experiment is 471,205 G$ and the off-peak time is 427,155 G$. The result is that costs were quite low in both cases. An experiment using all resources, without the cost optimization algorithm during the Australian peak, costs 686,960 G$ for the same workload. The cost difference indicates a saving in computational cost, and it is certainly a successful measure of our budget/deadline-driven scheduling on the Grid.

The number of computational nodes (CPUs) in use at different times during the execution of scheduling experimentation at Australian peak time is shown in Figure 17.14. It can be observed that in the beginning of the experiment (calibration phase), the scheduler had no precise information related to job consumption rate for resources; hence it attempted to use as many resources as possible to ensure that it could meet the deadline. After the calibration phase, the scheduler predicted that it could meet the deadline with fewer resources and stopped using more expensive nodes. However, whenever scheduler senses difficulty in meeting the deadline by using the resources currently in use, it includes additional resources. This process continues until deadline is met and at the same time ensures that the cost of computation is within a given budget.

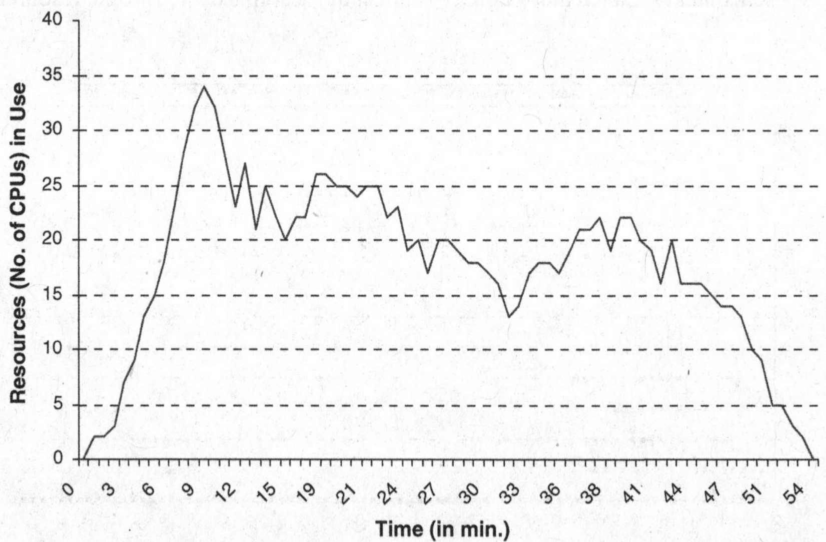

Figure 17.14 Number of resources in use during Australian peak-time scheduling experiment.

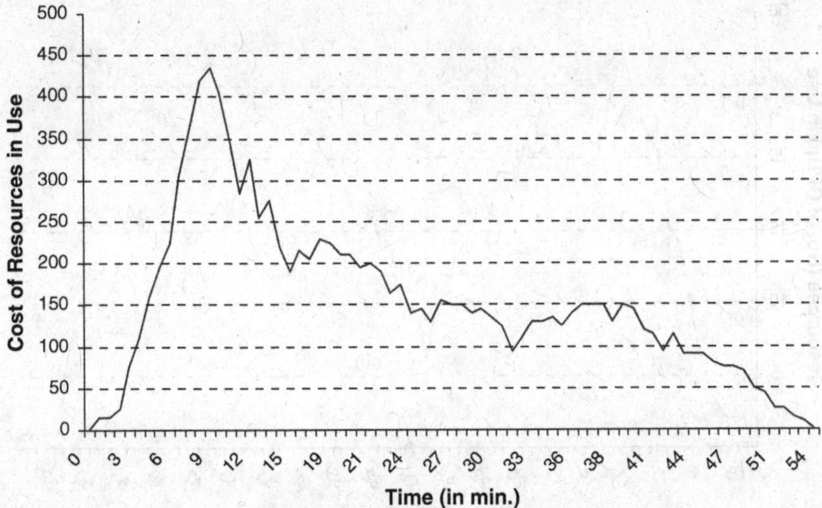

Figure 17.15 Cost of resources in use at Australian peak-time scheduling experiment.

The total cost of resources (sum of the access price for all resources) in use at different times during the execution of scheduling experimentation at Australian peak time is shown in Figure 17.15. It can be observed that the pattern of variation of cost during the calibration phase is similar to that of number of resources in use. However, this is not the same as the experiment progresses, and in fact the cost of resources decreased almost linearly although the number of resources in use did not decline at the same rate. The reason for this behavior is that a large number of resources selected by the scheduler were located in off-peak time zones (i.e., USA was in off-peak time when Australia was in peak hours) as they were less expensive. Another reason is that the number of resources used in these experiments contains more US resources compared to Australian resources.

Similar behavior did not occur in scheduling experiments conducted during Australian off-peak time (see Figs. 17.16 and 17.17). The variation pattern of total number of resources in use and their total cost is similar because the larger numbers of US resources were available cheaply. Although the scheduler has used Australian resources throughout the experiment (see Fig. 17.13), the scheduler had to depend on US resources to ensure that the deadline is met even if resources were expensive.

17.7.3 Cost and Time Optimization Scheduling Using Local and Remote Resources

This experiment demonstrates the use of cheap local resources and expensive remote resources together for processing a parameter sweep application (the same as that used in the previous scheduling experiment) containing 165 CPU-intensive jobs, each running approximately 5 min in duration. We have set the deadline of 2 h (120 mins)

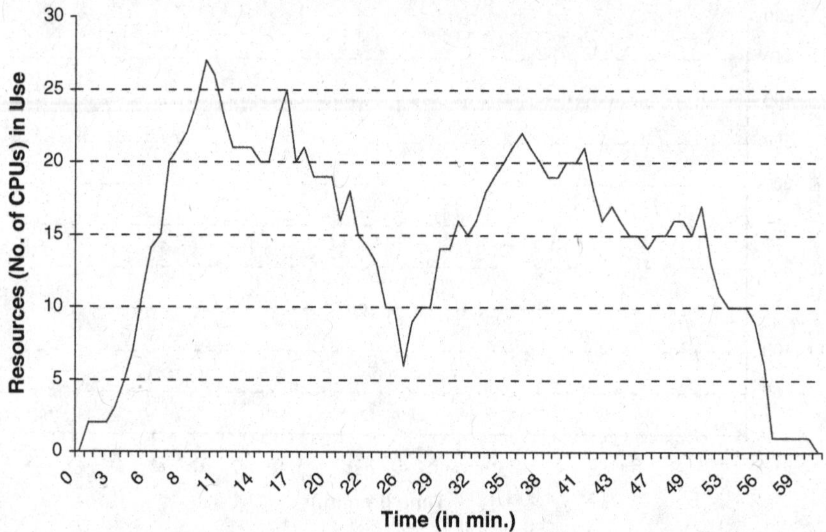

Figure 17.16 Number of resources in use at Australian off-peak time scheduling experiment.

and budget of 396,000 (G$ or tokens) and conducted experiments for two different optimization strategies:

- *Optimize for time*—this strategy produces results as early as possible, but before a deadline and within a budget limit.

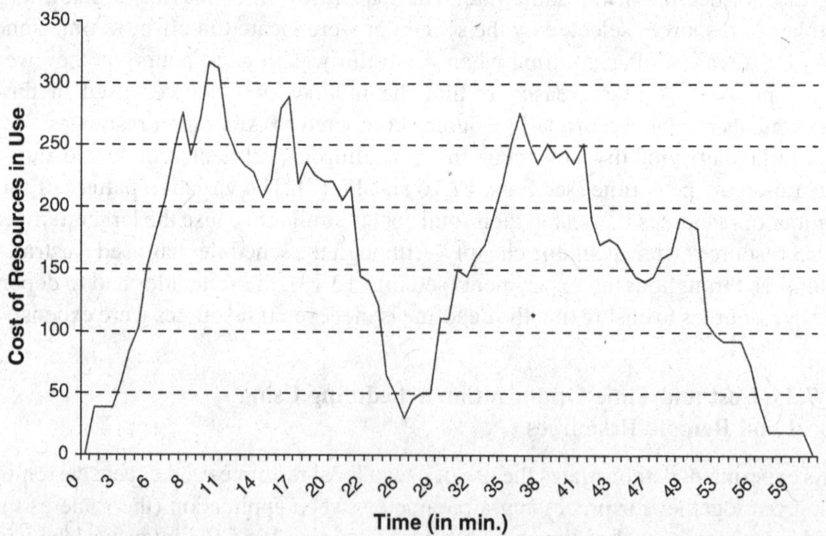

Figure 17.17 Cost of resources in use at Australian off-peak time scheduling experiment.

- *Optimize for cost*—this strategy produces results by deadline, but reduces cost within a budget limit.

In these scheduling experiments, the Nimrod/G resource broker employed the commodity market model for establishing a service access price. The broker established connection with the Grid Trader running on resource providers' machines to obtain service prices at runtime. The broker architecture is generic enough to use any of the protocols discussed by Buyya et al. [21] for negotiating access to resources and choosing appropriate ones. The access price varies for local and remote users; users are encouraged to use local resources since they are available at cheaper price. Depending on the deadline and the specified budget, the broker develops a plan for assigning jobs to resources. While doing so, it does dynamic load profiling to establish the user job consumption rate for each resource. The broker uses this information to adapt itself to the changing resource conditions including failure of resources or jobs on the resource.

We have used a subset of resources of the WWG testbed in these scheduling experiments. Table 17.6 shows resource details such as architecture, location, and

TABLE 17.6 The WWG Testbed Resources Used in Scheduling Experiments, Job Execution, and Costing

Resource Type and Size (Nr. of Nodes)	Organization and Location	Grid Services and Fabric	Price [G$/(CPU:s)]	Jobs Executed on Resources	
				`Time_Opt`	`Cost_Opt`
Linux cluster (60 nodes)	Monash, Australia	Globus, GTS, Condor	2	64	153
Solaris (Ultra-2)	Tokyo Institute of Technology, Japan	Globus, GTS, Fork	3	9	1
Linux PC (Prosecco)	CNUCE, Pisa, Italy	Globus, GTS, Fork	3	7	1
Linux PC (Barbera)	CNUCE, Pisa, Italy	Globus, GTS, Fork	4	6	1
Sun (8 nodes)	ANL, Chicago, USA	Globus, GTS, Fork	7	42	4
SGI (10 nodes)	ISI, Los Angeles, USA	Globus, GTS, Fork	8	37	5
Total experiment cost (G$)				237,000	115,200
Time to complete experiment (min.)				70	119

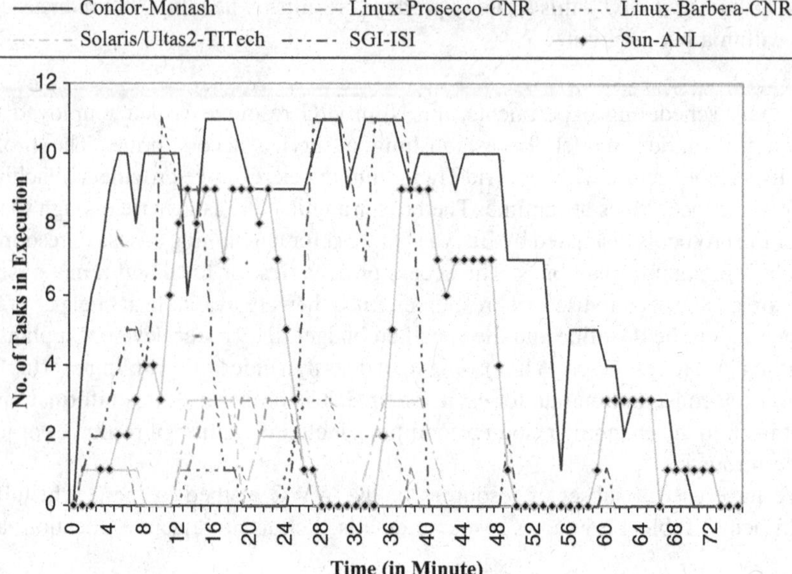

Figure 17.18 Resource selection in deadline and budget constrained time optimization scheduling.

access price along with type of Grid middleware systems used in rendering them Grid-enabled. These are shared resources, and hence they were not fully available to us. The access price indicated in the table is being established dynamically (commodity market model). The access price are artificial; however, they assigned to reflect the offering of differentiated services at different costs as in the real-world marketplace.

The number of jobs in execution on resources (*Y* axis) at different times (*X* axis) during the experimentation is shown in Figures 17.18 and 17.19 for the time and cost optimization scheduling strategies, respectively. In the first (time minimization) experiment, the broker selected resources in such a way that the whole application execution is completed at the earliest time for a given budget. In this experiment, it completed execution of all jobs within 70 min and spent 237,000 G$. In the second experiment (cost minimization), the broker selected cheap resources as much as possible to minimize the execution cost while still trying to meet the deadline (completed in 119 min) and spent 115,200 G$. After the initial *calibration phase*, the jobs were distributed to the cheapest machines for the remainder of the experiment. The processing expense of the time optimization scheduling experiment is much larger than the cost optimization scheduling experiment because of the use of expensive resources to complete the experiment early. The results show that our Grid brokering system can take advantage of economic models and user input parameters to meet their requirements.

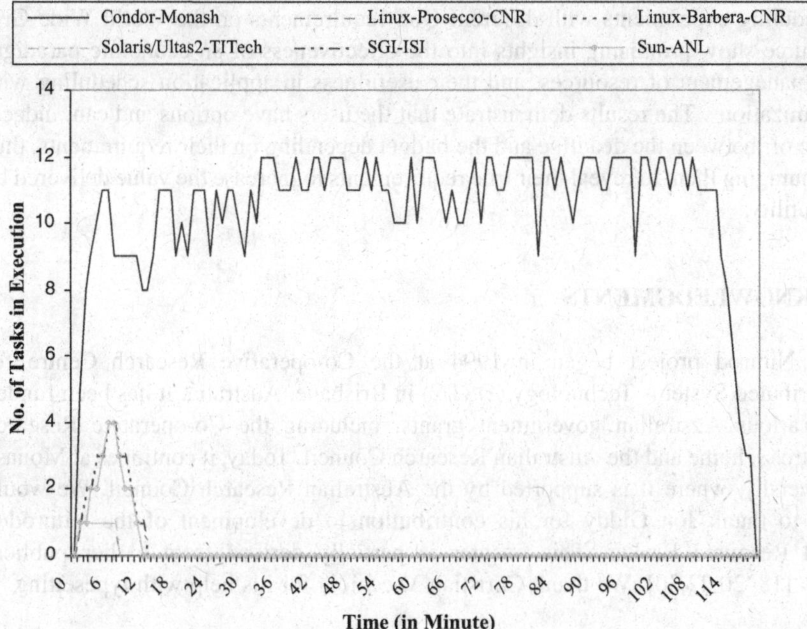

Figure 17.19 Resource selection in deadline/budget-constrained cost optimization scheduling.

17.8 SUMMARY AND COMMENTS

We have discussed the design, development, and experimental evaluation of the Nimrod/G Grid resource broker that supports deadline and budget constrained and quality of service requirements–driven application scheduling on worldwide distributed resources. The broker is able to dynamically adapt itself when there is change in the availability of resources and user QoS requirements during the application execution. It also supports scalable, controllable, measurable, and easily enforceable policies and scheduling algorithms for allocation of resources to user applications. It demonstrates that the computational economy approach for Grid computing provides an effective means for pushing Grids into mainstream computing and enables the creation of a worldwide Grid marketplace.

The Nimrod tools for modeling parametric experiments are mature and in production use for cluster and Grid computing. The Nimrod/G task-farming engine (TFE) services have been used in developing customized clients and applications. An associated dispatcher is capable of deploying computations (jobs) on Grid resources enabled by Globus, Legion, and Condor. The TFE jobs management protocols and services can be used for developing new scheduling policies. We have built a number of market-driven deadline- and budget-constrained scheduling algorithms, namely, time and cost optimizations with deadline and budget constraints. The results of scheduling experiments with different QoS requirements on the World Wide Grid resource show promising insights into the effectiveness of an economic paradigm for management of resources, and their usefulness in application scheduling with optimizations. The results demonstrate that the users have options and can, indeed, trade off between the deadline and the budget depending on their requirements, thus encouraging them to reveal their true requirements to increase the value delivered by the utility.

ACKNOWLEDGMENTS

The Nimrod project began in 1994 at the Co-operative Research Centre for Distributed Systems Technology (DSTC) in Brisbane, Australia. It has been funded by various Australian government grants, including the Co-operative Research Centres scheme and the Australian Research Council. Today, it continues at Monash University, where it is supported by the Australian Research Council. We would like to thank Jon Giddy for his contribution to development of the Nimrod/G Grid Resource Broker. This chapter is partially derived from earlier publications [18–20,22,30]. We thank Christian Vecchiola for his help with typesetting.

REFERENCES

1. B. Chun, *Market-based Cluster Resource Management*, PhD dissertation, Univ. California Berkeley, Oct. 2001.
2. C. Waldspurger, T. Hogg, B. Huberman, J. Kephart, and W. Stornetta, Spawn: A distributed computational economy, *IEEE Transactions on Software Engineering* **18**(2):103–117 (Feb. 1992).
3. D. Abramson, A. Lewis, and T. Peachy, Nimrod/O: A tool for automatic design optimization, *Proc. 4th International Conf. Algorithms & Architectures for Parallel Processing* (ICA3PP 2000), Hong Kong, China, Dec. 2000.
4. D. Abramson, A. Lewis, Peachy, and C. Fletcher, An automatic design optimization tool and its application to computational fluid dynamics, *Proc. Super Computing 2001 Conf.*, Denver, CO, Nov. 2001.
5. D. Abramson, I. Foster, J. Giddy, A. Lewis, R. Sosic, R. Sutherst, and N. White, The Nimrod computational workbench: A case study in desktop metacomputing, *Proc. Australian Computer Science Conf. (ACSC 97),* Macquarie Univ., Sydney, Feb. 1997.
6. D. Abramson, P. Roe, L. Kotler, and D. Mather, ActiveSheets: Super-computing with spreadsheets, *Proc. 2001 High Performance Computing Symp. (HPC'01), Advanced Simulation Technologies Conf.,* April 2001.
7. D. Abramson, R. Sosic, J. Giddy, and B. Hall, Nimrod: A tool for performing parametised simulations using distributed workstations, *Proc. 4th IEEE International Symp. High Performance Distributed Computing*, Virginia, Aug. 1995, IEEE CS Press, 1995.
8. D. Ferguson, C. Nikolaou, J. Sairamesh, and Y. Yemini, Economic models for allocating resources in computer systems, in *Market-Based Control: A Paradigm for Distributed Resource Allocation*, S. H. Clearwater (ed.), World Scientific Press, Singapore, 1996.

9. G. Heiser, F. Lam, and S. Russell, Resource management in the Mungi single-address-space operating system, *Proc. Australasian Computer Science Conf.*, Perth, Australia, Feb. 4–6, 1998, Springer-Verlag, Singapore, 1998.
10. I. Foster and C. Kesselman, Globus: A metacomputing infrastructure toolkit, *International Journal of Supercomputer Applications* **11**(2):115–128 (1997).
11. J. Postel, C. Sunshine, and D. Cohen, The ARPA Internet Protocol, *Computer Networks* **5** (1981).
12. L. Gong, *Project JXTA: A Technology Overview*, Technical Report, Sun Microsystems Inc., April 2001, http://www.jxta.org/project/www/docs/TechOverview.pdf.
13. M. Litzkow, M. Livny, and M. Mutka, Condor—a hunter of idle workstations, *Proc. 8th International Conf. Distributed Computing Systems (ICDCS 1988)*, San Jose, CA, Jan. 1988, IEEE CS Press, 1988.
14. R. Buyya and M. Murshed, GridSim: A toolkit for the modeling and simulation of distributed resource management and scheduling for Grid computing, *Concurrency and Computation: Practice and Experience* **14**(13–15):1175–1220 (Nov.–Dec. 2002).
15. M. Stonebraker, R. Devine, M. Kornacker, W. Litwin, A. Pfeffer, A. Sah, and C. Staelin, An economic paradigm for query processing and data migration in Mariposa, *Proc. 3rd International Conf. Parallel and Distributed Information Systems*, Austin, TX, Los Alamitos, CA, Sept. 28–30, 1994, IEEE Computer Society Press, 1994.
16. Mojo Nation, http://www.mojonation.net/, June 2001.
17. N. Nisan, S. London, O. Regev, and N. Camiel, Globally distributed computation over the Internet: The POPCORN project, *Proc. International Conf. Distributed Computing Systems (ICDCS'98)*, Amsterdam, The Netherlands, May 26–29, 1998, IEEE CS Press, 1998.
18. R. Buyya, D. Abramson, and J. Giddy, A case for economy Grid architecture for service-oriented Grid computing, *Proc. International Parallel and Distributed Processing Symp.: 10th IEEE International Heterogeneous Computing Workshop (HCW 2001)*, San Francisco, CA, April 23, 2001, IEEE CS Press, 2001.
19. R. Buyya, D. Abramson, and J. Giddy, An economy driven resource management architecture for global computational power Grids, *Proc. 2000 International Conf. Parallel and Distributed Processing Techniques and Applications (PDPTA 2000)*, Las Vegas, NV, June 26–29, 2000, CSREA Press, 2000.
20. R. Buyya, D. Abramson, and J. Giddy, Nimrod/G: An architecture for a resource management and scheduling system in a global computational Grid, *Proc. 4th International Conf. High Performance Computing in Asia-Pacific Region (HPC Asia 2000)*, Beijing, China, May 2000, IEEE Computer Society Press.
21. R. Buyya, D. Abramson, J. Giddy, and H. Stockinger, Economic models for resource management and scheduling in Grid computing, *Concurrency and Computation: Practice and Experience* **14**(13–15):1507–1542 (2002).
22. R. Buyya, J. Giddy, and D. Abramson, An evaluation of economy-based resource trading and scheduling on computational power Grids for parameter sweep applications, *Proc. 2nd International Workshop on Active Middleware Services (AMS 2000)*, Kluwer Academic Press, Aug. 1, 2000, Pittsburgh, PA.
23. R. Buyya, The World-Wide Grid (WWG), http://www.buyya.com/ecogrid/wwg/, 1999–2002.
24. S. Bansal and G. Pal, The Web at your (machine's) service, *JavaWorld Magazine* (Sep. 28, 2001), http://www.javaworld.com/javaworld/jw-09-2001/jw-0928-smsservice.html.

25. S. Chapin, J. Karpovich, and A. Grimshaw, The legion resource management system, *Proc. 5th Workshop on Job Scheduling Strategies for Parallel Processing*, San Juan, Puerto Rico, April 16, 1999, Springer-Verlag Press, Germany, 1999.
26. S. Fitzgerald, I. Foster, C. Kesselman, G. von Laszewski, W. Smith, and S. Tuecke, A directory service for configuring high-performance distributed computations, *Proc. 6th IEEE International Symp. High-Performance Distributed Computing (HPDC 1997)*, Portland, OR, Aug. 1997.
27. TurboLinux, Using application programming interface, in *EnFuzion Manual*, 2002, Chapter 9, available at http://www.csse.monash.edu.au/cluster/enFuzion/api.htm.
28. W. T. Sullivan, III, D. Werthimer, S. Bowyer, J. Cobb, D. Gedye, and D. Anderson, A new major SETI project based on Project Serendip data and 100,000 personal computers, *Proc. 5th International Conf. Bioastronomy*, 1997.
29. Y. Amir, B. Awerbuch., A. Barak A., S. Borgstrom, and A. Keren, An opportunity cost approach for job assignment in a scalable computing cluster, *IEEE Transactions on Parallel and Distributed Systems* **11**(7):760–768 (July 2000).
30. R. Buyya, *Economic-Based Distributed Resource Management and Scheduling for Grid Computing*, PhD thesis, Monash Univ., Melbourne, Australia, 2002.
31. D. Abramson, J. Giddy, and L. Kotler, High performance parametric modeling with Nimrod/G: Killer application for the global Grid?, *Proc. 14th International Parallel and Distributed Processing Symp.* Cancun, Mexico, May 2000, pp. 520–528.
32. W. Sudholt, K. Baldridge, D. Abramson, C. Enticott, and S. Garic, Parameter scan of an effective group difference pseudopotential using Grid computing, *New Generation Computing* **22**(2):125–135 (2004).
33. A. Lynch, D. Abramson, K. Beringer, and P. Uotila, Influence of savanna fire on Australian monsoon season precipitation and circulation as simulated using a distributed computing environment, *Geophysical Research Letters* **34**(L20801):1–5 (2007).

18

TECHNIQUES FOR PROVIDING HARD QUALITY-OF-SERVICE GUARANTEES IN JOB SCHEDULING

PAVAN BALAJI, PONNUSWAMY SADAYAPPAN, AND MOHAMMAD ISLAM

18.1 INTRODUCTION

Batch job schedulers are commonly used to schedule parallel jobs at shared-resource supercomputer centers. The typical model for these supercomputer centers is to allocate resources (processors, memory) to a job on submission, if available. If the requested resources are not currently available, the job is queued and scheduled to start at a later time (when the resources become available). The turnaround time or response time of a job is the sum of the time for which it has to wait in the job queue (for resources to be available) and the actual runtime after the job starts executing. Users are typically charged as a function of the total resources used (*resources* × *runtime*).

Together with the standard working model described above, there has also been a lot of more recent interest in hard quality of service (QoS) in job scheduling in terms of guarantees in the job's turnaround time [1–5]. Such QoS capability is useful in several instances. For example, a scientist can submit a job before leaving work in the evening and request a deadline in the job's turnaround time for 8:00 a.m. the next morning; that is, she needs the job to complete and the results to be ready by the time she is back the next morning.

Market-Oriented Grid and Utility Computing Edited by Rajkumar Buyya and Kris Bubendorfer

The overall issue of providing QoS for job scheduling can be viewed in terms of three related aspects, which, however, can be decoupled:

1. *Job Scheduling with Response Time Guarantees.* Providing a scheduler that allows users to specify hard QoS requirements in terms of when they want their job to complete, and enforcing such QoS requirements during job submission; that is, once accepted, the system should guarantee to meet the promised QoS requirement.
2. *Modeling User Tolerance in QoS Requirements.* Several users can tolerate different deadlines for their jobs. For example, a user might want her job to complete by the time she gets back the next morning (8 a.m.). If meeting this deadline is not possible, a lesser desired but acceptable deadline might be after lunch the next day (1 p.m.).
3. *Opportunity Cost of Hard QoS Guarantees on System Resource Usage.* One of the primary issues with providing hard QoS guarantees is that accepting a job requires the resources promised to that job be locked down and not reallocated to some other job. This means that if a user estimates the runtime of the job to be an hour, but the job finishes in 5 mins, the resources might have to be idle for 55 mins. Further, suppose that there are resources available to only accept one job. If a job arrives and offers to pay $ 10, the system might accept it. Two minutes later, if a second job arrives and offers to pay $ 100, this new job cannot be accepted since the first job has already been promised the resources. Thus, by accepting every job, the system is implicitly paying an opportunity cost by tying down the resources for this job.

In this chapter, we discuss each of these three aspects. We first present three different approaches that aim at meeting the first goal of providing response time guarantees and provide comparative studies between these approaches. Next, we model user tolerance in QoS using a bid-butler kind of mechanism; that is, the user specifies by when the job needs to be finished and how much she/he is willing to pay for the additional QoS requirement. The bid-butler (a software agent running on the user system) performs the bids on behalf of the user till a bid is accepted by the system. Finally, we present the drawbacks in hard QoS-based scheduling, primarily the ones caused by opportunity cost. In other words, since the scheduler does not know what kind of jobs will get submitted in future, it has to use some kind of greedy approach to accept submitted jobs. However, if it is too greedy and accepts any submitted job, it might miss out on later arriving more expensive jobs.

18.2 TECHNIQUES FOR HARD QoS GUARANTEES

Most current schemes used in Grid and supercomputing that have been proposed for scheduling independent parallel jobs dealt with maximizing system metrics such as the system utilization and throughput [11,12] and minimizing user metrics such as turnaround time, wait time, and slowdown [19,20]; or both [14,15]. Some other schemes have also looked at prioritizing the jobs according to a number of statically or dynamically determined weights [6]. However, schemes that provide hard QoS guarantees are not as common in practice.

In this section, we present three approaches that provide hard QoS guarantees to users. The first two approaches (modified slack-based approach and modified real-time approach) are variants of previously proposed approaches that have been modified to provide hard QoS guarantees, while the third approach (QoS for parallel job scheduling) is a new algorithm specifically built to provide hard QoS guarantees.

18.2.1 Modified Slack-Based (MSB) Approach

The slack-based (SB) algorithm, proposed by Feitelson [6], is a backfilling algorithm used to improve the system throughput and the user response time. The main idea of the algorithm is to allow a slack or laxity for each job. The scheduler gives each waiting job a precalculated slack, which determines how long it may have to wait before running: "important" jobs will have little slack in comparison with others. When other jobs arrive, this job is allowed to be pushed behind in schedule time as long as its execution is within the initially calculated laxity. The calculation of the initial slack involves cost functions taking into consideration certain priorities associated with the job. This scheme supports both user-selected and administrative priorities, and guarantees a bounded wait time for all jobs.

Compared to the original SB algorithm, MSB (illustrated in Algorithm 18.1) differs in the way the slack is determined for a given job. The original SB algorithm uses weighted user and political priorities to determine the slack. However, to provide hard QoS, this is changed by setting the slack to be

$$\text{Slack} = \text{deadline} - (\text{ arrival time} + \text{runtime})$$

The rest of the algorithm follows the approach taken by the SB algorithm. The jobs present are arranged in an order decided by a heuristic function (such as earliest deadline first, or least laxity first). Once this order is fixed, the new job is inserted in each possible position in this arrangement. Thus, if there are N jobs existing in the schedule, when the new job arrives, $N+1$ different schedules are possible. A predecided cost function is used to evaluate the cost of each of these $N+1$ schedules and the one with the least cost is accepted. We can easily see that MSB is an $O(N)$ algorithm considering the evaluation of the cost function to be a constant cost. In practice, evaluating the cost function of the schedule depends on the number of jobs in the schedule and thus can be a function of N.

The following is a formal pseudocode for this algorithm:

```
function MSB (J, S_org, S_cheap)
  Input: New job J, existing schedule S_org
  Output: Updated schedule S_cheap
  Returns: Whether Job J is accepted or rejected
  cheapPrice ← ∞
  S_cheap ← S_org
  S_new ← S_org
  for each time slot t_s of S_org do
      Remove all waiting jobs from t_s to the end of S_new and
        place them into a Temporary List (TL)
      Schedule the job J in S_new
      Sort the TL using the scheduled time order
      Add each job from TL into the schedule S_new
      price ← Cost(S_new)
      if price < cheapPrice then
          cheapPrice = price
          S_cheap ← S_new
          Update slack of all jobs in S_cheap
    end if
  end for
  if cheapPrice ≠ ∞ then
      return ACCEPTED
  else
    S_cheap ← S_org
    return REJECTED
  end if
end function
```

Algorithm 18.1 Admission control mechanism followed in modified slack-based scheme.

18.2.2 Modified Real-Time (MRT) Approach

For dynamic systems with more than one processor, a polynomial time optimal scheduling algorithm does not exist [7–9]. The real-time algorithm, proposed by Ramamritham et al. [10], is an approach to schedule uniprocessor tasks with hard real-time deadlines on multiprocessor systems. The algorithm tries to meet the specified deadlines for the jobs by using heuristic functions. The tasks are characterized by worst-case computation times, deadlines, and resource requirements. Starting with an empty partial schedule, each step in the search extends the current partial schedule with one of the tasks yet to be scheduled. The heuristic functions used in the algorithm actively direct the search for a feasible schedule; that is, they help choose the task that extends the current partial schedule. Earliest "deadline first" and "least laxity first" are examples of such heuristic functions.

In order to accommodate this algorithm into the domain of scheduling dynamically arriving parallel jobs, two modifications are made to the algorithm. The first one is to allow parallel jobs to be submitted to the algorithm, and the other is to allow dynamically arriving jobs.

The real-time algorithm assumes that the calculation of the heuristic function for scheduling a job into a given partial schedule takes constant time. However, this assumption holds true only for sequential (single processor) jobs. The scenario we are looking at in this chapter relates to parallel jobs, where holes are possible in the partial schedule. In this scenario, such an assumption would not hold true.

```
function MRT(J, S_org, S_new)
    Input: New job J, existing schedule S_org
    Output: Updated schedule S_new
    Returns: Whether Job J is accepted or rejected
    S_new ← S_org
    backTrackCount ← 0
    Remove all waiting jobs from S_new and place them into
        a Temporary List (TL)
    Add the new job J into the TL
    Sort the TL using the appropriate heuristic
        function (e.g. EDF)
    S_new ← Ø
    for each job J_i from TL do
        Determine whether the job J_i is strongly
            feasible in current partial schedule S_new
      if J_i is strongly feasible then
          Add job J_i into S_new
          Remove job J_i from TL
          continue
      else
        Backtrack to the previous partial
        schedule of S_new
        backTrackCount ← backTrackCount + 1
        if backTrackCount > MAX_BACKTRACK then
            S_new ← S_org
            return REJECTED
        else
            continue
        end if
      end if
    end for
    if all jobs are placed in the schedule then
        return ACCEPTED
    else
        return REJECTED
    end if
end function
```

Algorithm 18.2 Admission control mechanism followed by MRT scheme.

The modified real-time algorithm (MRT), as illustrated in Algorithm 18.2, uses the same technique as the real-time algorithm but accommodates parallel jobs as well. When a new job arrives, all the jobs that have not yet started (including the newly arrived job) are sorted using some heuristic function (e.g., earliest deadline first, least laxity first). Each of these jobs is inserted into the schedule in the sorted order. A partial schedule at any point during this algorithm is said to be feasible if every job meets its deadline. A partial schedule is said to be strongly feasible if the following two conditions are met:

- The partial schedule is feasible.
- The partial schedule would remain feasible when extended by any one of the unscheduled jobs.

When the algorithm reaches a point where the partial schedule obtained is not feasible, it backtracks to a previous strongly feasible partial schedule and tries to take a different path. A certain number of backtracks are allowed, after which the scheduler rejects the job.

18.2.3 QoPS Approach

The *Q*o*S* for *p*arallel job *s*cheduling (QoPS) [3] algorithm is a new algorithm that has been designed specifically for the purpose of QoS in job scheduling and hence provides specific optimizations pertaining to this domain. It uses a heuristic approach to find feasible schedules for jobs.

The scheduler ideally considers a system where each job arrives with a corresponding completion time deadline requirement. When each job arrives, it attempts to find a feasible schedule for the newly arrived job. A schedule is said to be feasible if it does not violate the deadline constraint for any job in the schedule, including the newly arrived job. However, it does allow a flexibility of reordering the jobs in any order as long as the resultant schedule remains feasible. Algorithm 18.3 presents the pseudocode for the QoPS scheduling algorithm.

The main difference between the MSB and the QoPS algorithms is the flexibility the QoPS algorithm offers in reordering the jobs that have already been scheduled (but not yet started). For example, suppose that jobs $J_1, J_2, \ldots, J_N$ are currently in the schedule but not yet started. The MSB algorithm specifies an order for the jobs as calculated by some heuristic function (such as least laxity first, earliest deadline first). This ordering of jobs specifies the order in which the jobs have to be considered for scheduling. For the rest of the algorithm, this ordering is fixed. When a new job J_{N+1} arrives, the MSB algorithm tries to fit this new job in the given schedule without any change to the initial ordering of the jobs.

On the other hand, QoPS allows flexibility in the order in which jobs are considered for scheduling. The amount of flexibility offered is determined by the *K-factor* denoted in the pseudocode illustrated by Algorithm 18.3.

```
function QoPS(J, S_org, S_new)
    Input: New job J, existing schedule S_org
    Output: Updated schedule S_new
    Returns: Whether Job J is accepted or rejected
    S_new ← S_org
    for each pos of S_org in position (0, N/2, 3N/4, 7N/8, ...) do
        status ← scheduleAtPos(pos, S_new)
        if status = TRUE then
            return ACCEPTED
        end if
    end for
    S_new ← S_org
    return REJECTED
end function

function scheduleAtPos(J, pos, S_new)
    Input: New job J, position pos, existing schedule
        S_new
    Output: Updated schedule S_new
    Returns: Whether Job J is accepted or rejected
    Remove all waiting jobs from pos to N and place
        them into a Temporary List (TL)
    Add the new job J into TL
    Sort TL using any heuristic function (e.g. EDF)
    ViolationCount ← 0
    for each job J_c in TL do
        Add job J_c into schedule S_new in the earliest
            possible position
        if CompletionTime(Jc) > Deadline(Jc) then
            ViolationCount ← ViolationCount + 1
            if ViolationCount > K-FACTOR then
                return FALSE
            end if
            Failed_pos ← position where violation occurs
            Remove jobs of S_new from position (pos+Failsdpos)/2
                to Failed_pos and add them into TL
            Sort TL again using the same heuristic used.
            Add the failed (critical) job J_c at the top
                of TL to make sure it is scheduled
            first
        end if
    end for
    return TRUE
end function
```

Algorithm 18.3 Admission control mechanism used in QoPS scheme.

When a new job arrives, it is given $\log_2 N$ points in time where its insertion into the schedule is attempted, corresponding to the reserved start times of jobs (0, $N/2$, $3N/4$, ...) respectively, where N is the number of jobs currently in the schedule. The interpretation of these options is as follows. For option 1 (corresponding to job 0), we start by removing all the jobs from the schedule and placing them in a temporary list (TL). We then the sort the TL according to some heuristic function (e.g., least laxity first, earliest deadline first). Finally, we try to place the jobs in the order specified by the TL. For option 2, we do not start with an empty schedule. Instead, we only remove the latter $N/2$ jobs in the original schedule, chosen in scheduled start-time order, place them in the temporary list TL, and sort this temporary list (on the basis of the heuristic function). We then create a reservation for the newly arrived job, and finally generate reservations for the remaining $N/2$ jobs in the order specified by TL. Thus, there would be $\log_2 N$ options of placement.

For each option given to the newly arrived job, the algorithm tries to schedule the jobs according to this temporary ordering. If a job misses its deadline, it is considered as a critical job and is pushed to the head of the list (thus altering the temporary schedule). This altering of the temporary schedule is allowed at most K times; after this the scheduler decides that the new job cannot be scheduled while maintaining the deadline for all of the already accepted jobs and rejects it. This results in a time complexity of $O(K \log N)$ for QoPS.

18.2.4 Comparison of Different Scheduling Algorithms

Figure 18.1 shows the percentage of unadmitted jobs and unadmitted processor seconds (product of the job's runtime and number of processors) for the three schemes (MSB, MRT, QoPS) in the case where all submitted jobs have deadlines associated with them. As shown in the figure, all three schemes perform within 10% of each other, with QoPS performing slightly better in most cases.

Figure 18.2 shows the percentage of unadmitted jobs and unadmitted processor seconds for the three schemes in the case where only 20% of the submitted jobs have

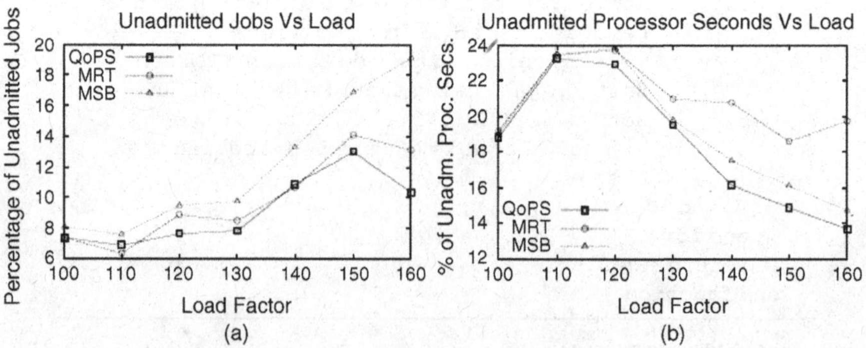

Figure 18.1 Admittance capacity measurements using the Cornell Theory Centre trace when 100% of the jobs have deadlines associated with them: (a) unadmitted jobs; (b) unadmitted processor seconds.

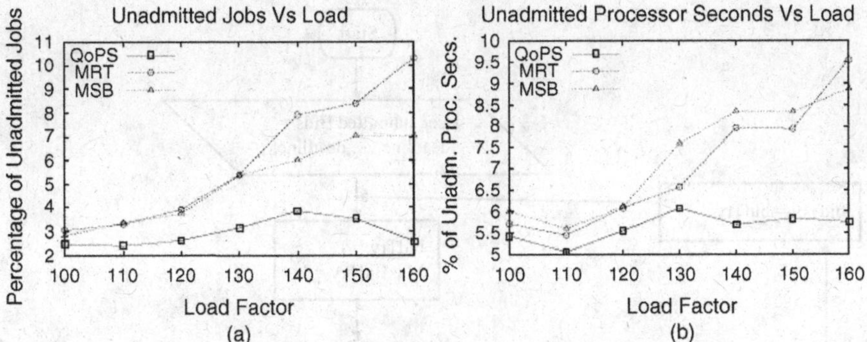

Figure 18.2 Admittance capacity measurements using the Cornell Theory Centre trace when 20% of the jobs have deadlines associated with them: (a) unadmitted jobs; (b) unadmitted processor seconds.

deadlines associated with them. The remaining jobs are given artificially assigned deadlines to avoid starvation. In this case, we notice the same trend, with QoPS performing about 5–10% better than the other schemes.

18.3 BID-BROKER APPROACHES FOR MULTIGRAINED QoS

Hard QoS approaches only provide different ways of scheduling jobs such that the turnaround time requested by the user is guaranteed at admission time. However, often the users have some tolerance to what deadline a system can provide; that is, if one deadline is not accepted by the system, a second deadline, although less desirable, might be acceptable. Thus, it is intuitive to have a bid-broker approach (Fig. 18.3) [4,13,16–18] where the user provides a set of deadlines to a software agent that bids different deadlines and amounts on behalf of the user until a bid is accepted by the system.

While bid-broker approaches provide a lot of flexibility to the user, they have a significant impact on different aspects of the system, such as the percentage of job and processor-seconds that are accepted, and consequently the revenue generated by the supercomputer center. In this section, we present various experiments that demonstrate the impact of such bid-broker approaches on the system resource usage.

18.3.1 Impact of User Tolerance

We first study the behavior of QoPS with respect to admittance capacity, resource charge and QoS charge metrics as a function of user tolerance [illustrated as a tolerance factor (TF)]. We assume that all users have the same amount of tolerance (equal TF for all jobs). The TF parameter shows the general characteristics of the users in this case, for example, a high value of TF would create a scenario where the users are more tolerant, while a low value of TF would create a scenario where the users are less tolerant.

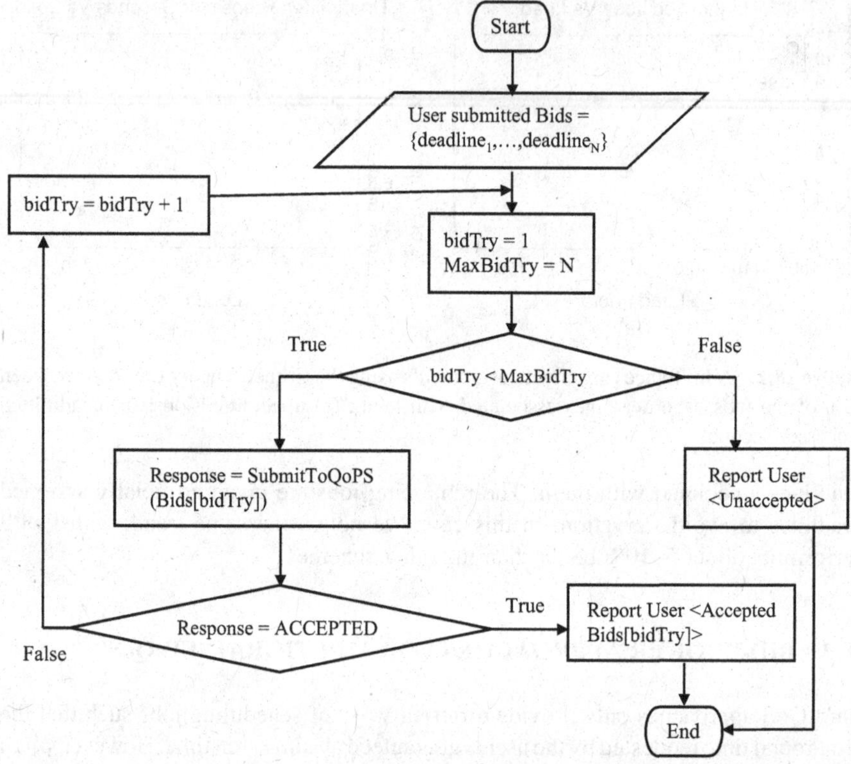

Figure 18.3 High-level bid-broker flowchart.

Figure 18.4 shows the variation in the number of jobs accepted with respect to TF. We can see that fewer jobs are accepted as the TF increases initially; after that the number of accepted jobs increases monotonically and can reach to 100% acceptance for even higher TF. The reason for the initial downward trend is attributed to the acceptance of many heavy jobs (with respect to processor seconds). The same TF

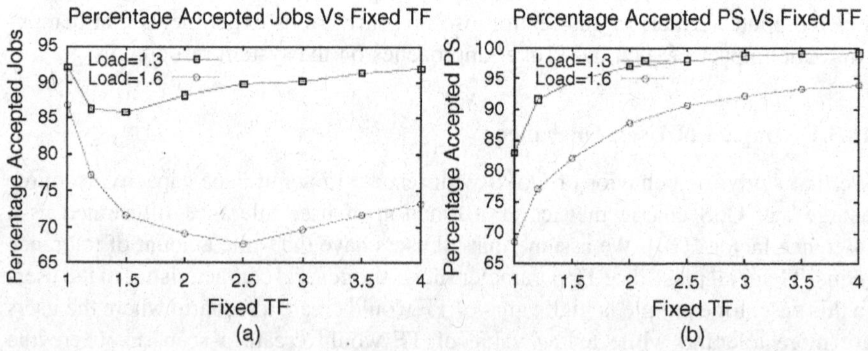

Figure 18.4 Impact of tolerance factor on (a) job admittance capacity; (b) processor seconds acceptance.

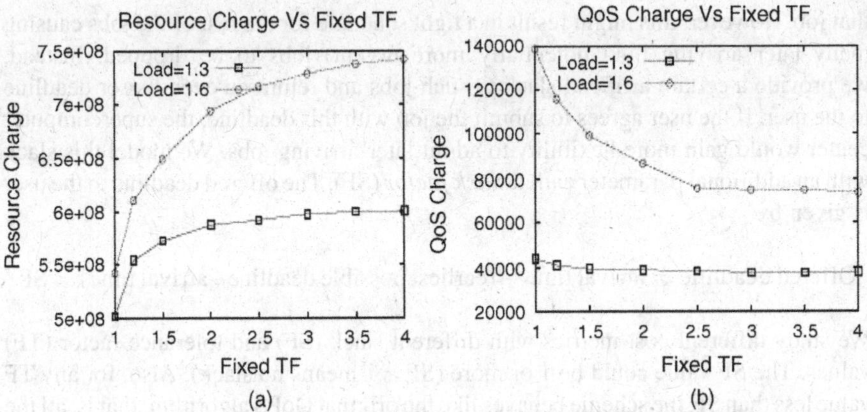

Figure 18.5 Two charges at different loads with stringency factor = 0.2: (a) resource charge; (b) QoS charge.

value would provide a higher absolute tolerance for larger jobs when compared to smaller jobs. When the absolute tolerance was less (for small TF values), earlier arriving small jobs could use up the space in the schedule and force the larger jobs to be dropped. When the tolerance increases, the large jobs can still be accepted because of the additional absolute tolerance available. This, however, would mean that later arriving smaller jobs would be dropped since the large job would use up the space in the schedule. This hypothesis is strengthened by the variation of the accepted processor seconds as shown in Figure 18.4b. As the TF value increases, the overall accepted processor seconds increase. When the TF value becomes sufficiently large, the trend is more intuitive with more and more jobs being accepted.

Figure 18.5b shows the QoS Charge as a function of TF for different loads. This figure shows a counterintuitive result of a monotonic drop in the QoS charge with user tolerance; thus, if the users are more tolerant, the supercomputer center gets lesser profit from the jobs! This is attributed to the per-job profit achieved with increasing user tolerance. With an increase in the TF value, jobs that would have failed in the original no-tolerance scheme are now accepted. Therefore, later-arriving jobs that would have been accepted with the user-requested deadlines cannot be admitted with this deadline. However, because of the increased user tolerance, they are still admitted with a looser deadline; that is, the later-arriving jobs are still admitted, but for a lesser QoS charge. This effect cascades for later-arriving jobs causing an overall decrease in the QoS charge the supercomputer center can get.

We next look at the variation of the resource charge of the system with TF (Fig. 18.5a). The resource charge increases as the TF increases. This is intuitive as the resource charge is directly proportional to the accepted processor seconds.

18.3.2 Impact of Artificial Slack

To handle the loss of revenue due to user tolerance, "artificial slack" is used in schedulers [4]. If we are not able to accept a job with the user requested deadline, providing the best possible deadline would maximize the revenue achievable from that job. However, this might result in a tight schedule for the rest of the jobs causing many later arriving (and potentially more urgent) jobs to be dropped. Instead, we provide a certain artificial slack to such jobs and return an even looser deadline to the user. If the user agrees to submit the job with this deadline, the supercomputer center would gain more flexibility to admit later-arriving jobs. We model this slack with an additional parameter called *slack factor* (SF). The offered deadline to the user is given by

$$\text{Offered deadline} = \text{arrival time} + (\text{earliest possible deadline} - \text{arrival time}) \times \text{SF}$$

We study different cost metrics with different slack (SF) and tolerance factor (TF) values. The SF value could be 1 or more (SF = 1 means no slack). Also, for any TF value less than SF, the scheme behaves like the original QoPS algorithm; that is, all the jobs whose initially requested deadline could not be met are dropped immediately. Further, in general, an increase in the value of SF tends to negate user tolerance; increasing SF tends to be equivalent to decreasing TF. We evaluate the metrics for both moderate load (30% duplicated jobs in a standard Cornell Theory Centre trace) and high load (60% duplicated jobs in a standard Cornell Theory Centre trace).

Figure 18.6a shows the variation of the resource charge with the slack factor (SF) for different tolerance factors. With increasing SF larger jobs have a higher absolute slack value. This allows more small jobs to be admitted by utilizing this slack. The admittance of these small jobs, however, uses up the slack present in the schedule and causes later-arriving larger jobs to be dropped. So, in general, increasing SF has the inverse effect of increasing TF.

Figure 18.6b shows the variation of the QoS charge with the slack factor for different tolerance factors. Again, we see a similar effect as the previous graph—increasing SF has the inverse effect of increasing TF (i.e., QoS charge increases with increasing SF).

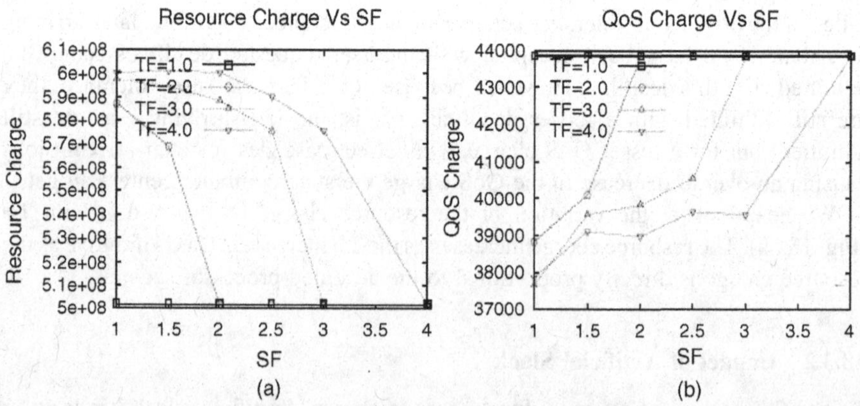

Figure 18.6 Impact of slack factor variation: (a) resource charge; (b) QoS charge.

18.4 OPPORTUNITY COST IN HARD QoS

Hard QoS approaches such as QoPS attempt to accept as many jobs as possible and do not analyze the costs of the jobs that are being submitted. Let us consider a situation where there is a set of jobs that are already running in the system and that there are four idle processors available. Suppose that a four-processor job J_4 arrives, requests for a deadline in 4 h, and offers to pay $100. In this situation, QoPS checks whether it can accommodate this job into the system and accepts it. Immediately after this job is accepted, another four-processor job J_5 arrives, requests the same deadline (4 h) and offers to pay $200 (a higher price than J_4). Since J_4 has already been accepted, the system cannot accept J_5 and hence has to forgo the more profitable job. This demonstrates that it may not always be beneficial to admit all revenue-generating jobs, because of consequent potential future loss of revenue, namely, *opportunity cost*. In other words, while each job pays an explicit price to the system for running it, the system may also be viewed as paying an implicit opportunity cost by accepting the job. Accordingly, accepting the job is profitable only when the job's price is higher than its opportunity cost.

Formally, the *opportunity cost* of a job is defined as the difference between the highest revenue possible for the entire workload, with and without accepting the job. If the opportunity cost of a job is known upfront, the system can easily derive the potential benefit in accepting the job. However, knowing the opportunity cost of a job upfront is impossible. In this section, we present analysis on the impact such opportunity cost can have on the overall revenue of the supercomputer center and predictive techniques that attempt to minimize such effects. Specifically, we first present an extension of QoPS, termed *value-aware QoPS* (VQoPS) [5] that analyzes job prices with various statically assumed opportunity cost values for the jobs. As we will show later in the section, no single statically assumed opportunity cost value does well for all kinds of job mixes.

In the second part of the section, we introduce *dynamic value-aware QoPS* (DVQoPS)—a self-learning variant of VQoPS to analyze past jobs and predict opportunity costs for future jobs [5]. However, if the opportunity cost is decided on the basis of a very long history, the mechanism will lose sensitivity to small pattern changes in the jobs. Similarly, if the opportunity cost decision is based on a very short history, the sample set of previous jobs might be too small and the results obtained might be noisy and unstable. To add to the complexity, the optimal history length to be considered might be different for different days (e.g., there are more jobs when there is a paper deadline, and hence short histories might be sufficient) or for different parts of the day (e.g., there are more jobs in the day time as compared to nights or weekends). Thus, the length of the history needs to be dynamically adapted to balance sensitivity (not too long a history) and stability (not too short a history).

Job Workload Characteristics: Opportunity cost of a job depends on two broad aspects: job characteristics and workload characteristics.

- *Job Characteristics.* Two primary characteristics of a job impact its opportunity cost: job shape and job urgency. *Job shape* determines how many later jobs must be dropped. Large jobs (in processor seconds) typically cause more later-arriving jobs to be dropped; thus, their opportunity cost will likely be high. *Job urgency* determines how stringent the schedule is, and how easy it is to accommodate other jobs. Thus, the opportunity cost of stringent jobs will likely be high.

- *Workload Characteristics.* Three primary workload characteristics impact a job's opportunity cost: offered load, job mix, and job pricing. When there are few jobs in the system (i.e., low offered load), acceptance of a non-urgent job is less likely to prevent admittance of future urgent jobs. Thus, the opportunity cost would typically be low. Similarly, if all jobs had the same urgency and pricing, opportunity cost of every job will be zero, since it is not possible for a later job to have better pricing. But when there are some urgent (and high-paying) and some non-urgent (and low-paying) jobs in the system, opportunity cost is no longer zero; opportunity cost of admitting a nonurgent job increases with the percentage of urgent high-paying jobs since there is a high probability that its admittance could prevent admission of a future high-paying job. Finally, the higher the relative premium paid by urgent jobs compared to non-urgent jobs, the greater the cost of losing an urgent job, and greater the opportunity cost of non-urgent jobs.

18.4.1 Value-Aware QoPS (VQoPS)

Quality of service for parallel job scheduling does not differentiate between jobs according to their price. However, in an environment that allows users to offer price on the basis of responsiveness, some jobs will offer more revenue than others. Similarly, some jobs will have tighter deadlines than others. For an algorithm that is expected to improve the overall revenue of the system, the following two properties are desirable:

- During backfilling, it should reorder the job queue so as to give higher priority for more urgent jobs and attempt to reduce their turnaround time, thus increasing revenue.
- It should maximize overall system revenue during job acceptance by considering both the explicit revenue benefit and the implicit loss of opportunity for the system.

Value-aware QoPS (VQoPS) utilizes some of the characteristics of the job (job shape), to identify its opportunity cost. It uses a static system parameter [opportunity cost (OC) factor], assumes the opportunity cost of the job to be OC factor × job size and analyzes the impact of different OC Factors on system revenue. Figure 18.7 shows a high-level VQoPS flowchart. VQoPS utilizes QoPS as a pluggable module to verify when a new job can be accepted. Since QoPS just provides a recommendation on whether a job should be accepted or rejected, VQoPS adapts it to instead provide the list of all the acceptable schedules that it finds. VQoPS weighs the statically assumed opportunity cost of the new job with its price and decides whether the job should be accepted. In particular, if the revenue gain obtainable can offset the opportunity cost,

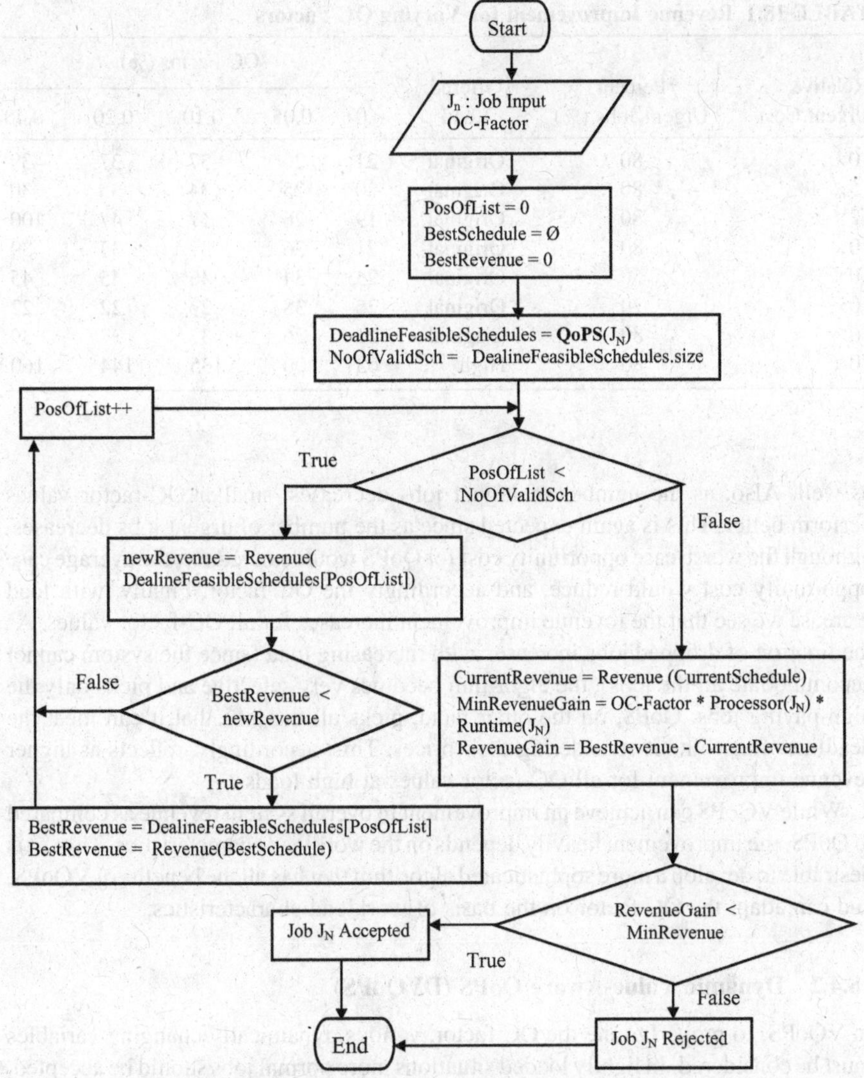

Figure 18.7 VQoPS algorithm flowchart.

VQoPS accepts the job. It is worthy to note that the OC-factor input in VQoPS is constant (static) throughout the job processing and is expected to be defined by an administrator as a system parameter. The time complexity of our approach for N jobs is $(K{\cdot}N^2{\cdot}\log(N))$, where K specifies maximum number of violations allowed in QoPS.

As we can see in Table 18.1, as the relative cost of the urgent jobs decreases, we see that the smaller OC-factor values perform better. This is expected, since the opportunity cost of turning away a future urgent job decreases as the cost of the urgent job decreases. Accordingly, the OC factor providing the best performance decreases

TABLE 18.1 Revenue Improvement for Varying OC Factors

Relative Urgent Cost	Percent Urgent Jobs (%)	Offered Load	OC Factor (%) 0.0	0.05	0.10	0.20	0.40
10×	80	Original	21	26	37	37	39
5×	80	Original	20	25	34	35	30
2×	80	Original	19	26	27	47	100
10×	80	Original	21	26	37	37	39
10×	50	Original	23	34	46	45	45
10×	20	Original	26	38	22	22	22
10×	80	Original	21	26	37	37	39
10×	80	High	63	90	135	144	160

as well. Also, as the number of urgent jobs decreases, smaller OC-factor values perform better. This is again expected since as the number of urgent jobs decreases, although the worst-case opportunity cost for QoPS would not reduce, the average case opportunity cost would reduce, and accordingly the OC factor. Finally, with load increase we see that the revenue improvement increases for all OC-factor values. As the fraction of dropped jobs increases with increasing load (since the system cannot accommodate all the jobs), the algorithm becomes very selective and picks only the high-paying jobs. QoPS, on the other hand, picks all the jobs that it can meet the deadlines for, without considering their prices. This, accordingly, reflects as higher revenue improvement for all OC-factor values at high loads.

While VQoPS can achieve an improvement in overall system revenue as compared to QoPS, the improvement heavily depends on the workload characteristics. Thus, it is desirable to develop a more sophisticated algorithm that has all the benefits of VQoPS, and can adapt the OC factor on the basis of workload characteristics.

18.4.2 Dynamic Value-Aware QoPS (DVQoPS)

In VQoPS, to properly tune the OC factor, various dynamically changing variables must be considered. In lightly loaded situations more normal jobs should be accepted, and a lower OC factor should be used. As the load increases, the OC factor should be increased. If the expected price difference between urgent and nonurgent jobs is small, the scheduler should be more aggressive and accept cheaper jobs. As the expected revenue difference increases, the OC factor should be increased to be more selective in jobs accepted. Finally, as the percent of urgent or expensive jobs increases, the OC factor should also increase. When there are only a few urgent jobs, it is not desirable to reject a large number of normal jobs waiting for an urgent job to arrive. However, as it becomes more likely an urgent job will arrive in the near future, the OC factor should increase. It is very difficult to manually account for these considerations and their interactions, especially as they change over time. Thus, it is desirable for the scheduler to automatically generate and adjust the OC factor.

Dynamic VQoPS [5] aims at achieving this goal by performing a number of *what-if* simulations over a limited backward window in time, called the *rollback window*. The idea is to periodically adjust the OC factor by looking backward and performing simulations to estimate the revenue that would have been realized for various choices of OC factors. Such simulation is feasible since the history of arrived jobs (accepted and rejected jobs) is available at any time. For each choice of OC factor, it utilizes the revenue of each job accepted by the simulated schedule, and thereby estimates the total revenue. The OC factor giving the best overall revenue over the window is chosen for immediate future use (until the next OC factor change event).

The basic premise of the adaptive OC-factor selection procedure is that the best OC factor depends on time-varying workload characteristics. If DVQoPS is to be effective in adapting to such variations, clearly the rollback window must not be too large, such as one month, because the time variance in load will be averaged out over the long rollback window. At the other extreme, if the rollback window is very small, the results of the what-if simulations may be extremely sensitive and not robust.

18.4.2.1 Balancing Sensitivity and Stability in DVQoPS. The choice of rollback window involves a judicious balance between *sensitivity* and *stability*. The rollback window should be short enough to be sensitive to changes in workload characteristics (e.g., load–job mix). Similarly, the rollback window should not be so short that specific jobs affect the best what-if OC factor, and rather be stable with respect to identifying aggregate characteristics of the jobs in the window.

To assess the effect of the rollback window on trace variation, the average offered load is computed over segments of duration equal to the rollback window, and the variance of these averages computed. At one extreme, if the rollback window size is the entire trace duration, the variance is zero since a single average load is computed. At the other extreme, when the rollback window is minimized, the variance of the average loads is maximized. As the rollback window size increases, the load variance is expected to decrease.

To understand the impact of rollback window on stability of OC-factor choice, consider the following example. Suppose that a set of N consecutively arriving jobs were considered for the what-if simulations in a rollback window, and the best OC-factor choice determined. Let us then slightly change the front end of the window to exclude the latest of these N jobs, but move back the rear end of the rollback window to include the last arriving job outside the currently chosen window. If the best choice of OC factor for the two rollback windows is very different, it implies that the choice procedure is very unstable.

Table 18.2 shows the impact of rollback window choice on the variance of OC-factor choice for adjacent window groups, variance of the average offered load and overall revenue. By varying the length of the rollback window from 1 to 128 h, the revenue varies from 414M (million) units to 716M units. That is, rollback window size has a large impact on the overall revenue. The second column of the table shows the average of the variance of each set of 5 consecutive OC-factor choices. With a small rollback window, a small change in the considered jobs will result in a very different OC factor. This reflects as a higher average variance for the OC factor.

TABLE 18.2 Impact of Rollback Window Size

Rollback Window Size	Avgerage OC Factor Variance (* 10^{-5})	Load Variance	Revenue
1	3.15	10.60	473,631,718
4	6.18	2.89	508,341,077
16	7.84	0.62	555,062,813
32	2.99	0.34	692,266,945
48	1.36	0.24	715,606,095
64	1.03	0.17	715,733,110
128	1.13	0.04	701,476,009

The third column shows the variance of the average offered load over the window size. As the variance in average offered load decreases, important variations in the load are being missed and the historical simulation will not be able to *see* the variations. The rollback window size needs to be large enough to have a low average OC-factor variance (so the historical OC factor has meaning), but small enough to capture significant workload differences. Therefore, each scenario may require a different rollback window size that may vary over time.

Thus, a max rollback window is used to dynamically vary the rollback window size. Every maximum rollback window hours the scheduler runs historical simulations (using rollback window sizes of 1 h, 2 h, 4 h, 8 h, 16 h, 32 h, 64 h) to determine what rollback window would have yielded the best revenue over the last maximum rollback window hours and uses it for the next maximum rollback window hours.

Dynamic VQoPS asynchronously evaluates the rollback interval and OC factor after every fixed interval (Fig. 18.8a). Figure 18.8b demonstrates the basic steps used to determine the best rollback interval. This is used in Figure 18.8c when evaluating the best OC factor. For each candidate rollback interval, DVQoPS runs the simulation starting *candidate rollback interval* hours in the past. The *rollback interval* is set to the candidate rollback interval that would have produced the best revenue. This best rollback interval is used for the next maximum rollback window hours. The OC factor is set by running *what-if* simulations for different values of candidate OC factors. The current OC factor is set to the candidate OC factor that yields the maximum revenue. DVQoPS uses the new OC-Factor for the next rollback window hours.

Since DVQoPS dynamically determines the best choices from a set of T OC factors and R rollback windows, its time complexity would increase to $\Theta(T \cdot R \cdot K \cdot N^2 \cdot \log N)$. While the time complexity of the scheme seems to be high, in practice experimentation has shown that the scheduling event takes an average of less than one second for each job. Given that job arrival times are typically in the order of several minutes in most supercomputer centers, this is not a concern.

18.4.3 Performance Analysis of DVQoPS

Figure 18.9 illustrates the percentage revenue improvement (compared to QoPS) for VQoPS (with different static OC factors) and DVQoPS. VQoPS achieves about

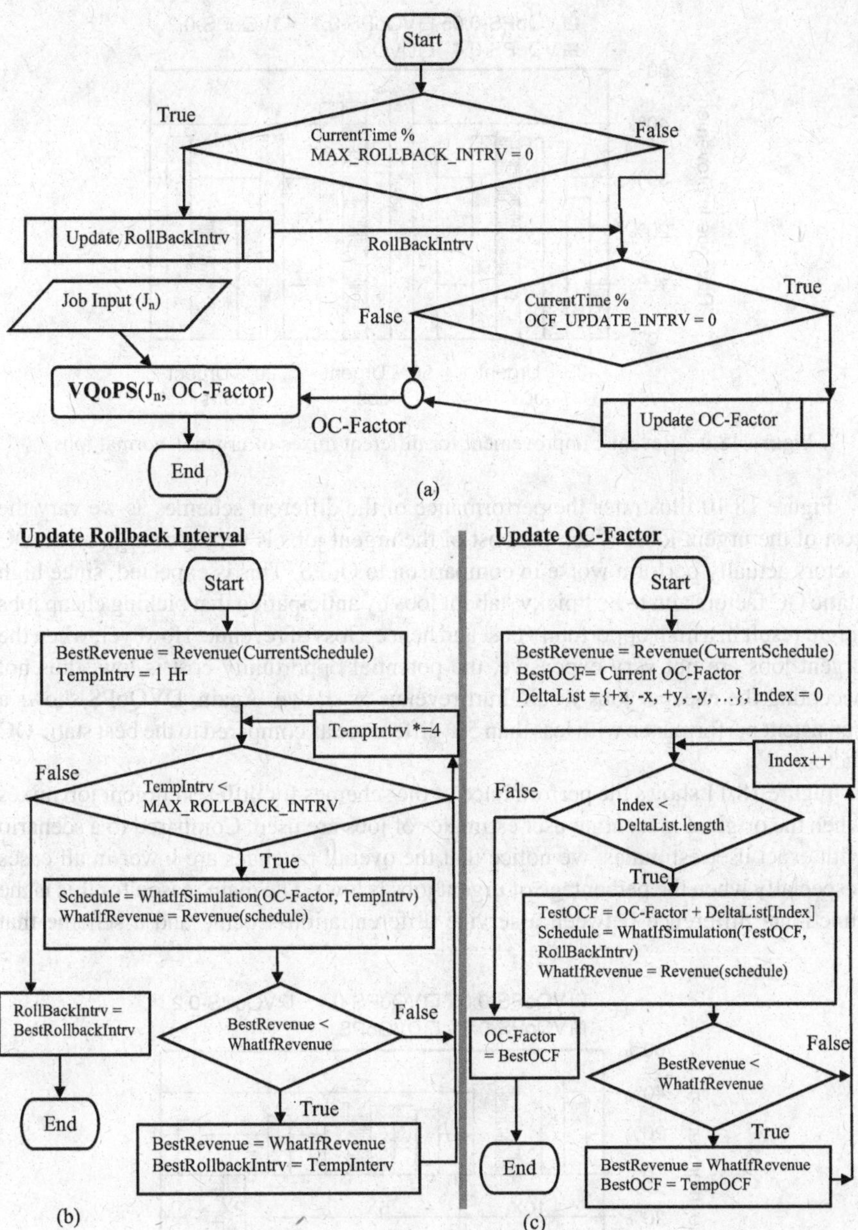

Figure 18.8 DVQoPS algorithm flowchart.

20–45% improvement with different OC factors performing the best for different workload characteristics (i.e., percentage of urgent jobs)—there is no consistently superior OC-factor value. DVQoPS, on the other hand, consistently achieves within 5% of the best VQoPS implementation for all workloads.

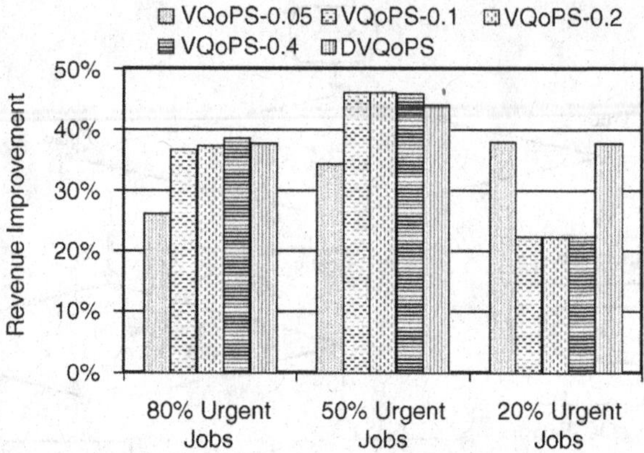

Figure 18.9 Revenue improvement for different mixes of urgent—normal jobs.

Figure 18.10 illustrates the performance of the different schemes as we vary the cost of the urgent jobs. When the cost of the urgent jobs is very low, high static OC factors actually perform worse in comparison to QoPS. This is expected, since high static OC factors aim to be "picky" about jobs by anticipating that picking cheap jobs might result in a high opportunity cost and hence a loss of revenue. However, when the urgent jobs are not very expensive, the potential opportunity cost is low; thus not accepting the cheaper jobs would hurt revenue as shown. Again, DVQoPS shows a consistent performance with less than 5% difference as compared to the best static OC factor.

Figure 18.11 shows the performance of the schemes for different urgent job mixes when the original inaccurate user estimates of jobs are used. Compared to a scenario with exact user estimates, we notice that the overall revenues are lower in all cases (especially when the percentage of urgent jobs is low). The main reason for this is the functional difference between a service differentiation scheme and a scheme that

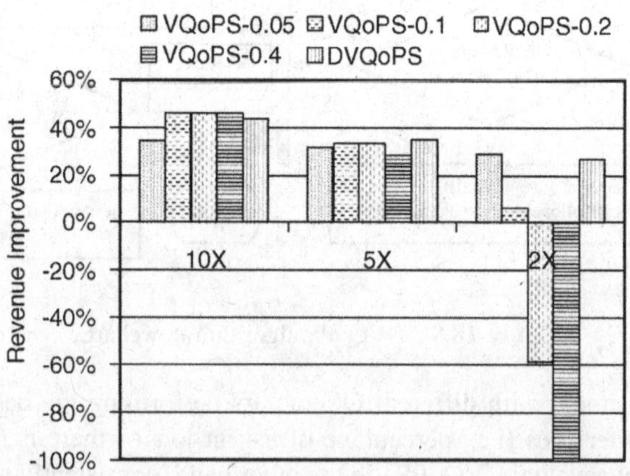

Figure 18.10 Revenue improvement for different relative urgencies of urgent—normal jobs.

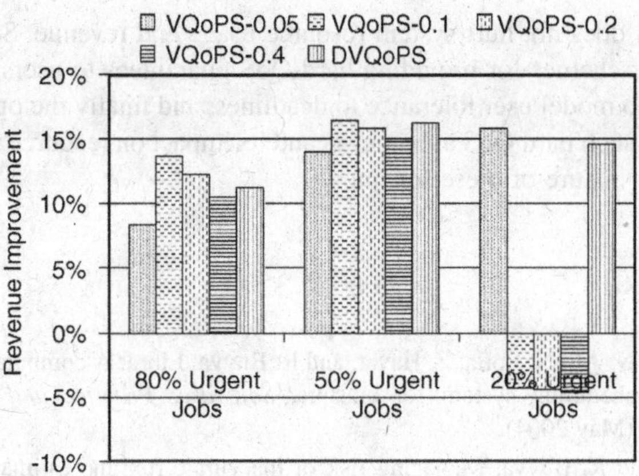

Figure 18.11 Revenue improvement for different job mixes of urgent—normal jobs where job's runtime is inaccurately estimated.

maintains deadline guarantees. Specifically, a scheme that maintains deadline guarantees has to be conservative with respect to its estimates about a job's runtime. For example, if a one-minute job estimates its runtime as one hour, the scheme has to assume that it is going to run for the entire hour and find a feasible schedule before accepting the job. Because of this conservative nature of deadline guarantee schemes, the number of accepted jobs is much less than what the system could potentially accept. Further, for all the accepted jobs, if most jobs terminate early and thus pay the maximum amount that they had promised, no real differentiation can be achieved for these jobs. Only for the jobs that are accepted and have to wait in the queue, can we provide efficient mechanisms to improve the overall revenue of the system. Since, with inaccurate estimates, such jobs are fewer, we see that the overall revenue is less as well. In general, with inexact user estimates, it may appear that little profit can be made, but because jobs complete early, running jobs earlier can actually make more profit and the effect of the opportunity cost is reduced. Therefore, it is often better to be more lax with the OC factor and accept jobs that appear to only modestly increase revenue.

Also, for low percent of urgent jobs, high OC-factor values actually perform worse than QoPS. The reason for this is, when the static OC factor is high, VQoPS rejects all the normal jobs; since the number of urgent jobs is very low, the system is left underutilized as compared to schemes with lower static OC factor values. This reflects in lower revenue than even basic QoPS in some cases.

18.5 SUMMARY

There has been a growing amount of interest in providing hard QoS guarantees for users in job scheduling, in terms of job completion time. In this chapter, we discussed different techniques that are used within this realm to allow flexibility to the user in such a way that does not hurt system resource usage and revenue. Specifically, we discussed three schemes for providing hard QoS guarantees to users, extensions to these schemes to model user tolerance to deadlines, and finally the opportunity cost associated with such hard QoS approaches and its impact on resource wastage due to the conservative nature of these schemes.

REFERENCES

1. J. Sherwani, N. Ali, N. Lotia, Z. Hayat, and R. Buyya, Libra: A computational economy based job scheduling system for clusters, *Software: Practice and Experience* **34** (6):573–590 (May 2004).
2. C. S. Yeo and R. Buyya, Managing risk of inaccurate runtime estimates for deadline constrained job admission control in clusters, *Proc. 35th International Conf. Parallel Processing*, Columbus, OH, Aug. 14–18, 2006.
3. M. Islam, P. Balaji, P. Sadayappan, D. K. Panda, QoPS: A QoS based scheme for parallel job scheduling, *Job Scheduling Strategies for Parallel Processing workshop* (JSSPP) [held in conjunction with *IEEE International Symp. High Performance Distributed Computing (HPDC)]*, Seattle, WA, June 24, 2003.
4. M. Islam, P. Balaji, P. Sadayappan, D. K. Panda, Towards provision of quality of service guarantees in job scheduling, *Proc. 6th IEEE International Conf. Cluster Computing*, San Diego, CA, Sept. 20–23, 2004.
5. M. Islam, P. Balaji, G. Sabin, P. Sadayappan, Analyzing and minimizing the impact of opportunity cost in QoS-aware job scheduling, *Proc. 36th International Conf. Parallel Processing*, XiAn, China, Sept. 10–14 2007.
6. D. Talby and D. G. Feitelson, Supporting priorities and improving utilization of the IBM SP2 scheduler using slack based backfilling, *Proc. 13th International Parallel Processing Symp.*, 1999, pp. 513–517.
7. A. K. Mok, The design of real-time programming systems based on process models, *Proc. IEEE Real Time Systems Symp.*, Dec. 1984, pp. 5–16.
8. A. K. Mok, *Fundamental Design Problems of Distributed Systems for the Hard Real-Time Environment*, Massachussetts Institute of Technology (MIT), Cambridge, MA, 1983.
9. A. K. Mok and M. L. Dertouzos, Multi-processor scheduling in a hard real-time environment, *Proc. Texas Conf. Computing Systems*, 1978.
10. K. Ramamritham, J. A. Stankovic, and P. Shiah, Efficient scheduling algorithms for real-time multiprocessor systems, *IEEE Transactions on Parallel and Distributed Systems*, 1:184–194 (April 1990).
11. S. -H. Chiang and M. K. Vernon, Production job scheduling for parallel shared memory systems, *Proc. 15th International Parallel and Distributed Processing Symp.*, CA, April 2001.
12. D. Feitelson, L. Rudolph, and U. Schwiegelshohn, Parallel job scheduling—a status report, *Proc. 10th Workshop on Job Scheduling Strategies for Parallel Processing*, New York, June 2004.
13. A. Byde, M. Salle, and C. Bartolini, *Market-Based Resource Allocation for Utility Data Centers*, Technical Report, HP Laboratories, Bristol, 2003.

14. R. Kettimuthu, V. Subramani, S. Srinivasan, T. Gopalasamy, D. K. Panda, and P. Sadayappan, Selective preemption strategies for parallel job scheduling, *Proc. 31st International Conf. Parallel Processing*, Vancouver, BC, Canada, Aug. 18–21, 2002.
15. B. Jackson, B. Haymore, J. Facelli, and Q. O. Snell, Improving cluster utilization through set based allocation policies, *Proc. 2001 International Conf. Parallel Processing Workshops*, 2001, pp. 355–360.
16. B. Chun and D. Culler, User-centric performance analysis of market-based cluster batch schedulers, *Proc. 2nd IEEE International Symp. Cluster Computing and the Grid*, 2002.
17. D. Irwin, L. Grit, and J. Chase, Balancing risk and reward in a market-based task service, *Proc. 13th IEEE International Symp. High-Performance Distributed Computing*, Honolulu, HI, June 4–6, 2004.
18. C. S. Yeo and R. Buyya, Pricing for utility-driven resource management and allocation in clusters, *International Journal of High Performance Computing Applications* **21**(4):405–418 (Nov. 2007).
19. P. Keleher, D. Zotkin, and D. Perkovic, Attacking the bottlenecks in backfilling schedulers, *Cluster Computing: The Journal of Networks, Software Tools and Applications* **3**:245–254 (March 2000).
20. A. W. Mualem and D. G. Feitelson, Utilization, predictability, workloads and user estimated runtime estimates in scheduling the IBM SP2 with backfilling, *IEEE Transactions on Parallel and Distributed Systems* 529–543 (June 2001).

19

DEADLINE/BUDGET-BASED SCHEDULING OF WORKFLOWS ON UTILITY GRIDS

JIA YU, KOTAGIRI RAMAMOHANARAO, AND RAJKUMAR BUYYA

Grid technologies provide the basis for creating a service-oriented paradigm that enables a new way of service provisioning based on utility computing models. For typical utility computing-based services, users are charged for consuming services on the basis of their usage and QoS level required. Therefore, while scheduling workflows on utility Grids, service price must be considered while optimizing the execution performance.

In this chapter, the characteristics of utility Grids and the corresponding scheduling problems are discussed, followed by descriptions of two scheduling heuristics based on two QoS constraints: deadline and budget. Two different workflow structures and experiment settings are also presented for evaluation of the proposed scheduling heuristics.

19.1 INTRODUCTION

Utility computing [19] has emerged as a new service provisioning model [6] and is capable of supporting diverse computing services such as servers, storage, network, and applications for e-business and e-science over a global network. For utility computing-based services, users consume required services, and pay only for what they use. With economic incentive, utility computing encourages organizations to

Market-Oriented Grid and Utility Computing Edited by Rajkumar Buyya and Kris Bubendorfer

TABLE 19.1 Community Grids versus Utility Grids

Attributes	Community Grids	Utility Grids
Availability	Best effort	Advanced reservation
QoS	Best effort	Contract/service-level Agreement (SLA)
Pricing	Not considered or free access	Usage, QoS level, market supply and demand

offer their specialized applications and other computing utilities as services so that other individuals/organizations can access these resources remotely. Therefore, it facilitates individuals/organizations to develop their own core activities without maintaining and developing fundamental computing infrastructure. In the more recent past, providing utility computing services has been reinforced by service-oriented Grid computing, which creates an infrastructure for enabling users to consume services transparently over a secure, shared, scalable, sustainable, and standard worldwide network environment.

Table 19.1 shows different aspects between community Grids and utility Grids in terms of availability, quality of services (QoS), and pricing. In utility Grids, users can make a reservation with a service provider in advance to ensure service availability, and users can also negotiate service level agreements with service providers for the required QoS. Compared with utility Grids, service availability and QoS in community Grids may not be guaranteed. However, community Grids provide access based on mutual agreement driven by partnership (LHCGrid [23]) or free access (e.g., SETI@Home [24]), whereas in utility Grids users need to pay for service access. In general, the service pricing in utility Grids is based on the QoS level expected by users and market supply and demand for services.

Typically, service providers charge higher prices for higher QoS. Therefore users do not always need to complete workflows earlier than they require. They sometimes prefer to use cheaper services with a lower QoS that is sufficient to meet their requirements. Given this motivation, cost-based workflow scheduling is developed to schedule workflow tasks on utility Grids according to users' QoS constraints such as deadline and budget.

19.2 GRID WORKFLOW MANAGEMENT SYSTEM

Scientific communities such as high-energy physics, gravitational-wave physics, geophysics, astronomy, and bioinformatics, are utilizing Grids to share, manage, and process large datasets [18]. In order to support complex scientific experiments, distributed resources such as computational devices, data, applications, and scientific instruments need to be orchestrated while managing the application operations within Grid environments [13]. A workflow expresses an automation of procedures wherein files and data are passed between procedures applications according to a defined set of rules, to achieve an overall goal [10]. A workflow management system defines, manages, and executes workflows on computing resources. The use of the workflow paradigm for application composition on Grids offers several advantages [17], such as

- Ability to build dynamic applications and orchestrate the use of distributed resources
- Utilization of resources that are located in a suitable domain to increase throughput or reduce execution costs
- Execution spanning multiple administrative domains to obtain specific processing capabilities
- Integration of multiple teams involved in managing different parts of the experiment workflow—thus promoting interorganizational collaborations

Realizing workflow management for Grid computing requires a number of challenges to be overcome. They include workflow application modeling, workflow scheduling, resource discovery, information services, data management, and fault management. However, from the users' perspective, two important barriers that need to be overcome are (1) the complexity of developing and deploying workflow applications and (2) their scheduling on heterogeneous and distributed resources to enhance the utility of resources and meet user quality-of-service (QoS) demands.

19.3 WORKFLOW SCHEDULING

Workflow scheduling is one of the key issues in the management of workflow execution. Scheduling is a process that maps and manages execution of interdependent tasks on distributed resources. It introduces allocating suitable resources to workflow tasks so that the execution can be completed to satisfy objective functions specified by users. Proper scheduling can have a significant impact on the performance of the system. In general, the problem of mapping tasks on distributed resources belongs to a class of problems known as "NP-hard problems" [8]. For such problems, no known algorithms are able to generate the optimal solution within polynomial time. Even though the workflow scheduling problem can be solved by using exhaustive search, the time taken for generating the solution is very high. Scheduling decisions must be made in the shortest time possible in Grid environments, because there are many users competing for resources, so timeslots desired by one user could be taken by another user at any moment.

A number of *best-effort* scheduling heuristics [2,12,21] such as min–min (minimum–minimum) and heterogeneous earliest finish time (HEFT) have been developed and applied to schedule Grid workflows. These best-effort scheduling algorithms attempt to complete execution within the shortest time possible. They neither have any provision for users to specify their QoS requirements nor any specific support to meet them. However, many workflow applications in both scientific and business domains require some certain assurance of QoS (see Fig. 19.1). For example, a workflow application for maxillofacial surgery planning [10] needs results to be delivered before a certain time. For these applications, the workflow scheduling applied should be able

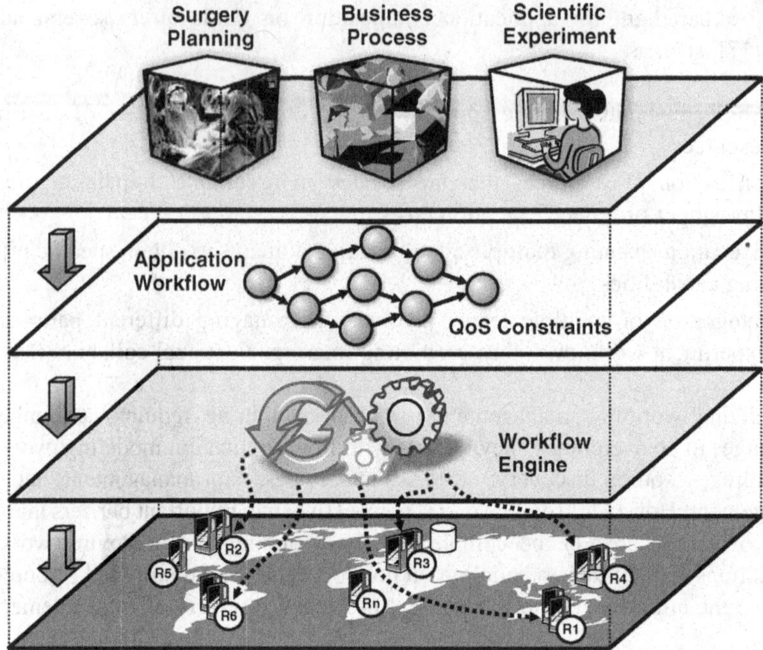

Figure 19.1 A high-level view of a Grid workflow execution environment.

to analyze users' QoS requirements and map workflow tasks onto suitable resources such that the workflow execution can be completed to satisfy their requirements.

Several new challenges are presented while scheduling workflows with QoS constraints for Grid computing. A Grid environment consists of large number of resources owned by different organizations or providers with varying functionalities and able to guarantee differing QoS levels. Unlike best-effort scheduling algorithms, which consider only one factor (e.g., execution time), multiple criteria must be considered to optimize the execution performance of QoS constrained workflows. In addition to execution time, monetary execution cost is also an important factor that determines quality of scheduling algorithms, because service providers may charge differently for different levels of QoS [3]. Therefore, a scheduler cannot always assign tasks onto services with the highest QoS levels. Instead, it may use cheaper services with lower QoS that is sufficient to meet the requirements of the users.

Also, completing the execution within a specified QoS (e.g., time and budget) constraints depends not only on the global scheduling decision of the workflow scheduler but also on the local resource allocation model of each execution site. If the execution of every single task in the workflow cannot be completed as expected by the scheduler, it is impossible to guarantee QoS levels for the entire workflow. Therefore, schedulers should be able to interact with service providers to ensure resource availability and QoS levels. It is required that the scheduler be able to determine QoS requirements for each task and negotiate with service providers to establish a service-level agreement (SLA), which is a contract specifying the minimum expectations and obligations between service providers and consumers.

This chapter presents a number of workflow scheduling algorithms based on QoS constraints such as deadline and budget while taking into account the costs and capabilities of Grid services.

19.4 QoS-BASED WORKFLOW SCHEDULING

19.4.1 Problem Description

A workflow application can be modeled as a directed acyclic graph (DAG). Let Γ be the finite set of tasks $T_i (1 \leq i \leq n)$. Let Λ be the set of directed edges. Each edge is denoted by (T_i, T_j), where T_i is an immediate parent task of T_j and T_j is the immediate child task of T_i. A child task cannot be executed until all of its parent tasks have been completed. There is a transmission time and cost associated with each edge. In a workflow graph, a task that does not have any parent task is called an *entry task*, denoted as T_{entry}, and a task that does not have any child task is called an *exit task*, denoted as T_{exit}. In this thesis, we assume there is only one T_{entry} and T_{exit} in the workflow graph. If there are multiple entry tasks and exit tasks in a workflow, we can connect them to a zero-cost pseudoentry or exit task.

The execution requirements for tasks in a workflow could be heterogeneous. A service may be able to execute some of workflow tasks. The set of services capable of executing task T_i is denoted as S_i, and each task is assigned for execution on only one service. Services have varied processing capability delivered at different prices. The task runtimes on all service and input data transfer times are assumed to be known. The estimation of task runtime is presented in Section 19.4.2. The data transfer time can be computed using bandwidth and latency information between the services. t_i^j is the sum of the processing time and input data transmission time, and c_i^j is the sum of the service price and data transmission cost for processing T_i on service $s_i^j (1 \leq j \leq |S_i|)$.

Let B be the cost constraint (budget) and D be the time constraint (deadline) specified by a user for workflow execution. The budget-constrained scheduling problem is to map every T_i onto a suitable service to minimize the execution time of the workflow and complete it with the total cost less than B. The deadline constrained scheduling problem is to map every T_i onto a suitable service to minimize the execution cost of the workflow and complete it before deadline D.

19.4.2 Performance Estimation

Performance estimation is the prediction of performance of task execution on services and is crucial for generating an efficient schedule for advance reservations. Different performance estimation approaches can be applied to different types of utility services. We classify existing utility services as either resource services, application services, or information service.

Resource services provide hardware resources such as computing processors, network resources, storage, and memory, as a service for remote clients. To submit tasks to resource services, the scheduler needs to determine the number of resources and duration required to run tasks on the discovered services. The performance estimation for resource services can be achieved by using existing performance estimation techniques (e.g., analytical modeling, empirical and historical data) to predict task execution time on every discovered resource service.

Application services allow remote clients to use their specialized applications, while *information services* provide information for the users. Unlike resource services, application and information services are capable of providing estimated service times on the basis of the metadata of users' service requests. As a result, the task execution time can be obtained by the providers.

19.5 WORKFLOW SCHEDULING HEURISTICS

Workflow scheduling focuses on mapping and managing the execution of interdependent tasks on diverse utility services. In this section, two heuristics are provided as a baseline for cost-based workflow scheduling problems. The heuristics follow the divide-and-conquer technique, and the steps in the methodology are listed below:

1. Discover available services and predict execution time for every task.
2. Distribute users' overall deadline or budget into every task.
3. Query available timeslots, generate an optimized schedule plan, and make advance reservations on the basis of the local optimal solution of every task partition.

19.5.1 Deadline-Constrained Scheduling

The proposed deadline constrained scheduling heuristic is called *greedy cost–time distribution* (GreedyCost-TD). In order to produce an efficient schedule, GreedyCost-TD groups workflow tasks into task partitions and assigns subdeadlines to each task according to their workload and dependences. At runtime, a task is scheduled on a service, which is able to complete it within its assigned subdeadline at the lowest cost.

19.5.1.1 Workflow Task Partitioning. In workflow task partitioning, workflow tasks are first categorized as either synchronization tasks or simple tasks. A *synchronization task* is defined as a task that has more than one parent or child task. In Figure 19.2, T_1, T_{10}, and T_{14} are synchronization tasks. Other tasks that have only one parent task and child task are simple tasks.

In Figure 19.2, $T_2 - T_9$ and $T_{11} - T_{13}$ are simple tasks. Simple tasks are then clustered into a *branch*, which is a set of interdependent simple tasks that are executed sequentially between two synchronization tasks. For example, the branches in Figure 19.1b are $\{T_2, T_3, T_4\}$, $\{T_5, T_6\}$,$\{T_7\}$, $\{T_8, T_9\}$, $\{T_{11}\}$, and $\{T_{12}, T_{13}\}$.

After task partitioning, workflow tasks Γ are then clustered into partitions. As shown in Figure 19.2b, a *partition* $V_i (1 \leq i \leq k)$ is either a branch or a set of one

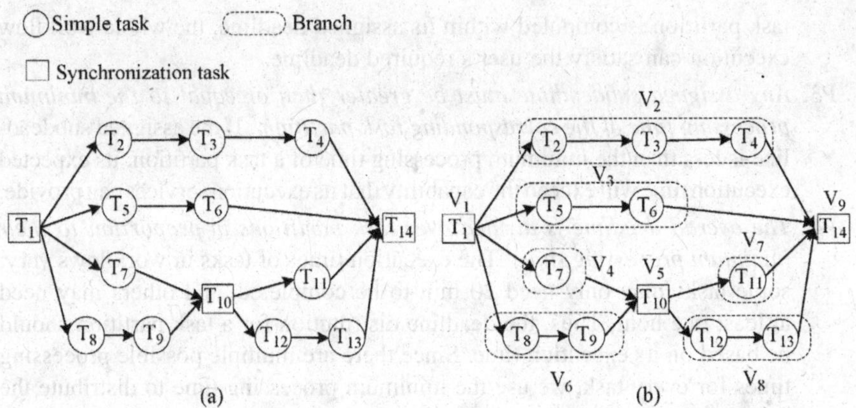

Figure 19.2 Workflow task partition: (a) before partitioning; (b) after partitioning.

synchronization task, where k is the total number of branches and synchronization tasks in the workflow. For a given workflow $\Omega(\Gamma, \Lambda)$, the corresponding task partition graph $\Omega'(\Gamma', \Lambda')$ is created as follows

$$\begin{cases} \Gamma' = \{V_i | V_i \text{ is a partition in } \Omega, \text{ where } 1 \leq i \leq k\} \\ \Lambda' = \{(v_i, w) | v \in V_i, w \in V_j, \text{ and } (v, w) \in \Lambda\} \end{cases}$$

where Γ' is a set of task partitions and Λ' is the set of directed edges of the form (V_i, V_j), and V_i is a parent task partition of V_j and V_j is a child task partition of V_i.

19.5.1.2 Deadline Distribution. After workflow task partitioning, the overall deadline is distributed over each V_i in Ω'. The deadline assigned to any V_i is called a *subdeadline* of the overall deadline D. The deadline assignment strategy considers the following facts:

P1. *The cumulative expected execution time of any simple path between two synchronization tasks must be the same.* A simple path in Ω' is a sequence of task partitions such that there is a directed edge from every task partition (in the simple path) to its child, where none of the task partitions in the simple path is repeated. For example, $\{V_1, V_3, V_9\}$ and $\{V_1, V_6, V_5, V_7, V_9\}$ are two simple paths between V_1 and V_9. A synchronization task cannot be executed until all tasks in its parent task partitions are completed. Thus, instead of waiting for other simple paths to be completed, a path capable of being finished earlier can be executed on slower but cheaper services. For example, the deadline assigned to $\{T_8, T_9\}$ is the same as $\{T_7\}$ in Figure 19.2. Similarly, deadlines assigned to $\{T_2, T_3, T_4\}$, $\{T_5, T_6\}$, and $\{\{T_7\}, \{T_{10}\}, \{T_{12}, T_{13}\}\}$ are the same.

P2. *The cumulative expected execution time of any path from $V_i(T_{\text{entry}} \in V_i)$ to $V_j(T_{\text{exit}} \in V_j)$ is equal to the overall deadline D.* P2 ensures that once every task partition is computed within its assigned deadline, the whole workflow execution can satisfy the user's required deadline.

P3. *Any assigned subdeadline must be greater than or equal to the minimum processing time of the corresponding task partition.* If the assigned subdeadline is less than the minimum processing time of a task partition, its expected execution time will exceed the capability that its execution services can provide.

P4. *The overall deadline is divided over task partitions in proportion to their minimum processing time.* The execution times of tasks in workflows vary; some tasks may only need 20 min to be completed, and others may need at least one hour. Thus, the deadline distribution for a task partition should be based on its execution time. Since there are multiple possible processing times for every task, we use the minimum processing time to distribute the deadline.

The deadline assignment strategy on the task partition graph is implemented by combining breadth-first search (BFS) and depth-first search (DFS) algorithms with critical-path analysis to compute start times, proportion, and deadlines of every task partition. After distributing overall deadline into task partitions, each task partition is assigned a deadline. There are three attributes associated with a task partition V_i: deadline ($\mathrm{dl}[V_i]$), ready time ($\mathrm{rt}[V_i]$), and expected execution time ($\mathrm{eet}[V_i]$). The ready time of V_i is the earliest time when its first task can be executed. It can be computed according to its parent partitions and defined by

$$\mathrm{rt}[V_i] = \begin{cases} 0 & T_{\mathrm{entry}} \in V_i \\ \max\limits_{V_j \in PV_i} \mathrm{dl}[V_j] & \text{otherwise} \end{cases} \tag{19.1}$$

where PV_i is the set of parent task partitions of V_i. The relation between three attributes of a task partition V_i follows that

$$\mathrm{eet}[V_i] = \mathrm{dl}[V_i] - \mathrm{rt}[V_i] \tag{19.2}$$

After deadline distribution over task partitions, a subdeadline is assigned to each task. If the task is a synchronization task, its subdeadline is equal to the deadline of its task partition. However, if a task is a simple task of a branch, its subdeadline is assigned by dividing the deadline of its partition according to its processing time. Let P_i be the set of parent tasks of T_i. The assigned deadline of task T_i in partition V is defined by

$$\mathrm{dl}[T_i] = \mathrm{eet}[T_i] + \mathrm{rt}[V] \tag{19.3}$$

where

$$\mathrm{eet}[T_i] = \frac{\min\limits_{1 \le j \le |S_i|} t_i^j}{\sum\limits_{T_k \in V} \min\limits_{1 \le l \le |S_k|} t_k^l} \times \mathrm{eet}[V] \tag{19.4}$$

$$\mathrm{rt}[T_i] = \begin{cases} 0 & T_i = T_{\text{entry}} \\ \max\limits_{T_j \in P_i} \mathrm{dl}[T_j] & \text{otherwise} \end{cases} \tag{19.5}$$

19.5.1.3 Greedy Cost–Time Distribution (TD). Once each task has its own subdeadline, a local optimal schedule can be generated for each task. If each local schedule guarantees that their task execution can be completed within their subdeadline, the whole workflow execution will be completed within the overall deadline. Similarly, the result of the cost minimization solution for each task leads to an optimized cost solution for the entire workflow. Therefore, an optimized workflow schedule can be constructed from all local optimal schedules. The schedule allocates every workflow task to a selected service such that they can meet its assigned subdeadline at low execution cost. Let $\mathrm{Cost}(T_i)$ be the sum of data transmission cost and service cost for processing T_i. The objective for scheduling task T_i is

$$\begin{aligned} &\text{Minimize } \mathrm{Cost}(T_i) = \min_{1 \le j \le |S_i|} c_i^j \\ &\text{subject to } t_i^j \le \mathrm{eet}[T_i] \end{aligned} \tag{19.6}$$

The details of GreedyCost-TD heuristic are presented in Algorithm 19.1. It first partitions workflow tasks and distributes overall deadline over each task partition and

---

Input: *A workflow graph* $\Omega(\Gamma, \Lambda)$, *deadline* D
Output: *A schedule for all workflow tasks*

```
Request processing time and price from available services for
∀T ∈ Γ
Convert Ω into task partition graph Ω′(Γ′, Λ′)
Distribute deadline D over ∀V_i ∈ Γ′ and assign a sub-deadline to
each task
Put the entry task into ready task queue Q
while there are ready tasks in Q do
   Sort all tasks in Q
   T_i ← the first task from Q
   Compute ready time of T_i
   Query available time slots during ready time and
   sub-deadline
   S ← a service which meets Equation 4-6
   if S = φ then
      S ← S_i^j such that j = arg min_{1≤j≤|S_i|} t_i^j
   end if
   Make advance reservations of T_i on S
   Put ready child tasks into Q whose parent tasks have been
   scheduled
end while
```

Algorithm 19.1 Greedy cost–time distribution heuristic.

then divides the deadline of each partition into each single task. Unscheduled tasks are queued in the ready queue waiting to be scheduled. The order of tasks in the ready queue is sorted by a ranking strategy that is described in Section 19.5.3. The scheduler schedules tasks in the ready queue one by one. The entry task is the first task that is put into the ready task and scheduled. Once all parents of a task have been scheduled, the task becomes ready for scheduling and is put into the ready queue (line 15). The ready time of each task is computed at the time it is scheduled (line 9). After obtaining all available timeslots (line 9) on the basis of the ready time and subdeadline of current scheduling tasks, the task is scheduled on a service that can meet the scheduling objective. If no such service is available, the service that can complete the task at earliest time is selected to satisfy the overall time constraint (lines 11–12).

19.5.2 Budget-Constrained Scheduling

The proposed budget-constrained scheduling heuristic is called *greedy time–cost distribution* (GreedyTime-CD). It distributes portions of the overall budget to each task in the workflow. At runtime, a task is scheduled on a service that is able to complete it with less cost than its assigned subbudget at the earliest time.

19.5.2.1 Budget Distribution. The budget distribution process is to distribute the overall budget over tasks. In the budget distribution, both workload and dependencies between tasks are considered when assigning subbudgets to tasks. There are two major steps:

Step 1: Assigning Portions of the Overall Budget to Each Task. In this step, an initial subbudget is assigned to tasks according to their average execution and data transmission cost. In a workflow, tasks may require different types of services with various price rates, and their computational workload and required I/O data transmission may vary. Therefore, the portion of the overall budget each task obtains should be based on the proportion of their expense requirements. Since there are multiple possible services and data links for executing a task, their average cost values are used for measuring their expense requirements. The expected budget for task T_i is defined by

$$\text{eec}[T_i] = \frac{\text{avgCost}[T_i]}{\sum\limits_{T_i \in \Gamma} \text{avgCost}[T_i]} \times B \tag{19.7}$$

where

$$\text{avgCost}[T_i] = \frac{\sum\limits_{1 \le j \le |S_i|} c_i^j}{|S_i|}$$

Step 2: Adjusting Initial Subbudget Assigned to Each Task by Considering Their Task Dependences. The subbudget of a task assigned in the first step is based only on its average cost without considering its execution time. However, some tasks could be completed at earliest time using more expensive services based on their local budget, but its child tasks cannot start execution until other parent tasks have been completed. Therefore, it is necessary to consider task dependences for assigning a subbudget to a task. In the second step, the initial assigned subbudgets of tasks are adjusted. It first computes the approximate execution time on the basis of its initial expected execution budget and its unit time per cost so that the approximate start and end times of each task partition can be calculated. The approximate execution time of task T_i is defined by

$$\text{aet}[T_i] = \text{eec}[T_i] \times \frac{\text{avgTime}[T_i]}{\text{avgCost}[T_i]} \tag{19.8}$$

where

$$\text{avgTime}[T_i] = \frac{\sum\limits_{1 \le j \le |S_i|} t_i^j}{|S_i|}$$

Then it partitions workflow tasks and computes approximate start and end times of each partition. If the end time of a task partition is earlier than the start time of its child partition, it is assumed that the initial subbudget of this partition is higher than what it really requires and its subbudget is reduced. The spare budget produced by reducing initial subbudgets is calculated and is defined by

$$\text{spareBudget} = B - \sum_{T_i \in \Gamma} \text{eec}[T_i] \tag{19.9}$$

Finally, the spare budget is distributed to each task on the basis of their assigned subbudgets. The final expected budget assigned to each task is

$$\text{eec}[T_i] = \text{eec}[T_i] + \text{spareBudget} \times \frac{\text{eec}[T_i]}{\sum\limits_{T_i \in \Gamma} \text{eec}[T_i]} \tag{19.10}$$

*19.5.2.2 **Greedy Time–Cost Distribution (CD).*** After budget distribution, CD attempts to allocate the fastest service to each task among those services that are able to complete the task execution within its assigned budget. Let $\text{Time}(T_i)$ be the completion time of T_i. The objective for scheduling task T_i is

$$\begin{aligned} &\text{Minimize Time}(T_i) = \min_{1 \le j \le |S_i|} t_i^j \\ &\text{subject to } c_i^j \le \text{eec}[T_i] \end{aligned} \tag{19.11}$$

The details of greedy time–cost distribution are presented in Algorithm 19.2. It first distributes the overall budget to all tasks. After that, it starts to schedule first-level tasks of the workflow. Once all parents of a task have been scheduled, the task is ready for scheduling and then the scheduler put it into a ready queue (line 17). The order of

```
Input: A workflow graph Ω(Γ,Λ), budget B
Output: A schedule for all workflow tasks

1  Request processing time and price from available services for
   ∀T_i ∈ Γ
2  Distribute budget B over ∀T_i ∈ Γ
3  PlannedCost=0; acturalCost =0
4  Put the entry task into ready task queue Q
5  while there are ready tasks in Q do
6      Sort all tasks in Q
7      S← the first task from Q
8      Compute start time of T_i and query available time
   slots
9      eec[T_i]=PlannedCost-acturalCost +eec[T_i]
10     S← a service which meets Equation 4-11
11     if S= φ then
12        S ← S_i^j such that j = arg min_{1≤j≤|S_i|} t_i^j
13     end if
14     Make advance reservations with of T_i on S
15     acturalCost = acturalCost +c_i^j
16     PlannedCost = PlannedCost +eec[T_i]
17     Put ready child tasks into Q whose parent tasks have been
       scheduled
18 end while
```

Algorithm 19.2 Greedy time–cost distribution heuristic.

tasks in the ready queue is sorted by a ranking strategy (see Section 19.5.3). The actual costs of allocated tasks and their planned costs are also computed successively at runtime (lines 15–16). If the aggregated actual cost is less than the aggregated planned cost, the scheduler adds the unspent aggregated budget to subbudget of the current scheduling task (line 9). A service is selected if it satisfies the scheduling objective; otherwise, a service with the least execution cost is selected in order to meet the overall cost constraint.

19.5.3 Ranking Strategy for Parallel Tasks

In a large-scale workflow, many parallel tasks could compete for timeslots on the same service. For example, in Figure 19.2, after T_1 is scheduled, T_2, T_5, T_7, and T_8 become ready tasks and are put into the ready task queue. The scheduling order of these tasks may impact on performance significantly.

Eight strategies are developed and investigated for sorting ready tasks in the ready queue:

1. *MaxMin-Time*—obtains the minimum execution time and data transmission time of executing each task on all their available services and sets higher scheduling priority to tasks which that longer minimum processing time.

2. *MaxMin-Cost*—obtains the minimum execution cost and data transmission cost of executing each task on all their available services and sets higher scheduling priority to tasks that require more monetary expense.
3. *MinMin-Time*—obtains minimum execution time and data transmission time of executing each task on all their available services and sets higher scheduling priority to tasks that have shorter minimum processing time.
4. *MinMin-Cost*—obtains minimum execution cost and data transmission cost of executing each task on all their available services and sets higher scheduling priority to tasks that require less monetary expense.
5. *Upward ranking*—sorts tasks on the basis of upward ranking [20]. The higher upward rank value, the higher scheduling priority. The upward rank of task T_i is recursively defined by

$$\text{Rank}(T_i) = \bar{\omega}_i + \max_{T_j \in succ(T_i)} (\bar{c}_{ij} + \text{rank}(T_j))$$

$$\text{Rank}(T_{\text{exit}}) = 0$$

where $\bar{\omega}_i$ is the average execution time of executing task T_i on all its available services and $\bar{c}_{ij}$ is the average transmission time of transfering intermediate data from T_i to T_j.
6. *First Come—First Serve (FCFS)*—sorts tasks according to their available time; the earlier available time, the higher the scheduling priority.
7. *MissingDeadlineFirst*—sets higher scheduling priority to tasks that have earlier subdeadlines.
8. *MissingBudgetFirst*—sets higher scheduling priority to tasks that have fewer subbudgets.

19.6 WORKFLOW APPLICATIONS

Given that different workflow applications may have different impacts on the performance of the scheduling algorithms, a task graph generator is developed to automatically generate a workflow with respect to the specified workflow structure, the range of task workload, and the I/O data. Since the execution requirements for tasks in scientific workflows are heterogeneous, the service-type attribute is used to represent different types of service. The range of service types in the workflow can be specified. The width and depth of the workflow can also be adjusted in order to generate workflow graphs of different sizes.

According to many Grid workflow projects [2,11,21], workflow application structures can be categorized as either balanced or unbalanced structure. Examples of *balanced structure* include neuroscience application workflows [22] and EMAN (Electron Micrograph Analysis) refinement workflows [12], while examples of *unbalanced structure* include protein annotation workflows [4] and montage workflows [2]. Figure 19.3 shows two workflow structures, a balanced-structure application and an unbalanced-structure application, used in our experiments. As shown in

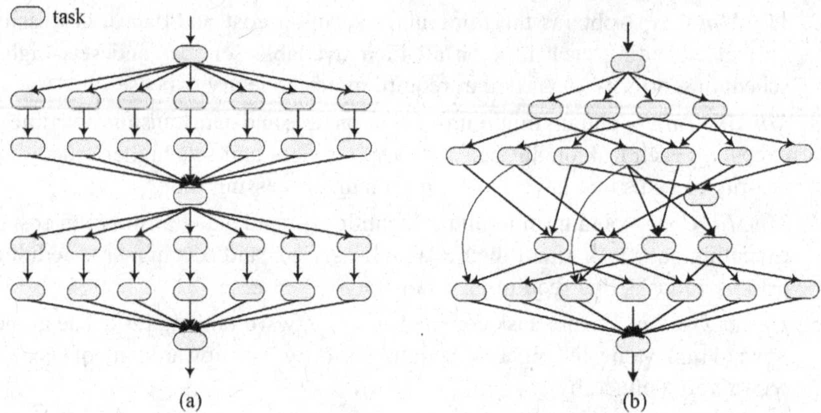

Figure 19.3 Small portion of workflow applications: (a) balanced-structure application; (b) unbalanced-structure application.

Figure 19.3a, the balanced-structure application consists of several parallel pipelines, which require the same types of service but process different datasets. In Figure 19.3b, the structure of the unbalanced-structure application is more complex. Unlike the balanced-structure application, many parallel tasks in the unbalanced structure require different types of service, and their workload and I/O data vary significantly.

19.7 OTHER HEURISTICS

In order to evaluate the cost-based scheduling proposed in this chapter, two other heuristics that are derived from existing work are implemented and compared with the TD and CD.

19.7.1 Greedy Time and Greedy Cost

Greedy time and *greedy cost* are derived from the cost and deadline optimization algorithms in Nimrod/G [1], which is initially designed for scheduling independent tasks on Grids. *Greedy time* is used for solving the time optimization problem with a budget. It sorts services by their processing times and assigns as many tasks as possible to the fastest services without exceeding the budget. *Greedy cost* is used for solving the cost optimization problem within the deadline. It sorts services by their processing prices and assigns as many tasks as possible to cheapest services without exceeding the deadline.

19.7.2 Backtracking

Backtracking (BT) is proposed by Menasce and Casalicchio [14]. It assigns ready tasks to least expensive computing resources. The heuristic repeats the procedure until all tasks have been mapped. After each iterative step, the execution time of the current assignment is computed. If the execution time exceeds the deadline, the heuristic backtracks to the previous step and removes the least expensive resource from its resource list and reassigns tasks with the reduced resource set. If the resource list is empty, the heuristic continues to backtrack to the previous step. It reduces the corresponding resource list and then reassigns the tasks. The backtracking method is also extended to support optimizing cost while meeting budget constraints. Budget-constrained backtracking assigns ready tasks to fastest computing resources.

19.8 PERFORMANCE EVALUATION

19.8.1 Experimental Setup

GridSim [4] is used to simulate a Grid environment for experiments. Figure 19.4 shows the simulation environment, in which simulated services are discovered by querying the GridSim index service (GIS). Every service is able to provide free slot query, and handle reservation request and reservation commitment.

There are 15 types of services with various price rates in the simulated Grid testbed, each of which was supported by 10 service providers with various processing capabilities. The topology of the system is such that all services are connected to one another, and the available network bandwidths between services are 100, 200, 512, and 1024 Mbps (megabits per second).

For the experiments, the cost that a user needs to pay for a workflow execution consists of two parts: processing cost and data transmission cost. Table 19.2 shows an example of processing cost, while Table 19.3 shows an example of data transmission cost. It can be seen that the processing cost and transmission cost are inversely proportional to the processing time and transmission time, respectively.

In order to evaluate algorithms on reasonable budget and deadline constraints, we also implemented a time optimization algorithm, *heterogeneous earliest finish time* (HEFT) [20], and a cost optimization algorithm, *greedy cost* (GC). The HEFT

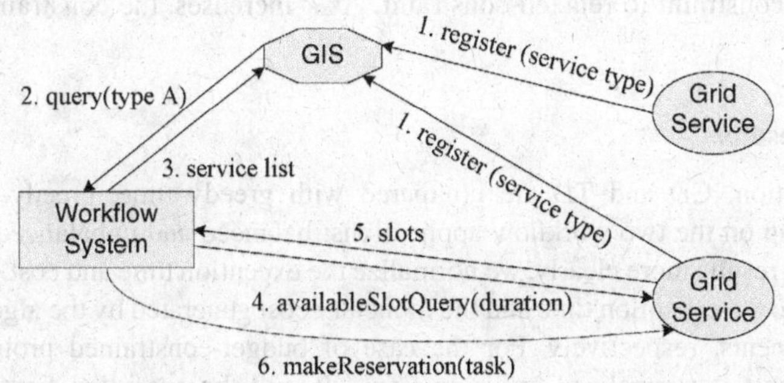

Figure 19.4 Simulation environment.

TABLE 19.2 Service Speed and Corresponding Price for Executing a Task

Service ID	Processing Time (s)	Cost (G$/s)
1	1200	300
2	600	600
3	400	900
4	300	1200

TABLE 19.3 Transmission Bandwidth and Corresponding Price

Bandwidth (Mbps)	Cost (G$/s)
100	1
200	2
512	5.12
1024	10.24

algorithm is a list scheduling algorithm that attempts to schedule DAG tasks at minimum execution time on a heterogeneous environment. The GC approach is to minimize workflow execution cost by assigning tasks to services of lowest cost. The deadline and budget used for the experiments are based on the results of these two algorithms. Let $C_{\min}$ and $C_{\max}$ be the total monetary cost produced by GC and HEFT, respectively, and $T_{\max}$ and $T_{\min}$ be their corresponding total execution time. Deadline D is defined by

$$D = T_{\min} + k(T_{\max} - T_{\min}) \tag{19.12}$$

and budget B is defined by

$$B = C_{\min} + k(C_{\max} - C_{\min}) \tag{19.13}$$

The value of k varies between 0 and 10 to evaluate the algorithm performance from tight constraint to relaxed constraint. As k increases, the constraint is more relaxed.

19.8.2 Results

In this section, CD and TD are compared with greedy time, greedy cost, and backtracking on the two workflow applications: balanced and unbalanced. In order to show the results more clearly, we normalize the execution time and cost. Let C_{value} and T_{value} be the execution time and the monetary cost generated by the algorithms in the experiments, respectively. For the case of budget-constrained problems, the execution cost is normalized by using C_{value}/B, and the execution time by using $T_{\text{value}}/T_{\min}$. The normalized values of the execution cost should be no greater than one

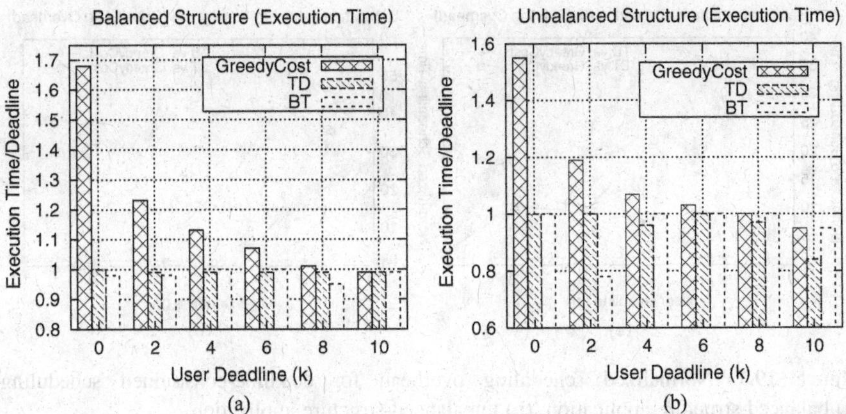

Figure 19.5 Execution time for scheduling balanced-structure (a) and unbalanced-structure (b) applications.

($\leq$1) if the algorithms meet their budget constraints. Therefore, it is easy to recognize whether the algorithms achieve the budget constraints. By using the normalized execution time value, it is also easy to recognize whether the algorithms produce an optimal solution when the budget is high. In the same way, the normalized execution time and the execution cost are normalized for the deadline constraint case by using T_{value}/D and $C_{\text{value}}/C_{\min}$, respectively.

19.8.2.1 Cost Optimization within a Set Deadline. A comparison of the execution time and cost results of the three deadline-constrained scheduling methods for the balanced-structure application and unbalanced-structure application is shown in Figures 19.5 and 19.6, respectively. The ranking strategy used for TD is FCFS. From Figure 19.5, we can see that it is hard for greedy cost to meet deadlines when

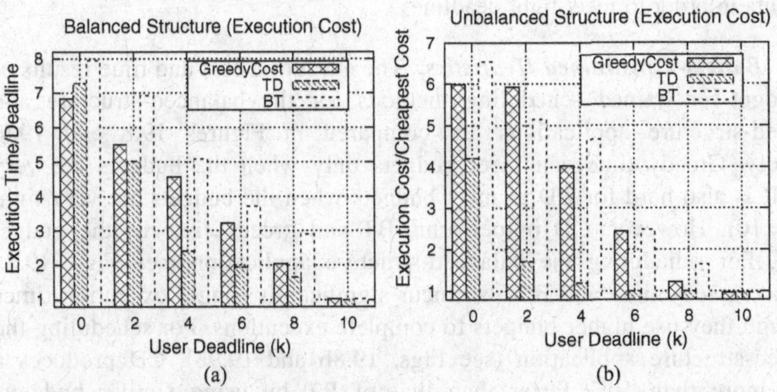

Figure 19.6 Execution cost for scheduling balanced-structure (a) and unbalanced-structure (b) applications.

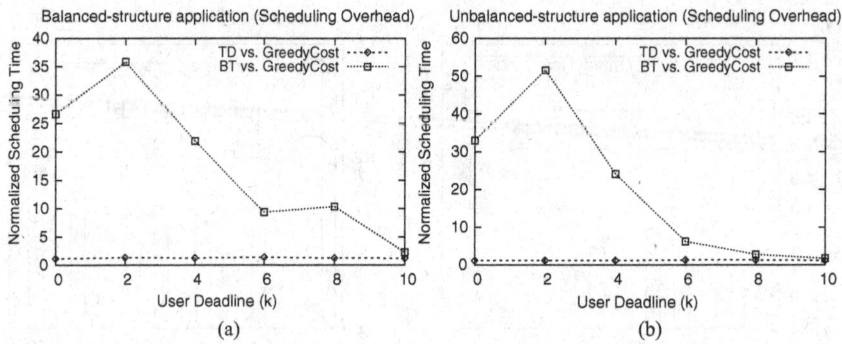

Figure 19.7 Normalized scheduling overhead for deadline-constrained scheduling: (a) balanced-structure application; (b) unbalanced-structure application.

they are tight, TD slightly exceeds deadline when $k = 0$, while BT can satisfy deadlines each time. For execution cost required by the three approaches shown in Figure 19.6, greedy cost performs worst while TD performs best. Even though the processing time of the greedy cost is longer than TD, its corresponding processing cost is much higher. Compared with BT, TD saves almost 50% execution cost when deadlines are relatively low. However, the three approaches produce similar results when deadline is greatly relaxed.

Figure 19.7 shows scheduling running time for three approaches. In order to show the results clearly, the scheduling time of BT and TD is normalized by the scheduling time of greedy cost. We can observe that greedy cost requires the least scheduling time, since the normalized values of BT and TD are higher than 1. The scheduling time required by TD is slightly higher than greedy cost but much lower than BT. As the deadline varies, BT requires more running time when deadlines are relatively tight. For example, scheduling times at $k = 0, 2, 4$ are much longer than at $k = 6, 8, 10$. This is because it needs to backtrack for more iterations to adjust previous task assignments in order to meet tight deadlines.

19.8.2.2 Budget-Constrained Heuristics. The execution cost and time results of three budget-constrained scheduling methods for the balanced-structure and unbalanced-structure applications are compared in Figures 19.8 and 19.9, respectively. Greedy time can meet budgets only when the budgets are very relaxed. It is also hard for CD to meet budgets when the budgets are very tight (i.e., $k = 10$). However, CD outperforms BT and greedy time as the budget increases. For scheduling the balanced-structure application (see Figs. 19.8a and 19.9a), greedy time and BT also incur significantly longer execution times even though they use higher budgets to complete executions. For scheduling the unbalanced-structure application (see Figs. 19.8b and 19.9b), CD produces a schedule more than 50% faster than that of BT by using similar budgets. However, CD performs worse than BT and greedy time when the budget is very relaxed (i.e., $k = 10$).

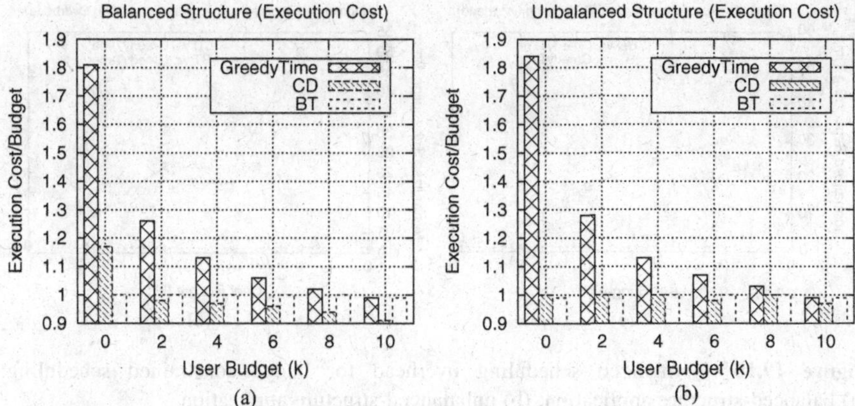

Figure 19.8 Execution cost for scheduling balanced-structure (a) and unbalanced-structure (b) applications.

Figure 19.10 shows scheduling runtime for three approaches: greedy time, CD, and BT. In order to show the results clearly, we normalize the scheduling time of BT and CD by using the scheduling time of greedy time. We can observe that greedy time requires the least scheduling time, since the normalized values of BT and CD exceed 1. The scheduling time required by CD is slightly higher than that of greedy time but much lower than that of BT. Similar to the deadline constrained cases, the runtime of BT decreases as the budget increases.

19.8.2.3 Impact of Ranking Strategy. The FCFS strategy is used as the ranking strategy for the experiments comparing CD and TD with other heuristics. In order to investigate the impact of different ranking strategies, experiments comparing five different ranking strategies for each constrained problem are conducted. In these

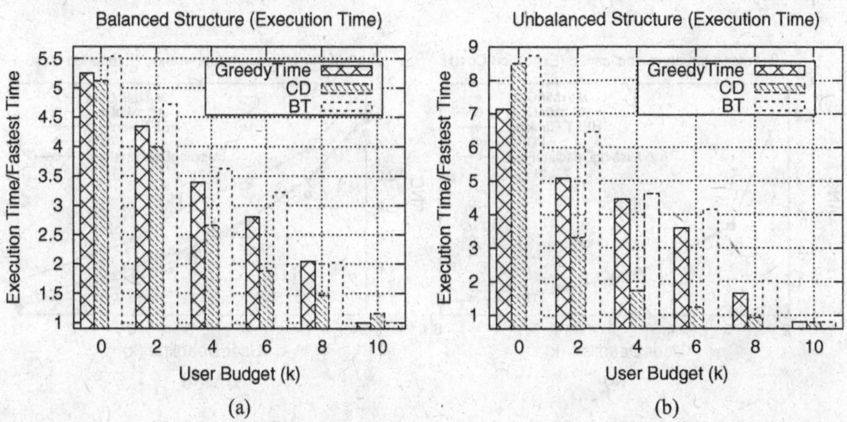

Figure 19.9 Execution time for scheduling balanced-structure (a) and unbalanced-structure (b) applications.

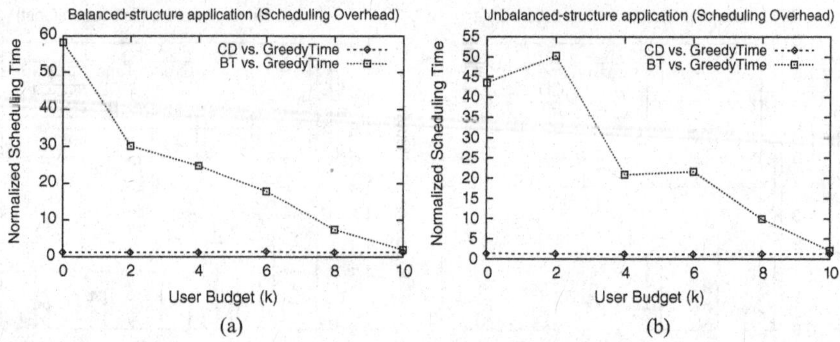

Figure 19.10 Normalized scheduling overhead for budget-constrained scheduling: (a) balanced-structure application; (b) unbalanced-structure application.

experiments, each ranking strategy is carried out to schedule 30 random generated balanced-structure and unbalanced-structure workflow applications. The average values are used to report the results.

Figure 19.11 shows the total execution costs of TD by employing different ranking strategies: `MaxMinCost`, `MinMinCost`, HEFT ranking, FCFS, and `Missing-DeadlineFirst`. Their cost optimization performances are measured by the average normalized cost (ANC) which is the average value of execution cost for executing 30 different randomly generated workflow graphs. The execution cost is normalized by the cheapest cost generated by greedy cost (GC).

For the balanced-structure (see Fig. 19.11a) application, five ranking strategies produce similar results. However, for the unbalanced-structure (see Fig. 19.11b), application, `MinMinCost` performs better than others while `MissingDeadline` incurs significantly higher cost. The scheduling running time is also investigated and showed in Figure 19.12. Among five strategies, HEFT ranking produces highest complexity, while FCFS and `MissingDeadlineFirst` produce lowest complexity.

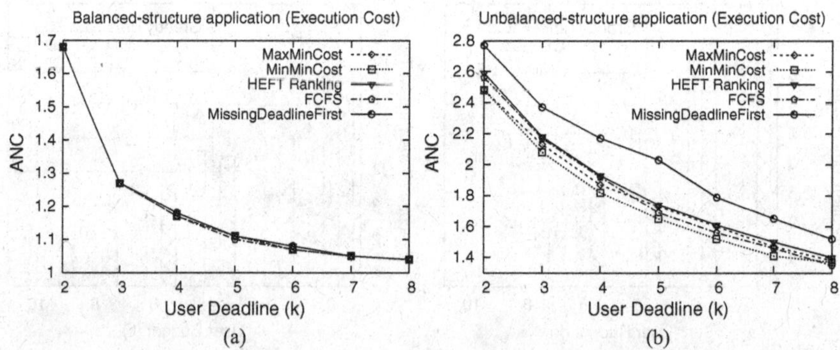

Figure 19.11 Comparison of execution costs among five different ranking strategies for scheduling deadline-constrained workflow: (a) balanced-structure application; (b) unbalanced-structure application.

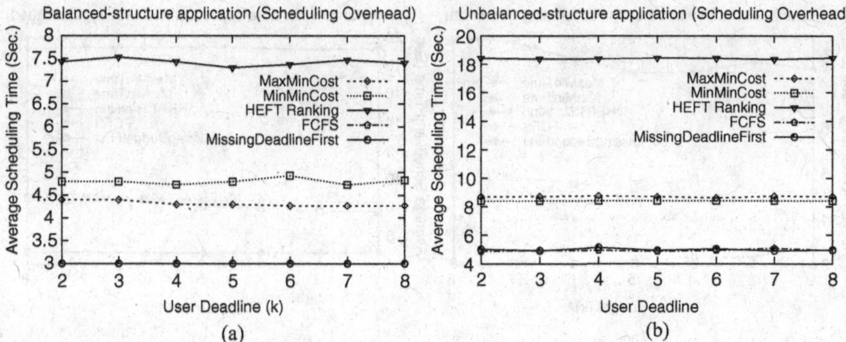

Figure 19.12 Scheduling overhead of five deadline-constrained ranking strategies: (a) balanced-structure application; (b) unbalanced-structure application.

The scheduling running time of `MinMinCost` is slightly higher than that of `MaxMinCost` for balanced-structure applications, but they are similar for the unbalanced-structure applications. Therefore, FCFS and `MissingDeadlineFirst` are good enough for scheduling balanced-structure applications, since they incur similar execution cost but less scheduling running time.

Figure 19.13 shows the total execution time of CD employing different ranking strategies: `MaxMinTime`, `MinMinTime`, HEFT ranking, FCFS, and `MissingBudgetFirst`. Their time optimization performances are measured by the average normalized time (ANT), which is the average value of execution time for executing 30 different random generated workflow applications. The execution time is normalized by the fastest time generated by HEFT.

For the balanced-structure application (see Fig. 19.13a), five ranking strategies produce similar results. However, for the unbalanced-structure application (see Fig. 19.13b), HEFT ranking produces faster schedules while `MinMinTime` performs slightly worse than `MaxMinTime`, FCFS, and `MissingBudgetFirst`.

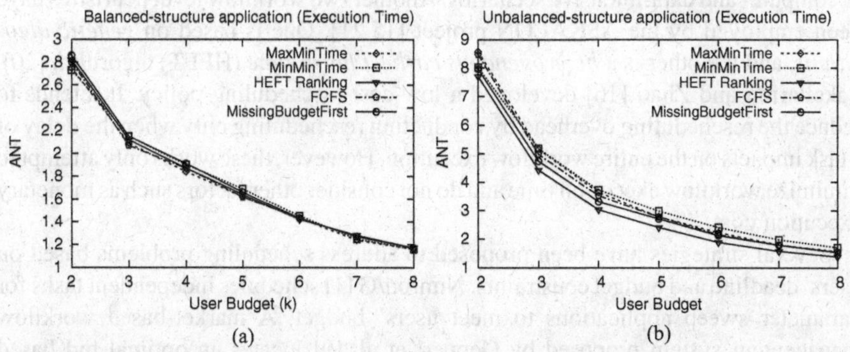

Figure 19.13 Comparison of execution costs among five different ranking strategies for scheduling budget-constrained workflow: (a) balanced-structure application; (b) unbalanced-structure application.

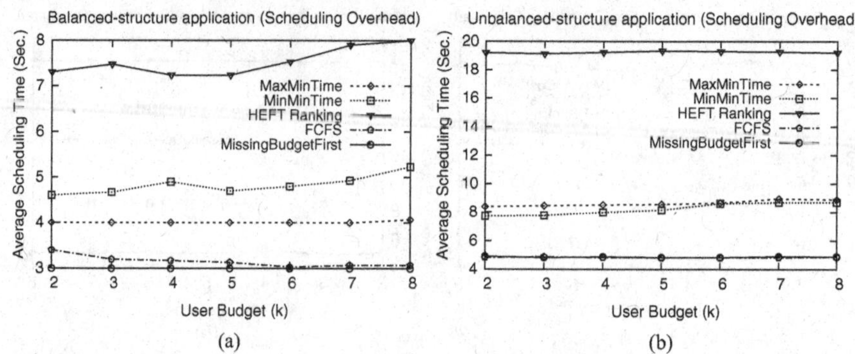

Figure 19.14 Scheduling overhead of five budget-constrained ranking strategies: (a) balanced-structure application; (b) unbalanced-structure application.

However, as shown in Figure 19.14, it also takes longer for HEFT ranking to return the results.

19.9 RELATED WORK

Many heuristics have been investigated by several projects for scheduling workflows on Grids. The heuristics can be classified as either task level or workflow level. *Task-level* heuristics scheduling decisions are based only on the information on a task or a set of independent tasks, while workflow-level heuristics take into account the information of the entire workflow. *Min-Min*, *Max-Min*, and *Sufferage* are three major task level heuristics employed for scheduling workflows on Grids. They have been used by Mandal et al. [12] to schedule EMAN bioimaging applications. Blythe et al. [2] developed a workflow-level scheduling algorithm based on the *greedy randomized adaptive search procedure* (GRASP) [7] and compared it with Min-Min in compute- and data-intensive scenarios. Another two workflow level heuristics have been employed by the ASKALON project [15,21]. One is based on *genetic algorithms*, and the other is a *heterogeneous earliest finish time* (HEFT) algorithm [20]. Sakellariou and Zhao [16] developed a low-cost rescheduling policy. It intends to reduce the rescheduling overhead by conducting rescheduling only when the delay of a task impacts on the entire workflow execution. However, these works only attempt to minimize workflow execution time and do not consider other factors such as monetary execution cost.

Several strategies have been proposed to address scheduling problems based on users' deadline and budget constraints. Nimrod/G [1] schedules independent tasks for parameter sweep applications to meet users' budget. A market-based workflow management system proposed by Geppert et al. [9] locates an optimal bid based on the budget of the current task in the workflow. However, the work discussed in this chapter schedules a workflow that consists of a set of interdependent tasks, according to a specified budget and deadline of the entire workflow.

19.10 SUMMARY

Utility Grids enable users to consume utility services transparently over a secure, shared, scalable, and standard worldwide network environment. Users are required to pay for access services according to their usage and the level of QoS provided. In such "pay per use" Grids, workflow execution cost must be considered during scheduling on the basis of users' QoS constraints.

This chapter has presented characteristics of utility Grids and modeled their workflow scheduling problems formally. Deadline- and budget-constrained scheduling heuristics have also been investigated. Deadline-constrained scheduling is designed for time-critical applications. It attempts to minimize the monetary cost while delivering the results to users before a specified deadline. Budget-constrained scheduling is intended to complete workflow executions according to the budget available for users.

The heuristics discussed in this chapter distributes overall deadline and budget over each task and then optimizes the execution performance of each task according to their assigned subdeadline and subbudget. The heuristics have been evaluated against others, including greedy time, greedy cost, and backtracking heuristics through simulation in terms of performance and scheduling time.

REFERENCES

1. D. Abramson, R. Buyya, and J. Giddy, A computational economy for Grid computing and its implementation in the Nimrod-G resource broker, *Future Generation Computer Systems* **18**(8):1061–1074 (Oct. 2002).
2. J. Blythe, S. Jain, E. Deelman, Y. Gil, K. Vahi, A. Mandal, and K. Kennedy, Task scheduling strategies for workflow-based applications in Grids, *Proc. 5th IEEE International Symp. Cluster Computing and the Grid (CCGrid'05)*, Cardiff, UK, 2005.
3. R. Buyya, D, Abramson, and J. Giddy, Nimrod/G: An architecture of a resource management and scheduling system in a global computational Grid, *Proc. 4th International Conf. High Performance Computing in Asia-Pacific Region (HPC Asia 2000)*, Beijing, China, May 2000.
4. R. Buyya and M. Murshed, GridSim: A toolkit for the modeling and simulation of distributed resource management and scheduling for Grid computing, *Concurrency and Computation: Practice and Experience* **14**(13–15):1175–1220 (Nov.–Dec. 2002).
5. A. O'Brien, S. Newhouse, and J. Darlington, Mapping of scientific workflow within the e-Protein project to distributed resources, *Proc. UK e-Science All Hands Meeting*, Nottingham, UK, 2004.
6. T. Eilam, K. Appleby, J. Breh, G. Breiter, H. Daur, S. A. Fakhouri, G. D. H. Hunt, T. Lu, S. D. Miller, L. B. Mummert, J. A. Pershing, and H. Wagner, Using a utility computing framework to develop utility systems, *IBM System Journal* **43**:97–120 (2004).
7. T. A. Feo and M. G. C. Resende, Greedy randomized adaptive search procedures, *Journal of Global Optimization* **6**:109–133, (1995).
8. D. Fernández-Baca, Allocating modules to processors in a distributed system, *IEEE Transactions on Software Engineering* **15**(11):1427–1436 (Nov. 1989).

9. A. Geppert, M. Kradolfer, and D. Tombros, Market-based workflow management, *International Journal of Cooperative Information Systems* **7**(4):297–314 (Dec. 1998).

10. T. Hierl, G. Wollny, G. Berti, J. Fingberg, J. G. Schmidt, and T. Schulz, Grid-enabled medical simulation services (GEMSS) in oral & maxillofacial surgery, *Jahrestagung der Deutschen Gesellschaft für Computer- und Roboterassistierte Chirurgie (CURAC 2004)*, Munich, Germany, 2004.

11. D. Hollinsworth, *The Workflow Reference Model, Workflow Management Coalition*, TC00-1003, 1994.

12. A. Mandal, K. Kennedy, C. Koelbel, G. Marin, B. Liu, L. Johnsson, and J. Mellor-Crummey, Scheduling strategies for mapping application workflows onto the Grid, *Proc. IEEE International Symp. High Performance Distributed Computing (HPDC 2005)*, Research Triangle Park, NC, 2005.

13. Mayer, S. McGough, N. Furmento, W. Lee, M. Gulamali, S. Newhouse, and J. Darlington, Workflow expression: Comparison of spatial and temporal approaches, *Proc. Workflow in Grid Systems Workshop (GGF-10)*, Berlin, March 9, 2004.

14. D. A. Menasce and E. Casalicchio, A framework for resource allocation in grid computing, *Proc. IEEE Computer Society 12th Annual International Symp. Modeling, Analysis, and Simulation of Computer and Telecommunications Systems*, Volendam, The Netherlands, Oct. 5–7, 2004.

15. R. Prodan and T. Fahringer, Dynamic scheduling of scientific workflow applications on the Grid: A case study, *Proc. 20th Annual ACM Symp. Applied Computing (SAC 2005)*, New Mexico, ACM Press, New York, March 2005.

16. R. Sakellariou and H. Zhao, A low-cost rescheduling policy for efficient mapping of workflows on Grid systems, *Scientific Programming* **12**(4):253–262 (Dec. 2004).

17. D. P. Spooner, J. Cao, S. A. Jarvis, L. He, and G. R. Nudd, Performance-aware workflow management for Grid computing, *The Computer Journal* **48**(3):347–357 (May 2005).

18. I. Tayler, E. Deelman, D. Gannon, and M. Shields, eds., *Workflows for E-Science: Scientific Workflows for Grids*, Springer-Verlag, London, Dec. 2006.

19. G. Thickins, Utlity computing: The next new IT model, *Darwin Magazine* (April 2003).

20. H. Topcuouglu, S. Hariri, and M. Wu, Performance-effective and low-complexity task scheduling for heterogeneous computing, *IEEE Transactions on Parallel Distributed Systems*, **13**:260–274 (2002).

21. M. Wieczorek, R. Prodan, and T. Fahringer, Scheduling of scientific workflows in the ASKALON Grid environment, *ACM SIGMOD Record* **34**:56–62 (2005).

22. Y. Zhao, M. Wilde, I. Foster, J. Voeckler, T. Jordan, E. Quigg, and J. Dobson, Grid middleware services for virtual data discovery, composition, and integration, *Proc. 2nd Workshop on Middleware for Grid Computing*, Toronto, Ontario, Canada, 2004.

23. W. Hoschek, J. Jaen-Martinez, A. Samar, H. Stockinger, and K. Stockinger, Data management in an international data Grid project, *Proc. 1st IEEE/ACM International Workshop on Grid Computing*, India, Springer-Verlag Press, Germany, 2000.

24. W. T. Sullivan, III, D. Werthimer, S. Bowyer, J. Cobb, D. Gedye, and D. Anderson, A new major SETI project based on Project Serendip data and 100,000 personal computers, *Proc. 5th International Conf. Bioastronomy*, Bologna, Italy, 1997.

20

GAME-THEORETIC SCHEDULING OF GRID COMPUTATIONS

Yu-Kwong Kwok

20.1 INTRODUCTION

Computational Grids are no longer simply experimental artifacts but are being used for many commercial and industrial applications around the world. The lofty goal of Grid computing [10,11] is to leverage on the interconnection of a large number of geographically distributed machines to solve computational problems faster and on a gigantic scale [4]. However, this goal is based on the premise that the interconnected machines are *cooperative* in the sense that they are willing to execute remote jobs. We believe that as the Grid scales up, this premise may no longer hold. Note that the Grid is a large-scale peer-to-peer (P2P) system at the server level (rather than at the desktop level as in file-sharing P2P applications). Thus, the "peers" (i.e., the Grid sites, owned and managed by different organizations) may not always want to cooperate with each other. Indeed, the various computers *within* a Grid site may not even cooperate with each other. This scenario resembles the situation in the noncooperation among states of a large country, or the noncooperation among departments in a large organization.

Thus, modeling the Grid and its constituents by taking into account the potential noncooperativeness at various levels is an important research problem. With such modeling, we can then study the impact of *selfishness* and subsequently design proper strategies to avoid its adverse impacts. This can, in turn, lead to a much more efficient utilization of the Grid processing resources. However, although there have been several more recent attempts in scrutinizing the Grid from a "market"-oriented

Market-Oriented Grid and Utility Computing Edited by Rajkumar Buyya and Kris Bubendorfer

perspective [6] (as detailed in Section 20.3), the modeling problem of the Grid with realistic selfishness concepts is relatively unexplored. Indeed, traditional nonstrategic job scheduling techniques may generate inefficient resource allocation results because Grid scheduling [46,52] works in a unique environment where the Grid sites are autonomous and may give unpredictable performance which is out of the scheduler's control.

Game theory [30] has been widely used in many resource allocation problems, and Grid job scheduling is no exception. In this chapter, we first present a brief tutorial on game-theoretic techniques in Section 20.2. Our game-theoretic discussions include noncooperative games, mechanism design, auctions, cooperative games, and bargaining. In Section 20.3, we discuss in detail several more recently proposed techniques for game-theoretic Grid job scheduling. We then make a few suggestions in Section 20.4 for Grid administrators as to how we can make better use of Grid resources applying these game-theoretic results. In Section 20.5, we suggest some future research avenues. We conclude this chapter in Section 20.6.

20.2 BACKGROUND

Game theory [30,31] has been applied to tackle resource allocation problems involving autonomous agents in a wide range of application scenarios [7–9,34,37,38]. In this section, we provide a brief tutorial on introductory game theory that is useful for understanding the salient features of the Grid scheduling techniques described in the next section. Specifically, in the following, we present an overview of noncooperative game, mechanism design, auctions, cooperative game, and bargaining.

20.2.1 Noncooperative Game

A noncooperative game is characterized by a set of players denoted by $N = \{1, \ldots, n\}$. Each player independently chooses a particular strategy from its strategy space. The Cartesian product of the strategy space $S = S_1 \times \cdots \times S_n$ represents all possible outcomes of the game. If player i chooses the strategy s_i from its strategy space S_i, we denote the outcome of the game as $s = \{s_1, \ldots, s_n\} \in S$. The preference of a player is determined by its utility function (also called *payoff function*) u_i, which maps an outcome to a numerical value, called the *payoff*. For example, we represent player i's payoff as $u_i(s)$ when the outcome is s. As it is an autonomous agent (e.g., a volunteer site in a computational Grid), each player is modeled as a selfish but rational entity that independently optimizes its payoff. Usually manifested itself as a multiobjective optimization problem, the "optimal" strategy of a player that maximizes its payoff may also depend on the strategies of other players.

In noncooperative game theory, the most commonly used solution concept is called the *Nash equilibrium* [30]. Specifically, a particular strategy combination $s^* = \{s_1{}^*, \ldots, s_n{}^*\}$ is said to attain the Nash equilibrium state when no player can improve its payoff by unilaterally deviating from its chosen strategy. This requires the following conditions to be satisfied simultaneously:

$$u_i(s^*) \geq u_i(s_1{}^*, \ldots, s_{i-1_{i-1}}{}^*, s_i, s_{i+1_{i+1}}{}^*, \ldots, s_n{}^*), \quad \forall s_i \in S_i, i \in N. \quad (20.1)$$

We note that players are assumed to know the utility functions of one another, but there is no coordination among themselves. In other words, each player independently chooses the strategy that maximizes its own payoff. In general, a game may have any number of Nash equilibria, that is, from none to infinitely many. To model a specific scenario as a noncooperative game, we should first design a utility function that generates more than one Nash equilibria. Then, we should design a specific protocol that leads players to the desired Nash equilibrium. Let us consider the following illustrative example.

Consider the scenario where there are two prisoners being interrogated separately. They cannot communicate with each other and can either deny or confess the charges against them. This is the well-known *Prisoner's dilemma* game [30], which is a classical two-person noncooperative game. The players in this game are the two prisoners, denoted by A and B. The strategy space of each player consists of two actions: deny or confess. We represent the payoffs of the game in the payoff matrix as shown in Table 20.1, where (x, y) represents that A's payoff is x and B's payoff is y.

We note that a, b, c, d are some constants, and we have $a > b > c > d$. It is clear that the globally "optimal" outcome of the game is that both prisoners deny the charges, resulting in an outcome of (b, b). However, this outcome is unstable because either prisoner could improve its own payoff by switching from deny to confess (note that $a > b$). If one prisoner has switched to confess, then the other prisoner should also switch to confess because $c > d$. Thus, both prisoners should choose confess, which is the unique Nash equilibrium of this game.

20.2.2 Mechanism Design and Auctions

Mechanism design [29] is commonly considered as complementary to noncooperative game theory. Indeed, as we have illustrated, the major focus of non-cooperative game theory is the analysis of the equilibrium state given the strategies and utility functions of the players. By contrast, mechanism design concerns about what "external measures" we can impose or implement in the system to drive players to converge to a desirable equilibrium state. Usually, such external measures are implemented in the form of certain payment functions administered by a certain central authority; that is, each player, on top of its own utility gained in the game,

TABLE 20.1 Payoff Matrix of the Prisoner's Dilemma Game

	B Chooses "Deny"	B Chooses "Confess"
A chooses "deny"	(b, b)	(d, a)
A chooses "confess"	(a, d)	(c, c)

can receive payment from a central authority if the player's strategy outcome conforms to the desired outcome of the central authority.

One important aspect of the payment function is that its computation requires inputs from the players (e.g., by observing their strategies or by receiving messages from them). Thus, if the inputs from some players are inaccurate (i.e., the players lie to the central authority), then the payments, and hence the system state, may become suboptimal. To avoid converging to a suboptimal state, the central authority must use a protocol that is incentive compatible—a rationally selfish player will always tell the truth as enticed by the protocol (e.g., in the form of some rules and messages from the central authority). In other words, the protocol drives the players to make telling the truth their "dominant" (locally optimal) strategy. Such a protocol is called a *truth-revealing mechanism*. Auctions [18] serve as good examples to illustrate these interesting features of mechanism design. We briefly describe the second-price sealed-bid auction below (a simple variant of the well-known Vickrey auctions [47]).

In a second-price sealed-bid auction of a single indivisible object, each bidder i submits a sealed bid b_i. Bidder i assigns a value x_i to the object. If bidder i wins the auction, the overall payoff of a bidder i is then given by $x_i - p_w$, where p_w is the amount bidder i needs to pay the auctioneer. On the other hand, if bidder i loses the auction, the overall payoff is 0. Now, an interesting unique aspect of second-price sealed-bid auction is that the bidder who submits the highest bid will win the auction but the amount he/she needs to pay is the value of the second highest bid; that is, $p_w = \max_{j \neq i} b_j$ if bidder i wins the auction, i.e., $b_i \geq \max_{j \neq i} b_j$. We can show that this auctioning policy (i.e., the winning rule and the payment function) is truth-revealing; that is, all bidders will bid at their true valuations x_i of the object. This is obviously of the best interest to the auctioneer.

Consider, without loss of generality, bidder 1's bid b_1. Suppose that $y = \max_{j \neq 1} b_j$ is the highest bid from the remaining bidders. Now, if bidder 1 bids at x_1 (i.e., $b_1 = x_1$), then he/she will win if $x_1 > y$ and the payment is y, independent of x_1. On the other hand, if bidder 1 bids at $z < x_1$, then he/she will still win provided $x_1 > z > y$. Most importantly, the payment is still y, independent of z and, thus, there is no incentive for bidder 1 to bid at z instead of x_1 because doing so may actually make him/her lose the auction. Indeed, consider that bidder 1 bids at $z < y$ and he/she will lose. Now, if we have $y > x_1$, then bidder 1 should also bid at x_1 because bidding lower than that will also lose the auction anyway. In summary, bidding lower than the true valuation will never increase the maximum possible profit. Similar arguments also apply when we consider the cases of overbidding (i.e., bidding at $z > x_1$).

With the salient features of simplicity and effectiveness, the second-price sealed-bid auctions are commonly used for modeling resource allocation problems in distributed systems.

20.2.3 Cooperative Game and Bargaining

A cooperative game consists of a set of players denoted by $N = \{1, \ldots, n\}$. However, unlike the scenario in a noncooperative game, the players do not act independently.

Instead, players form different groups, called *coalitions*, among each other. As there are n players, there are 2^n possible coalitions. Each coalition, which consists of a set of players $C \subseteq N$, is associated with a value determined by a characteristic value function $v(C)$. By convention [30], it is assumed that the empty set has zero value: $v(\phi) = 0$. We note that $v(C)$ represents the utility created from the cooperation of players in C only. Since the value function is assumed to be nondecreasing, $v(N)$ is the maximum utility created by the cooperation of all the players. We are interested in value functions that satisfy the following superadditive property:

$$v(C_1 \cup C_2 \cup \cdots) \geq \sum_{\forall i} v(C_i) \tag{20.2}$$

The solution to a typical cooperative game consists of two parts: (1) formation of a coalition and (2) allocation of the value of the coalition $v(C)$ to the set of constituent players. Specifically, the value allocated to player i is denoted as v_i. Players are also modeled as selfish but rational entities in that the objective of each player is to maximize its allocated value. As such, the question we need to answer in a cooperative game is how we should allocate $v(C)$ such that the constituent players of the coalition would not leave the coalition according to their self-interests. One of the most commonly used solution concept is called the *core*. An allocation is said to be in the core of the game if the following two conditions are satisfied:

$$\sum_{\forall i \in C} v_i = v(C) \tag{20.3}$$

$$\sum_{\forall i \in C'} v_i \geq v(C'), \quad \forall C' \subseteq C \tag{20.4}$$

The first condition ensures that the value of the coalition is completely allocated to all constituent players. Obviously, this is a requirement for stability. The second condition means that a subset of constituent players cannot improve their values by forming another coalition. In other words, the best strategy is to cooperate in the original coalition. Thus, the players would leave the coalition neither alone nor as a group. This suggests that the coalition is stable. We illustrate these features with an example below.

Consider the scenario with three workers and a project, which cannot be completed by any one of the workers alone. If all three workers take part in the project, they create one unit of overall payoff. If only two of them participate, the payoff is reduced to α. We can model this scenario as a cooperative game, in which each worker is a player. Now, the characteristic value function is given by

$$v(C) = \begin{cases} 1, |C| = 3 \\ \alpha, |C| = 2 \\ 0, |C| = 1 \end{cases} \tag{20.5}$$

We denote the payoff value to player i as v_i, where $i = \{1,2,3\}$. If the three players form a coalition, we would like to know how they should split the unit of payoff: (1) we must have $v_1 + v_2 + v_3 = 1$ and (2) we have $v_i + v_j \geq \alpha$, for any i, j. If $\alpha \leq \frac{2}{3}$, then the players can always arrive at an allocation such that the coalition is stable, that is, the core of the game.

With the interesting stability features based on the core, cooperative game is also commonly used in modeling resource allocation situations where selfish but rational agents cooperate to achieve a common goal. For example, such a model can be used for studying the formation of coalitions in a peer-to-peer (P2P) file-sharing network where users have a common goal of maximizing the availability of desirable files [19].

Apart from the core, another commonly used model in cooperative game theory is bargaining [30], which is useful for capturing the characteristic of a resource allocation situation where multiple rationally selfish agents need to share a piece of resource (or work) in a globally efficient yet fair manner.

A very commonly used solution concept is the Nash bargaining solution [30], which is an axiomatic characterization of the bargaining outcomes, and where we denote U_i as the utility function of each player i. Initially, the utility value of each player is zero. The vector $U = \{U_1, \ldots, U_N\}$ (where N is the number of players in the system) denotes the system state in terms of the utilities. The initial vector is then denoted by $U^0 = \{U_1{}^0, \ldots, U_N{}^0\}$, called the *disagreement point* [30]. To solve the fair contribution problem is then equivalent to finding a *Pareto-optimal* utility vector. The definition of a Pareto-optimal solution is that there does not exist an alternative solution that leads to strictly superior utility values for all the players.

Now, we can define a bargaining problem to determine a Pareto-optimal solution. Define S to be the set of all possible utility vectors. The goal of the bargaining problem is that the players negotiate to come to a Pareto-optimal solution vector. Now, the Nash bargaining solution states that there exists a unique solution U^* satisfying the following axioms:

1. *Individual rationality*: $U_i{}^* \geq U_i{}^0$.
2. *Feasibility*: $U^* \in S$.
3. *Pareto optimality*: U^* is Pareto-optimal.
4. *Independence of irrelevant alternatives*: If $U^* \in S' \subset S$ and U^* is a solution to the problem (S, U^0), then U^* is also a solution to the problem (S', U^0).
5. *Independence of linear transformations*: For any linear transformation ϕ on the problem, $\phi(S, U^0) = (\phi(S), \phi(U^0))$.
6. *Symmetry*: If S is invariant under all exchanges of players, then two players having the same disagreement point and utility function will get the same utility.

The Nash bargaining solution is then given by solving the following optimization problem

$$\arg\max \prod_{i=1}^{N} (U_i - U_i^0) \tag{20.6}$$

subject to the following constraints

$$U_i > U_i^{\,0} \tag{20.7}$$

$$U_i \leq U_i^{\,m} \tag{20.8}$$

where $U_i^{\,m}$ represents the maximum possible utility of player i.

Now, a crux in the Nash bargaining solution is that the utility U_i is concave and injective, $\ln(U_i)$ is strictly concave. This optimization problem can then be solved by maximizing the following Lagrangian J using the Karush-Kuhn-Tucker conditions:

$$J = \sum_{i=1}^{N} \ln(U_i - U_i^{\,0}) + \sum_{i=1}^{N} \lambda_i (U_i - U_i^{\,0}) + \sum_{i=1}^{N} \beta_i (U_i^{\,m} - U_i) \tag{20.9}$$

With the generality of the Nash bargaining solution, it is very useful in modeling many resource allocation problems.

20.3 GAME-THEORETIC JOB ALLOCATION IN GRIDS

In this section, we describe in more detail several more recently proposed game theoretic techniques for allocation of jobs to a computational Grid with selfish machines.

20.3.1 Bidding-Based Grid Load Balancing

Grosu and Chronopoulos [14] studied the global load-balancing problem in a network of n heterogeneous machines, each of which can handle any job but possibly with different processing rates. Furthermore, each machine i is modeled as an $M/M/1$ queue, with processing rate μ_i, $i = 1, \ldots, n$. The total job arrival rate is denoted by Φ so that $\Phi < \sum_{i=1}^{n} \mu_i$. The load balancing problem is to determine the load λ_i for each machine so as to minimize the expected response time. Now, the expected response time at machine i is given by

$$F_i(\lambda_i) = \frac{1}{\mu_i - \lambda_i} \tag{20.10}$$

Consequently, the overall expected response time is given by

$$D(\lambda) = \frac{1}{\Phi} \sum_{i=1}^{n} \frac{1}{\mu_i - \lambda_i} \tag{20.11}$$

Then, using the theoretical result in [2], Grosu and Chronopoulos showed that the following simple algorithm is a truthful mechanism generating optimal load allocations:

1. Each machine i sends its bid (i.e., the processing rate μ_i) to the central allocator.
2. The central allocator solves the optimization problem of minimizing $D(\lambda)$.

3. The central allocator then assigns load λ_i to each machine i and the corresponding payment:

$$P_i(b_{-i}, b_i) = b_i\lambda_i(b_{-i}, b_i) + \int_{b_i}^{\infty} \lambda_i(b_{-i}, x)dx \qquad (20.12)$$

In this payment function, the notation (b_{-i}, b_i) denotes the vector of bids with all bid values fixed except b_i. Here, if a machine bids at its true value, then $b_i = (1/\mu_i)$. Now, the first term in the payment function represents the cost incurred by machine i, and the second term represents the expected profit of machine i.

Penmatsa and Chronopoulos [32,33] extended the framework for job allocation in a computational Grid. Subrata et al. [44] further extended the framework by including the inter-Grid site communication factors. A similar formulation is also employed by Ghosh et al. [13] for the job allocation problem in a mobile Grid. In their model, there is a wireless access point (WAP) that mediates the requests from different mobile devices constituting the Grid. Using the Nash bargaining solution [30], they devised a framework for unifying network efficiency, fairness, utility maximization, and pricing. A payment scheme similar to Equation (20.12) above is used.

20.3.2 Auditing the Execution of Jobs

Yurkewych et al. [53] presented an interesting theoretical study on the auditing of voluntary execution of jobs in a peer-to-peer Internet computing environment, which can be considered as a particular form of open computational Grid. In the model, the job allocation system (on behalf of some users) issues a payment to a machine for each job whose result is accepted by the allocation system (i.e., the result is correct). However, machines are possibly selfish, and, hence, can cheat in the execution of the job by fabricating a result instead of computing it. Thus, the job allocation system must perform auditing and possibly carry out a punishment for a machine that cheats. The job allocation system's strategy is to allocate jobs redundantly to multiple machines. The job allocation system can then compare the results returned for a given job by using some sort of voting scheme. Now, as the machines are aware of the fact that redundant allocation is being employed, they might form a collusion group in order to enhance their return for the resources used.

Specifically, the job allocation system S allocates a job redundantly as follows. S randomly chooses a set of machines with size $M \leq N$ (called the *poll size*), and a number $\varepsilon > 0$, called the *poll tolerance*. If S chooses to audit, then it sends the job to a particular trusted machine (which may be S itself). Knowing the correct result, S penalizes all machines whose results are incorrect. If S chooses not to audit, then it carries out a result voting process. If there is a set of machines with size $> \frac{1}{2}M + \varepsilon$ producing consistent results, then S accepts the majority result as a correct one. S then rewards all the machines giving the majority result. If there is no consensus, then S reassigns the job to a new set of machines and repeat the voting process.

Theoretical and simulation results showed that redundancy can eliminate the need for auditing (and thus, the cost of incorporating trusted machines) when collusion is prevented. Furthermore, it was found that poll sizes remain small in the case for a unanimous consensus, but increase for smaller consensus sizes.

20.3.3 Scheduling Jobs to Selfish Grid Machines

Kwok, Hwang, and Song recently proposed an interesting and practical analysis of game-theoretic scheduling strategies in selfish Grids [21].

20.3.3.1 A Hierarchical Semiselfish Grid Model. It is beyond doubt that the ultimate scale of a computational Grid is gigantic, and thus, the Grid, pretty much like the Internet itself, will cross organizational and national boundaries. An open question is how such a gigantic distributed computing platform, which is likely to be composed of hundreds of thousands of processors, is to be structured and maintained. Kwok et al. suggested that a hierarchical structure, as depicted in Figure 20.1a, is the only feasible solution.

In their study, they envision that each "Grid site" will be not a single computer but rather a network of computers, each of which is a cluster of machines or a tightly coupled massively parallel machine. Thus, eventually there may be hundreds of Grid sites, each of which consists of tens of multiprocessors (i.e., clusters and parallel machines). Indeed, such a structure, again resembling the Internet itself, closely matches the "administrative" structure of computing resources in organizations.

For instance, the computer science department of a university might own a large cluster of PCs, the electrical engineering department might possess another, and the physics department might manage a massively parallel supercomputer. Yet, all these computing resources participate in the global Grid community according to the university's mandate. Thus, at the intra-site level, the participating computers, each of which is autonomous, form a *federation*. At the intersite level, the participating Grid sites form another level of federation.

With the hierarchical structure shown in Figure 20.1a, there are also two levels of job scheduling and dispatching, depicted in Figure 20.1b. Specifically, the job submission system, which is implemented as a global middleware, channels user-submitted jobs to the global scheduling system. Such a job submission middleware can be easily constructed using Web services tools (e.g., WSDL and SOAP messages [3]). Equipped with a global Grid processing resources registry (which again could be based on the UDDI protocol), the global scheduler performs job allocation, according to a certain scheduling algorithm.

Most importantly, at the inter-site level, the scheduler has only the knowledge of the processing capability of each Grid site as a whole, without regard to the details within the site. In this manner, the scalability of scheduling at the global Grid level can be efficiently handled. Furthermore, again this scheduling model conforms well to the administrative structure of the Grid community in the sense that the global scheduler probably should not "micromanage" the execution of jobs down to the

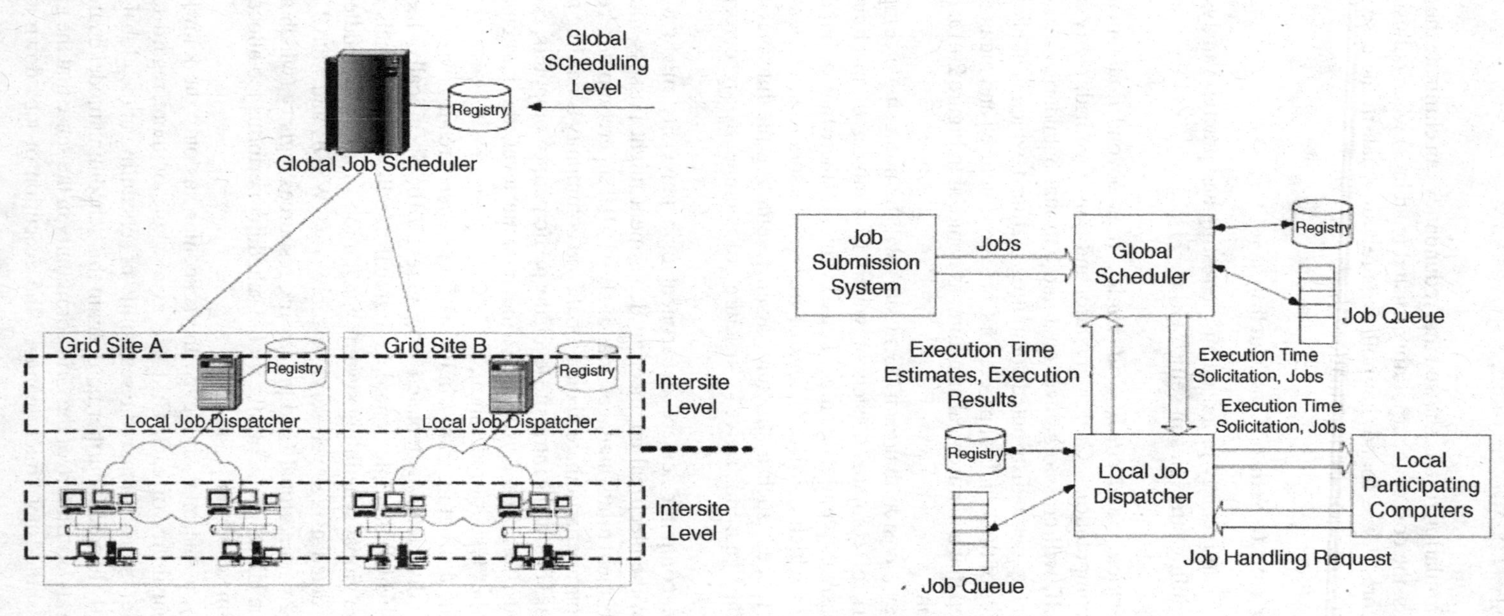

Figure 20.1 System model of an open Grid computing platform: (a) hierarchical structure of an open Grid; (b) control flow in open Grid job scheduling.

machine level. The global scheduler makes use of the "capability parameters" supplied by the Grid sites as the inputs to the scheduling algorithm. These capability parameters are, in turn, mediated by the local job dispatcher at each Grid site according to its information about the local participating machines.

As described above, this hierarchical model, while capturing the realistic administrative features of a real-life large-scale distributed computing environment, is also generic in nature. Indeed, this federation-based Grid model opens up a large variety of interesting research issues. First, any efficient online job scheduling algorithm can be used. Furthermore, it is an important to study how the various parameters are generated and communicated. Indeed, from the hierarchical model, three different game-theoretic job allocation and execution problems can be formulated [21]:

1. *Intrasite Job Execution Strategies.* This problem concerns the strategies of the participating computers inside a Grid site. Specifically, although the various computers participate in the makeup of the Grid site, each individual computer is selfish in that it only wants to execute jobs from local users but does not want to contribute to the execution of remote jobs. For example, even though a cluster of PCs in the computer science department is designated as one of the member computer of a university-based Grid site, the cluster's administrators and/or users may still prefer to dedicate the computing time to process local requests as much as possible. However, if every participating computer does not contribute, the Grid site as a whole will fail to deliver its promise as a serving member of the Grid community, thereby defying the original motive of forming the Grid. Thus, one of the participating computers eventually has to take up a job assigned to the Grid site by the global scheduler. This problem is interesting in that we need to determine how a participating computer should formulate its job execution strategy so as to maximize its own utility (i.e., execute more local jobs) in a selfish manner without rendering the whole site nonoperational. We focus on this problem in this section.
2. *Intrasite Bidding.* This problem concerns the determination of the advertised "execution capabilities" for jobs submitted to the global scheduler. Recall that for the scheduler to allocate jobs using a certain scheduling algorithm, it needs to know all the sites' execution capabilities—in the Kwok et al. study, these are modeled as the execution times needed for the pending jobs. To determine the execution time needed for a certain job, within a Grid site each participating computer can make a "declaration"—a notification to the local job dispatcher specifying the time needed to execute the job. The local job dispatcher can then "moderate" all these declarations to come up with a single value to be sent to the global scheduler. For example, if the local job dispatcher is aggressive in job execution, it could use the "minimization" approach—taking the minimum value of the declarations from all the member computers. On the other hand, a conservative approach is to perform "maximization"—taking the maximum value instead. This problem is also interesting in that we need to analyze, possibly using auction theory, to determine the best "bidding" (i.e., making

execution time declarations) strategies for each member computer. Specifically, we need to determine whether *truthful revelation* is the best approach in the bidding process.

3. *Intersite Bidding.* Similar to the intrasite situation, at the intersite level, the various local job dispatchers also need to formulate game-theoretic strategies for computing the single representative value of the job execution time to be sent to the global scheduler.

Another exciting avenue of research is to study the interplay of these three games, that is, how the selfishness of each individual computer affects the intrasite bidding, which, in turn, will impact the intersite bidding in a complicated manner.

Indeed, different combinations of the abovementioned games will result in different Grid structures. For a *semiselfish* Grid, the intrasite games are noncooperative while the intersite game is cooperative. This model fits most current Grid situation because a Grid is usually formed after some cooperative negotiations at the organization level. However, the individual machines operated by bottom-level departments may not cooperate among each other. For a *fully selfish* Grid, the games are assumed to be noncooperative at all levels. This model is the most general model. Finally, the *ideal* Grids are modeled by cooperative games at all levels.

In this section, because of space limitations, we focus on the formulation, analysis, and results on the first problem introduced above [21]. Specifically, to simplify the model, we assume that for the inter- and intra-site bidding processes, truthful mechanisms [24] are used.

20.3.3.2 Semiselfish Mechanisms and Mixed Strategies. In this section, we present Kwok et al.'s analytical formulation of the game-theoretic framework for the intrasite job execution mechanism. We first describe the job model and execution policies. We then formulate the two-player case, which was shown to be generalized to the general n-player case [21]. Table 20.2 summarizes the notation used throughout this section.

In the game-theoretic study of Grid job scheduling, we consider a class of malleable jobs [16], each of which has the following execution time model: $T(J_k) = a_k + (b_k/P)$, where a_k is the serial portion of the job J_k and b_k is the parallel portion that can be shortened (hence, rendered malleable) if more processors are available. In other words, the execution time decreases in a linear manner as the number of processors allocated to the job increases. Thus, we assume that each job is a parallel application that can be executed using multiple processors. Consequently, the "cost" for each participating computer (e.g., possibly a cluster of PCs) in executing a job is the number of processors, denoted by P, devoted to the job during its execution time period.

To model the "selfish" behavior of each participating computer (i.e., each player) in a Grid site j, Kwok et al. [21] propose the following *utility function*:

$$U_i = \frac{P_i^t}{P_i^r} \tag{20.13}$$

TABLE 20.2 Notation in Game-Theoretic Formulation

Symbol	Definition
$T(J_k)$	Execution time of job J_k
a_k	Serial fraction of job J_k
b_k	Parallel fraction of job J_k
U_i	Utility function of machine i (i.e., player i)
s_i	Degree of cooperation of machine (i.e., the *mixed strategy* [31] of player i)
P_i^t	Total number of processors available at machine i
P_i^r	Number of processors used for executing a job at machine i
τ	Duration of a job dispatching round
P_o	Fixed overhead component of P_r
Q	Variable component of P_r
P	Minimum number of processors used to finish a job
P_w	Extra number of processors needed for a job after τ units of time
α	Selfishness penalty factor
R_j	Reputation index (RI) of Grid site j
n	Number of players at each Grid site
m	Number of Grid sites
W_j^1	Workload accepted in the first round by site j
W_j^2	Workload accepted in the second round by site j
W_j^r	Workload rejected eventually by site j
β_1, β_2, γ	Weighting factors in updating RI

where U_i is the utility of player i, P_i^t is the total umber of processors of player i, and P_i^r is the total umber of processors it used for a remote job. Here, we assume that $P_i^r > 0$ because there is always some overhead for a computer to participate in the Grid (e.g., need to expend some processing resources to monitor the Grid status, or to advertise its capabilities).

Kwok et al. suggested that this simplistic selfish utility function is able to model a real-life situation. Essentially, each machine is selfish in the sense that it does not want to contribute to the Grid community if possible by minimizing the utilization of the machine by remote jobs. Thus, the machine can spend more time to handle local jobs. This is realistic even in the current Grid computing environment because although machines are "assigned" to contribute in a Grid on the institutional or departmental level, local users may not be too concerned about this and would simply like to utilize the machines as much as they can.

However, the Grid site as a whole would like to maximize its *reputation index* (RI), which quantifies the contributions of the site (intuitively, a higher RI would lead to a better reputation of the organization as a whole). Specifically, the RI value R_j will be incremented if an assigned job is successfully executed at site j and decremented if the job fails (the failure of a job will be elaborated below). In the following, we present Kwok et al.'s novel formulation of this assigned job execution mechanism as a noncooperative game [28] to study the dynamics of the conflicting goals of the selfish machines and the Grid site as a whole.

In this model, we assume that after a job is assigned to a Grid site, the job is associated with an *execution deadline* in that the job can be held in the job queue at the local job dispatcher for a certain period of time. Let us denote this time by 2τ. We elaborate the rationale behind this policy [21] below. Thus, in the execution game, there are two rounds of "moves." Within each round, each computer acts according to its selfish strategy, and it can choose to either ignore or tackle the job.

Kwok et al. considered *mixed strategies* [27,31] in their study. Essentially, each computer uses a probabilistic "wait and see" approach—try to avoid the work by waiting, with a certain probability, for some other computer to take it up. Now, consider that if a job is taken up immediately after it is assigned, the amount of resources occupied is given by: $P^r = P_o + Q$, where P_o is the fixed overhead component of resources and Q is a variable component that depends on how much time is left for the job (here, the player index indicated by the subscript is dropped for clarity).

Specifically, if the job is executed immediately after assignment, then $Q = P$, where P is the number of processors needed in order to finish the job using the amount of time advertised by the Grid site to the global scheduler. On the other hand, if the job is executed after one round (i.e., τ units of time) because no computer executes it in the first round, then the number of processors involved becomes $P^r = P_o + Q = P_o + P + P_w$. In other words, the waiting time τ has to be compensated by "throwing in" P_w more processors to the job so that the deadline of the job can still be met. Let us consider a simple scenario first—only two computers are involved.

20.3.3.2.1 The Two-Player Game. Let us consider two participating computers, denoted by M_1 and M_2, having mixed strategies s_i, where $0 \le s_i \le 1$ for $i = 1,2$. Here, s_i, called the *degree of cooperation* in Kwok et al.'s study, is the probability (i.e., the mixed strategy) that the assigned job is executed by computer M_i. Now, in the first round, if M_1 chooses not to perform the job, there are two possible outcomes: (1) M_2 performs it or (2) M_2 does perform it. Suppose that after the first round, if the job is not executed, M_1 will do so with probability 1. As such, we have

$$Q = s_1 P + (1 - s_1)(1 - s_2)(P + P_w) \tag{20.14}$$

By symmetry, a similar expression can also be derived for M_2. Suppose $P_w = \alpha P$, where $0 < \alpha < 1$ (i.e., τ is not a long period of time with respect to the job's execution time [21]). Here, α is called the *selfishness penalty factor* because it quantifies the amount of extra resources incurred should the machine refuse to execute the job earlier. Differentiating U_1 with respect to s_1 gives

$$\frac{\partial U_1}{\partial s_1} = -\frac{P^t P}{(P^r)^2}(s_2(1+\alpha) - \alpha) \tag{20.15}$$

Depending on the value of s_2, $(\partial U_1/\partial s_1)$ assumes different values:

1. $s_2 < (\alpha/(1+\alpha)) \Rightarrow (\partial U_1/\partial s_1) > 0$: M_1's best "execution strategy" is "always do it" (i.e., $s_1 = 1$).

2. $s_2 > (\alpha/(1+\alpha)) \Rightarrow (\partial U_1/\partial s_1) < 0$: M_1's best "execution strategy" is "always ignore it" (i.e., $s_1 = 0$).
3. $s_2 = (\alpha/(1+\alpha)) \Rightarrow (\partial U_1/\partial s_1) = 0$: M_1's best "execution strategy" is either of the two possible actions (i.e., it is indifferent).

Theorem 20.1. The strategy combination

$$(s_1, s_2) = \left(\frac{\alpha}{1+\alpha}, \frac{\alpha}{1+\alpha}\right)$$

achieves a Nash equilibrium [27,31] in the two-player game in that no player can benefit by unilaterally deviating from this strategy combination (i.e., $U_i(s_i^*) < U_i(\alpha/(1+\alpha))$ for any $s_i^* \neq (\alpha/(1+\alpha))$.

Proof. Theorem 20.1 is true because $Q = P$ and thus, U_i does not depend on the value of s_1 (for $i = 1,2$) under this symmetric combination. Thus, any deviation of s_1 from $\alpha/(1+\alpha)$ would not affect U_i. □

It should be noted that deviating from the Nash equilibrium strategy does not make the utility worse. In fact, the only requirement of the Nash equilibrium is that unilateral deviation does not lead to a better utility. However, this equilibrium, albeit unique, is a weak one (i.e., unstable) and the solution is degenerated [31,36] in that each player i can choose any strategy provided the other player fixes its strategy to be $\alpha/(1+\alpha)$.

Now, let us consider the case where each of the two computers is patient enough to wait for one more time interval τ (i.e., the absolute deadline) before committing itself to take up the job. Thus, the variable component of the number of processors involved becomes

$$Q = s_1 P + (1-s_1)(1-s_2)[s_1 P + P_w + (1-s_1)(1-s_2)(P + 2P_w)] \tag{20.16}$$

The terms in square brackets account for the total cost for the two-round waiting. With some sample numerical values (i.e., $P_{\text{total}} = 256$, $P_o = 4$, $P = 32$, and $\alpha = 0.5$), Figure 20.2a shows the relationships between, s_1 and s_2. We can draw a number of conclusions [21]:

- If M_1 always executes the job (i.e., $s_1 = 1$), its utility is independent of M_2's strategy s_2.
- The maximum value of the utility increases with s_2.
- For small values of s_2, the optimal strategy for M_1 is to always perform the job.
- For large values of s_2, the optimal strategy for M_1 is to always wait.
- For some values of s_2, the optimal strategy for M_1 is the interior of the strategy space, [i.e., $s_1 \in (0,1)$].

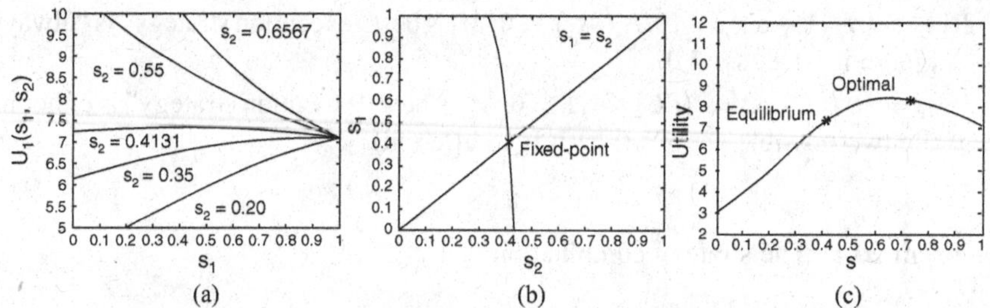

Figure 20.2 Relationships among the utility function U_1 and degree of cooperation s_1 of machine M_1, and the degree of cooperation s_2 of machine M_2: (a) $U_1(s_1, s_2)$ versus s_1 with various values of s_2; (b) s_1 versus s_2; (c) utility versus s.

Furthermore, by performing partial differentiation with respect to s_1, we can see that the best execution strategy with variable s_2 for M_1 is

$$s_1 = \frac{2(1+2\alpha)(1-s_2)^2 - (1-\alpha)(1-s_2) - 1}{2(1+2\alpha)(1-s_2)^2 - 2(1-s_2)} \tag{20.17}$$

If we take $s_1 = s_2$ and $\alpha = 0.5$ so as to solve this cubic equation, we can get only one real root: $s_1 = s_2 = 0.4131$. Indeed, Figure 20.2b shows a plot of Equation (20.17) when $\alpha = 0.5$. We can see that there is only one *fixed-point* solution within the feasible strategy space, namely, $s_1 = s_2 = 0.4131$, which is the unique equilibrium strategy of the game.

However, again this Nash equilibrium is suboptimal, as evident by the following analysis. To obtain the global optimal utility value, let us take $s_1 = s_2$ in Equation (20.16) and substitute it into the utility function U (here, the subscript is dropped because of symmetry). We then consider the case of setting $\partial U/\partial s = 0$ under this "enforced" symmetrical strategy combination. We have

$$4(1+2\alpha)^3 - 3(3+8\alpha)s^2 + 2(4+13\alpha)s - 2(1+5\alpha) = 0 \tag{20.18}$$

Solving this cubic equation with $\alpha = 0.5$, we also get only one real root: $s = 0.6567$. Figure 20.2c shows the variation of the utility function with symmetric strategies (i.e., $s_1 = s_2$). We can see that the optimal strategy is $s_1 = s_2 = \hat{s} = 0.6567$, while the Nash equilibrium strategy is $s_1 = s_2 = 0.4131$. Thus, the Nash equilibrium utility is *Pareto-inefficient* [31], which is a common characteristic in noncooperative game models. Fortunately, under the proposed hierarchical scheduling model, it is feasible to make use of the local job dispatcher to guide the players (i.e., the participating computers) to use the optimal strategy [21].

It should be noted that "optimality" is defined with respect to the utility of the machines. Thus, an optimal strategy is one that "satisfies" optimally the "selfishness" of the local machines. Consequently, according to the "self-interest" of the local machines, each machine would then be willing to use the "optimal" strategy values for local job execution decision making.

In the analysis above, we assume that there are only exactly two rounds of moves. We can easily extend the analysis to the general case where there are an infinite number of rounds [21]. In this general case, the variable resource component Q of M_1 is given by

$$Q = P\left(\frac{\alpha\Omega}{(1-\Omega)^2} + \frac{s_1}{(1-\Omega)}\right) \tag{20.19}$$

where $\Omega = (1-s_1)(1-s_2)$. Here, again by partial differentiation with respect to s_1, we find that the equilibrium strategy of M_1 is given by

$$s_1 = \frac{(\alpha-1)(s_2)^2 - 3\alpha s_2 + 2\alpha}{(\alpha-1)(s_2)^2 + (1-2\alpha)s_2 + \alpha} \tag{20.20}$$

Solving Equation (20.20) with $s_1 = s_2$ (i.e., symmetric equilibrium) and $\alpha = 0.5$, we have $s_1 = s_2 = 0.4707$. On the other hand, the optimal strategy for the "enforced" symmetric case is given by the solution of the following equation:

$$s^4 - 2(\alpha+1)s^3 + 6\alpha s^2 - 8\alpha s + 4\alpha = 0 \tag{20.21}$$

For $\alpha = 0.5$, the only legitimate root of this equation is $s = 0.6579$. We can see that the Nash and optimal strategy values for the two-round case are both slightly smaller than those of the ∞-round case. Nevertheless, as argued from a practical perspective [21], in the proposed model the system would consider a job as rejected by the assigned site if it is not accepted after two rounds. Thus, the job execution game would not be played indefinitely for each allocated job at a site.

20.3.3.2.2 The Two-Round Policy. In the analysis above, the selfishness penalty factor α is defined as $\alpha = P_w/P$. It can be shown that $\alpha/(1+\alpha) = \tau/\Gamma$, where Γ is the execution time for the parallel fraction of the job. Here, we can see that (1) with a fixed value of α, τ assumes different values for different jobs; and (2) as α increases, τ becomes a larger fraction of Γ.

Indeed, with $\alpha = 0.1$ (i.e., 10% more processors are needed to finish the job after each round), τ is equal to 9.1% of Γ. On the other hand, with $\alpha = 0.5$ (i.e., with 50% more processors needed to finish the job after each round), τ is equal to 33.3% of Γ. Thus, with $\alpha = 0.5$, after two rounds of waiting, 66.7% of originally useful execution time is wasted and 200% of the originally needed resources are needed to finish the job. Therefore, it is deemed to be reasonable to consider that the job is rejected if it is not executed by any player after two rounds. As detailed by Kwok et al. [21], a rejected job is rescheduled by the global scheduler to a possibly new site in the next batch. Kwok et al. then generalized the two player situation to an n-player scenario. They provided algorithms and protocols to guide the scheduling process [21]. They performed simulations using the numerical aerodynamic simulation (NAS) and parameter sweep application (PSA) workloads to study the overall job execution performance of the Grid system under a wide range of parameters. Specifically, they found that the socially optimal selfish strategy significantly outperforms the Nash selfish strategy.

20.3.4 Related Work on Game-Theoretic Job Allocation

Using game-theoretic approaches for resource allocation in a distributed system has generated intensive interests in the research community [7–9,34,37–39,42,43,49,51]. Regev and Nisan [35] suggested a system called Popcorn market for trading online CPU time among distributed computers. In their system, a virtual currency called "popcoin" was used between buyers and sellers of CPU times. The social efficiency and price stability were studied using the Vickrey auction theory [30]. Wolski et al. [50] proposed a model called *G-commerce*, in which computational resources among different Grid sites are traded in a barter manner. The efficiency of two different economic models—commodities markets and auctions—were studied by simulations. They concluded that a commodity market is a better choice for controlling Grid resources compared with auctions. Larson and Sandholm [23] pioneered the consideration of the computation cost involved in determining the valuations that are essential inputs to the auction system. They defined the notion of "miscomputing ratio," which characterizes the impact of selfishness on the efficiency of the auction. Volper et al. [48] proposed a game-theoretic middleware called GameMosix. Selfish behaviors are modeled by "friendship relationships" in that computers will help each other only when they have established friendship relationships before. Quantitatively, a unit of friendship is accumulated if a computer takes a job from another computer. Sender and receiver algorithms were then devised to handle remote job executions based on friendship values. Khan and Ahmad [17] performed a detailed and interesting performance comparison study on three simple game-theoretic job allocation schemes with different design rationales: noncooperative, semicooperative, and cooperative. They found that the cooperative scheme outperformed the other two game-theoretic strategies. There is also a plethora of relevant work from the multiagent research community [41,45]. Much work has been proposed for resource allocation in a multiagent system [1,12,25,26]. Coalition formation by multiple agents for collusive execution of tasks has also been studied [5,15,40].

20.4 VISIONARY THOUGHTS FOR PRACTITIONERS

Grid computing is all about pooling autonomous processing resources together to solve large problems. A major merit of autonomy of Grid sites is that management and maintenance is highly decentralized, making it more cost-effective. However, a downside is that each individual Grid site inevitably has self-interests, probably about, for instance, how much time it is willing to contribute, what type of jobs it is willing to execute, how much storage it is willing to share, and what level of security risk it is willing to take. Even though some incentives are in place (e.g., in the tangible form of storage or processing time reciprocity trading, or in the intangible form of just sharing of fame), traditional nonstrategic ways of scheduling jobs to a fully cooperative distributed system may be inefficient. On the basis of the techniques we surveyed in this chapter, we offer the following suggestions to Grid computing practitioners (in particular, Grid administrators):

1. *Accounting System.* It is important for the Grid computing system to keep track of the job execution statistics: execution times, storage consumed, communication times, failure rates, and deadline miss rates. These statistics, open to all users of the Grid, can serve two purposes: (a) the Grid scheduler can make use of them to make better scheduling decisions (possibly based on auctioning, as explained below); (b) an individual site can monitor the performance of its own machines to detect possible hardware and software problems. Such an accounting system, more importantly, can help realize the "complete information" criterion required in many game-theoretic modeling of resource allocation. Specifically, each Grid site can compare and contrast its statistics against those of other sites to deduce the "strategies" employed by other sites.
2. *Internal Reputation System.* On the basis of the accounting system, an internal reputation system (i.e., not open to external Grid users) can be set up to keep track of some reputation scores for the sites. Such reputation scores can be computed in the central administration site directly from the job execution statistics (e.g., using a weighted sum of the parameters) or maintained by individual sites through a distributed reputation aggregation process [20]. The reputation scores can be useful to serve as an intangible form of "payment" that is required in a mechanism design setting (e.g., job auctioning).
3. *Job Auctioning.* A job auctioning mechanism is highly recommended. Auctions, if properly designed, have salient features such as optimality in job allocation with respect to heterogeneity of machines and jobs, simplicity of job scheduling, and robustness (a job will still be run even if some Grid sites fail because some other sites can win the auction). However, the auction must be carefully articulated to achieve "truth revelation." A properly designed payment system can help. Indeed, in a real Grid site, even real monetary payments can be considered because each Grid site can possibly expend much money for paying electricity and maintenance staff. Thus, the rationale is that if the Grid site has some idle time during which the fixed cost of electricity and staff is still required, it has a high incentive to win the auction (tell the truth) and then has its fixed cost subsidized by executing the remote jobs.
4. *Execution Auditing.* As discussed in the previous section, some Grid sites could possibly generate wrong results for a job (may be due to intentional cheating or unintentional errors caused by a virus infection). Thus, it is important for the Grid to perform auditing of job execution. However, auditing implies redundant execution of jobs, representing a potential waste of resources. Consequently, we may also need to consider implementing auditing in a game-theoretic manner. Specifically, we can develop a Nash bargaining solution–based allocation mechanism to distribute the jobs that are to be audited.

20.5 FUTURE RESEARCH DIRECTIONS

The existing game-theoretic Grid scheduling techniques presented in this chapter have several limitations. For one thing, it is common that analysis is focused on symmetric mixed strategies. It would be interesting to analyze situations where heterogeneous strategies and deterministic actions are used by the machines. Moreover, the simulation study would provide more insights if we integrate all three levels of Grid scheduling (i.e., global intersite level, intrasite level, and individual machine level) together with intelligent algorithms used at each level. Furthermore, most simulation results are based on a small-scale Grid due to various constraints in the testbeds used. An important future research goal would be to perform more extensive simulations to study the performance of the integrated scheduling system under large-scale Grids or even a real Grid.

There are some other interesting avenues of further research:

1. It is important to devise an algorithm (possibly game-theoretic) for the site manager to determine an accurate representative value of job execution time, based on the objective of successfully bidding the job without over committing its resources.
2. The job deadlines in most performance studies are governed by the underlying application and are not under control of an individual site. However, if the deadline of a job can be manipulated by a site, it would be interesting to design a game-theoretic deadline setting strategy in order to maximizing the successful remote execution probability.
3. Linking the selfish factors with appropriate trust negotiation models for Grid computing is still a wide-open research problem.

Another future research direction is to consider integrating job execution in a mobile Grid based on hybrid wireless networks (i.e., cellular plus WiFi networks) [22] with job execution in wired Grids. The presence of wireless Grid peers extends the reach of Grid computing, which creates new application scenarios. For example, a wired Grid site may provide transcoding services to wireless peers with different energy consumption constraints, which are important considerations for mobile Grid machines. Each wireless peer should pay the wired Grid site for transcoding the job data content. Alternatively, the originating wired Grid site can delegate such transcoding services to some capable peers in the wired network. These peers convert the data content in a suitable format for wireless peers. Instead of paying the originating wired Grid site, wireless peers should reward those wired peers providing the transcoded data content. This creates a market-like scenario for trading different resources between wired and wireless peers. On the other hand, wireless peers can improve the resilience of Grid job execution because they provide different paths for distributing job data items. As such, both wired and wireless peers would benefit from the services provided by each other.

20.6 CONCLUSIONS

In this chapter, we have presented a brief tutorial on game-theoretic techniques (noncooperative games, mechanism design, auctions, cooperative games, and bargaining) and a detailed discussion on several more recently proposed game-theoretic Grid job scheduling techniques. We have also provided some thoughts for Grid computing practitioners on the basis of these existing research results. Much work needs to be done to advance the field of scheduling jobs in an open computational Grid. One particular direction that we firmly believe is promising is to adopt more economic and financial concepts in scheduling jobs to an open computational Grid. Indeed, apart from the basic game-theoretic tools that we have surveyed in this chapter, we believe that fruitful results can be derived using more sophisticated game theoretic tools such as Bayesian games (incomplete information), evolutionary games, and multiobjective repeated games. Financial derivative tools such as "options" can also be considered for implementation in a computational Grid because they could be useful for modeling "speculative job execution" in a distributed system with the objective of maximizing the potential gain in performance.

REFERENCES

1. S. Abdallah and V. Lesser, Learning the task allocation game, *Proc. 5th ACM International Joint Conf. Autonomous Agents and Multiagent Systems* (*AAMAS 2006*), May 2006, pp. 850–857.
2. A. Archer and E. Tardos, Truthful mechanism for one-parameter agents, *Proc. 42nd IEEE Symp. Foundations of Computer Science, Oct.* 2001, pp. 482–491.
3. D. K. Barry, *Web Services and Service-Oriented Architectures*, Morgan Kaufmann, 2003.
4. F. Berman, G. Fox, and T. Hey, eds., *Grid Computing: Making the Global Infrastructure a Reality*, Wiley, 2003.
5. B. Blankenburg, R. K. Dash, S. D. Ramchurn, M. Klusch, and N. R. Jennings, trusted kernel-based coalition formation, *Proc. 4th ACM International Joint Conf. Autonomous Agents and Multiagent Systems* (*AAMAS 2005*), July 2005, pp. 989–996.
6. R. Buyya,*Economic-Based Distributed Resource Management and Scheduling for Grid Computing*, PhD thesis, Monash Univ., Melbourne, Australia, April 2002.
7. A. Czumaj, P. Krysta, and B. Vocking, Selfish traffic allocation for server farms, *Proc. 34th ACM Annual Symp. Theory of Computing* (*STOC*), May 2002, pp. 287–296.
8. A. Czumaj and A. Ronen, On the expected payment of mechanisms for task allocation, *Proc. 23rd ACM Annual Symp. Principles of Distributed Computing* (*PODC*), July 2004, pp. 98–106.
9. M. Feldman, K. Lai, and L. Zhang, A price-anticipating resource allocation mechanism for distributed shared clusters, *Proc. 6th ACM Conf. Electronic Commerce* (*EC 2005*), June 2005, pp. 127–136.
10. I. Foster and C. Kesselman, *The Grid: Blueprint for a New Computing Infrastructure*, Morgan Kaufman, 1999.

11. I. Foster, C. Kesselman, and S. Tueke, The anatomy of the Grid: Enabling scalable virtual organizations, *International Journal of Supercomputing Applications* **15**(3): 200–222 (2001).
12. A. Galstyan, S. Kolar, and K. Lerman, Resource allocation games with changing resource capacities, *Proc. 2nd ACM International Joint Conf. Autonomous Agents and Multiagent Systems* (*AAMAS 2003*), July 2003, pp. 145–152.
13. P. Ghosh, N. Roy, S. K. Das, and K. Basu, A game theory based pricing strategy for job allocation in mobile Grids, *Proc. 18th International Parallel and Distributed Processing Symp.* (*IPDPS*), April 2004, pp. 82–91.
14. D. Grosu and A. T. Chronopoulos, Algorithm mechanism design for load balancing in distributed systems, *IEEE Transactions on Systems, Man, and Cybernetics—Part B: Cybernetics* **34**(1):77–84 (Feb. 2004).
15. L. He and T. R. Ioerger, Forming resource-sharing coalitions: A distributed resource allocation mechanism for self-interested agents in computational Grids, *Proc. 2005 ACM Symp. Applied Computing* (*SAC*), March 2005, pp. 84–91.
16. L.V. Kalé, S. Kumar, and J. DeSouza, A malleable-job system for time-shared parallel machines, *Proc. International Symp. Cluster Computing and the Grid* (*CCGrid 2002*), May 2002, pp. 230–237.
17. S. U. Khan and I. Ahmad, Non-cooperative, semi-cooperative, and cooperative games-based Grid resource allocation, *Proc. 20th International Parallel and Distributed Processing Symp.* (*IPDPS*), April 2006.
18. V. Krishna, *Auction Theory*, Academic Press, 2002.
19. Y.-K. Kwok, Incentives issues in peer-to-peer systems, in *The Handbook of Computer Networks*, Vol. 3, H. Bidgoli,ed., Wiley, Dec. 2007, pp. 168–188.
20. Y.-K. Kwok, Peer-to-peer systems, in *The Handbook of Technology Management*, H. Bidgoli, ed., Wiley, Dec. 2008.
21. Y.-K. Kwok, K. Hwang, and S. Song, Selfish Grids: Game-theoretic modeling and NAS/PSA benchmark evaluation, *IEEE Transactions on Parallel and Distributed Systems* **18**(5):621–636 (May 2007).
22. Y.-K. Kwok and V. K. N. Lau, *Wireless Internet and Mobile Computing: Interoperability and Performance*, Wiley, Sept. 2007.
23. K. Larson and T. Sandholm, Miscomputing ratio: Social cost of selfish computing, *Proc. 2nd ACM International Joint Conf. Autonomous Agents and Multiagent Systems* (*AAMAS 2003*), July, 2003, pp. 273–280.
24. D. Lehmann, L. I. O'Callaghan, and Y. Shoham, Truth revelation in approximately efficient combinatorial auctions, *Journal of the Association for Computing Machinery (ACM)* **49**(5):577–602 (Sept. 2002).
25. Z. Liu, V. Misra, and L. Wynter, Dynamic offloading in a multi-provider environment: A behavioral framework for use in influencing peering, *Proc. 4th IEEE International Symp. Cluster Computing and the Grid* (*CCGrid*), April 2004, pp. 449–458.
26. M. Li, S. Yang, Q. Fu, and J. Yang, Research on Grid resource reliability model based on promise, *Proc. 2005 IEEE International Conf. Information Technology: Coding and Computing* (*ITCC*), Vol. 1, April 2005, pp. 310–315.
27. J. F. Nash Jr., The Bargaining Problem, *Econometrica* **18**(2):155–162 (April 1950).
28. J. F. Nash Jr., Non-cooperative games, *Annals of Mathematics* (Series 2) **54**(2):286–295 (Sept. 1951).

29. N. Nisan and A. Ronen, Algorithmic mechanism design, *Games and Economic Behavior* **35**:166–196 (2001).

30. M. J. Osborne, *An Introduction to Game Theory*, Oxford Univ. Press, 2004.

31. M. J. Osborne and A. Rubenstein, *A Course in Game Theory*, MIT Press, 1994.

32. S. Penmatsa and A. T. Chronopoulos, Job allocation schemes in computational Grids based on cost optimization, *Proc. 19th IEEE International Parallel and Distributed Processing Symp.* (*IPDPS*), April 2005.

33. S. Penmatsa and A. T. Chronopoulos, Price-based user-optimal job allocation scheme for Grid systems, *Proc. 20th IEEE International Parallel and Distributed Processing Symposium* (IPDPS), April 2006.

34. R. Porter, Mechanism design for online real-time scheduling, *Proc. 5th ACM Conf. Electronic Commerce* (*EC 2004*), May 2004, pp. 61–70.

35. O. Regev and N. Nisan, The POPCORN market—an online market of computational resources, *Proc. 1st ACM International Conf. Information and Computation Economies* (*ICE*), Oct. 1998, pp. 148–157.

36. J. B. Rosen, Existence and uniqueness of equilibrium points for concave N-person games, *Econometrica* **33**(3):520–534 (July 1965).

37. A. L. Rosenberg, On scheduling mesh-structured computations for Internet-based computing, *IEEE Transactions on Computers* **53**(9):1176–1186 (Sept. 2004).

38. K. Rzadca and D. Trystram, Promoting cooperation in selfish grids, *Proc. 18th ACM Annual Symp. Parallelism in Algorithms and Architectures* (*SPAA 2006*), Aug. 2006, p. 332.

39. K. Rzadca, D. Trystram, and A. Wierzbicki, Fair game-theoretic resource management in dedicated Grids, *Proc. 7th IEEE International Symp. Cluster Computing and the Grid* (*CCGrid*), May 2007, pp. 343–350.

40. A. Shankaranarayanan, F. Dehne, and A. Lewis, A template based static coalition protocol—a^{3P}viGrid, *Proc. 2006 Australasian Workshops on Grid Computing and e-Research*, Jan. 2006, pp. 55–62.

41. W. Shen, Y. Li, H. H. Ghenniwa, and C. Wang, Adaptive negotiation for agent-based Grid computing, *Proc. ACM AAMS 2002 Workshop on Agentcities: Challenges in Open Agent Environments*, July 2002, pp. 32–36.

42. K. M. Sim, A survey of bargaining models for Grid resource allocation, *ACM SIGecom Exchanges* **5**(5):22–32 (Dec. 2005).

43. K. M. Sim, Relaxed-criteria G-negotiation for Grid resource co-allocation, *ACM SIGecom Exchanges* **6**(*2*)*:37–46 (Dec. 2006).*

44. R. Subrata, A. Y. Zomaya, and B. Landfeldt, Game-theoretic approach for load balancing in computational Grids, *IEEE Transactions on Parallel and Distributed Systems* **19**(1):66–76 (Jan. 2008).

45. K. Tumer and J. Lawson, Collectives for multiple resource job scheduling across heterogeneous servers, *Proc. 2nd ACM International Joint Conf. Autonomous Agents and Multiagent Systems* (*AAMAS 2003*), July 2003, pp. 1142–1143.

46. S. Venugoal and R. Buyya, An SCP-based heuristic approach for scheduling distributed data-intensive applications on global Grids, *Journal of Parallel and Distributed Computing*, **68**(4):471–487 (April 2008).

47. W. Vickrey, Counterspeculation, auctions, and competitive sealed tenders, *Journal of Finance*, **16**:8–37 (1961).

48. D. E. Volper, J. C. Oh, and M. Jung, GameMosix: Game-theoretic middleware for CPU sharing in untrusted P2P environment, *Proc. 17th ISCA International Conf. Parallel and Distributed Computing Systems* (*PDCS 2004*), Sept. 2004, pp. 448–454.
49. M. P. Wellman, J. K. MacKie-Mason, D. M. Reeves, and S. Swaminathan, Exploring bidding strategies for market-based scheduling, *Proc. 4th ACM Conf. Electronic Commerce* (*EC 2003*), June 2003, pp. 115–124.
50. R. Wolski, J. S. Plank, T. Bryan, and J. Brevik, G-commerce: Market formulations controlling resource allocation on the computational Grid, *Proc. 15th International Parallel and Distributed Processing Symp.* (*IPDPS*), April 2001, pp. 1–8.
51. Y. Yang, Z. Tian, Z. Zhai, and L. Liu, A novel auction algorithm for resource management in Grid environment, *Proc. 1st International Conf. Communications and Networking in China* (*ChinaCom 2006*), Oct. 2006, pp. 1–5.
52. C. S. Yeo and R. Buyya, Pricing for utility-driven resource management and allocation in clusters, *International Journal of High Performance Computing Applications* **21**(4):405–418 (Nov. 2007).
53. M. Yurkewych, B. N. Levine, and A. L. Rosenberg, On the cost-ineffectiveness of redundancy in commercial P2P computing, *Proc. 12th ACM Conf. Computer and Communications Security (CCS 2005)*, Nov. 2005, pp. 280–288.

21

COOPERATIVE GAME-THEORY-BASED COST OPTIMIZATION FOR SCIENTIFIC WORKFLOWS

RADU PRODAN AND RUBING DUAN

Scheduling large-scale applications on the Grid is a fundamental challenge that is critical to application performance and cost. In this chapter we present a cooperative distributed game-theory-based (game-theoretic) algorithm for cost optimization of scientific workflows characterized by a large set of homogeneous activities. We present both simulated and real-world results that demonstrate the effectiveness of our approach compared to other related algorithms.

21.1 INTRODUCTION

Since the late 1990s, Grid computing has evolved toward a worldwide infrastructure providing scientific applications with dependable, consistent, pervasive, and inexpensive access to geographically distributed high-end computational capabilities. One of the most challenging NP-complete problems that researchers try to solve is how to map complex scientific workflows onto the Grid such that certain objective functions, like makespan in academic Grids or cost in business or market-oriented Grids, are optimized. This problem was traditionally addressed in the Grid community in the form of a centralized metascheduling service [1] that tries to map activities (or jobs) of single or multiple applications to individual processors [2,3].

Market-Oriented Grid and Utility Computing Edited by Rajkumar Buyya and Kris Bubendorfer

This approach has the following drawbacks from the Grid perspective:

- There can be no single metascheduler in a distributed environment like the Grid, where individual applications are controlled and managed by different actors with potentially different goals and interests;
- Access to a Grid site is usually mediated by a resource manager or job queuing system [4] that prohibits direct access to processors. Moreover, in a business Grid the total number of processors available at a site may not even be public information.

Since there are potentially many workflows on the Grid that are competitors for the use of available resources, several issues arise and ought to be dealt with:

- The efficient resource allocation for different workflows taking into account their different performance and cost requirements
- The ability to implement allocation schemes in a distributed manner with no centralized decision point
- The fair use of resources from the system perspective and with respect to various metrics like performance or cost

In this chapter, we address these issues by proposing an optimization scheme for a class of scientific Grid workflows characterized by a large number of homogeneous parallel activities. We propose a cooperative game-theoretic algorithm that can minimize the cost of execution of multiple workflows while guaranteeing the user-specified deadline in two steps: workflow partitioning based on deadline assignment and cost optimization.

We compare the performance of our approach with six existing heuristics and show that, for this class of application, our algorithm is superior in complexity, cost, and fairness. However, our algorithm may not be suitable for highly heterogeneous applications when a scheduling problem cannot be properly formulated as a typical and solvable game, consisting of phases that can be specifically defined to enable game players to bargain with no dependences on each other.

21.2 BACKGROUND AND RELATED WORK

Scheduling workflow and parameter study applications is one of the most important and difficult research topics in Grid computing that leads to the development of many approaches and algorithms. We can therefore cover only the most important or relevant related work ones in this section.

The directed acyclic graph manager (DAGMan) [6] developed by the Condor project allows scheduling of workflows using opportunistic techniques such as matchmaking based on resource offers, resource requests, and cycle stealing with no support for advanced optimization heuristics.

The Grid Application Development Software (GrADS) project [2] continued the tradition of the AppLeS effort on developing techniques for scheduling MPI, iterative, master–slave, and workflow applications. Workflow scheduling is approached by adapting Max-Min, Min-Min, and Suffrage heuristics originally developed for throughput scheduling of independent tasks. We propose in this chapter an approach that proves to be more effective for the class of workflows consisting of large numbers of homogeneous and independent activities.

A comparison of eleven heuristics is also presented by Braun et al. [3]. All these methods, however, provide a centralized metascheduling approach in contrast to our distributed multiworkflow cost optimization method.

The scheduler in Gridbus [7] provides just-in-time mappings using Grid economy mechanisms. It makes scheduling decisions on where to place jobs on the Grid depending on the computational resources characteristics and users' quality-of-service (QoS) requirements. Yu and Buyya [8] introduce a new type of genetic algorithm for large-scale heterogeneous environments for which the existing genetic operation algorithms cannot be directly applied. Because of their high time complexity, genetic algorithms are not practical for large-scale workflow applications.

In terms of game-theoretic algorithms, other researchers in performance-oriented distributed computing focus on system-level load balancing [9,10] or resource allocation [11,12], which aims to introduce economic and game-theoretic aspects into computational questions. Penmatsa and Chronopoulos [10] formulate the problem as a cooperative game where Grid sites try to minimize the expected response time of tasks, while Kwok et al. [12] investigate the impact of selfish behaviors of individual machine by taking into account the noncooperativeness of machines.

The Imperial College e-Science Networked Infrastructure (ICENI) project [13] solves the scheduling problem using a game theory algorithm that eliminates strictly dominated strategies where the least optimal solutions are continuously discarded. The feasibility of this algorithm is questionable because of its high time complexity. Apart from the game theory algorithm, ICENI provides scheduling solutions using random, best of n-random, and simulated annealing.

Intra- and interworkflow cooperation is not considered by other systems. Our work differs in that we present a practical Grid system model and a common class of workflow applications characterized by a large number of homogeneous independent activities. We formulate the scheduling problem as a cooperative game among workflow managers controlling the execution of individual workflows and propose an algorithm that considers not only deadline and cost, but also provides fairness to all workflows.

21.3 MODEL

We describe in this section the abstract workflow and Grid models used as the main foundation for our cost optimization approach.

21.3.1 Real-World Application Examples

We focus on large-scale workflow applications that are characterized by a high number (thousands to millions) of homogeneous parallel (independent) activities that dominate the performance of applications.

For example, Figure 21.1 depicts two real-world applications that we use as case study in our work and that had an impact on our proposed application model: WIEN2k from theoretical chemistry and ASTRO from astronomy domains.

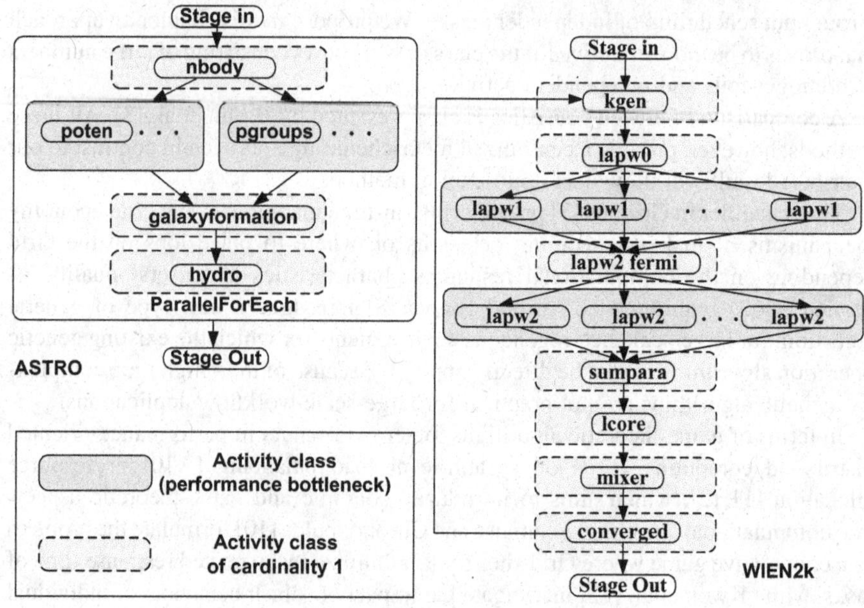

Figure 21.1 Real-world workflow examples.

WIEN2k [14] is a program package for performing electronic structure calculations of solids using density functional theory based on the full-potential (linearized) augmented plane-wave [(L)APW] and local-orbital (LO) method. We have ported the application onto the Grid by splitting the monolithic code into several coarse-grained activities coordinated in a workflow, as illustrated in Figure 21.1. The `lapw1` and `lapw2` activity classes can be solved in parallel by a fixed number of homogeneous activities called *k-points*. A final activity named *converged* applied on several output files tests whether the problem convergence criterion is fulfilled.

ASTRO [15] is an astronomical application that solves numerical simulations of the movements and interactions of galaxy clusters using an *N*-body system. The computation starts with the state of the universe at some time in the past and ends at the current time. Galaxy potentials are computed for each timestep, and then the hydrodynamic behavior and processes are calculated and described.

The sources of performance bottlenecks in such applications are large sets of homogeneous activities such as `lapw1` and `lapw2` in WIEN2k, or `poten` and `pgroups` in ASTRO. In ASTRO, the number of Grid cells (i.e., number of `pgroups` and `poten` activities) of a real simulation is 128^3, while in WIEN2k, the number of `lapw1` and `lapw2` parallel activities may be of several thousand for a good density of states. Sequential activities are relatively trivial in these applications and can be served and scheduled on demand on the fastest or cheapest available processor.

21.3.2 Application Model

From the previous analysis, we propose an abstract model to represent a Grid application as a special kind of workflow: Wf = (ACS, CFD), where

$\text{ACS} = \bigcup_{k=1}^{K} \text{AC}^{(k)}$ is the set of activity classes and

$$\text{CFD} = \{\text{AC}_{source} <^{c} \text{AC}_{\text{sink}} | \text{AC}_{\text{source}} \in \text{ACS} \wedge \text{AC}_{\text{sink}} \in \text{ACS}\}$$

is the set of control flow dependences. We define an *activity class* $\text{AC}^{(k)}$ as a homogeneous set of parallel activities $\text{AC}^{(k)} = \bigcup_{j=1}^{N_k} A_j^{(k)}$ which have the same activity type and can be concurrently executed, where N_k is the *cardinality* of the activity class. The term *activity type* refers to an abstract functional description of activities such as matrix multiplication, a fast Fourier transform, or `poten`, `pgroups`, `lapw1`, `lapw2` for our real-world pilot applications (see Fig. 21.1). We call *atomic* or *sequential activity* an activity class of cardinality 1.

21.3.3 Grid Model

We define an abstract Grid model based on the characteristics of the Austrian Grid [5], which is the real Grid infrastructure on top of which we carry out our research. A Grid environment consists of a set of *sites* connected to the Internet, where each site is a homogeneous parallel computer that can be a cluster, a network of workstations, or a distributed ccNUMA shared-memory machine. Access to each site is performed through a local queue implemented by the portable batch system, load-sharing facility, Sun Grid engine, Condor, or Grid resource allocation manager [4], and administered using local policies.

Activities or jobs arriving at each site may belong to multiple applications. The execution of each application is controlled by one *workflow manager* that competes with the other managers for resources (see Fig. 21.2).

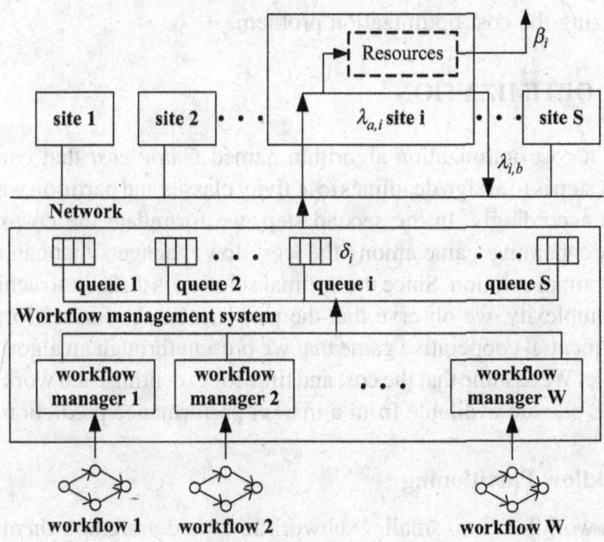

Figure 21.2 Grid system model overview.

TABLE 21.1 Notations

Notation	Meaning
$\Delta = \left(\delta_i^{(k)}\right)_{K \times S}$	Matrix of distribution
$\delta_i^{(k)}$	Number of activities of class k scheduled to site i
$p_i^{(k)}$	Predicted execution time of activity of class k on site i
$c_k(\Delta)$	Cost of activity class k for the distribution matrix Δ
$t^{(k)}(\Delta)$	Remaining execution time of activity class k for the distribution matrix Δ
$\Theta = \left(\theta_i^{(k)}\right)_{K \times S}$	Resource allocation matrix
$\theta_i^{(k)}$	Number of processors on site i allocated to each activity class k
d_{phase}	Deadline of phase *phase*
$w_i^{(k)}$	Importance weight of site i for activity class k
φ_i	Price of site i
m_i	Number of processors on site i
$St(l)$	lth game stage

Most of the existing scheduling approaches in the related work assume direct mapping of user jobs or workflow activities to individual processors that we consider inappropriate for Grid computing where sites are exclusively managed by such locally administered queuing systems. To support this more realistic model, the workflow manager maintains one queue for each Grid site to schedule and manage jobs according to the processing rate of activities on that site.

Table 21.1 summarizes a set of notations that we use in the remainder of the chapter when formalizing the cost optimization problem.

21.4 COST OPTIMIZATION

We introduce a cost optimization algorithm named *Game-cost* that consists of two steps. The first step is to assign deadlines to activity classes and partition workflows into subworkflows accordingly. In the second step, we formulate the cost optimization problem as a cooperative game among the workflow managers that can theoretically generate the optimal solution. Since the optimal solution is difficult to achieve because of the high complexity, we observe that the problem can be further formulated and solved as a sequential cooperative game that we present through an algorithm and one simple example. We assume that the cost and time for executing each workflow activity onto each Grid site are available from a market performance prediction service.

21.4.1 Workflow Partitioning

Partitioning a workflow into smaller subworkflows and assigning them to different games are the two key steps in the design of our cost optimization algorithms. Our

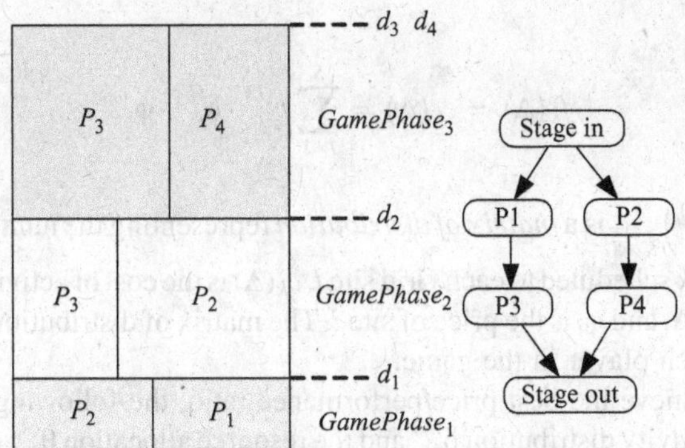

Figure 21.3 Sample workflow partitioning–deadline assignment.

partitioning method uses a static deadline assignment method called *effective deadline* [16], in which the deadline of any activity is the overall workflow deadline minus the total expected execution time of its subsequent activities. We describe this phase only intuitively because of space limitations.

Figure 21.3 presents one simple example of deadline assignment and partitioning of a workflow consisting of four activity classes. According to the user-specified deadline and work amount of each activity class, four deadlines—d_1, d_2, d_3, and d_4—are assigned to the partitions P_1, P_2, P_3, and P_4 by using the effective deadline method. Thereafter, we sort the deadlines and identify *game phases* between two adjacent deadlines. In case a partition spawns across multiple phases such as P_3 in Figure 21.3, we split the work evenly between phases. In this example, the optimization process is divided into three game phases, where each game phase is associated with one color in Figure 21.3, that is, phase 1 between 0 and d_1, phase 2 between d_1 and d_2, and phase 3 between d_2 and d_3 (where $d_3 = d_4$).

We apply our cost optimization algorithm on each game phase independently.

21.4.2 Cooperative Game Formulation

In this section, we formulate the cost optimization problem as a cooperative game that requires the definition of three important components:

$$\text{Game} = \text{players} + \text{strategies} + \text{specification of payoff}$$

We consider a K-player game in which K workflow managers as *players* attempt to minimize the cost c_k of executing their own activity class k, which depends on the number of activities in the activity class $\delta^{(k)}$ and their predicted execution time $p^{(k)}$, while guaranteeing a deadline. For the sake of clarity and without losing any generality, we assume that each workflow manager handles the execution of one activity class. The objective function for each workflow manager $k \in [1..K]$ can be expressed as

$$f_k(\Delta) = c_k(\Delta) = \sum_{i=1}^{S} p_i^{(k)} \cdot \delta_i^{(k)} \cdot \varphi_i$$

where $\Delta = \left(\delta_i^{(k)}\right)_{K \times S}$ is a *matrix of distribution* representing the number of activities from each class k scheduled to each Grid site i, $c_k(\Delta)$ is the cost of activity class k given the distribution Δ, and φ_i is the price of site i. The matrix of distribution represents the *strategies* of each player in the game.

When we achieve the best price/performance ratio, the following deadline constraint for the activity distribution $\delta_i^{(k)}$ and the resource allocation $\theta_i^{(k)}$ of activity class k on site i must be satisfied

$$d_{\text{phase}} \geq \frac{\delta_i^{(k)} \cdot p_i^{(k)}}{\theta_i^{(k)}} \tag{21.1}$$

where d_{phase} is the deadline of the phase represented by the current game.

The embodiment of *payoff* in our cooperative game is the *resource allocation matrix* $\Theta = \left(\theta_i^{(k)}\right)_{K \times S}$ representing the number of processors on site i allocated to each activity class k according to following equation

$$\theta_i^{(k)} = m_i \cdot \frac{\delta_i^{(k)} \cdot p_i^{(k)} \cdot w_i^{(k)}}{\sum_{x=1}^{K} \delta_i^{(x)} \cdot p_i^{(x)} \cdot w_i^{(x)}} \tag{21.2}$$

where $w_i^{(k)}$ is the *importance weight* of site i for activity class k, defined as

$$w_i^{(k)} = \frac{1/(\varphi_i \cdot p_i^{(k)})}{\sum_{y=1}^{S} (1/(\varphi_y \cdot p_y^{(k)}))}, \tag{21.3}$$

where S is the number of Grid sites.

We use this importance weight to improve the fairness of resource allocation because one Grid site may have preferences over a certain set of activity classes. For our cooperative cost optimization game, the solution is determined by the following optimization problem

$$\text{Minimize} \sum_{k=1}^{K} c_k(\Delta)$$

subject to the following constraint:

$$\max_{k \in \text{phase}} \left\{ t^{(k)}(\Delta) \right\} = \max_{k \in \text{phase}} \left\{ \frac{\delta^{(k)}}{\sum_{i=1}^{S} (\theta_i^{(k)} / p_i^{(k)})} \right\} \leq d_{\text{phase}}$$

In order to present the high complexity of the game, we introduce the Lagrangian for this optimization problem, which is a typical method for finding the extreme of a function of some variables subject to one or more constraints. The Lagrangian $L(\delta,\eta)$ for this problem, where η represents the Lagrange multipliers, is

$$L(\delta,\eta) = \sum_{k=1}^{K}\sum_{i=1}^{S} p_i^{(k)} \cdot \delta_i^{(k)} \cdot \varphi_i + \eta \cdot \left(\frac{\delta^{(k)}}{\sum_{i=1}^{S} \theta_i^{(k)}/p_i^{(k)}} \right) - d_{\text{phase}} \tag{21.4}$$

Unfortunately, the exact and direct solution (which is also optimal) to this optimization problem is in general difficult to obtain. Because the problem has high complexity and $K \cdot S$ variables, the solution depends on the distribution of activities in the same class on different sites, and the distribution of activities in different classes on the same site. In other words, the change of one variable impacts the values of all other variables. To circumvent this difficulty, we derive an approximate solution by further formulating this problem as a *sequential game* [17], in which players select a strategy following a certain predefined order, and in which some players can observe the moves of the players who preceded them. Although the optimal solution is not achievable directly from Equation (21.4), we can derive intermediate solutions based on a sequence of *game stages* according to the following decreasing sequence, where $St(l)$ denotes the lth game stage and Δ^* is the optimal distribution:

$$\sum_{k=1}^{K} c_k^{St(1)}\left(\Delta^{St(0)}\right) \geq \sum_{k=1}^{K} c_k^{St(2)}\left(\Delta^{St(1)}\right) \geq \ldots \geq \sum_{k=1}^{K} c_k^{St(l-1)}\left(\Delta^{St(1-2)}\right)$$
$$\geq \sum_{k=1}^{K} c_k^{St(l)}\left(\Delta^{St(1-1)}\right) \geq \sum_{k=1}^{K} c_k\left(\Delta^*\right)$$

The termination condition of the sequential cooperative game is as follows

$$\sum_{k=1}^{K} c_k^{St(l+1)}\left(\Delta^{St(1)}\right) \geq \sum_{k=1}^{K} c_k^{St(l)}\left(\Delta^{St(1-1)}\right)$$

which means that the algorithm can no longer reduce costs.

According to Equations (21.1) and (21.2), the resource allocation matrix in the lth stage denoted as $\Theta^{St(l)}$ is calculated from the distribution of the last stage $\Delta^{St(l-1)}$ and can be further used to produce the new distribution matrix in the same stage:

$$\Theta^{St(l)} = \Theta\left(\Delta^{St(l-1)}\right)$$
$$\Delta^{St(l)} = \Delta\left(\Theta^{St(l)}\right) = \frac{d_{\text{phase}} \cdot \theta_i^{(k)}}{p_i^{(k)}}$$

The main idea of our method is to accumulate the optimization effects across many game stages until we achieve a certain cost balance among activity classes on all Grid sites. Because of the demand of the cumulative effects,.we need a weight that is the normalized value of expected execution costs as defined in Equation (21.3) to generate positive impacts on the results of every game stage. The weight of one activity ought to be comparable with the weight of activities in the same activity class on different sites and the weight of activities in different activity classes on the same site. Furthermore, we need an intermediate variable that in our case is the resource allocation matrix Θ to accept and preserve the cumulative effects from the importance weights and transfer the them to the next stage to the activity distribution matrix Δ.

21.4.3 Game-cost Algorithm

The Game-cost algorithm outlined in pseudocode in Figure 21.4 receives as input a set of workflow partitions, the expected execution time $p^{(k)}$ and the number of activities $\delta^{(k)}$ in each activity class k, the number of processors m_i and the price φ_i of each Grid site i, as well as the deadline of the current phase d_{phase}. The algorithm consists of three steps:

1. The Grid sites are first sorted according to the price/performance ratio for each activity class. In Figure 21.5, for example, the ordered set of sites for activity classes A_0 and A_1 is $\{S_1, S_0\}$in both cases.
2. We add each activity class from the current partition to the set of players and sequentially compute the initial distribution of activities $\Delta^{St(1)}$ from the fastest to the slowest site in terms of price/performance ratio.
3. The algorithm searches for the optimal distribution of activities and the allocation of resources. At the beginning, activity classes are competitors on the site that has the highest price/performance ratio. After the competition of one stage, winners get more processors from one resource and in the next stage losers compete for resources with the second highest price/performance ratio. This process repeats until no more costs can be reduced (i.e., seven stages in our example). In addition, in case of some tight deadlines and the nonbacktracking nature of the algorithm, sometimes it might not be possible to meet the deadlines for all activity classes.

The time complexity of the cost optimization algorithm is $O(l{\cdot}K{\cdot}S)$ and the space complexity is $O(K{\cdot}S)$, where l is the number of game stages, K the number of activity classes, and S the number of Grid sites. The convergence process is very fast as shown in Figure 21.6 with few numbers of stages because of deadline constraint limits. In this experiment, we randomly generated five examples by assigning $10^2 \times 10^4$ activities to $10^2 \times 10^2$ processors. After about 20–30 stages, the optimization almost completed, whereas the entire processes need about 50 stages for this problem size.

```
algorithm game-cost;
input: ℘ = set of partitions;
       K = number of activity classes;
       S = number of Grid sites;
       m_i = number of processors on Grid site i;
       p_i^(k) = predicted execution time of activity class k on site i;
       δ^(k) = number of activities in the activity class k;
       φ_i = price of Grid site i;
       d_phase = deadline of current phase;
output:        Δ^St(1) = distribution matrix of activities;
               Θ^St(1) = allocation matrix of resources.

/* Step 1. Sort Grid sites for each activity class by increasing
           performance/price ratio */

/* Step 2. Initialize Δ^St(0) and the weights w_i^(k) of activity classes */
for each AC^(k) ∈ ℘ do
       add AC^(k) to the set of game players;
       for each sorted Grid site i do
              calculate w_i^(k) according to Equation 21.3;
              calculate δ_i^(k) = (m_i · d_phase) / p_i^(k);
              if δ_i^(k) > δ^(k) − Σ_{j=1}^{i−1} δ_j^(k) then δ_i^(k) = δ^(k) − Σ_{j=1}^{i−1} δ_j^(k);

/* Step 3. Search the final distribution of activities and the
           allocation of resources */
do
       for each AC^(k) ∈ ℘ do
              for each sorted Grid site i do
                     calculate Θ^St(n) = (θ_i^(k))_{K×S};
                     calculate Δ^St(n) = (δ_i^(k))_{K×S};
                     if all activities are allocated then break;
       if max_{k∈phase} {t^(k)(Δ)} > d_phase then continue; /* deadline is not met */
while Σ_{k=1}^{K} (c_k(St(n−1)) − c_k(St(n)) > ε);
```

Figure 21.4 The Game-cost algorithm.

We can observe in Figure 21.6 that the convergence curves can vary depending on the competition process and execution environment, exhibiting some peaks and troughs, and the total cost declines. The execution cost of workflows grows rapidly in the beginning to meet the deadline, then slows down and flattens until it reaches a peak. The first peak indicates completion of the competition on the site with the highest price/performance ratio. After the peak, the execution cost starts to decline

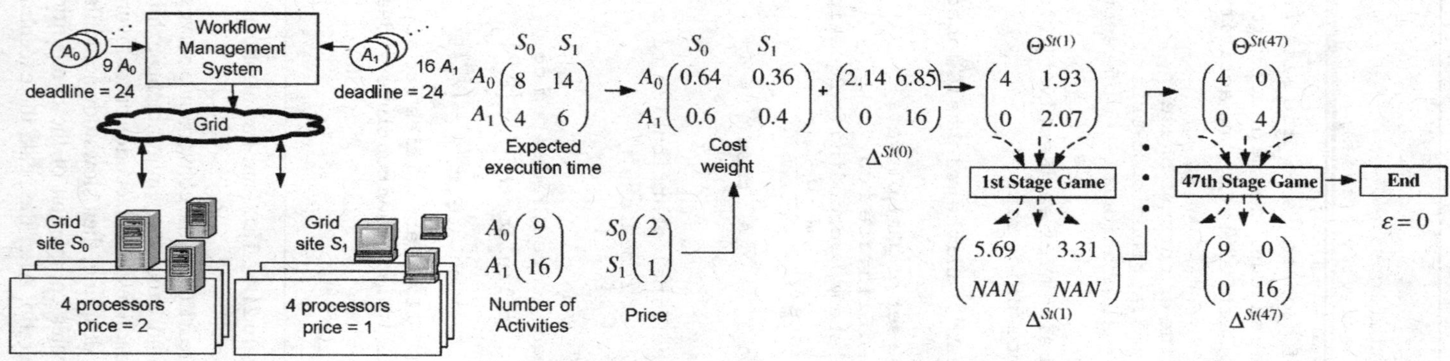

Figure 21.5 Game-cost intermediate data.

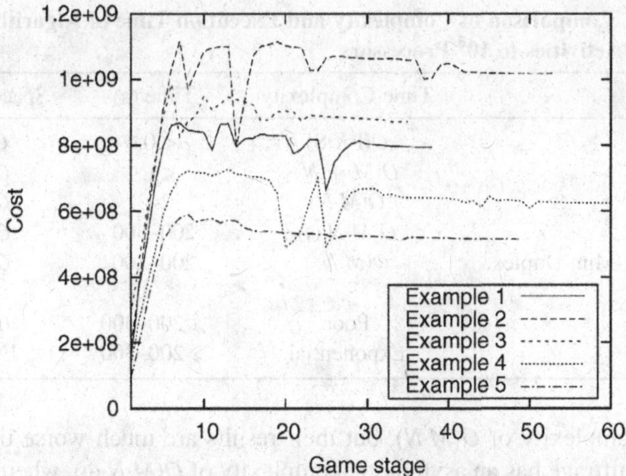

Figure 21.6 Cost optimization convergence process.

very rapidly because many activities are moved to the site with the second highest price/performance ratio, and reach a trough. This process repeats until no more optimization can be achieved and all activity classes can meet their deadlines.

21.5 EXPERIMENTAL RESULTS

In this section, we first compare the spatiotemporal complexity of different scheduling heuristics, and then show results for two real applications in the Austrian Grid [5] to explain the advances of our algorithm. To ensure the completeness of our experiments, we also evaluate and compare different algorithms over a more complex simulated environment using a large amount of activities based on different machine and activity heterogeneity.

21.5.1 Complexity and Execution Times

To compare the computational time and complexity of our algorithm, we implemented in our system the minimum execution time (MET), minimum completion time (MCT), Min-Min, Max-Min, Suffrage, and opportunistic load balancing (OLB) algorithms [18] slightly modified for deadline and cost optimization.

The execution time of the Game-cost algorithm is distinctly less than that for all other algorithms. The time complexity is related only to the number of activity classes K and the number of sites S. When we assign 10^5 activities to 10^3 processors, the execution time of our algorithm is less than 0.4 s on a dual-core 2.4-GHz Opteron processor, while other algorithms may need several hours to generate comparable solutions (see Table 21.2). MET, which has asymptotic complexity of $O(M + N)$, executes for less than one second, where M is the number of processors and N is the number of activities. However, the results of MET have serious problems because MET schedules most activities to the fastest Grid sites. OLB and MCT have

TABLE 21.2 Comparison of Complexity and Execution Time of Algorithms When Assigning 10^5 Activities to 10^3 Processors

Algorithm	Time Complexity	Time (s)	Space Complexity
Game-cost	$O(1 \cdot K \cdot S)$	< 0.4	$O(K \cdot S)$
MET	$O(M + N)$	<1	$O(M + N)$
OLB, MCT	$O(M \cdot N)$	2–3	$O(M + N)$
Suffrage	$O(M \cdot N \cdot \omega)$	200–300	$O(M + N)$
Min-Min, Max-Min, Duplex, HEFT	$O(M \cdot N^2)$	200–300	$O(M + N)$
GA	Poor	$\gg$200–300	$O(M + N)$
A*	Exponential	$\gg$200–300	Exponential

asymptotic complexity of $O(M \cdot N)$, but their results are much worse than those of Game-cost. Suffrage has an asymptotic complexity of $O(M \cdot N \cdot \omega)$, where $\omega \leq N$, and executes for an average of 200–300 s. Min-Min and Max-Min (and Duplex) have asymptotic complexity of $O(M \cdot N^2)$ and an average execution time of 200–300 s.

There are some other well-known algorithms to which we do not compare for various reasons such as work queue (WQ) [19], heterogeneous earliest finish time (HEFT) [20], genetic algorithms (GAs) [3], or A* [21]. WQ is designed for homogeneous parallel machines, HEFT degrades to Min-Min for large-scale applications, while GA-based solutions and A* scale poorly with the number of activities and processors (although they can decrease the makespans of Min-Min by 5–10% according to related work [3]).

For large-scale applications having a much larger total number of activities than activity classes (i.e., $M \gg K$), the space complexity of Game-cost [i.e., $O(K \cdot S)$] is much lower than that of other algorithms [i.e., $O(M + N)$ or exponential], which explains its lower execution time. For such applications characterized by a large number of homogeneous activities, the scheduling problem can be easily formulated as a typical and solvable game, although we cannot exclude the possibility that there will be large-scale applications with tens of thousands of different types of activities. Solving this latter problem will entail further research on game partitioning techniques.

21.5.2 Real-World Applications

In this section, we evaluate our algorithm using two real-world scientific workflow applications called WIEN2k [14] and ASTRO [15], which we introduced earlier in this chapter. We run the experiments in a subset testbed of the Austrian Grid infrastructure [5] consisting of a set of parallel computers and workstation networks accessible through the Globus toolkit and local job queuing systems as separate Grid sites. For the sake of clarity, we limit our testbed to two clusters, one at the University of Innsbruck and the other at the University of Linz, with only four processors available on each Grid site. The characteristics of these machines are summarized in Table 21.3.

In this experiment, we evaluate the performance of Min-Min (the best of the other heuristics) and Game-cost by comparing the cost and fairness of the executions. We

TABLE 21.3 The Austrian Grid Testbed

Site	Size	Gigahertz	Architecture	Manager	Location
hc-ma.uibk	4 (8)	2.2	EM64, COW	SGE	Innsbruck
altix1.jku	4 (64)	1.6	I2, ccNUMA	PBS	Linz

quantify the *cost fairness* by using a variation of the Jain's fairness index [22]

$$\text{Fairness} = \frac{\left(\sum_{w=1}^{W} c_w\right)^2}{W \cdot \sum_{w=1}^{W} c_w^2}$$

where W is the number of workflows and c_w is the total cost of executing the workflow w. The fairness value ranges from zero to one, where zero indicates the worst and one the best fairness when all workflows need approximately the same cost to execute.

Figures 21.7 and 21.8 present a scenario in which Game-cost outperforms Min-Min. In this particular case Min-Min gives a cost of 2377 and a fairness of 0.88. Comparing the results of Game-cost with the results of Min-Min, we notice that Game-cost improved the cost by 7.15% and the fairness by 10%. It is important to notice that the fairness of Game-cost is almost perfect (0.9677).

Moreover, we can intuitively observe that in case of Min-Min the workflow activities are highly interleaved in the Gantt chart, which makes their completion time difficult to predict. Contrarily, Game-cost yields an execution plan in which activities belonging to the same class are grouped in contiguous slots on the same sites, which make their execution more predictable.

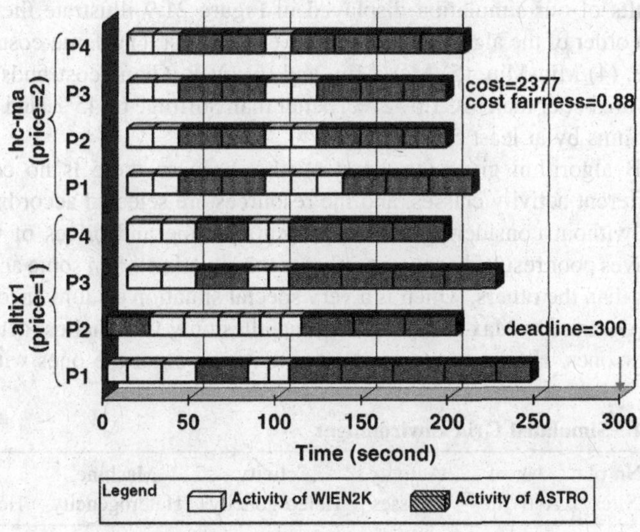

Figure 21.7 Min–min Gantt chart.

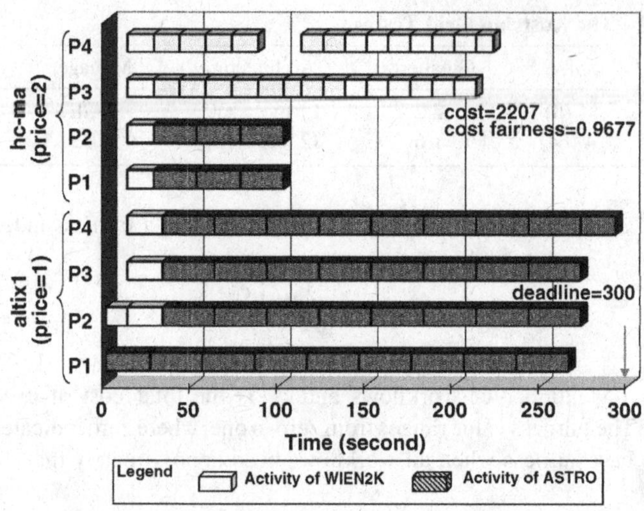

Figure 21.8 Game-cost Gantt chart.

21.5.3 Simulation-Based Comparison

In this section we compare the results delivered by the Game-cost algorithm with the MCT, OLB, Min-Min, Max-Min, and Suffrage heuristics [18] modified and extended to incorporate cost and deadline control. We performed the experiments in a simulated environment summarized in Table 21.4, where the generation of expected execution times of activities is based on activity and machine heterogeneity, which are selected from a uniform distribution in the specified ranges.

The results of our simulation displayed in Figure 21.9 illustrate the following relative cost order of the algorithms from the best to worst: (1) Game-cost, (2) MCT, (3) Suffrage, (4) Min-Min, (5) Max-Min, and (6) OLB. Game-cost finds mappings whose costs are better than MCT by 27%, better than Suffrage by 45%, and better than other algorithms by at least 50%.

The OLB algorithm gives the worst results, because there is no cooperation between different activity classes, and the resources are selected according to their availability without considering activity execution time and prices of Grid sites. Max-Min gives poor results because it only fits the situation when some activities are much larger than the others, which is a very special situation seldom encountered in practice. In contrast to Max-Min, Min-Min handles only the smallest activities and ignores lager ones. However, the smallest activities are not the ones with the best

TABLE 21.4 Simulated Grid Environment

Nr. of Processes	Nr. of Sites	Nr. of Activities	Activity Classes	Activity Heterogeneity	Machine Heterogeneity	Price Heterogeneity
1023	10	13,272	10	[1,10]	[1,10]	[1,10]

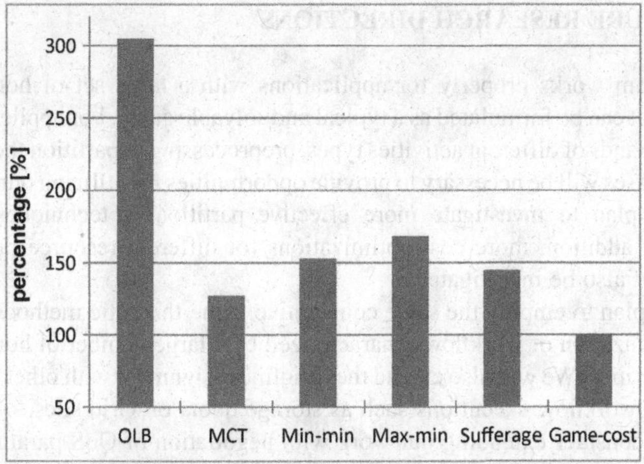

Figure 21.9 Comparison of Game-cost with other heuristics.

performance/price ratio and, therefore, Min-Min cannot perform well. Suffrage performs in much the same way as to Min-Min for similar reasons. MCT performs well, giving the second best results because it unconsciously selects activities with average sizes, and there is a greater likelihood that those activities have the statistically best performance/price ratio. The Game-cost scheduling algorithm provides the best cost because it makes globally intelligent decisions.

21.6 VISIONARY THOUGHTS FOR PRACTITIONERS

Game-cost is a novel scheduling algorithm suited for multiple large-scale workflow applications in the Grid characterized by a large number of homogeneous parallel activities. The algorithm successfully utilizes some properties of Grid and large-scale workflows that cannot be utilized by other heuristics, such as access to Grid sites through local job management systems, or decentralized decisionmaking between multiple independent workflow managers owned by different actors. Undoubtedly, Game-cost has the potential to become an important Grid scheduling algorithm, which we illustrated in this chapter by applying it on real-world applications rather than simulated environments only. The distributed nature of the algorithm based on the cooperative negotiation of multiple workflow managers is a more realistic model that is expected to replace the traditional centralized workflow metascheduling and management schemes.

Obviously, no method can solve all problems, and similarly, Game-cost cannot solve all cost optimization problems. However, it covers an important class of applications, has large potential to be extended, and can be easily mutated to be applied to many different cases because of its good flexibility. On the basis of the new management model, new fault tolerance techniques and load balancing mechanisms can be explored to make the Grid more manageable and efficient.

21.7 FUTURE RESEARCH DIRECTIONS

Our algorithm works properly for applications with a large set of homogeneous activities that can be formulated as a typical and solvable game. For applications with tens of thousands of different activities types, preprocessing to partition the game into different phases will be necessary to provide opportunities for utilizing our algorithm. Hence, we plan to investigate more effective partitioning techniques in future research. In addition, more cost optimizations for different resource provisioning modes could also be investigated.

We also plan to employ the same cooperative game-theoretic method for performance optimization of workflows characterized by a large number of homogeneous parallel activities. We will also extend the deadline assignment with other constraints imposed on workflow executions such as storage quota on Grid sites.

We also consider extending our work with negotiation of QoS parameters (e.g., deadline, maximum budget) between the participating actors that must be preserved for the entire execution of the application in a dynamic and unreliable Grid environment in the form of service-level agreements.

21.8 CONCLUSIONS

With increasing focus on large-scale workflow applications on the Grid, it is important for a Grid middleware to efficiently and effectively schedule and dynamically steer execution of workflows. We analyzed the main bottleneck of a special class of workflows characterized by a large number of homogeneous activities, and presented a solution for cost optimization based on a sequential cooperative game algorithm.

We presented a set of experiments for two real-world applications in the Austrian Grid infrastructure, as well as for randomly generated application scenarios with various activities and machine heterogeneity. The results obtained demonstrate that our approach delivers better solutions in terms of cost and fairness with fewer algorithm execution times than do other existing approaches such as Min-Min, Max-Min, or Suffrage. Furthermore, we observed that the larger-scale the experiments are, the better results we achieve.

REFERENCES

1. S. S. Vadhiyar and J. J. Dongarra, A metascheduler for the Grid, *Proc. 11th International Symp. High Performance Distributed Computing*, Edinburgh, UK, July 24–26, 2002.
2. F. Berman et al., New Grid scheduling and rescheduling methods in the GrADS project, *International Journal of Parallel Programming* **33**:209–229 (2005).
3. T. D. Braun et al., A comparison of eleven static heuristics for mapping a class of independent tasks onto heterogeneous distributed computing systems, *Journal of Parallel and Distributed Computing* **61**(6):810–837 (2001).
4. K. Czajkowski, I. Foster N. Karonis S. Martin W. Smith, and S. Tuecke, A resource management architecture for metacomputing systems, *Proc. Job Scheduling Strategies for Parallel Processing Workshop*, Orlando, FL, March 30, 1998.

5. J. Volkert, Austrian Grid: Overview on the project with focus on parallel applications, *Proc. International Symp. Parallel and Distributed Computing*, Timisoara, Romania, July 6–9, 2006.
6. G. Malewicz I. T. Foster A. L. Rosenberg, and M. Wilde, A tool for prioritizing DAGMan jobs and its evaluation, *Journal of Grid Computing* **2**(5):197–212 (2007).
7. R. Buyya and S. Venugopal, The Gridbus toolkit for service oriented Grid and utility computing: An overview and status report, *Proc. 1st International Workshop on Grid Economics and Business Models*, Seoul, South Korea, April 23, 2004.
8. J. Yu and R. Buyya, A budget constrained scheduling of workflow applications on utility Grids using genetic algorithms, *Proc. 1st Workshop on Workflows in Support of Large-Scale Science*, Paris, June 19–23, 2006.
9. C. Kim et al., An algorithm for optimal load balancing in distributed computer systems, *IEEE Transactions on Computers* **41**(3):381–384 (1992).
10. S. Penmatsa and A. T. Chronopoulos, Cooperative load balancing for a network of heterogeneous computers, *Proc. 21st International Parallel and Distributed Processing Symp.*, Rhodes Island, Greece, April 25–29, 2006.
11. J. Bredin et al., A game-theoretic formulation of multi-agent resource allocation, *Proc. 4th International Conf. Autonomous Agents*, Barcelona, Spain, June 3–7, 2000.
12. Y.-K. Kwok K. Hwang, and S. Song, Selfish Grids: Game theoretic modeling and NAS/PAS benchmark evaluation, *IEEE Transactions on Parallel and Distributed Systems* **18**(5):621–636 (2007).
13. L. Young S. McGough S. Newhouse, and J. Darlington, Scheduling architecture and algorithms within the ICENI Grid middleware, *Proc. UK e-Science All Hands Meeting (EPSRC)*, 2003.
14. K. H. Schwarz P. Blaha, and G. K. H. Madsen, Electronic structure calculations of solids using the WIEN2k package for material sciences, *Computer Physics Communications* **147**(1):71–76 (1Aug. 2002).
15. W. Kapferer et al., Metal enrichment of the intra-cluster medium over a Hubble time for merging and relaxed galaxy clusters, *Astronomy and Astrophysics* **466**(3):813–821 (2007).
16. B. Kao and H. Garcia-Molina, Deadline assignment in a distributed soft real-time system, *IEEE Transactions on Parallel and Distributed Systems* **8**(12):1268–1274 (1997).
17. R. B. Myerson, *Game Theory: Analysis of Conflict*, Harvard Univ. Press, 1997.
18. M. Maheswaran et al., Dynamic mapping of a class of independent tasks onto heterogeneous computing systems, *Journal of Parallel and Distributed Computing* **59**:107–131 (1999).
19. R. L. Graham, Bounds for certain multiprocessor anomalies, *Bell System Technical Journal* **45**:1563–1581 (1966).
20. H. Zhao and R. Sakellariou, An experimental investigation into the rank function of the heterogeneous earliest finish time scheduling algorithm, *Proc. Euro-Par Conf.*, Klagenfurt, Austria, Aug. 26–29, 2003.
21. S. Russell and P. Norvig, Artificial Intelligence: A Modern Approach, Prentice-Hall, 2003.
22. R. Jain D. Chiu, and W. Hawe, *A Quantitative Measure of Fairness and Discrimination for Resource Allocation in Shared Computer Systems*, DEC Research Report TR-301, Sept. 1984.

22

AUCTION-BASED RESOURCE ALLOCATION

BJÖRN SCHNIZLER

22.1 INTRODUCTION

Since the early 1990s, the integration of computers into parallel and distributed systems has become common practice. In this context, the Grid denotes an infrastructure in which computer resources (e.g., disk space, processors) are organized in a cohesive distributed system [1]. Within the Grid, distant computers are dynamically linked over either public or virtual private networks. The establishment of such Grids has major ramifications in business applications, since organizations that have computational demand are not required to purchase and maintain computer resources on their own. Instead, it is possible that computation can be performed on demand by using resources from the Grid that are not under permanent control of the temporary user. The demand for computation is covered by resource owners that have temporarily idle computers. The suppliers of computer resources in Grids are either small-scale owners or large-scale owners who strive for an increased utilization of existing resources.

Much research effort has been devoted to the development of Grid middleware that provides the technical infrastructure to share resources over multiple geographic and administrative domains. However, the allocation of supplied resources to jobs is studied in less detail. Current state-of-the-art systems for resource management typically use idiosyncratic cost functions for scheduling jobs [2]. Those mechanisms are controlled centrally and work well only if information about supply and demand is truthfully reported. Since Grid addresses resource sharing not only within the borders

Market-Oriented Grid and Utility Computing Edited by Rajkumar Buyya and Kris Bubendorfer

of one organizational unit but also cross-organizationally, centrally controlled mechanisms suffer untruthful revelation of job-related data.

Market mechanisms are known to attain fairly efficient allocations in situations where the participating agents may conceal their private information about costs and valuations. If the market mechanism is properly defined, users may be provided incentives to express their true values for service requests and offers. This, in turn, marks the prerequisite for attaining an efficient allocation of services, which maximizes the sum of aggregate valuations [3].

In more recent times, the idea of incorporating market mechanisms into Grid technology has increasingly gained attention. Despite this interest in market-based approaches, research regarding market mechanisms for Grid resources remains in its infancy. The canon of available market mechanisms only insufficiently copes with the requirements imposed by the Grid [3]. The contribution of this chapter is to tailor a market-based Grid exchange that can attain efficient allocations. This is achieved by a multiattribute combinatorial exchange (MACE).

The remainder of this chapter is structured as follows. The economic and technical properties that the proposed market mechanism should satisfy are presented in Section 22.2 and reflected on with regard to related work in Section 22.3. On the basis of the requirements, Section 22.4 describes the design of an auction mechanism for the Grid. In Section 22.5, the proposed mechanism is evaluated by means of a numerical simulation. Section 22.6 concludes the chapter with a brief summary.

22.2 REQUIREMENTS

The objective of an adequate market mechanism for the Grid is the efficient and reliable provision of resources to satisfy demand. A critical step in designing such a market is to understand the nature of the trading object [4]. This chapter considers services that respect resource functionalities (e.g., storage) and quality characteristics (e.g., size), dependences, and time attributes. Relying on services instead of computational resources removes many technical problems. For instance, the resource CPU may technically not be offered without an appropriate amount of hard-disk space on the same computer, while a computation service offering CPU cycles already includes the complementary resources. In the remainder of the chapter, it is abstracted from those technical details by treating resources and services as synonyms.

The following subsections present the design objectives and the Grid-specific requirements for the market mechanism.

22.2.1 Design Objectives

The theoretical basis for designing mechanisms has emerged from a branch of game theory called *mechanism design* [5]. Within the scope of practical mechanism design, the primary design objective is to investigate a mechanism that has desirable properties. The following comprises common economic properties of a mechanism's outcome:

Allocative Efficiency. An allocation is efficient if the sum of individual utilities is maximized. A mechanism can attain allocative efficiency only if the market participants report their valuation truthfully. This requires incentive compatibility in equilibrium.

Incentive Compatibility. A mechanism is incentive-compatible if every participant's expected utility-maximizing strategy in equilibrium with that of every other participant is to report her/his true preferences [6].

Individual Rationality. The constraint of individual rationality requires that the utility following participation in the mechanism be greater than or equal to the previous utility.

Budget Balance. A mechanism is budget balanced if the prices add up to zero for all participants [7]. In case the mechanism runs a deficit, it must be subsidized by an outside source and is therefore not feasible per se.

Computational Tractability. Computational tractability considers the complexity of computing a mechanism's outcome. With an increasing number of participants, the allocation problem can become very demanding and may delimit the design of choice and transfer rules [8].

For the scenario at hand, allocative efficiency meets the general design goal that the mechanism designer wants to achieve, whereas the remaining categories are constraints on the objective.

22.2.2 Domain-Specific Requirements

In addition to those mechanism properties pertaining to the outcome, the mechanism must also account for the underlying environment. The constraints of the market participants impose very rigid requirements on the design [3]:

Double-Sided Mechanism. A Grid middleware usually provides a global directory enabling multiple service owners to publish their services and multiple service requesters to discover them. Since a market mechanism replaces these directories, it has to allow many resource owners (henceforth sellers) and resource consumers (buyers) to trade simultaneously.

Language Including Bids on Attributes. Participants in the Grid usually have different requirements for the quality characteristics of Grid services and require these in different timespans. For example, a data-mining job could require a storage service with at least 250 GB of free space for 4 h in any timeslot between 9 a.m. and 4 p.m. The Grid community takes these requirements into account by defining service-level agreement protocols, such as WS-Agreement [9]. To facilitate the adherence of these agreement protocols, a market mechanism is required to support bids on multiple quality attributes of services as well as time objectives.

Language Including Combinatorial Bids. Buyers usually demand a combination of different Grid services as a bundle in order to perform a task [10]. As such,

Grid services are *complementarities*, meaning that participants have superadditive valuations for the services, since the sum of valuations for single services is less than the valuation for the whole bundle. Suppose that a buyer requires services for storage, computation, and rendering. If any service is not allocated to her, the remaining bundle has no value for her. In order to avoid this exposure risk, the mechanism must allow for bids on bundles. In addition, the buyer may want to submit more than one bid on a bundle as well as many that exclude each other. In this case, the resources for the bundles are substitutes; that is, participants have subadditive valuations for the services. For instance, a buyer is willing to pay a high price for a service during the day and a low price if the service is executed at night. However, this service may be computed only once. To express this, the mechanism must support XOR (exclusive OR) bids to express substitutes. For simplicity, a seller's bid is restricted to a set of OR bids. This simplification can be justified by the fact that Grid services are nonstorable commodities; for instance, a computation service currently available cannot be stored for a later time.

Language Including Coallocation Constraints. Capacity-demanding jobs often require the simultaneous allocation of several homogenous service instances from different providers. For example, a large-scale simulation may require several computation services to be completed at one time. The literature often refers to the simultaneous allocation of multiple homogenous services as *coallocation*. A mechanism for the Grid has to enable coallocations and provide functionality to control it. In this context, two cases must be considered: (1) it is desirable to limit the maximum number of service coallocations, that is, the maximum number of service divisions; and (2) it may be logical to couple multiple services of a bundle in order to guarantee that these resources are allocated from the same seller and will be executed on the same machine.

An adequate market mechanism for the Grid must satisfy these requirements stemming from the economic environment and ideally meet the design objectives.

22.3 RELATED WORK

Waldspurger et al. [11] and Regev and Nisan [12] propose the application of Vickrey auctions for allocating homogenous computational resources in distributed systems. Vickrey auctions achieve truthful bidding as a dominant strategy and hence result in efficient allocations.

Buyya et al. [13] were among the first researchers to motivate the transfer of market-based systems from distributed systems to Grids. Nonetheless, they propose classical one-sided auction types that cannot account for combinatorial bids. Wolski et al. [14] compare classical auctions with a bargaining market, concluding that the bargaining market is superior to an auction-based market. This result is less surprising since the authors consider only classical auction formats where buyers cannot express bids on bundles. Eymann et al. [15] introduce a decentralized bargaining system for resource allocation in Grids. In their simulation the bargaining systems work fairly well; however, bids on bundles are largely ignored.

Subramoniam et al. [10] account for combinatorial bids by providing a tatonnement process for allocating and pricing Grid resources. Furthermore, Ng et al. [16] propose repeated combinatorial auctions as a microeconomic resource allocation in distributed systems. Nonetheless, the resources are still considered to be standardized commodities. Standardization of the resources would imply that either the number of resources is limited compared to the number of all possible resources or there are many mechanisms that are likely to suffer because of meager participation. Both implications result in rather inefficient allocations.

Additionally, state-of-the-art mechanisms widely neglect time attributes for bundles and quality constraints for single resources. Hence, the use of these mechanisms in the Grid environment is considerably diminished. The introduction of time attributes redefines the Grid allocation problem as a scheduling problem. To account for time attributes, Wellman et al. [17] model single-sided auction protocols in order to allocate and to schedule resources with regard to different time constraint considerations. However, the proposed approach is single-sided. Installing competition on both sides is deemed superior, since no particular market side is systematically given an advantage. Demanding competition on both sides suggests the development of a combinatorial exchange. In the research literature, Parkes et al. [6] introduce the first combinatorial exchange as a single-shot sealed-bid auction. As payment scheme, Vickrey discounts are approximated. The approach results in approximately efficient outcomes; however, it accounts for neither time nor quality constraints. It is thus not directly applicable to the Grid allocation problem. Counteractively, Bapna et al. [18] propose a family of combinatorial auctions for allocating Grid services. Although the mechanism accounts for quality and time attributes and enables the simultaneous trading of multiple buyers and sellers, there is no competition on the sellers' side as all orders are aggregated to one virtual order. Moreover, the mechanism does not account for coallocation constraints.

In reviewing the related mechanisms according to the requirements presented in Section 22.2, it is revealed that no market mechanism installs competition on both sides, includes combinatorial bids, allows for time constraints, manages quality constraints, or considers coallocation restrictions. This chapter intends to address these deficiencies by outlining the design of a multiattribute combinatorial exchange for allocating and scheduling Grid services.

22.4 A MULTIATTRIBUTE COMBINATORIAL EXCHANGE

The design of MACE follows common assumptions of mechanism design and auction theory; agents are assumed to be risk neutral, have quasilinear utility functions as well as independent private valuations and reservation prices. The valuation functions of agents satisfy free disposal and $v_i(\emptyset) = 0$. The valuation functions of sellers allow a linear transformation in case of partial executions. For instance, a seller who values a storage service with 300 GB capacity with 10 also values a partial execution of the service with 150 GB with 5. In contrast, buyers do not accept partial executions of their requests or their applications. Furthermore, it is assumed that buyers can specify their resource requirements in terms of quality characteristics and job duration. For instance, it is assumed that a buyer can specify the amount of storage space that is required for executing a job. In addition, the buyer can specify how long the job has to be executed. Likewise, a seller of resources can specify the characteristics of those resources that he can offer in the future. The elicitation of the resource characteristics can be supported by prediction models such as proposed by Smith [19]. In addition, it is assumed that jobs can be paused and be resumed at a later time.

Resource allocations are interpreted as contracts. This means that a seller has to provide the allocated resources. In case of failure, the seller has to offer alternative resources or compensate the buyer for the failed allocation.

As in any combinatorial auction, the design of MACE affects three main components: (1) the communication language which defines how bids can be formalized, (2) the winner determination problem, and (3) the pricing scheme to determine net payments. As such, the following description of MACE is structured as follows: (1) a bidding language is introduced that supports multiattribute combinatorial bids including coallocation constraints, (2) a winner determination model (allocation rule) is proposed that attains an efficient allocation if agents bid truthfully, and finally, (3) a pricing schema is outlined to incentivize agents to reveal their private information.

22.4.1 Bidding Language

The design of an auction that meets the requirements requires an expressive bidding language. The following notation is used to define such a language. Let N be a set of N buyers and M be a set of M sellers, where $n \in N$ defines an arbitrary buyer and $m \in M$ an arbitrary seller. There are G discrete resources $G = \{g_1, \ldots, g_G\}$ with $g_k \in G$ and a set of D bundles $S = \{S_1, \ldots, S_D\}$ with $S_j \in S$ and $S_j \subseteq G$ as a subset of resources. For instance, $S_j = \{g_k, g_l\}$ denotes that the bundle S_j consists of two resources, g_k and g_l, where g_k could be a computation service and g_l a storage service.

A resource g_k has a set of A_k cardinal quality attributes $A_{g_k} = (a_1^k, \ldots, a_{A_k}^k)$ where $a_i^k \in A_{g_k}$ represents the $i.th$ attribute of the resource g_k. For instance, in the context of a Grid resource, a quality attribute can be the *size* of a storage service. A buyer n can specify the minimal required quality characteristics for a bundle $S_j \in S$ with $q_n^N(S_j, g_k, a_i^k) \geq 0$, where $g_k \in S_j$ is a resource of the bundle S_j and $a_i^k \in A_{g_k}$ is an attribute of the resource g_k. For instance, the minimal required size of a storage service $g_k \in S_j$ can be denoted by $q_n^N(S_j, g_k, a_i^k) = 200\,\text{GB}$. Accordingly, a seller m can specify the maximum offered quality characteristics with $q_m^M(S_j, g_k, a_i^k) \geq 0$. The quality attributes are assumed to be cardinal numbers. The characteristics have to satisfy $\underline{q_n^N(\cdot)} \geq \overline{q_n^N}(\cdot)$ if the first quality characteristic $q_n^N(\cdot)$ satisfies at least the second one $\overline{q_n^N}(\cdot)$. These quality characteristics are also used to specify a value for the agent's network connection. For instance, this can be used to denote the uplink and downlink rates of the given network connection.

For each resource $g_k \in S_j$, a buyer n can specify the maximum number of coallocations in each timeslot with $\gamma_n(S_j, g_k) \geq 0$. This means that a buyer n can limit the number of sellers that provide the required resource g_k. Let $\gamma_n(S_j, g_k) = K$ if the resource g_k has no divisibility restrictions, where K is a large enough constant.[1] The coupling of two resources in a bundle is represented by the binary variable $\phi_n(S_j, g_k, g_l)$, where $\phi_n(S_j, g_k, g_l) = 1$ if resources g_k and g_l have to be allocated from the same bundle bid of a seller and $\phi_n(S_j, g_k, g_l) = 0$ otherwise. It is assumed that all resources offered in a bundle are located on the same machine.

Resources in the form of a bundle S_j can be assigned to a set of maximal T discrete timeslots $T = (0, \ldots, T-1)$, where $t \in T$ specifies one single timeslot. A buyer n can specify the minimum required number of timeslots $s_n(S_j) \geq 0$ for a bundleS_j. The earliest timeslot for any allocatable bundle S_j can be specified by $e_n^N(S_j) \geq 0$ for a buyer n and $e_m^M(S_j) \geq 0$ for a seller m; the latest possible allocatable timeslot, by $l_n^N(S_j) \geq 0$ for a buyer n and by $l_m^M(S_j) \geq 0$ for a seller m.

A buyer n can express the valuation for a single slot of a bundle S_j by $v_n(S_j) \geq 0$, whereat $v_n(S_j)$ denotes the maximum price for which the buyer n is willing to buy. The reservation price for allocating a single slot of a bundle S_j is denoted by $r_m(S_j) \geq 0$. This price represents the minimum price for which the seller m is willing to sell.

On the basis of these parameters, an atomic bid of a buyer is defined as follows.

Definition 22.1: MACE Atomic Buyer Bid. In MACE, an atomic bid B_n of a buyer n is defined as

$$\begin{aligned} B_n(S_j) = (&v_n(S_j), s_n(S_j), e_n^N(S_j), l_n^N(S_j) \\ &(q_n^N(S_j, \bar{g}_1, a_1^1), \ldots, q_n^N(S_j, \bar{g}_l, a_{A_{\bar{g}_l}}^l)), (\gamma_n(S_j, \bar{g}_1), \ldots \gamma_n(S_j, \bar{g}_l)) \\ &(\phi_n(S_j, \bar{g}_1, \bar{g}_2), \phi_n(S_j, \bar{g}_1, \bar{g}_3), \ldots, \phi_n(S_j, \bar{g}_1, \bar{g}_l), \ldots, \phi_N\text{agent}(S_j, \bar{g}_{l-1}, \bar{g}_l))) \end{aligned}$$

where $G_{S_j} = \{\bar{g}_1, \ldots, \bar{g}_l\}$ are the resources of the bundle S_j.

The atomic bid can also be represented in a more compact way. For instance, the encoding of the coupling conditions $\phi_n(\cdot)$ can be restricted to cases with $\phi_n(\cdot) = 1$. For better readability, however, the atomic bid is formalized in this detailed way.

In order to allow buyers to express substitutes over a set of resources, MACE supports the submission of XOR concatenated atomic bids.

Definition 22.2: MACE XOR Buyer Bid. A XOR bid of a buyer n is defined as

$$B_n = (B_n(S_j) \oplus \ldots \oplus B_n(S_k)).$$

The total number of atomic bids that are concatenated by the XOR operator can be restricted by the auctioneer.

[1]The constant K has to be greater than the total number of seller bids.

The sellers' bids are formalized similarly to those of the buyers. However, they do not include maximum divisibility and coupling properties and assume that the number of time slots is equal to the given time range. An atomic bid for a seller is defined as follows.

Definition 22.3: MACE Atomic Seller Bid. An atomic bid B_m for a seller m is defined as

$$B_m(S_j) = (r_m(S_j), e_m^M(S_j), l_m^M(S_j), q_m^M(S_j, \bar{g}_1, a_1^1), \ldots, (q_m^M(S_j, \bar{g}_l, a_{A_{\bar{g}_l}}^l)))$$

where $G_{S_j} = \{\bar{g}_1, \ldots, \bar{g}_l\}$ are the resources that are part of the bundle S_j.

For sellers as resource providers, a XOR operator is not necessary. Grid resources are nonstorable commodities. For instance, a computation service currently available cannot be stored and used at a later time. As such, the bidding space for sellers is restricted to OR bids.

In the following subsections, it is assumed that the bid elicitation has already taken place. This means that buyers and sellers submitted their preferences by means of the bidding language to the auctioneer. For formulating bids, agents may use preference elicitation techniques to formalize their preferences [20] or may use an autonomous bidding agent that takes over their bidding strategies.

22.4.2 Winner Determination

On the basis of this bidding language, the winner determination problem of MACE [MACE allocation problem (MAP)] can be formulated. Following the previous winner determination models, MAP is formulated as a linear mixed-integer program.

For formalizing the model, the decision variables $x_n(S_j)$, $z_{n,t}(S_j)$, $y_{m,n,t}(S_j)$, and $d_{m,n,t}(S_j)$ have to be introduced. The binary variable $x_n(S_j) \in \{0, 1\}$ denotes whether bundle S_j is allocated to buyer $n(x_n(S_j) = 1)$ or not $(x_n(S_j) = 0)$. Furthermore, the binary variable $z_{n,t}(S_j) \in \{0, 1\}$ is assigned to a buyer n and is associated in the same way as $x_n(S_j)$ with the allocation of S_j in timeslot t. For a seller m, the real-valued variable $y_{m,n,t}(S_j)$ with $0 \leq y_{m,n,t}(S_j) \leq 1$ indicates the percentage contingent of bundle S_j allocated to the buyer n in timeslot t. For example, $y_{m,n,t}(S_j) = 0.5$ denotes that 50% of the quality characteristics of bundle S_j are allocated from seller m to buyer n in timeslot t. Suppose that a seller is offering a storage service $S_2 = \{g_2\}$ with 30 GB of free space. A partial allocation of 15 GB from seller m to buyer n in timeslot t would lead to $y_{m,n,t}(S_2) = 0.5$. The binary variable $d_{m,n,t}(S_j) \in \{0, 1\}$ is linked with $y_{m,n,t}(S_j)$ and denotes whether the seller m allocates bundle S_j to buyer n in timeslot $t(d_{m,n,t}(S_j) = 1)$ or not $(d_{m,n,t}(S_j) = 0)$.

Using these variables, MAP is formulated as follows [21]:

$$\max \sum_{n \in N} \sum_{S_j \in S} \sum_{t \in T} v_n(S_j) z_{n,t}(S_j) - \sum_{m \in M} \sum_{n \in N} \sum_{S_j \in S} \sum_{t \in T} r_m(S_j) y_{m,n,t}(S_j) \qquad (22.1)$$

$$\text{s.t.} \sum_{S_j \in S} x_n(S_j) \leq 1, \forall n \in N \tag{22.2}$$

$$\sum_{t \in T} z_{n,t}(S_j) - x_n(S_j) s_n(S_j) = 0, \forall n \in N, \forall S_j \in S \tag{22.3}$$

$$\sum_{n \in N} y_{m,n,t}(S_j) \leq 1, \forall m \in M, \forall S_j \in S, \forall t \in T \tag{22.4}$$

The objective function 1 maximizes the surplus V^*, which is defined as the difference between the sum of the buyers' valuations $v_n(S_j)$ and the sum of the sellers' reservation prices $r_m(S_j)$. Assuming bidders to be truthful, the objective function reflects the goal of maximizing social welfare. The first constraint, in Equation (22.2), guarantees that each buyer n can be allocated to one only bundle S_j. This constraint is necessary to fulfill the XOR constraint of a buyer bid. Constraint (22.3) ensures that for any allocated bundle S_j, a buyer n receives exactly the required slots within the time set T. For each timeslot t, constraint (22.4) ensures that each seller cannot allocate more than the seller possesses. The formulation of this constraint implicates that a seller cannot fully allocate two resources to two different buyers in timeslot t. For instance, suppose a seller offers the bundle $S_j \doteq \{g_k, g_l\}$. An allocation of the resource g_k to buyer 1 (with $y_{m,1,t}(S_j) = 1$) and an allocation of g_l to buyer 2 (with $y_{m,2,t}(S_j) = 1$) is not possible. This restriction is applied to simplify the model. However, the abovementioned allocation can be attained by submitting an OR concatenated bid on the bundles $S_n = \{g_k\}$ and $S_i = \{g_l\}$.

Constraints (22.2)–(22.4) consider the basic allocation functionality of the exchange. In designing an adequate mechanism for the Grid, quality characteristics and dependences between resources must also be addressed:

$$\sum_{S_{j3} \ni g_k} z_{n,t}(S_j) q_n^N(S_j, g_k, a_i^k) - \sum_{S_{j3} \ni g_k} \sum_{m \in M} y_{m,n,t}(S_j) q_m^M(S_j, g_k, a_i^k) \leq 0,$$

$$\forall n \in N, \forall g_k \in G, \forall a_i^k \in A_{g_k}, \forall t \in T \tag{22.5}$$

$$\sum_{S_{j3} \ni g_k} \sum_{m \in M} d_{m,n,t}(S_j) - \sum_{S_{j3} \ni g_k} \gamma_n(S_j, g_k) z_{n,t}(S_j) \leq 0,$$

$$\forall n \in N, \forall g_k \in G, \forall t \in T \tag{22.6}$$

$$\sum_{S_{j3} \ni g_k, g_l} \phi_n(S_j, g_k, g_l) \Big(\sum_{S_{j3} \ni g_k} d_{m,n,t}(S_j) - \sum_{S_{j3} \ni g_l} d_{m,n,t}(S_j) \Big) = 0,$$

$$\forall n \in N, \forall m \in M, \forall g_k, g_l \in G, \forall t \in T \tag{22.7}$$

$$\sum_{S_{j3} \ni g_k, g_l} \phi_n(S_j, g_k, g_l) \Big(\sum_{S_{j3} \ni g_k} \sum_{m \in M} d_{m,n,t}(S_j) + \sum_{S_{j3} \ni g_l} \sum_{m \in M} d_{m,n,t}(S_j) - 2 z_{n,t}(S_j) \Big)$$

$$\leq 0, \forall n \in N, \forall g_k, g_l \in G, \forall t \in T \tag{22.8}$$

Constraint (22.5) guarantees that for any allocated bundle in an arbitrary timeslot t, all required resources have to be fulfilled in the same slot in at least the qualities demanded. Constraint (22.6) ensures that a resource will be provided by at most $\gamma_n(S_j, g_k)$ different suppliers. For simplicity, it is assumed that a resource g_k with restricted coallocations is not part of further XOR concatenated bids of the buyer n. Furthermore, resources with coallocations cannot be allocated as free-disposal items. As an example, suppose that a buyer n values $S_j = \{g_k\}$ with $v_n(S_j) = 1$ and $S_i = \{g_l\}$ with $v_n(S_i) = 10$. For bundle S_j, the buyer has coallocation restrictions with $\gamma_n(S_j, g_l) = 1$. A seller m that offers $S_t = \{g_k, g_l\}$ cannot allocate the resource g_l to buyer n as this would imply a free-disposal allocation of the restricted resource g_k.

Constraints (22.7) and (22.8) are both responsible for the coupling of two resources. Constraint (22.7) ensures that two resources must be provided by the same seller, in case they should be coupled. This constraint alone does not suffice the coupling requirements since it would be possible for two sellers to coallocate a coupled computation service with 3000 MIPS (million instructions per second) and a storage service with 30 GB in different quality characteristics. For instance, MAP could allocate a computation service with 2998 MIPS and a storage service with 1 GB from one seller, and a computation service with 2 MIPS and a storage service with 29 GB from another. To exclude these undesirable allocations, constraint (22.8) imposes the restriction that coupled resources cannot be coallocated. Simplifying the model, this also includes free-disposal resources. For instance, if the computation service with 3000 MIPS and the storage service with 30 GB are allocated from one particular seller as a bundle, another seller cannot allocate a bundle containing a rendering service and another storage service to the same buyer. However, the seller may allocate any bundle without a storage and computation service to the buyer, such as the rendering service alone. Furthermore, it is assumed that coupled resources are only part of one particular atomic bid $B_n(S_j)$ in case a buyer submits two XOR concatenated bids containing coupled resources.

The time restrictions of the bids are given by

$$(e_n^N(S_j) - t) z_{n,t}(S_j) \leq 0, \forall n \in N, \forall S_j \in S, \forall t \in T \tag{22.9}$$

$$(t - l_n^N(S_j)) z_{n,t}(S_j) \leq 0, \forall n \in N, \forall S_j \in S, \forall t \in T \tag{22.10}$$

$$(e_m^N(S_j) - t) \sum_{n \in N} y_{m,n,t}(S_j) \leq 0, \forall m \in M, \forall S_j \in S, \forall t \in T \tag{22.11}$$

$$(t - l_m^M(S_j)) \sum_{n \in N} y_{m,n,t}(S_j) \leq 0, \forall m \in M, \forall S_j \in S, \forall t \in T \tag{22.12}$$

Essentially, constraints (22.9)–(22.12) indicate that slots cannot be allocated before the earliest and after the latest timeslot of either a buyer [constraints (22.9) and (22.10)] or a seller [Constraints (22.11) and (22.13)].

Finally, the establishment of the relationship between the real-valued decision variable $y_{m,n,t}(S_j)$ and the binary variable $d_{m,n,t}(S_j)$ needs to be addressed and the decision variables of the optimization problem have to be defined:

$$y_{m,n,t}(S_j) - d_{m,n,t}(S_j) \leq 0, \forall n \in N, \forall m \in M, \forall S_j \in S, \forall t \in T \quad (22.13)$$

$$d_{m,n,t}(S_j) - y_{m,n,t}(S_j) < 1, \forall n \in N, \forall m \in M, \forall S_j \in S, \forall t \in T \quad (22.14)$$

$$x_n(S_j) \in \{0,1\}, \forall n \in N, \forall S_j \in S \quad (22.15)$$

$$z_{n,t}(S_j) \in \{0,1\}, \forall n \in N, \forall S_j \in S, \forall t \in T \quad (22.16)$$

$$y_{m,n,t}(S_j) \geq 0, \forall n \in N, \forall m \in M, \forall S_j \in S, \forall t \in T \quad (22.17)$$

$$d_{m,n,t}(S_j) \in \{0,1\}, \forall n \in N, \forall m \in M, \forall S_j \in S, \forall t \in T \quad (22.18)$$

Constraints (22.13) and (22.14) incorporate an `if-then-else` constraint. If a seller m partially allocates a bundle S_j to a single buyer n ($y_{m,n,t}(S_j)$>0), the binary variable $d_{m,n,t}(S_j)$ has to be $d_{m,n,t}(S_j) = 1$ [constraint (22.13)]; otherwise, it has to be $d_{m,n,t}(S_j) = 0$ [constraint (22.14)]. Finally, constraints (22.15)–(22.18) specify the decision variables of the optimization problem.

As multiple solutions may exist that maximize the objective function, ties are broken in favor of maximizing the number of traded bundles and then at random. A special case of tie breaking occurs if the total surplus is zero. This can be the case if buyers and sellers balance their payments or if no possible trade can be matched. In such a scenario, the allocation with the balanced traders is selected.

Following related work on combinatorial auctions and exchanges [22], the presented winner determination problem is also NP-complete.

Theorem 22.1: MAP Complexity.The MACE allocation problem (MAP) is NP-complete.

Proof. The combinatorial allocation problem (CAP) can be reduced to MAP. Obviously, any CAP instance (multiple buyers, one seller with a zero reservation price, no attributes and no coupling constraints) can be solved by MAP. CAP is known to be NP-complete [22]. As such, MAP is also NP-complete. □

22.4.3 Pricing

The outcome of MAP is allocative efficient as long as buyers and sellers reveal their valuations truthfully. The incentive to set bids according to the valuation is induced by an adequate pricing mechanism.

The implementation of an adequate price mechanism for an exchange is a challenging problem. The Vickrey–Clarke–Groves (VCG) schema cannot be applied as it runs a deficit and requires outside subsidiary [23]. On the other hand, alternative pricing schemas such as the approximated VCG mechanism are budget-balanced and approximately efficient [6]. However, the pricing scheme still requires $I+1$ instances of MAP to be solved if I agents are part of the allocation. As a consequence, an alternative pricing scheme is designed that is computationally more efficient and still attains desirable economic properties. The underlying idea of the k-pricing scheme is to determine prices for a buyer and a seller on the basis of the difference between their bids [24]. For instance, suppose that a buyer n wants to purchase a storage service for $v_n(\cdot) = 5$ and a seller m wants to sell a storage service for at least $r_m(\cdot) = 4$. The difference between these bids is $\beta = 1$, where β is the surplus of this transaction that can be distributed among the participants. For a single commodity exchange, the k-pricing scheme can be formalized as follows. Let $v_n(S_j) = a$ be the valuation of a buyer n and $r_m(S_j) = b$ be the reservation price of the buyer's counterpart m. It is assumed that $a \geq b$, which indicates that the buyer has a valuation for the commodity that is at least as high as the seller's reservation price. Otherwise, no trade would occur. The price for a buyer n and a seller m can be calculated by $p(S_j) = ka + (1-k)b$ with $0 \leq k \leq 1$.

The k-pricing schema can also be applied to a multiattribute combinatorial exchange: In each timeslot t in which a bundle S_j is allocated from one or more sellers, the surplus generated by this allocation is distributed among a buyer and the sellers. Suppose that a buyer n receives a computation service $S_1 = \{g_1\}$ with 1000 MIPS in timeslot 4 and values this slot with $v_n(S_1) = 5$. The buyer obtains the computation service $S_1 = \{g_1\}$ by a coallocation from seller 1 (400 MIPS) with a reservation price of $r_1(S_1) = 1$ and from seller 2 (600 MIPS) with $r_2(S_1) = 2$. The distributable surplus of this allocation is $\beta_{n,4}(S_1) = 5-(1+2) = 2$. Buyer n gets $k\beta_{n,4}(S_1)$ of this surplus; thus, the price buyer n has to pay for this slot $t = 4$ is

$$p^N_{k,n,4}(S_j) = v(S_1) - k\beta_{n,4}(S_1)$$

Furthermore, the sellers have to divide the other part of this surplus: $(1-k)\beta_{n,4}(S_1)$. This will be done by considering each proportion a seller's bid has on the surplus. In the example, this proportion $0 \leq o_{m,n,t}(S_j) \leq 1$ for seller 1 is $o_{1,n,4}(S_1) = \frac{1}{3}$ and for seller 2 is $o_{2,n,4}(S_1) = \frac{2}{3}$. The price that a seller m receives for a single slot $t = 4$ is consequently calculated as

$$p^M_{k,n,4}(S_j) = r_m(S_1) + (1-k)\beta_{n,4}(S_1)o_{m,n,4}(S_1).$$

Expanding this scheme to a set of timeslots, coallocations, and the allocation of different bundles to a buyer results in the following formalization. Let $\beta_{n,t}(S_j)$ be the surplus for a bundle S_j of a buyer n with all corresponding sellers for a timeslot t:

$$\beta_{n,t}(S_j) = z_{n,t}(S_j)v_n(S_j) - \sum_{m \in M} \sum_{S_l \in S} y_{m,n,t}(S_l)r_m(S_l)$$

The iteration over $\sum_{S_l \in S} y_{m,n,t}(S_l)r_m(S_l)$ is required, as one seller may allocate a subset S_l of the required bundle S_j to a buyer. For instance, this is the case if a buyer requires $S_3 = \{g_1, g_2\}$ and two sellers allocate $S_1 = \{g_1\}$ and $S_2 = \{g_2\}$.

For the entire job (i.e., all timeslots), the price for a buyer n is calculated as

$$p_{k,n}^{N}(S_j) = x_n(S_j)v_n(S_j)s_n(S_j) - k\sum_{t\in T}\beta_{n,t}(S_j)$$

This means that the difference between the valuation for all slots $v_n(S_j)s_n(S_j)$ of the bundle S_j and the kth proportion of the sum over all timeslots of the corresponding surpluses is determined.

The price of a seller m is calculated in a similar way. First, the proportion $o_{m,n,t}(S_j)$ of a seller m allocating a bundle S_j to the buyer n in timeslot t is given by

$$O_{m,n,t}(S_j) = \left\{ \frac{y_{m,n,t}(S_j)r_m(S_j)}{\sum_{m\in N}\sum_{S_l\in S} y_{m,n,t}(S_l)r_m(S_l)} \right.$$

The formula computes the proportion of a seller's allocation compared to all other allocations made by any seller to the particular buyer n. In case a buyer is allocated a bundle S_j, it is ensured that it is not allocated any other bundle (XOR constraint). As a consequence, any allocation of a seller to buyer n correlates with this bundle S_j. Having computed $\beta_{n,t}(S_j)$ and $o_{m,n,t}(S_j)$, the price a seller receives for a bundle S_j is calculated as follows:

$$p_{k,m}^{M}(S_j) = \sum_{n\in N}\sum_{t\in T} y_{m,n,t}(S_j)r_m(S_j) + (1-k)\sum_{n\in N}\sum_{S_l\in S}\sum_{t\in T} o_{m,n,t}(S_j)\beta_{n,t}(S_l)$$

Using the k-pricing schema, the exchange does not have to subsidize the participants, since it fulfills the budget balance property in a way that no payments toward the mechanism are necessary.

Theorem 22.2: Budget Balance and Individual Rationality. MACE is budget-balanced and individually rational [3].

Following the Myerson–Satterthwaite theorem [23], it is obvious that MACE cannot be incentive-compatible. In order to evaluate these implications of the pricing schema in different settings, further analyses need to be investigated.

22.5 EVALUATION

The application of the k-pricing schema implicates that agents can gain a higher utility by misrepresenting their private information. This raises the question of whether this utility gain can be measured and whether it can serve as a metric for the loss of incentive compatibility. Let $\tilde{I}$ be a set of agents that can manipulate their valuations and reservation prices. In a benchmark scenario with an outcome o, all agents $\tilde{i} \in \tilde{I}$ honestly reveal their preferences. Consequently, their utility $u_{\tilde{i}}(o)$ from bidding truthfully can be calculated as $\sum_{\tilde{i}\in\tilde{I}} u_{\tilde{i}}(o)$. In a second setting with an outcome $\bar{o}$, agents $\tilde{i} \in \tilde{I}$ manipulate their bids, whereas the input parameters (i.e., the characteristics of the underlying bids) remain the same. The resulting utility due to manipulation is calculated as $\sum_{\tilde{i}\in\tilde{I}} u_{\tilde{i}}(\bar{o})$. Thus, the utility gained due to manipulation can be measured as

$$UG^{O}_{n,k}(S_j) = \sum_{\tilde{i}\in\tilde{I}} u_{\tilde{i}}(\bar{o}) - \sum_{\tilde{i}\in\tilde{I}} u_{\tilde{i}}(o) \tag{22.19}$$

where k stands for the k-pricing schema and O stands for an optimal winner determination algorithm. The metric reflects the difference between the utility gained by manipulation and the utility gained in a truthful scenario. If this value is positive, agents have an incentive to manipulate their bids. In case the value is negative, agents do worse by manipulating.

22.5.1 Data Basis

As a data basis, a random bid stream including "decay" distributed bundles is generated. The "decay" function has been recommended by Sandholm [8] because it creates hard instances of the allocation problem. At the beginning, a bundle consists of one random resource. Afterward, new resources are added randomly with a probability of $\alpha = 0.75$. This procedure is iterated until resources are no longer added or the bundle already includes the same resource. The effects that can be obtained by the decay distribution will be amplified. Hence, the decay function is used to create a benchmark for upper bounds of the effects.

As an order, buyers and sellers submit an atomic bid, where a bundle is decay-distributed from five possible resources. Each resource has two different attributes drawn from a uniform distribution within a range of $[1, \ldots, 2000]$. The time attributes are each uniformly distributed where the earliest and latest timeslots each have a range of [0,. . .,4], and the number of slots lies in [1,. . .,3]. For simplicity, neither coallocation restrictions nor coallocations constraints are taken into account. The corresponding valuations and reservation prices for a bundle are drawn from the same uniform distribution and multiplied by the number of resources in a bundle. In any problem instance, new orders for buyers and sellers are randomly generated. Subsequently, demand and supply are matched against each other, determining the winning allocation and corresponding prices.

22.5.2 Results

Following Equation (22.19), the measured metric reflects the difference between the utility gained by manipulation and the utility gained in a truthful scenario. Consequently, the following results reflect absolute values. In case a manipulating agent $\tilde{i}$ is neither part of the allocation in the truthful scenario o nor in the manipulating scenario $\bar{o}$, the resulting utilities ($u_{\tilde{i}}(o) = u_{\tilde{i}}(\bar{o}) = 0$) are neglected.

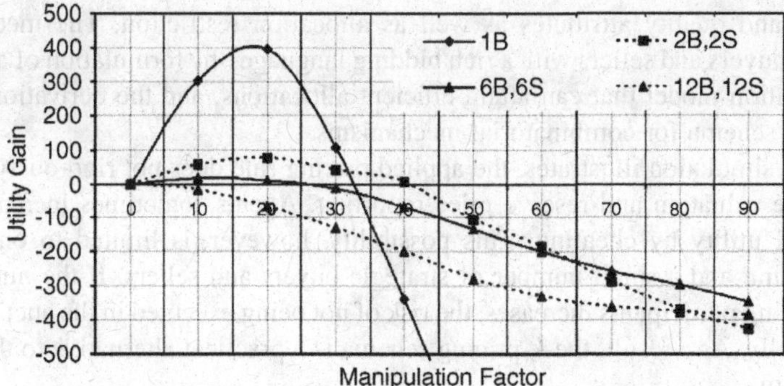

Figure 22.1 Utility gain of manipulating agents with the application of the k-pricing schema.

Figure 22.1 depicts the utility gain of agents as a function that depends on the manipulation factor $\beta\%$. The input data are generated using the baseline setting I_1 for domain-independent bids. The graph points out that agent can increase their utility by manipulation. For instance, if one agent underbids her valuation by $\lambda = 20\%$, her average utility gain is $UG_k^O = 394.15$. However, if the agent manipulates by more than $\lambda = 20\%$, her average utility gain continuously decreases. This reasoning is based on the fact that she increases the risk of not being allocated in the final outcome. In settings with a manipulation factor greater than $\lambda = 35\%$, she has a negative utility gain. Consequently, she has no incentive to underbid her valuation by more than $\lambda = 35\%$. Utility losses greater than 500 ($UG_k^O \leq -500$) are truncated in the graph.

If more agents deviate from bidding truthfully, the average utility gain of each agent decreases. In settings where half of the agents manipulate their bids by more than $\lambda = 30\%$, no agent has a positive utility gain on average. Moreover, if all agents manipulate their bids, none of them can attain a positive utility. This can be explained by the fact that the total number of potential counterparts decreases as the price span between buyers and sellers increases.

The results show that agents can gain a positive utility by manipulating their bids. The gains, however, are restricted to settings in which only a few agents manipulate their bids by a low factor. Although a single agent can gain a positive utility by not revealing his true preferences, the gain decreases if more agents start to manipulate their bids. If only one agent manipulates by a low factor, the overall efficiency losses are small. The simulation results suggest that the k-pricing schema has accurate incentive properties resulting in fairly mild allocative efficiency losses. As a consequence, the k-pricing schema can be a practical alternative to the VCG mechanism for combinatorial auction mechanisms.

22.6 CONCLUSION

This chapter proposed the derivation of a multiattribute combinatorial exchange. In contrast to other combinatorial approaches, the proposed mechanism also accounts for time and quality attributes as well as allocation restriction. The mechanism provides buyers and sellers with a rich bidding language, the formulation of a winner determination model that can attain efficient allocations, and the derivation of the k-pricing schema for combinatorial mechanisms.

As the simulation illustrates, the applied pricing rule does not rigorously punish inaccurate valuation and reserve price reporting. Agents sometimes increase their individual utility by cheating. This possibility, however, is limited to only mild misreporting and a small number of strategic buyers and sellers. If the number of misreporting participants increases, the risk of not being executed in the auction rises dramatically. As a result, the k-pricing schema is a practical alternative to the VCG mechanism.

Aside from topics related to the computational issues of the mechanism, future research needs to extend the expressiveness of the current bidding language. For instance, MACE only supports the specification of cardinal resource attributes. Although this is sufficient for most practical cases, there may be settings in which nominal attributes are also required. In addition, the bidding language is based on pairs of attributes and values that syntactically describe resources and their quality attributes. Consequently, demand and supply is matched on the basis of attribute-based matching functions. This may be insufficient if an agent is not only interested in one particular resource configuration but also willing to accept similar ones. To remedy this drawback, the use of ontology-based bidding languages has to be considered in the future [25].

REFERENCES

1. I. Foster and C. Kesselman, *The Grid—Blueprint for a New Computing Infrastructur*, 2nd ed., Elsevier, 2004.
2. R. Buyya, *Economic-based Distributed Resource Management and Scheduling for Grid Computing*, PhD thesis, Monash Univ., Melbourne, Australia, 2002.
3. B. Schnizler, *Resource Allocation in the Grid–A Market Engineering Approach*, Studies on eOrganisation and Market Engineering, Univ. Karlsruhe, 2007.
4. C. Weinhardt, D. Neumann, and C. Holtmann, Computer-aided market engineering. *Communications of the ACM* **49**(7):79–79 (2006).
5. P. Milgrom, *Putting Auction Theory to Work*, Cambridge Univ. Press, 2004.
6. D. Parkes, J. Kalagnanam, and M. Eso, Achieving budget-balance with Vickrey-based payment schemes in exchanges, *Proc. 17th International Joint Conf. Artificial Intelligence*, 2001, pp. 1161–1168.
7. M. O. Jackson, Mechanism theory, in *Encyclopedia of Life Support Systems*, Eolss Publishers, Oxford, UK, 2002.
8. T. Sandholm, Algorithm for optimal winner determination in combinatorial auctions, *Artificial Intelligence* **135**(1–2):1–54 (2002).
9. H. Ludwig, A. Dan, and B. Kearney, Cremona: An architecture and library for creation and monitoring of WS-Agreements, *Proc. 2nd International Conf. Service Oriented Computing*, 2004, pp. 65–74.

10. K. Subramoniam, M. Maheswaran, and M. Toulouse, Towards a micro-economic model for resource allocation in Grid computing systems, *Proc. 2002 IEEE Canadian Conf. Electrical & Computer Engineering*, 2002.

11. C. Waldspurger, T. Hogg, B. Huberman, J. Kephart, and W. Stornetta, Spawn: A distributed computational economy, *IEEE Transactions on Software Engineering* **18**(2):103–117 (1992).

12. O. Regev and N. Nisan, The POPCORN market: Online markets for computational resources, *Decision Support Systems* **28**(1–2):177–189 (2000).

13. R. Buyya, D. Abramson, J. Giddy, and H. Stockinger, Economic models for resource management and scheduling in Grid computing, *Concurrency and Computation: Practice and Experience* **14**(13–15):507–1542 (2002).

14. R. Wolski, J. Plank, J. Brevik, and T. Bryan, Analyzing market-based resource allocation strategies for the computational Grid, *International Journal of High-Performance Computing Applications* **15**(3):258–281 (2001).

15. T. Eymann, M. Reinicke, O. Ardaiz, P. Artigas, L. D. de Cerio, F. Freitag, R. Messeguer, and L. Navarro, Decentralized vs. centralized economic coordination of resource allocation in grids, *Proc. 1st European Across Grids Conf.*, 2003.

16. C. Ng, P. Buonadonna, N. B. Chun, A. C. Snoeren, and A. Vahdat, Addressing strategic behavior in a deployed microeconomic resource allocator, *Proc. 3rd Workshop on Economics of Peer-to-Peer Systems*, 2005.

17. M. P. Wellman, W. E. Walsh, P. R. Wurman, and J. K. MacKie-Mason, Auction protocols for decentralized scheduling, *Games and Economic Behavior* **35**:271–303 (2001).

18. R. Bapna, S. Das, R. Garfinkel, and J. Stallaert, A market design for Grid computing, *INFORMS Journal of Computing* **20**(1):100–111 (2008).

19. W. Smith, Improving resource selection and scheduling using predictions, in *Grid Resource Management—State of the Art and Future Trends*, J. Nabrzyski, J. M. Schopf, and J. Weglarz, J.,eds., Kluwer Academic Publishers, 2004.

20. W. Conen and T. Sandholm, Preference elicitation in combinatorial auctions, *Proc. 3rd ACM Conf. Electronic Commerce, ACM Press, New York*, 2001, 256–259.

21. B. Schnizler, D. Neumann, D. Veit, and C. Weinhardt, Trading Grid services—a multi-attribute combinatorial approach, *European Journal of Operational Research*, **187**(3): 943–961 (2008).

22. M. Rothkopf, A. Pekec, and R. Harstad, Computationally manageable combinational auctions, *Management Science* **44**:1131–1147 (1998).

23. R. B. Myerson and M. A., Satterthwaite, Efficient mechanisms for bilateral trading, *Journal of Economic Theory* **28**:265–281 (1983).

24. M. A. Sattherthwaite and S. R. Williams, The Bayesian theory of the k-double auction, in *The Double Auction Market—Institutions, Theories, and Evidence*, D. Friedman and J. Rust, eds., Addison-Wesley, 1993, pp. 99–123.

25. S. Lamparter and B. Schnizler, Trading services in ontology-driven markets, *Proc. 2006 ACM Symp. Applied Computing, ACM Press*, 2006, pp. 1679–1683.

23

TWO AUCTION-BASED RESOURCE ALLOCATION ENVIRONMENTS: DESIGN AND EXPERIENCE

ALVIN AUYOUNG, PHIL BUONADONNA, BRENT N. CHUN, CHAKI NG, DAVID C. PARKES, JEFF SHNEIDMAN, ALEX C. SNOEREN, AND AMIN VAHDAT

23.1 INTRODUCTION

Many computer systems have reached the point where the goal of resource allocation is no longer to maximize utilization; instead, when demand exceeds supply and not all needs can be met, one needs a policy to guide resource allocation decisions. One natural policy is to seek *efficient* usage, which allocates resources to the set of users who have the highest utility for the use of the resources. Researchers have frequently proposed market-based mechanisms to provide such a goal-oriented way to allocate resources among competing interests while maximizing overall utility of the users.

The emergence of several large-scale, federated computing infrastructures [2,3,5,7,49] creates an opportunity to revisit the use of market mechanisms to allocate computing resources. There are several common characteristics of federated systems that make a market-based approach appropriate: (1) the end users of these systems commonly have synchronized demand patterns (e.g., due to shared conference deadlines or other external events), which makes excess resource demand a common occurrence; (2) resource ownership is shared by the community, and therefore, there are many parties with a stake in the allocation policies used by the system; and (3) there are many resources, which means that resource contention cannot be resolved by human administration or simply by the result of an uncoordinated

Market-Oriented Grid and Utility Computing Edited by Rajkumar Buyya and Kris Bubendorfer

process. An allocation system designed around a market can lead to a socially optimal allocation outcome for users, which is particularly important during times of heavy resource contention. Markets also create a natural structure for globally desirable incentives and user behavior and can relieve system administrators of significant management burden.

In general, however, market-based allocation schemes have yet to catch on in practice. To understand why applying a market-based design to these systems is a challenging problem, and perhaps why markets have not been easily applied in the past, one can observe ways in which these computing environments differ from traditional markets:

1. Computing systems lack several natural market components. Since end users typically do not engage in the purchase or production of resources, they are not typically required to use currency or otherwise barter for resource use. Therefore, many users are not accustomed to—or comfortable with—determining their utility for a resource in terms of currency. Also missing in these systems is a means of resource production. Since the supply of resources is often fixed—due to external constraints—and cannot easily be summarily increased or decreased in response to global demand, both underdemand and overdemand of resources are common.
2. Another difference between computing systems and traditional markets relates to the behavior of participants. Rather than engage in strategic, sophisticated behavior (which can require costly modeling of other participants), end users in systems may prefer the simple interfaces and allocation policies of today's systems [e.g., first come–first serve (FCFS), best-effort], rather than needing to submit bids or otherwise provide richer information in order to achieve what may sometimes amount to only a slight utility gain [15].

We present two case studies of market-based mechanisms that were developed to support sophisticated usage policies in real computing environments and designed to address some of these challenges. First, we present *Bellagio*, a market-based resource allocator deployed for six months on the worldwide PlanetLab research network [5]. We then describe *Mirage*, an allocator deployed on a shared sensor network testbed [25], which is still in use as of this writing. We discuss our experiences with each system, and focus on both the initial challenges these systems were designed to address and the empirical successes and difficulties that we have observed since deployment. A key contribution of these systems is their user-centric design. Both Mirage and Bellagio use a resource discovery interface and a combinatorial bidding language to allocate resources; the former allows users to easily communicate domain-specific resource demand, and the latter allows users to express needs on bundles of resources, which is important in each of our applied domains. Both systems also use a virtual currency policy that attempts to create incentives similar to those created by currency in a real market economy.

Deployments such as these appear vital in understanding both the potential and limitations of market-based resource allocation in computer systems. While our deployments were mostly successful, our experience also highlights a few persistent challenges with applying markets to these systems. For example, the perishable nature of computer resources influenced the use of a sliding-window-based allocation mechanism. This formulation has side effects of making the system unusable for a portion of users, and also allowing it to be manipulated by others. In addition, choosing a level of system transparency to increase the usability of market mechanisms also allowed users to exhibit globally undesirable market behavior. We conclude with a set of suggestions to help guide future deployments of market-based resource allocation systems.

23.2 BACKGROUND

Since the mid-1990s, large-scale, federated computing infrastructures have emerged as the primary means for delivering significant network and computational resources. By time-sharing communal resources, users can harness the power of an otherwise unobtainable set of resources to perform a wide variety of tasks. Computation in Grid and cluster environments [6,7,12,20,22,51], wide-area distributed service development, deployment of network testbeds [2,5] and development in sensor networks [3,49] are all examples of common tasks in these emerging environments. Resource allocation continues to be the fundamental challenge in these systems.

23.2.1 Traditional Allocation Approaches

Perhaps the most natural resource allocation scheme in *time-shared* systems is proportional share, which provides equal, simultaneous access to time-shared resources to all users. In this model, multiple applications can run on a machine simultaneously. It is well known, however, that proportional-share scheduling alone does not function well in systems where overdemand for resources is common. In particular, as demand for resources increases, the time share per resource received by each user decreases, while overheads remain constant (or, in some cases, increase due to thrashing). In the end, the utility delivered to each user goes to zero as the number of competing users increases.

Batch scheduling is commonly used to schedule jobs in *space-shared* systems, such as supercomputers and Grid computing environments. As opposed to time-shared resources, space-shared systems are well suited for applications that require a large share of a system's resources (e.g., a CPU-intensive job), and therefore, run a single application on a machine at a time. Most space-shared systems schedule jobs to optimize system-level metrics such as total throughput or average job turnaround time. These approaches avoid the thrashing that can occur with high resource contention that occurs in proportional-share schemes. However, these systems typically do not account for the heterogeneity of users in their needs in regard to scheduling jobs. For example, simple batch scheduling systems do not distinguish between users with jobs that require timely completion and users with jobs that do not. More sophisticated schedulers like Maui [26] include multiple priority queues, but lack an automated method for preventing users from artificially inflating job priority. Also, the number of available job priorities is usually fixed, which restricts the amount of utility information that a user can express for a job. These systems offer no way to resolve contention for resources in the face of heavy demand—conflicts are generally resolved through human intervention.

23.2.2 Job Utility Functions

Maximizing aggregate *utility*, or value delivered by the system, requires eliciting user preferences for resources over time and space [32]. The fundamental shortcomings of existing approaches are rooted in the fact that they do not explicitly consider a user's utility for a job when making a scheduling decision. Consider the example of a student using a computing cluster who has a set of jobs associated with various course projects. The student has an internal prioritization for the relative importance of each job, based on the importance of each course and the various deadlines for each project. Therefore, she may be able to carefully craft her job submissions to create an ideal (i.e., utility-maximizing) execution sequence. However, if she is sharing the computing cluster with a group of like-minded students—each of them with their own job utility functions—it is unlikely that the entire set of students can coordinate to craft a mutually agreeable schedule. A study of over one hundred users at the San Diego Supercomputing Center (SDSC) supports the notion that real jobs exhibit sophisticated utility existing information [32], information that cannot be explicitly communicated to the scheduling system. Despite the fact that SDSC uses a sophisticated priority-based scheduler, the study highlights the fact that without explicitly considering the utility function of a job, a scheduling system cannot make automated decisions that maximize the overall utility of its users. A job utility function captures the value that a job has to its user, as well as how this value can vary over time, or other dimensions.

The idea of scheduling based on per-job utility functions is a well-trodden field. The Alpha OS [19] handles time-varying utility functions; Chen and Muhlethaler [14] discuss how to do processor scheduling for them; Lee et al. [31] look at tradeoffs between multiple applications with multiple utility dimensions; Muse [13] and Unity [48] use utility functions for continuous fine-grained service quality control; and Petrou et al. [40] describe using utility functions to allow speculative execution of tasks. Siena [9] considers the impact of user aggregate utility functions to control service provider behavior across multiple jobs. Kumar et al. [29] use a single utility function to aggregate data from multiple sources. These prior works assume the existence of mechanisms to elicit honest and comparable utility functions from a user. Similar to priority job schedulers, a shared scheduling system needs a mechanism to prevent self-interested users from artificially overstating their job utility.

23.2.3 Economic Approaches

A well-designed economic approach to resource allocation can provide a natural framework for users to communicate their job utility functions, and for the system to elicit true utility functions from users. The basic idea is that resources are priced by looking to balance global supply and demand, with users required to purchase resources using a personal budget of currency. In this case, resource prices force users to self-select a resource allocation on the basis of their utility for jobs, implying that the resources are allocated to the jobs that value them the most. Because users must provide payment (perhaps in a virtual rather than real-world currency) in return for the allocation of jobs, users will tend to be straightforward in describing their utility (measured in units of currency) for different allocations.

Market-based systems have long been proposed as solutions for resource allocation in these environments, yet integration of these systems into real computer systems has garnered little momentum. A number of previous efforts have explored market-based approaches for resource allocation in computer systems. The earliest work that we are aware of is Sutherland's futures market for CPU time on Harvard's PDP-1 [46]. Subsequent work can be categorized into two groups: pricing mechanisms and auction-based mechanisms. In *pricing mechanisms*, the system determines a price for each resource by using a combination of various signals, such as load and resource demand history; users acquire resources by purchasing them at market prices. In *auction-based mechanisms*, the system generates prices for resources dynamically by first collecting bids from users on resources that are then allocated, typically to maximize revenue to the bid-taker. Past effort on market mechanisms has been largely dominated by auction-based schemes and has been applied to resource allocation in a broad range of distributed systems including clusters [18,47], computational Grids [30,50,51], parallel computers [45], and Internet computing systems [33,41].

As with these systems, our designs (Bellagio and Mirage) also rely on an auction to allocate resources. An auction is an appealing model for dynamic domains in which resource demands can be expected to fluctuate rapidly [16]. Recognizing that users of large-scale computing environments often require the use of combinations of resources [16,21], we adopt the model of a *combinatorial* auction, in which users bid on bundles of resources as opposed to individual resources. This ability to bid on resource combinations in space and time allows users to more accurately express their preferences on different resources. For example, a user can indicate that some resources are interchangeable ("substitutes") or that some are required together ("complements"). To the best of our knowledge, Bellagio and Mirage are the first deployed systems that support allocation of combinations of heterogeneous computational resources via flexible auction methods.

Of course, there exist many alternatives to the use of markets in serving the purpose of resource allocation in computer systems. These include first come–first served (FCFS) allocation and also reservation systems that permit scheduling into the future. Despite our general belief in the importance of market-based methods, the ultimate success of a system is measured in usage, and usage depends on a number of factors that are easy to overlook. For example, ease of use may trump mechanism features. People may be willing to accept the limitations of simpler systems if market-based systems are seen as too complex, or if they fail in other ways. This is one reason why it seems especially important to deploy market-based systems and gain real experience.

Through such a deployment, one gains a rare opportunity to deploy a market and examine the interactions between participants in an isolated economic system. Uncovering practical issues in a deployed computational market can lead to observations about the need for new theory or design market, which may then help in bringing the benefits of efficient, market-based resource allocation to users of today's large-scale shared infrastructures.

23.3 SYSTEM DESIGN

In this section, we describe the high-level design used by both Bellagio and Mirage. We discuss the basic allocation method and virtual currency system used in both systems.

23.3.1 System Architecture

The goal of our market-based mechanism is to determine an allocation that maximizes user utility (as measured, e.g., in units of virtual currency). If the market is reasonably competitive and bids reflect the true utility of a user for a particular allocation, then, by clearing a market to maximize the total bid value, the market will tend to achieve this goal of maximizing total utility.

The basic design of both the Bellagio and Mirage systems is that of a repeated, sealed-bid combinatorial auction,[1] which allocates resources to competing users over time. Given that the *winner-determination problem* in a combinatorial auction is known to be NP-hard [42,43], we adopt a greedy algorithm to ensure that the auctions clear quickly irrespective of the number or size of user bids. For this purpose, we adopt a simple heuristic that greedily allocates bids in (also called a "first fit" schedule) order of a bid's *value density*, which is the bid value divided by its size and length [10]. We repeat this allocation algorithm k times, with a different ordering of the top k bid value densities, and select the best allocation among these k attempts. In our deployment we set $k = 10$. We adopt a first-price auction format, rather than an auction with a more complex payment rule, in part because of our intent to make auction clearing as fast as possible.[2]

In this setting, the auction is run periodically. Once bids are received the auction must determine winning bids and the associated resource allocation. A user in our systems submits bids to the auction using a two-phase process (Fig. 23.1). First, she adopts a *resource discovery service* to find candidate resources that meet her needs. Then, using the concrete resources identified from the first step, such a user can place bids using a system-specific bidding language.

[1]The initial deployment of Mirage used an open-bid English auction format, which was later changed to a sealed-bid format.

[2]Furthermore, it is well understood that the second-price, Vickrey style of payment rule does not immediately provide the incentive advantages enjoyed in static settings when these rules are adapted to dynamic settings [37].

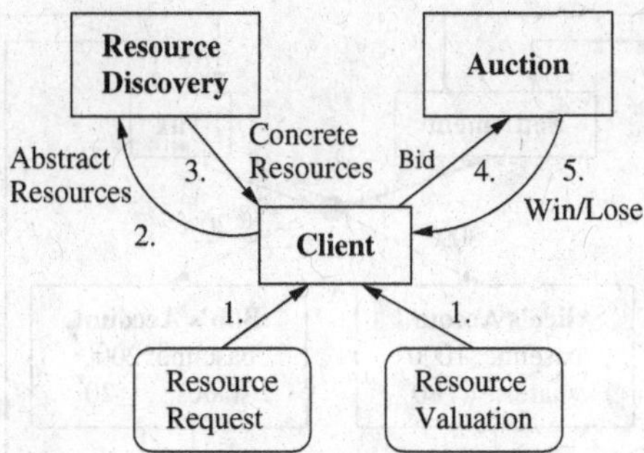

Figure 23.1 Bidding and acquiring resources. (Reproduced from [17, Fig. 2]).

23.3.2 Currency

Most existing computing systems lack any notion of currency. Because introducing real currency was not a feasible option in our target environments, we have designed a virtual currency system to be used in both Bellagio and Mirage.

The design of a good currency policy will encourage desirable behaviors and serve to discourage undesirable behaviors. The lack of proper policies can render the system useless. For example, if users can obtain large amounts of virtual currency very easily, they will, of course, bid arbitrarily high values all the time. Such a system reduces to resource allocation on the basis of social conventions, since there is no incentive for a user to not always bid the maximum possible value permitted within the bidding language. Simply stated, the currency must be "real enough" that users do not want to spend it because they will be able to benefit from saving unspent currency for future use. In order to support virtual currency, we rely on a central bank that enforces a currency policy by controlling the aggregate amount and flow of virtual currency in the system.

Since users have no direct way of earning virtual currency, the system must decide how to distribute the currency. Because users enter the system with no virtual currency, we also need to provide new users with some initial amount of currency. In addition, as users spend currency over time, we also need a way to infuse their accounts with new currency. Clearly, many virtual currency polices could be employed to meet these requirements, and different policies will result in very different economic systems and resource allocations.

Our virtual currency policy is based on two principles: (1) prioritizing users on the basis of an exogenous policy (we will describe the specific policies for Bellagio and Mirage in the next sections) and (2) penalizing/rewarding users on the basis of usage or lack of usage during times of peak demand. Examples of factors that may affect prioritization include the *types of usage* (e.g., research vs. coursework), the *amount of contribution* made to a system, and *fairness* concerns, which may be defined in terms of the cumulative resource consumption of an individual. Allowing the prioritization metric to be determined exogenously permits flexibility in crafting a good policy for a specific domain. In addition, it seems natural to reward the user who refrains from using the system during times of peak demand (or, more generally,

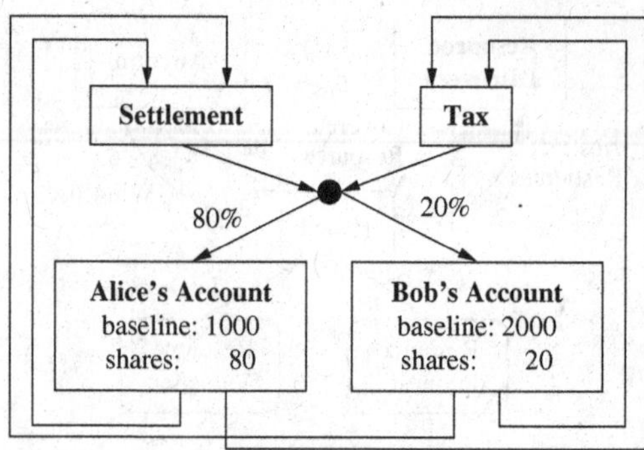

Figure 23.2 Virtual currency policy. (Reproduced from [17, Fig. 3]).

does not waste resources) and penalize the user who uses resources aggressively when resources are scarce. Consider a user who monopolizes the entire system for several days prior to a major deadline, for instance.

Each user is associated with an account at a central bank that stores virtual currency. Each bank account is assigned a baseline amount of currency according to priority, a number of *currency shares* that influence the rate that currency will subsequently flow into the account, and is also initialized with a baseline amount of currency. Given an initial currency allocation, users can begin to bid for resources in the auction. Each time the auction clears, trades are settled and revenue is collected from the accounts for winning bids. This currency is then distributed back to all accounts through profit sharing in a proportional-share fashion based on the number of shares in each account (Fig. 23.2). It is this profit-sharing policy that allows users who do not waste resources to save additional currency that can be used for a subsequent burst of activity later.

In addition to profit sharing, the system also imposes a fixed-rate savings tax on all accounts that have excess currency above their baseline values, again with proportional-share distribution. The motivation for the savings tax is based on expected resource consumption. For example, in other distributed systems testbeds such as PlanetLab [5], it has been observed [16] that resource consumption is often highly imbalanced with a small fraction of the users consuming the majority of the resources and many users often going idle for long periods of time. Similarly, parallel batch computing systems often exhibit a diurnal load pattern [4] varying between extremes of light utilization and heavy utilization. Assuming similar resource consumption patterns, and in the absence of additional policy, the implication would be that heavy users would eventually be working out of accounts with very little currency even if there is little demand for resources in the system. To mitigate this effect, we impose a fixed-rate *savings tax* that makes operational the concept of "use it or lose it" policy employed by agencies such as the Federal Aviation Administration in allocating scarce resources; in other words, it is fine to defer the consumption of currency for a while but at some point it is desirable to allow others to gain the benefit of resources that a user is not using by redistributing some of the currency via the savings tax. Users should be rewarded for not wasting resources, but such a reward should not last forever. In the absence of any activity in the system, the savings tax works such that all accounts eventually converge back to their baseline values. The savings tax is collected every 4 hours, at a rate of 5% of an account's savings. These parameters were chosen such that an exhausted bank account can recover half of its balance within a few days, and the full amount in a week.[3]

By controlling the distribution of wealth in a virtual economy, the systems are able to indirectly control the share of resources received by individual participants over different timescales, despite artifacts introduced by the virtual currency and the continued presence of load imbalance. In order to control the distribution of wealth among users, there are two policies that we must determine: how users will be able to earn virtual currency, and how (if at all) the system will limit the wealth of users. We discuss the policies chosen for our specific implementations, Bellagio and Mirage, next.

23.4 BELLAGIO

In this section we describe the Bellagio architecture and our deployment experience on PlanetLab.

23.4.1 Target Platform

PlanetLab [5] is a distributed, wide-area, federated testbed consisting of over 800 machines hosted by more than 400 sites across the world (removed due to copyright issues). Machines are owned and operated locally by each site, but primarily administered centrally by PlanetLab Central (PLC). PLC performs access control and maintains a consistent software image on each machine. Each site is in charge of the physical upkeep of its machines, such as uptime and providing adequate and persistent network bandwidth. Additionally, each site pays a periodic fee to PLC to support the central administration. In return, a site's members, such as research scientists and graduate students, are granted access to use any machine in the system. Each user can obtain a *slice*, which grants her access to the resources of any PlanetLab machine. The instantiation of a slice on a particular machine is called a *sliver*. A sliver shares basic information about its associated slice, such as authentication keys and basic configuration files, and is the physical manifestation of the user's isolated environment on a machine. A sliver is therefore intended to export an interface similar to that of a virtual machine or other virtualization technology [38]. As of this writing, PlanetLab implements virtualization using the Linux V-Server technology.

A typical scenario for a PlanetLab user is that she will first obtain a slice from her local administrator (by way of PLC). Once she has a slice, she creates slivers on any number of machines. The most common use for the machines is as part of a wide-

[3]Kash, Friedman, and Halpern [23,28] have initiated a research agenda on developing a theory for how to allocate virtual currency within "scrip" systems in which agents both contribute and consume resources.

area network experiment, with each component machine acting as an endpoint or providing some other function within the experiment. The value a user has for these machines is not only in their local resources but also their geographic location; a wide-area configuration of machines provides a realistic setting for many distributed systems and network experiments. At any point in time, a particular machine can be multiplexing its resources across processes from many different slivers. These tasks can vary in length (i.e., from a few minutes to months) and in size (i.e., a few nodes vs. all nodes). Each machine's resources are time-shared among active slivers using an equal-weight, proportional-share scheduling policy. For example, if there are n active slivers on a machine, each active sliver is expected to receive a $1/n$th time slice of a machine's CPU cycles and network bandwidth over every scheduling window. We call this type of scheduling *work-conserving*, since resource access is multiplexed among active slivers. PLC performs limited admission control such that the number of active slivers on a machine is limited to $n = 1000$ (i.e., no more than 1000 simultaneous slices can run on a machine). This constraint is imposed due to the physical limitations on memory and disk space on each machine.

The need for a more sophisticated resource allocation policy became apparent during deadlines for the major systems and networking conferences in 2003 and 2004, when resource contention became a persistent problem in PlanetLab. Figure 23.3 illustrates a common occurrence for PlanetLab users. Owing to synchronized conference paper deadlines among users, the system experiences large spikes in resource demand in the days leading up to a deadline. The proportional-share resource allocation policy provides users with little control over their share of resources during such times, little incentive to reduce consumption, and even less means to coordinate usage with one another. The end result is that significant resource contention leaves the system unusable for the majority of users.[4] Bellagio was designed to help address this problem.

23.4.2 Architecture

Bellagio makes allocation decisions using a combinatorial auction. We need to provide additional mechanisms on PlanetLab to allow users to bid for these resources. In this section, we describe these mechanisms.

23.4.2.1 Resource Discovery. The decision to use a combinatorial auction rather than a series of single-item auctions is motivated by the fact that most users on PlanetLab require simultaneous use of a large number of machines. Selecting these machines poses a challenge to users because there is a large set from which to choose, and machines—while largely homogeneous in resource capacity—often exhibit dynamic characteristics. For example, a typical usage scenario would involve

[4]Since the Bellagio deployment and discontinuation, PlanetLab has continued to rely on Sirius, a resource reservation service. Current evidence suggests that resource contention may no longer be a serious problem [39].

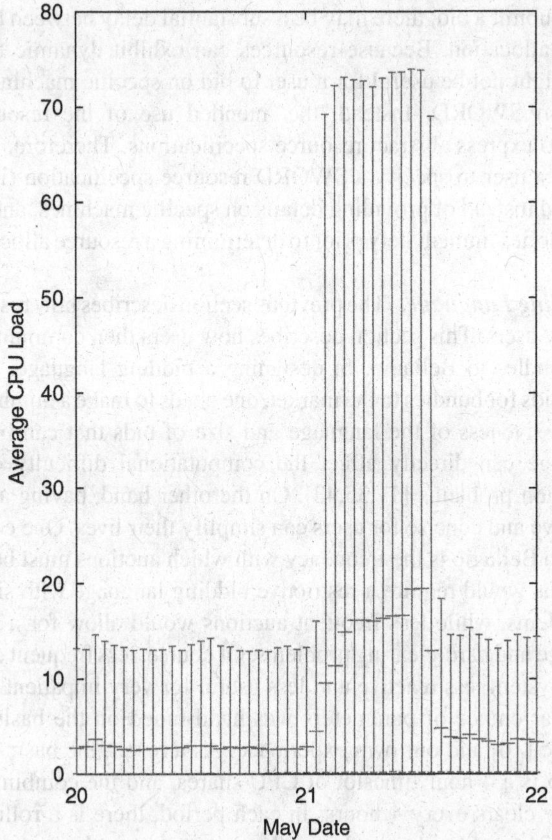

Figure 23.3 The 5th, average, and 95th percentile loads on 220 PlanetLab nodes leading up to the May 2004 OSDI deadline. (Reproduced from [8, Figure 13]).

selecting machines that exhibit low load and an abundance of network capacity. In addition, a user might want machines that have a particular physical network topology of interest, such as within the same continent, or explicitly spanning continents.

Distributed resource discovery allows end users to identify available resources on the basis of both of these characteristics. Bellagio uses a Sealable Wide-Area Overlay-based Resource Discovery Service (SWORD) [36] for this purpose, which is a resource discovery service implemented on PlanetLab. It exports an interface that allows PlanetLab users to locate particular resources matching various criteria. For example, users can search for resources based on resource-specific attributes (e.g., machines with low CPU load and large amounts of free memory), interresource attributes (e.g., machines with low internode latency), and logical (e.g., machines within a specific administrative domain) or physical attributes (e.g., geographic location). SWORD returns a set of candidate machines matching the user's description.

Once users submit a bid, there may be a substantial delay between bid submission and the actual allocation. Because resources can exhibit dynamic temporal characteristics, it might not be useful for a user to bid on specific machines that she has discovered from SWORD. Instead, the intended use of the resource discovery mechanism is to express abstract resource specifications. Therefore, Bellagio alternatively allows a user to specify a SWORD resource specification (i.e., a SWORD query) in her bid instead of providing details on specific machines, and Bellagio will resolve these queries immediately prior to determining a resource allocation for users.

23.4.2.2 ***Bidding Language.*** The previous section describes how resources bundles are identified by users. This section describes how users then communicate demands for resource bundles to Bellagio. In designing a bidding language, which enables users to report bids for bundles to the market, one needs to make a number of tradeoffs. First, the expressiveness of the language and size of bids that can be submitted in a given language can directly affect the computational difficulty of solving the induced allocation problems [11,35,43]. On the other hand, having a language that is both expressive and concise for users can simplify their lives. One consideration of relevance within Bellagio is the frequency with which auctions must be cleared. Very frequent auctions would require a restrictive bidding language with simple, induced allocation problems, while less frequent auctions would allow for a more complex bidding language and hard-clearing problems. Of course, less frequent auctions would also make the system less reactive and less useful for very impatient users.

The particular choice of parameters was hand-tuned on the basis of studies of PlanetLab usage [16] and our own experience. As a result, the basic unit of allocation in Bellagio is a 4-hour timeslot of CPU shares, and the combinatorial auction correspondingly clears every 4 hours. In each period, there is a rolling window of $T=\{1,2,3...,42\}$ timeslots forward from the current time in the auction (where $T=1$ denotes the immediately next timeslot that will be available). We let N denote the set of resources available to allocate (i.e., different Planet for Lab nodes). Note that immediately prior to running the auction clearing algorithm, any bid that contains an abstract resource specification (SWORD query), Bellagio translates the resource specification to a set of concrete candidate machines. The bidding language allows a user to specify a required allocation duration, from the set $D=\{1,2,4,8\}$ which represents the number of time-slots to reserve. A component of a bid b_i from a user is constructed as follows:

$$b_i = (s_{i,0}, t_{i,1}, d_i, \{n_{i,1}, n_{i,2}, \ldots\}, \{ok_{i,1},\ ok_{i,2}, \ldots\}, v_i),$$

where $s_{i,0}$, $t_{i,1} \in T$ denote the range of possible start times for the bid to be valid, $d_i \in D$ is the duration of the job, $\{n_{i,1},\ n_{i,2},\ \ldots,\ n_{i,k}\}$ and $\{ok_{i,1},\ ok_{i,2},\ \ldots, ok_{i,k}\}$ denote the required quantities $n_{i,j} \geq 1$ on resource equivalence classes $ok_{i,j} \subseteq N$. An example of equivalence class is $ok_{i,j}=\{$`*.princeton.edu`$\}$, where $ok_{i,j}$ represents the subset of PlanetLab nodes located in the `princeton.edu` domain. The corresponding $n_{i,j}$ parameter represents the desired quantity of nodes satisfying this equivalence class. $v_i \geq 0$ is the bid price (willingness to pay) for any bundle of resources that satisfy this bid. These parameters allow PlanetLab users to reserve CPU shares for a duration of up to 32 h, and up to a week in advance. For example, a user might request "any 10 nodes from Princeton, and any 10 nodes from Berkeley, for 32 consecutive hours anytime in the next 24 hours." A corresponding bid of value v would be

$$b_i = (1, 6, 8\{10, 10\}, \{\{\texttt{*.princeton.edu}\}, \{\texttt{*.berkeley.edu}\}\}, \texttt{v}\}.$$

23.4.2.3 Currency Policy. The currency distribution policy in Bellagio is performed at a per-organization basis. Each site begins with an initial balance of virtual currency that is proportional to the number of machines it has contributed to PlanetLab. This policy was designed to encourage contributions to PlanetLab, and in particular to reward those who contribute the most. If new sites joined PlanetLab, they were assigned currency in this way. This endowment is the only way that currency can be introduced into the economy. In PlanetLab, individual users and slices are associated with a particular site or institution. All users and slices associated with that institution have rights to the site's bank account. When a user makes a bid, her balance is temporarily frozen into an intermediate Bellagio account. Each time an auction clears, revenue is collected from the accounts of winning bidders.

As described earlier, each bank account is also associated with a currency share that determines the site's portion of profit sharing. Initially, the currency share for a bank account was the same as its initial balance—the number of machines that their site has contributed to PlanetLab. However, we modified this policy on observation that certain machines in the system were used much more often than other machines. We wanted a policy that would reward organizations that contribute the most valuable (highly utilized) resources. Therefore, we revised profit sharing such that it is divided only among each organization that owns a machine in a winning allocation; profit (revenue) from each auction-clearing period is funneled directly back to the account of the PlanetLab organization that owns the machine. One implication of this policy is the promotion of long-term system growth. Users wishing to receive a larger revenue share will now have incentive to contribute useful resources to the shared infrastructure.

Once the payment amount for each winning bid has been determined, the user's bank account is charged by the appropriate amount, and resource bindings are performed by returning resource capabilities in the form of tickets to the winning bidders using a system such as SHARP (Service Highly Available Resoure Peening) [24].

23.4.3 Deployment

In the summer of 2004, PLC provided the opportunity for research groups on PlanetLab to experiment with more sophisticated scheduling policies. Beginning in December 2004, timed with the release of PlanetLab kernel version 3.0, Bellagio was given a fraction of each PlanetLab machine's CPU resources, which it could then allocate to different user slices. For example, if a machine has n active slices, each slice receives *1/n* time share of the machine's CPU. A full allocation of Bellagio's share of resources to a single slice would provide the slice with $3(n+2)$. For large n, the relative boost that a slice could receive is 200% Therefore, for a single machine, the full allocation of Bellagio's resource can double or triple a slice's relative CPU scheduling share. We stress that the use of Bellagio was strictly optional: PlanetLab users automatically received a default proportional share allocation; our system sold an increase only in these soft resource shares. This particular resource boost is an artifact of the scheduling technology used by PlanetLab, and the amount of resources that we were provided to allocate within our market.

Because we were introducing a market-based allocation scheme to a live system that previously had no notion of markets, we anticipated the learning curve for new users to be high. The Bellagio user interface was designed to encourage early adoption by the PlanetLab user community and promote frequent use. In order to lower the barrier for the user community, every registered PlanetLab user was automatically registered to use Bellagio; a user simply supplied her authentication credentials to the Bellagio Web interface, which were then verified against the central PlanetLab database. The Web interface was deployed on a cluster of Linux machines with a PHP frontend and a PostgreSQL database backend. The database contained account balances for virtual currency and managed user authentication.

Once authenticated by the Web interface, a user could view the status of her account and previous bids and allocations. To facilitate the bidding process, we provided several useful guides. First, to address the issue of "valuation uncertainty," which is an issue related to whether users will understand how to value resources in units of the virtual currency, we provide historical prices in Bellagio as a reference point to the current level of demand in the system. Then, to help formulate bids, we provided several "one click" bidding options, such as "bid on any *N* nodes in my slice" or "any *N* nodes from *K* distinct autonomous systems." Users also had the option of formulating complex queries by defining equivalence classes of resources on which to bid. Also, as mentioned, Bellagio provided an interface to SWORD to perform these queries, which is a tool familiar to many PlanetLab users.

Bellagio was released for public use in February 2005. Each site was given a balance of 100 units of virtual currency per node; the initial balance of sites ranged from 100 to 2200. During its lifetime, it saw 23 bids from PlanetLab users representing 13 different organizations, which resulted in a total of 242,372 allocated hours of CPU shares. Bellagio was taken offline in the summer of 2005.

23.5 MIRAGE

In this section we describe the Mirage architecture and our deployment experience on the Intel Research Sensor Network Lab.

23.5.1 Target Platform

The initial motivation for this work became apparent during the construction of a 148-node testbed at the Intel Research (laboratory in) Berkeley California) (IRB). This testbed consists of 97 Crossbow MICA2 and 51 Crossbow MICA2DOT series sensor nodes, or *motes*, mounted uniformly in the ceiling of the lab. The motes incorporate an Atmel ATmega128 8-bit microcontroller, with 4 kB of random-access memory (RAM), 128 kB of flash memory, and a Chipcon CC1000 frequency shift keying (FSK) radio chip. The MICA2 series devices in the testbed operate in the 433-MHz industrial–scientific–medical (ISM) band and incorporate a sophisticated sensorboard that can monitor pressure, temperature, light, and humidity. The MICA2DOT devices operate in the 916-MHz ISM band and do not include sensorboards.

Users of a sensor-network testbed such as IRB's are frequently interested in acquiring combinations of resources that meet certain constraints. For example, consider a machine learning researcher who is interested in testing distributed inference algorithms in sensor networks. Such a user might be interested in evaluating algorithms at a moderate scale while performing inference over temperature and humidity readings of the environment. The user's code might also be tailored to a particular type of device (e.g., a MICA2 mote) and needs to run on a different, appropriately spaced frequency to avoid crosstalk from other experiments. Thus, a user's abstract resource requirement might be something like "any 64 MICA2 motes, operating on an unused frequency, that have both a temperature and a humidity sensor."

23.5.2 Architecture

As described in the Bellagio architecture, Mirage makes allocation decisions using a combinatorial auction. In this section we describe the methods that we provide in Mirage to allow users to bid for motes.

23.5.2.1 Resource Discovery. Similar to Bellagio, Mirage allows users to specify the type of resources they are interested in using as abstract resource specifications. A resource discovery service then maps these specifications to concrete resources that meet the desired constraints. We use this level of indirection for three reasons: (1) it frees the user from having to manually identify candidate resources; (2) it allows users to automatically take advantage of new resources as they are introduced into the system; and (3) as mentioned, testbed users are frequently interested in acquiring sets of nodes and are often indifferent to which specific nodes they are allocated as long as the candidate resources meet the user's constraints. The resource discovery service allows users to discover all possible candidates and thus provide the system with the maximal amount of information on substitutes when clearing the auction.

Abstract resource specifications allow users to specify constraints on the types of resources they seek to acquire. For example, testbed users often need to specify constraints on per-node attributes. In the machine learning example described earlier, for instance, a logical conjunction on per-node attributes (mote type and sensorboard type) combined with a desired number of nodes is required. In other cases, constraints on internode attributes may be necessary. For example, a user might wish to acquire "8 motes where each pair of motes is at least 10 meters apart" to ensure that the network causes a multihop routing layer to form. Currently, Mirage supports resource discovery using per-node attributes including mote type, sensorboard type, and supported frequency range.

23.5.2.2 ***Bidding Language.*** The bidding language allows users to express desired resources and the value for those resources. More specifically, a bid in the bidding language includes combinations of concrete resources, obtained via the resource discovery service, that are equally acceptable to the user and the maximum amount that the user is willing to pay for those resources. Since time is a critical aspect of resource allocation (e.g., resources near a conference deadline), resource combinations specify resources in both space and time. Formally, a bid b_i in Mirage is specified as follows:

$$b_i = (v_i, s_i, t_i, d_i, f_{\min}, f_{\max}, n_i, ok_i)$$

Bid b_i indicates that the user wants any combination of n_i motes from the set ok_i (obtained through resource discovery) for a duration of d_i hours with a start time anywhere between times s_i and t_i and a frequency anywhere in the range $[f_{\min}, f_{\max}]$. The associated bid price is v_i, representing the units of virtual currency that the user is willing to pay for these resources. Continuing with the distributed inference example, a user thus might say: "any 64 MICA2 motes, which have both a temperature and a humidity sensor, operating on an unused frequency in the range [423 MHz, 443 MHz], for 4 consecutive hours anytime in the next 24 hours." Suppose that the user used the resource discovery service and found 128 motes meeting the desired resource specification and valued the allocation at 99 units of virtual currency. The corresponding bid in this case would be

$$b_i = (99, 0, 20, 4, 423, 443, 64, \text{ list of 128 motes})$$

Mirage uses a greedy heuristic algorithm to compute the set of winning bids, similar to the algorithm used by Bellagio.

The resources that a user of the IRB testbed cares about can exhibit both substitutes and complements. For example, in the machine learning example, the user does not care which specific MICA2 motes are allocated as long as a total of 64 of them are allocated. Hence, MICA2 motes are substitutes for one another. Similarly, the user does care that 64 motes are allocated simultaneously. A partial allocation of, say, 8 motes would not meet the user's needs in this case since the user's intention was to test at a moderate scale. (The extreme case would be a partial allocation of a single mote.) Thus, the 64 motes can be viewed as being complimentary to one another.

23.5.2.3 ***Currency Policy.*** As in Bellagio, each user is associated with a project that has an account at a central bank that stores virtual currency. Each project's bank account is assigned a baseline amount of currency based on priority, a number of currency shares, which influences the rate at which currency flows into the account, and is initialized with a baseline amount of currency. Priority and currency shares are determined exogenously, and are based mostly on the type of usage (e.g., research vs. coursework). Most accounts have a baseline balance and currency share of 1000, while two local users have a balance and share of 2000. Note that the profit-sharing policy differs from the one used in Bellagio. In Mirage, the sensor nodes are all owned by the IRB lab, and therefore, profit cannot be associated with a particular project, whereas in PlanetLab a resource can be directly attributed to a particular site.

23.5.3 Deployment

We deployed Mirage on IRB's 148-mote sensor-network testbed in December 2004, and it is still in operation as of this writing. The implementation consists of three types of components: clients, a server, and a frontend machine that users log in to and which provides controlled physical access to the testbed (Fig. 23.4). Clients provide users with secure, authenticated command-line (the `mirage` program) and Web-based access to a server (`miraged`) that implements a combinatorial auction, bank, and resource discovery service. The server provides service to clients by handling secure, authenticated XML-RPC requests using the Secure Sockets Layer (SSL) protocol with persistent state stored in a PostgreSQL database. Finally, the frontend physically enforces resource allocations from the auction using Linux's per-uid `iptables` packet-filtering capabilities. By default, all users are denied access to all motes. According to the outcome of the auction, rules are added as needed to open up access to users of winning bids for specific periods of time.

The auction is parameterized by several variables: number of resource slots, resource slot size, and acceptable bid durations. Our deployment includes 148 motes where access to those motes is based on 1-hour slots, the minimum time unit of

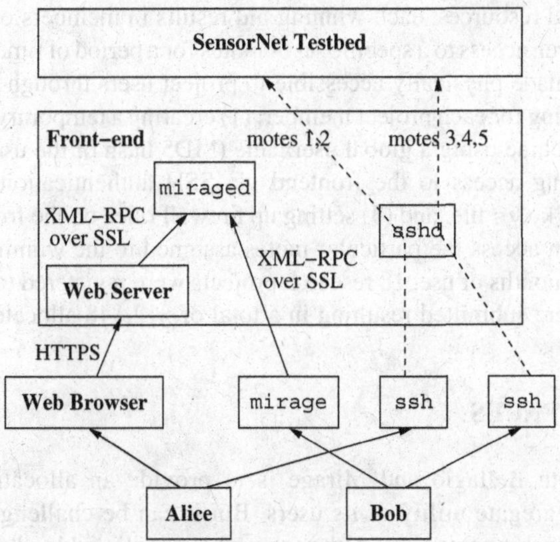

Figure 23.4 Mirage implementation. (Reproduced from [17, Fig. 4]).

resource allocation. To accommodate users who might require a range of different times with the motes, users may bid for either 1-, 2-, 4-, 8-, 16-, or 32-hour duration blocks. To allow users who wish to plan ahead (e.g., perhaps near a conference deadline), the auction will sell resources for up to 3 days into the future. Given our slot size of 1 hour, this works out to a total of 72 slots. Thus, we can view the resources being allocated as a matrix of 148 motes by 72 timeslots. When the system boots, all slots are available. Over time, slots become occupied as bids are allocated resources and new slots become available as the window of slots opens up over time.

To use the system, users register for an account at a secure Website by providing identifying information, contact information, a project name, and by uploading Secure Shell (SSH) public key. Each user is associated with a project, and each project has an owner. An administrative user is responsible for enabling accounts for project owners and assigning each project a baseline virtual currency value and a number of virtual currency shares. Project owners can subsequently enable their own users, thereby eliminating the administrative user as a centralized bottleneck.

Users bid securely in the auction using either the command-line tool `mirage`, which acts as an XML-RPC/SSL client, or through the Web-based interface, where PHP scripts on the backend act as XML-RPC/SSL clients to the relevant servers. The command-line tool provides full access to the entire RPC interface exposed by `miraged`. Use of this program is useful for various types of scripting and automation. To accommodate users who prefer a graphical interface, the Web-based interface provides a simple, integrated interface to the system where users specify what resources they want and how much they are willing to pay using an HTML form. The Web server, in turn, maps the user's abstract resources to concrete resources using the resource discovery service and places a bid in the auction on the user's behalf.

To use testbed resources, each winning bid results in members of the associated project being given access to a specific set of motes for a period of time specified in the bid. Motes are made physically accessible to project users through the frontend by doing the following for each project member: (1) creating a temporary UNIX login on the frontend machine using a global username (MD5 hash of the user's SSH public key), (2) enabling access to the frontend via SSH authentication using an SSH `authorized_keys` file, and (3) setting up firewall rules on the frontend such that only the user can access the particular motes assigned to the winning bid.

In the first 6 months of use, 18 research projects were registered to use the system and 322 bids were submitted resulting in a total of 312,148 allocated node hours.

23.6 EXPERIENCES

The goal of both Bellagio and Mirage is to provide an allocation policy that increases the aggregate utility of its users. But it can be challenging to measure our success in reaching this goal. Although we have real workload data from which we can quantify the aggregate utility (in units of virtual currency) of our scheduling

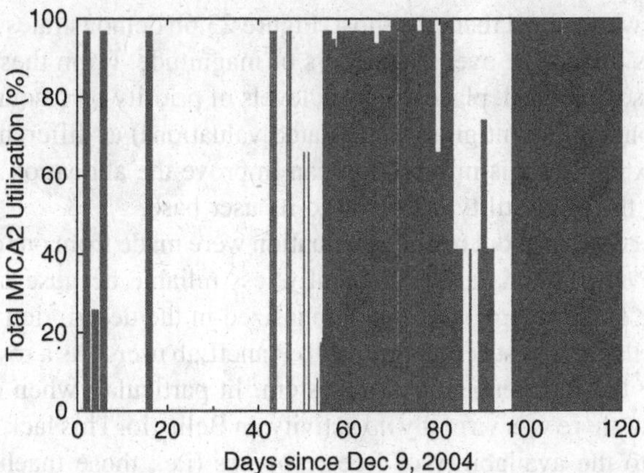

Figure 23.5 Testbed utilization for 97 MICA2 motes. (Reproduced from [17, Fig. 1a]).

policy on our target users, it is difficult to quantify the aggregate utility of a different scheduling policy using the same workload data. The problem is that there may have been bids that were withdrawn, repeated, or simply not submitted in the Bellagio and Mirage workload data. If we cannot account for the absent (or duplicated) resource requests, we cannot accurately reconstruct a workload stream that would have been presented to a more traditional scheduling policy, such as FCFS or proportional-share schedulers. Nevertheless, our data contain sufficient information that demonstrates that our market-based systems likely *do* increase utility in both domains. We explain this next.

Figure 23.5 indicates that resource contention continues to persist on the IRB sensor network testbed, as it had prior to the deployment of Mirage. We can see that during times of heavy system load, the bidding process is able to allocate resources at a higher price (Fig. 23.6a), and resolves contention by allocating the scarce resource

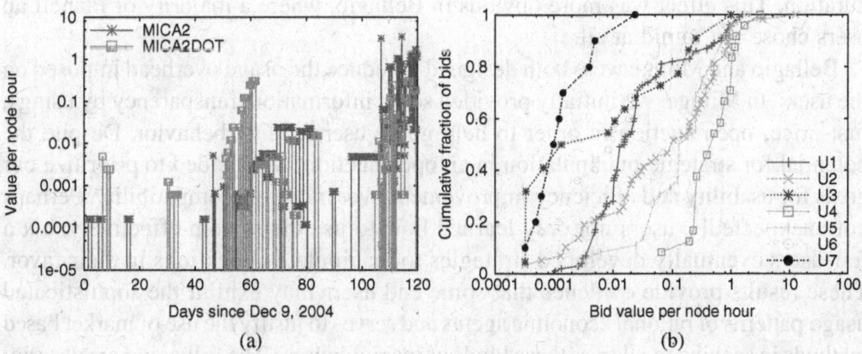

Figure 23.6 Mirage data: (a) Median node-hour market prices. (Reproduced from [34, Fig. 3]). (b) Bid value distribution per user. (Reproduced from [37, Fig. 2]).

supply to users who valued them the most. Figure 23.6b demonstrates that individual users place bids that range over four orders of magnitude. From these data, we can conclude that users, indeed, place different levels of priority on resources (assuming that the bids don't represent grossly misstated valuations) at different times, which suggests that extracting this information can improve the allocation efficiency of a system, that is, the total utility delivered to its user base.

Similar observations about resource valuation were made from our deployment on Bellagio; however, the data are significantly less reliable because of the few data points available from deployment. As emphasized in the description of the deployment, use of Bellagio was strictly optional to PlanetLab users. As a result, the market did not capture the full demand of the system. In particular, when overall system demand was low, there was virtually *no* activity on Bellagio. This lack of activity was due primarily to the availability of free resources (i.e., those machine shares not allocated by the market), and in fact ultimately led to Bellagio being taken offline. We see this result as an artifact of the opt-in nature of Bellagio, and not a negative result about the applicability of a market-based scheduler on the PlanetLab domain.

This example also serves to illustrate that users will often choose an easier-to-user approach, even if it results in slightly less utility. One particular burden of our auction-based approach is the artificial delay to node allocations. Since auctions are run every hour, allocations to winning bids are correspondingly delayed until the hour. There is a tradeoff here between imposing little delay on users and maximizing the efficiency of an allocation; increasing the frequency of auctions reduces the delay imposed on users, but it also reduces the amount of demand information captured in an auction, potentially reducing the quality of the allocation.

In Mirage, the auction-clearing period of one hour was designed to mitigate the impact of the imposed auction delay. However, from the available data, we observe that a significant fraction of the bids from users could not be satisfied given the one-hour delay. Each bid in Mirage includes both a delay field and a patience field, indicating an earliest start time and latest start time allowed for an allocation. These fields are used to communicate time-based constraints such as a deadline for an allocation. Figure 23.7 indicates that 10% of user bids could not wait for the one-hour duration. This effect was more obvious in Bellagio, where a majority of PlanetLab users chose not to bid at all.

Bellagio and Mirage were both designed to reduce the usage overhead imposed on the users. In Mirage, we initially provided some information transparency by using a first-price, open auction in order to help guide user bidding behavior. Despite the potential for strategic manipulation in an open auction, we decided to prioritize our goals for usability and efficiency improvement over incentive compatibility. Perhaps not unexpectedly, users not only learned how to use the system effectively, but a few users eventually developed strategies to manipulate allocations in their favor. These results provide evidence that some end users may exhibit the sophisticated usage patterns of rational economic agents and serves to justify the use of market based methods in seeking to address these kinds of manipulations. The following are descriptions of the four primary bidding behaviors that we observed during the initial Mirage deployment:

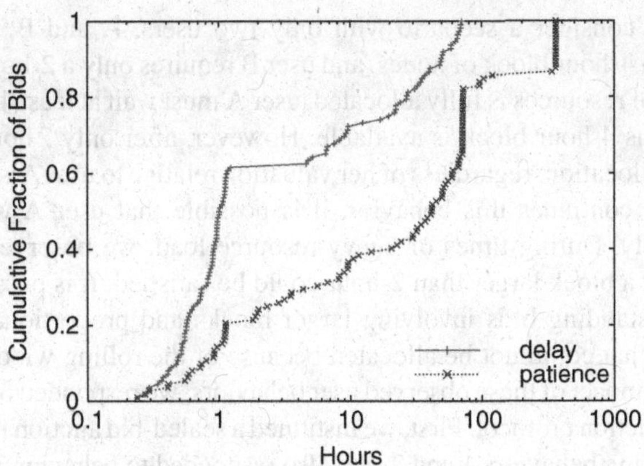

Figure 23.7 Distribution of delay and patience from bids submitted to Mirage between January 20 and March 22, 2005.

Behavior 1: Underbidding Based on Current Demand. Since all outstanding bids in our initial deployment were publicly visible, users could observe periods with low demand and submit low-valued bids in these periods. For example, one user would frequently bid a low value, such as 1 or 2 when no other bids were present. Underbidding is not necessarily a problem in this situation, because it can still result in a utility-maximizing allocation; For instance, if supply exceeds demand, then all interested users receive an allocation. This can be a problem in for-profit systems, however, where it would be important to use a reserve price to provide good revenue properties. Moreover, it suggests that users need to be strategic in thinking about how and when to bid, which indicates that such a system might be difficult to use.

Behavior 2: Iterative Bidding. The possibility of user underbidding coupled with uncertainty about the bid values of other users results in "iterative" bidding—a behavior in which a user adjusts her bids while an auction remains open and in response to price feedback. This poses a problem for system performance in Mirage because the auctions need to have a definite closing time (because the associated resources are perishable), and users may still be adjusting their bids when an auction closes. The impact of this strategy is a potential efficiency loss in the allocation.

Behavior 3: Rolling-Window Manipulation. Unlike auctions for tangible goods, resource allocation in computer systems are not allocated permanently, but rather allocated for particular intervals of time. Since many experiments by Mirage users can span several days, we permitted users to bid for allocation blocks of 1, 2, . . ., or 32 hours in size. In order to allow users to plan in advance, we auction off resources over a rolling window of 72 hours into the future. In periods of overdemand (e.g., during the SenSys 2005 conference deadline) the entire window of resources becomes fully allocated, and we found that the design of the rolling window can lead to unintended consequences. For example, consider a scenario with only two users, A and B, where user A requires a 4-hour block of nodes, and user B requires only a 2-hour block. If the window of resources is fully allocated, user A must wait at least 4 hours before a contiguous 4-hour block is available. However, after only 2 hour, user B will win her allocation, regardless of her valuation relative to user A's. Furthermore, if user B continues this behavior, it is possible that user A will be starved indefinitely. During times of heavy resource load, we observed that no bids involving a block larger than 2-hour could be satisfied. It is possible that there were outstanding bids involving larger blocks and proportionally larger bid amounts that could not be allocated because of the rolling window. Given the negative impact of these observed user behaviors, we responded by adjusting the Mirage auction protocol. First, we instituted a sealed-bid auction format, thereby discouraging behaviors 1 and 2. We also responded to behavior 3 by increasing the allowable time window to be 104 hours, with bid start times constrained to be within the next 72 hours. To understand the rationale for this change, consider the following example. Assume that we have users A and B, where user A requires a 32-hour block of nodes (the maximum allowed), and user B requires a 16-hour block of nodes. If the entire 72-hour window is allocated, the next available 32-hour block occurs 104 hour in the future. By expanding the rolling window to 104 hours and restricting the last 32 hours (of the window) from being reserved, bids from users A and B will be considered for the next available 32-hours block. Under the original auction format, the bid from user B would win the allocation before the bid from user A could even be considered.

Behavior 4: Auction Sandwich Attack. While our changes eliminated behavior 3 and significantly reduced behaviors 1 and 2, a fourth behavior exploited the available information about awarded allocations. In the so-called auction sandwich attack, a user exploits two pieces of information: (1) historical information on previous winning bids to estimate the current workload and (2) the greedy nature of the auction-clearing algorithm. In this particular case, we observed a user employing a strategy of splitting a bid for 97 MICA2 motes across several bids, only one of which has a high value per node hour. During times of high resource demand, most users request a majority of nodes (usually all 97 MICA2 motes, since a conference deadline requires large-scale experiments). Since Mirage uses a greedy (first-fit) heuristic in its auction-clearing algorithm, the user's single high value bid is likely to win, and because the bids from other users are then blocked and unable to fit in the remaining available slots, her other low-valued bids fill the remaining slots. We produce an actual occurrence of this behavior in Table 23.1. Here, user A submits three bids, the main one being a bid with value 130 (value per node hour $130/(4{\cdot}40) = 0.813$) and used to outbid a bid from user B, with value 1590 (value per node hour $1590/(32{\cdot}97) = 0.0512$). Once the high-valued 40-node bid has occupied its portion of the resource window, no other 97-node bids can be matched. Consequently, the user wins the remaining 57 nodes using two bids: a 24-node bid and a 33-node bid, both at low bid prices.

TABLE 23.1 Behavior 4 on 97 MICA2 Motes

Time	Project	Value	Nr. of Nodes	Nr. of Hours
04-02-2005 03:58:04	User B	1590	97	32
04-02-2005 05:05:45	User A	5	24	4
04-02-2005 05:28:23	User A	130	40	4
04-02-2005 06:12:12	User A	1	33	4

23.7 CONCLUDING REMARKS

From our deployments, we have seen that a market-based allocation system can significantly reduce the management burden and simultaneously improve user satisfaction on large-scale federated infrastructures.

The allocation decisions in Bellagio and Mirage are autonomously driven by user-provided job utility information, with very limited human intervention; when user behavior is properly constrained, the scheduling policies can lead to utility-maximizing resource allocations. While market-based systems have not yet seen widespread adoption, we believe that further efforts to deploy and study live systems will promote more support in the research and systems community, and can ultimately achieve the goal of more efficient utilization of today's computing platforms.

Overall, we made the following observations in this chapter:

1. *Markets can increase allocation efficiency, but only if users behave properly.* It can be difficult to rigorously compare the efficiency of two different allocation policies because the workload data that would be generated by each policy are different. However, from the Mirage deployment, we have demonstrated several scenarios where markets can be expected to outperform traditional allocation policies. One important aspect of this is the observation that even in large-scale infrastructures, resource demand often exceeds resource supply; in both Mirage and Bellagio, there are unavoidable periods of time where users' resource demands overlap, creating a situation where the system must arbitrate among them. We have observed user bids that vary by several orders of magnitude, indicating that there is room to make intelligent (and therefore, unintelligent) allocation decisions. Well-designed markets will promote a socially optimal allocation for the actual supply and demand conditions. In the case of Mirage, we saw that strategic behavior from a subset of users could potentially decrease the utility of the allocation to other users. By adjusting the allocation policy, we were able to limit the opportunities for strategic manipulation, and mitigate this negative impact on well-behaved Mirage users.

2. *Users are able to utilize market-based methods and will follow sophisticated behaviors if given sufficient incentive.* There exist many simpler alternatives to markets for the design of methods for resource allocation, such as, traditional methods that do not require the provision of bid information to describe demands by users. We have hypothesized that users might sometimes prefer this simplicity over the potential benefits of a market. But we have also observed that given enough incentive, users are

willing to put forth the effort to use a market system. In Bellagio, we saw that there was neither enough pressure nor sufficient incentive to use the market, and the vast majority of users opted for the simpler proportional allocation scheme in PlanetLab and were willing to forego any additional resources that Bellagio could provide. On the other hand, users in Mirage were given no alternative for obtaining a sensor node allocation. While finding that users were able to utilize the market-based system, we also observed both simple and strategic behavior, with the latter providing a (sometimes successful) attempt to manipulate allocations in their favor.

Our deployment experience has also highlighted a few key obstacles that can be addressed by future research:

Mechanisms with Faster Response Time. In the course of the Bellagio deployment, we learned that many users prefer immediate use (i.e., standard best-effort, proportional-share) over a potentially larger resource allocation (acquired from bidding). In Mirage, we also observed that many users required more immediacy for a significant fraction of their resource requests. As alluded to earlier, there is a tradeoff between offering a resource immediately and the efficiency gained from delaying an allocation decision. A hybrid mechanism, such as buy-it-now pricing on eBay [1], may provide a compromise between these desired properties.

Low-Cost Mechanism or Highly Valued Resources. In the Bellagio deployment, we learned that the resources made available through the auction were not valuable enough to users to justify expending the effort to obtain them. Many PlanetLab experiments are bottlenecked by other resources such as memory or disk bandwidth, and obtaining a few extra soft CPU shares is of little value. A market mechanism must either provide a resource of obvious and significant value to the end user, or impose a low enough cost to a user to justify its adoption. In Mirage, the market is the only means to obtain a sensor node, but having a market with a low cost of use was nevertheless important in promoting its adoption in the first place.

Strategyproof Methods. As we saw in behavior 4 from the Mirage deployment, some users will try to exploit, and can also succeed in exploiting, the particular characteristics of a market design. In promoting simplicity for users and also robustness and predictability for system designers, it can be helpful to deploy nonmanipulable "strategyproof" methods. There is a developing literature on the design of such mechanisms for dynamic environments (see Parkes [37] for a more recent survey), and it will be of interest to continue to seek to adopt these methods within computer systems [27].

ACKNOWLEDGMENTS

This chapter is based on four of the authors' previous publications [8,17,34,44].

REFERENCES

1. eBay, inc, http://www.ebay.com/.
2. EmuLab, http://www.emulab.net/.
3. Millennium sensor cluster. http://www.millennium.berkeley.edu/sensornets/.
4. Parallel Workloads Archive, http://www.cs.huji.ac.il/labs/parallel/workload/.
5. PlanetLab, http://planet-lab.org/.
6. San Diego Supercomputing Center, http://www.sdsc.edu/.
7. TeraGrid, http://teragrid.org/.
8. A. AuYoung, B. N. Chun, A. C. Snoeren, and A. Vahdat, Resource allocation in federated distributed computing infrastructures, *Proc. 1st ACM Workshop on Operating System and Architectural Support for the On Demand IT Infrastructure (OASIS 04)*, Boston, MA, Oct. 9, 2004.
9. A. AuYoung, L. E. Grit, J. Wiener, and J. Wilkes, Service contracts and aggregate utility functions, *Proc. 13th IEEE International Symp. High Performance Distributed Computing*, Paris, France, June 19–23, 2006.
10. S. Baruah, G. Koren, D. Mao, B. Mishra, A. Raghunathan, L. Rosier, D. Shasha, and F. Wang, On the competitiveness of on-line real-time task scheduling, *Real-Time Systems* **4**(2):125–144 (1992).
11. C. Boutilier, Bidding languages for combinatorial auctions, *Proc. 17th International Joint Conf. Artificial Intelligence*, Seattle, WA, Aug. 4–10, 2001.
12. A. Byde, M. Salle, and C. Bartolini, *Market-Based Resource Allocation for Utility Data Centers*, Technical Report HPL-2003-188, HP Laboratories, 2003.
13. J. S. Chase, D. C. Anderson, P. N. Thakar, A. M. Vahdat, and R. P. Doyle, Managing energy and server resources in hosting centers, *Proc. 18th ACM Symp. Operating Systems Principles (SOSP 01)*, Chateau Lake Louise, Banff, Canada, Oct. 21–24, 2001.
14. K. Chen and P. Muhlethaler, A scheduling algorithm for tasks described by time value function, *Real-Time Systems* **10**(3):293–312 (1996).
15. N. Christin, J. Grossklags, and J. Chuang, *Near Rationality and Competitive Equilibria in Networked Systems*, Technical Report 2004-04-CGC, Univ. California Berkeley, 2004.
16. B. N. Chun and A. Vahdat, *Workload and Failure Characterization on a Large-Scale Federated Testbed*, Technical Report IRB-TR-03-040, Intel Research Berkeley, CA, 2003.
17. B. N. Chun, P. Buonadonna, A. AuYoung, C. Ng, D. C. Parkes, J. Shneidman, A. C. Snoeren, and A. Vahdat, Mirage: A microeconomic resource allocation system for SensorNet testbeds, *Proc. 2nd IEEE Workshop on Embedded Networked Sensors (EmNetsII)*, Sydney, Australia, May 30–31, 2005.
18. B. N. Chun and D. E. Culler, User-centric performance analysis of market-based cluster batch schedulers, *Proc. 2nd IEEE International Symp. Cluster Computing and the Grid*, Berlin, Germany, May 21–24, 2002.
19. R. K. Clark, E. D. Jensen, and F. D. Reynolds, An Architectural overview of the alpha real-time distributed kernel, *Proc. USENIX Winter Technical Conf.*, San Diego, CA, Jan. 25–29, 1993.
20. J. Dean and S. Ghemawat, MapReduce: Simplified data processing on large clusters, *Proc. 6th Conf. Operating Systems Design & Implementation*, San Francisco, CA, Dec. 6–8, 2004.

21. D. Feitelson, L. Rudolph, and U. Schwiegelshohn, Parallel job scheduling—a status report, *Proc. 10th Workshop on Job Scheduling Strategies for Parallel Processing*, New York, NY, June 13, 2004.
22. I. Foster and C. Kesselman, *The Grid: Blueprint for a New Computing Infrastructure*, Morgan Kaufmann, 1999.
23. E. J. Friedman, J. Y. Halpern, and I. Kash, Efficiency and Nash equilibria in a Scrip system for P2P networks, *Proc. 7th ACM Conf. Electronic Commerce (EC 06)*, Ann Arbor, MI June 11–15, 2006.
24. Y. Fu, J. Chase, B. Chun, S. Schwab, and A. Vahdat, Sharp: An architecture for secure resource peering, *Proc. 19th ACM Symp. Operating Systems Principles (SOSP 03)*, Bolton Landing, NY, Oct. 19–22, 2003.
25. Intel Research Berkeley, Mirage: Microeconomic Resource Allocation for SensorNet Testbeds, http://mirage.berkeley.intel-research.net/.
26. D. Jackson, Q. Snell, and M. Clement, Core algorithms of the Maui scheduler, *Proc. 7th Workshop on Job Scheduling Strategies for Parallel Processing*, Cambridge, MA, June 16, 2001.
27. L. Kang and D. C. Parkes, A decentralized auction framework to promote efficient resource allocation in open computational Grids, *Proc. Joint Workshop on Economics of Networked Systems and Incentive-Based Computing (NetEcon-IBC 07)*, San Diego, CA, June 11, 2007.
28. I. A. Kash, E. J. Friedman, and J. Y. Halpern, Optimizing Scrip systems: Efficiency, crashes, hoarders, and altruists, *Proc. 8th ACM Conf. Electronic Commerce (EC 07)*, San Diego, CA, June 11–15, 2007.
29. V. Kumar, B. F. Cooper, and K. Schwan, Distributed stream management using utility-driven self-adaptive middleware, *Proc. 2nd International Conf. Autonomic Computing*, Seattle, WA, June 13–16, 2005.
30. K. Lai, B. A. Huberman, and L. Fine, Tycoon: *A Distributed Market-Based Resource Allocation System*, Technical Report cs.DC/0404013, HP Laboratories, 2004.
31. C. Lee, J. Lehoczky, D. Siewiorek, R. Rajkumar, and J. Hansen, A scalable solution to the multi-resource QoS problem, *Proc. 20th IEEE Real-Time Systems Symp.*, Phoenix, AZ, Dec. 1–3, 1999.
32. C. B. Lee and A. Snavely, On the user-scheduler dialogue: Studies of user-provided runtime estimates and utility functions, *International Journal of High-Performance Computing Applications* **20**(4):495–506 (2006).
33. L. Levy, L. Blumrosen, and N. Nisan, On-line markets for distributed object services: The MAJIC system, *Proc. 3rd USENIX Symp. Internet Technologies and Systems*, San Francisco, CA, March 26–28, 2001.
34. C. Ng, P. Buonadonna, B. N. Chun, A. C. Snoeren, and A. Vahdat, Addressing strategic behavior in a deployed microeconomic resource allocator, *Proc. 3rd Workshop on the Economics of Peer to Peer Systems (P2PEcon 05)*, Philadelphia, PA, Aug. 22, 2005.
35. N. Nisan, Bidding and allocation in combinatorial auctions, *Proc. 2nd ACM Conf. Electronic Commerce*, Minneapolis, MN, Oct. 17–20, 2000.
36. D. Oppenheimer, J. Albrecht, D. Patterson, and A. Vahdat, Design and implementation tradeoffs for wide-area resource discovery, *Proc. 13th IEEE International Symp. High Performance Distributed Computing*, Research Triangle Park, NC, July 24–27, 2005.

37. D. C. Parkes, Online mechanisms, in *Algorithmic Game Theory*, N. Nisan, T. Roughgarden, E. Tardos, and V. Vazirani, eds., Cambridge Univ. Press, 2007.

38. L. Peterson, D. Culler, T. Anderson, and T. Roscoe, A blueprint for introducing disruptive technology into the Internet, *Proc. 1st Workshop on Hot Topics in Networks (HotNets-I)*, Princeton, NJ, Oct. 28–29, 2002.

39. L. Peterson, V. Pai, N. Spring, and A. Bavier, *Using PlanetLab for Network Research: Myths, Realities, and Best Practices*, Technical Report PDN-05-028, PlanetLab Consortium, 2005.

40. D. Petrou, G. R. Ganger, and G. A. Gibson, Cluster scheduling for explicitly speculative tasks, *Proc. 18th ACM International Conf. Supercomputing*, Saint-Malo, France, June 26 – July 1, 2004.

41. O. Regev and N. Nisan, The POPCORN market—an online market for computational resources, *Proc. 1st International Conf. Information and Computation Economies*, Charleston, SC, Oct. 25–28, 1998.

42. M. H. Rothkopf, A. Pekec, and R. M. Harstad, Computationally manageable combinational auctions, *Management Science* **44**(8):1131–1147 (1998).

43. T. Sandholm, S. Suri, A. Gilpin, and D. Levine, Winner determination in combinatorial auction generalizations, *Proc. 1st International Joint Conf. Autonomous Agents and Multiagent Systems*, Bologna, Italy, July 2002.

44. J. Shneidman, C. Ng, D. Parkes, A. AuYoung, A. C. Snoeren, A. Vahdat, and B. N. Chun, Why markets could (but don't currently) solve resource allocation problems in systems, *Proc. 10th USENIX Workshop on Hot Topics in Operating Systems (HotOS-X)*, Santa Fe, NM, June 12–15, 2005.

45. I. Stoica, H. Abdel-Wahab, and A. Pothen, A microeconomic scheduler for parallel computers, *Proc. 1st Workshop on Job Scheduling Strategies for Parallel Processing*, Santa Barbara, CA, April 25, 1995.

46. I. E. Sutherland, A futures market in computer time, *Communications of the ACM* **11**(6): 449–451 (1968).

47. C. A. Waldspurger, T. Hogg, B. A. Huberman, J. O. Kephart, and S. Stornetta, Spawn: A distributed computational economy, *IEEE Transactions on Software Engineering* **18**(2): 103–177 (1992).

48. W. E. Walsh, G. Tesauro, J. O. Kephart, and R. Das, Utility functions in autonomic systems, *Proc. 1st International Conf. Autonomic Computing*, New York, NY, May 17–18, 2004.

49. G. Werner-Allen, P. Swieskowski, and M. Welsh, MoteLab: A wireless sensor network testbed, *Proc. 4th International Conf. Information Processing in Sensor Networks*, Los Angeles, CA, April 25–27, 2005.

50. R. Wolski, J. S. Plank, T. Bryan, and J. Brevik, G-commerce: Market formulations controlling resource allocation on the computational Grid, *Proc. 15th International Parallel and Distributed Processing Symp.*, San Francisco, CA, April 23–27, 2001.

51. C. S. Yeo and R. Buyya, Pricing for utility-driven resource management and allocation in clusters, *International Journal of High-Performance Computing Applications* **21**(4): 405–418 (2007).

24

TRUST IN GRID RESOURCE AUCTIONS

KRIS BUBENDORFER, BEN PALMER, AND WAYNE THOMSON

24.1 INTRODUCTION

Trust is a concept that we humans implicitly understand, but we have difficulty in applying our understanding digitally. Trust takes into account the role of the entity, the degree of potential loss, and sometimes prior experience or experience of those trusted by you (referral). However, trust can be misplaced, and the degree of risk underestimated. Essentially, just because something is trusted does not mean that it is also trustworthy.

Consider the collapse of the 1995 Barings Bank [1] in which Nick Leeson, a floor manager for Barings Trading, abused his position of trust by hiding losses made in the futures and options markets over 3 years. The mechanism he used was cross-trades made to a special error account that was not visible to auditors in the main London office. Leeson was also head of settlement operations for his unit, which short-circuited normal accounting and auditing safeguards. As in most cases, the employee had a satisfactory history within the company before being placed in this position of trust. Without a perfect oracle, it is probably not possible to make better trust evaluations. What was really missing in the Barings Bank collapse were additional mechanisms (checks and balances) to ensure that its employees could not act in an unauthorized way.

We draw an analogy here to resource allocation mechanisms. Even if a community broker or auctioneer is trusted, we still cannot have confidence in its trustworthiness without additional mechanisms to audit and constrain its actions. Within the scope of a single organization this may not be an issue; however, when we cross organizational boundaries and potentially include the potential for profit or loss, then we need better mechanisms than traditional *blind trust* for a market-oriented Grid.

Market-Oriented Grid and Utility Computing Edited by Rajkumar Buyya and Kris Bubendorfer

24.1.1 The Need for Trustworthy Resource Auctions

Imagine that two independent resource providers (let's call them Bob and Jane) have surplus resources and wish to sell the rights to use these resources via Alice, their friendly local auctioneer. The auction is a sealed-bid reverse auction (or tender), where clients issue requests for resources and resource providers bid (and compete) to supply. The auction house itself is hosted on resources provided by Sam. When a client submits a resource request to Alice, Alice creates an auction and advertises the new auction to Bob and Jane. Bob and Jane respond by submitting their bids to Alice. At the end of the auction, Alice examines the bids and declares the winner of the auction.

There are a number of potential problems with this auction. Alice can freely examine the bids from Bob and Jane. She can then reveal this information to others, giving them a competitive advantage, or she can simply collect bid information over time to manipulate the market by setting reserves and so on. The bid information, as such, represents commercially sensitive information from the resource providers, and this information should ideally be kept private. Even if Alice is willing to keep the bid information private, Sam could extract the information directly from memory or if it were encrypted, extract the key from memory. Alice might also favor Jane over Bob, by discarding all or a portion of Bob's bids—at the expense of Bob and the clients. Likewise, Sam could filter bids preventing Alice from including them in the auction. If Alice or Sam were also a resource provider, then the incentive to cheat would be considerable. As stated by Hal Varian [2], "even if current information can be safeguarded, records of past behavior can be extremely valuable, since historical data can be used to estimate the willingness to pay."

The first step in solving these problems is to ensure that bids are kept private, that is, hidden from Alice or Sam. At first this seems to be impossible, as Alice would be unable to compute the winner of the auction. However, we can exploit certain cryptographic techniques that allow Alice to compute the outcome of the auction, without revealing anything other than the winner and the final price. Such schemes are known as a *privacy-preserving* scheme, whereby Alice (or Sam) cannot reveal or use the bid information to manipulate the market. In addition, in a second-price or Vickrey auction [3], Alice cannot inflate the prices to obtain a higher commission—a problem known as the *corrupt auctioneer*. We will discuss these techniques later in this chapter.

The second step is to ensure that the auction protocol has been executed correctly and that all bids have been considered to preclude the possibility of filtering or favoritism. This can be achieved using a *verification* scheme—some of which permit any party in the auction to verify offline that the auction was held correctly.

Essentially, we have three main requirements for the holding trustworthy resource auctions in a multiorganizational (or open) Grid:

1. We should be able to avoid having to trust a single auctioneer.
2. We should be able to provide strong bid privacy.
3. We should be able to verify that the auction was conducted correctly.

24.2 SECURE AUCTION PROTOCOLS FOR THE GRID

Removing the need to establish trust enables Grid allocation architectures that are user-centric, peer-oriented, open, and dynamic. From this flexibility we should see improvements in reliability, availability, and accessibility. Resource auctions can be executed safely using *any* computing resources contributed by *any* provider. As such, as the size of the Grid increases, additional untrustworthy computing resources can be deployed or redeployed dynamically to meet any subsequent growth in the number of resource auctions.

Table 24.1 presents our taxonomy of auction protocols that feature some form of cryptographic security. The first column shows whether the auction protocol is verifiable by anyone (public) or whether it is verifiable only by specific participants of the protocol (group). The next column shows whether the auction protocol supports combinatorial auctions. The bid privacy trust model is shown in the next column and indicates whether the auction protocol uses a single trusted auctioneer, two-party trust, or a multiparty trust scheme. Finally our table shows the bid privacy provided by the protocols using the following privacy levels (adapted from Suzuki and Yokoo [4]):

- Level 0: Only the winning bidder/s and the price they paid are revealed.
- Level 1: In addition to the information revealed by level 0, one other piece of information is revealed.
- Level *s*: In addition to the information revealed by level 0, it is also possible to recover bid statistics. For example, the average bid and the standard deviation of bids.
- Level *: All of the bids are revealed to the auctioneer after the auction closes.

Consider the three requirements outlined in Section 24.1.1:

1. *We should be able to avoid having to trust a single auctioneer*. Schemes that use a single trusted auctioneer [9,19] are not in themselves trustworthy protocols. Some other schemes use two-party trust [5,7,8,16] where bids are kept private unless there is collusion between these two parties. All remaining schemes use some form of multiparty trust, where the operation is spread over many independent parties normally implemented using multiparty trust. Undermining this form of auction would require collusion between a significant number of corrupt parties. A two-party trust scheme has the practical advantage that it is often easier to find two servers from separate organizations than it is to find a large group of independent servers as is used in a multiparty trust scheme. On the other hand, multiparty trust can provide increased reliability, availability, and accessibility.
2. *We should be able to provide strong bid privacy.* In the schemes described by Lipmaa et al. [5] and Parkes et al. [19] a trusted auctioneer learns bids after the bid-opening phase of the auction. This requires that a large amount of trust be placed in the auctioneer to not sell or otherwise leak bid information. Rather than releasing specific bids, the schemes described by Lipmaa et al. [5] and

TABLE 24.1 Privacy-Preserving Auction Taxonomy

Auction Scheme	Verifiability		Combinatorial	Bid Privacy Trust Model			Bid Privacy Level			
	Group	Public	Auction Support	Single Trusted Auctioneer	Two Party Trust	Multiparty Trust	0	1	s	*
Franklin and Reiter [30]	•					•				•
HKT[a] [6]						•	•			
Two-server [7]	•				•			•		
Garbled circuits [8]	•		•		•		•			
Noninteractive [9]				•			•			
Polynomial [10]	•					•	•			
No threshold trust [5]	•				•				•	
Polynomial GVA[b] [11]			•			•	•			
Homomorphic [12]			•			•	•			
Extended HKT [13]		•				•	•			
Five models [14]		•				•			•	
SGVA[c] [4]			•			•	•			
Yet another [15]		•				•	•			
Receipt-free [16]		•			•		•			
Combinatorial bidder resolved [17]			•			•	•			
GW Micali [18]		•				•	•			
Verifiable scheme [19]		•		•						•
Bidder resolved [20]		•				•	•			
Extended verifiable homomorphic [21]		•	•			•	•			

[a]Harkavy–Tygar–Kikuchi.
[b]Generalized Vickery auction.
[c]Secure GVA.

Peng et al. [14] leak bid statistics, while the scheme proposed by Cachin [7] leaks a partial ordering of bids. To provide the requirement of strong bid privacy, we should look at using one of the schemes with the highest level of bid privacy (level 0).

3. *We should be able to verify that the auction was conducted correctly.* Apart from providing confidence in the result of auctions, verifiability can increase the robustness of the solution by allowing participants to check intermediate results. For example, an auction evaluator conducting threshold decryption can prove that his/her share of the decryption is correctly calculated. Most verifiable auctions were initially group verification, where *involved* parties could verify the outcome of the auction. A more recent development has been public verifiability, where *any* entity can verify the result of the auction. Public verification can also be added to existing schemes [13,21] using techniques such as zero knowledge proofs.

24.3 AUCTION PROTOCOL CASE STUDIES

As can be gathered from reading the taxonomy in Section 24.2, there are many secure auction protocols of varying capability that can be used as the basis for a trustworthy Grid auction. In this section we present three of the most Grid-suitable protocols as worked examples.

24.3.1 How to Represent Combinatorial Auctions

Combinatorial auctions have been represented in a number of ways, including graphs, matrices, and circuits. Two of the auction protocols presented in this chapter represent auctions using graphs, while the third uses a circuit. Up to this point in the chapter we have used the *resource* as the object of an auction. However, from this perspective, we will use the term *good* as this is the standard term in auction theory.

A graph can be used to solve combinatorial auctions where nodes represent unallocated goods, edges between nodes represent the allocation of a subset of goods to bidders, and each complete path represents an allocation of the goods. Figure 24.1 provides an example auction graph for three goods {G1,G2,G3} with two bidders B1 and B2. Edge allocations are shown under edges, bids are presented above edges and nodes are labeled n_0 to n_{N-1}, where N is the number of nodes in the graph. The highest path cost from n_5 to n_i is represented by its f value $f(i)$. The highest bid for edge (n_5, n_2) is \$4, and as node n_5 has no incoming edges, $f(5) = 0$ and so $f(2) = 4$. The other f values are $f(3) = 9$, $f(4) = 1$, and $f(1) = 10$. To determine $f(0)$, each of the incoming edges are compared, and (n_3, n_0) provides the highest-cost path with (n_3, n_0) $+ f(1) = 19$. The highest bids are recorded at each step and the winning allocation is B2 wins G2 for \$9 and B1 wins G1 and G3 for \$10.

An auction circuit can also be used to represent a combinatorial auction and is composed of a series of Boolean gates. The circuit has a set of inputs, the gates of the circuit, and a set of outputs.

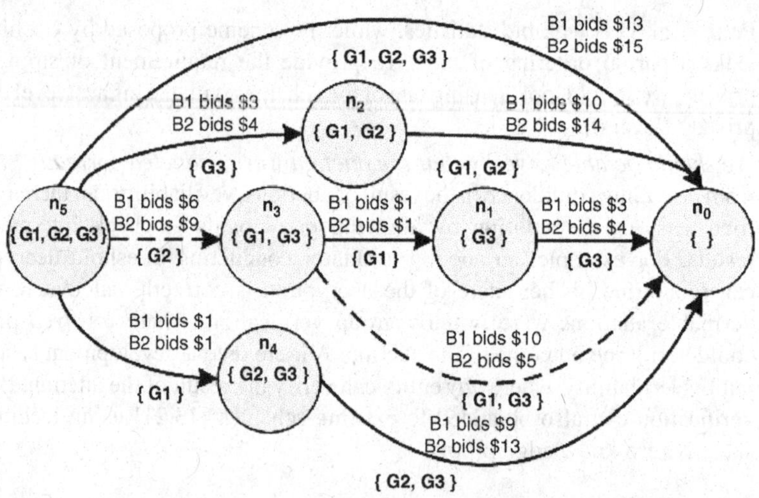

Figure 24.1 An auction graph for three goods G1, G2, and G3. The optimal path is indicated by the dashed line.

Figure 24.2 shows a Boolean circuit that is being used for a trivial auction with one good, two bidders, and two bits representing the price. The circuit has inputs of the bids for the two bidders represented by two bits. The outputs are composed of two Boolean values that indicate whether Bidder 1 was the winner or if Bidder 2 was the winner. The other two outputs indicate the bits of the maximum or winning price.

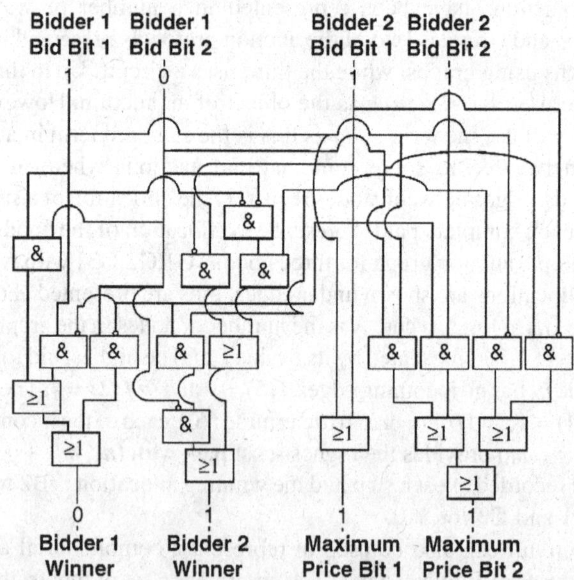

Figure 24.2 A simple auction circuit.

The example in Figure 24.2 shows Bidder 2 winning the auction with a maximum price of 11. To further illustrate this point, consider a further example where Bidder 1's input is 10 and Bidder 2's input is 01, the output is Bidder 1 Winner = 1, Bidder 2 Winner = 0, Maximum Price Bit 1 = 1, and Maximum Price Bit 2 = 0.

24.3.2 The Garbled Circuits Scheme

The principal idea of a garbled circuit is to act as a replacement for the "trusted party" in transactions between mutually distrustful parties. Garbled circuits were presented in Yao's seminal 1986 paper [22] as a solution to the "millionaire's problem," in which two millionaires wish to determine who is richer—without revealing their actual wealth to the other. In essence, a garbled circuit acts as a black box, which will evaluate an input without revealing anything but the output for that one value. A garbled circuit involves the creation of a set of Boolean gates to compute a function, and then the garbling of this circuit to obfuscate the input and intermediate values but still allow execution of the function given the garbled inputs.

To achieve privacy on the input and intermediate values of the circuit, the circuit creator assigns random values and a permutation to wires in the circuit while keeping these hidden from the party that will execute the circuit. If these values are known to the circuit executor, then the privacy of inputs is lost.

To garble a circuit, the circuit creator assigns every wire connecting the gates a random value (W^1), corresponding to the 1 value of the wire and a random value (W^0) corresponding to the 0 value of the wire. Every wire is also assigned a random permutation over {0, 1} π: $b \rightarrow c$ from the actual value of the wire b to the permutated value c. The garbled value of a wire with an actual value of b is defined as $\langle W^b, c \rangle$ where the random value associated with b is concatcenated with the result of the permutation of b.Figure 24.3 shows a wire with an actual ungarbled value of b. The random values and permutation tables are shown above the wire and the garbled values, below.

A gate table is then constructed for each Boolean gate in the circuit that can output the garbled value of the output wire when given the garbled input values. Finally, a table is constructed to map the garbled outputs of the circuit to the actual outputs. Construction of the gate tables and output tables requires knowledge of the random values and the random permutation assigned to the wires, which are kept private by the garbled circuit constructor. Without knowledge of these random values and permutation, it is difficult to work out any intermediate values in the circuit. To execute the circuit, the garbled input values for the circuit are needed. The garbled inputs are found using a protocol called *verifiable proxy oblivious transfer* (VPOT) [23]. Once the garbled input values are known, the gate tables are used to find the garbled outputs by applying the XOR (exclusive OR) function over the output of a random function on the garbled inputs and the entry in the gate table. When all the garbled outputs have been calculated, the output tables are used to work out the actual output.

24.3.2.1 Worked Example. Figure 24.4 illustrates a small garbled circuit with an AND gate and an OR gate. The garbled circuit creator produces the random values

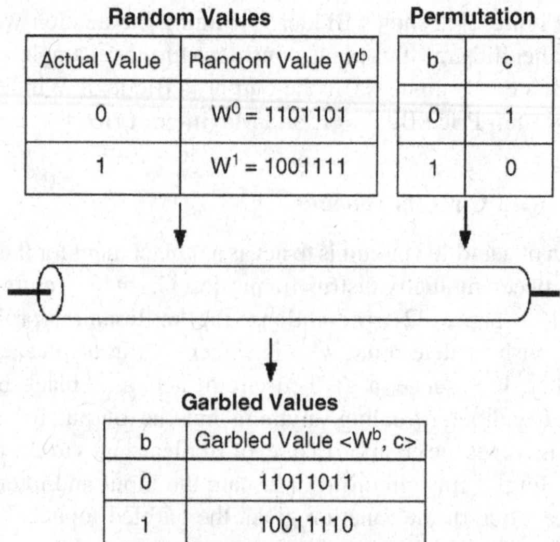

Random Values
Actual Value
Random Value W^b
0
W^0 = 1101101
1
W^1 = 1001111
Permutation
b
c
0
1
1
0
Garbled Values
b
Garbled Value <W^b, c>
0
11011011
1
10011110

Figure 24.3 Garbled circuit wire.

assigned to wires, the gate tables, and the garbled output to output mapping. The random function F is available to any party in the protocol. The garbled value of a wire is set to $\langle W^b, c\rangle$ so for wire Z the garbled value of 0 is $\langle W^0, C_0\rangle = \langle 01,0\rangle = 010$. We set the input values to $V=1$, $W=1$, and $Y=0$. With these input values, the output of this circuit should be 1.

To execute this circuit, the circuit executor would take the following steps:

1. Ascertain the garbled input values. The garbled input value for $V=001$, for $W=010$, and for $Y=010$. The garbled input value is the garbled value of the wire for the input value.

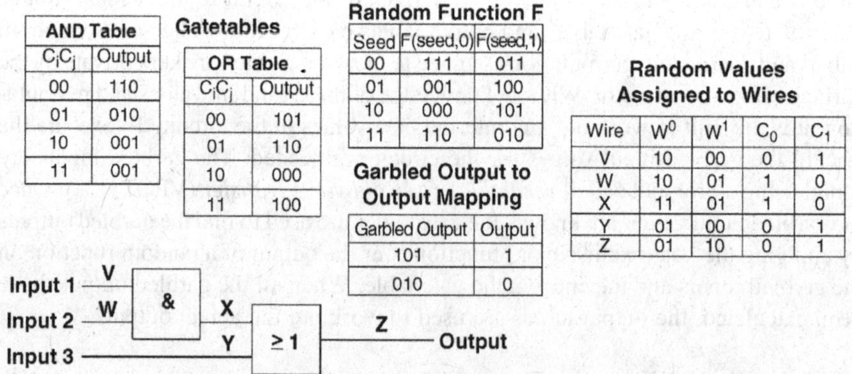

Figure 24.4 A simple garbled circuit.

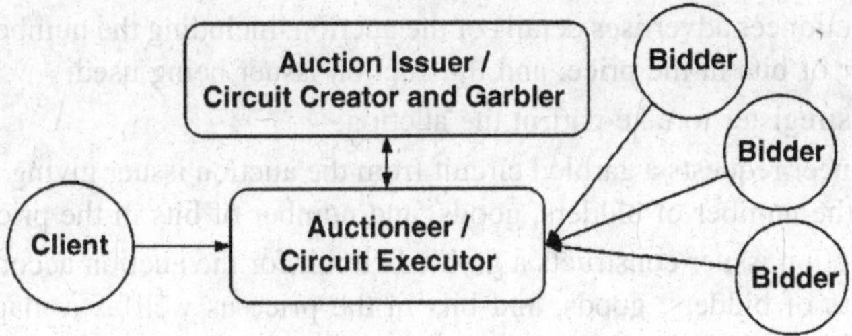

Figure 24.5 Garbled circuit interaction diagram.

2. Now we need to execute the gates. To execute the AND gate we use our garbled inputs and the gatetable. The equation used to calculate the garbled output is $\texttt{GarbledOutput} = \texttt{F}(W^b, c_j) \oplus \texttt{F}(W^b, c_i) \oplus \texttt{Gatetable}(c_i, c_j)$. So, the output is $001 \oplus 111 \oplus 100 = 010$.
3. Now we need to execute the OR gate. The output is $101 \oplus 001 \oplus 001 = 101$. Using the garbled output to output mapping, we can see the output of the garbled circuit is 1.

(*Note*: A real circuit that executes an auction has many thousands of gates.)

24.3.2.2 Garbled Circuits for Auctions. Naor et al. [8] introduced the two-party garbled-circuit-based protocol for a sealed-bid, two-server auction using oblivious transfer. The protocol features an auctioneer and an auction issuer as the two parties. This protocol is an efficient single-pass protocol that also preserves the communication pattern of traditional auctions (see Fig. 24.5).

The bidders and the client only need to have a connection to the auctioneer, and the auctioneer is the only party that needs a connection to the auction issuer. In addition, bidders do not have to encrypt values, which can be computationally expensive.

Figure 24.6 shows the views for each party when conducting the protocol to learn the garbled input values for the auction circuit.

24.3.2.3 The Garbled Circuit Auction Protocol. The basic steps of a sealed-bid auction using the garbled auction circuit protocol are

- The client contacts the auctioneer with details of the auction she/he wishes to run.

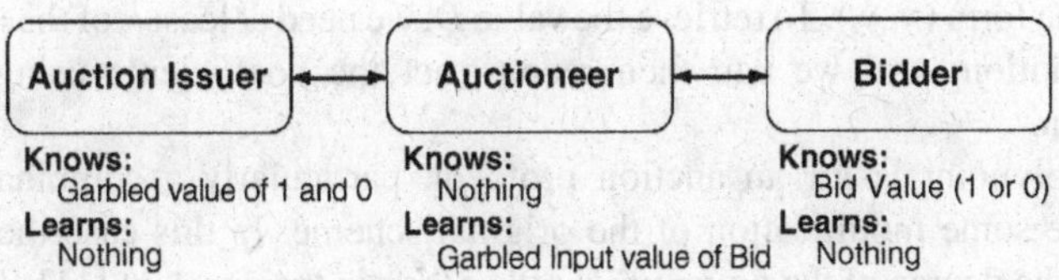

Figure 24.6 Views for each party.

- The auctioneer advertises details of the auction, including the number of goods, number of bits in the price, and the auction issuer being used.
- Bidders register to take part in the auction.
- Auctioneer requests a garbled circuit from the auction issuer giving the auction issuer the number of bidders, goods, and number of bits in the price.
- The auction issuer constructs a garbled circuit for the auction according to the numbers of bidders, goods, and bits in the price as well as a mapping from garbled outputs to outputs.
- The auctioneer receives the garbled circuit and output mapping.
- The auction issuer, auctioneer, and bidders use the VPOT protocol, which results in the auctioneer learning the garbled values of the inputs, and the auction issuer and bidders learning no new information.
- The auctioneer executes the garbled circuit using the garbled input and decodes the output using the output mapping sent by the auction issuer.

24.3.3 The Polynomial Scheme

The idea of using polynomials to efficiently share a secret between a group of people originated with Shamir [31] in his seminal paper "How to share a secret." The following question set by Liu [32] captures the essence of the problem:

> *Eleven scientists are working on secret project. They wish to lock up the documents in a cabinet so that the cabinet can be opened if and only if six or more of the scientists are present. What is the smallest number of locks needed? What is the smallest number of keys each scientist must carry?*

The answer to this is 462 locks and 252 keys per scientist. Clearly this is not a practical situation and scales exponentially as the number of scientists increases. This is a (k,n) threshold scheme, where we divide the secured data D into n pieces and require at least k of those pieces to reconstruct the original. The choice of k and n determine the strength of the system and, of course, $k < n$. Such threshold schemes are ideal when we wish to establish cooperation within a group of mutually untrusted and possibly competing entities. Shamir's breakthrough was to solve this problem efficiently using polynomials. Shamir's algorithm is based on the idea that a polynomial of degree $k - 1$ can be uniquely identified by k points. Therefore we can construct a polynomial $f(x)$ of degree $k - 1$ using $k - 1$ random coefficients and the secret D as the constant. We then pick n random x values and solve the polynomial creating n points (or key shares) of the form (x_i,y_i). To retrieve the value D, we need at least k of these shares (in any combination) and we can then reconstruct the coefficients using Lagrange interpolation.

Using polynomials for an auction protocol, particularly a combinatorial one, does require some modification of the original scheme. In this case the secret bid is stored in the degree of the polynomial rather than in the constant [11]. This has the nice property that two secret bids (encoded as polynomials A and B) can be compared using only local information with the following formulae: max{deg(A), deg(B)} = deg($A + B$), deg(A) + deg(B) = deg($A \cdot B$). Hence, each auction evaluator (with key share ks) can compute locally its share of $A + B$ by computing $A(x_{ks}) + B(x_{ks})$, or of $A \cdot B$ by taking the product $A(x_{ks}) \cdot B(x_{ks})$.

24.3.3.1 The Polynomial Auction Protocol. This protocol was developed by Yokoo and Suzuki [11] and is more fully described in Reference 24 with implementation performance results. It is outlined here in the following five steps:

1. The client publishes information about goods under auction with an auction graph. Also published is a set of evaluator resolve values by E evaluators for generating polynomial shares, a constant value c for weight resolution, and a threshold value t is published that is used to prevent interference from less than t corrupt auctioneers.
2. Bidders calculate valuations and generate weights for each edge from the auction graph they are interested in. To form a weight w a threshold modifier $t \cdot (j - i)$ is added to the valuation, where j is the identification number of the larger node and i is the identification number of the smaller node. This modifier ensures that t evaluators are required to decrypt any edge and it is weighted against node identifiers so that costs are consistent over paths of different lengths. A random polynomial of degree w and constant 0 is solved with each evaluator's resolve value and sent to the respective evaluator to be recorded as an edge on her/his copy of the auction graph.
3. The optimal value of the auction is the sum of bidder valuations on the greatest path through the graph. As bids are distributed amongst the evaluators, valuations must be reconstructed by interpolating shares published by evaluators. The cost of node n_0, denoted $f(0)$, is the sum of all paths in the graph, which each evaluator calculates using dynamic programming and publishes.
4. Evaluators use binary search to collaboratively discover the optimal value o. Using Lagrange interpolation a polynomial can be recovered with a degree of 1 less than the number of shares used, and it is this number that the search discovers. At each iteration, evaluators publish shares masked with shares from M mask publishers generated in a similar ways as bids. The polynomial degree for the mask is equal to the number of shares to use and the constant equal to c. If the Lagrange polynomial has a constant equal to $M \cdot c$, the optimal value is less than or equal to 1 less than the number of shares; otherwise the optimal value is greater than the number of shares. The optimal value d is therefore found where $d \leq o$ and $d + 1 > o$.
5. An optimal path is traced from n_0 to n_{N-1}. As the cost of an optimal node n_i is the greatest path cost from n_i to n_0, the cost of an edge added to $f(j)$ of connected node j is $f(i)$. Beginning with $i = 0$, an optimal path is found by iteratively checking whether $f(j) + f(n_i, n_j) > f(i) - 1$. A comparison is carried out as in step 4: $f(i) - 1$ evaluators publish masked shares of $f(j) + f(n_i, n_j)$ and interpolation is used to check for a constant not equal to $M \cdot c$. When an optimal

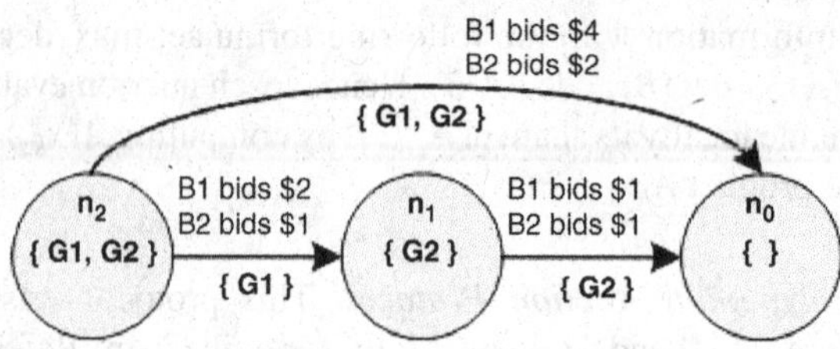

Figure 24.7 The initial auction graph with corresponding valuations.

node n_j is found, binary search is used to determine $f(j)$, and the cost of the previous optimal edge is the difference between the two nodes $f(i) - f(j)$.

24.3.3.2 Worked Example. Assume that 10 evaluators $\{e_1,e_2,...,e_9,e_{10}\}$ publish resolve values $\{1,2,3,...,9,10\}$. The client publishes details of two goods G1 and G2 with the initial graph as per Section 24.3.1 and the constant value $c = 100$. The threshold is set as 1 for simplicity of examples, but note that this compromises security by removing threshold properties. The initial graph with corresponding valuations is shown in Figure 24.7.

Complete valuations and bid weights for two bidders ($B1$ and $B2$) are given in Table 24.2. Bidder $B1$ generates a set of polynomials with a fixed coefficient of one corresponding to the weights: $x^6 + x^5 + x^4 + x^3 + x^2 + x$, $x^2 + x$, and $x^2 + x$ for edges (n_2,n_0), (n_2,n_1), and (n_1,n_0), respectively. The resolved polynomials sent to evaluators for both bidders are shown in Table 24.3. The weakness of using a fixed coefficient of 1 is apparent, as bids for the same value are identical. With random coefficients, interpolation is still possible and bids for the same value will differ.

The evaluators compute f values for each node using their bid shares and publish $f(0)$. Evaluator e_0 finds $f(1) = 3 + 5 = 5$ and $f(0) = (2 + 2)\,5 + (4 + 6) = 30$. The shares for all evaluators are provided in Table 24.4.

The minimum optimal value is set to zero, the maximum to nine and so initially $d = 4$. Resolved random polynomials of degree 4 and constant of 100 are sent to the evaluators from the mask publishers. Because random coefficients are not used in this example, both mask publishes generate the same masking polynomial $x^4 + x^3 + x^2 + x$. The total masks received by each evaluator added to evaluator

TABLE 24.2 Bidder Valuations and Weights for Each Combination of Goods

Edge	Goods	$B1$ Valuation	$B1$ W	$B2$ Valuation	$B2$ W
(n_2, n_0)	{G1, G2}	4	6	2	4
(n_2, n_1)	{G2}	2	3	1	2
(n_1, n_0)	{G1}	1	2	1	2

TABLE 24.3 Bids for Bidders 1 and 2

	*B*1			*B*2		
Evaluator	(n_2,n_1)	(n_1,n_0)	(n_2,n_0)	(n_2,n_1)	(n_1,n_0)	(n_2,n_0)
e_1	$1^3+1^2+1=3$	2	6	2	2	4
e_2	$2^3+2^2+2=14$	6	126	6	6	30
e_3	$3^3+3^2+3=39$	12	1092	12	12	118
...	...	...	...	...	...	...
e_9	$9^3+9^2+9=819$	90	597,870	90	90	7,380
e_{10}	$10^3+10^2+10=1110$	110	1,111,110	110	110	11,110

shares for $f(0)$ are

e_1	$208+30=238$
e_2	$260+396=656$
e_3	$440+2436=2876$
...	...
e_9	$14,960+768,870=783,830$
e_{10}	$22,420+222,420=1,413,040$

The Lagrange polynomial of these five points is $1988x^4 - 15{,}211x^3 + 46{,}185x^2 - 60{,}334x + 28{,}480$. The polynomial's constant is not equal to 200 $o > 4$. Table 24.5 shows a complete binary search for the optimal value, determined to be six, using evaluator shares.

Once the complete optimal path has been traced to n_{N-1}, the highest bid valuations can be computed by subtracting the threshold modifier from each respective edge cost. The edges from n_0 are checked, and all except (n_2,n_0) are less than or equal to $f(0) - 1$. Once this edge is found, the search ends as the destination is n_2. The actual cost is $6 - 1{\cdot}(2 - 0) = 4$ and the optimal allocation is published as B_0 wins {G1, G2} for $4.

TABLE 24.4 Evaluator Shares of the *f* Values

Evaluator	$f(2)$	$f(1)$	$f(0)$
e_1	0	5	30
e_2	0	20	396
e_3	0	51	2436
...	...	...	...
e_9	0	909	768,870
e_{10}	0	1220	1,390,620

TABLE 24.5 Evaluator Shares of the f Values

d	Polynomial	Constant	
4	$195x^4 - 1293x^3 + 3784x^2 - 4808x + 2360$	2360	$o > 4$
7	$2x^7 + 3x^6 + 5x^5 + 10x^4 + 12x^3 + 8x^2 + 4x + 200$	200	$o \leq 7$
5	$26x^5 - 165x^4 + 747x^3 - 1616x^2 + 1768x - 520$	-520	$o > 5$
6	$3x^6 + 5x^5 + 10x^4 + 12x^3 + 8x^2 + 4x + 200$	200	$o \leq 6$

24.3.4 The Homomorphic Scheme

There is much in common between this protocol and the previous polynomial example; both are threshold trust schemes and encode the auction in a graph. However, they use different cryptographic techniques: polynomial encryption and homomorphic encryption, respectively. Homomorphic cryptosystems maintain an algebraic operation between cipher text and plaintext, where the operation on the cipher text applies to the plaintext accordingly. Current cryptosystems provide only one operation, usually addition or multiplication, and this chapter uses a system with multiplication such as El-Gamal.

In more recent years electronic elections have received much focus from cryptographers. The problem of computing an election outcome while maintaining voter anonymity is well known. The following version of the popular *Mafia* party game captures the essence of the problem:

> The population is divided into the Mafia and the townspeople. The Mafia's goal is to rob the townspeople, while the town's goal is to imprison the Mafia. The members of the Mafia are aware of each other's identities; however, the townspeople are not aware of anything other than their own role. The game is played in two phases. In the first phase the Mafia discusses and then votes by secret ballot to choose the townsperson to rob. The victim is then eliminated from the game. In the second phase the entire town (including the Mafia) discuss who to imprison and then vote by secret ballot. The prisoner is eliminated from the game. The secret ballot allows the Mafia to misdirect the townspeople, and indeed the Mafia can likewise become involved in their own subgame.

We can build a simple voting protocol to preserve anonymity using homomorphic encryption for small-scale voting. A vector of homomorphic cipher text is offered to voters for each option to be voted on, and the maximum length of each vector is the maximum number of voters. Each element in a vector corresponds to a potential voter and starts as an encrypted zero. One at a time each voter retrieves the current vectors and removes an encrypted one from the right side of the vector that they wish to vote for, adding an encrypted value not equal to zero to the left side (called *left-shifting*). A required property of the cryptosystem is randomizability, where two encryptions of the same plaintext should not produce the same cipher text. Voters can therefore multiply each element in the vectors by a cipher text of 1, to hide the modifications. Once voting has closed, vectors can be decrypted and the outcome determined by counting the number of elements not equal to 0. This provides a solution that computes the outcome without revealing individual votes.

Of course, a corrupt official with the decryption key could decrypt two consecutive sets of votes and determine the difference. To ensure that vectors are not decrypted prematurely, threshold encryption can be used so votes can only be opened by consensus. One complication that is not dealt with here is techniques to prevent voters from cheating by incrementing multiple vectors or a vector by more than one. Assuming that everyone voted, the votes will not add up to the expected numbers, but it is not possible to determine who rigged the vote.

This homomorphic vector approach can be applied to combinatorial auctions in a similar manner as polynomial encryption was used in polynomial auctions. Bids are represented by threshold homomorphic vectors, where the value of the vector is a series of encrypted common values followed by encrypted ones. Evaluators are divided into groups which each evaluate a node in the auction graph. Secure dynamic programming is performed by recursively evaluating nodes; each group left-shifts outgoing edges by the highest incoming path cost, which is found by multiplying alternative incoming edges together. Bid vector preliminaries are provided before the protocol is described.

24.3.4.1 Bid Vector Representation. As already stated, homomorphic bid vectors are made from a series of encrypted constants followed by a series of encrypted ones. Each element in the vector is encrypted with the public key PK^+ of the relevant evaluator group. The value of the vector is equal to the number of elements not equal to 1. For example, a bid of 3 in a vector with a maximum bid of 5 and constant Z encrypted with the key for an evaluator group 0, is represented by $PK_0^+(Z), PK_0^+(Z), PK_0^+(Z), PK_0^+(1), PK_0^+(1)$.

24.3.4.2 Bid Vector Comparison. Vectors need to be compared for alternate bidders on edges and alternate paths to nodes. Two vectors cannot be directly compared without decrypting; however, the highest of the two can be found using multiplication if they have been encrypted with the same key. For instance, if two bidders bid 4 and 2 for the same edge, then they would be multiplied as follows:

$$\begin{array}{rl} & PK_0^+(Z),\ PK_0^+(Z),\ PK_0^+(Z),\ PK_0^+(Z),\ PK_0^+(1) \\ \times & PK_0^+(Z),\ PK_0^+(Z),\ PK_0^+(1),\ PK_0^+(1),\ PK_0^+(1) \\ \hline & \boldsymbol{PK_0^+(Z^2),\ PK_0^+(Z^2),\ PK_0^+(Z),\ PK_0^+(Z),\ PK_0^+(1)} \end{array}$$

The result shows that the higher of the two vectors is 4.

It is also possible to check whether a vector represents a number greater than or equal to a given value without decrypting the entire vector. This is performed by decrypting only the element located at the given value and checking for plaintext not equal to 1.

24.3.4.3 Bid Vector Addition. A constant value v can be added to an encrypted vector by left-shifting the vector by the value required. v elements are removed from the right side, and v common values encrypted with the same key as the vector are added to the left side. The vector is randomized by multiplying the unchanged elements by an encrypted one. When a modified vector is added to the public bulletin board, randomization prevents participants from counting the number of changed elements.

24.3.4.4 The Homomorphic Auction Protocol. This auction protocol is another scheme designed by Suzuki and Yokoo [4]. The protocol is further described in Reference 25 and includes measured performance results. It is described here in the following four steps:

1. An auction graph is generated and published in the same manner as for polynomial auctions. Evaluators are divided into groups of E evaluators, and each group is assigned one of N nodes from the graph. Depending on security requirements, a threshold t, evaluators are required to decrypt bid vectors. For each node v, a shared public key PK_v^+ is generated along with E private keys $PK_v^{-1}, PK_v^{-2}, PK_v^{-3} \ldots PK_v^{-E}$ for each evaluator. Information published for bidders is as follows: the graph with public keys mapped to edges, maximum bid vector length B, and common value Z.
2. Bidders value each combination of goods, generating bids for each edge in which they are interested, submitting them to a public bulletin board. Each bid contains a homomorphic bid vector encrypted with public key PK_v^+ of the edge (the shared public key of the destination node) with a reference to the edge. Once bidding has closed, evaluation using dynamic programming begins by recursively discovering the optimal values of each node. The optimal value of a node $i, f(i)$, is the sum of the edges on the highest-cost path from the end node n_{N-1} to n_i. The optimal value of the graph is the optimal value of the root node n_0, which provides the total of the highest-cost path in the graph. An optimal edge value is the optimal value of its source node added to the highest bid vector for that edge. Although individual edge values are not discovered at this point, the highest incoming optimal edge value needs to be, and it is the decryption of the multiplicative sum of all incoming bid vectors left-shifted by the optimal value of their source nodes. Node evaluators decrypt the highest incoming optimal edge value (the multiplicative sum of incoming edges) using their private keys, and publish their shares. Once t shares have been published, the optimal value of the node can be decrypted and is added to all outgoing edges by left-shifting and randomizing.
3. The total optimal value is used to trace back the optimal path through the optimal bid vectors. An edge is on the optimal path, if its optimal bid vector is equal to $d = f(v)$, where v is the edge's destination node. It is possible to discover this without releasing bid values of edges not on the winning path by checking position d only for a value not equal to 1. The process starts from the root node n_0 and works backward towards n_{N-1}. When an optimal edge is found, its source node is published and the incoming edges of that node are checked. When n_{N-1} is reached, and the optimal path is found. The decryption is performed in the same manner as in step 3, with evaluators publishing shares of the bid vector position.

TABLE 24.6 Bids for Bidders 1 and 2

	Edge	Goods	Valuation	Bid Vector
$B1$	(n_2,n_0)	{G1,G2}	4	$PK_0^+(3), PK_0^+(3), PK_0^+(3), PK_0^+(3), PK_0^+(1)$
	(n_2,n_1)	{G2}	2	$PK_0^+(3), PK_0^+(3), PK_0^+(1), PK_0^+(1), PK_0^+(1)$
	(n_1,n_0)	{G1}	1	$PK_0^+(3), PK_0^+(1), PK_0^+(1), PK_0^+(1), PK_0^+(1)$
$B2$	(n_2,n_0)	{G1,G2}	2	$PK_0^+(3), PK_0^+(3), PK_0^+(1), PK_0^+(1), PK_0^+(1)$
	(n_2,n_1)	{G2}	1	$PK_0^+(3), PK_0^+(1), PK_0^+(1), PK_0^+(1), PK_0^+(1)$
	(n_1,n_0)	{G1}	1	$PK_0^+(3), PK_0^+(1), PK_0^+(1), PK_0^+(1), PK_0^+(1)$

4. Once the optimal path has been traced back bidders for each optimal edge can be found. Using the original bid vectors for each optimal edge, the same technique used in step 4 to identify optimal edges is used to identify optimal bid vectors and hence the winning bidders. The position to check is the value that the edge provides, specifically, f (destination) – f (source).

24.3.4.5 Worked Example. An auction graph is created for two goods {G1,G2} and is published with $B = 5$ and $Z = 3$. Bidders $B1$ and $B2$ generate and post valuations and bid vectors for each of the edges, given in Table 24.6. The graph with corresponding valuations is shown in Figure 24.8.

As there are no incoming edges for n_2, $f(2) = 0$, and so the bid vectors on the outgoing edges from n_2 do not need to be left-shifted by anything. The corresponding bid vectors are multiplied together:

$$\begin{array}{rl} & PK_0^+(3),\ PK_0^+(3),\ PK_0^+(3),\ PK_0^+(3),\ PK_0^+(1) \\ * & PK_0^+(3),\ PK_0^+(3),\ PK_0^+(1),\ PK_0^+(1),\ PK_0^+(1) \\ \hline & PK_0^+(9),\ PK_0^+(9),\ P\bar{K}_0^+(3),\ PK_0^+(3),\ PK_0^+(1) \end{array}$$

$$\begin{array}{rl} & PK_1^+(3),\ PK_1^+(3),\ PK_1^+(1),\ PK_1^+(1),\ PK_1^+(1) \\ * & PK_1^+(3),\ PK_1^+(1),\ PK_1^+(1),\ PK_1^+(1),\ PK_1^+(1) \\ \hline & PK_1^+(9),\ PK_1^+(3),\ P\bar{K}_1^+(1),\ PK_1^+(1),\ PK_1^+(1) \end{array}$$

These resulting vectors are published as the highest bid vectors from n_2 to n_0 and n_1, respectively. The evaluators for n_1 can now find the optimal value as the only incoming

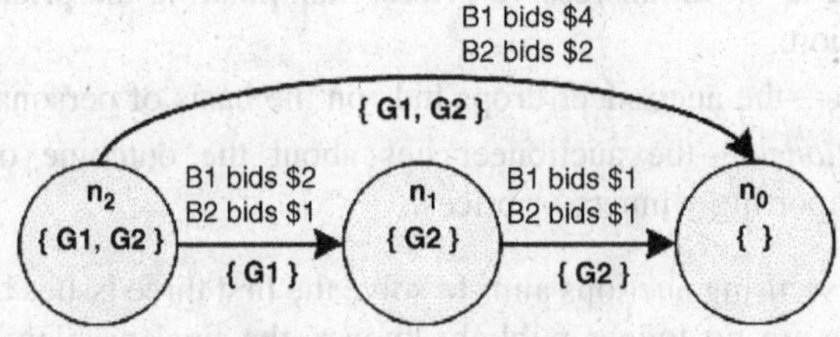

Figure 24.8 The initial auction graph with matching valuations.

optimal bid vector has been published. The evaluators each use their private key to decrypt a share of the bid vector. Once t shares have been published, the optimal value is decrypted from the shares to find that $f(1) = 2$. The outgoing edge to n_0 is left-shifted by 2, randomized, and then published. The evaluators of n_0 multiply the two incoming edges together:

$$\begin{array}{rl} & PK_0^+(3), PK_0^+(3), PK_0^+(3), PK_0^+(3), PK_0^+(1) \\ * & PK_0^+(3), PK_0^+(3), PK_0^+(3), PK_0^+(1), PK_0^+(1) \\ \hline & PK_0^+(9), PK_0^+(9), PK_0^+(9), PK_0^+(3), PK_0^+(1) \end{array}$$

They then perform shared decryption, finding that $f(0) = 4$. This value is published as the optimal value of the graph.

Position 4 of n_0's incoming optimal bid vectors are checked for a value not equal to 1. The evaluators each publish their shares, and the decrypted values are found as 3 and 1 for edges (n_2,n_0) and (n_2,n_1) respectively. n_1 is published as not optimal, n_2 is published as optimal, and because $n_2 = n_{N-1}$, the optimal path has been found and it is also published as the single edge (n_2,n_0).

Position 4 (4 – 0) in edges (n_2,n_0) and (n_1,n_0) are checked for a value not equal to one. The value from $B1$'s vector is 3, and the value from $B2$'s vector is 1, so the result is published; $B1$ has won both goods {G1,G2} for $4.

24.4 COMPARISON OF PRIVACY-PRESERVING PROPERTIES

Each of the three protocols introduced in this chapter differs in what privacy-preserving properties are offered. For example, privacy in garbled circuits relies on only two parties (the auctioneer and the issuer) not collaborating, while the other two schemes can require a variable number of parties to not collaborate. This section compares the properties that the schemes offer against Bob and Jane's problems outlined in step 1 of section 24.1.1. These problems are as follows:

- *Insider trading*—the auctioneer misuses information about current auction state (i.e., current valuations) for competitive advantage. This information could be provided (possibly sold) to a bidder in a sealed bid auction to enable the bidder to bid the minimum valuation possible to win.
- *Private information revelation*—the auctioneer gathers a history of information such as minimum bids for use in future auctions. This information may be used for example to set unfair reserve prices, manipulating the pricing in a second priced auction.
- *Bid filtering*—the auctioneer drops bids on the basis of personal interests.
- *Lying auctioneer*—the auctioneer lies about the outcome of the auction, either misreporting winners or prices.

This first step to securing auctions aims to solve the first three issues by sealing bids; however, as bids are no longer publicly known, the final problem is introduced.

All three protocols solve the insider trading problem as no bids are decrypted until the auction is over. Garbled circuits prevents information leakage provided the two participants do not collude. This is effectively equivalent to a (2,2) threshold scheme. The polynomial and homomorphic schemes both provide a variable (t,n) threshold scheme, but differ in what can be released. In polynomial, the cost of each node can be determined without any decryption of edges, and so the longest path is found without leakage. However, in the homomorphic protocol, because addition is not offered by the cryptosystem, evaluator groups must decrypt the multiplicative sum of incoming edges. It requires only one evaluator in each group to publish the maximum cost for that node. If two connected nodes have their maximum cost released then the maximum edge cost between them can be calculated. For an edge not on the optimal path, this is private information that should not be revealed.

There are two classifications of bid filtering: bids may be dropped according to (1) their values or (2) who made them. Auctioneers in each of the three protocols obviously cannot drop bids according to the value before evaluation, and once evaluation starts, evaluators cannot drop bids without other evaluators noticing. In the garbled circuits protocol, the auction issuer can publish hash values of the data it receives from bidders that bidders can use to ensure that their bid was included. The polynomial and homomorphic protocols do nothing to stop bids from being dropped according to who placed them, but they could be used with an anonymity service.

In the garbled circuit auction protocol, a corrupt auction issuer could create an invalid circuit that does not correctly compute the result of the auction. A corrupt auctioneer could also not even execute the circuit given to it by the auction issuer. Several methods have been suggested to verify these steps of the garbled circuit auction protocol.

It is not possible for an auctioneer to lie about the outcome at any of the decryption steps in the polynomial and homomorphic protocols, because evaluators can rerun their final decryption steps. They can, however, publish fake shares that may affect the outcome if used. These may be able to be detected if enough combinations of different shares are used to check the outcome at each decryption. However, a better protocol would offer verification to ensure that active interference is discouraged and detected.

24.5 PERFORMANCE COMPARISON

Figure 24.9 shows the timeline for conducting an auction. The auction starts when the client requests the auctioneer to perform the auction, and ends when the winner of the auction has been determined. There are four phases: auction creation, bidder registration, bid submission, and winner determination.

Each auction protocol uses different cryptographic techniques that exhibit different performance characteristics. In the garbled circuit protocol there is potential for considerable communication overhead in transmitting the garbled circuit. In the polynomial protocol there is potential for a high overhead when increasing the

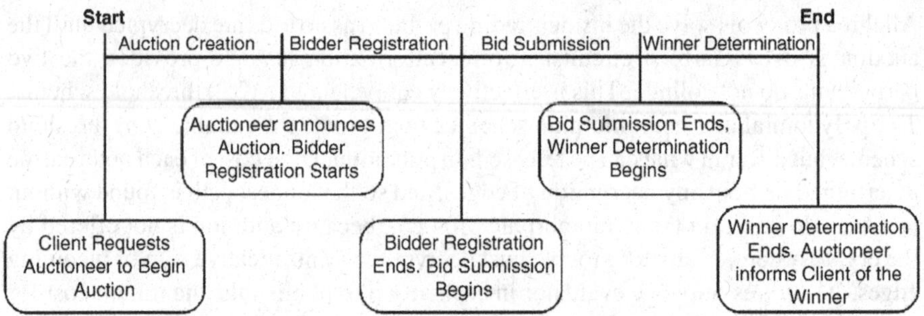

Figure 24.9 Auction timeline.

threshold of auctioneers needed to decrypt a value. In the homomorphic protocol overhead will increase with the key size.

As the number of goods in an auction increases, so must the complexity of the garbled circuit. Figure 24.10 quantifies the relationship between the number of goods in the auction and the size of the garbled circuit. The size of the circuit increases exponentially with the number of goods. For an example auction with three goods, a maximum bid of 16, and 10 bidders the size of the circuit is about 600 kB.

In order for the polynomial auction to tolerate more corrupt auctioneers, the threshold must be increased ($t = 2$, meaning that we can tolerate one corrupt auctioneer). Figure 24.11 shows the exponential effect of increasing this threshold. This exponential increase is due to the time required to do the Lagrange interpolation as the degree of the polynomial storing the secret increases.

To improve the security of the homomorphic scheme, the size of the encryption keys must increase. Figure 24.12 shows the implication of increasing the key size on the winner determination time. This exponential increase is due to the additional overhead of performing modulo operations in a larger group (Z_p).

Figure 24.13 illustrates the overall performance of each protocol with respect to the number of goods. As the combinatorial allocation problem (CAP) is NP-complete, such exponential growth will come as no surprise. However, in general,

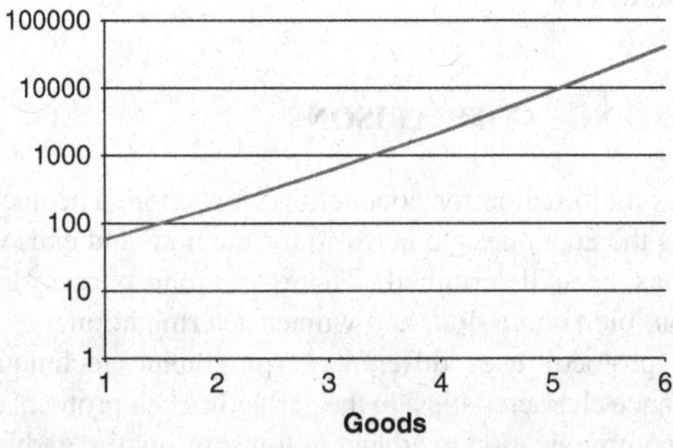

Figure 24.10 Size of circuit versus number of goods.

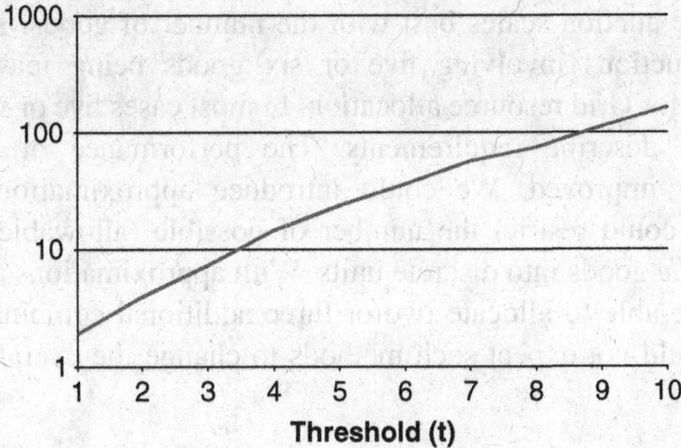

Figure 24.11 Polynomial threshold value versus time.

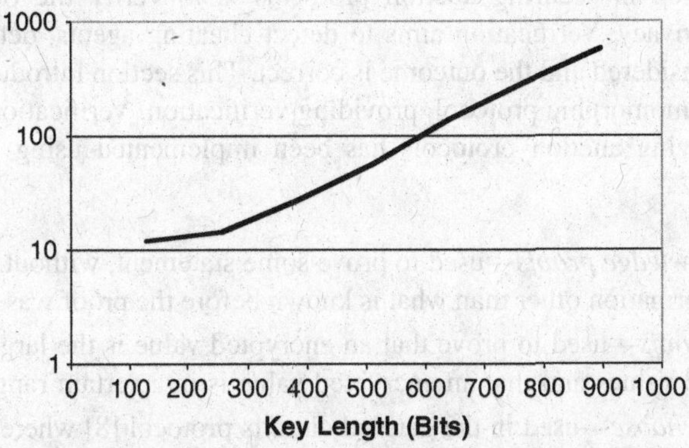

Figure 24.12 Homomorphic key size versus time.

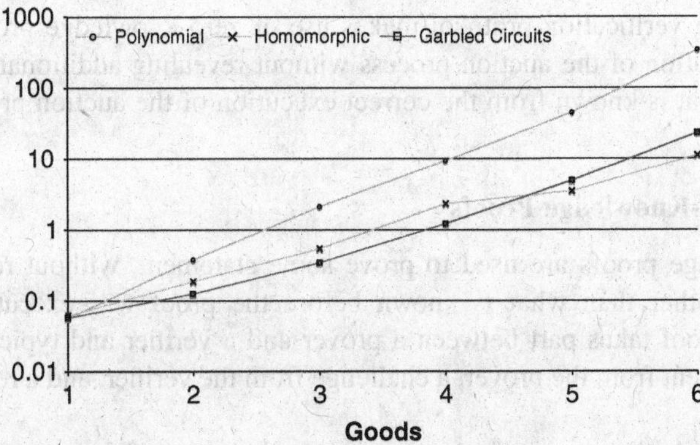

Figure 24.13 A performance comparison of the three auction protocols.

the homomorphic auction scales best with the number of goods. As the protocols stand, we see auctions involving five or six goods being feasible within the typical timescale for Grid resource allocation. In most cases five or six combinations are sufficient to describe requirements. The performance of these protocols could be further improved. We could introduce approximations to the CAP; for instance, we could restrict the number of possible (allowable) combinations, or we could *bundle* goods into discrete units. With approximations and bundling we would perhaps be able to allocate two or three additional combinations of goods. However, we would not expect such methods to change the overall ranking of the protocols.

24.6 VERIFIABLE AUCTION PROTOCOLS

The second step in securing auction protocols is to verify the outcome while maintaining privacy. Verification aims to detect cheating agents, determining that all bids are considered and the outcome is correct. This section introduces modifications to the homomorphic protocol, providing verification. Verification for use with privacy-preserving auction protocols has been implemented using the following techniques:

- *Zero-knowledge proofs*—used to prove some statement, without revealing any other information other than what is known before the proof was executed [26]
- *Range proofs*—used to prove that an encrypted value is the largest in a set of encrypted values and that an encrypted value is in a certain range [5]
- *Cut and choose*—used in the garbled circuits protocol [8] where x copies of a garbled circuit are constructed for the auction and x-1 randomly chosen copies are opened before the auction to check they have been correctly constructed
- *Verifiable secret sharing*—used to verify shares of a secret have been correctly calculated [10]

The following verification protocol makes use of zero-knowledge proofs to allow public verification of the auction process without revealing additional information other than what is known from the correct execution of the auction protocol.

24.6.1 Zero-Knowledge Proofs

Zero-knowledge proofs are used to prove some statement, without revealing any information other than what is known before the proof was executed. A zero-knowledge proof takes part between a prover and a verifier and typically consists of a commitment from the prover, a challenge from the verifier, and a response from the prover.

Figure 24.14 illustrates a famous zero knowledge proof known as Ali Baba's cave. Alice wants to convince the verifier Bob that she knows the secret password

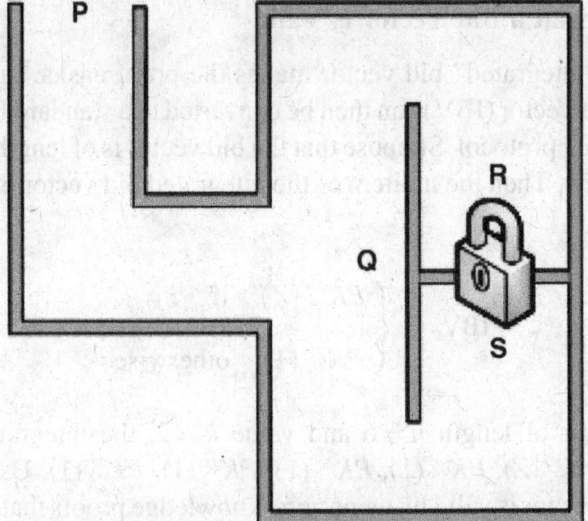

Figure 24.14 Ali Baba's cave.

to open a door between *R* and *S*. To prove this while not revealing the secret password used, Alice and Bob conduct the following steps:

- Bob waits at *P* while Alice goes to either *R* or *S* (commitment).
- Bob goes to *Q* so that Alice may not move from *R* to *S* other than by the locked door (which she needs to know the secret to pass through).
- Bob chooses either the top (*R*) or bottom (*S*) tunnel.
- Bob challenges Alice to come out of the tunnel of his choice. Alice can exit the correct tunnel 100% of the time only if she knows the password.
- If Alice does not know the secret words, there is a 50% chance she will exit from the wrong tunnel.
- Bob can then repeat this process as many times as he wants to convince himself that Alice knows the secret word, but Bob will never learn the secret word himself.

This verification process is divided into several operations:

1. Prove that a bid vector is valid. When a bidder submits a bid vector, the auctioneers and bidder prove that the bid vector is a valid bid vector.
2. Prove a maximum bid from a set of bids. While calculating the result of the auction, auctioneers can prove that a bid is the maximum bid in a set of bids without revealing the value of any of the encrypted bids.
3. Prove that shift and randomization have been done correctly. The homomorphic protocol uses a technique called *shift and randomize* to add a constant to a bid vector; a proof can be published showing that this operation has been done correctly.

24.6.2 Proving that a Bid Vector is Valid

Constructing an "integrated" bid vector makes the proof easier and more efficient. This integrated bid vector (IBV) can then be converted to a standard bid vector as used in the homomorphic protocol. Suppose that the bid vector is of length n and the bidder wants to bid value k. Then the ith item of the integrated bid vector is of the following form:

$$\mathrm{IBV}_i = \begin{cases} PK^+(Z) & \text{if} \quad i = k \\ PK^+(1) & \text{otherwise} \end{cases}$$

So for a bid vector of length $n = 6$ and value $k = 2$, the integrated bid vector is IBV $= PK^+(1)$, $PK^+(Z)$, $PK^+(1)$, $PK^+(1)$, $PK^+(1)$, $PK^+(1)$. Using this IBV, we can prove the bid vector is valid by using zero-knowledge proofs that every item in the bid vector is an encryption of 1 or a Z [27] and that the product of every item in the bid vector decrypts to Z [28].

The encrypted IBV is then converted to a standard bid vector by performing the following operations on the items in the bid vector:

$$\mathrm{BV}_i = \begin{cases} \mathrm{IBV}_i & \text{if} \quad i = n \\ \mathrm{BV}_{i+1} \times \mathrm{IBV}_i & \text{otherwise} \end{cases}$$

So IBV $= PK^+(1)$, $PK^+(Z)$, $PK^+(1)$, $PK^+(1)$, $PK^+(1)$, $PK^+(1)$ becomes $BV = PK^+(Z)$, $PK^+(Z)$, $PK^+(1)$, $PK^+(1)$, $PK^+(1)$, $PK^+(1)$.

To verify that the bid vector is valid, a verifier will check the proofs to determine whether every item in the "integrated" bid vector is 1 or Z, as well as the proof that the decryption of the product of all the items is Z. The verifier can then check that the standard bid vector was constructed correctly, due to the homomorphic nature of the encryption used.

24.6.3 Proving a Maximum Bid from a Set of Bids

To prove that one encrypted bid vector is the maximum from a set of encrypted bid vectors, an auctioneer publishes a verifiable shuffle of the set of encrypted bid vectors using techniques from the paper by Furukawa and Sako [29]. Bid vectors should all be shuffled using the same permutation that is known only to the auctioneer. The auctioneer then proves that one of the entries in the maximum bid vector decrypts to Z while all other bids decrypt to 1 at the same index in the shuffled bid vectors. The bid vectors can be shuffled in such a way that the first item in the shuffled bids decrypts to Z for only one of the bids. The auctioneer can arrange the shuffling this way, knowing the maximum bid value before shuffling.

As all the other bids are shown to decrypt to 1 and we can verify the shuffle of the encrypted values, this proves the maximum bid from the set of encrypted bid vectors without revealing the value of the maximum bid.

For example, suppose that we have three bids:

Bid 1: $PK^+(Z)$, $PK^+(Z)$, $PK^+(Z)$, $PK^+(1)$.

Bid 2: $PK^+(Z)$, $PK^+(Z)$, $PK^+(1)$, $PK^+(1)$.

Bid 3: $PK^+(1)$, $PK^+(1)$, $PK^+(1)$, $PK^+(1)$.

Bid 1 is the maximum bid. To prove this, an auctioneer applies a permutation π to the bids, say, $\pi = \{3,4,1,2\}$. The modified vectors are

Shuffled bid 1: $PK^+(Z)$, $PK^+(1)$, $PK^+(Z)$, $PK^+(Z)$.
Shuffled bid 2: $PK^+(1)$, $PK^+(1)$, $PK^+(Z)$, $PK^+(Z)$.
Shuffled bid 3: $PK^+(1)$, $PK^+(1)$, $PK^+(1)$, $PK^+(1)$.

The auctioneer then proves that this shuffle has been done correctly [29] and that the elements at position 0 decrypt to Z, 1, and 1, respectively.

24.6.4 Putting It All Together

This section outlines the process for a verifiable homomorphic combinatorial auction. Figure 24.15 illustrates a simple auction with two bidders bidding for two goods. The winner of the auction should be Bidder 1 who has the maximum bid of $3 for the two items together.

Execution of the protocol involves the following steps:

- Bidders publish their bids for every good. Bidders also publish proof that every item in their bid vector decrypts to a 1 or a Z.
- Auctioneers publish a proof that the product of all the items in the "integrated" bid vector decrypts to Z.
- Auctioneers conduct the auction. If they need to add constants to bid vectors, they publish a proof this is done correctly using the 'shift and randomise' zero knowledge proof [21], from section 6.5.

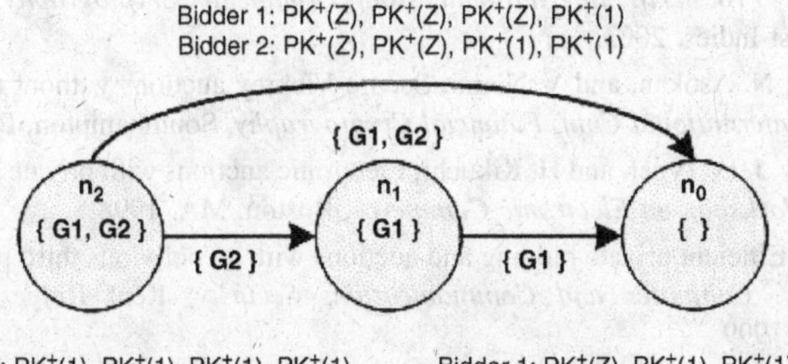

Figure 24.15 Example auction.

- The auctioneers have found and published the optimal path and the winning bids in the optimal path. They now prove that the optimal path is, indeed, optimal and that the winning bids were the maximum using the proof from Section 24.6.3 above.

24.7 SUMMARY

When Grids cross organizational boundaries to become ad hoc collections of resources with multiple owners, we strike the problem of establishing how we can trust other organizations and their software during resource allocation. This is especially true in on-demand Grids and market-oriented Grid or utility computing, where such allocation decisions will have very real financial implications. Privacy-preserving auction protocols prevent an auctioneer from identifying bidders and acting to advantage, or to disadvantage certain bidders. These auctions also prevent the auctioneer from stealing and distributing commercially sensitive bid information. Verifiable auction protocols allow independent verification of an auctioneer's actions and therefore provide cryptographic guarantees that the outcome of the auction includes all bids and that the outcome of the auction was computed correctly. In effect, the auctions become on-demand auditable by any participant rather than operating as black boxes. Combining both privacy-preserving and verifiable auction protocols removes the need to place trust in any auctioneer—whether they are actually trustworthy or not.

REFERENCES

1. S. Fay, The Collapse of Barings, Richard Cohen Books, London, 1996.
2. H. R. Varian, Economic mechanism design for computerized agents, *Proc. Usenix Workshop on Electronic Commerce*, New York, 1995.
3. W. Vickrey, Counterspeculation, auctions, and competitive sealed tenders, *The Journal of Finance* **16**(1):8–37 (1961).
4. K. Suzuki and M. Yokoo, Secure generalized Vickery auction using homomorphic encryption, *Proc. 7th International Conf. Financial Cryptography*, Guadeloupe, French West Indies, 2003.
5. H. Lipmaa, N. Asokan, and V. Niemi, Secure Vickrey auctions without threshold trust, *Proc. 6th International Conf. Financial Cryptography*, Southhampton, Bermuda, 2002.
6. M. Harkavy, J. D. Tygar, and H. Kikuchi, Electronic auctions with private bids, *Proc. 3rd USENIX Workshop on Electronic Commerce*, Boston, MA, 1998.
7. C. Cachin, Efficient private bidding and auctions with an oblivious third party, *Proc. 6th ACM Conf. Computer and Communications Security*, Kent Ridge Digital Labs, Singapore, 1999.
8. M. Naor, B. Pinkas, and R. Sumner, Privacy preserving auctions and mechanism design, *Proc. 1st ACM Conf. Electronic Commerce*, Denver, CO, 1999.

9. O. Baudro and J. Stern, Non-interactive private auctions, *Proc. 5th International Financial Cryptography Conf.*, Grand Cayman, British West Indies, 2001.
10. H. Kikuchi, (M + 1)St-price auction protocol, *Proc. 5th International Conf. Financial Cryptography*, Grand Cayman, British West Indies, 2001.
11. K. Suzuki and M. Yokoo, Secure combinatorial auctions by dynamic programming with polynomial secret sharing, *Proc. 6th International Conf. Financial Cryptography*, Southampton, Bermuda, 2002.
12. M. Yokoo and K. Suzuki, Secure multi-agent dynamic programming based on homomorphic encryption and its application to combinatorial auctions, *Proc. 1st Joint International Conf. Autonomous Agents and Multiagent Systems*, Bologna, Italy, 2002.
13. K. Peng, C. Boyd, E. Dawson, and K. Viswanathan, Robust, privacy protecting and publicly verifiable sealed-bid auction, *Proc. 4th International Conf. Information and Communications Security (ICICS '02)*, Singapore, 2002.
14. K. Peng, C. Boyd, E. Dawson, and K. Viswanathan, Five sealed-bid auction models, *Proc. Australasian Information Security Workshop Conf. ACSW Frontiers*, Adelaide, Australia, 2003.
15. W. Ham, K. Kim, and H. Imai, Yet another strong sealed-bid auction, *Proc. Symp. Cryptography and Information Security*, Japan, 2003.
16. X. Chen, B.-Y. Lee, and K. Kim, Receipt-free electronic auction schemes using homomorphic encryption, *Proc. 6th International Conf. Information Security and Cryptology, Bristol, UK*, 2003.
17. J. Nzouonta, *An Algorithm for Clearing Combinatorial Markets*, Technical Report. CS-2003-23, Florida Institute of Technology, 2003.
18. K. Peng, C. Boyd, and E. Dawson, A multiplicative homomorphic sealed-bid auction based on Goldwasser-Micali encryption, *Proc. 8th International Conf. Information Security, Singapore*, 2005.
19. D. C. Parkes, M. O. Rabin, S. M. Shieber, and C. A. Thorpe, Practical secrecy-preserving, verifiably correct and trustworthy auctions, *Proc. 8th International Conf. Electronic Commerce*, Fredericton, New Brunswick, Canada, 2006.
20. F. Brandt, How to obtain full privacy in auctions, *International Journal of Information Security* **5**(4): 201–261 (2006).
21. B. Palmer, Verifiying privacy preserving combinatorial auction, Msc Thesis, Victoria University of Wellington, New Zealand, 2008.
22. A. C. Yao, How to generate and exchange secrets, *Proc. 27th IEEE Symp. Foundations of Computer Science*, 1986.
23. A. Juels and M. Szydlo, A two-server, sealed-bid auction protocol, *Proc. 6th International Conf. Financial Cryptography*, Southampton, Bermuda, 2002.
24. K. Bubendorfer and W. Thomson, Resource managment using untrusted auctioneers in a Grid econonmy, *Proc. 2nd IEEE International Conf. e-Science and Grid Computing*, Amsterdam, The Netherlands, 2006.
25. K. Bubendorfer, I. Welch, and B. Chard, Trustworthy auctions for Grid-style economies, *Proc. 6th IEEE International Symp. Cluster Computing and the Grid (CCGrid06)*, Singapore, 2006.
26. S. Goldwasser, S. Micali, and C. Rackoff, The knowledge complexity of interactive proof systems, *SIAM Journal of Computing* **18**(1): 186–208 (1989).

27. R. Cramer, R. Gennaro, and B. Schoenmakers, A secure and optimally efficient multi-authority election scheme, *Proc. Workshop on the Theory and Application of Cryptographic Techniques on Advances in Cryptology (EUROCRYPT)*, Konstanz, Germany, 1997.
28. D. Chaum and T. P. Pedersen, Wallet databases with observers, *Proc. 12th Annual International Cryptology Conf. Advances in Cryptology*, Santa Barbara, CA, 1993.
29. J. Furukawa and K. Sako, An efficient scheme for proving a shuffle, *Proc. 21st Annual International Cryptology Conf. Advances in Cryptology*, Santa Barbara, CA, 2001.
30. M. Franklin and M. Reiter, The design and implementation of a secure auction service, *IEEE Transactions on Software Engineering* **22**(5): 302–312 (1996).
31. A. Shamir, How to share a secret, *Communications of the AEM* **22**(11): 612–613 (1979).
32. C. Liu, Introduction to combinatorial mathematics, McGraw-Hill, 1968.

25

USING SECURE AUCTIONS TO BUILD A DISTRIBUTED METASCHEDULER FOR THE GRID

KYLE CHARD AND KRIS BUBENDORFER

25.1 INTRODUCTION

The previous chapter introduced a number of different techniques for establishing trustworthy Grid resource or service auctions. These protocols permit new architectures that are community- or peer-oriented to be developed without compromising the integrity of the resource or service allocations. In this chapter we will look at an architecture that is designed to take advantage of trustworthy protocols in a Grid context. Distributed Resource Infrastructure for a Virtual Economy (DRIVE) [1] is a community metascheduler implemented within a virtual organization (VO) [2], using resources contributed by the members of the VO to conduct the auction. This distribution of effort decentralizes and shares the computational burden of allocation over all participating resource providers.

DRIVE uses auction protocols to quickly and efficiently establish the market price for a resource or service. DRIVE is designed to allocate jobs to multiple local resource managers (LRMs) in both small- and large-scale Grids. This flexibility is achieved in part through a modular auction protocol plug-in architecture, allowing users to define and select protocols on the basis of context specific requirements.

The allocation mechanism is dynamically composed from a set of *obligation* Grid services individually contributed by resource providers. As these services are hosted by potentially untrusted members of dynamic VOs, there are obvious risks in terms of trust and security. These risks can be mitigated by choosing an appropriate protocol

Market-Oriented Grid and Utility Computing Edited by Rajkumar Buyya and Kris Bubendorfer

while also considering the tradeoff between security and cost. For example, within a single organization there is an inherent level of trust in the members of the VO; thus a simple open-auction protocol could be used to quickly allocate resources, whereas in a global Grid this trust does not exist and users may wish to use secure and trustworthy auction protocols, such as those presented in Chapter 24, to ensure that the allocation is done fairly and sensitive information is not disclosed.

DRIVE is built from a collection of Globus Toolkit version 4 (GT4) [3]-WSRF (Web Services Resource Framework) compliant Web services with a Java-based client-side broker. Importantly, the broker has no requirement for GT4 or any form of Web service container.

25.2 BACKGROUND

Economic allocation mechanisms commonly use some form of market abstraction to efficiently determine the price for a good (or service). There are various types of appropriate market abstractions, including commodity markets, posted price, and auctions. Single-bid auctions are most often preferred in distributed system resource allocation auctions as they are an efficient means of producing optimal allocations with minimal communication and usually minimal computation. To meet quality of service (QoS) criteria, an auction for a single *representative* resource (e.g., CPU time is only one of the many resources required for execution) is not normally sufficient. This problem is solved by using combinatorial auctions where bidders bid on collections of goods. Auctions in general have been shown to provide some QoS advantages over other methods [4].

A *virtual organization* (VO) [2] is a dynamic collaboration of administratively and geographically disjoint individuals or institutions who share computing resources to meet a common goal. A Grid can be organized into a number of VOs, each with different policy requirements. As such, the VO provides a way to manage complex Grid systems by establishing and enforcing agreements between resource providers and the VO, and the VO and its members. The virtual organization membership service (VOMS) [5] is used to manage authorization information within multiorganization collaborations (VOs). VOMS defines user groups, roles and capabilities, and includes tools to provide much of the VO management functionality DRIVE requires. Users may be members of any number of VOs, with any number of roles assigned in each VO. The structure of a VO is somewhat representative of the Grid, it can support complex hierarchical structures containing groups and subgroups under separate administration.

Globus Toolkit [3], the predominant Grid toolkit, uses a decentralized scheduling model in which scheduling decisions are made by application-level schedulers and brokers. Resource brokers translate application or user requirements into appropriate Grid-specific resource requirements. Brokers often include schedulers and perform many aspects of metascheduling. Globus brokers are responsible for discovering available resources using the monitoring and discovery system (MDS). Jobs are passed to the appropriate Grid resource allocation and management (GRAM) service, which, in turn, interacts with the LRM to execute the job.

25.3 RELATED WORK

Nimrod/G [6] is a Grid resource broker that uses market-based mechanisms for resource allocation. Distribution is achieved through interaction between hierarchical schedulers. The *Gridbus broker* [7] is a metascheduler that extends Nimrod/G to take a data-centric approach to scheduling; in particular, it is able to access remote data repositories and optimize allocation on the basis of data transfer. Nimrod/G and the Gridbus Broker are discussed in more detail in chapters 17 and 26.

EMPEROR [8] provides a framework for implementing scheduling algorithms focusing on performance criteria. The implementation is based on the open grid services architecture (OGSA) and makes use of common Globus services for tasks such as monitoring, discovery, and job execution. EMPEROR is focused on resource performance prediction and does not use distributed allocation, nor does it support economic allocation mechanisms.

GridWay [9] is a lightweight client-side metascheduler that facilitates large-scale resource sharing across administrative domains. GridWay provides support for simple scheduling mechanisms with the ability for user-defined extensions through its modular architecture. GridWay utilizes common Globus components for data transfer, resource discovery, and job execution. Unlike many metaschedulers, GridWay has a single site-level installation that users can connect to without requiring local GridWay or Globus installations. However, it does not support market-based allocation and uses an organization-level server for each domain.

The *community scheduler framework* (CSF) [10] is an open-source framework for implementing metaschedulers (community schedulers) using a collection of Grid services. CSF provides a queuing service where job submissions are assigned to resources by applying policies, the scheduling mechanisms are user-defined and implemented using a plug-in architecture. This method can support limited economic scheduling via the queuing mechanism. Advanced reservation is supported through a reservation service that interacts directly with reservation-compliant LRMs.

DRIVE is radically different from current metascheduling technology. Existing metaschedulers are typically deployed per client or using an organization-level server implementation. DRIVE is not centered about a single client or client domain, but rather abstracts over collections of resource providers that are members of a VO. DRIVE also provides a rich economic model for allocations, including support for secure combinatorial allocations, privacy, and verifiability.

25.4 USE CASES

In the process of designing DRIVE, a number of use cases have been considered that typify common usage of Grids. A range of situations, infrastructures, and application complexities have been investigated to ensure flexibility in the architecture. A major goal of the DRIVE architecture is to facilitate use in a wide variety of Grid scenarios ranging from single-user single-organization Grids to large-scale collaborations using resources provisioned from a global Grid. The following section outlines three use cases: a small-scale single institution computation of the Tutte polynomial [11], CyberShake [12], a large-scale multiprovider geophysics computation, and a potential utility computing scenario.

25.4.1 Tutte Polynomial

As the first use case we consider the needs of a single scientist (or small group of scientists) operating within their organization. Imagine that our scientist wants to compute Tutte polynomials [11], which are used in a number of different disciplines. For a single researcher it would take weeks to set up and run each of the algorithms against a test suite of graphs. When these experiments are broken into Grid jobs, they can be run on a small single organizational Grid over a weekend.

In graph theory Tutte polynomials can be used to find the number of spanning trees, forests, or connected spanning subgraphs. Tutte polynomials can also be used in areas such as microbiology to classify knots, where a knot is a form somewhat like a tangled cord with its ends joined. An interesting application of knots is in the study of DNA where the double helix can be viewed as two tangled strands forming a knot. The computation of Tutte polynomials is computationally intensive and is well suited to running on a Grid.

The algorithms presented by Haggard et al. [11] provide a way to compute the Tutte polynomial of large graphs. In order to develop the proposed algorithms, a variety of graph sizes and complexities are considered. The Grid used to test the three Tutte algorithms contained approximately 150 desktop machines running the Sun Grid engine [13]. Each experiment tested a single algorithm and was made up of a few hundred jobs (207, 144, and 428, respectively), with each job performing analysis on 100 different-sized graphs. Each graph took between a few seconds and a few hours to compute because of the wide range of size and complexity. The total runtime of the three experiments was less than 60 h, with less than 1 MB of data moved between nodes for each job and a resulting dataset of approximately 50 MB for all three experiments.

In this use case the requirements for security, trust, and privacy are minimal because the jobs are running within the user's organization. There are no hard deadlines or QoS constraints, and the jobs have relatively short runtimes with no dependences between them. For this scenario we can use a simple First-price auction protocol that does not need to support advanced reservation, deadlines, QoS constraints, trust, or privacy.

25.4.2 CyberShake

The second use case considered is the Southern California Earthquake Center (SCEC), a large-scale VO encompassing 50 earth science research institutions across the world. SCEC has a production Grid infrastructure used to share participating institution resources among collaborating parties. This infrastructure provides the ability for researchers to utilize a large pool of resources; however, for many projects the SCEC capabilities are not sufficient. An example is the CyberShake project [12], which involves calculation of probabilistic seismic hazard analysis (PSHA) maps, which can be used when designing buildings. More recent advancements in geophysics models allow calculation of these PSHA maps on the basis of earthquake wave propagation simulations; however, these calculations require a large amount of computation and storage. In order to facilitate such large-scale calculations, large portions of the computation must be outsourced to high-end facilities such as TeraGrid.

The PSHA calculations are conducted for each site of interest in stages, with some stages containing thousands of individual jobs. To produce a hazard map of a region, at least 1000 sites need to be calculated. The first stage of "strain green tensor" (SGT) generation runs over a period of days using 144 or 288 processors and producing up to 10 TB of data. The second stage runs several thousand (average 5000) individual rupture forecasts each on a single processor for intervals ranging from a few minutes to 3 days. The third stage calculates the spectral acceleration and involves the same number of jobs each running for a matter of minutes. Finally the spectral acceleration values are combined and hazard maps are constructed.

The experiments shown in the paper by Deelman et al. [12] are based on calculation of PSHA maps for two sites of interest using resources provisioned from SCEC and TeraGrid. The resulting experiments involve over 250,000 individual jobs with a total runtime equivalent to 1.8 CPU years. The reservation of nodes at two major computing centers for 9.5 and 7 days, respectively, are sufficient to perform the calculations.

Scenarios like CyberShake show common infrastructural requirements for large-scale science applications. Providing QoS guarantees and enforcing deadlines is much more important than in small-scale experiments because of the need for coordinated computation and storage over a large pool of resources. In order to support scenarios like CyberShake, DRIVE must be able to provision resources from dynamic VOs spanning multiple organizations. As there is no expectation of inter-organizational trust, we need to adopt an auction protocol that acts in place of a trusted third party to establish trustworthy resource allocation. In this case we would use a verifiable, privacy-preserving auction protocol such as those presented in Chapter 24. Additionally advanced reservations and contracts are vital in assuring deadlines are met and levels of QoS can be specified and provided.

25.4.3 Utility Computing Wholesale Markets

The third use case is a hypothetical utility computing scenario. In a utility computing model computation and storage is viewed as a commodity in which users pay for the resources that they use in much the same as we currently pay for electricity. Although a true utility computing infrastructure remains unrealized, we might imagine that such a scheme could be implemented on a global scale using a tiered approach. In this scheme there would be three tiers: a wholesale computation market, a retail computation market, and an optional organizational market. Wholesalers buy large chunks of computation from resource providers and later sell it to retailers, who, in turn, sell it to organizations or individuals. An organization may also choose to use auctions to divide their allocation among their users. The requirements at each of these tiers are different and can be separately met by different scheduling and trust arrangements:

- *Wholesale to Retail.* The requirements at the wholesale-to-retail tier are secure, verifiable, privacy-preserving allocations. This market represents a very competitive environment in which allocations are for huge quantities of resources worth large amounts of money. Ensuring that the correct allocations are made without any sensitive data being released, is imperative. Because of the large quantities of resources being reserved and exposure to risk, it is essential to use a more complex yet safer allocation process. The cost for this may be more than that for a simple allocation mechanism, but in a large-scale case this represents a small fraction of the total resources provisioned. The allocation process should be secure and verifiable while also keeping commercially sensitive information private.
- *Retail to Organization.* The requirements at the retail-to-organization tier are more relaxed; allocations will be of a fine- to medium-grained nature with less risk than in the wholesale market. Resources may be allocated using mechanisms different from those used at the wholesale level; for example, a provider might use a fixed-price model. The allocation mechanism in the most part should be faster with less emphasis placed on trust, security, and privacy.
- *Organization to User.* The requirements at the organization-to-user level are very fine-grained with little to no risk. The organization-level tier would be commonly seen within organizations but is not an essential part of the overall utility computing model. The main concern of the allocation mechanism within the organization is efficient allocation with minimal overhead. As the allocation takes place within a trusted domain, a simple First-price auction protocol could be used with no regard for trust or privacy. Specialized subschedulers such as Falkon [14] may also be used to allocate resources within the organization.

25.4.4 Summary

These use cases show a range of requirements placed on Grid systems. The allocation infrastructure needs to scale to support dynamic multiorganization collaborations while also providing efficiency in small-scale Grid scenarios. In order to do this, mechanisms are required to deal with trust, security, and privacy while also providing the ability to reserve resources and enforce contracts between participants. The range of use cases shows that no one mechanism will satisfy every scenario; in order to provide the required flexibility, DRIVE must have a modular architecture that is capable of supporting different allocation plug-ins. Generally when provisioning large quantities of resources, the overhead associated with secure allocation protocols is tolerable considering the benefits gained. However, for smaller allocations this overhead could be a significant percentage of the total job, and therefore a simpler protocol may be more suitable.

25.5 DRIVE ARCHITECTURE

Ideally a metascheduler should be flexible in terms of suitability for use in different Grid scenarios, ranging from small-scale local Grids within single organizations to large-scale global Grids that span administrative boundaries. DRIVE achieves this flexibility through the use of a VO model to represent Grid systems and an auction plug-in architecture for allocating resources. The VO model is used to group resource providers and users to specific Grid systems, and a VO membership service controls VO access to services and resources by authenticating participants.

The plug-in auction protocol is vital in tailoring allocation mechanisms to specific scenarios. For instance, within an organization internal trust may exist—in this case DRIVE users can achieve maximum allocation performance by choosing a conventional sealed-bid auction plug-in that does not utilize expensive trust or privacy-preserving mechanisms. In a global utility Grid no such trust exists. The same DRIVE architecture can be used with a secure auction protocol [15] plug-in ensuring that the allocation is carried out fairly and bid details are kept private. Because of the high overhead of secure protocols, we suggest the use of subscheduling tools such as Falkon [14] to provide rapid execution of many smaller tasks and amortize overhead. To permit the deployment of different auction mechanisms (both secure and insecure), we make use of the *general auction framework* (GAF) [16] to provide a protocol-independent shell for a wide range of auction types. This is important as it allows protocols to be seamlessly selected for different tasks, due to the wide-ranging complexity of privacy-preserving, trustworthy, and verifiable auction protocols.

25.5.1 High-Level Description

Figure 25.1 shows the high-level DRIVE architecture. The cloud outlines the scope of the VO. Resource providers 2 and 3 are members of the VO, while resource provider 1 is attempting to join the VO. On joining the VO, a resource provider exposes a set of *obligation* services that it contributes to the VO for the running of the metascheduler.

Obligation services, shown by resource provider 3, can include the auction manager, auction context, auction component, and MDS. Once a member of the VO, the resource provider also exposes *participation* services, which are needed to bid for, accept, and schedule jobs on the resource provider. Participation services, shown by resource provider 2, include the bidding service, reservation service, and GRAM. The remaining *trusted core* services: VOMS, category manager, and contract service, are in the current architecture hosted by a set of trusted hosts, although it is our aim to redesign these services to also run on hosts without needing to establish trust. The actual obligation services are defined by the use case. For instance, within an organization where internal trust exists, all trusted core services could be deployed as obligation services to achieve a wide distribution of load within the VO.

The client-side broker provides a transparent interface to DRIVE, supporting job monitoring and submission to allocated resource providers (via GRAM). The broker requires no specific Grid components or Web service containers and can be set up as a client-side application or deployed as a domain-level server. All correspondence

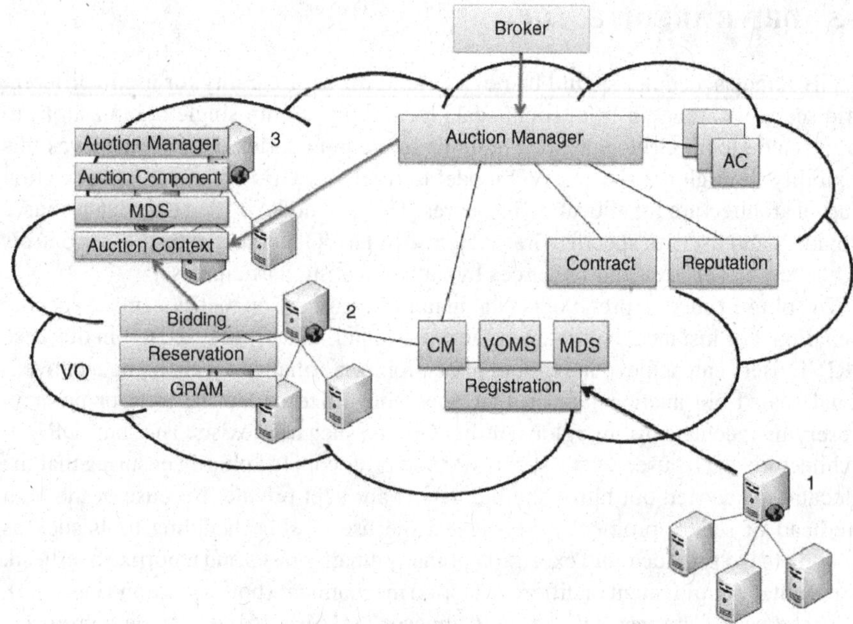

Figure 25.1 Overview of the DRIVE architectural components.

between the broker and a DRIVE VO is through Web service interfaces. The broker is able to discover metascheduler services via DRIVE using the standard Globus MDS and is free to choose services on the basis of reputation [17]. The broker submits job requests to an auction manager, which instantiates an auction context for the duration of the auction. At the end of the auction, the winner and broker receive contracts (containing SLAs) describing the agreed on commitments, and the job is dispatched to the GRAM service on the allocated hosts.

25.5.2 Architectural Components

The DRIVE architecture is built from WSRF Web services. Each service has a well-defined task and is accessible through a standard interface. These services collectively perform resource allocation through plug-in auction protocols. The services listed below are categorized into trusted core, obligation, and participation services. For brevity, the list excludes standard Globus services such MDS and GRAM:

Trusted Core Services

- *Category Manager*. This service provides registration for resource providers. Resource providers register their bidding profile when joining the VO. This profile is used to categorize the type of job that a resource is interested in hosting. When an auction is conducted, the category manager is consulted and appropriate resource providers are selected according to their resource profiles. This has the effect of reducing auction size and therefore increasing the efficiency of the allocation process.

- *Contract Service.* This service stores contracts that have been issued within the VO. This service is used in the contract hardening process before redemption, ensuring that the contract can be honored. It is also used to monitor SLAs contained in the contracts.

Obligation Services

- *Auction Manager.* This is the central auction service; it manages the auction process and advertises the auction to suitable bidders. The broker starts an auction by passing the job description (JSDL) to the auction manager, which then creates the appropriate auction resources and selects the services required for the particular auction protocol.
- *Auction Context.* This service stores state for individual auctions, including status/protocol-specific state. Clients can register for notifications or poll the service for status, results, and contracts.
- *Auction Component.* This is a universal component that can be used for different auction protocols; it is a shell that wraps protocol-specific services. The auction component takes different forms depending on the protocol; for example, in a verifiable secure generalized Vickery auction (vSGVA) the auction component is an auction evaluator used to compute the winner of the auction. In the garbled circuit protocol the auction component is an auction issuer used to garble the circuit and is required for the VPOT protocol [18].

Participation Services

- *Bidding Service.* This service responds to auction events from the auction manager and computes bids for jobs that it wishes to host using pricing algorithms, local policy, and consideration of future commitments.
- *Reservation Service.* This service stores any commitments made by the provider, normally in the form of contracts. This service is the key component for supporting advanced reservation in DRIVE; the bidding service is able to check resource commitments using its reservation service prior to bidding on advanced reservation auctions.

25.5.3 Contract Structure

There is potential for considerable latency in the allocation process between the bidding phase and auction completion. This latency greatly impacts utilization when resources are reserved while waiting for the result of the auction; this problem is exaggerated by the fact that all but one of the bidders will not win the auction. Overbooking can be used to minimize this problem by allowing resources to bid on auctions that may exceed their capacity in the knowledge it is unlikely that they will win all auctions. To permit overbooking, DRIVE makes use of a progressive contract structure [19] to ensure that resources are available at the time of the bid and when the contract is finalized. Backup resources are used to reduce the impact of overbooking in the case of unexpected changes to resource availability.

In DRIVE an agreement is returned by the auction manager to the client on the result of the auction. This agreement does not guarantee resource availability; rather, it is a strong indication that the resources will be available at the specified time and can be regarded as a placeholder for the eventual contract containing service-level agreements (SLAs). A group of backup resource providers is computed by the auction manager to allow for the possibility that an agreement may not be honored. Before a client can use the resources, the agreement must be converted into a contract. To do this, the resource providers are contacted to check the current resource availability.

This approach is also applicable to the problem of advanced reservation. It increases the likelihood that resources will bid on advanced reservation auctions in the knowledge that they will not be penalized as harshly if their resource state changes. Penalties may apply for breaking an agreement; for example, the party that breaks the agreement may have to pay the difference of price between its bid and the backup options computed by the auction manager.

Service-level agreements are specified in the hardened contract to ensure that the agreed on QoS is delivered by the resource providers. The details of the SLA tie specific user requirements with resource provider capabilities as detailed in the contract. The SLA is made up of a number of measurable properties that are monitored for the duration of usage. These properties map to specific QoS parameters. The SLA may also define a set of penalties in the event that a certain capability cannot be met by the resource provider. SLAs are discussed in more detail earlier in this book.

25.5.4 Coallocation

Coallocation is the process of simultaneously allocating resources in predetermined capacities over a group of resource providers. Coallocation is often required in Grid computing because of requirements for QoS, replication, and parallelism. Consider, for example, a large-scale science application that has data sites worldwide. Overall efficiency can be greatly improved by running an application in parallel using many processing resources close to the individual data sites. Coallocation auctions are performed in the same way as conventional single auctions, but rather than a single contract, a number of contracts are created for each coallocated task. Coallocated tasks are listed in the auction description, which is taken into account during the bidding phase, and multiple winners (and backup resources) are accepted for the auction. The construction of the subsequent coallocative contracts is done via *coallocative oversubscribing resource allocation* (CORA) [19] through the contract service.

25.5.5 Advanced Reservation

Advanced reservation is a key component in Grid resource provisioning, as jobs often require particular resources to be available at certain times in order to run efficiently. An example would be a requirement for a large amount of data storage as an intermediary stage in a workflow in order to temporarily store results of a job. This storage must be available when the job completes and for the duration of the subsequent processing stage. To support advanced reservation, DRIVE makes use of a reservation service per resource provider; this service stores commitments made by providers, allowing future commitments to be considered prior to bidding. We expect to extend the reservation service to leverage existing functionality in advanced reservation-compliant LRMs and GRAM.

25.5.6 Job Description

There are a number of distributed resource management systems designed to deploy jobs to remote Grid resources; unfortunately most use proprietary languages and interfaces to describe and deploy jobs. Grid environments commonly require communication between different types of job management systems running on heterogeneous hosts. For this reason there have been efforts to define a standardized job description language in order to provide transparency over distributed resource managers.

DRIVE makes use of the *job submission description language* (JSDL) to describe jobs submitted to the VO. JSDL is a language designed to describe requirements of jobs for submission to Grids. JSDL is an XML-based language with an XML schema that allows the expression of requirements as a set of XML elements. The JSDL Working Group is in the process of extending the language to encompass a wider range of jobs and is producing translation tables to and from scheduling languages (job requirements and resource descriptions) used by the major distributed resource managers and Grid projects.

25.5.7 VO Security

Security is a major issue to be considered in DRIVE. Globus security mechanisms rely on certificates to authenticate access to resources and use policy decision points to decide permissible actions. DRIVE relies heavily on VOs to group users and provide the infrastructure required for general VO functionality such as allocation and management. In order for users to join VOs and prove that they are a member of the VO, we use the *virtual organization membership service* (VOMS) [5], a database-based mechanism used to manage authorization information within multiinstitutional collaborations. User roles and capabilities are stored in a database, and a set of tools are provided for accessing and manipulating data. Users join a VO by contacting the VOMS service to gain credentials Resources then check local access control lists to determine whether these credentials are appropriate.

Credentials for users and providers are generated when required on the basis of authorization information stored in the database. These credentials extend authorization information stored in standard X.509 Grid proxies by including role and capability information as well as VOMS server credentials. The resource provider authenticating the certificate keeps an access control list to make authorization decisions based on groups, roles, or capabilities. VOMS has the advantage that resource sites do not need to retrieve all VO lists multiple times a day; rather, VO information is pushed through the certificate. We use VOMS in DRIVE to take advantage of single-signon, backward compatibility with standard certificates, and the ability for users to join multiple VOs. Another important aspect of VOs is the ability to define policy. Although VOMS does not provide a standard way to define fine-grained policy, this can be achieved by adding policy tables to the database or through a separate policy management service.

25.5.8 Interaction Phases

There are three major interaction phases for participants in a DRIVE VO. First, resource providers register with a VO making obligation and participation services available to other entities of the VO. Having joined the VO, users can request resource allocations using the contributed services to determine suitable resource providers. Finally, jobs can be submitted and executed on members of the VO.

25.5.8.1 Registration. Before a resource provider can offer its services, it must first be a member of a VO. The process of registration is as shown in Figure 25.2:

1. The first step of registration is joining the VO. To do this, each resource provider registers with VOMS. VOMS records user information and issues certificates to be used when authenticating access. The resource provider is then able to pull authentication information from VOMS and use it to maintain an access control list containing VO/user rights.

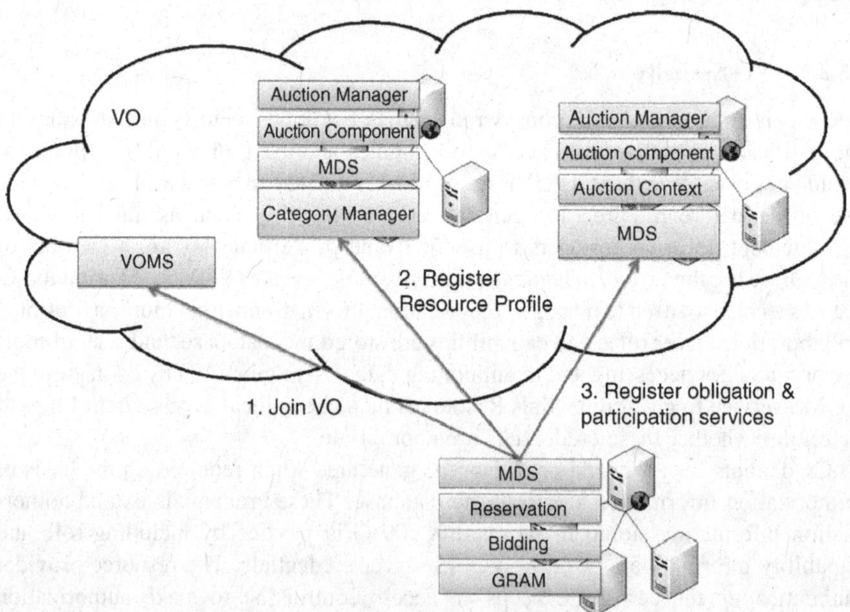

Figure 25.2 DRIVE resource provider registration.

2. Participation service details and high-level resource profiles are then submitted to a category manager in order to categorize providers according to the type of auctions that they are interested in bidding on, for example, CPU-intensive jobs.
3. Finally, the address of any contributed services and the address of the participation services are registered in the MDS index service for discovery purposes by clients, providers, or other services in the VO.

25.5.8.2 Resource Allocation. Resource allocation is performed in the VO using auction-based mechanisms and is conducted using a subset of the contributed obligation services. From a user's perspective, jobs are described using JSDL (job submission definition language) documents and are submitted to a client broker. The process of economic allocation (auctioning) is transparent to the user. The DRIVE architecture does not specify the type of job that can be submitted, only that it is defined using JSDL. Workflows can be decomposed into a set of jobs each described with a JSDL document; the set of JSDL documents is passed to the broker to be submitted to the Grid. The allocation process is shown in Figure 25.3:

1. First, the broker must authenticate itself on behalf of the user with VOMS. Then a working proxy is created and subsequent access to VO services is provided via this proxy.
2. The broker locates a viable auction manager using the MDS index service. The choice of auction manager can be based on protocol support, reputation, location,

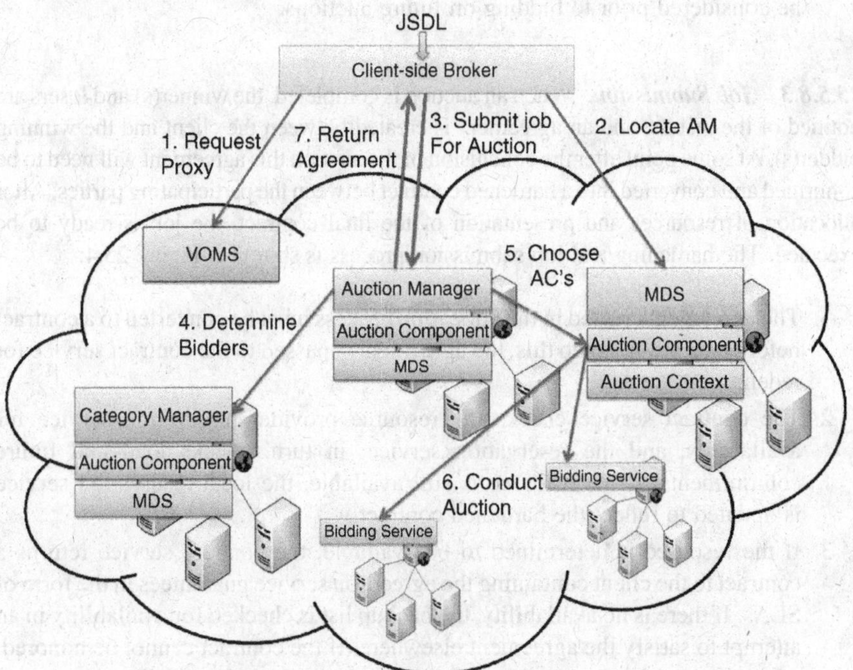

Figure 25.3 DRIVE resource allocation.

or any other user requirements. After selection of a suitable auction manager, all allocation is now performed though this service.

3. The job is submitted to the chosen auction manager to coordinate the auction process.
4. Suitable resource providers are selected by consulting category manager resource profiles. These selected resource providers are then notified of the auction. Resource providers that are not explicitly chosen are still able to bid, but must discover the auction through the auction publishing services.
5. Depending on the auction protocol selected, different auction components will be instantiated and used. For example, for the garbled circuit protocol, an auction issuer is constructed, while for the homomorphic and polynomial auction protocols, a group of auction evaluators will be created.
6. Resource providers each host a bidding service, which is responsible for implementing bidding policies, pricing goods in the auction according to a user-defined pricing function, and following the auction protocol to submit bids. The bidding service is invoked by the auction manager or auction component depending on the protocol.
7. When the auction is complete, a winner is determined and an agreement is created by the contract service and returned to the client by the auction manager. A list of alternative resource providers is maintained in case the agreement cannot be honored. The resource provider records the successful allocation and subsequent agreement through its reservation service; this information can then be considered prior to bidding on future auctions.

25.5.8.3 Job Submission. When an auction is completed, the winner(s) and losers are notified of the results, and an agreement is created between the client and the winning bidder(s). At some point after the conclusion of the auction this agreement will need to be confirmed and converted into a hardened contract between the participating parties. After allocation of resources and presentation of the final contract, the job is ready to be executed. The hardening and job submission process is shown in Figure 25.4:

1. The agreement created in the allocation process must be converted to a contract before execution. To do this, the agreement is passed to the contract service for redemption.
2. The contract service checks the resource provider reservation service for availability, and the reservation service, in turn, checks load and future commitments. If the resource is still available, the local reservation service is updated to reflect the hardened contract.
3. If the resource is determined to be available, the contract service returns a contract to the client containing the agreed-on service guarantees in the form of SLAs. If there is no availability, the backup list is checked for availability in an attempt to satisfy the agreement elsewhere. If the contract cannot be honored, some form of penalty may be imposed (reputation or financial).

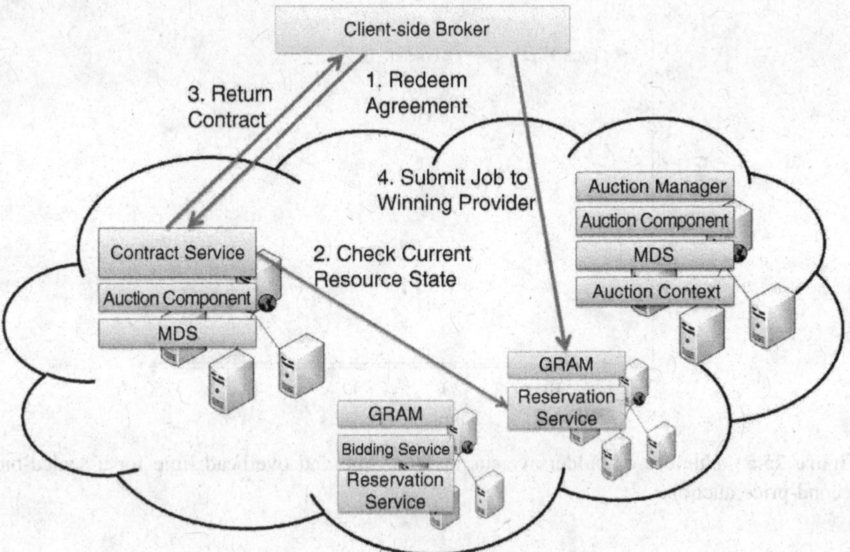

Figure 25.4 DRIVE job submission and execution.

4. The final contract is then redeemed by the client at the appropriate resource provider, and the job is submitted to the LRM through GRAM. If there is no suitable backup, a new auction will be conducted.

25.6 PROTOTYPE AND EVALUATION

The DRIVE prototype is built using a collection of WSRF Grid services deployed to GT4 containers. A simple Java client acts as an external resource broker to request allocations and submit jobs to GRAM. The focus of this initial implementation is to experiment with auction protocols in a distributed Grid service environment and to serve as a proof of concept for the viability of the DRIVE auction architecture. The prototype supports two distributed auction protocols: a standard sealed-bid second-price auction and a privacy-preserving, verifiable garbled circuit. The following experiments focus on total auction time and resource/protocol overhead when increasing the number of bidders participating in an auction and the number of goods represented.

25.6.1 Number of Bidders

To support global-scale Grid computing, a large number of resource providers must be considered in the resource allocation process; when using auctions, this translates into a large number of bidders. The time taken to solicit bids and determine a winner in both the sealed-bid (Fig. 25.5) and garbled circuit (Fig. 25.6) protocols is shown to be almost linear.

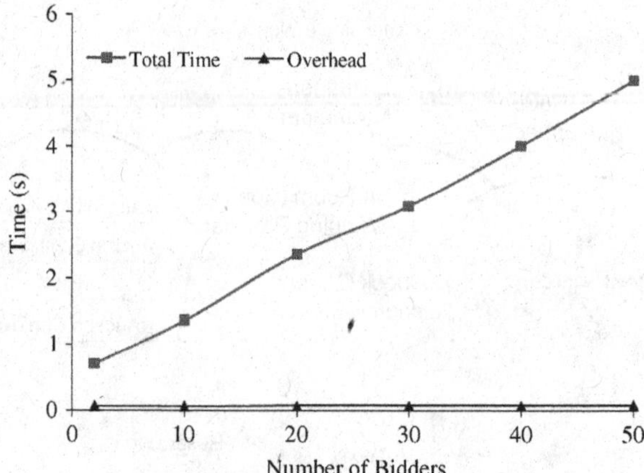

Figure 25.5 Number of bidders versus auction time and overhead time for a sealed-bid second-price auction.

Both graphs (in Figs. 25.5 and 25.6) also show the overhead associated with the auction process. In this case overhead is measured as the time taken to set up auction components, such as the creation of the WSRF resources storing auction state and protocol-specific computation that is performed before the auction commences (circuit creation).

The measured overhead of the sealed-bid auction protocol is near constant as only a single simple WSRF resource is created and minimal preliminary computation is required by the protocol. This overhead is only a small fraction of the total auction time, showing that the use of WSRF resources does not greatly impact the auction

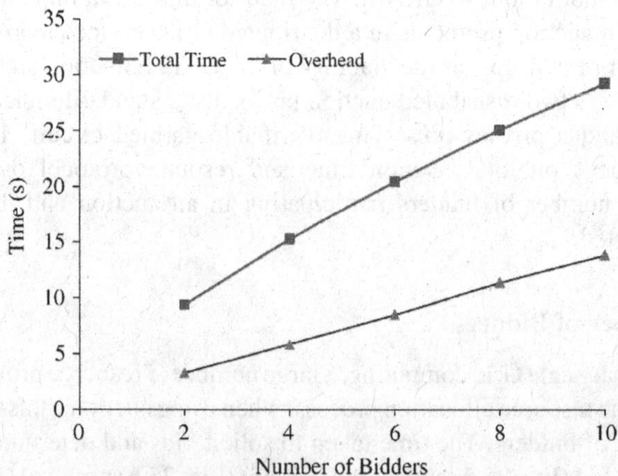

Figure 25.6 Number of bidders versus auction time and overhead time for garbled circuits.

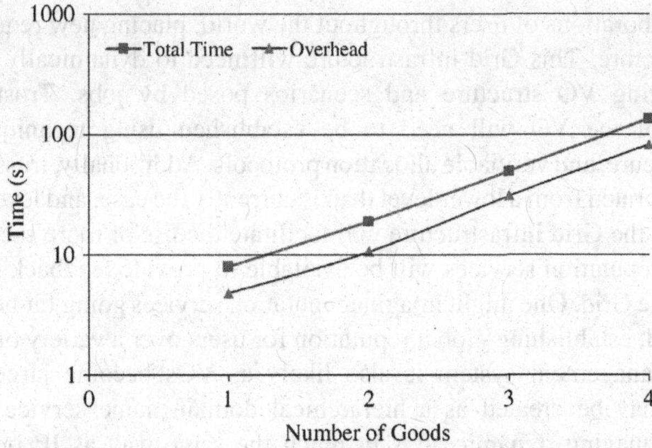

Figure 25.7 Number of goods versus auction time and overhead time for garbled circuits.

time. The garbled circuit protocol, on the other hand, has considerable overhead, due to circuit creation, and increases linearly with the number of bidders.

A comparison of the sealed-bid and garbled circuit protocols shows the substantial computational cost in terms of auction time and overhead when using complex trustworthy protocols. With the sealed-bid auction, it takes 5 s to determine a winner with 50 bidders, whereas with the garbled circuit protocol, it takes almost 30 s with only 10 bidders. As mentioned previously, we envision the use of more complex trustworthy protocols in larger-value auctions where you would expect fewer bidders and would be willing to sacrifice auction time for trustworthy results.

25.6.2 Number of Goods

Combinatorial auctions can be used to describe complex resource dependences often required in Grid systems [e.g., combinatorial allocation problem (CAP)] when expressing QoS constraints. Figure 25.7 shows the winner computation time using the garbled circuit protocol and the associated overhead.

The auction time and overhead are exponential with the increase in the number of goods represented, as is expected because of the NP-complete nature of the CAP. These results show the importance of limiting the number of combinations of goods represented in computational auctions because of the exponential increase in cost. The overhead also increases exponentially with the number of goods represented as the graph size is proportional to the number of combinations.

25.7 FUTURE TRENDS

As Grid computing evolves toward the vision of a global utility Grid infrastructure, a wider range of applications will be seen. We will see an increase in the number of large dynamic collaborations of users throughout the world, placing new requirements on Grid infrastructure. This Grid infrastructure will need to dynamically adapt to the rapidly changing VO structure and scenarios posed by jobs. Trust within the components of the VO will need to be established using techniques such as distributed, secure, and verifiable allocation protocols. Additionally, trust and security will be incorporated from a lower level than is currently the case, and leveraging these capabilities in the Grid infrastructure will facilitate the use of more secure mechanisms. Global reputation services will be available to provide feedback on users and providers in the Grid. One might imagine reputation services going far beyond that of the Grid world, establishing global reputation for users over a variety of domains. A global VO management system is also likely as VOs become larger and more dynamic. It may be created as a hierarchical domain name service (DNS)-type system for managing dynamic VOs in much the same way as IP information is dynamically updated today.

25.8 SUMMARY

Grid metaschedulers turn the focus of resource allocation from the resource to the client; global resource allocation is achieved by submitting workload to numerous LRMs. Most metaschedulers are implemented on a per-client basis and are therefore concerned only with their own allocations rather than achieving globally optimal allocation across LRMs. Client-oriented metaschedulers compete by submitting jobs to resources with no knowledge of, or coordination with, other metaschedulers' actions, potentially reducing system efficiency. Current metascheduling technology requires dedicated resources to be set aside for allocation rather than exploiting the large pool of available VO resources.

DRIVE is a distributed economic metascheduler based on a dynamic VO model, in which VO members collaboratively conduct resource allocation using services in the VO. Resource providers contribute a set of obligation Grid services to the VO as a condition for joining, and these services are used to host allocation and management services This collaborative resource allocation has the effect of spreading the burden of allocation across participating entities while also providing the ability to define distributed allocation protocols. A group of trusted services is hosted in a secure section of the VO, providing a trust anchor for security throughout the VO. Resource providers also have a set of participation services used to bid on auctions and manage local allocation. All services are designed using GT4-compliant WSRF Web services. The client-side broker is lightweight with no dependence on Web service containers or Grid middleware.

DRIVE makes use of a plug-in auction mechanism that facilitates the use of arbitrary auction protocols, making it a suitable metascheduler for various Grid topologies. Users are able to select protocols on the basis of specific requirements, infrastructure availability, and their trust relationships with the entities participating in the auction. This flexibility allows the same DRIVE infrastructure to be used within a trusted organization or on a global Grid where no such trust exists.

REFERENCES

1. K. Chard and K. Bubendorfer, A distributed economic meta-scheduler for the Grid, *Proc. 8th IEEE International Symp. Cluster Computing and the Grid (CCGrid '08)*, Lyons, France, 2008.
2. I. Foster, C. Kesselman, and S. Tuecke, The anatomy of the Grid: Enabling scalable virtual organizations, *Lecture Notes in Computer Science* **2150**:1–4 (2001).
3. I. Foster and C. Kesselman, Globus: A metacomputing infrastructure toolkit, *The International Journal of Supercomputer Applications and High-Performance Computing* **11**(2):115–128 (1997).
4. S. Krawczyk and K. Bubendorfer, Grid resource allocation: Utilisation patterns, *Proc. 6th Australasian Symp. Grid Computing and e-Research (AusGrid)*, Wollongong, Australia, 2008.
5. R. Alfieri, R. Cecchini, V. Ciaschini, L. dell'Agnello, A. Frohner, K. LHrentey, and F. Spataro, From gridmap-file to VOMS: Managing authorization in a Grid environment, *Future Generation Computer Systems*, **21**(4):549–558 (2005).
6. R. Buyya, D. Abramson, and J. Giddy, Nimrod/G: An architecture for a resource management and scheduling system in a global computational grid, *Proc. 4th International Conf. High Performance Computing in Asia-Pacific Region (HPC Asia 2000)*, 2000.
7. S. Venugopal, R. Buyya, and L. Winton, A grid service broker for scheduling distributed data-oriented applications on global grids, *Proc. 2nd Workshop on Middleware in Grid Computing (MGC '04)*, 2004.
8. L. Adzigogov, J. Soldatos, and L. Polymenakos, EMPEROR: An OGSA Grid meta-scheduler based on dynamic resource predictions, *Journal of Grid Computing*, **3**(1–2): 19–37 (2005).
9. E. Huedo, R. S. Montero, and I. M. Llorente, A framework for adaptive execution on Grids, *Software—Practice and Experience* **34**(7):631–651 (2004).
10. Open source metascheduling for virtual organizations with the community scheduler framework, *White Paper, Platform Computing Inc.* (2003).
11. G. Haggard, D. Pearce, and G. Royle, *Computing Tutte Polynomials*, Victoria Univ. Wellington, 2007.
12. E. Deelman, S. Callaghan, E. Field, H. Francoeur, R. Graves, N. Gupta, V. Gupta, T. H. Jordan, C. Kesselman, P. Maechling, J. Mehringer, G. Mehta, D. Okaya, K. Vahi, and L. Zhao, Managing large-scale workflow execution from resource provisioning to provenance tracking: The CyberShake example, *Proc. 2nd IEEE International Conf. e-Science and Grid Computing*, 2006.
13. W. Gentzsch, Sun Grid Engine: Towards creating a compute power Grid, *Proc. 1st International Symp. Cluster Computing and the Grid*, 2001.
14. I. Raicu, Y. Zhao, C. Dumitrescu, I. Foster, and M. Wilde, Falkon: A Fast and Light-weight tasK executiON framework, *Proc. SuperComputing*, 2007.
15. K. Bubendorfer, B. Palmer, and I. Welch, Trust and privacy in grid resource auctions, *in Handbook of Research on Grid Technologies and Utility Computing: Concepts for Managing Large-Scale Applications*, E. Udoh and F. Wang, eds., IGI-Global, 2009, Chapter IX.
16. W. Thomson, *A Framework for Secure Auctions*, MSc thesis, Victoria Univ. Wellington, 2008.

17. J. Sonnek and J. Weissman, A quantitative comparison of reputation systems in the Grid, *Proc. 6th IEEE/ACM International Workshop on Grid Computing*, 2005.
18. A. Juels and M. Szydlo, A two-server, sealed-bid auction protocol, *Proc. 6th Financial Cryptography Conf. (FC 2002)*, 2003.
19. K. Bubendorfer, Fine grained resource reservation in open grid economies, *Proc. 2nd IEEE International Conf. e-Science and Grid Computing (e-Science '06)*, Amsterdam, The Netherlands, 2006.

26

THE GRIDBUS MIDDLEWARE FOR MARKET-ORIENTED COMPUTING

Rajkumar Buyya, Srikumar Venugopal, Rajiv Ranjan, and Chee Shin Yeo

26.1 INTRODUCTION

Grids aim at exploiting synergies that result from the cooperation of autonomous distributed entities. The synergies that result from Grid cooperation include the sharing, exchange, selection, and aggregation of geographically distributed resources such as computers, databases, software, and scientific instruments for solving large-scale problems in science, engineering, and commerce. For this cooperation to be sustainable, participants need to have economic incentives. Therefore, "incentive" mechanisms should be considered as one of the key design parameters for designing and developing end-to-end Grid architectures. Although several studies have investigated market-oriented management of Grids, they were limited mostly to specific aspects of the system design such as service pricing or price-aware scheduling. This chapter presents architectural models, mechanisms, algorithms, and middleware services developed by the Gridbus project for end-to-end realization of market-oriented Grid computing.

Grid technologies such as Globus provide capabilities and services required for the seamless and secure execution of a job on heterogeneous resources. However, to achieve the complete vision of Grid as a utility computing environment, a number of challenges need to be addressed. They include designing Grid services capable of distributed application composition, resource brokering methodologies, policies and strategies for scheduling different Grid application models, Grid economy for data and resource management, application service specification, and accounting of

Market-Oriented Grid and Utility Computing Edited by Rajkumar Buyya and Kris Bubendorfer

resource consumption. The application development and deployment services need to scale from desktop environments to global Grids and support both scientific and business applications.

The Gridbus project is engaged in the design and development of service-oriented cluster and Grid middleware technologies to support e-science and e-business applications. It extensively leverages related software technologies and provides an abstraction layer to hide idiosyncrasies of heterogeneous resources and low-level middleware technologies from application developers. In addition, it extensively focuses on the realization of the utility computing model scaling from clusters to Grids and to the peer-to-peer computing systems. It uses economic models that aids in the efficient management of shared resources and promotes commoditization of their services. Thus, it enhances the tradability of Grid services according to their supply and demand in the system. Gridbus supports the commoditization of Grid services at various levels:

- Raw resource level (e.g., selling CPU cycles and storage resources)
- Application level (e.g., molecular docking operations for drug design application)
- Aggregated services (e.g., brokering and reselling of services across multiple domains)

The computational economy methodology helps in creating a service-oriented computing architecture where service providers offer paid services associated with a particular application and users, on the basis of their requirements, would optimize by selecting the services that they require and can afford within their budgets. Gridbus hence emphasizes the end-to-end quality of services driven by computational economy at various levels—clusters, peer-to-peer (P2P) networks, and the Grid—for the management of distributed computational, data, and application services.

Gridbus provides software technologies that spread across the following categories:

- Enterprise grid middleware with service-level agreement (SLA)-based resource allocation (Aneka)
- Grid economy and virtual enterprises (Grid Market Directory)
- Grid trading and accounting services (GridBank)
- Grid resource brokering and scheduling (Gridbus Broker)
- Grid workflow management (Gridbus Workflow Engine)
- Grid application development tools (Visual Parametric Modeller)
- Grid portals (Gridscape)

26.2 ARCHITECTURE

The Gridbus project aims to develop software frameworks and algorithms to realize a market-driven Grid computing environment, an example of which is illustrated in

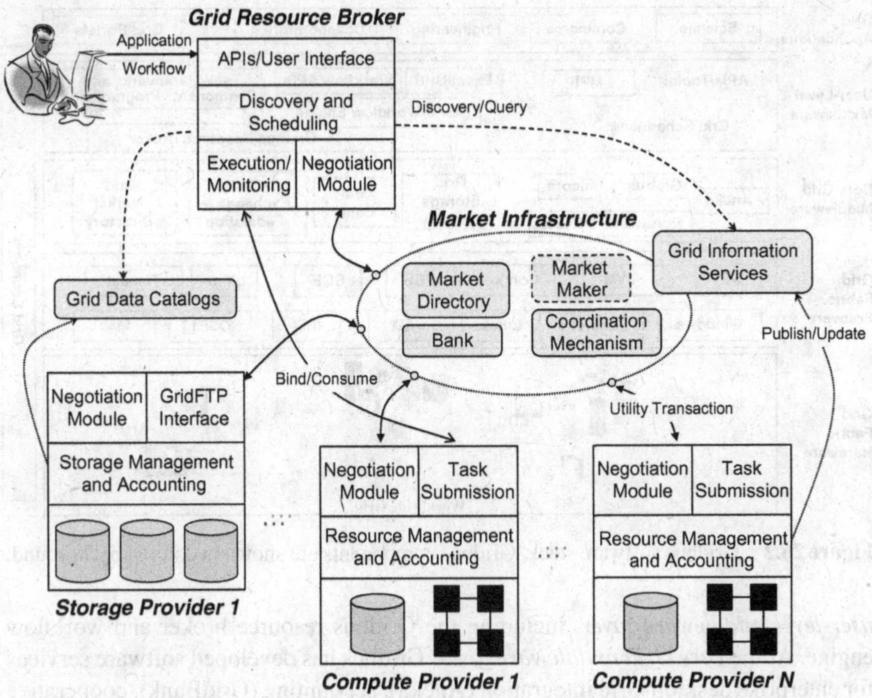

Figure 26.1 Architectural elements of market-based Grid computing.

Figure 26.1. The resource providers offer various resources, and are driven by the twin motivations of maximizing their profit and resource utilization. The requirement of the user is to execute her application given her requirements, such as accessing specific datasets for processing and/or a deadline for its completion. The user is constrained by her budget for accessing resources, and possibly by other factors such as access restrictions on certain storage resources and computing environments that can execute her application. The user operates through a Grid resource broker that, given user requirements and constraints, discovers appropriate resources, negotiates with them for access, executes the application, and returns the results to the user. The interface between the broker and the providers is enabled through the market infrastructure that provides functionalities such as directory of providers, and accounting and banking. In the following paragraphs, we will look at each participant and the related Gridbus components.

A layered view of its realization within the Gridbus middleware is shown in Figure 26.2. The Gridbus software stack is primarily divided into five layers: Grid applications layer, user-level middleware layer, core Grid middleware layer, Grid fabric software layer, and Grid fabric hardware layer. The notion of Grid economics is prevalent at each of these layers. At the *Grid applications layer*, the Gridbus project contributes through its monitoring and application composition Grid portals. These Grid portals have the capability to seamlessly interact with services running at the

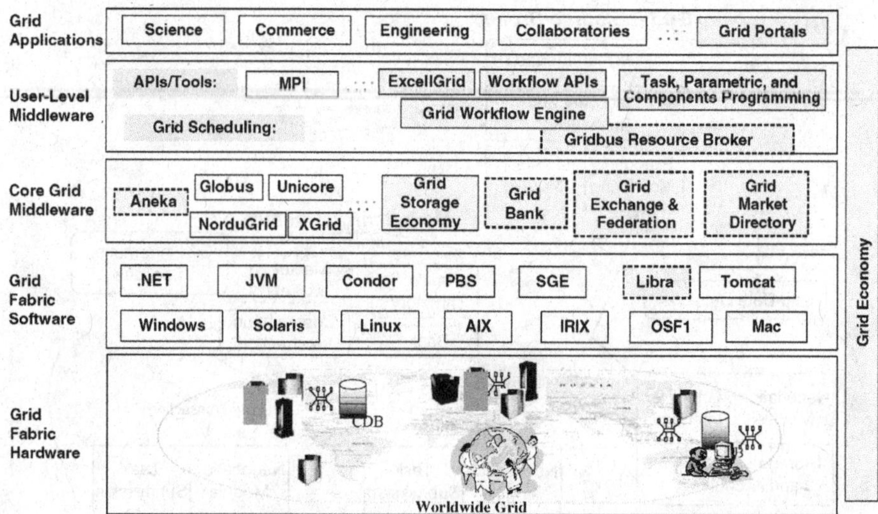

Figure 26.2 Gridbus software stack. Gridbus components are shown in colored background.

user-level middleware layer, including the Gridbus resource broker and workflow engine. At the *core Grid middleware layer*, Gridbus has developed software services for enterprise desktop Grid integration (Aneka), accounting (GridBank), cooperative resource management (Grid-Federation), and resource discovery (Grid Market Directory). The Libra system, which operates at the *Grid fabric software layer*, supports market-based allocation of cluster computing resources.

The Grid fabric hardware layer includes different kinds of computing, data, and storage facilities that belong to different Grid resource-sharing domains. There can be different types of providers offering different kinds of services to users. In Figure 26.1, we have depicted compute and storage providers, as these are the two basic resources required by any application. A compute provider leases highly capable computational resources such as supercomputers or clusters to the Grid environment. Such resources are generally managed by a queue-based scheduling system that allocates jobs to processors or nodes. However, most cluster management systems aim to improve system-centric metrics such as utilization. In contrast, Libra is an economy-based cluster scheduler that focuses on improving the quality of service (QoS) on a per-user basis. In addition, the resource may provide the ability to reserve nodes or processors in advance. The advance reservation is conducted through the negotiation interface that also enables the provider to participate in the market. These capabilities are provided in Aneka [10], a .NET-based enterprise Grid framework, in addition to the traditional cluster resource manager functions such as job submission and management. While the description so far relates to a compute provider, a storage provider would have similar components, except that the resource management would be replaced by storage management functions. Providers also track resource usage through accounting mechanisms to bill the users for their execution.

The Gridbus Grid resource broker [5] functions as a user agent in the market-oriented environment shown in Figure 26.1. The broker uses the user's requirements to discover appropriate Grid resources by querying Grid information services such as Globus' *Grid information indexing service* (GIIS) [12]. Market information such as prices and offers are queried from the market directory. Using this information, the broker identifies suitable providers and either carries out one-to-one negotiations or participates in auctions for resource shares. It then schedules user jobs over the acquired resource shares such that the deadline requirements of the user are met.

The primary components of the current market infrastructure are the Grid Market Directory (GMD) [6] and GridBank [7]. The GMD enables providers to advertise their services to the users through a registry service. Brokers can query the GMD to locate required services and query their attributes such as service addresses, pricing, and input methods. Other information services such as GIIS can also be considered as part of the market infrastructure as they allow the broker to discover capabilities and status of services, which, in turn, determine their value. GridBank is a accounting and micropayment service that provides an infrastructure for secure payments between the users and providers. GridBank can also be used as an accounting and authorization mechanism wherein only users with requisite credit in their accounts can enter into contracts with providers. It is important to note that there may be more than one instance of these components present in a Grid. As the scale of providers, brokers, and market components increases, it becomes necessary to connect these entities on the basis of a decentralized and scalable network model. Furthermore, these entities need to coordinate their activities in a scalable manner to achieve the desired systemwide objective functions. One such mechanism is the Compute Power Market [14], built using the JXTA infrastructure from Sun Microsystems, which allows the trading of computational power over peer-to-peer networks. Another more recent advancement with respect to coordinated Grid resource management has been the Grid-Federation [18] model, which encapsulates decentralized protocols and algorithms for efficient discovery and coordinated provisioning of resources in federated Grid and peer-to-peer systems.

26.3 GRID RESOURCE BROKER

The Gridbus broker is an advanced service-oriented metascheduler for compute and data Grids, with support for a wide range of Grid middleware and services. It accommodates many functions that Grid applications require, including discovering the right resources for a particular user application, scheduling jobs in order to meet deadlines, and handling faults that may occur during execution. In particular, the broker provides capabilities such as resource selection, job scheduling, job management, and data access to any application that requires distributed Grid resources for execution. The broker handles communication with the resources running different Grid middleware, job failures, varying resource availability, and different user objectives such as meeting a deadline for execution or limiting execution within a certain budget.

26.3.1 Architecture

The design of the Gridbus broker follows a layered architecture consisting of interface, core, and execution layers that together provide the capabilities shown for the market-oriented broker in Figure 26.1. The interface layer consists of application programming interfaces (APIs) and parsers for the input files through which external programs and users communicate with the broker, respectively. Resource discovery and negotiation, scheduling, and job monitoring are carried out in the core layer. The job execution is carried out through the execution layers in which middleware-specific adapters communicate with the target resources.

26.3.2 Input

There are many ways to specify the user requirements to the broker. Figure 26.3 shows a user application specified using the broker's own XPML (Extended Parametric Modeling Language) format. The qos tags enclose the user's QoS requirements, which, in the example, specify the deadline by which the job must be executed and the budget available for execution. The user wants the execution completed with the least

```
<xpml>
       <qos>
              <deadline value="2007-11-10T19 :30 :" />
              <budget value="10000.0"  />
              <optimisation value="COST" />
       </qos>
       <parametar name="X"  type=" integer"  domain=
          "range" >
              <range from="1"  to="10"  interval="1"  />
       </parameter>
       <parameter name="time_value"  type="integer"
          domain=" single">
              <single value="3000"  />
       </parameter>
       <job-requirements>
              <property name="estimatedTime"
                 value="60.00"  />
       </job-requirements>
       <task>
              <execute>
                     <command  value="calc"   />
                     <arg valuer="  $X  "  />
                     <arg value="  $time_value  "/>
              </execute>
       </tasK>
</xpml>
```

Figure 26.3 User requirement specification using XPML.

expense, which is indicated by the optimization value. XPML is used for specifying parameter sweep applications in which a single application is executed over a range of parameters. The `parameter` tags indicate the parameters, and the `task` tags specify the application to be executed.

Of interest to a market-oriented Grid is the QoS section. The values provided by the user in this section form the basis for the broker's resource discovery and scheduling mechanisms. While the only parameters recognized by the broker at present are the deadline, budget, and optimization values, the number of such inputs is limited only by the capabilities of the schedulers in the broker.

26.3.3 Discovery, Negotiation, and Scheduling

The broker queries resources for their capabilities and availability. Information about the resource costs is queried from the Grid Market Directory (GMD). Once the resources are identified, the broker may carry out one-to-one negotiations with them. The Gridbus broker has the ability to conduct bilateral negotiations with the resources by using the Alternate Offers Protocol [1]. The negotiation consists of the broker exchanging proposals with counter-proposals from the resource until both of them converge on an acceptable agreement, or one of them quits the process.

Figure 26.4 shows an extensible Markup Language (XML)-based negotiation proposal for reserving nodes in advance on a resource (with the values shown in bold). The broker creates this proposal according to the requirements given by the user. The reward field indicates the provider's gain for supplying the required number of

```
<xml - fragment xmlns: ws =" http: // www.gridbua.org/
   negotiation/ws">
   <ws : Reward>200.0</ws: Reward>
   <ws : Penalty>50.0</ws: Penalty>
   <ws: Requirements>
     <ws:ReservationRecordType>
         <ws:ReservationStartTime>
         2008-04-01T18:22:00.437+11:00
         </ws:ReservationStartTime>
       <ws:Duration>750000.0</ws:Duration>
       <ws:NodeRequirement>
         <ws:Count>4</ws:Count>
       </ws:NodeRequirement>
       <ws:CpuRequirement>
         <ws: Measure>Ghz</ws :Measure>
         <ws: Speed>2.5</ws:Speed>
       <ws:CpuRequirement>
     </ws:ReservationRecordType>
   </ws:Requirements>
</xml-fragment>
```

Figure 26.4 Negotiation proposal format.

resources. The penalty field denotes the penalty to be paid if the provider accepted the proposal but did not supply the required resources.

The requirements section here asks for four nodes with a minimum CPU speed of 2.5 GHz each for duration of 750 s starting from 6:22 p.m. on April 1, 2008. The provider (or resource) can, in turn, create a counterproposal by modifying sections of the broker's proposal and send that as a reply. The offers and counteroffers continue until one of the parties accepts the current proposal, or rejects it altogether. At present, the broker can negotiate only with Aneka [10], the resource management system covered in Section 26.6.

The broker enables different types of scheduling depending on the objectives of the user and type of resources. At present, the broker can accommodate compute, storage, network, and information resources with prices based on time (1 Grid dollar for 1 second), or capacity (1 Grid dollar for 1 MB). It can also accommodate user objectives such as the fastest computation within the budget (time optimization), or the cheapest computation within the deadline (cost optimization) for both compute and data-intensive applications. The compute-intensive algorithms are based on those developed previously in Nimrod/G [2]. A cost–time-minimizing algorithm for data-intensive applications is described in the following paragraphs. This algorithm was published and evaluated previously [3].

A distributed data-intensive computing environment consists of applications that involve mainly accessing, processing and transferring data of the order of gigabytes (GB) and upward. These operations are conducted over resources that are geographically distributed, and shared between different users. Therefore, the impact of data access and transfer operations on the execution time of the application and resource usage is equal to, if not more than, that of the compute-intensive processing operations. Transferring large volumes of data through the network can be very costly, and so can be processing it at an expensive compute resource. Therefore, the total cost can be defined as the sum of the processing cost, the data transfer (network) cost, and the storage cost. Likewise, the total time for execution is the sum of the job completion time and the data transfer time. A simple scheduling heuristic to reduce the total execution cost of the application can be expressed as follows:

1. Repeat for every scheduling interval while there are unprocessed jobs.
2. For every job, find the data file(s) that it is dependent on and locate the data hosts for those files.
3. Find a data-compute set (a set consisting of one compute resource for the execution and one data host for each file involved) that guarantees the minimum cost for that job.
4. Sort the jobs in order of increasing cost.
5. Assign jobs from the sorted list starting with the least expensive job until either all the jobs are allocated or all the compute resources have been allocated their maximum jobs.

Although this list shows only cost minimization, the same heuristic was followed in the case of time minimization except that the criterion in step 2 was changed to the *minimum execution time* required.

This scheduling algorithm was evaluated on resources distributed around Australia, listed in Table 26.1. The network connections between the compute resources were assigned artificial costs as given in Table 26.2. We used a synthetic application that transferred and processed large data files. These files were evenly distributed on the resources and were registered in a replica catalog [4]. The broker located the files by querying the catalog. For this experiment, we had 100 files, each 30 MB in size. Each job depended on one of the files, thus creating 100 jobs.

TABLE 26.1 Resources Used for Evaluation of Cost-Based Data-Intensive Scheduling

Organization[a]	Machine Details	Role	Cost [G$/ (CPU·s)]	Total Jobs Executed: Time	Total Jobs Executed: Cost
Dept. Computer Science, Univ. Melbourne (UniMelb CS)	belle.cs.mu.oz.au; IBM eServer, 4 CPU, 2 GB RAM, 70 GB HD, Linux	Broker host, data host, NWS server	NA (not used as a compute resource)	—	—
School of Physics, Univ. Melbourne (UniMelb Physics)	fleagle.ph.unimelb.edu.au; PC, 1 CPU, 512 MB RAM, 70 GB HD, Linux	Replica catalog host, data host, computer resource, NWS sensor	2	3	94
Dept. Computer Science, Univ. Adelaide (Adelaide CS)	belle.cs.adelaide.edu.au; IBM eServer, 4 CPU (only 1 available), 2 GB RAM, 70 GB HD, Linux	Data host, NWS sensor	NA (not used as a compute resource)	—	—
Australian National Univ., Canberra (ANU)	belle.anu.edu.au; IBM eServer, 4 CPU, 2 GB RAM, 70 GB HD, Linux	Data host, computer resource, NWS sensor	4	2	2
Dept. Physics, Univ. Sydney (Sydney Physics)	belle.physics.usyd.edu.au; IBM eServer, 4 CPU (only 1 available), 2 GB RAM, 70 GB HD, Linux	Data host, compute resource, NWS sensor	4	72	2
Victorian Partnership for Advanced Computing, Melbourne (VPAC)	brecca-2.vpac.org; 180-node cluster (only head node used), Linux	Compute resource, NWS sensor	6	23	2

[a]This column lists abbreviations used in Table 26.2.

TABLE 26.2 Network Costs between Data Hosts and Compute Resources (in G$/MB)[a]

Data Node Compute Node	ANU	UniMelb Physics	Sydney Physics	VPAC
ANU	0	34.0	31.0	38.0
Adelaide CS	34.0	36.0	31.0	33.0
UniMelb Physics	40.0	0	32.0	39.0
UniMelb CS	36.0	30.0	33.0	37.0
Sydney Physics	35.0	33.0	0	37.0

[a]See Table 26.1, "Organization" column, for abbreviations used in this table.

TABLE 26.3 Summary of Evaluation Results

Scheduling Strategy	Total Time Taken (min)	Compute Cost (G$)	Data Cost (G$)	Total Cost (G$)
Cost minimization	71.07	26,865	7560	34,425
Time minimization	48.5	50,938	7452	58,390

Table 26.3 summarizes the results that were obtained. As is expected, cost minimization scheduling produces minimum computation and data transfer expenses, whereas time minimization completes the experiments in the least time. The graphs in Figures 26.5 and 26.6 show the number of jobs completed against time for the two

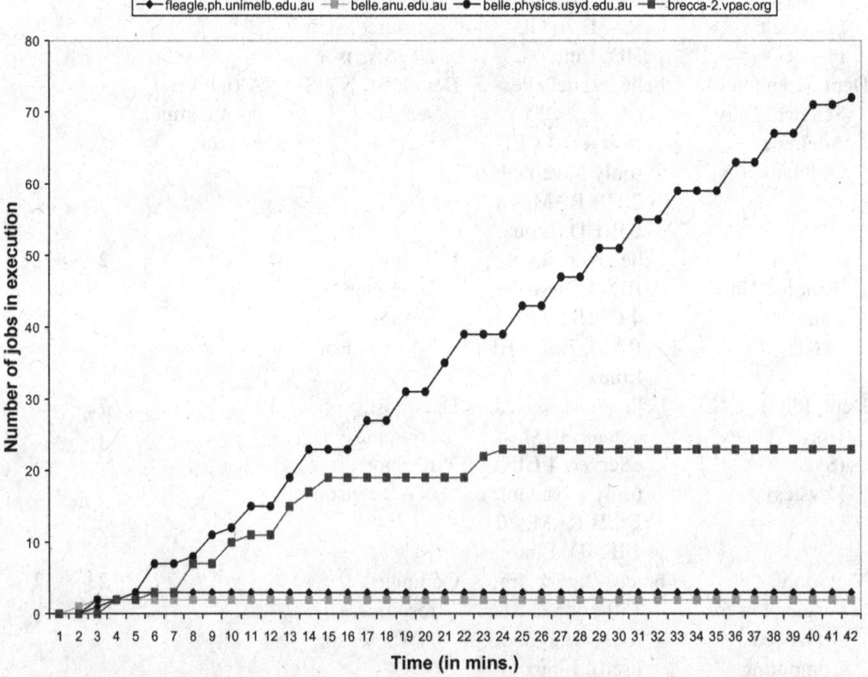

Figure 26.5 Cumulative number of jobs completed versus time for time minimization scheduling in data Grids.

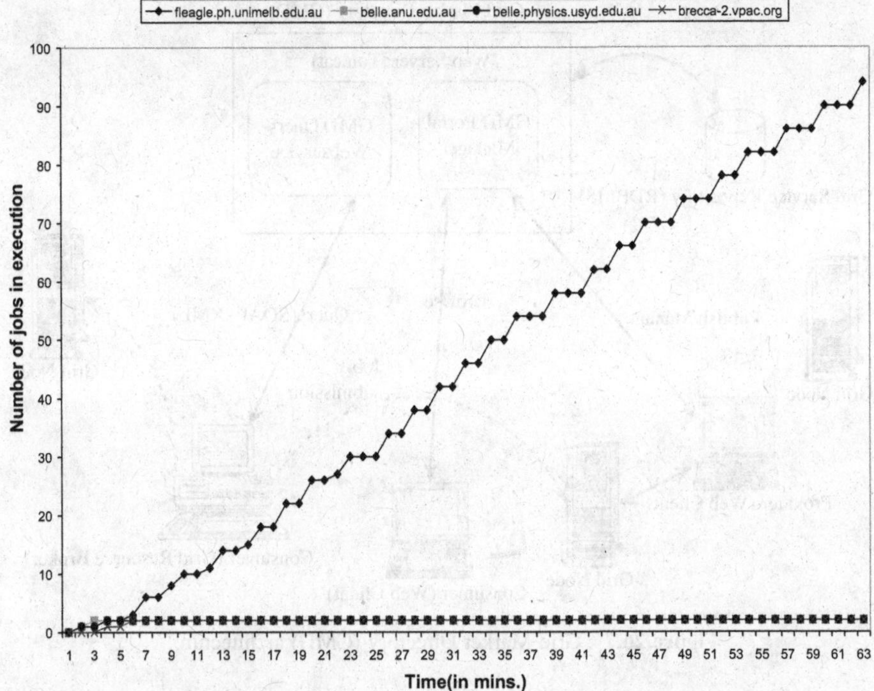

Figure 26.6 Cumulative number of jobs completed versus time for cost minimization scheduling in data Grids.

scheduling strategies. It can be seen that these mirror the trends for similar evaluations conducted with computational Grids [2]; that is, time minimization used the more expensive but faster resources to execute jobs, whereas cost minimization used the cheaper resource most to ensure a lower overall expense.

26.4 GRID MARKET DIRECTORY (GMD)

It has been envisioned that Grids enable the creation of virtual organizations (VOs) [11] and virtual enterprises (VEs) [13] or computing marketplaces [14]. In a typical marketbased model VO/VE, Grid service providers (GSPs) publish their offerings in a market directory (or a catalog), and Grid service consumers (GSCs) employ a Grid resource broker (GRB) that identifies GSPs through the market directory and utilize the services of suitable resources that meet their QoS requirements (see Fig. 26.7).

To realize this vision, Grids need to support diverse infrastructure/services [11], including an infrastructure that allows (1) the creation of one or more Grid market place (GMP) registries, (2) the contributors to register themselves as GSPs along with their resources/application services that they wish to provide, (3) GSPs to publish themselves in one or more GMPs along with service prices, and (4) Grid

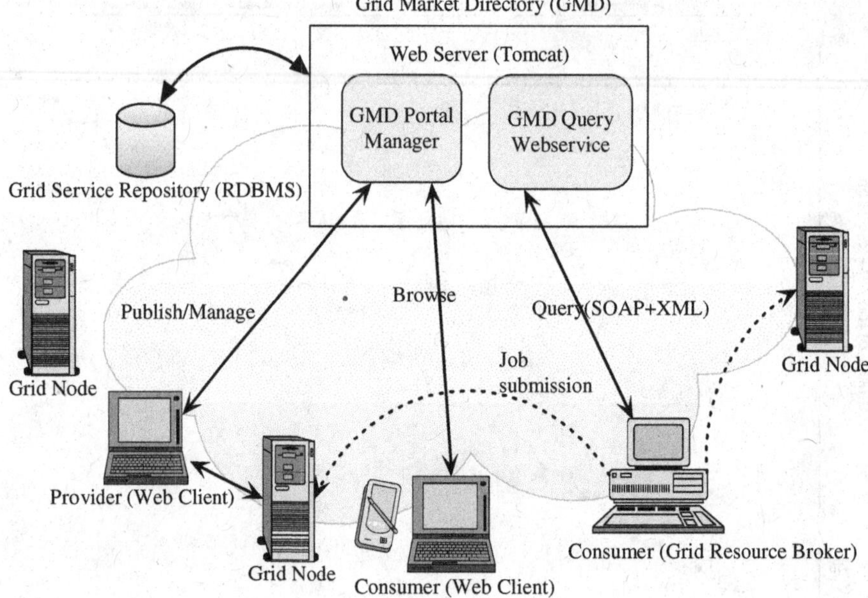

Figure 26.7 Grid Market Directory (GMD) architecture.

resource brokers to discover resources/services and their attributes (e.g., access price and usage constraints) that meet user QoS requirements. In this section, we describe a software framework called the *Grid Market Directory* (GMD) that supports these requirements.

The GMD [6] serves as a registry for high-level service publication and discovery in virtual organizations. It enables service providers to publish the services that they provide along with the costs associated with those services. Next, it allows consumers to browse the GMD for finding the services that meet their QoS requirements. The key components (refer to Fig. 26.7) of the GMD are

- *GMD portal manager* (GPM), which facilitates service publication, management, and browsing. It allows service providers and consumers to use a Web browser as a simple graphical client to access the GMD.
- *GMD query Web service* (GQWS), which enables applications (e.g., resource broker) to query the GMD to find a suitable service that meets the job execution requirements (e.g., budget).

Both components receive client requests through a HTTP server. Additionally, a database (GMD repository) is configured for recording the information of Grid services and service providers.

The GMD is built over standard Web service technologies such as Simple Object Access Protocol (SOAP) and XML. Therefore, it can be queried by programs irrespective of their operating environment (platform independent) and software libraries (language-independent). To provide with an additional layer of transparency, a client API has been provided to enable programs to query the GMD directly, so that the developers need not concern themselves with SOAP details. The Gridbus resource broker interacts with the GMD to discover the testbed resources and their high-level attributes such as access price.

26.5 GridBank

The early efforts in Grid computing and usage scenarios were mostly academic or exploratory in nature and did not enforce the Grid economy mechanisms. With the more recent move toward a multiinstitutional production-scale Grid infrastructure such as the TeraGrid facility [8], the need for Grid economy and accounting is being increasingly felt. In order to enable the sharing of resources across multiple administrative domains, the accounting infrastructure needs to support unambiguous recording of user identities against resource usage. In the context of the Gridbus project, an infrastructure providing such a service is called the *GridBank* [7].

GridBank is a secure Grid-wide accounting and (micro)payment handling system. It maintains the users' (consumers and providers) accounts and resource usage records in the database. It supports protocols that enable its interaction with the resource brokers of GSCs and the resource traders of GSPs. It has been envisioned to provide services primarily for enabling Grid economy. However, we also envision its usage in e-commerce applications. The GridBank services can be used in both cooperative and competitive distributed computing environments.

GridBank can be regarded as a Web service for Grid accounting and payment. GridBank uses SOAP over Globus toolkit's sockets, which are optimized for security. Clients use the same user proxy/component to access GridBank as they use to access other resources on the Grid. A *user proxy* is a certificate signed by the user that is later used to repeatedly authenticate the user to resources. This preserves the Grid's single-signin policy and avoids the need to repeatedly enter the user password. Using existing payment systems for the Grid would not satisfy this policy.

The interaction between the GridBank server and various components of Grid is shown in Figure 26.8. GSPs and GSCs first open an account with GridBank. Then, the user submits the application processing requirements along with the QoS requirements (e.g., deadline and budget) to the GRB. The GRB interacts with GSP's Grid Trading Service (GTS) or Grid Market Directory (GMD) to establish the cost of services and then selects a suitable GSP. It then submits user jobs to the GSP for processing along with details of its chargeable account ID in the GridBank or GridCheque purchased from the GridBank. The GSP provides the service by executing the user job, and the GSP's Grid resource meter measures the amount of resources consumed while processing the user job. The GSP's charging module contacts the GridBank with a request to charge the user account. It also passes information related to the reason for charging (resource usage record).

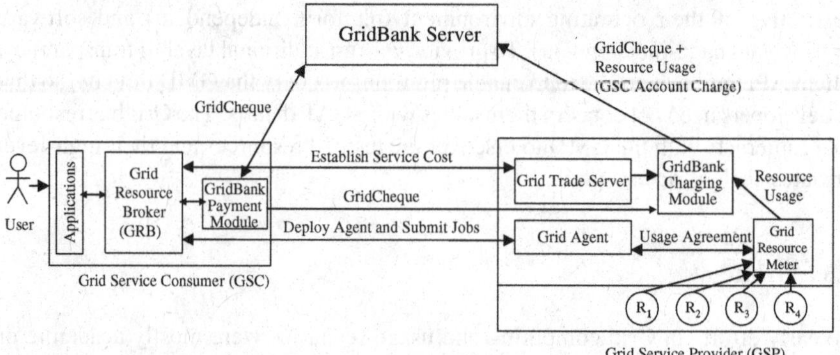

1) GRB negotiates service cost per time unit (e.g., $ per hour)
2) GridBank Payment Module requests GridCheque for the GSP whose service GSC wants to use. GridBank issues GridCheque provided GSC has sufficient funds.
3) GridBank payment module forwards GridCheque to GridBank Charging Module.
4) GRB deploys Grid Agent and submits jobs for execution on the resource.
5) Grid resource meter gathers resource usage records from all resources used to provide the service, optionally aggregates individual records into one resource usage record and forwards it to the GridBank charging module. Grid resource meter optionally performs usage check with grid agent.
6) GridBank charging module contacts GridBank and redeems all outstanding payments. It can do so in batches rather than after each transaction.

Figure 26.8 GridBank.

26.6 ANEKA: SLA-BASED RESOURCE PROVISIONING

This section describes how a service-oriented enterprise Grid platform called *Aneka* can implement SLA-based resource provisioning for an enterprise Grid using advanced reservations. An enterprise Grid [9] harnesses unused computing resources of desktop computers connected over an internal network or the Internet within an enterprise without affecting the productivity of their users. Hence, it increases the amount of computing resources available within an enterprise to accelerate application performance.

26.6.1 Design of Aneka

Aneka [10] is a .NET-based service-oriented platform for constructing enterprise Grids. It is designed to support multiple application models, persistence and security solutions, and communication protocols such that the preferred selection can be changed at any time without affecting an existing Aneka ecosystem. To create an enterprise Grid, the resource provider only needs to start an instance of the configurable Aneka container hosting required services on each selected desktop node. The purpose of the Aneka container is to initialize services, and to act as a single point for interaction with the rest of the enterprise Grid.

Figure 26.9 shows the design of the Aneka container on a single desktop node. To support scalability, the Aneka container is designed to be lightweight by providing the bare minimum functionality needed for an enterprise Grid node. It provides the base infrastructure that consists of services for persistence, security (authorization,

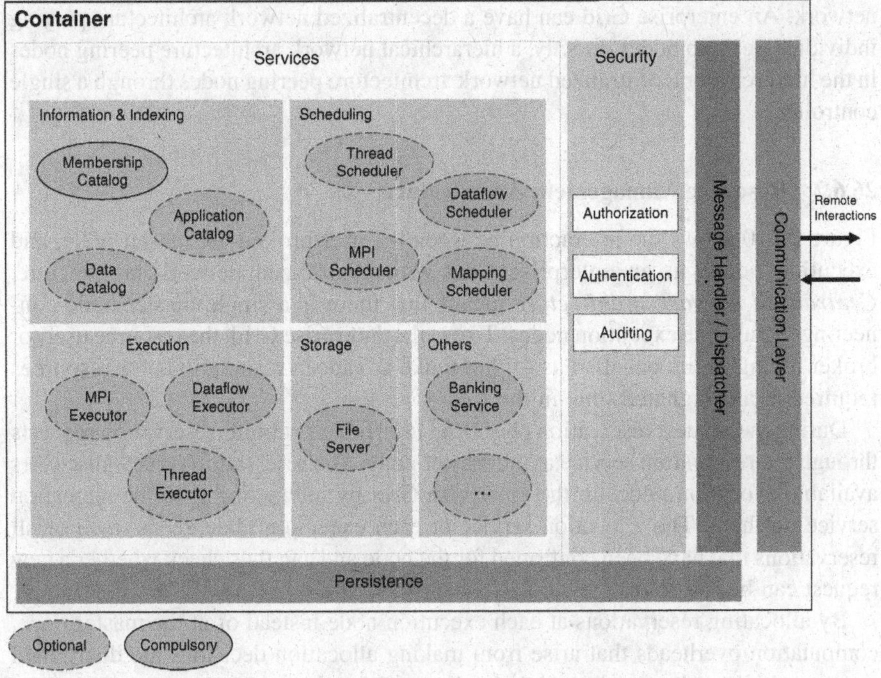

Figure 26.9 Design of Aneka container.

authentication, and auditing), and communication (message handling and dispatching). Every communication between Aneka services is treated as a message, handled and dispatched through the message handler/dispatcher that acts as a frontend controller. The Aneka container hosts a compulsory *membership catalog service*, which maintains the resource discovery indices (such as a .NET remoting address) of services currently active in the system.

The Aneka container can host any number of optional services that can be added to augment the capabilities of an enterprise Grid node. Examples of optional services are indexing, scheduling, execution, and storage services. This provides a single, flexible, and extensible framework for orchestrating different kinds of Grid application models.

To support reliability and flexibility, services are designed to be independent of each other in a container. A service can interact with other services only on the local node or other nodes through known interfaces. This means that a malfunctioning service will not affect other working services and/or the container. Therefore, the resource provider can seamlessly configure and manage existing services or introduce new ones into a container.

Aneka thus provides the flexibility for the resource provider to implement any network architecture for an enterprise Grid. The implemented network architecture depends on the interaction of services among enterprise Grid nodes since each Aneka container on a node can directly interact with other Aneka containers reachable on the network. An enterprise Grid can have a decentralized network architecture peering individual desktop nodes directly, a hierarchical network architecture peering nodes in the hierarchy, or a centralized network architecture peering nodes through a single controller.

26.6.2 Resource Management Architecture

Figure 26.10 shows the interaction between the user/broker, the master node, and execution nodes in an enterprise Grid with centralized network architecture. *Centralized network architecture* means that there is a single master node connecting to multiple execution nodes. To use the enterprise Grid, the resource user (or broker acting on its behalf) has to first make advanced reservations for resources required at a designated time in the future.

During the request reservation phase, the user/broker submits reservation requests through the reservation service at the master node. The reservation service discovers available execution nodes in the enterprise Grid by interacting with the allocation service on them. The allocation service at each execution node keeps track of all reservations that have been confirmed for the node and can thus check whether a new request can be satisfied.

By allocating reservations at each execution node instead of at the master node, computation overheads that arise from making allocation decisions are distributed across multiple nodes and thus minimized, as compared to overhead accumulation at a single master node. The reservation service then selects the required number of execution nodes and informs their allocation services to temporarily lock the reserved timeslots. After all the required reservations on the execution nodes have been temporarily locked, the reservation service feeds back the reservation outcome and its price (if successful) to the user/broker.

The user/broker may confirm or reject the reservations during the confirm reservation phase. The reservation service then notifies the allocation service of selected execution nodes to lock or remove temporarily locked timeslots accordingly.

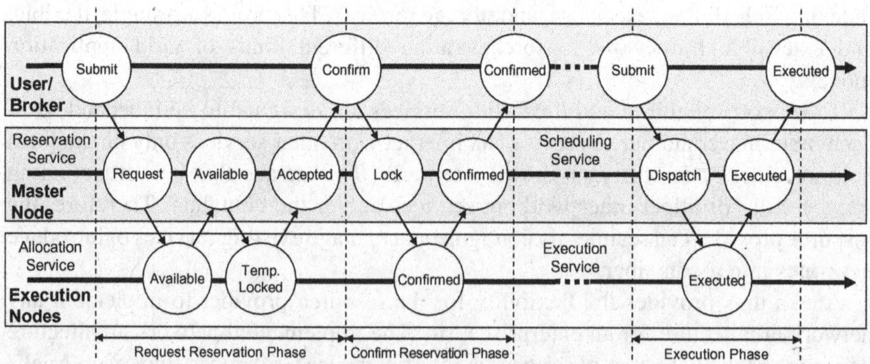

Figure 26.10 Interaction of enterprise Grid nodes.

We assume that a payment service is in place to ensure that the user/broker has sufficient funds and can successfully deduct the required payment before the reservation service proceeds with the final confirmation.

During the execution phase when the reserved time arrives, the user/broker submits applications to be executed to the scheduling service at the master node. The scheduling service determines whether any of the reserved execution nodes are available before dispatching applications to them for execution; otherwise applications are queued to wait for the next available reserved execution nodes. The execution service at each execution node starts executing an application after receiving it from the scheduling service and updates the scheduling service of changes in execution status. Hence, the scheduling service can monitor executions for an application and notify the user/broker on completion.

26.6.3 Allocating Advanced Reservations

Figure 26.11 shows that the process of allocating advanced reservations occurs in two levels: the allocation service at each execution node and the reservation service at the master node. Both services are designed to support pluggable policies so that the resource provider has the flexibility to easily customize and replace existing policies for different levels and/or nodes without interfering with the overall resource management architecture.

The allocation service determines how to schedule a new reservation at the execution node. For simplicity, the allocation service at each execution node can

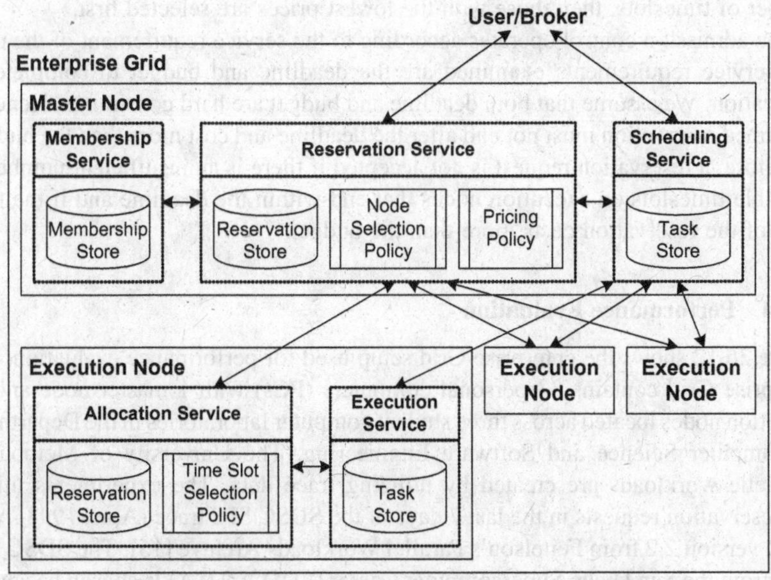

Figure 26.11 Interaction of services in enterprise Grid.

implement the same timeslot selection policy. The allocation service allocates the requested timeslot if the slot is available. Otherwise, it assigns the next available timeslot after the requested start time that can meet the required duration.

The reservation service performs node selection by choosing the required number of available timeslots from execution nodes and administers admission control by accepting or rejecting a reservation request. It also calculates the price for a confirmed reservation on the basis of the implemented pricing policy. Various pricing policies may be implemented. Available timeslots are selected with respect to the application requirement of the user.

The application requirement considered is the task parallelism to execute an application. A sequential application has a single task and thus needs a single processor to run, while a parallel application needs a required number of processors to concurrently run at the same time.

For a sequential application, the selected time slots need not have the same start and end times. Hence, available timeslots with the lowest prices are selected first. If there are multiple available timeslots with the same price, then those with the earliest start time are selected first. This ensures that the cheapest requested timeslot is allocated first if it is available. Selecting available timeslots with the lowest prices first is fair and realistic. In reality, reservations that are confirmed earlier enjoy the privilege of cheaper prices, as compared to reservation requests that arrive later.

However, for a parallel application, all the selected timeslots must have the same start and end times. Again, the earliest timeslots (with the same start and end times) are allocated first to ensure that the requested time slot is allocated first if available. If there are more available timeslots (with the same start and end times) than the required number of timeslots, then those with the lowest prices are selected first.

The admission control operates according to the service requirement of the user. The service requirements examined are the deadline and budget to complete an application. We assume that both deadline and budget are hard constraints. Hence, a confirmed reservation must not end after the deadline and cost more than the budget. Therefore, a reservation request is not accepted if there is an insufficient number of available timeslots on execution nodes that end within the deadline and if the total price of the reservation costs more than the budget.

26.6.4 Performance Evaluation

Figure 26.12 shows the enterprise Grid setup used for performance evaluation. The enterprise Grid contains 33 personal computers (PCs) with 1 master node and 32 execution nodes located across three student computer laboratories in the Department of Computer Science and Software Engineering, The University of Melbourne. Synthetic workloads are created by utilizing trace data. The experiments utilize 238 reservation requests in the last 7 days of the SDSC SP2 trace (April 1998–April 2000) version 2.2 from Feitelson's Parallel Workloads Archive [15]. The SDSC SP2 trace from the San Diego Supercomputer Center (SDSC) (USA) is chosen because it

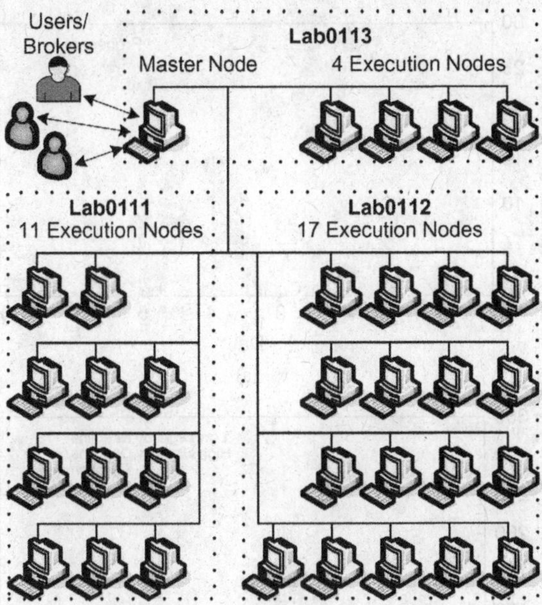

Figure 26.12 Configuration of Aneka enterprise Grid.

has the highest resource utilization (83.2%) among available traces to ideally model a heavy-workload scenario.

The trace only provides the interarrival times of reservation requests, the number of processors to be reserved as shown in Figure 26.13a (downscaled from a maximum of 128 nodes in the trace to a maximum of 32 nodes), and the duration to be reserved as shown in Figure 26.13b. However, service requirements are not available from this trace. Hence, we adopt a similar methodology [16] to synthetically assign service requirements through two request classes: (1) low-urgency and (2) high-urgency. Figures 26.13b and 26.13c show the synthetic values of deadline and budget for the 238 requests, respectively.

A reservation request i in the *low-urgency* class has a deadline of high $\text{deadline}_i/\text{duration}_i$ value and budget of low $\text{budget}_i/f(\text{duration}_i)$ value. $f(\text{duration}_i)$ is a function representing the minimum budget required on the basis of duration_i. Conversely, each request in the *high-urgency* class has a deadline of low $\text{deadline}_i/\text{duration}_i$ value and budget of high $\text{budget}_i/f(\text{duration}_i)$ value. This is realistic since a user who submits a more urgent request to be met within a shorter deadline offers a higher budget for the short notice. Values are normally distributed within each of the deadline and budget parameters.

We evaluate the performance of seven pricing mechanisms as listed in Table 26.4 for high-urgency reservation requests (with short deadline and high budget) from sequential applications (requiring one processor to execute) in the enterprise Grid. The enterprise Grid charges users only for utilizing the computing

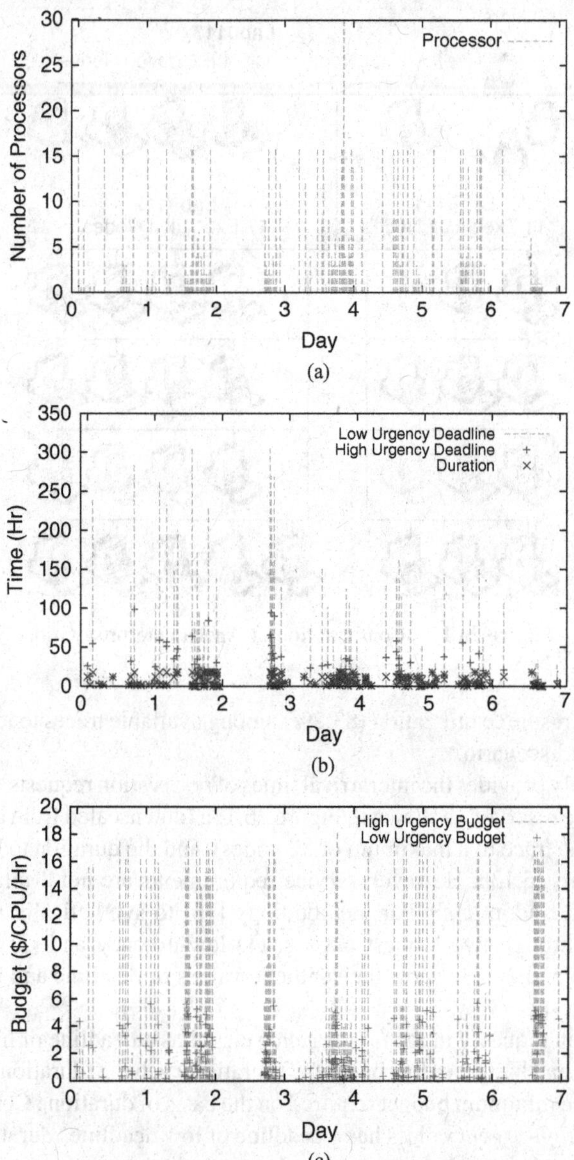

Figure 26.13 Last 7 days of SDSC SP2 trace with 238 requests: (a) number of processors (from trace); (b) duration (from trace) and deadline (synthetic); (c) budget (synthetic).

resource type on the basis of usage per processor (CPU) per hour (h). Thus, users are not charged for using other resource types such as memory, storage, and bandwidth. In addition, every user/broker can definitely accept another reservation timeslot proposed by the enterprise Grid if the requested one is not possible,

TABLE 26.4 Pricing Mechanisms

Name	Configured Pricing Parameters
FixedMax	\$3/(CPU·h)
FixedMin	\$1/(CPU·h)
FixedTimeMax	\$1/(CPU·h) (12 a.m.–12 p.m.) \$3/(CPU·h) (12 p.m.–12 a.m.)
FixedTimeMin	\$1/(CPU·h) (12 a.m.–12 p.m.) \$2/(CPU·h) (12 p.m.–12 a.m.)
Libra + \$Max	\$1/(CPU·h) ($PBase_j$), $\alpha = 1$, $\beta = 3$
Libra + \$Min	\$1/(CPU·h) ($PBase_j$), $\alpha = 1$, $\beta = 1$
Libra + \$Auto	Same as Libra + \$Min

provided that the proposed timeslot still satisfies both application and service requirements of the user.

The seven pricing mechanisms listed in Table 26.4 represent three basic types of pricing mechanism: (1) Fixed, (2) FixedTime, and (3) Libra + \$. Table 26.4 lists the maximum and minimum types of each pricing mechanism, which are configured accordingly to highlight the performance range of the pricing mechanism. The Fixed mechanism charges a fixed price at all times. The FixedTime mechanism charges a fixed price for different time periods of resource usage where a lower price is charged for off-peak (12 a.m.–12 p.m.) and a higher price for peak (12 p.m.–12 a.m.).

Libra + \$ [17] uses a more fine-grained pricing function that satisfies four essential requirements for pricing of resources to prevent workload overload: (1) flexibility, (2) fairness, (3) being dynamic, and (4) being adaptive. The price P_{ij} for per unit of resource utilized by reservation request *i* at compute node *j* is computed as $P_{ij} = (\alpha * PBase_j) + (\beta * PUtil_{ij})$. The base price $PBase_j$ is a static pricing component for utilizing a resource at node \$j\$ that can be used by the resource provider to charge the minimum price so as to recover the operational cost. The utilization price $PUtil_{ij}$ is a dynamic pricing component that is computed as a factor of $PBase_j$ based on the utilization of the resource at node *j* for the required deadline of request *i*: $PUtil_{ij} = RESMax_j / RESFree_{ij} * PBase_j$. $RESMax_j$ and $RESFree_{ij}$ are the maximum units and remaining free units of the resource at node *j* for the deadline duration of request *i*, respectively. Thus, $RESFree_{ij}$ has been deducted units of resource committed for other confirmed reservations and request *i* for its deadline duration.

The factors α and β for the static and dynamic components of Libra + \$, respectively, provides the flexibility for the resource provider to easily configure and modify the weightage of the static and dynamic components on the overall price P_{ij}. Libra + \$ is fair since requests are priced according to the amount of different resources utilized. It is also dynamic because the overall price of a request varies depending on the availability of resources for the required deadline. Finally, it is adaptive as the overall price is adjusted depending on the current supply and demand of resources to either encourage or discourage request submission.

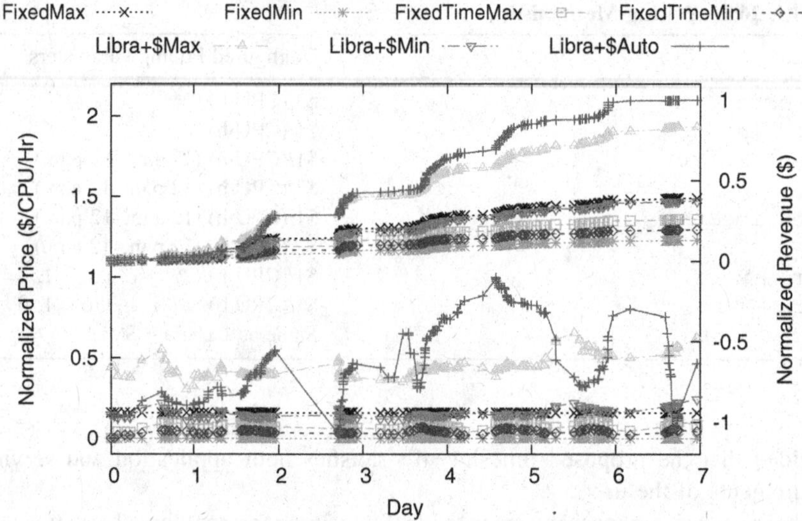

Figure 26.14 Price/revenue ratio of high-urgency requests.

However, these three mechanisms rely on static pricing parameters that are difficult to be accurately derived by the resource provider to produce the best performance where necessary. Hence, we propose `Libra + $Auto`, an autonomic `Libra + $` that automatically adjusts β per the availability of compute nodes. `Libra + $Auto` thus considers the pricing of resources across nodes, unlike `Libra + $`, which considers pricing of resources only at each node j via P_{ij}.

Figure 26.14 shows the performance results for the seven pricing mechanisms in an enterprise Grid for high-urgency requests from sequential applications over a 7-day time period that have been normalized to produce standardized values within the range of 0–1 for easier comparison. The performance metrics being measured are the price for a confirmed reservation [in \$/(CPU·h)] and the accumulated revenue for confirmed reservations (in \$). The revenue of a confirmed reservation is calculated using the assigned price (depending on the specific pricing mechanism) and reserved duration at each reserved node for all its reserved nodes. Then, the price of a confirmed reservation can be computed to reflect the average price across all its reserved nodes.

Of the four fixed pricing mechanisms listed in Table 26.4, `FixedMax` provides the highest revenue (maximum bound), followed by `FixedTimeMax`, `FixedTimeMin`, and `FixedMin` with the lowest revenue (minimum bound). Nevertheless, `FixedTime` mechanisms is easier to derive and more reliable than `Fixed` mechanisms since it supports a range of prices across various time periods of resource usage. However, all four mechanisms do not consider service requirements of users such as deadline and budget.

On the other hand, `Libra + $` charges a lower price for a request with longer deadline as an incentive to encourage users to submit requests with longer deadlines that are more likely to be accommodated than shorter deadlines. For a request with short deadline, `Libra + $Max` and `Libra + $Min` charge a higher price relative to their β in Table 26.4. `Libra + $Max` provides higher revenue than `Libra + $Min` because of a higher value of β.

Both `Libra + $Auto` and `Libra + $Max` are able to provide a significantly higher revenue than other pricing mechanisms through higher prices for shorter deadlines. Figure 26.14 shows that `Libra + $Auto` continues increasing prices to higher than that of `Libra + $Max` and other pricing mechanisms when demand is high such as during the latter half of days 1, 2, 3, and 5. But when demand is low, such as during the early half of days 2, 3, 5, and 6, `Libra + $Auto` continues to reduce prices to lower than that of `Libra + $Max` to accept requests that are not willing to pay more. Hence, `Libra + $Auto` is able to exploit budget limits to achieve the highest revenue by automatically adjusting to a higher β to increase prices when the availability of nodes is low and to a lower β to reduce prices when there are more unused nodes that will otherwise be wasted.

26.7 GRID-FEDERATION

As enterprise Grids grow to include a large number of resources (on the order of thousands), the centralized model for managing the resource set does not prove to be efficient as it requires the manager to coordinate a large number of components and handle a large number of messages on its own. This means that the central coordinator does not scale well, lacks fault tolerance, and warrants expensive server hardware infrastructure. Since participants in a Grid can join and leave in a dynamic fashion, it is also an impossible task to manage such a network centrally. Therefore, there is a need for an efficient decentralized solution that can gracefully adapt and scale to the changing conditions. This can be achieved by partitioning the resource set into smaller installations that are then federated to create a single, cooperative, distributed resource-sharing environment [18–20]. In a federated organization, an enterprise domain can deal efficiently with bursty resource requests through policy-based or opportunistic leasing of resources from the resource pool. This basically relieves an enterprise domain from the responsibilities of maintaining and administering different kinds of resources and expertise within a single domain. This section postulates how a Grid-Federation can be engineered, including its primary components and how existing Gridbus middleware can be used to realize such an environment.

26.7.1 Characteristics of a Grid-Federation

The unique challenges in efficiently managing a federated Grid computing environment include the following characteristics:

- *Distributed ownership*—every participant makes decisions independently.
- *Open and dynamic*—the participants can leave and join the system at will.
- *Self-interested*—each participant has distinct stakeholdings with different aims and objective functions.

- *Large-scale*—composed of distributed participants (e.g., services, applications, users, providers) who combine together to form a massive environment.
- *Resource contention*—depending on resource demand pattern and lack of cooperation among distributed users, a particular set of resources can be swamped with excessive workload, which significantly reduces the amount of useful utility that the system delivers.

We perceive that by designing appropriate scalable protocols for cooperation among users, allowing users to express preferences for resources, and letting providers decide their allocation policies, it is possible to overcome the problem of resource contention, distributed ownership, large scale, and dynamism in a large-scale federated Grid system. Therefore, our design of a Grid-Federation focuses on two important aspects: a distributed resource discovery system [21,25] and a market-based resource allocation system [26]. Grid-Federation allows cooperative sharing of topologically and administratively distributed Grid resources. To enable policy-based transparent resource sharing between resource domains, Grid-Federation instantiates a new RMS, called *Grid-Federation agent* (GFA). A GFA exports a resource site to the federation and is responsible for undertaking activities related to resource sharing, selection, and reporting. GFAs in the system interconnect using a *distributed hash table* (DHT) overlay [22–24], which makes the system scalable and decentralized. The Grid-Federation considers computational economy driven SLA negotiation protocol for enforcing cooperation and establishing accountability among the distributed participants (e.g., providers, users, schedulers) in the system.

We are realizing the Grid-Federation resource sharing model within the Aneka system by implementing a new software service, called *Aneka Coordinator*. The Aneka Coordinator basically implements the resource management functionalities and resource discovery protocol specifications defined by the GFA service. An *Aneka-Federation* integrates numerous small-scale Aneka desktop Grid services and resources that are distributed over multiple control and administrative domains as part of a single coordinated resource leasing abstraction. The software design of the Aneka-Federation system decouples the fundamental decentralized interaction of participants from the resource allocation policies and the details of managing a specific Aneka service.

26.7.2 Resource Discovery

The distributed resource discovery service in the Grid-Federation allows GFAs to efficiently search for available resources that match the user's expressed QoS parameters. The resource discovery service [25] organizes the information by maintaining a logical multidimensional publish/subscribe index over a DHT overlay [22–24] of GFAs (refer to Fig. 26.15). In general, a GFA service undertakes two basic types of queries [21]: (1) a *resource lookup query* (RLQ)—a query issued by a GFA service to locate resources matching the user's application QoS requirement and (2) a *resource update query* (RUQ), which is an update query sent to a resource discovery by a GFA (on behalf of the Grid site owner) about the underlying resource

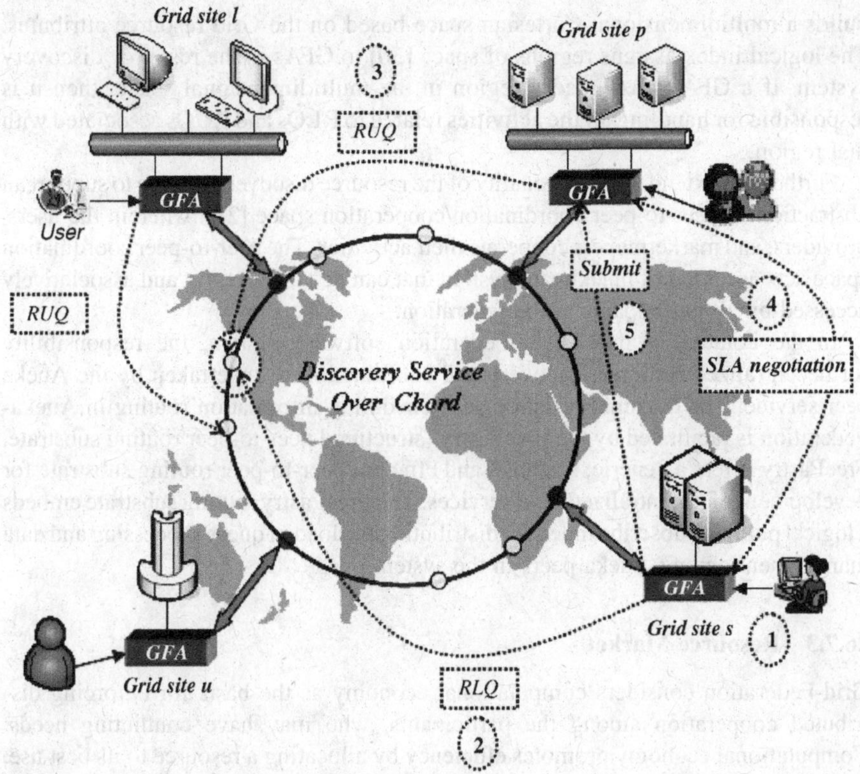

Figure 26.15 Grid-Federation – GFAs and Grid sites over Chord overlay. Dark dots indicate GFA services that are currently part of the Chord-based Grid network. Light dots represent the RUQ and RLQ objects posted by GFAs in the system.

conditions. Since a Grid resource is identified by more than one attribute, a RLQ or RUQ is always multidimensional.

Further, both these queries can specify different kinds of constraints on the attribute values depending on whether the value is a point or range query. A *point search query* specifies a fixed value for each resource attribute [e.g., `cpu_type` = `intel`, `processor_count` = `50`, `price` = `7` (Grid dollars/h)]. On the other hand, a range search query specifies a range of values for attributes (`e.g. cput_-type` = `intel` or `sparc`, `50` < `processor_count` < `100`, `5` < `price` < `10`). Currently, the resource discovery allows users to search for resources based on both point- and range-specifying RLQs. The providers can update the status (e.g, resource utilization, price, queue size, completion rate) with the service through point RUQs.

Because resources are dynamic, and can exhibit changing temporal characteristics, the providers can periodically update their status with the resource discovery service through RUQs. The mapping of RLQ and RUQ to the DHT-based overlay is accomplished through a multidimensional publish/subscribe index. The index builds a multidimensional Cartesian space based on the Grid resource attributes. The logical index assigns regions of space [30] to GFAs in the resource discovery system. If a GFA is assigned a region in the multidimensional space, then it is responsible for handling all the activities related to RLQs and RUQs associated with that region.

Further, we extend the functionality of the resource discovery service to support an abstraction of peer-to-peer coordination/cooperation space [28], wherein the users, providers, and marketmakers cooperate their activities. The peer-to-peer coordination space acts as a kind of blackboard system that can be concurrently and associatively accessed by all participants in the federation.

In the context of the Aneka-Federation software system, the responsibility for decentralized resource discovery and coordination is undertaken by the Aneka peer service. The dynamic resource and scheduling information routing in Aneka-Federation is facilitated by the FreePastry[1] structured peer-to-peer routing substrate. FreePastry offers a generic, scalable, and efficient peer-to-peer routing substrate for development of decentralized Grid services. The FreePastry routing substrate embeds a logical publish/subscribe index for distributing the load of query processing and data management among Aneka peers in the system.

26.7.3 Resource Market

Grid-Federation considers computational economy as the basis for enforcing distributed cooperation among the participants, who may have conflicting needs. Computational economy promotes efficiency by allocating a resource to its best use, giving incentives to resource providers for contributing their resources to the federation, and promoting further long-term investments in new hardware and software infrastructure by resource providers as a result of the economic gains that they receive from the system.

Grid-Federation applies a decentralized commodity market model for efficiently managing the resources and driving the QoS-based scheduling of applications. In the commodity market model, every resource has a price, which is based on the demand, supply, and value. A resource provider charges a unit of virtual or real currency, called *access cost*, to the federation users for letting them use his/her resources. All federation users express how much they are willing to pay, called a *budget*, and required response time, called a *deadline*, on a per-job basis. The providers and users maintain their virtual or real credits with accounting systems such as GridBank. The Grid-Federation scheduling method considers the following optimizations with respect to the economic efficiency of the system: (1) resource provider's objective function (e.g., incentive) and (2) user's perceived QoS constraints (e.g., budget and deadline).

Realizing a true cooperative resource-sharing mechanism between dynamic and distributed participants warrants robust protocols for coordination and negotiations. In decentralized and distributed federated Grid environments, these coordination

[1]See http://freepastry.rice.edu/FreePastry/.

and negotiation protocols can be realized through dynamic resource information exchanges between Grid brokers and site-specific resource managers (such as PBS, Alchemi, and SGE). Grid-Federation utilizes one such SLA-based coordination and negotiation protocol [27], which includes the exchange of QoS enquiry and QoS guarantee messages between GFAs. These QoS constraints include the job response time and budget spent. Inherently, the SLA is the guarantee given by a resource provider to the remote site job scheduler (such as GFA and resource broker) for completing the job within the specified deadline and agreed-on budget.

A SLA-based job scheduling approach has several significant advantages: (1) promotes cooperation among participants; (2) it inhibits schedulers from swamping a particular set of resources; (3) once a SLA is finalized, users are certain that agreed QoS shall be delivered by the system; (4) job queuing and processing delay are significantly reduced, thus leading to enhanced QoS; and (5) it gives every site in the system enhanced autonomy and control over local resource allocation decisions.

Our SLA model considers a collection of resource domains in the Grid-Federation as a contract-net. As jobs arrive, GFAs undertake one-to-one contract negotiation with the other GFAs that match the resource configuration requirements of the submitted job. Each GFA becomes either a manager or a contractor. The GFA to which a user submits a job for processing is referred to as the *manager GFA* (*scheduler GFA*). The manager GFA is responsible for successfully scheduling the job in the federated contract-net. The GFA, which accepts the job from the manager GFA and overlooks its execution, is referred to as the *contractor GFA* (*allocator GFA*). Individual GFAs are assigned these roles in advance. The role may change dynamically over time as per the resource management requirement, namely, scheduling or allocation. A GFA alternates between these two roles or adheres to both over the processes of scheduling and resource allocation.

The general Grid-Federation scheduling and resource allocation technique operates as follows. In Figure 26.15, a user who has membership to Grid site *s* submits her application to its local GFA (see step 1 in Fig. 26.15). Following this, the GFA at site *s* adheres to the role of manager GFA and submits a RLQ object to the Chord-based resource discovery service (refer to step 2 in Fig. 26.15). Consequently, the GFA at site *p* reports or updates its resource availability status by sending a RUQ object to the discovery service (shown as step 3 in Fig. 26.15). As the posted RUQ object matches the resource configuration currently searched by GFA at site *s*, the discovery service notifies the GFA accordingly.

Following this, the GFA at site *s* undertakes one-to-one SLA negotiation (refer to step 4 in Fig. 26.15) with the GFA at site *p* (contractor GFA) about possible allocation of its job. If site *p* has too much load and cannot complete the job within the requested SLA constraints (deadline), then a SLA fail message is sent back to the GFA at site *s*. In this case, the GFA at site *s* waits for future match notifications. Alternatively, if GFA at site *p* agrees to accept the requested SLA, then the manager GFA goes ahead and deploys its job at site *p* (shown as step 5 in Fig. 26.15). The one-to-one SLA-based negotiation protocol guarantees that (1) no resource in the federation would be swamped with excessive load and (2) users obtain an acceptable or requested level of QoS delivered for their jobs.

26.7.4 Performance Evaluation

We present an evaluation of the Grid-Federation system through a set of simulated experiments designed to test the performance of resource discovery and resource market services with regards to efficiency, scalability, and usability. We realize the simulation infrastructure by combining two discrete-event simulators: GridSim [31] and PlanetSim [32]. GridSim offers a concrete base framework for simulation of different kinds of heterogeneous resources, services, and application types. On the other hand, PlanetSim is an event-based overlay network simulator that supports routing of messages using well-known DHT methods, including Chord and Symphony. Next, we describe the simulation environment setup, including peer-to-peer network configuration, resource configuration, and workload.

The experiments run a Chord overlay with a 32-bit configuration, specifically, the number of bits utilized to generate GFA and key (RLQ and RUQ object) IDs. The Grid-Federation network includes 100 Grid resource domains. The Grid network processes 500 messages per second and can queue up to 10,000 messages at any given instance of time. GFAs inject RLQ and RUQ objects based on the exponential interarrival time distribution. The value for RLQ interarrival delay is distributed over [60,600] in steps of 120 s. GFAs update their host Grid site status after a fixed interval of time. In this study, we configure the RUQ interarrival delay to be 120 and 140 s.

Both RLQ and RUQ objects represent a Grid resource in a five-dimensional attribute space. These attribute dimensions include the number of processors, their speed, their architecture, operating system type, and resource access cost (price). The distributions for these resource dimensions are obtained from the Top 500 supercomputer list.[2] We assume that the resource access cost does not change during the course of simulation. Resource owners decide the access cost on the basis of a linear function whose slope is determined by the access cost and processing speed of the fastest resource in the federation. In other words, every resource owner charges a cost relative to the one offered by the most efficient resource in the system. The fastest Grid owner in the federation charges 6.3 Grid dollars/per hour for providing space for shared access to his/her resources. We generate the workload distributions across GFAs according to the model given by Lublin and Feitelson [29]. The processor count for a resource is fed to the workload model based on the resource configuration obtained from the Top 500 list.

26.7.5 Results and Discussion

To measure the Grid-Federation system performance, we use metrics such as resource discovery delay, response time on per-job basis, and total incentive earned by providers as a result of executing local and remote jobs of the federation users. The response time for a job summarizes the latencies for (1) a RLQ object to be mapped to the appropriate peer in the network per the distributed indexing logic, (2) waiting time until a RLQ object is hit by a RUQ object, (3) the SLA negotiation delay between the manager and contractor GFA, and (4) the actual execution time on the remote site machine.

[2]See http://www.top500.org/.

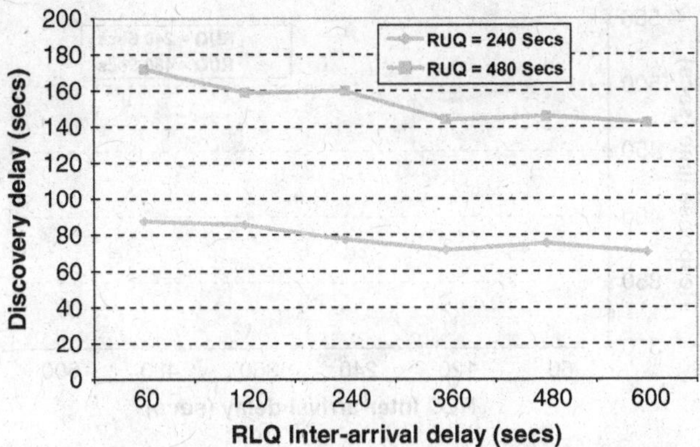

Figure 26.16 Average RLQ interarrival delay (secs) versus discovery delay (in seconds).

Figure 26.16 depicts the results of average resource discovery delay in seconds with increasing mean RLQ interarrival delay for different resource status update intervals (RUQ delay). The results show that at a higher RUQ update interval, with a large number of competing requests (high RLQ rate), the users have longer waiting time with regard to discovering resources that can satisfy their QoS metrics. The main reason behind this system behavior is that the RLQ objects for jobs have to wait for a longer time before they are hit by RUQ objects, because of the large number of competing requests in the system. Specifically, the distributed RLQ–RUQ match procedure also accounts for the fact that the subsequent allocation of jobs to resources should not lead to contention problems. Hence, with a large number of competing requests and infrequent resource update events, jobs are expected to suffer longer delay.

In Figure 26.17, we show the total incentive (in Grid dollars) earned by all providers in the federation. The providers earned almost similar incentive with varying rates of RLQ and RUQ objects, which is expected as we consider a static

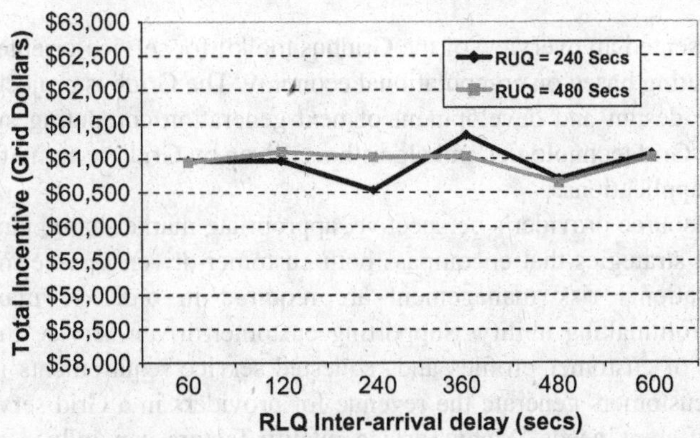

Figure 26.17 Average RLQ interarrival delay (in seconds) versus total incentive (in Grid dollars).

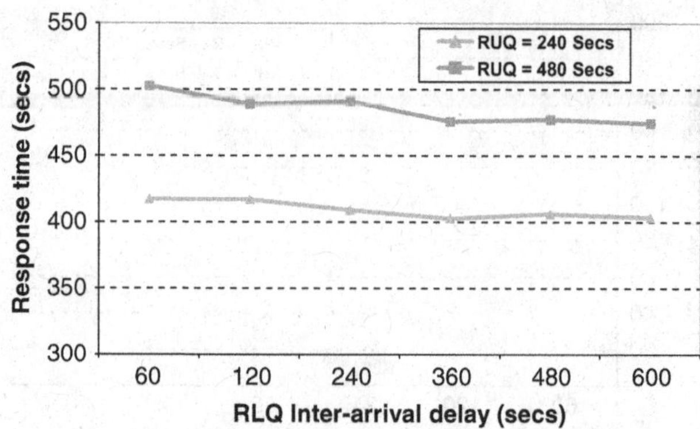

Figure 26.18 Average RLQ interarrival delay (in seconds) versus response time (in seconds).

resource access cost for the entire simulation period. However, the providers can dynamically vary their resource access cost with respect to the supply and demand in the federation. We intend to investigate this aspect of the system as part of our future work.

Figure 26.18 shows the average response time utility derived for federation users according to the resources they request and receive. The result shows that growth in the response time function for a user's job is similar to that for the resource discovery delay functions with varying RLQ and RUQ rates. For fixed RUQ rate, the result shows that at high RLQ interarrival delay, the jobs in the system face comparatively low resource discovery delay.

The main argument for this behavior is that under these settings, the RLQ objects encounter less network traffic and competing requests, which lead to an overall decrease in the discovery delay across the system.

26.8 CONCLUSION AND FUTURE DIRECTIONS

We have presented an overview of the Gridbus toolkit for service-oriented Grid and utility computing based on computational economy. The Gridbus project is actively pursuing the design and development of next-generation computing systems and fundamental Grid technologies and algorithms driven by Grid economy for data and utility Grid applications.

From a resource provider's perspective, appropriate market-based Grid resource management strategies that encompass both customer-driven service management and computational risk management are required in order to maximize the provider's profitmaking ability. Supporting customer-driven service management on the basis of customer profiles and requested service requirements is a critical issue since customers generate the revenue for providers in a Grid service market and have different needs. Many service quality factors can influence customer satisfaction, such as providing personalized attention to customers and encouraging trust and confidence in customers. Therefore, a detailed understanding of all possible customer characteristics is essential to address customer-driven service management issues. In addition, defining computational risk management tactics for the execution of applications with regard to service requirements and customer needs is essential. Various elements of Grid resource management can be perceived as risks, and hence risk management techniques can be adopted. However, the entire risk management process consists of many steps and must be studied thoroughly so as to fully apply its effectiveness in managing risks. The risk management process consists of the following steps: (1) establish the context; (2) identify the risks involved; (3) assess each of the identified risks; (4) identify techniques to manage each risk; and (5) finally, create, implement, and review the risk management plan. In the future, we expect to implement such a process into Aneka's resource management system so that it becomes more capable as a resource provisioning system.

Within a market-oriented Grid, consumers have to locate providers that can satisfy the application requirements within their budget constraints. They may prefer to employ resource brokers that are optimized toward satisfying a particular set of requirements (e.g., a time-constrained workflow execution) or a particular set of constraints (e.g., the most cost-effective workflow executions). In such cases, brokers have to predict capacity requirements in advance and form agreements with resource providers accordingly. The nature and form of Grid markets are still evolving, and researchers are experimenting with new mechanisms and protocols. Brokers may have to participate in different markets with different interaction protocols. Brokers may also eventually have their own utility functions depending on which they will accept user requests. Therefore, it can be said that future Grid brokers will require capabilities for negotiation and decisionmaking that are far beyond what today's brokers can support. We expect to provide such capabilities in the Gridbus broker, thereby enhancing it to function as an equal participant in future Grid markets. To this end, we will also apply results from research carried out in the intelligent agent community for these areas.

Markets strive for efficiency; therefore, it is imperative to have a communication bus that is able to disseminate information rapidly without causing message overload. It would be an interesting research topic to design and realize a completely decentralized auction mechanism, that has the potential to deliver a scalable market platform for dynamic interaction and negotiation among Grid participants. Such a mechanism would use existing research performed on decentralization in peer-to-peer networks. The auctioneers (resource owners) can advertise their items, auction types, and pricing information, while the buyers (resource brokers) can subscribe for the auctioned items. A resource provider can choose to hold the auctions locally or may distribute the work to a Grid marketmaker, which is also part of the peer-to-peer market system. We expect to extend our current work on peer-to-peer Grid-Federation to satisfy these requirements.

Composing applications for market-based Grids is radically different; therefore, we aim to investigate and develop algorithms, software framework, and middleware infrastructure to assist developers in exploiting the potential of such Grids. In particular, we intend to develop Grid middleware services that have the abilities to (1) coordinate resource usage across the system on the basis of market protocols (self-configuring); (2) interconnect participants (marketmakers, auctioneers, users) using on a decentralized overlay, such as a peer-to-peer network (self-organizing); (3) scale gracefully to a large number of participants; (4) make applications adapt to dynamic market, resource, and network conditions (self-managing applications); (5) take into account the application scheduling and resource allocation policy (pricing, supply, and demand) heterogeneity (self-optimizing); and (6) gracefully and dynamically adapt to the failure of resources and network conditions (self-healing). In this manner, applications and systems are expected to be autonomic, that is, run with minimal intervention from humans.

The Gridbus project is continuously enhancing and building on the various Grid technologies presented in this chapter. The project is also actively investigating and developing new Grid technologies such as the Grid Exchange, which enable the creation of a Stock Exchange–like Grid computing environment. For detailed and up-to-date information on Gridbus technologies and new initiatives, please visit the project Website: http://www.gridbus.org.

ACKNOWLEDGMENTS

This project was partially funded by Australian Research Council (ARC) and the Department of Innovation, Industry, Science and Research (DIISR) under Discovery Project and International Science Linkage grants, respectively. We would like to thank all members of the Gridbus project for their contributions. This chapter is partially derived from earlier publications [3–7,25,26].

REFERENCES

1. A. Rubinstein, Perfect equilibrium in a bargaining model, *Econometrica* **50**(1): 97–109 (1982).
2. R. Buyya, D. Abramson, and J. Giddy, A case for economy Grid architecture for service-oriented Grid computing, *Proc. 10th Heterogeneous Computing Workshop (HCW 2001): 15th International Parallel and Distributed Processing Symp. (IPDPS 2001)*, San Francisco, CA, April 23–27, 2001.
3. R. Buyya, D. Abramson, and S. Venugopal, The Grid economy, *Proceedings of the IEEE* **93**(3): 698–714 (2005).
4. B. Allcock, J. Bester, J. Bresnahan, A. Chervenak, I. Foster, C. Kesselman, S. Meder, V. Nefedova, D. Quesnel, and S. Tuecke, Data management and transfer in high-performance computational grid environments, *Parallel Computing* **28**(5): 749–771 (2002).
5. S. Venugopal, R. Buyya, and L. Winton, A Grid service broker for scheduling e-science applications on global data Grids, *Concurrency and Computation: Practice and Experience* **18**(6): 685–699 (2006).

6. J. Yu, S. Venugopal, and R. Buyya, A market-oriented Grid directory service for publication and discovery of Grid service providers and their services, *The Journal of Supercomputing* **36**(1): 17–31 (2006).

7. A. Barmouta and R. Buyya, GridBank: A Grid accounting services architecture (GASA) for distributed systems sharing and integration, *Proc. 3rd Workshop on Internet Computing and E-Commerce (ICEC 2003), 17th International Parallel and Distributed Processing Symp. (IPDPS 2003)*, Nice, France, April 22–26, 2003.

8. D. A. Reed, Grids, the TeraGrid, and beyond, *Computer* **36**(1): 62–68 (2003).

9. A. Chien, B. Calder, S. Elbert, and K. Bhatia, Entropia: Architecture and performance of an enterprise desktop Grid system, *Journal of Parallel and Distributed Computing* **63**(5): 597–610 (2003).

10. X. Chu, K. Nadiminti, C. Jin, S. Venugopal, and R. Buyya, Aneka: Next-generation enterprise Grid platform for e-science and e-business applications, *Proc. 3th IEEE International Conf. e-Science and Grid Computing (e-Science 2007)*, Bangalore, India, Dec. 10–13, 2007.

11. I. Foster, C. Kesselman, and S. Tuecke, The anatomy of the Grid: Enabling scalable virtual organizations, *International Journal of High-Performance Computing Applications* **15**(3): 200–222 (2001).

12. S. Fitzgerald, I. Foster, C. Kesselman, G. von Laszewski, W. Smith, and S. Tuecke, A directory service for configuring high-performance distributed computations, *Proc. 6th IEEE Symp. High Performance Distributed Computing (HPDC 1997)*, Portland, OR, Aug. 5–8, 1997.

13. L. Camarinha-Matos and H. Afsarmanesh, eds., *Infrastructures for Virtual Enterprises: Networking Industrial Enterprises*, Kluwer Academic Press, 1999.

14. R. Buyya and S. Vazhkudai, Compute power market: Towards a market-oriented grid, *Proc. 1st IEEE/ACM International Symp. Cluster Computing and the Grid (CCGrid 2001)*, Brisbane, Australia, May 15–18, 2001.

15. Parallel Workloads Archive, http://www.cs.huji.ac.il/labs/parallel/workload/, May 23, 2008.

16. D. E. Irwin, L. E. Grit, and J. S. Chase, Balancing risk and reward in a market-based task service, *Proc. 13th IEEE International Symp. High Performance Distributed Computing (HPDC 2004)*, Honolulu, HI, June 4–6, 2004.

17. C. S. Yeo and R. Buyya, Pricing for utility-driven resource management and allocation in clusters, *International Journal of High-Performance Computing Applications* **21**(4): 405–418 (2007).

18. R. Ranjan,*Coordinated Resource Provisioning in Federated Grids*, PhD thesis, Univ. Melbourne, Australia, July 2007.

19. N. Andrade, W. Cirne, F. Brasileiro, and P. Roisenberg, OurGrid: An approach to easily assemble Grids with equitable resource sharing, *Proc. 9th Workshop on Job Scheduling Strategies for Parallel Processing (JSSPP 2003), LNCS 2862/2003*, Seattle, WA, June 24, 2003.

20. D. Irwin, J. Chase, L. Grit, A. Yumerefendi, and D. Becker, Sharing networked resources with brokered leases, *Proc. 2006 Usenix Annual Technical Conf. (Usenix 2006)*, Boston, MA, May 30–June 3, 2006.

21. R. Ranjan, A. Harwood, and R. Buyya, Peer-to-peer resource discovery in global Grids: A tutorial, *IEEE Communication Surveys and Tutorials* **10**(2): 6–33 (2008).

22. I. Stoica, R. Morris, D. Karger, M. F. Kaashoek, and H. Balakrishnan, Chord: A scalable peer-to-peer lookup service for Internet applications, *Proc. 2001 ACM SIGCOMM Conf. Applications, Technologies, Architectures, and Protocols for Computer Communication (SIGCOMM 2001)*, San Diego, CA, Aug. 27–31, 2001.
23. S. Ratnasamy, P. Francis, M. Handley, R. Karp, and S. Schenker, A scalable content-addressable network, *Proc. 2001 ACM SIGCOMM Conf. Applications, Technologies, Architectures, and Protocols for Computer Communication*, San Diego, CA, Aug. 27–31, 2001.
24. A. Rowstron and P. Druschel, Pastry: Scalable, decentralized object location, and routing for large scale peer-to-peer systems, *Proc. 3rd IFIP/ACM International Conf. Distributed Systems Platforms (Middleware 2001)*, Heidelberg, Germany, Nov. 12–16, 2001.
25. R. Ranjan, L. Chan, A. Harwood, S. Karunasekera, and R. Buyya, Decentralized resource discovery service for large scale federated Grids, *Proc. 3rd IEEE International Conf. e-Science and Grid Computing (e-Science 2007)*, Bangalore, India, Dec. 10–13, 2007.
26. R. Ranjan, A. Harwood, and R. Buyya, A case for cooperative and incentive-based federation of distributed clusters, *Future Generation Computing Systems* **24**(4): 280–295 (2008).
27. R. Ranjan, A. Harwood, and R. Buyya, SLA-based coordinated superscheduling scheme for computational Grids, *Proc. 8th IEEE International Conf. Cluster Computing (Cluster 2006)*, Barcelona, Spain, Sept. 25–28, 2006.
28. R. Ranjan, A. Harwood, and R. Buyya,*Coordinated Load Management in Peer-to-Peer Coupled Federated Grid Systems*, Technical Report GRIDS-TR-2008-2, Grid Computing and Distributed Systems Laboratory, Univ. Melbourne, Australia, 2008.
29. U. Lublin and D. G. Feitelson, The workload on parallel supercomputers: Modeling the characteristics of rigid jobs, *Journal of Parallel and Distributed Computing* **63**(11): 1105–1122 (2003).
30. E. Tanin, A. Harwood, and H. Samet, Using a distributed quadtree index in peer-to-peer networks, *The VLDB Journal* **16**(2): 165–178 (2007).
31. R. Buyya and M. Murshed, GridSim: A toolkit for the modeling and simulation of distributed resource management and scheduling for Grid computing, *Concurrency and Computation: Practice and Experience* **14**(13–15): 1175–1220 (Nov.–Dec. 2002).
32. P. García, C. Pairot, R. Mondéjar, J. Pujol, H. Tejedor, and R. Rallo, PlanetSim: A new overlay network simulation framework, *Proc. 4th International Workshop on Software Engineering and Middleware (SEM 2004), Lecture Notes in Computer Science* **3437**: 20–21 (Sept. 2004).

INDEX

Market-Oriented Grid and Utility Computing Edited by Rajkumar Buyya and Kris Bubendorfer

WILEY SERIES ON PARALLEL AND DISTRIBUTED COMPUTING

Series Editor: Albert Y. Zomaya

Parallel and Distributed Simulation Systems / Richard Fujimoto

Mobile Processing in Distributed and Open Environments / Peter Sapaty

Introduction to Parallel Algorithms / C. Xavier and S. S. Iyengar

Solutions to Parallel and Distributed Computing Problems: Lessons from Biological Sciences / Albert Y. Zomaya, Fikret Ercal, and Stephan Olariu (*Editors*)

Parallel and Distributed Computing: A Survey of Models, Paradigms, and Approaches / Claudia Leopold

Fundamentals of Distributed Object Systems: A CORBA Perspective / Zahir Tari and Omran Bukhres

Pipelined Processor Farms: Structured Design for Embedded Parallel Systems / Martin Fleury and Andrew Downton

Handbook of Wireless Networks and Mobile Computing / Ivan Stojmenović *(Editor)*

Internet-Based Workflow Management: Toward a Semantic Web / Dan C. Marinescu

Parallel Computing on Heterogeneous Networks / Alexey L. Lastovetsky

Performance Evaluation and Characteization of Parallel and Distributed Computing Tools / Salim Hariri and Manish Parashar

Distributed Computing: Fundamentals, Simulations and Advanced Topics, *Second Edition* / Hagit Attiya and Jennifer Welch

Smart Environments: Technology, Protocols, and Applications / Diane Cook and Sajal Das

Fundamentals of Computer Organization and Architecture / Mostafa Abd-El-Barr and Hesham El-Rewini

Advanced Computer Architecture and Parallel Processing / Hesham El-Rewini and Mostafa Abd-El-Barr

UPC: Distributed Shared Memory Programming / Tarek El-Ghazawi, William Carlson, Thomas Sterling, and Katherine Yelick

Handbook of Sensor Networks: Algorithms and Architectures / Ivan Stojmenović *(Editor)*

Parallel Metaheuristics: A New Class of Algorithms / Enrique Alba (*Editor*)

Design and Analysis of Distributed Algorithms / Nicola Santoro

Task Scheduling for Parallel Systems / Oliver Sinnen

Computing for Numerical Methods Using Visual C++ / Shaharuddin Salleh, Albert Y. Zomaya, and Sakhinah A. Bakar

Architecture-Independent Programming for Wireless Sensor Networks / Amol B. Bakshi and Viktor K. Prasanna

High-Performance Parallel Database Processing and Grid Databases / David Taniar, Clement Leung, Wenny Rahayu, and Sushant Goel

Algorithms and Protocols for Wireless and Mobile Ad Hoc Networks / Azzedine Boukerche (*Editor*)

Algorithms and Protocols for Wireless Sensor Networks / Azzedine Boukerche (*Editor*)

Optimization Techniques for Solving Complex Problems / Enrique Alba, Christian Blum, Pedro Isasi, Coromoto León, and Juan Antonio Gómez (*Editors*)

Emerging Wireless LANs, Wireless PANs, and Wireless MANs: IEEE 802.11, IEEE 802.15, IEEE 802.16 Wireless Standard Family / Yang Xiao and Yi Pan (*Editors*)

High-Performance Heterogeneous Computing / Alexey L. Lastovetsky and Jack Dongarra

Research in Mobile Intelligence / Laurence T. Yang (*Editor*)

Advanced Computational Infrastructures for Parallel and Distributed Adaptive Applicatons / Manish Parashar and Xiaolin Li (*Editors*)

Market-Oriented Grid and Utility Computing / Rajkumar Buyya and Kris Bubendorfer (*Editors*)

Printed in the United States
By Bookmasters